Laughing Screaming

Film and Culture

John Belton, General Editor

Film and Culture   *A series of Columbia University Press*
Edited by John Belton

Laughing

What Made Pistachio Nuts
Henry Jenkins

Showstoppers: Busby Berkeley and the Tradition of Spectacle
Martin Rubin

Projections of War: Hollywood, American Culture, and World War II
Thomas Doherty

Laughing Screaming

Modern Hollywood Horror and Comedy

William Paul

Columbia University Press **New York**

Columbia University Press

New York   Chichester, West Sussex

Copyright © 1994   Columbia University Press
All rights reserved

Library of Congress Cataloging-in-Publication Data

Paul, William
        Laughing, screaming: modern Hollywood horror and
comedy / William Paul.
            p.   cm. — (Film and culture)
        Includes bibliographical references and index.
        ISBN 0-231-08464-1
        1. Horror films—History and criticism. 2. Comedy
films—History and criticism. 3. Sensationalism in motion pictures. 4. Sex in motion pictures. 5. Violence in motion pictures. 6. Motion pictures—Psychological aspects. I. Title. II.
Series.
PN1995.9.H6P35 1994
791.43'616—dc20   93-27388
                                                              CIP

∞

Casebound editions of
Columbia University Press
books are printed
on permanent and durable
acid-free paper.

Printed in the United States of America
c   10   9   8   7   6   5   4   3   2   1

To Lew—

By listening you taught me to hear,

by looking, to see.

Contents

3 *Growing Pains*

4 *The Case for Child Abuse*

5 *Revolting Bodies*

6 *Laughing Screaming*

Acknowledgments

I would like to thank all the people who talked to me about this project over the years of its composition and offered stimulation to my own thoughts about these films: Mark Feighn (who unsuspectingly set things in motion by urging me to see *Fast Times at Ridgemont High,* a film I might well have passed up, so that I might get a sense of what life in his new southern California environs was like), Richard Allen, Mike Anderegg, Jeanine Basinger, Phil Blumberg, Marcy Bohn, Tim Bohn, Nina Bouis, Randall Conrad, Christine Dahl, Ellen Draper, Pete Gurney, Jerry Herron, Val Kivelson, Andy Horton, Tim Johnson, Jim Knower, Ira Konigsberg, Julie Levinson, Marty Marks, Steve Mayer, Bruce McKenna, Roger Midgett, Charlie Musser, Gerry Peary, Ed Sikov, Joe Smith, Gaylyn Studlar, David Thorburn (especially for his insistence on keeping aesthetic issues alive in talking about popular culture), Susan White, Lewis Wurgaft, and Rafia Zafar.

I am grateful to Rob and Mary Joan Leith for early access to a VCR before it became a seemingly indispensable household item—particularly for their frequent good cheer during many bad movies. And I am certain that

Mary Joan's surprising pleasure in *Porky's* particularly in the shower scene, affected my own response to that very odd film, although she had the advantage of baking cookies the entire time she was watching it.

I was greatly helped by the expertise of the staffs and the resources at the New York Library for the Performing Arts, the Warner Brothers Archive at the University of Southern California, and the Margaret Herrick Library in Beverly Hills. Roy Thomas has been a wonderfully demanding and astute copyeditor; the book has greatly benefited from his work. Sean Cavazos-Kottke sped to the rescue with some last-minute fact checking and preparation of the index. Robert Rayher aided me in the not always easy work of frame enlargements, and Mike and Diane at Ivory Photo were efficient in the lab and attentive to the problems of making prints from motion picture film. The Office of the Vice President of Research at the University of Michigan generously provided funds for faculty release time, making it possible for me to finish this book.

I particularly want to thank five individuals who had far-reaching impact on the final shape and direction of this book, more, I think, than any of them might realize. My friend and former M.I.T. colleague Pete Donaldson offered early support and, as always with Pete, very cerebral ways of thinking about very noncerebral materials. I was also encouraged by the openness of this distinguished Elizabethan scholar to works of popular culture all too easily dismissed as crude. Pete would never settle for such simple formulations, nor would he let me. Tom Doherty, himself an astute commentator on popular culture, was an invaluable source of information on films, music, and more secondary material than I could ever manage, although I valiantly tried to keep up with him. A fine Classics scholar, Mike Moore helped me in my considerations of Old Comedy, Aristophanes, Plato, and Aristotle. He also profoundly affected my first viewing of *Revenge of the Nerds* by his giddily infectious delight in the good-natured humor of that film. Tom Gunning's writings on spectacle have had a general influence on my approach here, but he deserves special mention for directing me to Mikhail Bakhtin before Bakhtin became high fashion. And I greatly benefited from frequent discussions with Tom the one year we were both living in the Boston area and he was teaching a course on the horror film at Harvard. John Belton's thoroughgoing skepticism about this project in its early stages forced me to rethink and finally reshape much of the material in this book. And I greatly value three decades of an ongoing dialogue about film—challenging, lively, and often contentious—that John and I have shared since we were both undergraduates at Columbia College.

Finally, let me thank my wife, Rafia, and my son, Nathan, for their forbearance in accepting my frequent disappearing acts as I completed work on this book. And to my wife I would like to offer apologies for leaving her with an image she claims is indelible: looking up from her reading one night, she caught a glimpse of me sitting rapt before the television set, avidly taking notes as an infant in a snowsuit bloodily battered a woman's head with a kitchen mallet.

Laughing Screaming

Venerable Vulgarity

One would certainly have supposed that there could be no doubt as to what is to be understood by "sexual." First and foremost, what is sexual is something improper, something one ought not to talk about.

—*Sigmund Freud,* Introductory Lectures on Psychoanalysis

Chapter 1 *Rousing Rabble*

All movies are open wide, alike to moron and philosopher and to all that come between, with all the sanction and seeming approval that a broad and general public carries. There results are—the results. . . .

There is something socially wrong, something subversive to the best interests of society in the way a substantial number of present-day movies are made, written, conceived.[1]

Danger from Below

This is a book about movies that never won prestigious awards, movies that embraced the lowest common denominator as an aesthetic principle, movies that critics constantly griped about having to sit through. If any of these films garnered favorable comment, praise was generally limited by an obligatory remark noting the superiority of *this* one particular example over other, similar films.

This was at the best. More commonly, these films were taken as prime evidence of the vulgarity of mass taste, a neat tautology since the vulgar is precisely what belongs to the mass. In giving the public what it wanted, these films, alas, shirked their duty to elevate the mass to the critic's superior level of taste. In the worst light, these films were viewed as demonstrating the mind-numbing decadence of American culture, as an infinitely renewable sign that the end was near. In short, this is a book about "gross-out" comedy and horror, movies quite happy to present themselves to the public as spectacles in the worst possible taste.

Since critics who claim to have something to say about the nature of art are most likely to see that nature as noble—something that raises us above the gross physical existence that gross-out films celebrate—the films were generally not considered art at all. As a consequence, they were usually consigned to the less discriminatory realm of mere entertainment. But even driven back into lower depths by high-minded critics, they nonetheless fortified themselves by staking out a dominant position in the mainstream, an encampment that "noble" art often prefers to flee with a nice show of decorum. These films firmly held on to this dominant position for nearly two decades, commanding mainstream Hollywood production from the 1970s through the 1980s. This is a book, then, about movies that attracted large audiences as regularly as they repulsed critics. What those critics, dismayed by the sheer number of these films, regarded as endless and inane repetition, the audiences themselves saw as endless variation.[2]

Because these films attracted money as voluminously as complaints, they possessed a kind of economic power that at times made them seem more than a mere nuisance to the most disenchanted critics. At worst they seemingly threatened to overwhelm all commercial production. Did we really have to see another "slice-and-dice" fest, one more example of America's preference for violence over sex? And when there was sex, why couldn't Hollywood make movies about anything other than adolescent angst? That these movies were considered dangerous at all is not just because they made a lot of money, but because, in the process, they endowed the people who patronized them with a kind of power—the power to find pleasure in material that was not only offensive to the elite but also excluded the culture of the elite.

Many of the films I write about in this book are about young people, but not all. Still, although most of the films had a restricted rating that should have limited access to those under eighteen, the predominant audience for gross-out comedy and horror was young (roughly from adolescence to perhaps the late twenties). The target audience for the films often in turn became the target of attack in the popular press, which voiced the anxiety that these people not already fully formed might be deformed by such pernicious amusement. Arguments about the misguidance of art go back at least to Plato, but the advent of the mass media has made this seem of special concern with regard to children because the mass media purportedly can act on passive recipients unable to resist their blandishments.

Aggression is the keynote of gross-out as these films assaulted us with images of outrageously violent or sexual behavior, or violently sexual, or sexually violent. It is therefore easy to adopt the paranoiac strain that is a common response to popular culture and ask: Don't these films present something we ought to guard ourselves against? Doesn't the grossness these films present as a value in itself lay siege to all that is best in our culture and even best for the future of our society?[3] I must take these questions seriously, at the least as a point of departure, because I want to take these films seriously. Stated simply, I see these films not only as key expressions of their period but also as more fully achieved artistic expression than has generally been granted. In making this claim, I have set myself a difficult task because movies—especially if they are popular—remain something of a disreputable art. In this book, I am choosing to look at some of the most disreputable examples.

As a prelude to looking at the films themselves, I want to take a few detours along different paths that will eventually wend back to the films and provide the observant traveler with a sufficiently detailed landscape to make sense of this sudden efflorescence of gross-out. A *historical* path looks to the ways movies were viewed in the past and, especially for my concerns here, to the relationship of the young to movies. A more *theoretical* route encounters the role of the popular arts in society, particularly in a democratic society, and most particularly in a democratic society as large and complex as the United States. And a *cultural* approach provides a vista on the ways in which films serve to define the culture that has produced them, from which perspective the values of the culture itself may be spread out for view.

This last journey in effect returns to the historical and theoretical points of departure, but from a different aspect, one that sees our views of history and theory as necessarily conditioned by changes in the culture at large. We are all not only creatures of history, created by everything that has come before us, but also creatures of our culture, created by the terms for exploring and understanding our existence that the particular culture has given us. As the films themselves respond to changing history and a changing cultural climate, so too our historical perspective of their interaction with their audience necessarily changes. And, in turn, the way audiences actually interact with these films should serve to modify any theoretical view of popular culture.

I want to begin with a historical view because film offers the unique opportunity of an art form whose origins we can trace.[4] It is not that everything about movies was radically new, since they are, to their crowning glory, a bastard art, indiscriminately drawing on drama, literature, the fine arts, and music.[5] What was newest about film lay in a technological essence that made it infinitely reproducible.[6] Quite simply, there had never before been anything like the sheer scale and availability to the widest variety of audiences that film made possible. Had Chaplin remained a stage performer all his life, he no doubt would have been very popular and might well have achieved something of the legendary status of clowns from past centuries. But without film he could never have achieved the staggering popularity that has transformed the few props of derby hat, cane, and mustache into instantly recognizable symbols throughout the world. This extraordinarily wide dissemination of movies, the art form open "alike to moron and philosopher," must always be kept in mind because the audience necessarily affects the kind of art produced.[7] As the audience affects the art, the art has likewise been judged over the years by the nature of the audience. Almost inevitably, the horror films and comedies I am concerned with here have been dismissed because of the audience they address.[8]

Almost from the beginnings of movies, there was concern about what the movies were doing to the audiences who viewed them.[9] This concern reached its fullest expression in the early 1930s with what remains one of the most extensive sociological surveys on film: the studies of the impact of motion pictures undertaken by the Committee on Education Research of the Payne Fund, which brought together a battery of sociologists from leading universities across the country under the direction of Dr. W. W. Charters, professor of education and director of educational research at Ohio State University. The committee produced eleven volumes written by eighteen "social scientists—psychologists, sociologists and educators, representative of their fields in various universities across the country," with each volume covering different areas such as *Motion Pictures and the Social Attitudes of Children*; *Movies, Delinquency, and Crime*; and *Children's Sleep*.[10]

Although the study prided itself on the scientific seriousness of its endeavor, a twelfth volume, *Our Movie Made Children,* written by journalist and novelist Henry James Forman, appeared first in order to summarize the contents of the other books in a more popular and frankly more incendiary form. Before any of the actual studies could be seen, their complex and frequently inconclusive material became available to precisely the mass audience whose well-being motivated the initial inquiry.[11] Appearing at a time of increasing concern over the content of movies, the publication of *Our Movie Made Children* coincided with a movement to control that content. Because of this context, the book had an extraordinary impact at the time: it was a bestseller kept in circulation through quite a few printings over the next couple of years, generating a lot of discussion in the press, even to the point of being mentioned on the editorial page of the *New York Times*.[12] In all, it probably helped to prompt the new toughened censorship standards the major movie companies began enforcing on their own product in 1934.

The massiveness of the Payne Fund studies of mass art was formidable, but a number of strong answers to it were mounted. Notable was Mortimer Adler's book-length attack in *Art and Prudence,* which questioned not simply the scientific methodology but also some of the assumptions about the nature of art.[13] Adler did not move to place movies in the realm of great books, but he did see in them the poetry of a democratic society. He decried attacks on their alleged harmfulness, which he claimed was not demonstrable. Nevertheless, he subscribed to the notion that art could be weighed against prudence, that it might represent something harmful to the body politic, and in this case the "prudent man" might in fact be moved to action against art. To complement the popularization of the Payne Fund studies, Raymond Moley, former Assistant Secretary of State in Franklin D. Roosevelt's first administration, "at the suggestions of representatives of the motion picture industry," produced a slender and readable version of Adler's long, dense book to parallel *Our Movie Made Children*. The result was *Are We Movie Made?,* which provided the answer the interested sponsor wanted to hear: No![14]

Although the movie companies had commissioned Moley's response, they were already fighting a rear-guard action since they had caved in three years before to the kind of pressure *Our Movie Made Children* represented by tightening up their self-censorship. And, in any case, Adler and Moley did not entirely oppose the argument put forward by the Payne Fund studies. Their attitude was liberal, but not libertarian, so any acknowledgment of the need for "prudence" was in effect a concession to the right-wing position of the Payne Fund studies. Perhaps because movies present an art for the masses on a scale unlike anything ever possible before, the earliest sustained criticism came from the right, which possibly had more to fear from the free expression of a mass audience.[15] The right in this country has generally been more effective at exerting some kind of control over the content of popular arts than the left. This might be because they have mostly focused on such seemingly neutral cultural issues as sex and violence (the two chief bugbears of *Our Movie Made Children*), much as they continue nowadays to provide the focus for attacks on television. The left has more often been concerned with overt expressions of ideology, which has peculiarly led it to reject much of popular culture out of hand.

As noted, the concern for the potentially deleterious effects of art goes back at least to Plato, whom Adler specifically invoked in trying to sketch out the demands of "prudence." But the unprecedented size of the audience for movies gave a new urgency to this concern.[16] From fairly early on, then, as these studies indicate, movies were seen to have a power achieved through their wide dissemination, a power disturbingly not under the control of either the arbiters of taste, who generally found movies tasteless, or the government. In the past, Hollywood sought to evade the threat of government action, which had been instituted sporadically at a state and city level, by self-censorship, preferring to constrain its own freedom of expression rather than risk challenging the legality of outside constraints. And although the movie studios hired Raymond Moley to defend their right to free artistic expression, their willingness to embrace restriction perhaps signaled their own ambivalence about their audience. It is as if they accepted the right's fear of the adversarial potential of popular art.[17] The market determines the product: to stay popular, they have to give the people what they want, but the people might not want what the studios want to give them.

In considering the impact of the gross-out films in the 1970s, it is worth keeping this history in mind. Outwardly, Hollywood subscribed to Moley's liberalism through much of its history. Covertly, they accepted the right's repressiveness. Only in the late 1960s did they approach more of a libertarian attitude with the abandonment of self-censorship and the institution of the Ratings System. There are other important issues centering around this shift to freer expression for theatrical movies (which I will take up in later chapters), but for now I want to note that part of the reason for the change was economic. In 1964 the first film made for television, *The Killers*, was released theatrically instead. Especially after the Kennedy assassination, the film was considered simply too violent for television. This was also the year the first network television showing of *Psycho* (1960) had to be canceled for the same reasons. The demands of "prudence" held sway in both these instances, but they also serve to point

out that television, not the movie theater, was now the domain of prudence. The movie theater had become something else.

The Killers is important *both* because it was made for TV and also because it ended up playing in theaters first. The onset of television movies—movies that were explicitly made for the small screen—necessitated
a change in our attitude toward what we considered different about theatrical movies. By force of circumstances, *The Killers* inadvertently pointed
the way since the denial of a television broadcast said in effect the difference was censorship. *Psycho* had already extended the boundaries for
graphic violence four years before, so its unfitness for television made
clear that movie theaters were the appropriate venue for such explicitness.
Appropriately, the denial of its television showing immediately led to a
full-scale rerelease of the Hitchcock film. Throughout the 1960s, graphicness came to be associated with theatrical features.

Gross-out films represent the most extreme development of this change
because they embrace, as their grossness implies, explicitness as part of
their aesthetic. These are films of license, generally receiving what *Variety*
has called a "hard R," but occasionally stepping over the border into X-
rated territory and subsequently trimmed for reentry into R-land, as was
the case with *Fast Times at Ridgemont High* (1982) for its sex and many
of the horror films for their violence.[18] As these films are defined by their
sense of license and the aggressiveness with which they seem to abandon
all standards of decorum, they challenge the notion of "taste" as an indication of an art work's quality. And taste is a standard well worth challenging.

But I do not want simply to challenge. Rather, I would like to interrogate the notion of taste itself. Since arbiters of taste generally move toward
more spiritual matters when regarding culture, it is odd that physiology
should provide a standard for aesthetic pleasure. With food and drink,
taste is explicitly a matter of sensual pleasure; with art, works that aim
solely at such pleasure generally start to move into the realm of the tasteless. Taste as a concept applied to art seems to transcend the purely physiological, yet its basis in the physiological offers a kind of validation, as if
to suggest there is something essentially human to standards of taste. That
there are cultural determinants to taste in both gustatory and aesthetic
realms, however, should be evident from the sheer diversity of cuisine
throughout the world.[19] Still, I do not want to suggest that standards of
taste are entirely arbitrary because we can find at least one constant in
what is rejected.

As a physiological matter, we usually say something tastes bad if the taste itself is sufficiently strong to produce a response. Otherwise, it is merely bland. Translated into aesthetics, bad taste endows the object with an aggressiveness that must be defended against. With food, we spit it out. With art, we turn away and ignore the aggression or, in more repressive times, attempt to ban it. Aggression, then, is the essential element for gustatory and aesthetic bad taste. But the desire to censor aesthetic bad taste is where the physiological parallel breaks down and cultural determinants take over. We see no need for banning food that tastes bad, although there is probably general agreement that the public should be protected against poisonous food. In art, mere bad taste somehow escalates into something poisonous. "Gross-out" counters this escalation with a perverse reversal of these priorities. Not only does it embrace bad taste, it transforms revulsion into a sought-after goal.

Measured by the standards of contemporary films, many of the judgments made about movies in the early 1930s must seem quaint to the point of absurdity, like the strong condemnation of Greta Garbo for never having "portrayed what might be regarded as a good woman."[20] Much as the films might seem comparatively innocent to us, I want to look at this last great period of license for a number of reasons, not least of which is that a number of the films are now regarded as "classics." The films of the late 1920s and early 1930s might now seem practically decorous, yet for their time there was a strong sense they had gone too far, crossing over the point at which aggression becomes transgression. Many of the arguments used against these films at the time have been repeated against contemporary films and television programs, but the difference in the content of the films from the two periods makes the political attitudes underlying these objections the more pointed.

Objection to films of the early 1930s lay in their occupying a position of license, a license that seemed to merge easily into licentiousness for the period.[21] For Forman the theater itself is a terrible place, operating as a concomitant of the terrible things young people see on the screen "with large and eager eyes through the murk of the often stuffy theatre, watching the unfoldment of the ubiquitous themes—love, sex and crime" (p. 25). Forman can be quite precise about what he means by "ubiquitous" because this has all been carefully cataloged and calculated by the meticulous sociologists: for the years 1920, 1925, and 1930 "somewhere between seventy-five and eighty percent of all pictures dealt with love, sex, crime or mystery films [sic]" (pp. 29–30) whereas "thirty-six percent of all pictures were loaded with scenes of either crime or violence" (p. 34). As his title *Our Movie Made Children* indicates, Forman is chiefly concerned with the effects on youngsters of this horrific content, content he describes with a sensual luridness: "Killing and killing and more killing—that is the impression left upon these children. Their nerves ravaged and their nascent consciousness of the glorious new world into which they are being initiated marred and shocked by foolishly excessive violence" (pp. 37–38).

The reason for the emphasis on young audiences is that it grants Forman's polemic the alchemical power of transforming art into instruction. The insistently repeated fear here is that the movies have "really given us another educational system, alluring, persuasive, cogent and appealing, which involves all the childhood and youth of the country as completely, as thoroughly, in effect, as our long-built up educational system itself" (p. 157). Comparing movies to the public education system points to an anxiety not so much centered on teaching as on the enunciation of values which those in authority cannot control.

The underlying question here should be whether art does in fact instruct its audience. Much of the Payne Fund studies seemed intent on proving this was in fact the case, just as contemporary studies of violence on television take on the same ambition, although the results are always far less conclusive than would-be censors would like. If we grant for the moment it is in fact the purpose of art to instruct, we would have to consider the purpose of this instruction. Forman is quite explicit about this, but also fairly confused, and his confusion is valuable because it clarifies the problems involved in seeing art as education:

> What we call morality is conformity to mores. A nation may be possessed of the mores of Sodom and Gomorrah, or of the highest in the domains of culture and spirituality. The choice lies with the nation. Failure to conform to the existing standard of mores is immorality. . . . What is a good picture? A picture, leaving aside the quality of its art, is good if it complies with the national mores and bad if it conflicts. (p. 134)

The fissure that Forman opens up in his argument is the surprisingly anthropological turn he takes in granting morality to Sodom and Gomorrah, even if he assumes we will consider this bad morality. He hasn't fully embraced a relativistic position since he makes claims for a higher morality, but he has also inadvertently pointed out the problem of making value dependent on compliance "with national mores."

What if the mores themselves aren't moral? And are "national mores" definable in a society made up of different classes? Whose mores determine the national mores? The point is that no code to govern the content of art can ever be value neutral. The values of a specific class at a specific time inform every aspect of the Production Code that began to be stringently enforced in 1934. From a contemporary viewpoint, this is most forcefully clear in the Code's ban on miscegenation as subject matter for a movie.[22] This is not to say that many Americans today would not continue to object to miscegenation, but as a matter of public policy and "national mores" we have been moved to accept what had previously been banned. By invoking cities traditionally seen as immoral, Forman has implicitly opened up the possibility for an art that defines itself as moral by being oppositional, by going *against* the accepted mores. This is of particular interest to me here because "mores" as Forman uses the term seems to function much like "taste" as I have discussed it above—a concept determined by consensus.

As we look at the history of movies, a further problem emerges in trying to elevate a film's moral content into an educational experience. Even if any given film ultimately promulgates the "right" values (which is to say it promotes what the guardians of culture and the state would like the masses to think), there remains the possibility that the masses will, perversely, take the "wrong" values from the work at hand. Consider the case of *Public Enemy* (1931). In charting the rise and fall of a gangster, the film dealt with a subject of interest to public morality of the period, and it seemed to do so in a responsible way by instructing the audience that crime does not pay. Yet the reviewer for the *New York Times* found himself in the peculiar position of commending the film and condemning the audience:

> There is a prologue apprising the audience that the hoodlums and terrorists of the underworld must be exposed and the glamour ripped from them. There is an epilogue pointing [sic] the moral that civilization is on her knees and inquiring loudly as to what is to be done. . . . The audiences yesterday laughed frequently and with gusto as the swaggering Matt and Tom went through their paces, and this rather took the edge off the brutal picture the producers appeared to be trying to serve up.[23]

The problem here has to do with film's status as *spectacle*, an aspect of theatrical art in general that has long disturbed those inclined to be troubled by the direct emotional appeal of all forms of spectacle.[24] No matter what kind of attitudinizing one may try to encase them in, there always remains something of an appeal in the *shows* of violence and sexy behavior. Furthermore, all performance art contains elements of narcissistic display that grants it a quality of aggression. This combination of aggression with spectacle as an end in itself represents elements that gross-out films seem to glory in without scruple, and most often without presenting the attitudinizing framework generally thought necessary in the liberal period of the early 1930s.[25]

If the aggressive appeal of spectacle is a problem, the solution of *Our Movie Made Children* was to censor the show altogether because "the conclusion appears inescapable that to show certain types of pictures—so numerous in the current output—in what are known as high-rate delinquency areas, in cities, is in some measure like selling whiskey to the Indians, against which there are quite justly severe laws and sharp penalties" (p. 186).

The greatest threat that movies offer, then, is as a revolutionary force among a mass that is preferably kept passive and docile. Controlling movies is necessarily of importance to anyone who wants to control the social order. Forman's comparison of movies to alcohol is more revealing than he intended: after all, Dionysus is not only the god of the grape but also of the theater. And in both cases, the consumer may be moved to behavior dangerous to society by the simple consumption of the chosen product. The comparison at the least should suggest an acute awareness of the potentially subversive aspects of art—subversive of mores, standards, and taste.

This subversion might in fact be one of the chief appeals of art, or at least art that has a sufficient amount of aggression in it to propel it toward the circus of bad taste. I think this point is at least implicitly realized in a tag line frequently used in advertisements for broad comedy, billing them as "laugh riots" or even better, as "laff riots." Why is "laff" better than "laugh"? Because it politicizes spelling, turning it into a class issue with an aggressive assertion that the phonetic attempt of an uneducated writer, the "wrong" way, is in fact the right way. After all, we don't go to "laff riots" for schooling, so why should we bother with a ridiculous spelling system that can only be learned through long and arduous instruction? Maybe, in fact, we go to laff riots for the riot, to achieve the release, the breaking through of all constraints, that is fundamental to the aesthetics of gross-out.

The Danger from Above

If the right has feared a mass audience mobilized to immoral mores and threatening the stability of the social order, the left has generally conjured up a radically different creature, an audience that has seemingly lost all consciousness in a pleasurable mass ego disintegration. Much as these two mythic viewers are opposed, however, in both cases the audience is made an infinitely malleable thing, and in both cases paranoid scenarios dramatize what is most to be feared: on the right, an unruly mob endangering the privileges and property of the power structure; on the left, a narcotized mass drugged into an unthinking embrace of inimical values that are solely in the interest of the power structure.[26]

In this section I want to consider briefly a familiar position on the left. In principle, at least, the left should be more receptive than the right to the art that most appeals to the masses, and most particularly to an art that defines itself as oppositional to the dominant power structure, which in effect is the subject of the rest of this book. Yet the left has generally been as suspicious of popular culture as the right.

As the popularizer, within intellectual circles at least, of the terms "masscult" and "midcult," Dwight MacDonald is one of the most familiar spokesmen for the left's attitude toward popular culture.[27] In "A Theory of Mass Culture," his attack on popular culture proceeds along two tracks, economic and cultural. He wittily uses an economic argument to justify his terminology and point to the inevitably debased quality of the product: "It is sometimes called 'Popular Culture,' but I think 'Mass Culture' a more accurate term, since its distinctive mark is that it is solely and directly an article for mass consumption, like chewing gum" (p. 59).[28] MacDonald doesn't explain the simile, but it's a good one for his argument since chewing gum operates as something of a pacifier for its consumers, devoid of genuine nourishment but stilling the pangs of hunger by a mechanical imitation of eating, an eating that never allows swallowing. The underlying assumption is that means of production and distribution necessarily affect the quality of the product, a point that continues to be made even in writing on Hollywood that does not have an explicit political program. The point needs to be questioned.

The films I write about in this book could all reasonably be designated exploitation product, and as such they might be seen as the inevitable result of the rise in exploitation marketing in the 1970s whereby films open simultaneously in five hundred or more theaters (in recent years the number has escalated dramatically to as many as fifteen hundred or two thousand or more) and are promoted by massive television ad campaigns. The pattern is not new: it had been used occasionally in the past, mostly for exploitation fare like horror films.[29] But the exploitation marketing strategies of the 1970s did not initially lead to certain kinds of production. Rather, as my discussion of the release of *The Exorcist* in 1973 will demonstrate, these strategies were really a response to the kinds of films being made and most particularly to the ones garnering the greatest audiences after the bottom of the market for big-budget, reserved-seat films fell out in 1970–71. Once in place, exploitation marketing encouraged a continuance of exploitation product. Change is always possible in the future for the same reason that change took place in the 1970s: the exploitation marketing strategy was really a response to the successes of individual films—which is to say the marketing strategy was created by the market, and the product itself was not a function of the marketing.[30]

MacDonald's economic view leads him to a "conspiracy theory" familiar from much past writing on popular culture. He claims "mass culture" is "an instrument of political domination" because it is "imposed from above . . . fabricated by technicians hired by businessmen" (p. 60).[31] While the attack on businessmen marks this as a distinctly leftist view of popular culture, it has most recently been appropriated by former vice president Dan Quayle.[32] Movie producers might represent the only businessmen Quayle doesn't like, but the fact that this fervent right-winger can attack them as corrupters of society is enough to suggest how misguided is MacDonald's assumption that "businessmen" form a unitary group colluding to preserve the interests of the ruling class. At the least, MacDonald's business-oriented attack effectively ignored the entire exploitation market, which deliberately appeals to lower-class tastes, whereas the major studios more often sought a patina of bourgeois respectability. The shift of the entire industry to an exploitation market in the 1970s is of particular importance, then, because it took the major studios into areas they were in fact opposed to in the past.

Books on movies from the "New Hollywood" (as it came to be called in the popular press at the time) generally treat *Easy Rider* as the seminal film of the period.[33] Whatever its aesthetic values, its significance in terms of the market in 1969 was the fact that it was released by Columbia Pictures instead of American-International, the low-grade company that specialized in such biker exploitation fare.[34] In the following year all the major studios but Columbia had gone into the red because they had large portions of their budgets sunk into big-budget films intended for roadshow distribution, class acts that aspired to middle-class respectability by being limited to reserved seats and two shows daily in the big downtown theaters. These theaters would all but disappear by the next decade.[35] The fact that a major studio distributed *Easy Rider* had two effects of consequence for films in the 1970s. First, the film was taken more seriously than it probably would have been had it been presented under the usual aegis of American-International, receiving far more critical attention than any of the American-International biker films (although biker film cognoscenti debated its relative merits). Second, to the majors who were smarting from their big-budget disasters it pointed the way to one possible future, one that could embrace the oppositional and even offensive strategies of low-budget exploitation films.[36]

MacDonald seems to acknowledge the exploitation elements that are at least always potentially present in popular art when he moves from an economic to a cultural perspective. When he does so, however, the terms of his argument undergo a striking shift. Now "mass culture" becomes something more threatening to the guardians of culture, and the mass audience begins to take on a fearful quality that brings it a good deal closer to the audience described in Forman's *Our Movie Made Children*; "Like nineteenth-century capitalism, Mass Culture is a dynamic, revolutionary force, breaking down the old barriers of class, tradition, taste, and dissolving all cultural distinctions. . . . Mass Culture is very democratic: it absolutely refuses to discriminate against, or between, anything or anybody" (p. 62). Although MacDonald wants to save the masses from the manipulations of moneymen, he also feels he has to save them from themselves since they do not possess powers of discrimination. In an ideal world, then, there is still to be a culture "imposed from above," but now it will be imposed by those guardians of culture, the educated elite, who are able to set standards of taste beyond the ken of the people.

If we could grant that the purpose of art is solely to delight and give pleasure, not to instruct, then it might be easier to understand why a once strongly puritanical culture, one that mistrusts pleasure as an end in itself, sought to regard mass culture as a dangerous narcotic with the potential for corrupting all civilization. In similar fashion, all spectacle must be suspect for both the right and the left because it bypasses rationality to appeal directly to the desire for pleasure. In this regard at least, it must be more than coincidence that the radical shift away from the Puritan aesthetic in American culture in the 1960s and into more openly hedonistic philosophies was accompanied by a new appreciation for popular culture.[37] Indeed, any creative endeavor whose sole aim was the pleasure of immediate gratification came increasingly to be regarded as art; popular art was no longer the sociological artifact it had more commonly been reduced to in the past.

But what if the pleasure-seeking audience had in fact *not* been drugged into a state of dreamy narcolepsy? In *The Art of the Moving Picture* (first written in 1915, revised in 1922), Vachel Lindsay proposed a very different kind of mass audience, one that would be so engaged by what they were

looking at they would enter into a constant buzz of conversation throughout the film. He even advised local theater owners to start

> an advertising campaign in your town that says: "Beginning Monday
> and henceforth, ours shall be known as Conversational Theater." . . . At
> the door let each person be handed the following card:
> "You are encouraged to discuss the picture with the friend who accom-
> panies you to this place. Conversation, of course, must be sufficiently
> subdued not to disturb the stranger who did not come with you to the
> theater."[38]

Lindsay then goes on to list a series of questions friends might ask each
other while watching the film and concludes with a recommendation for
a kind of ballot on other recent films in which viewers can check off
"approved or disapproved."

Lindsay's utopian audience voting on what is really valuable in culture
would be deplored by most critics of mass culture like MacDonald because it would seem to reduce aesthetics to the kind of popularity contest
that sees artistic success in terms of commercial success. But Lindsay considered his suggestion for polling an audience as democracy's means of
turning the ordinary theater into a kind of art museum. This is a challenging position. Even Hollywood for all its venality is somewhat shy about
fully embracing the attitude that popularity equals artistic success. The
highest-grossing films of the year rarely win Academy Awards in major
categories unless they also had a good critical reception.[39] Because I myself am often likely to disagree with the mass audience, in trying to alter
some of the terms of familiar aesthetic debates on popular culture I do
not wish to throw out all standards of aesthetic judgment just to put in
their place commercial success as the chief measure of value. Many of the
films I praise in the following pages were not big hits, whereas I have
disliked a number of the biggest money-makers.

What I am claiming here is that the mass audience itself is not without
powers of discrimination (even though I might not always agree with its
choices). Much as Lindsay's audience seems utopian, he apparently based
it on actual experience of his own time, as indicated in his remarks on
"the buzzing commentary of the audience. There will be some people
who disturb the neighbors in front, but the average crowd has developed
its manners in this particular, and when the orchestra is silent, murmurs
like a pleasant brook" (p. 224).

Anyone today who has experienced a movie in a large crowded urban
theater (especially in the inner city, where audiences are often as vocal in

their responses to the screen as worshippers in Pentecostal churches) might even find the notion of a passive audience to be rather quaint. The fact of the matter is that the masses do discriminate all the time—much to the chagrin of the moneymen in Hollywood, who would much prefer it if the intellectual critics of popular culture were correct. Movie producers would be delighted to go with the lowest common denominator if it really were possible to find the sure-fire formula for it, but the public inevitably frustrates these attempts.[40]

Films have always had the power to rouse the rabble, and that is what is most disturbing about them—not only to the guardians of culture but necessarily to the guardians of the state as well.[41] And I have to admit my own disquiet over occasional responses, to the horror films in particular. During the end credits for *A Nightmare on Elm Street Part II: Freddy's Revenge* (1985), a man came up to me and, addressing me as "you kids," went into a harangue about what we kids thought we were getting away with, but we'd better watch out because he would get us. Since he was misjudging my age by at least two decades, none of this seemed very real, and he left as abruptly as he had come, venting the aggression the film had stirred up. This remains a singular experience for me, and how much the film caused the outburst or simply provided an appropriate environment for it is moot.

People make of movies what they will; given the often intensified emotional environment of many Hollywood movies and their ability to arouse strong emotions, aberrant responses are always possible, perhaps even likely. I certainly do not think the crazed viewer of *A Nightmare on Elm Street* should be taken either as a standard response or as an indication of the film's depraved quality.[42] What disturbed me most was not his threat, which was apparently delivered from some disconnected fantasy world, but the enforced recognition that anyone in the audience could actually have identified with the violently murderous Freddy. There is something in the *Nightmare* films that at least facilitates such an outburst, and it is unnerving to acknowledge that the more normative response I wish to ascribe to myself in experiencing the film's horror might have some connection to the aberrant response subsequently directed at me.

Even when the aberrations take place on a larger scale, I think it necessary *not* to set them in stark opposition to "normal" experience of the films. Movies have demonstrated the power to stir audiences to actual riot from time to time, most especially in the last couple of decades with *The Warriors* (1979) and *Krush Groove* (1985) when those audiences congregated in the larger inner-city theaters, where they seem most fully attuned to the oppositional strategies implicit in many action films. This might be more of a contemporary phenomenon because these films tend to be rawer and more aggressive in their energies than earlier Hollywood product. Nonetheless, intense arousal of emotion has been one of the key aims of dramatic art in the West at least up until the twentieth century.

Andrew Sarris reports that "Odetsian audiences in Manhattan balconies cheered wildly in the Forties when Ma Joad [in John Ford's *Grapes of Wrath* (1940)] dispensed her populist manifesto" at the end of the film.[43] There were no riots as far as I know and probably no direct political action, yet rousing the rabble seems precisely the point of the final speech in that film. Oddly, the ending has occasionally been attacked as an example of the worst in Hollywood censorship because of the changes it wrought on the John Steinbeck novel.[44] But the novel in fact moves toward a more conservative position than the film: it ends with a starving man, trapped in a flood, being suckled by a woman who has recently given birth.[45] The event plays against any genuine political understanding of the rest of the novel's narrative in two ways: the flood becomes a metaphorical extension of the Depression, retrospectively turning the Depression itself into an uncontrollable force of nature; second, any sense of mass and class is mitigated as a single act of explicitly Christian kindness between two individuals is elevated into the only kind of good the book can recognize. By transposing the "We the People" speech from the novel (taken over almost intact) to the end of the narrative, the film adopts a more militant stance than the novel—a point, as Sarris indicates, not lost on audiences in 1940.

Conspiracy theorists assume such things do not happen because it would not be in the interests of the banks controlling the studios, as the often reprinted article on *Young Mr. Lincoln* from *Cahiers du Cinema* argues.[46] Made just the year before (in 1939), that film is from the same studio, the same executive producer, and the same director as *The Grapes of Wrath*, yet the subject matter of *Young Mr. Lincoln* is by itself enough for *Cahiers* to assert the influence of the banks in promoting the Republican party on film. This in spite of the fact that the New Deal is presented in an almost beatific light in *The Grapes of Wrath*. I do not claim that the 1940 film had the power to move audiences to political action or even to change the manner in which they understood the problems of the nation. But it did (and still does, to a remarkable degree) have the power to move audiences to some sense of their collective unity, which is perhaps a reflection of the difference between the solitary experience of reading a novel and the communal experience of viewing a film.[47] The honor *The Grapes of Wrath* pays to the New Deal in the form of the federal workers camp (presided over by an FDR look-alike) puts the film in the mainstream of American political thought at the time. Yet underlying the stirring quality of the ending is the feeling that these federal programs did not, in fact, accomplish all they set out to do. The shift from passive acceptance in the novel to the film's more militant conclusion nevertheless does offer a way for the emotions of the theater audience to be aroused by sharing the communal nature of the film experience itself.

Gross-out films are looking for a comparably strong response from their audience. A gleeful uninhibitedness is certainly the most striking feature of these films—of both the comedies *and* the horror films—and it also represents their greatest appeal. At their best, these films offer a real sense of exhilaration, not without its disturbing quality, in testing how far they can go, how much they can show without making us turn away, how far they can push the boundaries to provoke a cry of "Oh, gross!" as a sign of approval, an expression of disgust that is pleasurable to call out. A scene in *Fast Times at Ridgemont High* effectively dramatizes this experience. Sean Penn, a drugged-out surfer, has accompanied a biology class he's not actually in on a field trip to a hospital. During the last part of the trip the teacher brings the students into a morgue and shows them a cadaver that has had its chest cut open. One student gets sick, various others want to turn away, and there is a vague suggestion of sadistic pleasure in the teacher's forcing his students to confront this gruesome sight since he keeps escalating how much of the grossness he exposes the students to. Finally, he reaches into the cadaver's chest and lifts out its heart, holding it up in the air for all to see. Most of the class is stunned except for Penn, who with certain amazement and apparent delight, cries out, "Oh, gnarly!" (the California equivalent to "Oh, gross!"). Clearly, this is why he has tagged along on the trip—to see a grossness not normally available to view.

I realize how disturbing this might sound to many readers, especially since the scene, for all its underlying brutality, is intended as comedy. Yet I would like to suggest that the very grossness of these films may in fact be salutary *because of* their willingness to confront things we normally feel compelled to look away from. These films offer a radical challenge to taste and value, but not in the programmatic way of self-consciously avant-garde art that could still make these works acceptable to arbiters of taste and value. They do it simply to make a buck, an aim that helps to define their ideology for the critics of mass culture. Yet I feel that to confuse ideology with economic ambition betrays a misunderstanding of how ideology intersects with aesthetics since similar aesthetic aims can serve differing ideological purposes.

Whatever the ideology—and this is often more varied than the frequently monolithic approaches to mass culture indicate—there is a perceived aesthetic need in Hollywood movies that is perhaps best signaled by our most common term for them, the one that has been most long-lasting. Earlier I cited a review that described audience behavior at the premiere showings of *Public Enemy*. Now consider the ad copy that ran alongside that review:

> *A PICTURE . . .*
> Not only a movie, not only a series of photographs on film. Not merely entertainment, to be forgotten a block from the theater.
> *A PICTURE . . .*
> A history within our history of a world within our world.
> *A PICTURE . . .*
> An unadorned, quivering, unparalleled slice of this life of ours.
> *A MOVING PICTURE . . .*
> That will appall some, thrill some, amaze some; that will anger a few, that will stir all.[48]

There is some contradiction here necessitated by hyperbole: although the first statement tells us this is "not only a movie," the last statement is very emphatic, by means of caps, italics, and underlining, that it is "a *moving* picture." But the statement is not really incoherent since it aims to shift the locus of movement from the screen *to the audience:* we find the movie very moving.

Today's movie audiences have long gotten beyond the wonder of early audiences that motion pictures move, but the term *movies* has remained primary (even over such terms as *film* and *cinema*), not so much because of the movement on the screen, I suspect, as because of the movement they cause *within* us. This is probably nowhere clearer than in the two genres I will consider here because their aims can be defined so simply: to move us to raucous laughter or equally raucous screaming. Henri Bergson has written that "laughter appears to stand in need of an echo."[49] The same is true of screaming. We may scream watching a horror film at home on television or we may let out a real belly laugh watching a comedy, but never as much as in a theater. Horror films and comedies represent preeminently theatrical genres—movies that work best within the context of a crowded theater—because their aesthetic aim *is* rousing rabble.

Chapter 2 *A New Language*

In Hollywood the collective enterprise engaged in making movies is known simply as "the industry." The appellation was perhaps inevitable since the movies, in creating a mass audience on a then unheard of scale, also made money in a way that could not have been previously imagined.[1] Since the Romantic period, the romantic notion of the artist has been that of someone in opposition to the dominant mores of society and adamantly opposed to any monetary motive by the sheer nobility of the calling. In this context, the very profitability of mass art forms has in itself probably been sufficient to render them suspect to guardians of culture.

And yet throughout Western history art that most definitely exists as economic production has been offered to the people for consumption: from the traveling theater troupes of the Roman Empire to the jongleurs, minstrels, and troubadours, to the commedia dell'arte, to the fairs of medieval and Renaissance England with their theatrical spectacles and puppet shows in which were "inserted as many extravagancies, vulgarities and obscenities as the play would accommodate . . . even when the story was drawn from the Bible."[2] The one thing these all have in common is that they represent arts of *performance*, and the most popular of the popular arts have all been performing arts.

High culture could accept performing arts when they could fit its forms, so theater could become acceptable by becoming drama to read. Contrasting the history of the theater with the history of drama in the West, as both are taught and written about, makes apparent the different ways cultural products achieve rank. The history of Western theater (that which is *performed*) presents a continuous flow from the Greeks onward. The history of Western drama (that which is printed and *read*) moves along in bumps and starts, with some gaps lasting for centuries.[3] Performing arts are by nature transitory, disappearing in the very act of performance, and this at least offers a rationale for the privileging of the printed over the performed in the records of Western culture. But the invention of film presented a radical challenge to this preference by its ability to record performance. Film transforms the transitory into the permanent.

Film's durability now makes it possible to begin sketching a *tradition* of performers and performance as no previous age could. But even without a permanent detailed record of such a tradition in the past, I want to stress the underlying continuity in the performing arts because the films considered here do *not* have their roots in a past literary culture that might confer greater respectability on them.[4] Rather, there are far different antecedents and finally a different tradition that can be traced here: for the horror films, possibly the Roman circus and public executions, probably plays performed on fairgrounds,[5] certainly the Elizabethan revenge tragedies and Grand Guignol; for the comedies, the popular forms that have their earliest recorded expression in Aristophanes, then in the burlesques and parodies of the Phlyakes of early Italian popular comedy,[6] to the traveling stage troupes and the theatrical parts of festivities like the Feast of Fools and Midsummer Eve through the clowns, fools, and comic acrobats that filled out the shows of the fairground and traveling circuses.[7]

For most of the forms listed above, money was at least the spur if not the driving force of the art. In the past this did not necessarily make a work of art suspect. In Shakespeare's *Twelfth Night*, for example, Feste the clown earns money through witticism; in fact he sees nothing wrong in charging for each witty remark.[8] While none of the arts and artists mentioned here could approach the scale and economic ambition of film (and I do not wish to minimize the effect that scale could have on the works produced), most nonetheless existed within as precisely a defined economic context as movies have in this century. In the understandable desire to look for what was newest about the new forms of popular culture in the twentieth century, we have tended to overlook what was oldest about them, losing sight of powerful continuities between past performance and present practice.

These are all, in short, art forms that speak in "the language of the marketplace," as Mikhail Bakhtin has described them in *Rabelais and His World*.[9] As Bakhtin uses the term, the marketplace represents a culture that belongs to the people and is set against the Middle Ages' official culture of high seriousness: "The marketplace was the center of all that is unofficial; it enjoyed a certain extraterritoriality. In a world of official order and official ideology, it always remained 'with the people' " (pp. 153–54).

I will have more to say about the oppositional stance Bakhtin finds in art of the marketplace shortly, especially because the kind of grotesquerie Bakhtin analyzes in Rabelais has particular significance for the aesthetics of gross-out. For now the concept of the marketplace is of key importance since it places the economic issues I have been outlining in a different light. The art of the marketplace is the art the people choose by choosing to purchase it, not the art that guardians of the state and culture impose on them. As such, for Bakhtin, it can become a tool for freedom.

By "marketplace" Bakhtin meant an actual geographical location. I use the term in its more extended sense, which demands some qualification since the marketplace today is at the center of the official ideology. How much can I ennoble the marketplace and how much can I locate oppositional strategies within it, when we live in a culture that itself glorifies the marketplace? This is a complex issue, made even more difficult in the age of television when films have in effect become an adjunct of the advertising industry.[10] One perhaps somewhat perverse answer to these questions is to say that the marketplace is *not* in fact at the center of official ideology since the most vocal defenders of the free market inevitably end up seeking controls that will protect their market position. In some ways, the conservative stance taken by Henry James Forman in *Our Movie Made Children* provides a good translation of this economic position into a cultural one since the desire to control the content of films is really a desire to control the free market of films and (as Forman's "like selling whiskey to the Indians" analogy makes clear) explicitly a desire to control the lower classes.

A more compelling answer might explore the complexities of an ideology based on the marketplace. First of all, I should note the radical nature of capitalism, which is not at all concerned with conserving[11] and would probably sell tickets to the spectacle of its own demise.[12] Consider for a moment the brief cycle of student revolt films in the early 1970s. To some degree their oppositional strategies anticipated the films that are the subject of this book. In Robert Mulligan's ironically titled *The Pursuit of Happiness* (1971), for example, Michael Sarrazin, in trouble with the police for no real criminal offense, decides to leave the country because, as he puts it, "There's a nervous breakdown going on out there, and I don't want to be part of it." The apocalyptic sensibility is accompanied by a final image that shows a small airplane carrying the fleeing Sarrazin past the Statue of Liberty, an explicit ironic inversion of the symbol of freedom that once greeted immigrants from foreign tyrannies now greeting an emigrant from domestic tyranny. It *is* possible to see something conservative here, but it is also stated in an oppositional way as an underlying bitterness over the transformation of values, a mourning for the best in American culture that has been lost in our postindustrial bureaucratized world. The rejection of the contemporary world is potently cast as a provocation that inverts the traditional meaning of hallowed symbolism.

Even more extreme, since it presents a direct attack on material culture, is Michelangelo Antonioni's *Zabriskie Point* (1970) with its more explosive apocalypse set off by a sympathetic character to blow all the material wealth of American culture to smithereens. In spite of contretemps over the film's purported anti-Americanism during production and attempts to cut and censor it, the then new president of MGM James Aubrey reported after seeing it, "I put my hands on Michelangelo's shoulders and I said, 'Maestro, that may be the best movie I've seen in my life.' "[13] Neither the critics nor the masses were as enthusiastic, and the whole youth-revolt cycle proved to be short-lived because the public, it turned out, was less interested in movies made from the headlines than in the headlines themselves. But had the individual films proved more successful, as a few other films of revolt finally did,[14] the cycle might have developed into a full-fledged genre. Hollywood executives were primed to welcome gross-out even if it threatened contemporary standards of taste and decorum since selling whatever the market will buy is the most potent ideology governing Hollywood production.[15]

This does mean that those who embrace the marketplace as an ideology necessarily embrace the products of the marketplace. Occasionally, unhappiness over this disparity can surface. When Coca-Cola made David Putnam head Columbia Pictures, they sought someone who could make the product of their motion picture division as reputable as that of their soft drink division. So they handed the reins over to a CEO with a reputation for "quality" (i.e., nonexploitation) product with serious mid-cult ambition. Even so, Coca-Cola hedged its bets by its investment in Tri-Star, which was not under Putnam's direction and offered another area for releasing product Coca-Cola could keep an apparent distance from.[16] None of this worked out well for Putnam, whose respectable films did not do well, or for Coca-Cola, which finally decided to pull out of the movie business entirely. It is easier to keep a respectable reputation with soft drinks. No film company can survive without making at least some films that are disreputable. And there are few films released by major studios as disreputable as the ones I am writing about in this book, so much so that most cannot be shown on TV (or with vast alterations if shown at all). Studios can take pride in the profits of these films, but not in the product.[17]

Without referring to him specifically, Leslie Fiedler has extended Bakhtin's notion of the marketplace into twentieth-century America by proposing that American popular art be viewed as a kind of supermarket that stocks the widest variety of products and brands at a range of prices to appeal to the widest variety of tastes.[18] Fiedler seems to me more on the mark than theoreticians who treat Hollywood cinema as univocal expression.[19]

Andrew Sarris's suggestion to look at the trees rather than the forest of American movies was directed against an earlier generation of sociological critics, but it still needs to be heeded.[20] For example, Tri-Star is the company that released *Rambo: First Blood Part II* (1985), a film that even elicited approval from President Reagan. Within a year this same company was marketing *Head Office* (1986), a sharp comedy about executive life in the fast lane of a multinational conglomerate that manufactures everything from laxatives to antiballistic missiles (with the film suggesting some kind of connection between the two). One of the most thoroughly left-wing comedies to come out of Hollywood in its analysis of the military-industrial complex, the film features as one of its satiric highlights an arms merchant's fashion show with well-oiled Rambo look-alikes modeling the latest in portable machine guns. Decked out with bandoliers and antiaircraft weaponry, they parade up and down a runway to the excited oohs and aahs of prospective buyers from Central American dictator governments. As the grosses made clear, audiences weren't buying this satire of values enshrined in the earlier film, but the same company was nonetheless willing to market both *Rambo* and this anti-*Rambo* in the great crap shoot of movie distribution.[21]

If, as I have been arguing here, there is a long and continuous tradition for popular culture, one that is often in opposition to official culture and ideology, then the disreputable art of movies has an honorable position within that tradition. Part of the problem in understanding this position stems from the relationship of high art to low art, a relationship that often seems to admit no relation. Yet low art often does have direct influences on high art—especially at critical moments in cultural history. The Renaissance presented radical transformations wrought by the use of the vernacular and, coincident with it, the introduction of festive forms of art, both from the marketplace and from festivals.[22] In the Romantic period the *Lieder* of Franz Schubert paid tribute to folk songs,[23] in much the same way that the *Kunstmärchen* of Ludwig Tieck, E. T. A. Hoffmann, Gottfried Keller, and others honored the folk art of fairy tales.[24] The twentieth century has witnessed, in the teens and 1920s, the ascension of jazz into middle-class pop music and, indeed, all the way up into the concert halls of America and Europe, as well as the importation of elements from the circus, commedia dell'arte, the music hall, and vaudeville into "serious" drama in early Soviet theater, and the influence of the movies themselves on "serious" literature throughout the West. Finally, and of key importance to me here, the rise of the youth culture in the 1950s brought with it lower-class rock 'n' roll's displacement of middle-class pop music.

By no means is this an exhaustive listing, yet I think it is enough to suggest more of a continuum rather than a set of oppositions between high and low in the hierarchy of arts. There is less a sense of exclusivity and originality for high art than opponents of pop culture have ever recognized. The continuum that I am suggesting here does not move in two directions, however. Contrary to "trickle down" theories of high culture, works of low culture seem to me more likely to influence what happens on high. If "high" and "low" could be stripped of their evaluative connotations, then I might say "low" is an appropriate term since low culture presents a seemingly bottomless well on which high culture draws whenever it is about to run dry. This process seems to happen more frequently the more elevated high art becomes since it is that much further removed from its original source of nourishment.

Conflation of high and low culture often occurs during periods of change in society at large. At the least, as art arrives at new modes of expression through this conflation, we achieve new ways of looking at ourselves through the mirror of art. Of the movement into the vernacular at the time of Rabelais, Bakhtin writes: "It is possible to place oneself outside one's own language only when an essential historic change of language occurs. Such precisely was the time of Rabelais. And only in such a period was the artistic and ideological radicalism of Rabelasian images made possible" (p. 471).

The advent of the mass media themselves have created a radical change in language in an extended sense of the term. In the process they have created a cultural revolution, a revolution from which the defenders of

older social forms and artistic expression are still reeling. Not coincidentally, a more specific revolution accompanied the rise of gross-out films.
The popular press dubbed it the "sexual revolution," which perhaps reflects the most striking aspect of the change. But to stick solely with that
term would minimize the extent of the social changes through the period,
which I do not want to do. In many ways the development of gross-out
reflects the sudden shifts in perspective that accompanied a move outside
conventions of speech and behavior, a movement toward a greater freedom of expression and thought.

The radical cultural changes that paved the way for the films discussed
in this book can probably be tied to two post–World War II booms: that
in babies, of course, but perhaps even more important, the explosion of
middle-class affluence, in which the American working class suddenly
found itself to be part of the middle class (with UAW members and plumb-
ers often earning far more than many white collar workers).[25] Exempli-
fying Bakhtin's idea that changes in language are central to cultural
changes, startling changes in language throughout this period mirrored
the upward movement of the working classes, especially in the middle-
class appropriation of black lower-class slang. Likewise, language became
freer, more uninhibited, signaling a radical change in what was acceptable
as *public* discourse. Uninhibitedness became a goal in itself in this period,
and not just in freer sexual relations but in more public manifestations:
streaking, public nudity, pornography. And aggressive uninhibitedness is
a key goal of gross-out.

The baby boom spelled another cultural change that quite literally rose
up from below, as teenagers more and more seemed to be taking over
culture at large. By the late 1950s and early 1960s, a number of books had
appeared charting the development of a "teen sub-culture."[26] Concomitant
with the rise of teen culture, and the most obvious expression of it, was,
as I have suggested, the rise of rock 'n' roll. In much of the critical responses to teen culture, as in earlier responses to popular culture in general, there was something of a paranoid quality, a dreaded fear that these
new cultural manifestations would corrupt all that was good and valuable
in culture, or, at any rate, *what was good for the masses.*

In 1963 Fred M. Hechinger, the *New York Times* education editor, and
his wife Grace gave fullest expression to this fear in an apocalyptically
titled *Teen-Age Tyranny,* a tirade against this touted tyranny that blamed
everything from permissive child-rearing to progressive education to the
by-now familiar villain of the culture industry.[27] One of the worst aspects
of teen culture for the Hechingers was the fear of cultural decadence. They

saw teenagers as corrupting unwitting elders with their appalling values. This was made most dreadfully evident for them by the fact that adults had begun to like rock 'n' roll and even to dance the Twist:

> The success of the Twist is a flagrant example of a teen-age fad dominating the adult world. . . . Probably the summit of success came for Joey Dee [a rock 'n' roll singer] when he was asked to play at the fashion industry's Party of the Year, a one-hundred-dollar-a-plate dinner held appropriately at the Metropolitan Museum of Art for the benefit of the museum's Costume Institute. Beside the serene pool and the classic columns, in the shrine of Rembrandt, New York's fashionable adults twisted to the tune of "You Can't Sit Down." (pp. 112–13)

The Hechingers might see a sacrilege in setting the twist against a background of Rembrandt and classic columns, but the models for those classic columns probably witnessed writhing Dionysian rituals that would make these twisting socialites in evening dress seem pretty sedate.[28] The Hechingers' sense of desecration is appropriate nonetheless since it fully registers the sense of radical cultural change taking place in this period.[29]

Language was of central importance in defining the cultural changes. The earliest sign of 1960s campus unrest, beginning at the University of California at Berkeley in 1964, centered on public discourse: the "Free Speech" movement was born out of a student response to the university administration's ban on political organizations using campus property to publicize their causes and recruit new members. The first *New York Times* report on this student revolt bore a striking title: "Berkeley Students *Stage* Sit-In to Protest Curb on Free Speech."[30] As my emphasis indicates, there was something theatrical—indeed, spectacular with its unexpected cast of thousands—in the way the movement presented itself to the public; there was even some official entertainment: Joan Baez was there to sing "We Shall Overcome." Furthermore, "There was an air of festivity accompanying the beginning of the sit-in. The student body at this campus is unusually picturesque in its dress and grooming. The beards and long hair and guitars were much in evidence along the corridors of Sproul Hall. At least one young man came in barefoot."

If free speech could be extended to include modes of dress and appearance, then clearly radical challenges were being issued here. Perhaps most forceful was the notion that it was possible to be serious without being solemn: "festivity" soon became a key mode of action for an entire generation, which seemed to recognize that festival signifies freedom. While politics always has an element of theatricality to it, the real challenge here was that the theater of politics was being co-opted (to use a popular word of the period) and moved in a reverse direction. Theatrical power was being taken by those without power—the barefoot and, as the *Times* reporter wanted us to note, probably the unwashed.

I will have more to say about the Berkeley events in the next chapter. For now, I want to shift the focus back to film and note another free speech movement. I mentioned earlier the theatrical release of *The Killers* and the rerelease of *Psycho*. As this indicated a greater openness about what could be shown on the big screen in public as opposed to the small screen in private, there was a strong movement toward breaking down screen censorship, partly dictated by the shrinking audiences for theatrical movies, but also reflecting changes in society at large. Just how radical these changes were perceived at the time may be seen in a memoir written by Jack Vizzard, who served in the Production Code office from the 1940s on. He entitled one of the chapters covering this period simply, "Götterdämmerung."[31]

Soon after *The Killers* and the *Psycho* reissue, the Code was loosened up. Starting with *Who's Afraid of Virginia Woolf* in 1966 (because playwright Edward Albee's scalding dialogue was left intact for the film), Hollywood began to release movies with the advertised warning, "Suggested for Mature Audiences." Then in 1968 the industry instituted the Ratings System, opening the screen up to far more frankness than the original planners of this system probably anticipated.[32] Initially, at the very least, the Ratings System changed the kind of language that could be heard on the screen, the spoken discourse. But if discourse could be extended to include actions as well as language, the ratings paved the way for other radical changes in acceptable actions.

Liberation of screen violence came first, fairly early in fact with *Psycho* (1960) and *The Birds* (1963). But it really escalated in the late 1960s with the technological development of the spurting blood capsule and its extraordinary—and, for many, excessive—uses in *Bonnie and Clyde* (1967) and *The Wild Bunch* (1969). The early liberation of violence is perhaps not surprising because American movies have always been less inhibited about violence than sex. But these extended scenes of bloodiness that seemed to revel in their own grossness were something new, possibly spurred on by the nightly newscasts of the Vietnam War (which at least is how critics at the time saw it).

As "Make love, not war!" became a popular slogan among college students, a reordering of past priorities moved screen violence ahead of screen sexuality as a cause of concern.[33] Stephen Farber, who at twenty-six was brought onto the Ratings System Board as part of a new student internship program so there could be "some representation of the views of younger people on the board," was especially critical of the board's liberal treatment of violence compared to its moralistic views on sex.[34] He quit within six months, complaining, "Pubic hair and breasts, that's what they're worried about."[35] Farber was especially upset that the board would consistently give softer ratings to films with gory violence, but snap rigidly to attention with a hard rating whenever it flushed out flesh and sniffed suggestiveness. Violence began to be seen increasingly as the real sickness in American culture, with the repressive attitudes toward sexuality as an inevitable neurotic complement. But even if a particular film intended a critical point of view toward violence, its presentation on-screen ran into the problem inherent in the screen's nature as spectacle (a problem I observed in the reception of *Public Enemy*). No matter how critical the framework, no matter how bloody the violence, the very extremity of the violence made it an object of attraction. The strong and contradictory reactions provoked by *Bonnie and Clyde* and *The Wild Bunch* centered on this ambivalence. Were the films condemnations of violence or in fact celebrations?

Aggressively uninhibited sexuality took longer to appear, perhaps because it needed the economic change brought about by the exploitation market in the 1970s. *The Graduate* (1967), *Bob and Carol and Ted and Alice* (1969), and a bit later *Shampoo* (1975) are the landmark sexual comedies of the period, but they have little do to with the comedies discussed in this book because they draw strongly on classier forms of romantic comedy. A pronounced sexual distaste underlies much of *The Graduate*, but this raises matters of subtext I will deal with later. *Bob and Carol and Ted and Alice* moves toward a reaffirmation of something like romantic love, while *Shampoo* ends with a sense of emptiness that it seems to imply is a result of free sexuality. In all three, sexual desire as a value in itself ends up compromised, although all these films were sold to the audience for their sexual content. The ad for *The Graduate* made its central attraction explicit by showing a woman's giant leg completely enclosing a dwarfed student in cap and gown to indicate the film's view of graduation.

Nonetheless, these films look downright polite next to the raucous *Animal House* (1978; aka *National Lampoon's Animal House*) and *Porky's* (1982). The decisive difference is that *Animal House* and *Porky's* draw on different traditions: in no way are these films romantic comedies. The driving force in the other films is still romantic longing. In these films it is quite simply sex. Since conventional Western hierarchies put sex below romance, these films must inevitably seem lower class to their romantic predecessors. This movement downward (a typical strategy of gross-out movies) becomes itself a challenge to hierarchical modes of thought. While never romanticized, the sex in these comedies is rarely just sex plain and simple. Rather, any romantic quality is even further diminished because sex often coincides with a drive for power. This conflation of sex with power gives these films a much higher degree of aggression than even the sexually explicit romantic comedy of the period.

If sex farce is lower class than romantic comedy, I may claim there are hierarchies in culture that parallel hierarchies in class. This is a point elitist critics implicitly recognize when they designate the art works they prefer as "High Culture." There may be some reason to use "high" and "low" as descriptive terms, as was suggested above, but they inevitably end up being evaluative as well. Even within film itself, which is necessarily a lower-class form in relation to "high culture," there are hierarchic divisions traced along genre lines: suspense films are classier than horror films, romantic comedies classier than slapstick. In the past these distinctions were signaled to audiences by performers (bigger name stars appeared in the more respectable genres), higher budgets (providing for a conspicuous consumption of greater production values), and ad campaigns that would stress the quality of the product.[36] These are markers to signal the differences in advance of the film, but there are also differences in manner and content determined by genre.

I have chosen the above pairs of genres because they parallel each other in dramatic goals. Both horror and suspense films aim to generate fear and tension in the audience, while slapstick and romantic comedy strive for laughter, but they go after their similar ends in different ways. From the high perch of an elitist view, the negative definition of the lower works would have it that they are less subtle than higher genres. More positively, it could be said they are more direct. Where lower forms are explicit, higher forms tend to operate more by indirection. Because of this indirection the higher forms are often regarded as being more metaphorical, and consequently more resonant, more open to the exegetical analyses of the academic industry. In fact, lower forms are no less interpretable, but their directness makes metaphoric significance seem secondary to the primary power of the object itself. The primary object can then be enjoyed by the mass audience as a thing in itself, while higher forms prompt a turning outward to extra signification.

It would take me far beyond my argument to explore these differences in manner fully, but I do not want to pass over them lightly because they are more than mere matters of style. By their inferential resonance, higher forms seem to point to a transcendence of the material world into more spiritual realms, while lower forms are more firmly entrenched in the materiality of existence. Generally, criticism in Western culture has valued the former over the latter. Hence the terms *high* and *low* necessarily spell a hierarchy that makes them difficult to employ as purely descriptive.[37] At this point, in any case, I want it to be clear that this preference in fact stakes out an ideological position that sees the spiritual as higher than the material.

In movies at least, a radical shift took place in these distinctions, beginning in the 1970s and going into the 1980s, when genres previously considered exploitation material were given higher budgets and bigger stars. *Psycho* in 1960 provided the earliest warning of this as Alfred Hitchcock began moving toward the horror film (but, significantly, with the lowest-budgeted film of his American career and the least glamorous stars).[38] The greatest initial impact of *Psycho* was on schlock horror movies (notably those from second-tier director William Castle), each of which tried to bill itself as scarier than *Psycho*. Still, the class distinctions in genres pretty much held through the 1960s as Hitchcock's more elegant persona remained the prime influence on such classy films as *Charade* (1963) and *Arabesque* (1966). But by the 1970s the Hitchcock films most imitated were *Psycho* and *The Birds*, the latter a big-budget fantasy-horror film—whereas *Psycho* is the only Hitchcock film to spawn sequels. Typical of the shifts during this period, the first two *Psycho* sequels had bigger budgets and far more elaborate production values than the original film. Starting in the 1970s, then, a striking inversion began to take place in which low-class genres became high-class product—an inversion of values not limited to films.

The ascendancy of the gross-out films in this period is clearly a reflection of this change, but it relates to larger changes in the culture, an elevation of the low that was taking place in various spheres of experience. It is perhaps the movement of the proletariat into the middle classes that made such materially oriented genres possible. Although in greater physical need, the lower classes are not necessarily more concerned with the materiality of the world. Spirituality itself can be a good weapon against physical wants, which is precisely why religion could be deemed the opium of the people. Freedom from want makes it more possible to enjoy the physicality of physical existence. It is perhaps only in a time of comfort that the utopian project of gross-out comedy is possible.[39]

Nonetheless, I think it likely there are important determinants other than the physical comfort of the middle class. For one thing, there seems to be more than a casual connection between the Free Speech movement and the ascension of black slang that is a striking phenomenon of the period. Many of the first people to become active in campus politics had spent summers working in the South in the civil rights movement. A *New York Times* article on Mario Savio, one of the leaders of the Free Speech movement, quoted him on the connection between the two experiences: "I spent the summer in Mississippi. I witnessed tyranny. I saw groups of men in the minority working their will over the majority. Then I came back here and found the university preventing us from collecting money for use there and even stopping us from getting people to go to Mississippi to help."[40]

The development of an oppositional stance toward the dominant culture, then, took place through an identification with the clearly oppressed black lower classes, an identification that enabled the privileged white students to see oppression where they had not noticed it before. Free speech in effect came to mean appreciating the differences of nonnormative forms of speech and moving them outside conventional hierarchies of value.

The Hechingers' fear of teens corrupting American culture at large echoed, covertly, fear of lower-class culture corrupting teens. In deploring rising teenage marriages, they noted, for example, that "modern middle-class America, until very recently, considered early marriage as something of a lower-class phenomenon"(p. 70). Most specifically, they feared the adoption of black lower-class culture, which they viewed paternalistically but nonetheless as clearly inferior: "To many citizens the car is a status symbol. For some of the minority groups, who are tragically denied equal opportunities in housing, the car is the only outward sign of equality. To youth, it is recreation hall, freedom and mobility, front porch and boudoir" (p. 93).

No matter that sudden affluence had made adolescent access to the car possible. The presentation here conflates teens' desires for *auto*mobility with blacks enforced immobility in the class structure. Having come under the sway of black music, twisting the night away, and corrupting adults with their uncontrolled behavior, teens also took over black values in other areas.

The influence of black culture on teen culture returns me to the changes in public discourse through the 1960s and 1970s, most specifically to the ascension of black slang. Along with this elevation came a familiar strategy of black English—the substitution of an opposite meaning whereby bad, for example, and most especially ba-a-a-a-d, quite literally becomes good.[41] This shift in conventional meaning comes from a class that must necessarily see itself as oppositional. One way of addressing the over-whelming power of the class structure is to invert the terminology by which it defines values. This is an important point for understanding gross-out as a value since the very term implies an oppositional stance. *Gross*, as I've demonstrated here, is an adjective appropriate to an elitist view of popular culture—not used as often as *vulgar* but almost synonymous with it. It is congruent with the other shifts I have been discussing, then, that *gross* should come to connote something good, and that *gross-out* (which seemingly has the aim of making the reader/audience feel the grossness in themselves) should transform disgust into pleasure. In a profound way, contradiction is built into the concept of gross-out.

Chapter 3 *Dirty Discourse*

Gross-out films, the products of a period of intense change in acceptable public discourse, redefined and extended that discourse. It is not simply that we can now talk about films of license, while no earlier films would support that appellation. Rather, our notion of license has itself changed as we constantly redraw the boundaries of the permissible. For example, the pre-Seal of Approval period of the early 1930s was fairly free in defining characters' sexual desire. *Wonder Bar*, a Warner Brothers Busby Berkeley film that appeared in 1934 just on the cusp of the Code, includes a cast of homosexuals, lesbians, and mid-Western matrons mating with French gigolos because their husbands are off whoring. To top all this off, it features the dramatic highlight of a sexually motivated murder that takes place on a dance floor and goes unpunished. The Paris setting, itself a place of license in the American mind, sanctions the deviant behavior and inconsequential immorality. Nonetheless, for all the knowledgeable prurience of the material, by comparison to films of the 1970s and 1980s the presentation is indirect. In effect, a sense of discretion becomes part of a discourse on licentious behavior. *Wonder Bar* is a film of license, but license itself was constrained by the manners and mores of the period.

The restrictions on speech enunciated in the Production Code of 1930 offers fine evidence of how cultural expectations may stake out the fence-posts of containment. The section forbidding "profanity" specifies what is outlawed in an alphabetized list that ranges from "alley cat (applied to a woman)" to "whore." The section on "obscenity" states simply "Obscenity in word, gesture, reference, song, joke, or by suggestion (even when likely to be understood only by part of the audience) is forbidden." There is no need here to spell out what is obscene because everyone knows what is and is not offensive in ordinary public discourse. Four decades later, the matter was no longer so simple. Writing in 1970 in response to the radical changes of the recent past, Richard S. Randall, in his book on film censorship, noted, "Obscenity has broken out of its former judicial confines and has done so largely because the judiciary has almost eliminated it as a legal concept."[1] Acceptable public discourse had changed so greatly in this period that obscenity could no longer be defined with an early 1930s certainty.

In pointing out the differences between these two periods, I do not intend that the movies be taken as an exact reflection of real-life behavior. In both Code-restricted films and those produced during later periods of license, there are real differences between how people behaved in private and how fictional characters behaved on the screen. The treatment of bathrooms in Hollywood movies reveals how these differences become encoded. Before the 1960s, the primary reason for entering a bathroom in a movie was to take a bath or a shower, those fixtures offering the merest suggestion of a nudity that could never be shown. *Psycho* sounded the first ominous rumblings of change with the flush heard across the nation when Janet Leigh tried to dispose of some incriminating evidence down a toilet. In showing this action, *Psycho* became the first film, to my knowledge, to provide a close-up of this bathroom fixture in an American movie.

By the beginning of the 1970s, the toilet seemed to replace the tub as the key bathroom fixture. Male stars increasingly entered bathrooms specifically to urinate and could even be seen playing out whole scenes while standing at urinals. Women, for the most part, were more discrete, but, in perhaps the most extreme inversion of Hollywood glamour, Jane Fonda holds a conversation with George Segal in *Fun With Dick and Jane* (1977) while sitting on a toilet with her skirt hiked up over her knees. Responding to the experience of a robbery she has just successfully pulled off with Segal, Fonda expresses her excitement by jabbering nonstop over the whizzing undercurrent of her urine hitting the toilet bowl.

It would be a mistake to regard the discovery of the bowl chiefly as a development in screen realism. For one thing, bathroom experiences in life are most likely to be solitary, which is why they are uninteresting, dramatically speaking. In films, however, a visit to the bathroom inevitably becomes an occasion for dialogue. Two further restrictions on bathroom scenes seem to have cropped up spontaneously, without the kind of formal legislation the Code once required. Both point to an apparent preference for standing up while attending to the needs of the lower body. With an occasional exception like Jane Fonda, the bathroom as a place of elimination seems to belong to men. And elimination itself is generally restricted to urination, while defecation apparently retains the taint of an indecorous activity. All this suggests we are now willing to look at more than we used to, but we do not necessarily want to look at everything.

There is a purpose to these distinctions that has very little to do with issues of realism: however much it may differ from actuality, screen behavior remains of interest because it reveals what a culture thinks may be made public as opposed to what should be kept private. This is a point central to the nature of the discourse I am concerned with here. Since some distinction between public and private behavior is inevitable in any society, looking at where the line is drawn in public discourse can help define the mores of that society. A particularly striking feature in the art of the last couple of decades is the concern with breaking down that distinction between public and private. Most often, dividing lines simply end up elsewhere. Even so, the impulse to move beyond the public-private opposition inevitably changes the terms of public discourse.

A good deal of post–World War II literature set out to tear down the fences, to test the limits of obscenity, particularly in works by "beat" poets and novelists. The culmination of this trend reached back into the past, however, when the Supreme Court in 1959 finally declared D. H. Lawrence's novel *Lady Chatterly's Lover* not obscene, in spite of its abundance of language generally considered precisely that. In all these instances, however, we are dealing with a fairly private discourse, since a work of literature is experienced in isolation. In the 1960s, however, obscenity increasingly became a *public* matter. Four months after the first student sit-in on the Berkeley campus, what the popular press dubbed the "Dirty Words" movement succeeded the Free Speech movement, a shift to the seemingly private chamber of intimate language from the public arena of political rights.

The Dirty Words movement first gained national notice when Clark Kerr, chancellor of the University of California, announced he was resigning his post. A front-page *New York Times* article reported: "For about 10 days, through signs and loudspeakers, some students have argued that they have a right to utter four-letter words not ordinarily used in polite conversation."[2] "Polite conversation" is a key phrase because it implicitly acknowledges there are other forms of conversation, other forms of public discourse. How men by themselves talk in groups has, at least in the past, been radically different from how they talk in the presence of women and children.[3] During the Code period, Hollywood films held to that most restricted form of public discourse—the one that included women and children—but Hollywood was not alone in this. The *Times* itself and other major news organizations covering the Berkeley demonstrations could not report all the news because the words that detonated the dispute were not fit to print. By the next decade, when it became a matter of public record that such deleted expletives frequently cropped up in White House policy discussions as well as on the Berkeley campus, restrictions of public discourse grew sufficiently lax that most of these deleted expletives could turn up (at least in *Time* and *Newsweek* if not in the staid *New York Times* itself, where asterisks continued as the preferred form of expression).

Our expectation of what we may hear and read as part of the public record has radically altered in the last three decades, obliterating distinctions that used to be taken for granted. Kerr's short-lived resignation as chancellor actually turned chiefly on a battle with the regents of the university, but at the time, possibly sensing an easy issue to win agreement on, he suggested the Dirty Words controversy had something to do with his move. He told the *Times* he hoped his "dramatic step" of resigning would end "the continuing and destructive degradation of freedom into license."[4] Kerr could make this distinction with the expectation that most listeners would side with him and freedom, yet the next couple of decades became a period increasingly given to license. I noted in the previous chapter how the loosening of the Production Code began to pave the way for increasingly licentious fare in movie theaters in the 1960s. The consequence of this transformation was soon evident in the supremely theatrical quality of this new Berkeley demonstration, which drew inspiration specifically from the movies. One student in a "campus contest" entered as "Pussy Galore" (a character from the 1964 James Bond movie, *Goldfinger*, based on the Ian Fleming book), "with the result that obscene signs appeared on campus in support of the contestant."[5] The fact that "Pussy Galore" could make the transition from novel to screen provided one of the most notorious examples of the weakening Code at the time.[6]

Initially, the Free Speech movement disassociated itself from the Dirty Words protesters and announced they were "shocked" over the resignation of Kerr. Later, when the original obscene pranksters faced dismissal and suspension, a rally in their support attracted former Free Speech leaders, including Mario Savio, who spoke on their behalf. The disciplinarian response of university officials inadvertently turned obscenity into a political issue. While the Free Speech movement was entirely political in its original aims, the Dirty Words movement, on the surface at least, was something else, but the two seem to have become fused in later perceptions of the events. In Daniel Yankelovich's study of *The New Morality*, he finds the early stages of campus radicalism "most vividly symbolized by the Free Speech Movement at Berkeley. It was just a decade ago that students were demonstrating on the California campus for the right to use four-letter words."[7] This confusion interests me because of the importance it grants the dirty words themselves. In other times, this use of obscenity might have been seen merely as a college prank, however *tasteless.* In the context of Berkeley in the mid-1960s, the uttering of obscenity became inescapably a political act.

This peculiar alliance of politics and obscenity offered enough of a threat to liberal thinking that Clark Kerr vainly tried to reestablish a separation: "Mr. Kerr noted that he had 'fought countless battles for 12 years to increase and preserve freedom within the university,' but he added, that 'the freedom we sought was not license for hardcore pornography.'"[8] The "hardcore pornography" that Kerr evokes here is nothing more than a few four-letter words. Ironically, within four years of this statement, real hardcore pornography would appear on public movie screens just across the Bay in San Francisco. In trying to separate obscenity from the right to free expression, Kerr was fighting a rear-guard action. "Freedom" did become tied to "license" in this period, and the making public of once private areas of experience could eventually be seen as an expression of radical politics.

Almost by accident, a series of Supreme Court decisions through the late 1950s and 1960s helped stake out obscenity as political expression by declaring no work of art obscene unless it was "*utterly* without redeeming social value."[9] Obscenity in effect would be permissible if it could claim social significance. With these guidelines it became possible to find a way even for hardcore pornography.[10] *Sexual Freedom in Denmark* (1969), the first pornographic film to play in a commercial theater in New York City, used the neat trick of presenting itself as a documentary about the legalization of sexually explicit material in Denmark. It gained redeeming social value by being a film *about* pornography, rather than a pornographic film. The distinction mattered little to patrons who were not interested in edification, but it did give the film a legal defense.

I want to cite one other important extension of public discourse because it illuminates this period's insistent connection of dirty words to political meaning. An early *New York Times* article on the Berkeley Free Speech movement compared one of its leaders, Mario Savio, to Mort Sahl for "manner of speech and occasionally hip, occasionally gamey turn of phrase."[11] Lacking Sahl's national reputation, but more aggressively foul-mouthed, Lenny Bruce became for the next generation, when most of the battles over obscenity had been won, one of the key figures of this period. By 1971 Bruce, who had died of a narcotics overdose in 1966 after a series of arrests and trials over his "obscene" performances, had become St. Lenny, Martyr of the Dirty Words. Two plays about him, one off-Broadway, one on, as well as a film biography, all appeared in that one year. A *Time* article on this sudden interest in Bruce set the proper hagiographic tone with a quote from his mother: "A prophet has arrived."[12] In the elevation of Bruce, nonetheless, no one wanted to claim he died to make us dirty. Rather, praise focused on something quite different. The *Time* article also quoted a "music director of a Boston FM station which plays Bruce records often: 'His satire is so relevant. All the things he martyred himself for are hot today.'" Or, put another way, Bruce had *redeeming social importance*—obscenity did not exist for its own sake in his act, but rather provided a means to something higher.

This view of obscenity underwent a further change over the next ten years—after dirty words, or at least some, had become an acceptable part of public discourse. A biography of Bruce written in the mid-1970s claimed, strikingly without much sympathy, that Bruce became obsessed with the redeeming aspects of his performances. As he worked on the defense for his final obscenity trial, "Lenny had to prove his act had redeeming social value; otherwise he would be just another foulmouthed burlesque comic, still a little boy caught in the middle of a dirty act."[13] I myself prefer to grant more to Bruce's claim than does his biographer, and in particular I want to stress the social aspect of Bruce's humor because it points to a contradictory impact on later gross-out films.

Much as the radical transformations worked on public discourse by Bruce and others in the late 1950s and early 1960s paved the way for gross-out, gross-out turned another corner by seeming to attack the whole notion of social value. This is not to say that political content cannot be found in these films—and often fascinating content, as I hope my later discussions will make clear. But it is content that appears in a more submerged fashion, a style Bruce's biographer, with the hindsight of the mid-

1970s, would seem to prefer for Bruce himself. Even if later gross-out turned away from politics, we cannot ignore this aspect of Bruce. Clearly what attracted so much attention for him at his height was the social charge of his material. I can make the distinction between Bruce and later gross-out clear in a fairly simple way: if I were a lawyer trying to make a case for redeeming social value, I would rather defend Lenny Bruce than *The Evil Dead* (1983) or *Hardbodies* (1984).

There is one other point on Bruce's significance for gross-out that I want to note. Together with Mort Sahl, Mel Brooks, Dick Gregory, Shelley Berman, and others, he was known as one of the "sick comics"—comedians who presented aggressively neurotic personas and made comedy out of material once considered taboo, "invit[ing] audiences to laugh at subjects like racial persecution, physical disabilities and mental deformities."[14] The ascent of these comedians parallels the development of the "sick joke" cycles in the period that folklorist Alan Dundes has chronicled.[15] Dundes makes a few remarks about the informants for a study of "dead baby" jokes that are worth mentioning here: "'Oh, how gross!' is a common (and evidently desired) response to a dead baby joke. Informants who were teenagers during the 1960s and 1970s indicate that dead baby jokes were often used in a 'gross out,' in which each participant tries to outdo previous joketellers in recounting unsavory or crude jokes" (p. 3).

Like it or not, and I can well understand reasons for resisting this notion, aesthetic impulses are being outlined here which anticipate later developments in film. Much as joke cycles can extend their communication across the entire nation, jokes represent a more private area of discourse than commercial art, especially if the jokes are of an outrageous nature that would make one cautious about who the listener is. These are jokes teenagers tell each other, not their parents. Gross-out movies transformed this kind of relatively private material into public discourse.

The Free Speech and Dirty Words movements took place at Berkeley in 1965. Lenny Bruce died in 1966. And the turbulent year 1968 proved to be a climactic one for massive student protests and campus riots. Rioting students at Columbia University taunted Tactical Patrol police by chanting words no newspaper could reprint. In this context, the Ratings System, introduced on November 1, 1968, must seem as much a reflection of changes taking place in society at large as it was an economic necessity for the industry to help differentiate theatrical from television films. The ratings offer a convenient way to demarcate changes in public discourse precisely because they categorize limits of what may be acceptable. Even a casual perusal of ratings given over the past few decades gives a fair measure of changes in that discourse. The most clear-cut example of this is the fact that *Midnight Cowboy* earned an X rating when it was first released in 1969; a year-and-a-half later it was rerated, moved down to an R (and it would probably go even further down if resubmitted in today's market). *Summer of '42*, originally an R in 1971, was rerated a simple PG for home-video release. As these shifts indicate, there is no eternal and objective process of valuation that automatically dictates what words call for what ratings, or what parts of the body may be unveiled for which category. The categories change as the social context changes.

Initially, the Ratings Board seemed to want to present itself as operating in a kind of value-neutral way, treating all comers alike. Something happened in 1970 to challenge this notion.[16] A love scene in *Ryan's Daughter* briefly exposed Sarah Miles's breast and the Ratings Board automatically gave the scene an R.[17] MGM, the producing studio, protested: the motivation for the protest was chiefly economic because the film was one of their most expensive releases that year and an R rating would have been overly restrictive in advance for what they hoped would be a blockbuster. The power of MGM and the size of the film's budget was probably not lost on the Ratings Board, although the argument was not presented to them in economic terms. Rather, MGM claimed, this was a serious artistic work, there was nothing leering about the brief nudity, and it was necessary to the artistic integrity of the film. MGM won its appeal.

Artistic integrity, discretion, ambition, and a film's budget (but only covertly)—in a word, "class"—entered the decision-making process in determining ratings. I am especially interested in tying the ratings not just to the change in discourse but also to the class sense that is connected to that discourse because it is in both perspectives that the ratings are important for the two kinds of films being considered in this book. An R rating is pretty much a prerequisite of gross-out, both for the comedies and the horror films, and in both genres there seems to have been something of an escalation. Where *Animal House* was a benchmark in raunchiness in 1978, it was far outstripped by *Porky's* just a few years later.

It wasn't just the explicit content of these films that gained them their restricted ratings. It was also a matter of manner, a clear-cut appeal to grossness that marked them as lower class. On this class issue Lenny Bruce's career offers a striking parallel. As has been noted, Bruce is generally grouped with a whole generation of "sick" comedians, but at the time he was the one most often singled out for persecution and prosecution. Bruce's material could go to further extremes than many of his colleagues, yet I suspect it was his manner that made him most disturbing. He was abrasive, aggressive, and decidedly lower class. His most extensive training ground proved to be cheap "burlesque bars" on the West

Coast, and even in moving up to more respectable venues like Town Hall and Carnegie Hall he never cut off his roots in humor aimed at lower-class patrons. More particularly, Bruce felt a close alliance to the black jazz musicians who shared the bill in the clubs he played, and in a way the free-form, improvisational style of his monologues invokes jazz. The aggressiveness of Bruce's lower-class stance and his connection to black culture probably has something to do with his becoming "the hero of the emergent youth culture."[18] Had Bruce stuck to the dives where he had originally gained popularity, he probably would have escaped his later notoriety.

After World War II, consumers of youth culture attending elite schools themselves reflected a class shift not unlike that of Bruce. There was a strong transformation in the demographics of college campuses in the postwar period; no longer chiefly the elite, these students were increasingly the sons and daughters of the working and middle classes. This new elite announced itself by appropriating black slang and addressing those in authority with the language of the gutter. It was in the context of this class ascent that Bruce brought his lower-class material up with him and that caused him trouble, but a decade later the changing cultural milieu would make this conflation of aesthetic classes more commonplace.

In films, the class issues can become fairly confused because budgets inevitably determine the classiness of a project. They also help suggest what the hoped-for rating might be because each more restricted rating limits the potential gross that can be recouped to cover the budget. When some of the imagery familiar from gross-out horror films turned up in 1984's *Indiana Jones and the Temple of Doom* in the form of a gross open-heart surgery performed without instruments or anesthetics on a living patient, the Ratings Board compliantly gave a PG to this super high-budget film with glossy production values. This also turned out to be one of the Ratings Board's biggest goofs: the uproar from disturbed parents who had brought young children to the film eventually led to the establishment of the PG-13 category ("Parents Strongly Cautioned"), a neat catchall for borderline films, especially when questions of budget and class are involved. The gross-out comedies and horror films, on the other hand, are almost always by definition low-class since their appeal is to what is openly announced as grossness.

In charting the changes in public discourse that these films represent and in trying to connect this to political and social changes in the period, I want to suggest a way of looking at gross-out as something other than proof of America's cultural decadence. In fact, I would argue there is something creative in the desire to break down inhibitions, to move away from the repressions of our traditional society, all during a time of powerful liberation movements in general: the civil rights movement, women's liberation, gay liberation, rights for the elderly or the disabled, new and open concern for protecting abused spouses and children. Through all these movements, there is an underlying intent to make the private public property, to bring out into the open "closeted" prejudices as a way to destroy them. At the least, gross-out also functions as a way of bringing out into the open precisely those things we have most been inclined to repress.

I may seem here to be approaching these works from sociological and policy perspectives that might give them a veneer of "redeeming social value", but I do not really want to turn them into "prudent" art, to strip them of their exhilarating trashiness just to demonstrate they really do serve a social good. I simply want to stress their connection to a larger discourse. Furthermore, there is an aesthetic dimension to these issues that is significant in itself and takes these works as something more than evidence of a decline into total vulgarity. Without ever losing sight of that vulgarity, venerating it in fact, I want to tie gross-out more directly to past traditions. The most positive way I can view these films is to note they offer evidence that Hollywood—for the first time in its history—has reached a level of explicitness on scatological and sexual matters that makes it possible to film adaptations of Rabelais and Aristophanes. That no one has done so yet is not so much a matter of impropriety as of the inevitable confusion between the seemingly high and the seemingly low, since the preservation of what was low in the past often becomes part of the high culture.[19] This transformation of the once low to the high offers a way of understanding the value in gross-out films by recognizing the value in the vulgarity of older, now more accepted works.

In *Rabelais and His World*, Mikhail Bakhtin points to a tradition of "grotesque realism" that he feels finds its fullest development in Rabelais. After this, it pretty much disappeared from most formal literature with the advent of the very different Romantic understanding of the grotesque: "the tradition of the grotesque is not entirely extinct: it continues to live and to struggle for its existence in the lower canonical genres (comedy, satire, fable) and especially in non-canonical genres (in the novel, in a special form of popular dialogue, in burlesque). Humor also goes on living on the popular stage."[20]

As Bakhtin invokes the popular stage here, I am tempted to add almost the whole of movies, certainly Hollywood movies, to his list, and most of all gross-out movies, the most noncanonical of noncanonical forms. Gross-out films have a good deal in common with Bakhtin's idea of "grotesque realism":

> The essential principle of grotesque realism is degradation, that is, the lowering of all that is high, spiritual, ideal, abstract; it is a transfer to the material level, to the sphere of earth and body in their indissoluble unity. . . . The people's laughter which characterized all forms of grotesque realism from immemorial times was linked with bodily lower stratums. Laughter degrades and materializes. (pp. 19–20)

Earlier I had suggested the emphatic physicality of physical existence that these films embrace. Now, in light of Bakhtin's remarks, I want to consider this physicality as a deliberate reversal, an intentional lowering of the high and the spiritual.

Much as these films draw on noncanonical traditions, they also embody challenges to commonplace modes of thought, seeing the body in a hierarchical manner that parallels the hierarchies of genre I discussed in chapter 2. Official culture sees the high, the "noblest" aspects of experience (mind and spirit) as superior to the low, the body in its most grossly physical terms (the mouth, the genitals, the anus). But Bakhtin believes it is precisely the point of grotesque art before the Romantic period to level this hierarchy by reversing it, by elevating the "material bodily lower stratum." In the process "the essential topographical element of the bodily hierarchy turn[s] upside down: the lower stratum replaces the upper stratum" (p. 309). In this reversal, the physical asserts itself over the spiritual and presses its demands to be placed at the top of the hierarchy.[21]

A similar reversal began to emerge in American culture in the 1950s. The Ratings System of 1968 came about because films in the late 1950s and early 1960s were increasingly pressing against the constraints of the Code. Initially this meant loosening up restrictions on such topics as drug addiction and miscegenation, but the lower body eventually became the key area in which the battleground was fought. As the age of the Hollywood audience went down (made up increasingly of high school and college age students), Hollywood movies moved down the body. But in American culture the elevation of the lower body really begins with rock 'n' roll, *the* art form for American youth. In the 1950s, Elvis Presley's gyrations earned him the name "Elvis the Pelvis," but the pelvis was itself subject to censorship. When Presley appeared on "The Ed Sullivan Show" in 1956, TV's watchdogs decided he should be seen only from the waist up.[22] To witness the pelvis in full action, you had to go to movie theaters. Movie theaters increasingly became the arena in which to celebrate the lower body.

The reversal Bakhtin finds in Rabelais (a reversal Hollywood movies increasingly embraced in the 1970s) suggests a radical challenge I can make most apparent by reworking Bakhtin's notion in Freudian terms.[23] I realize the arguments of both Bakhtin and Freud are too complex to force an exact fit, so I do not intend the Freudian terms to act as psychological analogues of Bakhtin. But Freud is close enough to Bakhtin in one striking regard: he elevates the low by seeing the physical drives of the body as primary. The demands of the libido, not of the divine spirit, are the driving force of existence.

As the libido is always doomed to disappointment, the demands it makes must be tempered through repression. "Where id was, there must ego be," is one of Freud's most concise—and for that reason most quoted—formulations.[24] And ego must be there since civilization itself is built on these repressions. Because Bakhtin's concept of the grotesque reverses this formulation by asserting the ascendancy of the body, it in effect offers a challenge to the very foundations of civilization. For this reason it is at least understandable why works that aggressively elevate the low may be regarded as dangerous since in Freudian terms they celebrate the return of the repressed. In a sense these works are dangerous to the ways we think of ourselves as civilized people.

As Freud sees the lower bodily stratum repressed for the advance of civilization, Bakhtin charts something of a parallel repression in the post-Renaissance view of Rabelais. In particular, the understanding of laughter itself changed. Bakhtin sees a "reduced" form of laughter taking hold of official culture from the Romantic period on: "laughter was cut down to cold humor, irony, sarcasm. It ceased to be a joyful and triumphant hilarity. Its positive regenerating power was reduced to a minimum" (p. 38).

Rabelais in particular and the grotesque in general came to be understood chiefly as satire. This might make such works more acceptable because satire irretrievably transforms the celebratory and challenging aspects of the grotesque into the tendentious. In the process, laughter gains a sense of purpose which serves the social good. However extreme, Rabelais's fancies turned out to produce prudent works after all. This is not to say that satire itself does not offer up challenges. Clearly it does, but the challenges benefit society since they offer a corrective to behavior the satirist views negatively. Grotesque humor as Bakhtin defines it is both less purposeful but ultimately more radical.

The movement to the Romantic period with its "reduced" forms of laughter offers a mirror inversion of the historical process I have described in charting the growth of gross-out. The earliest products of the new "sick" sensibility were valued for their tendentiousness, the redeeming value that could gain them the imprimatur of the Supreme Court. Later works, content to move into a realm of pure fancy, have been commensurately devalued because of that. Consequent to the development charted by Bakhtin, twentieth-century views of laughter see chiefly a kind of corrective. As a consequence we generally elevate comic modes like satire and irony over farce and ribaldry. This reduced notion of laughter dominates much Western thinking, providing the foundation for the different but complementary theories of laughter put forth by Henri Bergson and Freud, the two most influential writers on the subject.[25] The emergence of gross-out in the 1970s and the 1980s challenges this dominance. It suggests other ways of looking at laughter—and, for my purposes here, terror as well. The advent of our own dirty discourse has enabled us to reestablish ties to a repressed tradition of vulgar art.

Chapter 4 **The Greater Tradition**

Both Bergson and Freud considered laughter chiefly in terms of its purpose. For Bergson the emphasis is on the social, with the stability of society as a whole the aim of laughter. For Freud the emphasis is on the biological individual, with the aim much like other biological mechanisms—screaming, for example—of maintaining a balance in "the economy of the soul." Although Freud discusses different kinds of humor, he privileges "tendentious wit," chiefly, I suspect, because it is easiest to talk about goals when the *targets* are always clear. Paralleling this, Bergson most of all privileges social satire. A wide range of laughter is necessarily left out of these discussions because it cannot be made to fit their teleologies. Looking at laughter in terms of a teleology inevitably leads to a reduced understanding of it, much as the transformation of art into education leads to a reduction. In this chapter I want to reclaim some of the losses that take place in the face of these reductions. It is precisely what is lost that most clearly defines the aesthetics of gross-out.

There is a great tradition of vital art generally decried for its vulgarity if it is noticed at all. Occasionally, official culture takes up works previously embraced by the masses, but when this happens what had signified their mass appeal somehow vanishes. Although Charles Dickens achieved an early and extraordinary popularity, it took a good deal longer for his stature as a writer to be acknowledged. And even then, critical reception transformed his work to make him great *in spite of* his sentimentality. "In Dickens," Dwight MacDonald cautions, "superb comedy alternates with bathetic sentimentality, great descriptive prose with the most vulgar kind of theatricality."[1] What a nineteenth-century audience might have been seen as a key reason for reading these novels becomes something for us to overlook. We, of course, possess discriminatory sensibilities the masses are incapable of, even though the masses probably did discriminate in favor of Dickens's "sentimentality." By throwing out those qualities that made the novels most appealing to their audience, we can congratulate ourselves on our ability to locate the "true" merit of these works. This is a kind of "discrimination" as conformist in its aims as the mass audience it deplores is supposed to be.

"Sentimentality" is not much of an issue with gross-out films, of course, and placed next to their raucous vulgarity, Dickens must seem a writer of extraordinary gentility and restraint. More often lost in the critical transformations of popular art is the "bodily lower stratum." Although I feel there is a tradition of art intended for the *vulgus* that critical discourse inevitably overlooks, my concern in this chapter is not to establish that tradition by setting necessary criteria for inclusion or pointing to processes of transmission. Rather, to make visible the kinds of critical blind spots around popular art, I want to consider a number of instances of art once decried as vulgar but ultimately embraced by elite culture.

I recognize an element of arbitrariness in my selection, but I hope it will be seen as a deliberate arbitrariness: I want to range freely across centuries to suggest the extensiveness of what I am writing about, as I also want to suggest that none of these works and authors are isolated examples. While many substitutes are available, my selection does have a deliberateness nonetheless. I have chosen examples from the past whose content reveals a connection to gross-out films. Further, I have chosen examples from theater and painting rather than from prose fiction because theater and painting involve elements of spectacle that align them with film. As I suggested earlier, the root of most movie-bashing lies in suspicions about the value of spectacle in itself. Finally, in all instances, the high culture that determines their values ends up reducing the power of these works.

Three of the eleven extant plays of Aristophanes use names of animals for their titles (*The Wasps, The Birds, The Frogs*)—appropriately, because the plays are filled with a sense of animality. With their abundance of obscene sexual and scatological jokes, they present a joyous insistence on the "bodily lower stratum." This obscenity is essential to any experience of these plays, yet criticism has tended to treat it otherwise. Writing in 1975 (in a book aptly titled *The Maculate Muse*), Greek scholar Jeffrey Henderson noted: "Obscene humor has always been something of an embarrassment to writers on ancient comedy. . . . To this day there has been no study that attempts comprehensively to elucidate, evaluate, or even to discuss the nature and function of sexual and scatological language in Attic Comedy."[2] It is itself symptomatic of the period I am discussing here that a book centrally concerned with obscenity in Aristophanes should appear in the mid-1970s.[3] The spur of the Dirty Words movement and the subsequent changing public discourse provided the atmosphere in which obscenity could be interesting in itself, not as an adjunct to something else.[4]

In chapter 3, I discussed how the political value became related to obscenity in the early 1960s. This association might have grown attenuated later on, but even stripped of the direct satiric intent of a Lenny Bruce, obscenity can still carry an implicit political charge. In their challenge to the proprieties of public discourse, dirty words are overtly liberationist in their intent. During the Vietnam era Aristophanes' *Lysistrata* became one of the most frequently revived ancient plays, but not just because of its strong antiwar message.[5] Rather, its distinctive combination of antiwar sentiment with its riotously explicit sexuality gave it a special resonance for the period. It was timely all over again because it conjoined the liberationist politics of opposition with two other important liberations: the women's movement and the changing public discourse on the body, a discourse that insistently made public what bourgeois culture had previously kept private.

As a way of explaining its specific use in Aristophanes, Henderson has something to say on the use of obscenity in general that is central to the changing public discourse I discussed in the previous chapter: "to utter one of numerous words, to be found in any language, which openly (noneuphemistically) describe the tabooed organs or actions is tantamount to exposing what should be hidden. Our ability to expose the forbidden by using words gives these words a kind of magical power" (p. 2).

This sense of power, magical or otherwise, was unmistakable for both the Berkeley students behind the Dirty Words movement and Lenny Bruce. There is a similar power of aggression in the gross-out films that try to take public discourse into noneuphemistic directions. Occasionally

politics can be specifically invoked in these films (as in the epilogue to
Animal House), but most often this is not the case. Nonetheless, the aggressive "exposing what should be hidden" is always implicitly a political
act because it threatens the social order by contesting proper social behavior. Challenging what constitutes acceptable public discourse, which
is the key to the aesthetics of gross-out, inevitably carries with it deeper
challenges.

The bawdiness of Aristophanes has always been recognized (after all,
how could it be ignored?), but recognized in a way that in effect minimized
its significance and toned down the *riotous* fun of these plays. Earlier
critics generally lamented the obscenity, while more recent commentators,
keeping pace with the changing public discourse, have been more appreciative. Nonetheless, both groups have ended up making it a secondary attribute of the plays.[6] By insisting on the obscenity of these plays, I
am not trying to be a kind of smut sleuth, like a teenage boy looking up
"dirty" passages in a racy book. I am not focusing on prurient details at
the expense of an aesthetic whole. Rather, the distortions to these plays
more often moves in the other direction, with obscenity displaced from
its central position. Henderson notes: "The obscenity of Aristophanes is
almost always integrally connected with the main themes of the plays; it
is an important part of the stage action, the development of the plots, and
the characterizations of personae, and can no more readily be excised
from the plays than can any other major dramatic or poetic ingredients"
(p. x). The vulgar mass audience seems to understand the point better
than the critics. That, at least, seems implicit in the delight scholars take
in pointing out how thrill-seeking audiences will be disappointed by Aristophanes, even though *Lysistrata* keeps on being performed for precisely those thrills.[7]

Switching to matter appropriate to the horror films, I am going to make
a grand historical leap to the Renaissance and a change of venue from
theater to painting. In particular, I want to look at a painting by Caravaggio, *Judith and Holofernes* (ca. 1599), popular subject matter mentioned
earlier (chap. 2, note 5) in describing the theater of the English fairground.
The poster for the play (showing Judith beside the decapitated Holofernes) presents the same gruesome event that Caravaggio pictures—clearly
the main attraction of the story. As sensationalistic as the poster is, however, the act has already taken place. Caravaggio's painting moves to a
more extreme expression as it presents the actual moment of decapitation.
The violence, this severing from the lower body, is the most riveting feature of the painting, but it cannot be separated from the way the body
itself is depicted.

Before looking at this painting more closely, I want to pause briefly to consider the lower body in painting around the time of Caravaggio. Specifically, I have in mind Leo Steinberg's *The Sexuality of Christ in Renaissance Art and in Modern Oblivion*, which deals with a repression analogous to the repressions I am charting here. Steinberg begins his monograph by reinstating the lower body to a position of importance:

> The first necessity is to admit a long-suppressed matter of fact: that Renaissance art, both north and south of the Alps, produced a large body of devotional imagery in which the genitalia of the Christ Child, or of the dead Christ, receive such demonstrative emphasis that one must recognize an *ostentatio genitalium* comparable to the canonic *ostentatio vulnerum*, the showing forth of the wounds. . . . All of which has been overlooked for half a millennium.[8]

That it should finally be noticed and analyzed in 1983 after such a long silence is further evidence of concerns of our own time. Steinberg himself resolutely refuses any psychological speculations on this aspect of Renaissance painting, which is to say he declines to make it fully of our time.[9]

Probably with good reason because his central concern is to understand how the painters themselves viewed their subject matter, and this necessarily leads him into a theological explanation that is of some relevance here. Steinberg regards " 'incarnational theology' [as] characteristic of Renaissance thought," so that these works are precisely concerned with defining the "humanation" of Christ. To do so they had to present a Christ human in all his parts. In explaining this, Steinberg describes a hierarchical view of the body that parallels Bakhtin, although to different end:

> the conspicuous display of the privates, instead of resulting incidentally from the Child's total nudity, is more likely the motive that promoted this nudity. And the initial impulse must have derived from that pervasive medieval metaphor which localized Christ's divine nature symbolically in his upper body, his manhood beneath the girdle. The body assumed by the godhead was a hierarchic system, like the macrocosm itself. (p. 27)

Unlike the folk traditions that Bakhtin describes, here the hierarchy is maintained at the same time that the lower body is nonetheless venerated. The world of the spirit remains on a higher plane, but the grosser aspects of physical existence are treated in a celebratory way as human corporeal form is itself made miraculous.

The disturbed and disturbing vision of Caravaggio moves in a very different direction. Much of the power of *Judith and Holofernes* derives not just from the naturalistic presentation of the figures, although this is one of the familiar goals of Renaissance art and a feature for which Caravaggio is now justly praised. More to the point, I think, is the sheer power of the figure's physicality, a forceful physicality that honors the body at the very moment of its desecration. And it is possibly this gross physicality with no redeeming spirituality, only a kind of horror of all that flesh is heir to, that made Caravaggio seem vulgar to accepted taste until this century.[10] Caravaggio's stock has risen in the twentieth century, yet even reappraisal and higher valuation can involve certain denials.

When the Metropolitan Museum of Art in New York presented *The Age of Caravaggio* in 1985, it featured *Judith and Holofernes* as one of the posters made up for the vulgar exploitation of the paintings. The *vulgus* in this case, however, was predictably a more elite group than those that regularly view gross-out horror movies, so the resultant poster might have been more accurately named *Judith and Her Nurse*—because Holofernes was nowhere to be seen. The Metropolitan had taken the unusual step of reproducing only a detail of this painting (namely, the right half), so that the reaction to the horror was shown without the actual horror!

This bit of institutional censorship was no doubt economically necessary: one of Caravaggio's most powerful paintings rated a poster, but while wild teenage boys might like to cover their bedroom walls with bizarre and unsettling images from horror movies, Met patrons are not as likely to want a brutal execution complete with spurting blood adorning their living rooms. The motive for this tasteful execution of Caravaggio's painting may have been aesthetic as well as economic. At the least, there is a kind of critical statement made in severing the right half of the painting from the left. It weights the value of the painting toward the characters who react and pull away from the action. By concentrating on the psychology of the two reactive characters, the poster moves the painting toward the spiritual and away from the grossly physical.

This, of course, is merely a poster, and too much should not be made of it. Yet the substantial and scholarly article on this painting by Mina Gregori in the book published for the exhibition takes a similar strategy. She focuses far more descriptive attention on Judith and the nurse rather than Holofernes himself, and relates the extraordinary immediacy of the action to a genre convention, which serves to minimize it.[11] Finally, for all the work's power, she criticizes it in ways that should be familiar by now, setting the *merely* physical against the spiritual, which is never mere, and finding the work wanting because it does not have enough of the latter: Caravaggio "portrays . . . mere physical cruelty. Subjective implications, the artist's identification with the suffering of the victim, his stoic conception of grief—all this is absent" (p. 256). This is to say, the work is deficient because there is nothing that might give it spiritual value.

Such criticism is undoubtedly an attempt to make truly horrifying art defensible by praising its most easily defined virtues and censuring or censoring what is most disturbing about it. But praise is bought at the price of presenting literally half the picture. How many of us would feel entirely comfortable trying to explain what is *appealing* about the left half of that painting (as I shall try to explain the appeal of comparably gruesome scenes in horror films)? Most of us would probably be more at ease trying to locate quality in the right half. And yet the painting itself never really allows us such ease. Because Holofernes' head, as it is coming free of its torso, is actually moving into the center of the painting, pulled there by Judith's muscular arm, the greatest structural tension in the painting can be felt around the head. Much as we might want to look away, the centrality of the head being pulled into the safe right half, the tension in Judith's arm, the great spurt of blood, all these keep returning our eyes precisely to that which most disturbs our vision. In a sense, the postures of Judith and the nurse reflect our own state. Leaning back, they are trying to move away from this vision. Yet as Judith herself leans back, she is progressively pulling the head from its body, so that the motion of recoil brings with it the object that prompts the recoil.

It was possible to make up a poster of only the right half, but what of the opposite? What if there were no right half? We would, I think, be all the more likely then to cry out "Monstrous!" because we are offered no escape, no acknowledgment from the artist that our feelings are perceived and to some degree shared by him. Even if we succeed in looking away, as the Met poster and Gregori's description help us to do, I do not think we can forget that Caravaggio had to paint that left half, to confront the attraction implicit in the labor, in order to arrive at the expression of revulsion in the right half. Nor do I think we should forget, as we study the reactions of Judith and her nurse, that Judith had to commit the decapitation in order to shrink back from it. We might seek out denials that sever reaction from action, but the entire painting keeps pointing to a complicity that undercuts every denial we might try to make. The grossness is perhaps the key element in the painting's greatness.

Finally, I want to move on to film itself. Because of film's idiosyncratic conjoining of narrative and spectacle, I can most fully explore how much is lost when the vulgarity of a work is denied. Charlie Chaplin is my concern because the vulgar sources of his material are generally recognized—although usually just to point out how much he transcends them. As with Aristophanes, the vulgarity is often acknowledged in order to be dismissed. Chaplin is most often praised for his abilities as a mime, his pathos, his subtlety of expression, his humanism, and, whenever the comedy is addressed specifically, his satire. As far as I know, no one has ever thought to praise him for the *anality* of his humor. Something that touches on this might be mentioned in passing, but always in a way that ends up containing it. Anality is simply not regarded as fit for praise, certainly not to be made central to Chaplin's art. In effect, there is a kind of censoring here of what Bakhtin calls "the lower bodily stratum." This represents an astonishing distortion of Chaplin's films.

Consider the following scene from *City Lights* (1931): Charlie is visiting for the first time the home of a poor blind girl, whom he has met on the city streets where she was selling flowers, her meager means of earning a living. Because she has mistaken him for a handsome millionaire, Charlie tries to live up to the image she has formed of him by demonstrating his largess with the gift of grocery, including among other things a naked, fleshy goose that he tries to describe for her. One oddity I should mention in passing: since this is a silent film, Charlie inevitably describes things for the blind girl by means of mime, so there is paradoxically a suggestion that the girl has some power of sight. Importantly here it comes up in regard to the plucked goose, anticipating the denuding of Charlie that is soon to follow. I am not sure how much of this to ascribe to conscious intent on Chaplin's part, but the use of mime here nicely serves to underscore much of the tension in the scene between Charlie and the blind girl—the danger that she will be able to see him for the tramp he actually is rather than the millionaire she pictures him to be.

Appropriately, then, the central action in the scene revolves around an uncovering. As they sit down to talk, the blind girl asks Charlie if he will help her roll up a skein of yarn. As Charlie obligingly holds the wool, she inadvertently takes hold of a thread from his underclothes and winds that up instead. Too embarrassed to point out what is happening, Charlie allows the accidental unraveling to take place. Wiggling his hips back and forth to allow free movement of the thread and glancing down in dismay at his crotch, Charlie makes clear as can be, short of actual nudity, exactly what is being exposed.[12] Nonetheless, one critic who has written quite extensively and with great admiration on Chaplin has the blind girl unraveling Charlie's *undershirt*, thereby neatly censoring out the "lower bodily stratum" and most of the comic force of this scene.[13] The fear of exposure exists in all of Charlie's scenes with the girl, culminating in his actual exposure in the famous last scene when the girl's restored sight finally allows her to see Charlie for what he is. The earlier scene of unraveling has already specified and established the nature of that exposure by casting it in terms of the lower body.

This is not an incidental detail any more than the obscenity in Aristophanes is incidental detail. The sexual innuendo in *City Lights* deserves to be foregrounded because it has been so generally ignored in the past. But without the sexual content the film would be incoherent since Charlie in this film (in fact in all his films) rarely doubts himself in *social* terms. Indeed, the chief point of his seedy but upper-class costume (complete with the dandy affectation of the cane) is that he sees himself as superior to all other society, and, for the most part, he makes us the audience accept that view of him. For the fear of exposure to make sense here, it must be presented in sexual terms—for it is only in sexual terms that Charlie can be made to feel inferior. The sexual imagery in the unraveling scene's emphatic pointing to the lower body is something far more important to the film than a simple bit of titillation thrown to the *vulgus* to insure Chaplin's popularity. In fact, this "vulgar" humor both informs and forms the entire film through a richly articulated complex of sexual imagery.

The misunderstanding over this particular scene might be, appropriately, a blind spot, a lack of local insight that overlooks the connection between sight and sexuality the film is making here. Still, there are other instances in which the comedy of *City Lights* has been distorted and turned to "reduced forms of laughter," in order to make it more acceptable to dominant critical standards and take it out of the realm of "vulgar" comedy. I want to look briefly at the opening scene—the public dedication of a grotesquely monumental statue on which Charlie is discovered to be asleep—because it is one of the funniest set pieces in all Chaplin and, as such, one of the most frequently commented on. The critical commentary generally honors the scene for its satire, but if you come to the film from reading texts on it, the most striking thing about it is in fact the slightness of the satire.[14] Not that the scene *isn't* satirical, but next to, say, Swift, Shaw, or Brecht, it is pretty weak stuff, hardly the thing that I would want to base any claims for Chaplin's art on. Besides, I doubt that even the sharpest satire could ever produce the kind of belly laughs you get here, rumbling forth from the lower body into convulsions that go far beyond the more intellectual appeal of satire. *Belly* laughs are the appropriate response because what *is* very powerful about the scene, hilariously so, is the raucously insistent lower body imagery.

In a large public square, a statue to "Peace and Prosperity" is about to be unveiled. After a couple of pompous speeches by public figures (quacks and squawks on the soundtrack), the film's first image of uncovering occurs. A great black cloth rises to display a grouping of figures in the early 1930s monumentalist style—a seated woman in the center (is she peace or prosperity?)—surrounded by reclining male figures.[15] But more is revealed than the statue, for Charlie has apparently taken refuge here for the night: he is discovered asleep in a fetal position in the lap of the seated female. Whether peace or prosperity, she is clearly beneficent, although once revealed, she can no longer protect Charlie. Awakened by the uproar of the respectable gathering, he must emerge from this womb. The climb down sets his troubles in motion as it is interfered with by another figure in the grouping, a reclining male with an upended sword. There is—unfortunately or is it functional?—a hole in Charlie's trousers directly over his anus, and through this hole he is impaled on the erect sword. At one point during his struggles to free himself, the national anthem is played, which compels him to stand rigidly at attention until he can resume his struggle.

When he finally escapes from his impalement, he briefly sits on the head of the reclining male statue so that his anus fits directly onto the man's nose, a nice echo of the sword but also appropriate, albeit unconscious, revenge for it. Leaving this figure, he accidentally, although perhaps again with some unconscious intent, steps in the marble man's crotch. He tips his hat as if to excuse himself, but then as he leaves, he looks at his foot with a grimace, like someone who has just stepped in dog shit. He seems concerned that something might have rubbed off on his shoe. There is in fact a confusion around this action that is typical of Charlie: he had actually stepped in the crotch with his left foot, but then looked at his right as if that were the offending foot. Because the revenge against the phallic penetration of the statue must seem accidental, Charlie distances himself from the agent of his own aggression, suspecting that the passive foot is the one that was contaminated by what the active foot stepped in. One last accidental aggression occurs while he talks to a public official about how to get down: he places his face against an outstretched marble hand that brings about an unexpected "Kiss my ass" gesture. If all this anal and genital imagery represents satire, it is hard to see exactly what is being satirized. Something else is going on here, and quite insistently so.

It might be enough for my purposes here to limit my discussion to this scene alone because it is so insistent about something that has just as insistently been ignored in writing on Chaplin. Nonetheless, the raucous lower body imagery that informs all the comedy of this scene takes on a retrospective resonance from the rest of the film. What I want to stress here is why the scene with its emphasis on womb, anus, and genitals should be at the beginning of the film. This seems to me an especially problematic matter for criticism that sees the scene primarily as satire. Usually some attempt is made to relate it to the scenes with the millionaire since some social satire can be read into those sections of the film, but to do so effectively weakens the force of the opening. As the satire provides tepid laughter, it also carries little emotional resonance. If, in place of a focus on satire, the sexual imagery moves into the comic center, if the vulgar humor becomes the lens of Chaplin's vision, the scene has great importance for the rest of the film.

I can get at this most fully by looking at something else generally ig- nored in *City Lights*: the pronounced homosexual theme that runs throughout the film. Even the couple of critics who have mentioned this at all end up dismissing it.[16] Yet at the least, any homosexual theme in the body of the film should relate to the head of the narrative where there is an explicit invocation of homosexual intercourse in Charlie's troubles with an erect sword. If it were to recognize the homosexuality at all, the satiric view of the film might see an anticipation of Charlie's getting shafted by the millionaire, but this would still require explaining why the satirical thrust should be cast in sexual terms.

Beyond that, satire could not account for the one other scene in which the homosexual theme is explicit. Finding himself about to fight a boxer who towers over him, Charlie, to curry favor, simpers, minces, and even makes flirting gestures toward his powerful opponent. Here, then, is an- other scene in which there is an anxiety over an unveiling, and it does have a resonance for the film's opening scene. The boxer is so unnerved by this outrageous behavior that he hides behind a curtain to change into his boxing shorts, even though he has them on under his street pants. His sudden shyness is odd to the extent that the guy is clearly Charlie's su- perior physically, yet he feels genuinely threatened by this display of fem- inized behavior. The scene, then, suggests that sexualizing a nonsexual context endows Charlie with a surprising aggressive power. The homo- sexual theme generally invokes an issue of power in the film, and, as the confrontation with the boxer makes clear, it is something more than the opposition of social classes that satire would point to. In fact, homosexual anxiety is an issue that could extend beyond *City Lights* because Chaplin's films are always filled with men who are bigger and stronger than he, men against whom he always measures himself and generally finds some inadequacy which often expresses itself in something like coquettish behavior.

To get at what is going on with all these lower body issues in *City Lights* involves me in some speculation that I suspect will be resisted by those who admire the "beauty" and pathos of the ending. Let me state the proposition directly: Charlie loves the blind girl precisely because she is blind. If you look at the scene where they first meet, you can see him being flirtatious with her as Charlie would be with any pretty girl, but the point at which she becomes special for him is when he recognizes her defect. Suddenly his whole manner and bearing change, his face taking on an expression of deep concern, a solicitousness that signals how much he feels her lack. Still, I would question how much *we* in fact feel that defect. It seems to me one of the most important strategies of the film, both dramatically and thematically, that we never take the blindness seriously as an actual physical condition. Charlie's use of mime in talking to her, mentioned earlier, suggests the metaphorical status of the blindness. The ease with which the condition is cured drives the point home.

If this is metaphor, then, the insistent sexual imagery in the rest of the film should incline us to interpret the metaphor psychoanalytically. It is not too much of a leap to see that Charlie loves her for what she lacks, which is to say that Charlie loves her because he sees her as castrated. This is one way of making sense of the homosexual theme that has puzzled other writers, but also of the very structure of the film which alternates between nighttime scenes with the millionaire whom Charlie is dependent on and daytime scenes with the blind girl, who is dependent on Charlie. In the nighttime world of men, Charlie becomes a woman, but in the daytime world of women, he at least has the possibility of asserting himself as a man.

In the film's rich sexual imagery, this problematic opposition of masculine-feminine relates to central issues of sight and voyeurism, which might be seen as a kind of phallic privileging.[17] Once the sexual imagery is understood, what might seem like an unintegrated set piece becomes central to the film's concerns: I have in mind the scene that immediately follows the opening, well before the main narrative strands of the film take hold. Charlie is passing by an art gallery with two objects in its window, a rather small figure of a horse on the left and a large statue of a naked woman at the right. Charlie is immediately arrested by the sight of the naked woman, but doesn't want this to be apparent to the passing crowds, so he looks instead at the horse, every now and then stealing a glance at the larger statue. Finally, to indulge his gaze more fully, he adopts the pose of art connoisseur, hand under chin, stepping back to take the measure of the aesthetic experience. Unbeknownst to him, a sidewalk elevator has opened up, leaving a gaping hole behind him, but every time he steps back, the elevator returns to street level. The power of Charlie's gaze is of course dependent on a blindness—the fact that the statue cannot look back—but it is also placed in a context of danger.[18]

Much as the joke here revolves around the privileging of masculine vision, the capper to the scene foreshadows the homosexual theme. Stepping back one last time, Charlie finds himself on the elevator as it descends. Scampering back on the sidewalk for safety, he begins to yell and shake his fist at a workman who is riding back up on the elevator. When the elevator fully reaches sidewalk level, it turns out the workman is another one of Charlie's imposing giants. Facing this greater physical power, Charlie immediately loses his belligerent stance: he turns tail and runs. Facing the naked woman who cannot look back, Charlie possesses power but must express it surreptitiously because he is constrained by propriety. Facing another man, he sees himself as powerless and openly displays his lack of courage.

The ending of *City Lights* presents the culmination of these interlocking themes of sight and power. However consciously we might be aware of it, the insistent sexual imagery throughout the rest of the film amplifies the devastating emotional charge of the film's ending. The blind girl, having regained her sight, gains power through the physical transformation. She moves up the social scale, right into the bourgeois classes in fact: she now has her own flower shop. We next see Charlie after his release from prison, where he had been sent because of the money he had gotten for the blind girl's operation. The sequencing of events is important to our understanding of Charlie at this point because we see him in such an uncharacteristic fashion. For the first time in his screen life, Charlie really looks like a bum: his clothes now ragged, his entire body bent over in a posture of defeat. Most important of all, he is missing his cane, the most aggressively phallic part of his costume.[19] Precisely because we have just seen the blind girl's transformation into an independent woman, we must interpret Charlie's unusual appearance as a loss of power. Clearly, the power has gone elsewhere.

Just before Charlie meets this newly empowered woman, there is a gag, no longer funny, that deliberately echoes two earlier gags. Previously in the film, two newsboys had teased Charlie, but he displayed all his self-respect and dignity to them. They tease him once again, but now Charlie can no longer defend himself. This loss of dignity is the greatest defeat for Chaplin because it represents a loss of the self-image that has sustained him in all other films against the expectations of conventional society. The defeat is specifically tied in to the lower body imagery: as Charlie bends over, one of the newsboys pulls a rag of torn underwear through the anus hole in Charlie's pants.[20] With this one gesture, both the sword-impalement from the opening sequence and the blind girl's inadvertent baring of Charlie's privates are recalled. The film sets an odd play of anal aggression (which the opening makes something passive by always assigning to accident) against phallic aggression (which is understood as sight). It is in this context, then, that their final meeting and her recognition of him must be understood.

At their simplest, the crosscut close-ups that end the film—alternating shots of the once blind girl looking at Charlie, slowly recognizing him, and Charlie tremulously accepting the consequences of her recognition—serve to focus the central questions of the film: can Charlie allow the girl to see him as he really is, and commensurately can Chaplin allow us in the audience such a privileged view, without becoming emasculated? There is a fascinating stylistic figure in this final sequence in a jump-cut that effectively isolates the two shots that make up the scene. The shot that's angled toward the seeing woman is an over-the-shoulder two-shot, with Charlie's profile on the left side of the screen; the shot angled toward Charlie is effectively a single (although there is a slight indication of the woman's presence at the extreme right edge of the image). The sense of opposition gained by the two-shot/single contrast is extended by a mismatched action across the cut: In the single of Charlie, he holds the flower he had picked up from the sweepings of the shop directly in front of his mouth, defensively covering the bottom of his face. In the two-shot, his hand has dropped to expose his face fully to her view. This opposition, this play between wanting to expose and wanting to cover up, can never be resolved since the jump-cut fully separates the two shots and the two actions.[21]

There is an issue in this scene that connects with central questions in Chaplin's art. I have tried to get at this by suggesting an opposition between the vulgarity of the grossly material comedy and the more spiritual (or at times sentimental) impulses implicit in Chaplin's treatment of character. As the now-seeing woman confronts the flesh-and-blood reality of the man she could previously see only in her imagination, as she must confront the apparent disparity between the material and the spiritual, the following questions emerge: How can upper and lower body be made whole? How can the spiritual grace we accord the eyes be made commensurate with the other organs that bring us into contact with the outside world and with other people? There is no full embrace, no assurance of a future together. The film must end on a kind of suspension, a rift the jump-cut will not allow to mend, because this is a question that for Chaplin cannot be answered: the demands of upper and lower body remain apart, and yet they also remain within the same body.

Charlie is most at home in the world of material values. He is a character most fully defined by appetites, which accounts for the great emphasis on hunger in most of his films and the countless gags about eating.[22] Yet Charlie's appetite also extends to a hunger for the spiritual, which has enabled critical appreciation of Chaplin to emphasize the spiritual over the material. This is a severe distortion of Chaplin's comedy. The "vulgar" humor is not merely decoration necessary for an artist who sought widespread appeal, but is in fact close to the essence of his work. The kind of material-spiritual opposition that can be found in Chaplin has made it possible for critics to excuse his vulgarity. In focusing on the vulgar roots of Chaplin's art, the delight it takes in exploring the lower body, I have tried to establish that there are values inherent in the vulgarity itself.

A problem for conventional critical evaluation with many of the films I discuss in this book is that they are more inextricably located in the material world. In not utilizing the material-spiritual opposition of Chaplin's comedy, they lack the redeeming "compensations" of Chaplin. In arguing for the value of vulgarity, I do not want to suggest that I rate any of these works more highly or perhaps even on a level with Chaplin. But if I don't do this, it is not because of their vulgarity. Rather, film is a performing art, and few films can boast performances as extraordinary as Chaplin's. On the other hand, the frequent lack of subtlety in gross-out films is often a function of their uninhibitedness, and uninhibitedness can be prized as a thing in itself. Virtues generally contain their own specific faults. If Chaplin is able to explore an individual character with a greater sense of resonance and insight, that particular exploration is generally limited to his character. Many of the films to be considered here, on the other hand, focus less on individual character and more on groups to present concerns that extend beyond the solipsism of Chaplin and create a more fully articulated social vision.

The key question remains how much we value the virtues that any individual work offers. Maybe this will always remain a personal matter. But in positing a vulgar tradition in which to view gross-out films, I have tried to suggest virtues embedded in these works that need to be acknowledged. These are virtues that define communal art forms, art best experienced in a crowd. As such, gross-out films take us back to the origins of spectacle in ritual. In viewing them, we experience an art that openly defines itself as public spectacle, an art of festivity that has as its chief aim the inducing of celebratory frenzy.

Chapter 5   *A Festive Art*

If both laughing and screaming possess the echoing effect that Henri Bergson noted for laughter, gross-out movies are works that aim to transform theaters into giant echo chambers. However complex any individual work may be, the aesthetic aims of all are fairly simple: make the audience laugh, make the audience scream, make it scream with laughter, make it laugh in terror, create a "laff riot" or a "screamfest" to stir up the pleasure of pandemonium. In short, these films seek to create a *festive, communal* atmosphere in the theater. If these works are chiefly directed toward the young, that is because the young in our culture are particularly attuned to forms of festivity. The centrality of music to teen culture is probably the best evidence of this. Still, the most popular of the gross-out films have crossed age as well as ethnic and class lines, creating a genuinely communal experience every culture should find necessary.

In *Shakespeare's Festive Comedy*, C. L. Barber locates a special quality in Shakespearian comedy in "the use it makes of forms for experience which can be termed saturnalian." Demonstrating the extent to which Shakespeare drew on festive traditions of actual English holiday celebrations, Barber notes:

Release, in the idyllic comedies, is expressed by making the whole experience of the play like that of a revel. . . . The fundamental method is
to shape the loose narrative so that "events" put its persons in the position of festive celebrants: if they do not seek holiday it happens to
them. . . . A saturnalian attitude, assumed by a clear-cut gesture toward
liberty, brings mirth, an accession of wanton vitality.[1]

We can still see something of what's being described here in Mardi Gras,
where participants seek the release of excessive indulgence in a period
of license. But Barber is concerned specifically with how festivity may be
transformed into art. In contemporary culture, gross-out films present unusual examples of such festive creation.

However individual films might be valued, I do not anticipate objection
to my claim that gross-out comedy represents a kind of festive art complete with its own Lords of Misrule. Including gross-out horror in this
category might seem a little odd at first glance, however. I might note that
Greek tragedy was as much a part of a festival celebration as Greek comedy. But more importantly for the current context, there is always something of a carnival atmosphere in the theater around horror films. "Carnival" in fact suggests an affinity these films have with the "fun house" of
the fairground or amusement park. But how funny is a fun house? The
moniker might seem odd since the chief aim of such structures is to lead
the spectator through a maze of unexpected terrors. Still, the fun house
deserves its claims to fun since it denotes a special kind of pleasure that
derives from disruption, an abrupt challenge to the nervous system. This
is a pleasure akin to what a child feels when a parent suddenly says "Boo!"
There is a jolt of surprise, followed by giddy laughter, and then a desire
for the whole thing to happen all over again.

The fun of horror films follows the fun of the fun house by creating an
odd pleasure in disorientation, a challenge to the participant's sense of
mastery. The very architecture of the fun house, with its patterns of endless and confusing passageways, parallels one of the most common figures of style in the horror film. The fun house is generally laid out like a
maze so that visitors can never fully gain control of the space they move
through (although movement through it is precisely controlled). Consequently, visitors can never quite anticipate what they are going to see.
Similarly, there is always at least one sequence in a horror film in which
the camera accompanies a character in medium shot as he or she walks
through an unknown space. The closeness of the camera keeps us from
being able to determine the coordinates of the space with any certainty.

In this state of heightened receptivity, we experience fun in the surprise payoff that always ends this movement.

Fun house pleasure is not to be found solely in its terrors, and I think the same might be said of horror movies. Alongside its scare images, the fun house confronts the viewer with less frightening but equally disorienting experiences: a room full of mirrors that deliberately confuse reflection and reality; or infinitesimally long slides that turn what we might normally like to control into something close to free fall. These pleasures, then, present an undermining of our ordinary sense that we can process reality in a way that makes us certain of our place in it. Horror films aim for a similar kind of undermining and find a comparable pleasure in it.

Why the play of the fun house or the play of horror movies offers pleasure in what would truly be disturbing in ordinary life is an apparent contradiction that makes the experience analogous to comedy. In all three there is a kind of letting go, an indulgence that takes place within a safe environment which permits us to acquiesce without fear of consequence. Confronted with an actual situation of danger in real life, we might feel the impulse to scream and take no further action. But by adulthood, at least, we have usually learned that it is better to try to take action to move beyond the reach of the danger. The horror film allows us the pleasure of indulging our passivity, the pleasure of being liberated from the necessity of action. However disturbing the image on the screen may be, there is a certain comfort in knowing that we can deal with it solely by letting go, by screaming.

Laughter inevitably follows the most terrifying images in fright movies, especially if large numbers of the audience have been moved to scream. The laughter might be partly an expression of embarrassment, a recognition of the insubstantiality of the threat that had previously moved us to scream. Yet it is also a recognition of the pleasure in screaming itself. In both cases, the response is equally vocal, as the response to a horror film can be as raucous and audible as the response to a comedy. In no other films are we so aware of other people in the theater because in no other films are they so prompted by the film itself to make their presence known. There is, then, a kind of loss of individuality that parallels the spatial uncertainties I mentioned above, a loss that brings with it the gain of communal experience, a festive feeling akin to drunkenness.[2]

The alliance between the grossest horror and farcical comedy is far from new. The Grand Guignol, for example, generally alternated its buckets-of-blood horror playlets with broad farces.[3] But if horror has always worked in alternation with comedy, the 1970s and 1980s witnessed a new development as horror films began more and more to move to the rhythms of comedy. By the late 1980s a newspaper reviewer, decrying the "cheap thrills of splatter films," could note the following from the frequent experience of seeing these films in theaters: whatever the images of horror conjured up on the screen the "reaction was almost invariably the same— the audience laughed."[4] This shift in modern horror is perhaps most strikingly seen in the stratagem of the final scream instituted by *Carrie* (1976), which seems to parallel the final burst of laughter that generally brings comedy to a close.

There are further points in common between the gross-out comedy and horror films. At least one "type-scene" turns up in both genres:[5] the naked woman/women in the shower/bedroom, a scene inspired from two independent sources—*Psycho* (1960) for the horror films, *M*A*S*H* (1970) for the comedies. True to the sources, if the provocative sight arouses murder, it's a horror film; if it arouses sexual desire, it's a comedy. Much as these complementary scenes move to very different conclusions, gross-out horror and comedy present complementary dystopian-utopian visions. Like the fun house where we prefer to see distorted reflections of reality, gross-out films present us with a distorting mirror vision of culture and society by moving into positive and negative idealizations.

As the dystopian-utopian modes provide a complementary ambivalence across the two genres, the use of grotesque imagery provides the clearest nexus between the two types of film. The grotesque establishes an ambivalence within the films themselves: the horror films often become farcical in the extremity of their devices, while the comedies often move into nightmare sequences.[6] The two genres draw on different traditions of the grotesque to arrive at their respective gross-outs. The horror film generally follows what Bakhtin sees as the post-Renaissance tradition of viewing the grotesque as supernatural and demonic, while the comedies revert to earlier traditions of folk and popular culture that view the grotesque as natural and animal.[7] In both, the ambivalence of the image is the key.[8] We are drawn to gross-out at the same time that we are repulsed by it, or, rather, precisely because we are repulsed by it. Contradiction, then, is central to the mode of address in these films. Any attempt to render them as univocal, as criticism generally likes to do, is necessarily doomed. There is a complexity here necessitated by the mode of presentation that demands close attention, a point I will return to shortly.

Much as the two genres have in common, there has been an odd disparity between the critical writing on the gross-out horror films as opposed to the gross-out comedies. There is already a substantial body of serious criticism on the horror film, while the comedies have garnered little more than the usual reviews and a few longer pieces complaining about the sheer number of them.[9] Much as conventional expectations make me feel I have to justify including horror films in festive art, conventional expectations also make me want to justify finding "serious" meanings in the comedies. Much of the problem centers on how comedy is evaluated in our culture. Oscar Wilde gave the subtitle "A Trivial Comedy for Serious People" to *The Importance of Being Earnest*, By this, Wilde neatly deflected the expected criticism of any truly funny comedy, but the point may work in two ways. Triviality may exist as a remedy for seriousness, but only the truly serious can appreciate triviality. Taking my cue from Wilde, I intend to be very serious in looking at my very trivial comedies.

Writing on comedy is always a risky enterprise. If the critic doesn't sound like a stand-up comic, he's likely to be attacked for lacking a sense of humor, one of those serious people Wilde aimed his triviality at. Nevertheless, the statement "There's nothing deadlier than explaining a joke" is the utterance of fools. What is really intended in this familiar stricture is a bad joke that stands in need of explanation to be understood at all. In this regard there is some truth to the truism. Explaining a bad joke is almost as deadly as telling one. But explaining a good joke is a holiday trip, an invitation to linger over its brightest festivity by recreating it anew, at the same time discovering the sights of unscheduled and unexpected stops that explanation inevitably leads to. Only the richest metaphors are as resonant as a good joke, and both are equally open to interpretation.[10]

The horror films generally develop their meanings through metaphor, the comedies through jokes, with the former standing in higher critical repute certainly for their apparent meaningfulness than the latter. Through their different languages—the language of metaphor, the language of jokes—both project a fancy like dreams, and this I think is the key to why more has been written on the horror films.[11] Explaining a nightmare is comforting because the dream is disturbing, but explaining a pleasurable dream is not comforting because the explanation itself brings on a disturbance. In effect, we would like comedy to be meaningless because we would often rather not know what we're laughing at.[12] If laughter expresses an ambivalence, denying the seriousness of laughter becomes a way of denying its inherent ambivalence. It is likely the gross-out in horror films has attracted more critical attention because, on the surface at least, it presents a more unified stance, especially because the horror film seems to apply the grotesque in its modern understanding as demonic. Still, much as in the horror film, gross-out in comedy should be a key to its meaningfulness, not a denial of it.

Festivity, then, is not opposed to seriousness. But even raising this opposition brings me to one final intellectual strategy for dealing with the popular arts that became common in the 1960s and 1970s, perhaps appropriate to the changing public discourse in that period that I have charted. I need to recount it here because it seems close to the notion of accepting popular culture as a form of festivity at the same time that it backs away from the complete engagement that true festive art demands. A colleague, a professor of literature with a fine taste for cerebral and elitist prose, drama, and poetry, having spotted me at a screening of Howard Hawks's spear-and-sandal epic *Land of the Pharaohs* (1955), told me, with an odd expression of pride, that he must have seen this film about fifteen times. The pride was hard to square with his immediately proffered critique: it was, he beamed, a thoroughly moronic work. The man himself is definitely not a moron, yet he was quite precise about the kind of pleasure the movie gave him and, he expected, would continue to give him.

At the beginning of chapter 1, I cited the complaint from Forman's *Our Movie Made Children* that "all movies are open wide, alike to moron and philosopher." My colleague seems to have reworked this formula to suggest that the value of movies lies in their capacity for turning the philosopher into a moron. My own response to *Land of the Pharaohs*—that the film was clearly a failure, although not without an intelligence and skill that held some interest for me—he rejected out of hand. Rather, he seemed to embrace the film as an absurdist work, but conditionally, that is, only if the absurdism could be understood as unintentional (in contrast to the more cerebral and demanding absurdist theater of the 1950s). The film seems to represent some kind of celebratory experience for him, but one founded on finding nothing of value in the work itself.

Possibly the film was necessary for him as a kind of relief from the more intellectual art he has to deal with as part of his job, a kind of vacation whose festivity is dependent upon a perceived mindlessness. Movies, then, can be seen as a kind of summer camp for adults, and the underlying aesthetic enunciated here is, of course, "camp," in which the art object becomes something to celebrate at the same time that it is degraded.[13] This becomes a means of embracing the spectacle aspect of film, its sheer sensual appeal, at the same time holding to ancient suspicions against spectacle.[14] In this way, the elite critic not only gets to enjoy the work in all its degraded pleasure, he can also enjoy his own snobbery, which safely distances him from the source of pleasure. In its embrace of pleasure as a dominant aesthetic value, camp seems to embrace festive art. Yet at the same time, it represents a peculiar inversion of festive art since it builds on a split in sensibility between artist and audience that serves chiefly to celebrate the audience's status as intellectual elite.

True festive art, as both Bakhtin and Barber intend the term, can posit no such split for it is an art that ultimately celebrates communality, much as any festival does. Where camp is ultimately exclusionary, festive art is always inclusionary. And where camp condescendingly celebrates the vacuousness of the art work, festive art insists on the profundity of its festivity. Festivity is *not* opposed to depth of meaning. As Bakhtin has noted, certain truths are only available through festive art.[15] A worldview that sees a split between body and spirit limits the value of material existence. The highest value ultimately resides in the spiritual rather than the material. As gross-out films focus on the grossness of existence, they ultimately move material life into a position of seriousness that can never be obtained when the material is seen as divided from and inferior to the spiritual. The seriousness of this festivity, then, resides in the extent to which it inverts the most deeply rooted values of Western culture.

Most likely I was open to the aesthetic challenges offered by gross-out films precisely because my own critical interest has long been in the generally disreputable art form of Hollywood movies. Still, even within that lowly art, distinctions have been made, with some artists and some kinds of films receiving recognition as genuine art. In my past writing, I have generally paid most attention to this elite group of Hollywood films, the highest of the low. But even with this background, I freely admit that in the early stages of this project, I was myself surprised to be writing a book on gross-out at all. There were initially two spurs to my thoughts about these films—one aesthetic, one social—spurs that embedded themselves so deeply I felt compelled to look at what prompted my response. The first is the simplest to explain. A number of these films gave me real pleasure, even though serious critical commentary had generally ignored them. The movies had been overlooked because of their lowly generic origins, yet the more I looked at them, the clearer it seemed to me that an individual film's success derived from its dialogue with the genre, so I considered it necessary to look at the genre as a whole.

Second, the social point: startled as I was by the invasion of Czechoslovakia at the end of *Stripes* (1981), I was even more surprised to discover that hardly anyone had taken note of this. Some of this had to do with the nature of comedy, since we are so used to thinking a work is not worth taking seriously if it's comedy. As a consequence, there is little cause for concern about an invasion of Czechoslovakia so long as it's being led by Bill Murray, rather than, say, Sylvester Stallone.[16] But the more I looked at these films, the more apparent it became to me they had established a discourse with their audience so familiar and well understood that even the most extreme extensions of that discourse into outrageous areas could pass by without comment. The scene set in the black club in *Animal House* (1978) that I discuss later in this book is another good example of how these films were exploring issues central to American culture in ways that made more refined works of art seem timid.[17] It became increasingly clear to me, these films were not only worth looking at, but worth looking at *closely*.

That I want to look at these films closely might itself be a cause for surprise because it challenges a couple of familiar assumptions about popular culture. One has to do with how we understand individual works as cultural artifacts. We like to group films, much as I have done here with gross-out horror and comedy, and draw conclusions from those groupings as if the groupings by themselves tell us something significant about the culture. The popularity of violent films during certain periods tells us that we are a violent nation. But is that all they tell us? And why do we need films to tell us what must seem an obvious point? Any real probing of popular culture must attend to the tougher question of how individual films specifically articulate their concerns. It is by this articulation—a setting of parameters and defining of terms—that a culture engages in a discourse over, say, issues of violence. How we talk about something defines our concerns as much as the subject matter itself: whether we are dismissive or engaged, impassioned or cynical; whether we say something explicitly or keep it hidden; what kinds of associations particular thoughts and feelings give rise to. Individual films also have a distinctive way of talking, and we have to pay attention to manner as much as matter to understand what they are saying. By treating films solely as artifacts which we may slot into conceptual categories, we often end up scuttling not only what is most interesting about individual films but also what is most interesting about the historical periods they emerge from.[18]

A second point of concern arises from a more recent approach to popular culture that also sees oppositional strategies not unlike what I have been describing with gross-out. While founded on the old left view that works of popular culture conspire to control, it posits a counterforce. In doing so, this new theory substitutes the old left's view of an infinitely malleable mass with a kind of sentimental populism that grants all power to the people. It wholly accepts the manipulative aspirations of popular culture, but renders it impotent, bested by "excorporation," an oppositional strategy that transforms the individual work into something more useful to the popular audience. John Fiske has written:

> Excorporation is the process by which the subordinate make their own culture out of the resources and commodities provided by the dominant system, and this is central to popular culture, for in an industrial society the only resources from which the subordinate can make their own subcultures are those provided by the system that subordinates them. . . . This means that the study of popular culture requires the study not only of the cultural commodities out of which is it made, but also of the ways that people use them. The latter are far more creative and varied than the former.[19]

We have moved here from a paradigm of smart work/stupid audience to stupid work/smart audience. I think this new paradigm worth questioning because the notion of oppositional strategies in the audience depends upon a dubious aspiration to manipulation by the culture merchants. Furthermore, it denies the individual art work its agency and loses sight of a possible engagement between audience and art.

Any individual film does have agency to the extent that it uses a wide variety of devices—dramatic structure, performance, camera positioning, cutting, and so on—to produce definite responses in the audience. This is always clear with comedies and horror films since the reactions of laughing and screaming are so evident, but there are subtler ways in which a film cues its audience.[20] There is, for example, a scene from *Carrie* in which a shot that shows the complete shattering of a mirror precedes a shot showing the same mirror miraculously restored, with only two cracks through its glass. I will discuss this apparent discrepancy more extensively later, but it is enough to note now that it represents a moment that must prompt a response from even the most unreflective audience. We might simply think it strange, or we might try to find some explanation that will move us into the realm of interpretation. Whatever we do, the film has successfully set up its events in such a way that we must think something about this particular moment.

Determining exactly what an audience might be thinking is always a tricky thing. Still, using individual art works as evidence of the way a culture works inevitably ends up doing something like that. As I will discuss more extensively in a later chapter, there was a good deal of commentary on audience response to *The Exorcist* during its initial release in

1973. I want to consider briefly one contemporary observation about the audience because it says something about how we understand audience response. In a Sunday *New York Times* think piece on the success of the film ("Why the Devil Do They Dig 'The Exorcist'?"), Vincent Canby noted that audiences seemed to become restless during the quieter moments of the film, waiting solely for the most sensationalistic scenes.[21] This was implicitly a way of criticizing the work of the film, reducing it to the simple experience of its grossest moments—all sensation, no contemplation. Even if this wasn't necessarily a simple work, the writer assured us, that's what the mass audience made of it.[22]

But short of interviewing every member of the audience *during* the actual experience of the art work, how can we ever know for sure what an audience may be thinking? The apparent restlessness of the audience at *The Exorcist* could have in fact signified a number of things. It does not necessarily mean (as writers at the time claimed) that the audience solely sought the most horrifying moments of the film, completely bored with everything else. At the very least, the quieter moments are dramatically effective in setting off the horror. Even a supposedly inattentive audience must respond to the very different tone of those scenes. I think the only thing we can finally conclude from this is that the quieter scenes, in creating a context of contrast, condition how the audience experiences the most terrifying ones. In order to understand the impact of the film, then, we have to look at how the quiet scenes prepare for the noisy ones.

In trying to analyze how these films work, I am not forwarding definitive claims about what an audience thought and felt. I also doubt the value of statistical studies to do this. But I do think it possible to generalize from individual experience. Certainly, close attention to the way the film presents its characters and events can tell us a good deal about how a film conditions and anticipates audience reaction. By being attentive to my own responses as cued by the film, I expect I will have something to say that will resonate for the reader. What I do want to stress here is the following: we can understand the larger cultural discourse each film participates in only if we understand how the individual film articulates its own concerns.

The sum total of the individual films create a discourse, but the resultant discourse reciprocally defines the individual films.[23] My final task of this introduction is to define the nature of the discourse within which these films operate, what these films have to do to earn the unexpected approbation of "gross!" I cannot say when the word "gross-out" first came into existence or how it developed as a term of praise. One of the first examples I've been able to spot is in quotation from an obscure radio critic that appeared in the ads for *Animal House*: "A riot of a thing. One of the great gross-outs of all time. Raw, ribald, frantic, uproarious! You'll laugh till you cry."[24]

Not only is gross-out desirable; apparently so is a "riot." Even in the context of a horror film, "gross" is inevitably connected to what is pleasurable. A student review of *The Fly* (1986) in a college newspaper reported, "I attended this film gleefully expecting to be grossed out. And I was not disappointed."[25] By 1987 gross-out began to move outside its specific generic precincts as something to praise; a *New York Times* review of *Stakeout* (itself not a gross-out film) noted: "This cop team is a pleasure to be around. . . . We even find ourselves enjoying the gross-out competition between these big kids and the daytime shift."[26] It must be kept in mind that even as it has become commonplace, the term necessarily points to something oppositional in these works since it is a word that inverts its original meaning. This is perhaps clearest in an anecdote recounted in a *Variety* report of, appropriately enough, weekly grosses:

> "Have you seen the new version of 'The Fly'?" asked a woman in a North Side video store this weekend. "It was one of the most disgusting movies I've ever seen—I loved it!" . . . The late summer hit grossed (sorry!) $390,000 or near this week.[27]

Much as they can make lots of money for their makers, inversion and opposition are built into the aesthetic of these films by the very words we use to describe them.

As I have suggested in trying to point to the "seriousness" of these apparently frivolous works, some truths are more available to their mode of address. These are truths—befitting festive art—that are most fully focused on the relation of the individual to the community. If every community necessarily operates as a constraint on the individual, the oppositional quality in these works is centered on a questioning of those constraints. The testing of the limits of behavior is the dominant concern of both the comedies and the horror films, as it is the underlying concern of any attempt that seeks praise for being gross. Implicit in the testing of constraints is a reevaluation of what we mean by "high" and "low" in culture, since higher forms, like advanced civilizations for Freud, build on greater constraints. In a sense, these works are "barbaric" because they insist on a reversal of the hierarchy, but this is a barbarism that has been around our civilization for a long time. There might not have been such a precise word for it, but gross-out forms of expression have existed in the past, most notably in occasions like the medieval Feast of Fools (which quite explicitly inverted prevailing hierarchies).[28] The value of grossness lies in its inversion of accepted values.

"Hierarchy" generally has a specific social meaning, but as I have suggested in an earlier discussion of genre, there are hierarchies in art as well. In *The Life of the Drama*, Eric Bentley dealt with this issue by considering the low state into which melodrama and farce had fallen in the twentieth century. Theater critics are often more predisposed toward popular forms than literary critics, and Bentley generally sought a revaluation of disreputable art much as I have here. Titling one of his chapters "In Praise of Self-Pity," Bentley overtly offers a challenge to elite taste by praising farce and melodrama for outré values like violence and sentimentality.[29] Yet even as he offers this challenge, he continues to maintain a hierarchical view of dramatic art in ways that are of interest to me here. Invoking Freud, he suggests that higher forms are ruled by the "reality principle": "The higher forms—tragedy and comedy—are distinguished from the lower—melodrama and farce—by their respect for reality. 'Higher,' in this context, signifies adult, civilized, healthy; lower signifies childish, savage, sick. By this token, the lower forms are not excluded by the higher; they are transcended by them" (p. 257).

Lower forms, then, are clearly forms of indulgence that give in to our worst instincts. Bentley does grant this some value, just not as much as in the higher forms. I think Bentley's analysis provides an accurate statement of *why* there are hierarchical views of artistic modes. For all who see the arts hierarchically, the lower modes *merely* give pleasure, while the higher forms bring enlightenment, which is to say they function educationally. Yet we might question why any work of the creative imagination *should* find value by submitting to the reality principle.

Freud himself offers a way of rethinking these matters in *Civilization and Its Discontents* with a passage that considers the pursuit of pleasure and substitute satisfactions. In positing a "sublimation of the instincts," Freud wants to explore ways in which we gain control of our "instinctual impulses" and still derive pleasure from them. As examples of sublimation he offers "an artist's joy in creating, in giving his phantasies body, or a scientist's in solving problems or discovering truths."[30] With such examples, he is able to establish a familiar hierarchy, although he immediately notes a problem with it: "we . . . can say figuratively that such satisfactions seem 'finer and higher.' But their intensity is mild as compared with that derived from the sating of crude and primary instinctual impulses; it does not convulse our physical being" (pp. 79–80).

Now, it is clear I am concerned with works that deal in "crude and primary instinctual impulses," works that I have been arguing are intended to "convulse our physical being." But rather than seeing in these values and aesthetic aims clear markers of lowness, I would say the festivity of these works offer us a special commodity that belongs only to art.

Freud clearly identifies this when he writes of satisfaction "obtained from illusions":

> The region from which these illusions arise is the life of the imagination; at the time when the development of the sense of reality took place, this region was expressly exempted from the demands of reality-testing and was set apart for the purpose of fulfilling wishes which were difficult to carry out. At the head of these satisfactions through phantasy stands the enjoyment of works of art—an enjoyment which, by the agency of the artist, is made accessible even to those who are not themselves creative. (pp. 80–81)

Art, then, stands to some degree in opposition to the reality principle because it affords us satisfactions we gain knowingly through illusions. As such, it offers us the possibility of reaching our baser, cruder selves unencumbered by the demands of reality. This might seem of special importance in dealing with the utopian aspects of the comedies, since dystopias often seem more realistic. But I prefer to say that both operate clearly as fantasies of reality, and their value lies precisely in the ways they depart from reality.

It is worth keeping in mind that the pleasure principle itself occasions the reality principle. Yet, oddly, in evaluating art we have traditionally granted the latter priority. We talk about "indulging" pleasure, but we never indulge reality. Why not see pleasure itself as the highest good, a good that reality frequently opposes?[31] There is perhaps a kind of denial involved in placing artistic modes into a hierarchy, in which a secondary mental function, the reality principle, is made primary in products of the *imagination.* There is something self-congratulatory in the hierarchy of traditional elite culture: it is flattering because it makes man so noble, so raised above the beast. The notion that we can "transcend" our lower selves, as Bentley's high forms transcend their origins in low, is itself a flight from the reality principle. Freud himself would not accept such a notion of transcendence. In an attempt to define the way the mind works, he uses an extended metaphor of an imaginary Rome in which all of the past is preserved whole in its original state under the various new cities that are built on top of it. We never leave behind our primal instincts as we never leave behind our past.[32]

If it is the privilege of art that it can offer escape from the reality principle, why not elevate works that give imagination its freest reign? The best answer is probably that at times we want one, at times we want the other, but in neither case are we dealing with questions of value. Since all art is inherently festive, works that explicitly present themselves as festive art may well have a special value, may well present ways of looking at the world not available to a sensibility that embraces the reality principle. The extent to which "escapism" has become a negative term in this century for describing some kinds of art indicates how far we have come from any festive notion of art. Most of the works I consider in this book, even at their most dystopian, may be fairly labeled escapist. As a group, they are not likely to be praised for their realism. A small number of them do manage to achieve a degree of social authenticity and may be valued for this, but I hope never at the expense of the more fantastic works. Even at their most unrealistic and escapist, they are never divorced from experience.

On the contrary, precisely because they are so uninhibited, these films provide a reflection—and in many cases a more acute reflection than more prestigious works—of a period of radical social and cultural change. As the films themselves insistently tested the constraints of what is acceptable, they became an important part of a larger discourse that bespoke challenges to conventional assumptions and modes of behavior. These gross-out horror films and comedies do not speak in a single voice. Rather, they are generally raucous and contradictory in their free flights of fancy, from film to film, and just as often within individual films themselves. But taken together they do define a common discourse on power, sex, and the body that is the central concern of this book.

Even a cursory look at products of the past should make clear that no discourse is timeless for its terms are determined by assumptions and concerns of its culture. The different ways in which different discourses on similar issues speak is most evident with the comedies because they are so explicitly utopian in their aim. A utopian vision by its very nature strives for a timeless quality, yet in the terms it chooses to present itself it is inevitably time-determined. Much of the charm of Frank Capra's *Lost Horizon* (1937) for modern audiences, for example, lies in a kind of quaintness: even as it strives to create in Shangri-la a world outside of time, its utopianism is quite obviously not eternal since it comes complete with the latest in streamlined styles of architecture and dress to suggest a kind of futurism for 1930s audiences.

The discourse of its period defined the film's conception of utopia as precisely as the visuals. To a corporate industrial world poised on the brink of war, the film offered the escape of a peaceful communal existence based on a return to a more religious and agrarian order. For all its modernist visual trappings, this fantasy world really belongs to a past that antedates the film. The seeming contradiction between mode and appearance is central to the film's utopian scheme, a way to amalgamate contradictory impulses by combining a visual style that suggests the future with a societal model that idealizes the past. The gross-out comedies also posit a utopian communal existence, but it is one geared more toward the individual libido: these films find their utopianism in the unlimited expression of drives for power and sex, which consequently involves them in their own sets of contradictions. In at least one regard, then, these two utopias are antithetical since *Lost Horizon* creates a world that nullifies all expressions of individual power—that is, a world that nullifies precisely what the gross-out comedies glory in. And yet all these films may be fairly labeled utopian.

Even at their greatest remove from reality, gross-out comedy and horror films engage in a discourse that reflects the reality in which they are created. Both offer distorting mirror visions of culture and society, but the distortions are valuable in themselves because *the manner in which we seek to stylize reality is itself a comment on that reality.* The manner defines the discourse because it sets the terms that we use to understand reality. The horror films and comedies connect in that they share the desire to gross their audiences out, but my point in looking at the two genres together is that views of utopia and dystopia presented in the films combine to form different aspects of the same discourse, as the utopian view at times penetrates the horror films, while the dystopian view surfaces on occasion in the comedies. And because it is a discourse of gross-out, it is necessarily equivocal, ambivalent, contradictory.

These films are works that want to address us in a raucous, rude, even repulsive voice, and what's more, they take delight in the very objectionable qualities of this voice. In its freewheeling fancy and exuberant energy, this voice often speaks in obstreperous terms, trying to determine just how far it can go, what kind of license it can grant its own sense of freedom. Seeking to break down all constraints, even those of the rational mind, this is not a univocal mode of address, but one that often speaks in contradictions. As an example of the way the resulting contradictions surface, consider *Animal House*. On the one hand the film appears to be anti-institutional in its sustained attacks on the officials who run the college and the power structure of the fraternity council that rules social life. On the other hand, it embraces the institution of its own fraternity, which is itself defined hierarchically. The result is an odd inflection of familiar American concerns with individualism, presented in a distinctive discourse on power and freedom that this film shares with other gross-out films.

When *Animal House* first appeared, a number of critics treated it as satire and found it wanting.[33] In an interview given a week before the opening, the film's three screenwriters saw the matter very differently:

[DOUG] MILLER: . . . All that riotous fraternity behavior was just great. It was a tremendous explosion of—What was it an explosion of?

[HAROLD] RAMIS: The exhilaration of the 1950s. The rock 'n' roll energy that came to colleges in the early 1960s, the stuff that became the power of the late 1960s.[34]

That what was intended as celebration should be viewed as satire is probably a reflection of how we have learned to value comedy. There are clearly satiric moments in the film, but that does not render the whole as satire, nor does it have to be satire in order to be good. The festive mode is capacious: it can move in several different directions at once and never lose its air of celebration.

The festive air holds steady throughout *Animal House* precisely because the satire does not follow through. If the work were more fully satirical, it would be that much less festive. The film seems so much a product of its particular time and place precisely because it is filled with competing and contesting voices, much as any dynamic culture is. Consider, for example, the scene at the black roadhouse (to be examined in more detail in chapter 7). The first half of the scene has a stunning confrontational rawness in its clear-eyed presentation of how whites look at blacks in American society—yet by the end of the scene, the film's tone is something so different that it seems to openly contradict the satire that has gone before. It is perhaps inevitable that liberationist strivings do not finally destroy boundaries so much as draw new ones. For all that we desire freedom, we also need boundaries to function. But it is always worth looking at precisely where those boundaries are drawn as a way of defining a culture. Some of these works are more successful in realizing a liberationist spirit, some less so, but in no case is the way to liberation not compromised. A work of art is not a political platform, and only demagogues may achieve ideological purity.

As a discourse that became increasingly dominant through the 1970s and 1980s, gross-out films defined an important part of American life. To gain some perspective on the discourse of these films and the effect this has had on my life and the lives of those in my generation, I want in turn to define my experience of these films, individually and collectively, in the following pages. Gross-out speaks in a voice that demands to be heard because it represented a powerful strain in contemporary American culture. And it demands to be listened to closely: in the free-form give-and-take of its licentious manner, it speaks in the voice of festive freedom, uncorrected and unconstrained by the reality principle—fresh, open, aggressive, seemingly improvised, and always ambivalent.

A New Old Comedy

Old Comedy [is] difficult to treat in the terminology of cultured discourse. In these comedies we are constantly aware ... —not only in their riotous obscenities and irreverent travesties but in the carnival spirit that percolates through the most scathing abuse—of primordial values and elemental needs that continually threaten to smash the prevailing social order to smithereens.

—Robert M. Torrance, The Comic Hero

Chapter 6 *Animal Comedy*

Bringing Out the Beast

A bellydancer in traditional scanty costume slowly circles around a donkey making caressing gestures toward it in anticipation of their sexual encounter. She's been paid for it in advance and approaches her work with apparent pleasure, but the donkey has appetites of his own. As the dancer gets lost in her own seductive movements, he gobbles up a cornucopia of multicolored pills—uppers, downers, everything in between—and snorts about five rows of cocaine as a chaser. Before this encounter of a rare kind between beauty and the beast can take place, the beast keels over stone-cold dead.

Bachelor Party (1984)

When pornographic films won acceptance as theatrical entertainment in the early 1970s, bestiality became the one area where even the thick-skinned New York City police thought they should draw the line.[1] Still, the possibility of crossing that line could be played with in titillating fashion, as the scene described above shows. That scene, however, is *not* from a pornographic movie. Rather, it crops up in standard Hollywood fare deemed worthy of no more than an R rating. *Bachelor Party* was in fact one of the top-grossing comedies of 1984—not in the economic stratosphere of *Ghostbusters* or *Police Academy* perhaps, but boffo nonetheless. Its gags and jabs may be a bit cruder and a good deal more nasty-minded than many another comedy in the 1980s, but they are not very different in kind. *Bachelor Party* is merely one of a number of comedies that overtook American screens following the enormous popular success of *Animal House*, comedies that are defined by their raunchiness and an apparent desire to push beyond acceptable bounds of good taste.[2] While the films have enough in common to constitute a real genre, their power at the box office established them as the dominant comic genre for American audiences in the 1980s.

For the previous sixty years or so, romantic comedy had been *the* comedy style in Hollywood. While it did not become as dead as the Western in the 1980s, it certainly went into decline.[3] The new style that precipitated the decline I would like to dub "Animal Comedy" in honor of its primary progenitors, *Animal House* (1978) and *Porky's* (1982). Animals are never very far from these films—at least metaphorically, and occasionally literally, but in any case often enough to be presented in strikingly similar ways. In fact, the "overdosing donkey" gag from *Bachelor Party* described at the beginning of this chapter is pretty much a riff on the "horse has a heart attack" gag from *Animal House*. This insistent emphasis on animality points to physicality as a key attribute of these films. As a consequence, physical comedy generally receives pride of place over verbal comedy. Broad physical comedy is hardly new in American movies, of course, but in the sound period at least it has generally been limited either to isolated moments within a romantic comedy or relegated to the lower-class realm of B movies like the Bowery Boys and shorts like the Three Stooges. Animal Comedy represented a return to screen slapstick on a fairly grand and insistent scale.

Perhaps the surest sign that a new genre was emerging was that critics wearied of these films fairly quickly, generally dismissing them as comedies for adolescents. And it is probably true that the run-of-the-mill Animal Comedy found its largest audience among young males ranging in age from late adolescence to college age, which together represent a group our culture has called "animals"—kids aggressively pursuing the dictates of their newly felt hormonal urgings. Still, the most commercially successful of these films—and they account for some of the biggest grossers of the 1980s—had a far greater appeal. Most of them managed to have (and continue to hold) a successful afterlife in home video, perhaps drawing audiences even more consistently in this format than in theaters. However new, this development is not aberrational. These films have surfaced as mainstream comedy precisely because they reflect a trend in screen comedy that began in the 1960s.

Classical scholars make a distinction between Old Comedy and New Comedy that is relevant here.[4] In many ways what is newest about Animal Comedy is how old it is, reaching all the way back to Old Comedy. What we know of Old Comedy derives chiefly from the plays of Aristophanes, while New Comedy is essentially everything that comes after.[5] Old Comedy is very loosely plotted, episodic, developing through a series of contests or battles in which one character or group of characters triumphs over others. The sense of a contest (known as the *agon* in the Greek plays) is especially important for Animal Comedy, which usually pits groups of people against each other. In fact, a good number of the films made the contest metaphor literal by a sporting event that serves to bring an otherwise loosely structured narrative to some sense of resolution.[6] Appropriately enough, shortly before Animal Comedy burst on the scene, almost as if in preparation for it, there were a number of popular films about team sports in which the team players were often as gross as the animals in the later comedies: *The Longest Yard* (1974), *Slap Shot* (1977), even *The Bad News Bears* (1976) with its collection of foulmouthed little leaguers.

Old Comedy may be ruthlessly satiric in spirit (often with biting invective directed against actual people to a degree that has only been equaled with the early years of Dennis Miller's "Weekend Update" newscasts on "Saturday Night Live"). But satire is not really the essential matter of Old Comedy. More striking is its sense of license, an almost total lack of inhibition in its view of both sexual and social relations.[7] Old Comedy courts outrage in its insistent puncturing of taboos, whether it is man's ascension to power over the gods in *The Birds* or woman's ascension to power over men in *Lysistrata*. In part the breaking down of screen censorship in the 1960s was a necessary prerequisite for the subsequent flourishing of our New Old Comedy since the prohibitions of earlier decades were simply too powerful to challenge successfully. Comedies before the 1960s might have tickled taboos in fleeting fashion, but they rarely gave the impression that they might dare to speak the unspeakable. In the 1970s the unspeakable not only found a voice. Suddenly it wouldn't shut up.

From the 1920s on, New Comedy so dominated Hollywood's output that Northrop Frye could reasonably claim in 1949, "The average movie of today is a rigidly conventionalized New Comedy proceeding toward an act which, like death in Greek tragedy, takes place offstage, and is symbolized by the final embrace."[8] Frye's witty conjunction of sex and death implicitly points to an imbalance in earlier Hollywood films where death was presented explicitly, with some frequency, and almost always violently, while sex was generally kept under wraps. Yet thirty years after Frye wrote this, "the act" would no longer be offstage or offscreen, and it was just as likely to turn up in the middle of the movie as well as at the end. New Comedy had become old-fashioned.

New Comedy is essentially what we have come to know as romantic comedy, what Hollywood in its infinite wisdom has succinctly formulated as "Boy meets girls, boy loses girl, boy gets girl." This is the comic form that pretty much dominated American screens from the 1920s through the 1960s, and then staged something of a comeback in the late 1980s when Animal Comedy went into decline. While New Comedy isn't very new (it's at least as old as Menander), it deserves its name to the extent that it so successfully supplanted Old Comedy. Old Comedy has never completely disappeared: it is always present in slapstick, burlesque, and parody. A good number of silent comedy shorts might be reasonably called Old Comedy, but, significantly, when Charlie Chaplin, Buster Keaton, and Harold Lloyd sought to upgrade their image (and not coincidentally, their earning power as well) by moving into feature films, they also moved into the world of New Comedy, generally centering their films on romantic plots.[9] The broad farcical elements that would suggest Old Comedy certainly remained a *part* of these films, but they were no longer the whole show as they were in the shorts, which is probably why James Agee and other critics could repeatedly claim that the shorts of the great silent comedians were funnier than their features.[10]

In the mid-1960s a couple of films starring the Beatles and directed by Richard Lester appeared and instantly prompted comparisons to the Marx Brothers. While invocations of the Marx Brothers comedies were apt, the Beatles films actually appeared under the guises of different genres. *A Hard Day's Night* (1964) presented itself as a kind of documentary, but given to flights of fancy, while *Help!* (1965) parodied the spy genre suddenly made popular by the James Bond films. In neither case could the films be regarded as romantic comedy, but in order to escape the dominant comic mode of the time, both films had to invoke other genres, as if there were no formal precedent for what they were attempting. Even the Marx Brothers, having almost managed to escape romantic comedy plots in their Paramount period, found themselves saddled with and occasionally subservient to romantic comedy plots and the likes of Kitty Carlisle and Alan Jones when they moved to MGM and classier films in the mid-1930s.

The relationship between the move to romantic comedy and aspirations to class is an important notion I will return to shortly, but for now I want to point out that the Lester-Beatles films were in reality part of a trend and not quite the revolutionary break they appeared to be at the time. A couple of years before in 1962 Howard Hawks had directed *Hatari!*, a film that takes the form of "a hunting season, from beginning to end."[11] This basically describes the plot, which is nothing but a series of episodic segments alternating between exciting action scenes of capturing African game for shipment to European zoos and more relaxed scenes that develop romantic relations among the six main characters (with none of the character interactions given much weight). Hawks's decision to move away from rigidly structured plots was a conscious one in response to television. Perhaps less conscious was a decision to move away from the detailed exploration of character in favor of "typing"—that is, to make the variety of the group rather than any individual personality the key attraction. Hawks's decision also represented a return to the roots of silent film, and especially silent film comedy, where the plots (as much as there were plots) could develop by contingency more than formal dramatic structure and by character typing, as the commedia dell'arte provided the foundation on which improvisation could be worked.[12]

Silent comedy and especially silent comedy *shorts* were more and more evoked throughout this period, most notably by Blake Edwards with the very freely structured comedy, *The Great Race* (1965), dedicated to "Mr. Laurel and Mr. Hardy," and *The Party* (1968), which was entirely plotless. Other Edwards films of the mid-1960s—*The Pink Panther, A Shot in the Dark* (both 1964), and *What Did You Do in the War, Daddy?* (1966)—invoke other genres (mystery-suspense and war films), but like *Help!* they are comedies that rely on other genres to provide a sense of form for very loose structures. Edwards remains something of a specialized case because his films often seem an attempt to forge an alliance between Old and New Comedy. Still, he is part of a larger movement at the time away from romantic comedy as the dominant form in Hollywood movies.

What all these films have in common are ambling narratives, more episodic than dramatic, and an emphasis on *groups* of people brought together by some common activity or location. In all the films mentioned (as in the later gross-out comedies), it is often the activity or location that provides the film's coherence rather than tightly structured plots or complexly defined characters. There are possibilities for romance in these films, as there are possibilities for romance almost everywhere in the movies, but at best romantic interest always remains secondary. The real focus of the films is finally more social than individual.

A similar movement from the individual to the social group (with a complementary undermining of the notion of the lone hero) takes place around this time with the rise of the "buddy films." The presence of two glamorous leading men (Paul Newman and Robert Redford) made *Butch Cassidy and the Sundance Kid* (1969) something different from the hero-and-his-sidekick formula of earlier action films because the eye-catching equality of the stars undermined the recognizable hierarchy of casting in previous films. Almost lost in Newman and Redford's screen-stealing aura, Katharine Ross emerged, like romance itself, as a distinctly secondary concern. Or perhaps the old formula has been transmuted into something else. Implicitly locating this new formula in romantic comedy, Molly Haskell smartly observed that Newman and Redford were "on their way to becoming the Myrna Loy–William Powell of the 1970s."[13]

Nonetheless, the doubling up of the male stars points to a comic style ultimately different from romantic comedy as it simultaneously increases both aggression and regression. Writing in the early 1980s, Dave Kehr attributed the phenomenal success of *Animal House*, up to that time "the highest grossing comedy ever made," to "an unusual emotional subtext: the tight and cozy bonds of an all-male, post-adolescent pack."[14] As I have tried to indicate by invoking the buddy films, this "subtext" was not in fact unusual for the period. What struck the observant eye of this contemporary critic as unusual was its location in comedy, normally the domain of male-female relations. And it proved to be a good deal more common subsequently. From *Animal House* on, many of the comedies influenced by it have a duo (and occasionally a trio) at the center of the group. I think male bonding is less central to these films than Kehr would have it, but the foregrounding of male friendships does serve to move the films decisively away from romantic comedy traditions where the focus is entirely on heterosexual relations.

The emphasis on the group moves these films outside the realm of comedy to another generic tradition. The heterogeneous groups where individuals register as distinct types also suggest a comic reworking of the World War II combat genre. Jeanine Basinger claims the "unique group of mixed individuals" is the key feature that set these films apart from all earlier war films, and she sees in this new form both invocation and exaltation of "the melting pot tradition" and democracy.[15] With its leveling impulses and complementary attacks on the forces of authority, Animal Comedy also uses its groups as a way of honoring democratic ideals (a point I shall return to), but my specific purpose in invoking combat films here is as a lead-in to *M*A*S*H* (1970), a key film for the later gross-out comedies.

Four years before *M*A*S*H*, Blake Edwards had directed *What Did You Do in the War, Daddy?*, another wartime service comedy that focused on a group of people in the context of a loosely structured narrative. But *M*A*S*H* had three key differences that proved to be core elements for later Animal Comedy: (1) a far more caustic sense of humor, (2) a paradoxically exclusionary attitude toward those not considered fit for the heterogeneous group, and (3) a buddy relationship that held the center together. *M*A*S*H* and *American Graffiti* (1973), in which the combat group is in effect reconstituted among suburban high school students in the latter, are the two clearest progenitors of the later Animal Comedies. Many of the later films display a conscious awareness of these two films, which might be seen variously as imitation, parody, or homage. Whatever one makes of it, reference to these earlier works—often of a very specific nature—occurs frequently. For example, the public address announcement (complete with low-angle shots of speaker horn), used to give some sense of coherence to the episodic plot in *M*A*S*H*, turns up in *Car Wash* (1976) and *Meatballs* (1979), while the what-happened-to-them-after epilogue in *American Graffiti* turns up again in *Animal House*, *Stripes* (1981), *Fast Times at Ridgemont High* (1982), and *Heaven Help Us* (1985), among others.

The enormous success of both *M*A*S*H* and *American Graffiti* is particularly striking because of *their* generic roots. Service comedies and teenage comedies, particularly of the American-International variety, had offered movie companies dependable income in the past. Routine films churned out in routine fashion, they garnered a routine return on their investment. But they never earned anything on the scale of *M*A*S*H* or *American Graffiti* because neither category had been considered a classy genre in the past. They were essentially exploitation fare. In writing about the move of the silent comedians into feature films and the Marx Brothers' move to MGM, I raised the issue of class. Class is the key point here as well for it sets *M*A*S*H* and *American Graffiti* apart from their prototypes.

Perhaps the best way to get at this issue is to contrast several comic careers over the 1970s and 1980s. As Woody Allen's art became more ambitious, critics began invoking with greater frequency the names of Chaplin and Keaton. And for all his vulgarity, even Mel Brooks (who made his own silent-movie homage in 1976) clearly had the silent comedians in his art's mind. On the other hand, those of the first "Saturday Night Live" cast who moved successfully into feature films seemed to be aiming at a comic style pitched somewhere between the Three Stooges and the Bowery Boys. Here the coarseness of comedy in the style of the Three Stooges proved to be more popular than the subtleties of a Chaplin. The rise of the new gross-out comedy also saw the return of the Three Stooges to movie theaters in marathon showings of collections of their shorts and at midnight screenings, the favored hour for the grossest of gross-out movies.[16] Woody Allen's films have been successful within a fairly limited sphere, but he has never approached the popularity of Bill Murray or some of the other "Saturday Night Live" graduates.

In the way that grossness explicitly defined this new comic style and its willingness to confront what in the past had to be shied away from, Animal Comedies that focus on teenagers are set apart from the teenpix of the past by their stunning rawness. They are Andy Hardy with his pants down and his libido fully exposed for the first time (a spectacle that adults generally preferred to keep under wraps in the past). The key issue here, as in most gross-out movies, is graphic explicitness—an issue directly connected to notions of class. Paralleling a traditional critical preference for the spiritual over the material is a critical commonplace frequently used against popular art: that it is reputedly vulgar to show something directly, supposedly classier to "leave it to the imagination," to build on the resonances that accrue from suggestion and implication, as higher works of art generally do. The very rawness of Animal Comedy is part of its seemingly peculiar aspiration to *downward* mobility. By comparison, Woody Allen's art is yuppie comedy, aiming to efface his lower-class origins in stand-up comedy. (I mention Allen's upwardly mobile ambitions chiefly to point out what is so markedly different about Animal Comedy.) As it moves down the body, Animal Comedy also moves down in class—but, strikingly, it moves downward only in terms of content.

While genre itself in the past might have determined high or low class, class in the 1980s became entirely a matter of money. What is most striking about *Animal House* in the history of Hollywood comedy is not its vulgarity but rather the vulgarity within the wrappings of its slick and seemingly high production values. This film might have been an exploitation quickie in matter and attitude, but not in manner. And this difference in manner is the key importance of *M*A*S*H* and *American Graffiti*. *M*A*S*H* is a service comedy made classy by a cast of *dramatic* actors, a self-conscious highlighting of the ensemble performance through the extremity of its overlapping dialogue and a patina of seriousness that was signaled chiefly through grisly operation scenes and spurting blood. And *American Graffiti* is essentially an American-International teenybopper pic with a lot more spit and polish through its self-proclaimed attempt to catch the mood, style, and tone of a certain year—1962.

Also, in different ways, the Vietnam War hung over both these movies and endowed them with darker undercurrents for contemporary audiences and critics, undercurrents that have grown fainter in the intervening years. The films that came after them were not at all concerned with drawing on war as a way of enriching their status. Rather, they could act as if the class war had already been won, so that films of stature no longer had to be defined by their seriousness. By the time of *Animal House* and *Porky's*, the new comedies were quite content to celebrate their own apparent but joyous triviality.

This is not to say that these films are without challenges of their own. As the beast had been brought out of the closet, confusions in our conventional ways of determining class in movies spelled daunting confusions in standards of taste. The films themselves felt entirely comfortable with such confusions, in fact embraced them. Toward the beginning of *Bachelor Party*, when the five guys who form the core group meet for lunch, they repeatedly address each other as "you animal," allowing the film to point out right from the start how much it values inversions of values. Much as "bad" increasingly came to mean "good" in the 1960s and 1970s, "you animal" is a playful term of affection that casually reverses our traditional attitudes. In the world of this film, being animal commands more respect than being civilized. Being civilized in this film (as in most other Animal Comedies) has to be opposed because it promises a death-like existence of repression and a negation of spontaneous feeling.

For all that the discourse of Animal Comedy lauds the animal in man, oddly, once the beast is brought out, he acts, untamed creature that he is, in unexpected ways. Consider again the donkey dance from *Bachelor Party*. The premise of the scene is a promise that will never pay off. Without compromising its R rating, the film could have indicated that a sex act took place, but at some level it apparently suspects this would be too much, even for the anything-goes audience it posits. It would rather kill the donkey than follow through on its own freewheeling spirits. The beast, then, has been brought out of the closet to be killed, and uninhibitedness, once invoked, begins to set its own limitations. The actual parameters of repression are an infinitely changeable thing, but repression itself appears inescapable.

Even at its wildest, *Bachelor Party* is actually rather bashful about uninhibited sex. As far as I can tell, there are only two undeniable couplings at the party, and they are both presented indirectly. In one, a frustrated husband emerges with a satisfied smile on his face from a bedroom where one of the hired whores was apparently on duty, but we never actually see the woman. The absence is striking in the way it implicitly turns the sex act into a solitary experience. The second coupling is more fully dramatized, but it also takes a more bizarre turn. The wimpiest member of the group of five is caught by the sight of a woman across a crowded room: a tall bleached blonde—a good deal taller than the wimp, in fact—in a shiny tight evening gown, with broad shoulders and a husky voice. Their eyes meet, they go off into a bedroom, and an ellipsis shifts the scene to moments after the act when the wimp, overcome by the romantic circumstances of the meeting, passionately confesses to a friend that he's in love. At this point he wanders into a bathroom to discover his true love standing before a toilet with gown hiked up and urinating while standing. A reaction shot showing the wimp's realization that he has made love to a man is immediately followed by a shot of him in a shower, furiously scrubbing his chest and genitals to wash off the experience.

From a point of departure that seems to embrace all sex as good, clean fun, *Bachelor Party* then moves to a view of sex as indelibly dirty. *Bachelor Party* is in fact fairly dirty-minded throughout (not a typical feature of these films), and its tone is commensurately nastier than most Animal Comedy. Nonetheless, the confusions it arrives at in its attempts to strip off inhibitions do typify the genre. Animal Comedy is the product of an age that has tested the constraints of civilized behavior—but in this process of testing (and occasionally tearing down), these films almost inevitably (and for the most part unknowingly) end up constructing new constraints of their own.

Points of Departure

M*A*S*H and American Graffiti

At first glance, *American Graffiti* would seem to be the more direct influence on later films: the middle-class milieu that nonetheless opens itself up to other classes; the seemingly carefree existence of its aimlessly wandering young heroes, complemented by the aimlessly wandering plot; the plot line that centers on one character's quest for sexual initiation; a complementary striving for some kind of liberation in the other plot lines; and, in its most insistently repeated device, the what-happened-to-them-after epilogue that rounds off the seemingly open-ended narrative. Much as later gross-out comedies might borrow any of these elements, there are significant differences in tone that finally set *American Graffiti* apart from Animal Comedy. I want to consider briefly some of these differences as a way to throw the later films into relief.

Even when events become comparatively raucous, director George Lucas's personality always remains as sober-sided as a bookkeeper's, and there is relatively little sense of the high spirits that dominate the Animal Comedies. Rather, there is an underlying sense of disillusionment over the compromises life compels us to make and a concomitant nostalgia for the past. The epilogue makes evident what the tone of the film only evokes. Of the four boys we have followed in the course of the film, one dies while driving drunk; one is missing in action in Vietnam; the third becomes an insurance agent (which in terms of the rest of the film is something like a living death); and the fourth is a writer living in Canada, presumably in exile because of Vietnam. With this kind of future to look forward to, the past must truly seem a paradise lost.

"Where were you in '62?" the ads for *American Graffiti* asked on its first release. The nostalgic tone implicit in this question betrays the film's view of history. With a past defined chiefly as one of almost unlimited movement, of sporty cars and continuous music, indeed a nonstop party on wheels, any present must seem wanting. The explicit and implicit references to Vietnam in the epilogue contextualize the film to convey a sense of history as the final limiting constraint on all our freest aspirations. Many of the later Animal Comedies also take place in a not-too-distant past, with 1962 something of a favored year, but they have no need for the nostalgic fantasy of *American Graffiti.* Instead, because the libido possesses the power of magical thinking, the unconstrained libidinal drives that these films use to define their lead characters as heroic makes it possible to view the past anachronistically, as something that can be retroactively transformed by the libido.

The behavior of the kids in *Porky's* in particular would be inconceivable for the actual 1950s, the fictive date for the film. The only value the past maintains lies in the appeal of fifties' cars, fifties' rock 'n' roll, and a fondly remembered Eisenhower. In a very romanticized way, the spirit of the old commander-in-chief hovers over the film. He makes a brief appearance as an appropriately idealized Norman Rockwell portrait in a one-take scene when a frustrated and puritanical female gym instructor complains to her male colleagues and the school principle about a boy who has exposed his penis in the girls' shower room. As the men convulsively stifle their laughter throughout the scene, the camera slowly zooms in on the Rockwell portrait of a benignly smiling Ike. No matter that the real Eisenhower would likely have found it easy to express the disapproval that the other men in the scene find hard to share. As the zoom-in makes clear, it is the *image* of Eisenhower as kindly, indulgent grandfather that has become the important aspect of the 1950s for us. It is the images taken from the 1950s that count.

This is precisely the point: we appropriate the images of an earlier and seemingly more innocent age without their actual content. The rise of punk is as much an expression of our attitudes toward the 1950s as the rise of Reagan. We want to impose our own notions of behavior on the past as a way of regaining a past that we would really rather not return to. What was good about the 1950s, then, is chiefly the cars, the music, and the president—but not the sexual mores. So simply change the mores, and we can now feel more comfortable about who we are by fantasizing who we've been. As a consequence our identity becomes a matter of fantasy, a retreat from reality that itself appears real because of its seemingly historical perspective.

Much as the nostalgia itself signals fantasy, *American Graffiti* at least seems to honor the reality principle so cheerfully ignored by *Porky's* (which perhaps accounts for its higher critical standing). Inversely, what it does not honor is the animal drives of its characters, although there is certainly a sense of the animal in this film. Presiding over the entire narrative, weaving together the various strands, is a man-animal by the name of Wolfman Jack, a real-life disk jockey (playing himself) who provides running commentary between the rock 'n' roll cuts that play throughout the film. As the man who invokes the animal, he is defined in a way that will become familiar in Animal Comedy, and yet with a sense of qualification that will be absent from the later films. At one point in *American Graffiti*, Mackenzie Phillips tells Paul Le Mat that her parents won't let her listen to Wolfman because he's a Negro. The film immediately counters this remark by documenting the Wolfman's value through an elaborate montage sequence that shows all the various nightriders cruising the streets while listening to him on the radio. The positive value of this man-animal, then, is in a kind of social challenge: as a black, he rises up from the lowest classes; as a purveyor of rock 'n' roll he spreads the liberationist spirit of the music; as a radio personality he communicates across all social and individual boundaries.

And yet the film insists on putting all that is positive here in an ironic context. When Richard Dreyfuss, the one character destined to leave this town, wanders into the radio station, he discovers the real Wolfman: white, middle-aged, overweight, with a beard (the one concession to something different, something animal). In a discussion about getting out of town, the key thought occupying Dreyfuss on this his last night before leaving to go to college, he asks the Wolfman, "Why don't you leave?" The Wolfman's reply, "I'm not a young man anymore," is not exactly damning since the film itself has a deep ambivalence about what it means to leave home. Yet the unlimited freedom that he seems to represent in the earlier portions of the film and continually on its soundtrack is fully undercut by his response. Even he is bound to a place and a time.

What is animal and liberated in this film is pleasant only as an illusion, something to imagine more than to experience. When the animal enters reality, the film takes a turn toward the prudish. There is one other animal-man in the film, in fact another wolf. This wolfman also figures in another disillusionment, again witnessed by Richard Dreyfuss. The character is a teacher that Dreyfuss has apparently had a very close relationship with, a Mr. Wolfe. Dreyfuss talks to this other wolf as well, but Mr. Wolfe, who had gone "back East" to college, albeit for one semester only, has little advice to offer. Worse, the conversation is interrupted by Jane, a pretty student standing some way off in shadow, who calls Wolfe to her. After Wolfe walks over to her, Dreyfuss watches briefly as the older man makes a gentle, almost caressing gesture toward the girl's face.

It's not really clear what Dreyfuss sees in this, and he is soon distracted by the sight of a white Thunderbird. It's also not entirely clear what the film sees in this action. Is Mr. Wolfe really a wolf? Is he a seducer of his young charges or is the girl a seductress? The film seems to be somewhat uneasy about what it is showing. We catch only a glimpse of the inter-action between the two, in long shot, and the lighting is low key. The animal might be there, but it is better not to confront it directly. The film in fact ends up moving in a very different direction from later Animal Comedy. For all the seeming value accorded the free-spirited youngsters, the film finally exalts the ethereal over the physical.

The machine and not the animal offers the only real possibility for Eros in *American Graffiti*, as it seemingly offers the only real possibility for release. The reason Dreyfuss was distracted by the Thunderbird would seem to be his own sexual drives: earlier he had seen a blonde girl in just such a car beckoning to him, which causes him to spend the rest of the movie trying to find her again. Still, it is more accurate to say this has little to do with animal longing. The first time he sees her, he exclaims that she is "no woman!" By this he means she is no ordinary woman, but his actual phrase is right on target in other regards. Her appearance is ethereal: straw blonde, pale skin, the whiteness of the Thunderbird seemingly an exten-sion of her own coloring. This bird with its capacity to soar and transcend is preferable to the animal, which is why Dreyfuss can be distracted from his view of the big bad Wolfe by the promise of the mysterious, otherworldly bird.

By the end of the film, the object of his desire has fully metamorphosed into her car. As Dreyfuss looks out the window of the plane taking him East, he sees the white Thunderbird below speeding along a highway. There is a sense of regret here modulated by the irony of Dreyfuss looking down from a real height at a bird that is earthbound. Yet the irony is glancing, the regret dominant in support of the film's generally nostalgic tone. The car, and not a particular woman, is the appropriate symbol for all that is unfortunately left behind. Later films, like *Fast Times at Ridgemont High*, might also see cars as a source of liberation for their characters, but the films are just as likely to have those cars destroyed in surges of animal vitality. Animal feelings are displaced in *American Graffiti*, with the cars themselves carrying the strongest erotic charge (but an eroticism transformed into something spiritual). The halo of neon encircling Mel's Drive-In, the central meeting place for all the cars and kids, the spectral quality of light that seems to hover over all the cruising cars, in all this there is a sense of the sacred, which is really something different from festive art. The irrevocably lost times of this film are holy days, not holiday.

If specific narrative matter is derived from *American Graffiti*, it is nonetheless the rawer and more overtly sexual manner of *M*A*S*H* that makes it the more important influence on subsequent Animal Comedy. *M*A*S*H* is more fully an Old Comedy than *American Graffiti* in that it is built on a series of contests between the Elliott Gould–Donald Sutherland team and anybody who gets in their way, whether Army brass or women in authority. This could suggest a political content, yet the film insistently denies political meaning by denying that Gould and Sutherland seek power (unlike, for example, the women in *Lysistrata*). The us-versus-them opposition of *M*A*S*H* is something different from the anarchists versus conventionalists familiar from Old Comedy. The battle in this film deploys troops typical of later Animal Comedy: hip vs. square, the sexually liberated vs. the sexually uptight.

The virtues of Elliott Gould and Donald Sutherland over all the higher-ups in the army as well as their immediate adversary, fellow medic Robert Duvall, is chiefly a matter of attitude. They are cool, detached, able to escape from the insanity of their environment by their apparent indifference to it. However, this is not really the radical rejection of the world as it stands that it might at first appear to be because Sutherland and Gould have no wish to change that world. They have peculiarly accepted it as the necessary foil by which they might identify themselves. They in fact need this opposition to confirm the rightness of their own attitudes.

Robert Duvall, their chief opponent through the first half of the film, has responded to a crazy world by going crazy himself. In another context, his mad religiosity might be sympathetically regarded, without being endorsed, as an understandable reaction to the impossibility of his situation. Yet the film brutally rejects him, finally sending him off in a straitjacket. Madcap in the person of Gould or Sutherland is okay, but madness in the person of Duvall is not. In this rejection of Duvall, confusions at the center of the film come to the surface. The most damning scene against Duvall has him blaming a young orderly, Bud Cort, for the death of a patient. Throughout the scene Elliott Gould is shown in the background of the shot, wincing at Cort's pain in being told he has killed a patient by his neglect. The audience has already been encouraged to see Cort in all his winsome innocence as blameless and Duvall as the real villain. Consequently, a mise-en-scène that makes Gould the pivotal figure also makes him the most positive figure because of his empathy for Cort.

There are, however, limits to Gould's empathy. It does not occur to him to comfort the truly distraught Cort, who is very obviously in need of comforting. Instead, he goes into the next room, out of Cort's view, and slugs Duvall. In this way he provides himself—and the audience incidentally—with the satisfactions of his *own* violence, while leaving Cort entirely on his own to endure his distress. The film sentimentalizes Gould's concern at the beginning of the scene by having him act in a way that does nothing for the apparent object of his concern, although it does do a great deal for himself. Gould's empathy for Cort is really solipsistic and self-congratulatory since it quickly loses sight of Cort to go after the real object of its desires. The aggrandizement of the self is rarely carried to this extreme in the later films, but it is nonetheless important for them.

The extent to which the film shies away from acknowledging the real selfishness of its lead characters is best measured by the way it uses attitudes toward minorities as a test of virtue. This is a sentimentalized virtue because devoid of any real content, but it is important and worth looking at a little more closely here because the *correct* attitude toward minorities as a sign of virtue comes up with some frequency in the later Animal Comedies as well. Liking Jews is a sign of grace in the original *Porky's*; liking blacks takes on a similar function in *Porky's II: The Next Day* (1983); liking blacks in *Animal House* is something more hip, in fact a sign of hipness. In much the same way that a group of guys in *Porky's* casually tries to kid a redneck friend out of his redneck anti-Semitic response to a

Jew who has just entered their high school, Gould and Sutherland kid
redneck Tom Skerritt out of his objection to sharing a tent with a Negro
officer who is about to join their company. And yet minorities are almost
never key members of the central groups in any of these films. The democratic impulse rarely extends to forming close ties across racial and social
boundaries.

The democratic impulse doesn't extend to women either. In the treatment of women, the later Animal Comedies walk a line somewhere between *American Graffiti* and *M*A*S*H*. On the surface, *American Graffiti*
appears more gallant to its female characters to the extent that it seems to
take their emotions seriously and doesn't subject them to the kinds of
humiliations that the women in *M*A*S*H* have to endure repeatedly. But
one of the oddest features of the epilogue in Lucas's film is that it tells us
only what happened to the men.[17] It is as if the future of the women isn't
even worth mentioning because their future had only two possibilities
anyway—to get married or stay single—and it isn't very difficult to predict
the appropriate status for the appropriate characters. Strikingly, most of
the later Animal Comedies maintain the male bias in their epilogues as
well, with mention of the women made chiefly if it relates to the future
of the men. For example, Mandy figures in the epilogue of *Animal House*
solely because she marries Bluto (and because it is such an unlikely
match). Only in *Fast Times at Ridgemont High*, directed by a woman, are
the fates of the female characters granted status equal to those of the
men.[18]

The world of *M*A*S*H* is male-dominated to the point of being indif-
ferent to women except for sex. Its attitudes roughly outline the direction
the later films will take, although an underlying punitive attitude toward
sex makes the film more stridently callous toward its women than the later
Animal Comedies. Possibly one of the strangest episodes in *M*A*S*H* has
Donald Sutherland persuading his lover Jo Ann Pflug to sleep with a suicidal soldier to save his life. It seems the soldier (a dentist named Painless), famed among the troops both for the stupendous size of his penis
and the way he has used it on hundreds of women, has taken to worrying
about the nature of his own sexuality because a psychology book he has
just read says Don Juanism is a cover for latent homosexuality. The implicit
anti-intellectualism of this—not only does the film prove the book false,
it suggests a book can actually deceive this man about experiences he has
had—is not unusual in Altman's work, and it is also fairly typical of later
Animal Comedy as well. After all, the animals in both *Animal House* and
Porky's may be attending school, but the most important things they learn

have nothing to do with schooling. Experience (which inevitably means sexual experience) is opposed to formal education and always more highly valued.

Moreover, sexual experience should be read in these films as *male* sexual experience. Although women are certainly the object of masculine pursuit and are often sufficiently liberated to be available to male desire, female desire is at best a nebulous business. No woman in these films would consider killing herself because of sex as Painless does in *M*A*S*H*, but that is finally because sex supposedly doesn't mean very much to women. For the male animal in Animal Comedy, sex is *always* a matter of life and death. Sutherland uses a peculiar argument to convince Pflug to have sex with Painless. Appealing to some motherly impulse she ought to have, he insists it is her duty as a nurse, and he scores his most persuasive point by asking: "Is your virtue more important than his life?" In a very anti-Victorian way, sex has been transformed into Victorian-like duty. Any consideration of what Pflug herself might get out of the experience is limited to something that is of most interest to men. When Sutherland lifts up the sheets for her to view the presumably naked body of Painless with its outlandish penis, Pflug seems impressed to the point of submission, as if this penis were indeed painless in spite of its size. The view of her pleasure is presented in male terms.

The only time the film allows emotion about the women is when they have made themselves completely subservient to the men. The film suddenly goes squishy lyrical when a dazed and dreamy-eyed Pflug, the morning after doing her "duty" with the soldier she hardly knows, gets ready to leave the camp. Returning to home and husband, she has been magically transformed by the oversized penis. On the other hand, a completely recovered Painless hungrily sits down to a hearty breakfast as Pflug flies off, apparently already having forgotten about her. Sex might be a matter of life and death for men, but once they have had the experience, it can be neatly filed away, much as Sutherland himself had filed Pflug away in handing her over to the amorous dentist. Because women must necessarily be subordinate to men when it comes to sex, their own sexual desire is at best secondary in Animal Comedy. Men are the real animals.

Even if women are allowed to express sexual desire, the desire usually ends up contained in some way. A scene in *Fast Times at Ridgemont High* has two girls openly talking about fellatio, but the capper to the scene is that a group of guys, who have been listening to them the entire time, burst out laughing. Even in this film, which generally does honor its female characters' sexuality, it would be difficult to imagine the girls calling each other "you animal" in the approving manner of the guys in *Bachelor Party*. Generally, the only sexually liberated women in any of these films are not animals. Rather, they are entrepreneurs. This is at least anticipated by *M*A*S*H* where the women learn to render unto man what is man's rightful due (albeit without getting paid for it). Women's business sense improved in later comedies that saw the rise of the prostitute—*Night Shift* (1982), *Doctor Detroit, Risky Business, Trading Places* (all 1983), *Bachelor Party, Police Academy*, and so on—a development that oddly paralleled increasing public concern over the image of women in movies. The women in these films might be more overtly sexual than heroines in earlier comedies—and strikingly they often are paired with sexually inexperienced or reticent men—but their sexuality exists chiefly to be dominated, a commodity the women are never allowed to call their own because men always maintain the financial power to possess it. This contradiction between apparent sexual liberation and actual sexual subordination is central to Animal Comedy.

In an article on the underlying patterns of comic form, Northrop Frye has described a familiar movement toward "social integration" in comedy, a conciliatory gesture by which the opposing world is finally made to come around to the position of the comic hero. The conciliatory aspect of this movement is absent from *M*A*S*H* since the rightness of the heroes' position is often established by force, but in other aspects Frye's pattern applies here and has suggestive implications for both the sexual and social aspects of Animal Comedy. Frye describes those who stand in the way of the comic hero as "*people who are in some kind of mental bondage*, who are helplessly driven by ruling passions, neurotic compulsions, social rituals, and selfishness." The standard comic plot attempts to deliver these "humors" from their state of bondage: "The essential comic resolution, therefore, is an individual release which is also a social reconciliation. . . . The freer the society, the greater the variety of individuals it can tolerate, and the natural tendency of comedy is to include as many as possible in its final festival. The motto of comedy is Terence's 'Nothing human is alien to me.' "[19]

The ruthlessness with which comedy can reject varieties of human behavior—and *M*A*S*H* is particularly ruthless in this regard—might make Frye's final point on embracing all that is alien questionable, but I think his notion of movement from bondage to liberation is of key importance for Animal Comedy. The celebration of the animal in man that underlies these films makes liberation—and specifically liberation from social constraints—one of the key aims of the films. But as the confusion in Frye's last point suggests, the liberation often comes at some expense, bought by an acquiescence in other kinds of constriction, a point that has both social and sexual implications for Animal Comedy. How this works in the sexual sphere is clearest in the treatment of the Sally Kellerman character in *M*A*S*H*.

The episode with Pflug occupies a single narrative event and Pflug's role is less important than Sally Kellerman's, but between Pflug and Kellerman, *M*A*S*H* establishes the two types of women that most often turn up in Animal Comedy. They are not exactly whore and virgin but rather something close to these in their opposition of sexual compliance and sexual hypocrisy. Kellerman is the prime butt of jokes throughout the film because she is a sexual hypocrite, and hypocrisy is precisely the kind of bondage from which comedy seeks to liberate its characters. The very existence of the character *type*, then, sets up certain expectations. As comedy always has it, the hypocrisy will be exposed, and in the exposure the character will find herself freed from the constraints of her behavior. In the terms the film presents, Kellerman is in fact freed by an action that earns her the name "Hot Lips." Nonetheless, as the name suggests, she moves from one form of typing to another and in fact from one form of bondage to another.

Initially, the Kellerman character is set up as strictly army, a fiend for order, rigid in her application of the rules, and sexually uptight. Her humiliation comes through the broadcast of her lovemaking with Robert Duvall, her male counterpart in punctiliousness, over the public address system to the entire camp. It is a fitting comic deflation because this one action exposes everything that is hypocritical about both characters. Still, the film wants us to laugh at both Kellerman and Duvall not simply because they are exposing their hypocrisies, but precisely because they demonstrate some sexual appetite, because they are animal. It would be one thing if they were in fact delivered from their bondage by their public exposure, and more in keeping with the conciliatory tone that Frye has noted in comedy. But there is no real conciliation in this film. In fact, the film punishes the characters further for their one moment of liberation. Duvall enters more deeply into bondage as he is literally bound up in a straitjacket and led off to the loony bin. Kellerman almost completely disappears from the film, brought back later solely for further humiliations. Duvall almost gets off easy by being led off in a straitjacket; Kellerman's real problem for the film is that she is a woman.

The visual possession of women becomes a fairly common feature in Animal Comedy, and the scene most frequently repeated is established in

M*A*S*H (although usually inflected in the later films in a strikingly different manner). This key "type scene" is the public exposure of Hot Lips stark naked in her shower as all the guys and some of the gals watch and cheer as if they had just witnessed a theatrical performance. Animal Comedy picks up this scene and transmutes it often by multiplying the number of naked women. The setting may still be a shower or a dormitory room and the viewer may be alone or in a group, but the implication of theatricality usually remains. But there is an important shift in motivation in the later films. There the viewers are almost always male, and they are provoked to their voyeurism chiefly by sexual desire; in *M*A*S*H* the motivation is revenge, plain and simple.

Why further revenge this late in the film, when Hot Lips has already been humiliated—devastatingly—much earlier for her sexual hypocrisy? Moreover, after that earlier putdown, she gains Gould's approval during a difficult operation ("Hot Lips, you may be a pain in the ass, but you're a damn good nurse"). Since the approbation, qualified but not really grudging, indicates her progressive integration into the community, the continued need to humiliate her suggests there might be other characters in bondage. When Gould and Sutherland arrive in Japan for an emergency operation, Gould brusquely instructs a hospital official, "And give me *one* nurse who knows how to work in close without getting her tits in the way." The animosity here is directed not so much at the competency of the nurse, but at the "tits," the real problem with women. Breasts and nurses go together conventionally not just because nurses are mostly female, but because we associate both with caring nurturance. As such, Gould's rejection of the nurse's "tits" is for the film a rejection of dependency.

The central issue in the shower humiliation of Hot Lips is control. By desexualizing the voyeurism and heightening what Freud called the "component instinct" of sadism to replace sexual interest and enshrining revenge, the film places its voyeurs in a superior position where they themselves cannot be affected by the actual content of the spectacle. At the time of its release, one critic was moved to "salute *M*A*S*H* for its contribution to the art of talking dirty,"[20] and "dirty" is perhaps the best word for the way sexuality is viewed throughout the film. The sadistic impulses that dominate sexual expression here suggests a punitive response, an activity that needs to be cleaned up. This can happen in the later films as well. I noted earlier that *Bachelor Party* is dirty-minded, but unusually so. For the most part, however, Animal Comedy, much as it derives from *M*A*S*H*, moves in an opposite direction in its view of sexuality, striving to create a liberated world in which nothing sexual is dirty. In *Porky's*, as we shall see, there is at least the desire to make sexuality equal cleanliness.

I want to emphasize the difference in the way the scopophilic scenes are handled because it points to what is most distinctive about the later films. In *M*A*S*H* male bonding is central to the narrative, almost as if to compensate for the general sexual distaste that underlies much of the film. In the later films, male bonding, as Dave Kehr suggests, might offer a strong appeal, but it always remains a secondary concern. *M*A*S*H* does allow Donald Sutherland a brief love interest in Jo Ann Pflug, although it is barely sketched in and has little suggestion of any emotional interaction. Gould, on the other hand, has no dramatized interest in women at all. The real emotional center of the film is in the Sutherland-Gould friendship. The situation is quite different in *Animal House*: both Tim Matheson and Peter Riegert have sexual involvements which grant them major scenes apart from each other. Further, their sexual interests offer the key to their characters, with Matheson's promiscuity playing off Riegert's monogamy. The boys in the later films might join together for pranks (rarely directed specifically against women), but they are likely to go their separate ways in their individual romantic pursuits. In the terms of *M*A*S*H*, "tits" never get in the way in the later films.

There is one other scene of shower voyeurism in *M*A*S*H* that has attracted, surprisingly, less attention, but it should be mentioned here because it more closely anticipates the voyeuristic scenes in the later films—with one important difference: the sex object in this case is a man, in fact Painless, the suicidal dentist. Oddly, this time the interest is more genuinely scopophilic than in the scene with Hot Lips in that sex, rather than sadism, now provides the focus of voyeuristic concern. At a point early in the film, the men in the camp line up to catch a glimpse through a peep hole of Painless as he showers because, as we learn through dialogue not image, he has an extraordinarily large penis. The men's involvement in the spectacle is made explicit by two guys, one played by innocent Bud Cort, walking away from the show. As they express their pleasure over what they've just seen, his buddy excitedly says to Cort, "Man, I'd purely love to see *that* angry!" In the frequently sadistic context of the rest of the film, "angry" seems the appropriate word for sexual arousal. There is nonetheless something different here because the attraction is specifically sexual. "Tits" might offer an object for attack, but a large penis is magnetic.

In noting the sexual interest of this scene, I do not intend to dismiss it in preference to the later reworkings of Animal Comedy because they recast the voyeurism in heterosexual terms. In fact, considering the extent to which the rest of *M*A*S*H* works to keep homoeroticism far beneath the surface of the male camaraderie, I think what is best about this particular scene is its frank and easy admission of homoerotic interest. And because the scene determines a male as sex object, it provides a way of thinking about voyeurism that moves it away from sadism.[21] The pleasure of Hot Lips as object lies principally in the control granted the voyeurs, which is why it is important for the voyeurs to make their presence known to their victim. With Painless, who apparently remains unaware he is on display, there is never any question of control. The desire to see the penis "angry," a wish not granted by the performance, is tacitly an admission of the inability to control the spectacle. The seer's relationship to the seen, then, is more one of passivity. Pleasure lies in the eye's capacity not only to receive but also to conceive, to give life in fantasy to what remains inert in reality. The wish that sight provokes ties imagination to perception.

Precisely because the scene is more specifically sexual than the one with Hot Lips, there must remain questions about its intended impact. Since the film clearly does not intend us to regard the majority of the men in the camp as homosexual, why the desire to see the penis erect in an otherwise nonsexual context, or at best an autoerotic one? And why is erect defined as "angry"? The passivity in viewing is the key to what is taking place here: a kind of regression, in which the viewer feels something incommensurate between his own size and the size of the object. Clearly, the penis has been turned into a kind of aesthetic object, something that rewards contemplation with pleasure, with beauty determined chiefly by size. The fact that one man is looking at another does not make the voyeurism entirely a matter of identification since the desire to see the superpenis in the first place is based entirely on a sense of difference, a sense further enlarged by the desire to see it erect.[22] If the male viewer hopes to possess the potency of the male object by taking visual possession, the desire functions to conceal a perceived lack in himself. This felt absence behind the wish to enlarge the penis is the key to understanding the desire to see the penis "angry" and its term of expression.

What pleasure can the voyeur find in the penis's anger? Perhaps more exactly, where is the anger to be directed? The fact that the voyeuristic relationship here is dyadic serves to remove the anger from any possible heterosexual context in which sadism otherwise flourishes in this film. Because the voyeur in the film is as solitary as his object, if there is anger here, it must be directed toward the voyeur himself. The desire to see the penis angry, then, is a suppressed desire for punishment, and the position of the spectator is most precisely defined as masochistic.[23] The pleasure of viewing superpenis is not so much one of identification as regression, a return to an infant's helplessness in which the infant feels his own lack of power when confronting the object.[24] It is for this reason that comparable scenes of voyeurism in Animal Comedy are likely to present the voyeur in a precarious position. John Belushi in *Animal House*, for example, becomes so excited by the sight of a sorority sister masturbating that he falls off the ladder he had climbed up to gain this privileged sight. Whatever the specifics of gender, the passive position suggested in the voyeuristic regard of Painless is closer to the direction taken by the later films.

The scene with Painless is presented in glancing fashion, no doubt necessarily because the film is directed to a broad audience that would not want to linger over the homoerotic content. The heterosexual context in later versions of this scene make possible the more sexually explicit approach typical of Animal Comedy. To get at what is derived from *M*A*S*H* and what is discarded, consider the most exact re-creation of this scene in a later film. In doing so we come fairly close to scraping the bottom of a barrel that most cultured people would not want to open in the first place. Still, there is a pleasant consequence of Animal Comedy's seeming lack of inhibition: on occasion even the worst of films lights on startling images and scenes, however fleeting, that for their resonant outrageousness would challenge the most extreme Dadaism. *Hardbodies* (1984), I have little doubt, *is* one of the worst of movies, the kind of drudgery I could harden myself to only after I had become committed to my topic. Yet it does manage two scenes charged with such wild grotesquerie that they briefly breathe life into the general torpor. One of them, a reworking of the Painless-in-the-shower scene from *M*A*S*H*, typically recasts the scene in a heterosexual mode. Atypically, the man is kept as a sex object and those lining up to admire his endowments are women.

The bizarreness of the episode does not lie in inverting conventional male-female roles of voyeur–sex object. That's an inversion not at all uncommon in the 1980s, most obviously in the rise of the beefcake poster but also in movies themselves, where leading men have begun to find fitness trainers more important than acting coaches.[25] In that context what is comically strange about *Hardbodies* is the choice of male sex object: short, fat, both hirsute and balding, the least prepossessing male animal Animal Comedy could imagine. Yet this nebbish also inspires the film to its two wildest flights of fancy. To get at what happens in the second scene, the reworking from *M*A*S*H*, I have to look briefly at the first, in which the nebbish figures in literally fantastic form.

In this scene, two sisters who have been changing their clothes find themselves at one point both stripped to the waist and facing a mirror. As they look at themselves, they puzzle over why men are so attracted to breasts, noting that breasts don't do much of anything other than just lie there. Getting increasingly giggly from their speculations, they engage in a mutual fantasy of what the nebbish character might look like if he had breasts. At this point there is something best described as a "breast wipe," a wipe of interconnecting ovals, to a brief depiction of their fantasy: the nebbish lies horizontally across the screen, stark naked but with the left frame line discreetly blocking out his pubic area. Superimposed on his plump, hairy body are two large, floppy breasts, appropriate to his physical type.

Because the fantasy proceeds from the sisters looking at *themselves* in the mirror, it serves them as a means of understanding the transformation of their own bodies since puberty and the commensurate increase in sexual differentiation. The fantasy, then, signals a simultaneous movement toward maturity, which recognizes the sexually changed and charged body, complemented by a regression to infancy, a period in which greater sexual indeterminacy allows for commonplace confusions over sexual parts. In a number of essays, Freud notes the phenomenon of little boys imaginatively endowing their mother with a penis.[26] For Freud, this is a matter of primary narcissism, a need to maintain a sense of integrity when confronting the reality of castration that the mother's body actually presents.

The confusion in this scene provides a parallel that endows the father's masculine and hairy body with breasts, but also leaves the actual sexual organ indeterminate (or, perhaps more accurately, cut off—by the frame line). Further, since the fantasy proceeds from a mirror image, it also signals the dreamers' narcissistic investment in the dream. On the other hand, the regression to a childlike curiosity distances the women from their own reflected images. In effect, the image of their mother is reflected back to their regressed selves, in which a lack in their own bodies is complemented by the mother's abundance. This is similar to the regression and concomitant sense of inadequacy that lies behind the voyeur's narcissistic investment in Painless's penis.

The difference in *Hardbodies* comes in the double movement, which regresses the viewers to a childlike vision at the same time that it propels them into adult sexuality (with a strong suggestion that the infantile is never very far from the adult). This conflation of the infantile and the adult is central to Animal Comedy. In *M*A*S*H* the voyeurism prompts a fantasy that reinforces the scopophile's sense of inadequacy. In *Hardbodies* the inadequacy prompts a fantasy that in effect endows everyone with breasts, almost as if to confirm the rightness of the adult's body. The regression might initially distance the two sisters from their bodies as they wonder about the value of breasts, but ultimately it paves the way for an identification with the mother because their reflected images confirm their new, adult selves. What is being honored in the fantasy of the man with breasts is the resilience of the narcissistic ego in rebounding from its potential wounds and imposing its vision of self on the rest of the world.

The second scene, the one that derives directly from *M*A*S*H*, also builds on a narcissistic regression. This time, the nebbish character who was the subject of the sisters' fantasy is granted a triumphant reassertion of his masculinity by being turned into an image of male abundance. A group of women line up on a flight of stairs waiting their turn to catch a glimpse of a spectacular display located in the privacy of a bedroom. On display is the nebbish, totally naked but wearing a crown and holding a scepter, the symbolic substitute for what we are not allowed to see since the one view of him the audience is granted has him posed with his legs coyly crossed. This man who had previously failed to attract women has become an object of adoration because, like Painless, he possesses an exaggerated organ that transforms him into a totem. But since the character here is aware of the gaze and takes pleasure in it, the focus of the scene is as much on exhibitionism as voyeurism, what Freud saw as the passive and active forms of the same impulse.[27]

The pleasure of the exhibitionism lies in what is mirrored back to the character, a confirmation of narcissistic dreams of potency that acts as a counter to his earlier transformation in the sisters' fantasy. Again, the scene indulges a regression inasmuch as it points to a passivity of the character: he sits there waiting for definition of self in the admiring gaze of each woman. The regression is made explicit in the scene's conclusion. The nebbish's mother arrives for a visit and is told to wait in line. When she gets into the bedroom, she expresses outrage at what she sees and pulls him away from his adoring throng after making him get dressed. The effect is much like a mother who indulges her child's narcissistic exhibitionism until she decides she's had enough and puts a stop to it.

The exhibitionism in this scene itself parallels the central project of Animal Comedy—the attempt to determine how far one can go before some repressive force steps in. The double movement toward infantile and adult sexual expression I noted in these two scenes provides a developmental parallel to this project, with the infantile suggesting the unlimited realm, the adult the realm of the contained. If many of these films focus on characters in their late teens and early twenties, it is because this is the period of life most concerned with testing the limits of free expression: the freedom of infancy has only recently been left behind, the responsibilities of adulthood lay ahead. Repression, it often turns out in these films, is lurking just around the corner to punish the most outlandish expressions of liberation. Free sexual expression generally ends up contained in these films, but only *after* it has been *indulged.* The indulgence itself remains a primary pleasurable goal—and an aesthetic goal for the films themselves—because it enables a regressive reassertion of the narcissistic ego.

Animal Comedy is generally more directly focused on sexuality than is *M*A*S*H*, and even a truly marginal film like *Hardbodies* can provide these brief, explosive insights into sexual feeling that *M*A*S*H* is not really interested in. In making these comparisons, I have tried to establish what is distinctive about Animal Comedy by showing how it departs from the films it most fully derives from. As a prelude to a consideration of individual films, let me note the key features of the genre, the elements that find the most insistent repetition from film to film:

- As the above comparison to *M*A*S*H* should make clear, characters in Animal Comedy are defined chiefly in terms of their sexual desires. It is probably inescapable that guys attending a bachelor party should think of sex, but in these films high school and college students think chiefly of sex, summer campers think chiefly of sex, workers and members at a country club think chiefly of sex, soldiers think chiefly of sex, police trainees think chiefly of sex, even kibutzniks think chiefly of sex.[28] Only humans can be animal as these films use the term, which is to say that only humans can be so single-mindedly concerned with sex. The donkey in *Bachelor Party* wants food, not sex.
- Character typology concomitantly moves along lines of sexual interest. Unlike animal sexuality, which has biological regulation, human sexuality depends on inhibitions and repressions. But because animality in the films is regarded as freedom from inhibition, characters are defined negatively or positively by the extent to which they have embraced their animal natures, ranging from the anally repressed to the genitally aggressive, from tight-assed to cock of the walk.

- There is an element of the grotesque in all these films that derives in part from the insistent animality of the characters, although the general tone and feel of individual films may differ. When animality is its primary feature, the grotesque is generally celebratory.
- A more derisive use of the grotesque is made for figures of authority and power. They are usually the most overtly stylized in presentation, even in films like *Fast Times at Ridgemont High* and *Heaven Help Us*, where character is given a more realistic definition than is common in the genre. Even in these films, however, most students are preoccupied with sex, while the teachers move into the realm of grotesque caricature, comically in *Fast Times*, demonically in *Heaven Help Us*.
- As a complement to the insistent sexual dimension, character definition is often extended to a generalized desire for liberation. This might act in some of the softer core films as a substitute for specifically sexual desire.
- Characters are generally aligned to an institution, which may be construed as loosely as a country club (or even a bachelor party), but is most often seen as high schools (with summer camp a seasonable variation), prep schools, college, or the armed forces.
- The alignment of characters with an institution keeps the focus of the films more on groups of people rather than individuals. Individuals may stand out from the group, but they are nonetheless identified by their participation in the group.
- The group is generally defined in the mode of the World War II combat film by a variety of types. As a consequence, there is an underlying, and occasionally explicit, concern with defining a pluralistic society as a desired goal, although the pluralism does not encompass figures of authority.
- The structure of the narrative reflects the focus on a social group by being episodic, contingent, always retaining the possibility of veering off with a character who might have previously seemed minor.
- There is a revenge motif in at least one plot strand, the resolution of which (marked by the triumph of the group of animals) signals the end of the plot for the entire film.
- The plot moves through a series of random or interconnected contests, generally marking victories for the various protagonists along the way. These little contests culminate in a final contest

that is the most fully elaborated (and usually involves the entire cast), either in the form of a sporting event (derived from the concluding football game in *M*A*S*H* and the drag race in *American Graffiti*) or as an elaborate prank that is usually motivated by the revenge plot (*Animal House* and *Porky's*).[29]

- An us-versus-them mentality pervades all these films, providing the only real forward dynamic in the loose plot structure. The central group generally defines itself by values inimical to its opponents, who are often the ruling power structure.

This list is not exhaustive. Nor does it claim to account for the most notable elements of individual films. By it I have merely tried to establish a community drawn together from some of the most popular comedies over the last decade or so, something like a linguistic community which provides a discourse that each individual film utilizes for its own particular enunciation.[30] Not every element will appear in every film, and some that are foregrounded in one film may well move into the background in another. Finally, not every element is exclusive to Animal Comedy.[31] This could hardly be the case considering the ancient traditions Animal Comedy draws on. But more particularly there are points of overlap between Animal Comedy and what came to be known in this period as "teenpix"— in part because both have youthful casts (frequently in the case of Animal Comedy, always with the teenpix). For this reason, my discussion will occasionally segue into a consideration of the presentation of adolescence in other teenpix and other genres. But still there are very real differences here that mark Animal Comedy as a separate genre. Most simply stated, works like *Bachelor Party*, *Police Academy*, and *Moving Violations* (1985), all of which have adult casts, have far more in common with *Animal House* and *Porky's* than with, say, *Pretty in Pink* (1986).[32] How those points in common were first enunciated and what they signify are the subject of the next chapter, which looks at the two films that set the flattering standard of imitation that later works paid to them.

Chapter 7 **Sex and Power**

Porky's (1982)

As I suggested in the last chapter, the emphasis on animality in both *Animal House* and *Porky's* establishes them as the key influences on the subsequent comedies and places them all securely in the domains of farce. *Animal House* (1978) is not entirely without the kind of punitiveness associated with sex that shows up in *M*A*S*H* (1970), which in effect criticizes characters for the nature of their sexuality. Still, the grounds for the criticism are different because no one in *Animal House* is a sexual hypocrite like Sally Kellerman and Robert Duvall's characters. There is a jokey scene of a Wasp brother and sister sitting in a car parked in lover's lane and talking about the stressful events of the day while the sister solicitously masturbates (out of camera view) the harried brother, who is so upset by the behavior of the Animal House brothers that he just can't get into the sex. The sister's pumping arm stops only when she asks him to relax. The punch line to the scene comes with the revelation that she has been wearing surgical gloves throughout the "operation."

There are two comic barbs here: the nature of the sex (an early 1960s aversion to "going all the way") and the manner in which the sex is practiced (a prissily antiseptic hygiene—in the days before "safe" sex—at the opposite extreme of the let-it-all-hang-out shenanigans of the Animal House brothers). Since there is no middle ground here, the polarizations of behavior become unfair in the way that comedy is often unfair. Even so, *all* the characters in this film see themselves as sexual. It is finally ironic (but not entirely incongruous) that the woman is this scene will eventually end up with John Belushi. In the film's terms, this destiny offers her a level of sexual liberation never really granted Sally Kellerman in *M*A*S*H.*

Porky's is more generous toward its characters to the extent that it assumes *uninhibited* sexual desire for most, if not all, of them—good guys and bad guys alike. Further, *Porky's* is one of the few gross-out films that strives for something like sexual equality between men and women (even to the point of objectifying the guys as well as the gals). The film might have become initially well-known for its girls' shower scene, but it also presents a surprising amount of male nudity. More than that, it has an almost obsessive concern with what penises look like, right from the very opening scene when a character aptly named Pee Wee wakes up and measures his erection only to discover (he thinks) that it is growing shorter. Action films often have a male bias similar to Animal Comedy. In action films of the period just preceding Animal Comedy, Leo Braudy noted a movement toward a new explicitness: "The phallic guns function in the films of the 1960s and 1970s precisely as penis substitutes."[1] What's going on in *Porky's* is related to these changes, yet is something of a different nature. There is little phallic imagery in *Porky's*. The film is simply too literal for that, rarely finding a substitute as good as the real thing. Rather, *Porky's* is obsessed with penises, plain and simple.

There is a frequent strangeness to this film, strange in the original sense of the word—that so much in it seems foreign to actual experience, much as its sense of the 1950s is foreign to the actuality of the 1950s. There are plenty of jokes about erections and outsized sexual equipment in Mel Brooks's comedies, but I would guess that only homosexual pornography surpasses *Porky's* in its explorations of the variety of penile expression. The strangeness of *Porky's*, for American culture at least, is to present men as sex objects within a certifiably heterosexual context and to exult in Dionysian fashion in the penis as an erotic delight. The penis obsession of the film becomes a dreamlike inversion of our more culturally acceptable breast obsession.

The sense of a dream is important here because it makes acceptable the various inversions worked in the film. Speaking the unspeakable does give it the liberating quality of a dream; but there are so many troubling aspects to this dream, so many restraints thrown off, that the film occasionally threatens to become a nightmare—at least for its characters. One of the film's strangest scenes (one that occurs well before the better-known shower scene of naked girls) presents a group of naked guys in a specifically sexual context. This comes about when three boys play a practical joke on a group of their classmates: Promising a treat, they take them all out for an evening of sexual initiation with "Cherry Forever" (Susan Clark). The classmates are made to sit stark naked on Cherry's porch while they politely wait their turn. Meanwhile, the three jokesters, still clothed, claim the right to go first and retire inside with Cherry where they make all sorts of sexual sounds, moaning, groaning, and bouncing on the bed springs, without ever actually making love. By crosscutting back and forth, the film undermines the increasingly excited expectations of the classmates with the elaborate hilarity of the jokesters. The topper to the joke comes in the form of a huge black man who bursts in on the scene, apparently in a murderous rage at all these naked boys about to have their way with his wife.

What exactly is the point of this joke? The pleasure of the guys who have planned and elaborately executed the ruse is specifically not sexual since they only play at having sex with Cherry. Rather, the pleasure to be had is of a sadistic nature. It lies in arousing sexual desire in their buddies and then subjecting them to a particular punishment for that arousal. By the end of the scene it seems clear how "Cherry Forever" has earned her name, for neither the original jokesters nor their victims actually gain her sexual favors. This extremely sexualized situation finally offers no sexual fulfillment. The only pleasure from staging this caper must reside in an allegiance with the rampaging husband (an implied punishing "father figure"). Yet the husband/father is cast in conventional American terms as the "other," a character whose sexuality literally rages to set him apart from these more innocent white boys. The nightmare of the scene lies in the displacement of sexual desire into terror. Sexual arousal itself seems to conjure up the black superstud, the most awesome threat the endangered white male ego can imagine.[2]

Even before the scene becomes specifically nightmarish, it forces its characters into a dreamlike passivity, a virtual helplessness in confronting a sexually aggressive female. At the beginning of the scene, the boys are told to strip so that Cherry, playing nurse, can inspect them for venereal disease. As she does so, she studies each boy carefully and gives an incisive appraisal of the variety of sex organs she encounters, ranging from the expected belittling comments about Pee Wee to a slightly mocking astonishment about "Meat" (whose name is apparently as appropriate as Pee Wee's). While there is plenty of full frontal male nudity in the rest of the scene, at this point the camera is relatively discreet, shooting the boys from the waist up. Cherry's descriptions, however, are so exact and responsive to what she sees, that the viewer seems encouraged to conjure up the appropriate image. The penises become what the dominant woman makes them out to be.

Much of the comedy in this scene comes from the boys' responses to the descriptions, responses predicated on an enforced passivity that reverses male and female sex roles to make the woman the predator and the men the sex objects. Cherry, of course, is quite a bit older than the boys, and the way she is treating them at this also has a perverse maternal quality, so that the pure sense of fun the scene is after quickly segues into slapstick that seeks to allay the Oedipal nightmare. Thus, the admiring ministrations of the nurse-mother-whore leads to helpless arousal that in turn leads to the unwanted emergence of the castrating father, a superego figure appearing in the id disguise of black monster (who takes over the "primitive" quality of the instinctual energies he punishes). The whole scene ends appropriately with the common nightmare situation of finding oneself naked in a public place. Pee Wee, the character with the most to lose because he starts off with the least, runs for his life stark naked down the road toward town, where he is picked up by two cops out on patrol.

Porky's certainly upped the stakes on raunchiness in adolescent comedies—even *Animal House* began to seem a bit tame in retrospect—and I find much that is liberating in its exuberant directness and openness about sex. Much of the sexual comedy in the film (like that in the penis-inspection scene) has a naughty innocence that suggests the fun of boy and girls playing doctor together. The shower scene (the centerpiece of the advertising campaign) dramatizes a sweetly childlike "you show me yours and I'll show you mine" exchange, in which the girls take as much delight in inspecting the boys as vice versa. Still, even as the film joyously celebrates its own sexual liberation, over and over again the liberation oddly invokes its own constraints, most often by the way the comedy repeatedly takes on the elements of a nightmare.

Consider the case of the young male gym teacher in steadfast pursuit of a young female coach who ardently refuses his advances. An older coach, who, inexplicably, always refers to the young woman coach as

"Lassie," advises his younger colleague to take her up to the boys' locker room. Once there, he says meaningfully, everything will become clear. The young man remains skeptical, but he finally maneuvers the woman into the boys' locker room, where she is so turned on by the smell of sweaty gym clothes that she immediately initiates sex. This should of course be the fulfillment of the young coach's desires, but instead, as soon as the sexual activity begins, he unpleasantly discovers the reason for her nickname. In ecstasy, "Lassie" begins to howl wildly like a dog. The howl reverberates through the entire gymnasium where it is heard by smirking boys, startled girls, and a suspicious older female coach. The male coach's fear of discovery, then, immediately undercuts the pleasure of the sex. Sexual desire, in the logic of a nightmare, is married to frustration. Wanting to continue the sex, but also wanting to silence his partner, the male coach stuffs her mouth with the gym clothes. In quieting her expression of pleasure with the original source of the turn-on, he tries to build *his* pleasure on a denial of *hers*. Arousal carries within it the seeds of its own frustration.

Porky's repeatedly finds it difficult to be entirely uninhibited about its lack of inhibitions, however, and contradictions arise in the very terms the kids use to define their play. Even in the girls' shower scene, which most fully achieves the exhilaration of high-spirited boys and girls having sexual fun together, the film exposes contradictions in its most liberated attitudes. Pee Wee and two cohorts sneak into a passageway behind the girls' shower room (fortuitously equipped with three peepholes) and arrive just in time to witness the girls' shower after gym class. Pee Wee's peephole, unfortunately, gets blocked off by a very chubby girl taking a shower. In frustration, Pee Wee shouts for her to get out of the way, which causes all the girls to realize they are being observed. None of them takes this as badly as Sally Kellerman in *M*A*S*H*—partly because humiliation is not really the point here and partly because the girls *enjoy* being sex objects. The status of women as sex objects in this instance is not a matter of putting them in their place, as it was in *M*A*S*H*. Everybody in this film, male and female alike, is a sex object and quite happy to be so.

The girls might initially be the ones on display in the shower scene, but at least one boy manages to make it a mutual display, and in a fairly objectifying way. After their shock at being discovered is followed by amusement, the girls decide it best to leave, so one of Pee Wee's cohorts, in an attempt to keep them there, sticks his penis through the peephole, staging a piece of improvisational theater starring a character named "Polly the Penis," who speaks with a falsetto voice, a sex object with a personality. The girls are in fact delighted by this performance and stay on to watch, but their gym teacher Miss Balbricker (leading to the fateful nickname Miss Ballbreaker) rushes in and grabs hold of the penis, hoping to apprehend and convict the boy attached to it.

Being uninhibited has its risks, of course, and not just for boys who stick their penises through peepholes in shower walls. In the outrageous hilarity of this scene there is a sense that writer-director Bob Clark has let *himself* go to produce something like the filmic equivalent of automatic writing. The free play of fancy is probably what made the scene work so effectively for audiences in the first place, but Clark's fancy here (as elsewhere in the film) also leads him in directions that cancel out some of the premises of the scene. First, the act of *male* aggression that leads to the final action in the scene is presented in *female* terms. The sociable penis gives itself a woman's name and speaks in a high-pitched voice; but because he has detached his penis from his body, it is almost as if the boy were in fact inviting the dismemberment that the "ballbreaking" woman threatens him with.

In addition, there is the odd fact that after a few tempting long shots of girls with endowments you are not likely to find in the average gym class, the camera then chooses to look mostly at the fat girl who is blocking Pee Wee's peephole. The point might be to make the audience feel some of Pee Wee's frustration, but it also keeps us from seeing what the two other guys see. Instead the fat girl becomes the center of the camera's interest and, by implication, an object of disgust. The point is, apparently: there are limits to uninhibitedness, not all nudity is desirable, and some repression threatens at every point and, strikingly, often in the guise of a fat person. By first encouraging us to join the boys in the delights of viewing a naked bevy of shapely girls, then deliberately blocking our view and forging an identity with Pee Wee that we would rather reject, the film encourages our frustration. Actual repression in the person of a ballbreaker necessarily follows our own desires for repression as we realize we would prefer to have the fat girl both clothed and away from the peephole.[3]

In effect, the film evokes arousal chiefly to establish constraints. The fat girl is brought into the film solely to block our view of the svelte girls we've already been encouraged to enjoy. We never see the fat girl in any other scene, but her visual presence is echoed by other characters who take on the same thematic function of frustrating desire. Miss Balbricker, who puts the ultimate damper on this scene, is fat, and her appearance at the end of the scene provides quite a dramatic escalation. The first fat person merely frustrates the feeling of sexual desire, but the second threatens dismemberment. Finally—and most importantly since he gives the film its title—Porky is also fat.

That Porky does in fact give the film its title would seem surprising from any simple synopsis of the plot. He appears in only two sequences and is never established as the kind of presence that could linger over the other sections of the film. Initially, he might stand for uninhibitedness and sexual license because he runs a saloon-cum-whorehouse on the other side of the county line where such things are beyond the reach of conventional law. The opening shot of the film that identifies both Porky's place and the title of the film itself through an illuminated sign suggests this. Outlined in neon next to the letters of the name, and standing next to each other, are male and females pigs, their sex identified by appropriate human clothing. The sign then flashes to their next position, which has the female raising the back of her skirt to expose her haunches, and the male with a skipping gesture moving toward her. In other words, they are characters engaged in the same kind of fun and games that occupy the boys and girls of this film.

For all that his place promises unlicensed high jinks, Porky is in fact quite a repressive figure. When a group of boys from the high school show up one night to gain the privilege of losing their virginity, he takes their money and leads them into a dark room from which they are dumped into the lake over which Porky's is built. The action perhaps suggests an equation of the boys with feces that fits in with the ambivalence about the body felt at other points in the film. After literally treating the boys "like shit," Porky and his place pretty much disappear from the picture until the final sequence which shows the revenge the students take against their nemesis. It is really quite a revenge. They totally destroy the rather large building that houses the establishment, and that's just for starters.

If you wanted to establish a dramatically coherent plot here, you would find it difficult to justify Porky's presence in the film at all. Given that the girls, primarily in the person of Wendy (Kaki Hunter), are presented as sexually adventurous and willing, atypical for the 1950s (the period in which the film is set), why should the guys feel the need of a whorehouse for their first sexual experience, which was more typical of the 1950s? At the end of the film, Pee Wee is in fact initiated into sex as a generous act by Wendy, much like Jo Ann Pflug's mission of mercy for Painless in *M*A*S*H.* So forget about dramatic coherence. If you were willing to settle for thematic coherence, you'd still find it hard to justify Porky's presence in the film since the boys seek out his whorehouse as a place of absolute liberation, while the film ends up making it a place of repression. Underlying these surface inconsistencies may be a psychological reality that, in making sex both readily available and inaccessible, plays directly on the ambivalences the film's celebratory mode inadvertently invokes and subsequently tries to work through.

Porky is something of a Falstaff turned inside out, more a figure of terror than of fun, his wide girth signaling a dour oppressiveness much as Falstaff's signals a vital joyousness. Like Falstaff, Porky is a lord of misrule, but peculiarly where Falstaff's misrule offers an anarchic challenge to the demands of the real world, Porky's misrule suggests the oppressive rule of the real world itself. This is not quite an inversion of the opposing worlds in *Henry IV*, but close enough. A whorehouse could hardly be made to stand for the sense of responsibility that the real world of political conflict in *Henry IV* does, but Porky's does specifically invoke the constraints of the real world in its references to money and power, two issues the high school boys are blessedly delivered from in their far more heavenly "Angel Beach High School." When you are already living in paradise, why would you ever want to stray down to Porky's swamp? The boys' ultimate revenge against Porky is precipitated by an act of violence against a classmate, but the revenge itself becomes so extreme that it transcends its original purpose to become an end in itself. In the rousing destructiveness of the final scene, there is in fact a good deal of anger working itself out for the audience's pleasure, but anger against what?

Well, Porky is fat, and Porky's brother (a sheriff who enforces his misrule), is fat; Miss Balbricker is fat, and the girl in the shower who blocked our view of the pinup beauties is fat. The rest of the cast for the most part ranges from trim and well-built to extremely well-built. This film that seems to celebrate the joys of the flesh is in fact quite hostile to people who have a good deal of flesh. In some ways it is hostile to flesh itself. When Porky's collapses, a whore-dancer whom Pee Wee had found attractive on the boys' first visit, is made to fall from a tumbling pier and lands spread-eagled in her scanty costume on her backside, looking particularly ugly in her awkwardness. Because Porky is an evil wizard of Oz of the flesh, he offers only illusory visions of physical beauty. What these kids finally learn in their confrontations with him is that there's no place like home—especially not if you live in the paradisiacal precincts of an haute bourgeois Florida community where the majority of people are trim, attractive, and, after all those showers, squeaky clean.

By the bright sunlight of Angel Beach's days, sex is clean, healthy, and normal, but at night it takes a more horrific turn. The visit to Cherry Forever, which invokes both disease and a punitive black monster, takes place in the dead of night, as do two visits to Porky's. Porky himself is a monster, monstrously fat and monstrously animal. His first appearance in the film comes in a shot that begins with an enormous hog with swollen testicles, for whom Porky then substitutes in the image. The seemingly uncomplicated delight in sex that the film puts forth is in fact compromised by the way it constantly verges on nightmare and even on the horror film itself.

Since the film began with Pee Wee dispiritedly measuring the length of his erection, so it appropriately ends with his discovering the delights of having a penis (whatever the size) as he's sexually initiated by Wendy. Director Clark's camera is rarely discreet, but it becomes quite shy about Pee Wee's initiation. Rather than give us any indication of what it's like, Clark opts for a direct parody of *Jaws* (1975). Right at the moment Pee Wee's initiation begins, Clark cuts to a sequence of the now-crazed Miss Balbricker emerging from the woods like some kind of monster terrestrial shark, with subjective camera movement directly echoing the earlier horror film, hunting down penises to take them in for trial.[4]

Sexual delight, then, gives way to sexual fear, and the joy of having a penis is offset by the dread of losing it. It is for this reason that the final act of revenge against Porky is a symbolic castration. A kindly young cop, enforcing his healthy rule against Porky's evil misrule, lops off the pig hood ornament that stands erect on the front of Porky's car. The sequencing of events suggests a pattern: the symbolic castration of the threatening father leads to Pee Wee's initiation, which in turn leads to the crazed mother hunting penises for capture. Freud might have wondered what women *really* want, but for these films female sexuality is always presented as a much simpler thing than the male's. Men may never have to face the consequences of sexual activity in pregnancy and its life-risking potential, but these films nevertheless manage to see sex as a matter of life and death for men precisely because the delight of arousal arouses the fear of loss.

Ghostbusters (1984) had the genius to downplay the animal in Animal Comedy for the sake of a PG rating and then explicitly conjugate it with the horror film, in the process making more money than any of these other aforementioned high-grossing comedies. But the underlying attitudes toward sexuality are strikingly similar. When Sigourney Weaver is her normal self in the first part of the film, she allows none of the men to approach her sexually. But as soon as she becomes "possessed," which happens to mean it's dangerous to come near her, she also becomes sexually inviting. Sexual allure equals sexual threat. The men want women to respond to their sexual advances in the film, but that doesn't necessarily mean they want women who are sexually aggressive in an uninhibited way. Uninhibited aggression is something to fear, as perhaps female sexuality is something to fear, for which reason sexual liberation in a fair number of these films implies its own form of bondage.

At their best, these films can achieve moments of real exhilaration in their characters' sexual high jinks that I find salutary. At the least, they offer something better than the sexual hostility implicit in the demeaning view of women that dominates *M*A*S*H* or the nostalgic longing for the purity of adolescence that colors *American Graffiti*. By making sex the great dividing line that separates children from adults, these films finally celebrate the process of growing up, however confused and ambivalent the celebration might become.[5] In a sense, these films might all seem a response to the radical change in sexual mores that took place in this country in the 1970s and the 1980s, and the response is as confused as Americans themselves seem to be on these issues.[6]

It is perhaps for this reason that the films are so often set in the past. They do not really attempt to gain a historical perspective on the changes in our collective behavior so much as to make up for past mistakes by changing the past. Much of the confusion in *Porky's*, in fact, derives from its attempt to rewrite sexual attitudes and behavior in the past while still staying within a period that was a good deal more repressive than the film is willing to recognize. By making sex finally so easy, the films necessarily have to deny a great deal of actual experience. And liberation built on denial is not really liberation. Rather, it is another form of bondage, as the wildly contradictory attitudes underlying *Porky's* make clear.

Animal House (1978) and *Blazing Saddles* (1974)

Much as Animal Comedy celebrates sexual liberation, it also celebrates an antiauthoritarian social liberation. The authority figures in these films are inevitably repressive and almost as inevitably male. They are also inevitably adults trying to keep youngsters in line, so that a parent-child relationship is implicitly invoked. The real nexus of the sexual and social here is in an Oedipal battle against adult authority by people who are about to become adults and want to appropriate the authority for themselves. The rebellion is antiauthoritarian only to the limited extent that it is directed against specific authority figures. It never seeks to overturn the *notion* of authority itself. On the surface, the sheer exuberance and chaotic energy of these films might make them seem celebrations of the anarchic spirit in man. Yet the world of the films and the characters in them are indelibly defined by institutions, and often fairly repressive ones like the army or the police force. Anarchic energies, always contained within larger orders, are paradoxically presented as a stage en route to the assumption of power.

The resulting confusions in political attitudes mirror the confusions in sexual attitudes. In *Stripes* (1981) the aptly named Sgt. Hulka (Warren Oates), whose physical prowess is in itself the threat used to enforce his position, must teach discipline to his unruly children-recruits (Bill Murray and Harold Ramis among them) during a brutal basic training session. Most of the comedy through the bulk of the film centers on points, slyly covert or daringly direct, that apparently anarchic Murray can score against the tight-assed Oates. Nonetheless, by the end of the film Murray can stage a successful mini-invasion of Czechoslovakia, an action sufficiently heroic to make Papa Oates proud.

Murray is finally an anarchist in spite of himself, unlike the eternal adolescents Gould and Sutherland in *M*A*S*H*. *M*A*S*H* is a more fully anarchic film, in which the characters can never grow up but must re-peatedly identify themselves by their battles against father-authority fig-ures. The real issue in *Stripes* and other Animal Comedies, then, is not so much anarchy as power. The revolution these films posit is not so much a change in the power structure itself as in the occupants of the seats of power. In its seemingly contradictory impulses, the film anticipates the confusions of the Reagan revolution, trying to marry the gains in libera-tionist mores from the 1960s and 1970s to a more conservative notion of power and political order as represented in the 1980s.

Animal House best sums up the whirlwind of political attitudes found in these films because of the various social and political hierarchies it establishes for its characters. First of all, there are explicit and parallel oppositions—one between characters of different fraternities, the other between the animal house fraternity and the university administration.[7] Both cases present an us-versus-them mentality typical of Old Comedy. We are clearly meant to side with the Delts in part because they are the underdogs, in part because they claim to represent a more open and lib-eral existence that challenges the repressiveness of the dominant power structure. As in any *agon* in Old Comedy, much of the laughter is tickled from us by the delight of watching the characters we side with triumph over those we despise.

But inasmuch as Old Comedy asks us to take sides, the comic strategies of the genre inherently create problems for any work that presents itself overtly as a democratic celebration of human variety à la Terence. The fact that some characters are *by their very natures* despicable undercuts from the beginning the vision of a free and open society.[8] Like *M*A*S*H,* *Animal House* is antiauthoritarian to the extent that we are encouraged to side with the group that is in some way disenfranchised, but it is hardly populist. Like *M*A*S*H* as well, it is possible to see a reverse kind of elitism in *Animal House.* If we are finally made to cheer the rejection of specific and individual personality traits, then we can hardly say that either film really does celebrate the variety of human existence.

While the film employs the us-versus-them strategy of Old Comedy, it also builds an unexpected division of the characters within the "us"— that is, within the Animal House fraternity itself. Even this apparent bastion of free expression is not quite so free as it first seems. Unlike *M*A*S*H* but more typical of later Animal Comedy, *Animal House* presents a peculiarly close alliance between the haves and the have-nots signaled through casting and performance. The casting establishes a critical distinction in the way we view characters in this film that I can best get at by considering the presence of John Belushi. Belushi received star billing, and he seems intended as a reigning spirit of misrule for the film since he appears at the toga party explicitly as Dionysus. At the least, he is the most animal-like character in the film. He stuffs his face rather than eats; he always looks in need of a bath and a shave; he has a prodigious capacity for booze; and he enjoys spying on naked women through dormitory windows. All in all, he is quite an uninhibited character—yet his pleasure in women is *entirely visual* for he is never directly involved with a woman in the course of the film.

His passivity in looking at women actually mirrors the audience's relation to the film itself, a point made explicit when Belushi turns from the naked woman to look directly at us and acknowledge our complicity in his action. But when confronted with something that should be arousing, his seemingly immutable passivity points to ways in which the apparent freedom of the character is in fact hedged in. He might be a Dionysus, but the film simply cannot countenance the idea of Belushi actually making physical contact with a woman. By any conventional standards of casting—and the film is a good deal more conventional on this issue than might appear at first glance—there was something inherent in Belushi's persona that made it impossible for him to play romantic leads—and it was not just a matter of looks. The one real romantic lead he tried in his film career, in *Continental Divide* (1981), Lawrence Kasdan's attempt to update the Spencer Tracy–Katharine Hepburn comedies, invoked Tracy as the homely romantic hero to make Belushi acceptable in this role, but audiences didn't buy it. Without his manic energy Belushi is as dull on the screen as Dan Aykroyd. Oddly, the manic energy itself finally denies sex, which requires the kind of concentration that lies outside the grasp of a character who seems always on the verge of going out of control.

Animal House, like many of the films that followed after it, took the lead of *M*A*S*H* by establishing a central duo within a larger group, and it is this central duo that becomes the chief focus for the film's action. The real leads of *Animal House*, the characters around whom most of the plot moves, are Tim Matheson and Peter Riegert, and while they might belong to the same fraternity as Belushi, they seem to be living in a different universe. Belushi has escaped from a Three Stooges short, while Matheson and Riegert seem to be auditioning for a romantic comedy. Introduced as the fraternity's two most important members, they actually have minimal interaction with their brothers in the course of the film—with good reason, for in outline they sound more like the members of the despised opposing fraternity. They are good looking, always well-dressed and clean-shaven, and their behavior is fairly polite and refined (in fact polished in comparison to Belushi); while they might share a toke with a hip teacher, they never engage in the prodigious drinking of their brothers. Just after the Animal House charter has been revoked by the Fraternity Council, Matheson, in a commiserating gesture, tosses a full bottle of bourbon to Belushi, who incredibly drinks the whole thing in one swig. Matheson is there solely to toss the bottle; not one drop touches his chaste lips. Belushi's lips are merely the passageway to his gullet, while Matheson's are kept pure for more exciting pursuits.

For the most part the film simply accepts the hierarchy of character implied by the casting as an inevitability, and perhaps even sees it as something desirable. Do we really want to watch an entire movie of Belushi stuffing his face, spitting out food, belching, drinking, spying on women but keeping his distance, and nothing else? The closest the film comes to an ironic distance on its character hierarchy occurs at the toga party when Matheson shows up in both toga and a neatly knotted tie. Whatever irony the costume expresses is lost, however, in the conflicting messages of the symbol. Does the tie undercut the meaning of the toga, or does the toga cancel the social status implied by the tie? Is Matheson tight-assed like his other tied brethren in the more acceptable fraternities or is he simply cool in his combination of roles? As comic as the tie looks, it also shows that Matheson never loses sight of his proper place and always finds appropriate ways to set himself apart from his animal brothers. Through the rest of the party, Belushi merely gets drunk, while Matheson successfully seduces the dean's wife. His tie, then, appropriately signals his powers of usurpation *within* the power structure.

If casting sets Matheson and Riegert apart from their ally brothers, then casting also sets them apart from their enemy brothers, with implications of a Wasp-minority opposition. The Waspy frat is all blonde and blue-eyed, while Matheson and Riegert are dark-haired. And while the script never mentions it, their looks strongly suggest Irish and Jewish. They are, however, far more assimilated than Belushi, who remains indelibly ethnic, and, perhaps for that reason, must remain indelibly separate. The aberration of an early 1960s fraternity with Irish and Jewish brothers *plus* the large ethnic fruit salad of the supporting cast might itself be a source for comedy, but the film doesn't aim at a hip college version of *Abie's Irish Rose*. It is content with going against sociological probability to engineer a power struggle that puts the ethnics on top of the heap. Not all ethnics have this destiny, however. Only those who demonstrate their acceptability can make it.

The spirit of Animal Comedy, then, is not truly anarchic, even though the films seem to court anarchy at times. The problem for these films is not power itself, but rather with who wields the power.[9] Fairly often in these films power politics finds its nexus with sexual politics in race. *Trading Places* (1983), also directed by John Landis, makes the underlying political strategies of *Animal House* explicit by tying them to a racial issue. In this later film, the two characters on the outs, Dan Aykroyd and Eddie Murphy, also end up becoming like their oppressors, Ralph Bellamy and Don Ameche. *Trading Places* might present Eddie Murphy in a starring role that in effect raises him to the top of the social heap, but it still has a kind of double standard in the way it treats him. A romantic plot is presented in great detail for white costar Aykroyd, but Murphy goes it alone for most of the film, even though he is a performer with far greater sexual presence on-screen than Aykroyd.

Much the same thing happens even in *Beverly Hills Cop* (1984), Murphy's breakthrough hit where he doesn't have to share billing with a white male costar as he did in both *48 HRS.* (1982) and *Trading Places*. In *Cop* Murphy might turn a bastion of white power upside down, but his sexuality is again hemmed in. This time he does have a white female costar in Lisa Eilbacher, but he retains a chastely platonic friendship with her throughout. Eilbacher's position in the film is quite oddly defined, as if she should be a romantic lead but never becomes one. This is probably a confusion left over from earlier versions of the screenplay when the film was supposed to star Sylvester Stallone. This suggests that at some point a conscious choice had to be made to eliminate a romance from the picture. Stallone might have become romantically involved with the woman, but not Murphy. A film that celebrated his ascension to sexual as well as social power was probably deemed simply too all-embracing in its reversals for white audiences to accept.[10]

Race is rarely a central issue in these films, but it can take on central importance for the larger political attitudes of the films. In *M*A*S*H* one of the ways that we know Elliott Gould and Donald Sutherland are good guys is that they like blacks in such an automatic way that they seem completely divorced from the values of their own culture. With kneejerk alacrity they reject Southerner Tom Skerritt's objection to sharing living quarters with a black officer. *Porky's* expands on this. Two guys correct a friend who uses the word "nigger," saying he should either say "Negro" or "colored man" (much as Gould and Sutherland "correct" Skerritt). In addition, the latter film presents an extended subplot about an anti-Semite and a Super Jew who has so many virtues that only a complete nincompoop could not like him. Not only does he have the virtue of shrewdness often granted Jews (however disparagingly in anti-Semitic jokes), he comes up with the plans for the final revenge against Porky. He also seems to be something of a 97-pound weakling transformed: he can beat the hell out of the redneck. He explains his highly developed pugilistic skills to his new friends in this modest way: "When you're Jewish, you learn to fight or you take a lot of shit. I don't like shit."

Much as *Porky's* encourages us to side with the plight of the persecuted, it also suggests that choosing not to fight back is also choosing to "like shit." Power is always the key issue, and if we are made to side with the Jew here, it is simply because he is powerful. The terms by which the film defines its issues gives us no other options: could we possibly like a character who likes to take a lot of shit? The only thing that makes him distinctly Jewish in the film's stereotypical terms is his possession of a premeditated prowess: his muscles get developed at the behest of his overdeveloped brain. In a sense, *Porky's* strives to rewrite sociopolitical history much as it has rewritten the history of 1950s sexual mores, making its fantasy decade more enlightened and benign than the actuality. The sequel, *Porky's II: The Next Day* (1983), features a prejudice plot that comes closer to key issues of the period by focusing on blacks and the Ku Klux Klan, but everybody is so right-minded on this issue that it is hard to understand how there ever could have been any problem with integration in the South. No wonder Eisenhower was smiling in *Part I*. *Porky's* is a fantasy of how the world *should* have been.

In spite of the sentimentalized good-hearted thinking on race issues in these films, blacks always remain in subsidiary positions in them. *Ghost-busters* can add a black (Ernie Hudson) to the terrific trio of Bill Murray, Dan Aykroyd, and Harold Ramis, but the trio never really becomes a quartet. Hudson's character has the quality of an afterthought, a figure for black audiences to notice and white audiences to ignore. Blacks in fact occupy a fairly ambivalent position in these films. They are implicitly honored in that they are representatives of a "hip" culture the whites in these films frequently seek to emulate, but there is also no doubt it's a "lower" culture, much as slapstick is a lower form than romantic comedy. *Animal House* exposes this implicit confusion in its comic modes: the film might embrace slapstick, but it does so equivocally because the romantic heroes retain the real power in the plot and they themselves are never directly involved in the gross-out physical humor. Similarly, much as blacks in the film may be enjoyed for the energy they express, they never fully escape the rigidly stereotyped position that they have held in the imagination of white culture, a role that automatically makes them inferior.

If these films celebrate the animal in man, then blacks must hold a special position in them because, along with Indians in Westerns, blacks represent the supreme incarnation of the animal side of man for white culture. But there is still a problem here that I had touched on in discussing the Cherry Forever sequence from *Porky's*. Even in an open and liberated society, the driving force of black sexuality is in fact something to be feared. In the Eddie Murphy films, his sexual energy is rendered anodyne by being in effect stripped of a sexual context. He finally ends up as the happy black menial, using all his energy to support the power structure he initially seems to be subverting. In *Animal House* the contradictions are made even more explicit precisely because the film has a sharp satirical sense of white culture's relation to black culture, but *also* because the film itself ends up supporting stereotypes its satire seems to reject.

Blacks appear twice in the film, the first time on the periphery, the second time directly involved in the action. Much as the film seems to celebrate the possibility of an open society, it ends up finding reasons why it is better to keep blacks on the periphery. Blacks are first seen in the figures of a band, "Otis Day and the Knights," who perform at the fraternity's "toga party," the most explicitly Dionysian sequence in the film. Black music finds a specific association in the kind of release the animals of Animal House seek, a siren call to dropping inhibitions and conventions.[11] Yet even as the blacks sound the siren, they hardly heed its call. While the white boys and girls are all wearing togas (with the girls decorously sporting bras underneath), the gallant Otis (DeWayne Jessie)

and his Knights are dressed in flashy but classy evening suits. The difference in costume is striking. Blacks are fine as performers, live-action stim-
ulants to reckless behavior for the whites, but as performers they also stay
at a distance, and in line. Alone among the partygoers, Peter Riegert directly addresses the band by calling out his appreciation, a gesture that
has an element of self-display in it. Nowhere does he actually interact with
them.[12] Segregation seems the underlying point here. Black music might
invoke togas, with or without bras, but there are no black students at this
party. Even the wild ethnic mix of Animal House has its restrictions.

The whole situation changes when the black band reappears in the
film—chiefly because the scene changes to an entirely black environment. The plot gets rather complicated at this point, but I want to recount
it in some detail because it most fully invokes the conflicting political
attitudes that underlie much of the film. Matheson has come up with a
ruse for getting dates with "Emily Dickinson College" girls for himself and
three of his friends (Riegert, Tom Hulce, and Stephen Furst). He will present himself at a dorm as "Frank," the Amherst-attending boyfriend of a
girl who had been improbably killed the previous week in an accident
with an exploding kiln while working on perilous pottery. Shelly, a friend
of the perished potter, tries to comfort "Frank" by agreeing to go out with
him and even to provide dates for his three friends. The whole group ends
up at the Dexter Lake Club, where Otis Day and the Knights happen to
be playing.

The scene at the Dexter Lake Club begins with satirical barbs directed
against our heroes, and most especially Peter Riegert. As their car pulls
up to the club and they see the sign announcing Otis Day, Riegert joyfully
cries out to Matheson: "Otter, oh shit! Otis Day and the Knights! I don't
believe this." As they are about to enter the club, Riegert becomes more
specific about his ecstasy: "Wait till Otis sees us! He loves us!" Riegert has
oddly reversed priorities here in that he has made the performer's response to the audience more important than the audience's response to
the performer. Now this is partly a matter of the boy trying to impress his
date with an unexpected personal connection that validates his importance: if Otis loves us, then you should love us too. As at the party, black
music and musicians are invoked as a kind of prelude to uninhibitedness
for whites, but again the blacks are implicitly placed in a subsidiary role
by the way the whites view them.

That the film intends a criticism of Riegert's attitude is clear enough
from the sequence of shots that follows the group's entrance into the club:
long shot of dancing blacks who suddenly stop and look up as the music

stops in response to the entrance of the white college students; long shot of blacks at bar who look up startled; medium shot of the group of whites by the door who are equally startled; closer-in medium shot of Otis and some of his band looking surprised; close-up of Hulce, Matheson, and Shelly as Matheson says: "We are gonna die!" As if the point of all this weren't clear enough, Hulce then moves to the right to Riegert, the camera panning with him, as if to emphasize his already overly emphatic remark: "Boon, we're the only white people here."

The way the whole sequence is shot makes *us* feel the intrusiveness of the white group through the series of reaction shots of blacks at the same time that we share, via the closer camera distance, the viewpoint of the whites. The satiric point here is sharp. The white boys who assume an automatic closeness to blacks, much like Gould and Sutherland in *M*A*S*H*, are made to confront the fact that their assumptions are based on a fantasy of the actual social structure. The sense of closeness immediately evaporates as soon as they step into an all-black environment. Confronted with all this negritude, they just as automatically assume not only an understandable discomfort in a room full of strangers, racial as well as social, but more specifically danger: "We're gonna die!" The white relationship to black culture is in fact an equivocal thing, embracing solely what can be contained.

Some things are better seen from a distance, but whether this is finally the view of the white characters or of the film itself remains an open question. At one point in this scene, Hulce asks his date what she is majoring in. When she replies, "Primitive cultures," Landis cuts directly to a shot of the band just as Otis is singing a nonsense refrain (". . . the ooooh-mau-mau . . ."), which, in this context, maybe isn't nonsense at all. What is not so clear is Landis's view of the attitudes. Does the cut extend the satire or does it confirm the sense of danger with the implicit, however comic, suggestion of black uprising? The central dramatic issue of the scene is that the whites have lost a power so automatic they wouldn't think about it in dealing with blacks on their own turf. But how does the film finally want us to view this abrupt change in power relations? Comedy often celebrates rebellion that turns the power structure upside down, and there is certainly the potential for that here. The beginning of the scene does in fact have a real bite in the way it views the characters' interactions. But the film finally moves in a very different direction from its original destination by having satire segue into nightmare and from nightmare into celebration.

Satire ordinarily requires a definite and restricted point of view that tells us where we stand in relation to the characters in a scene. Since satire in itself implies a distance from character, we ordinarily cannot share a character's point of view and also look at him satirically. Nonetheless, this scene does initially achieve this precarious balance by generally granting the whites the closer camera placement. Initially, at least, the combination of distance and involvement gives the scene a complex and disturbing resonance. As the group of white kids take their seats around a small table, Riegert tries to express the confidence of a white who thinks he's at home in black culture. "Don't worry about this, man," he tells the group, and then casually saunters up to the bar where he calls out in a loud voice, "Hey, Otis, my man!" A close-up reaction shot of Otis shows he is clearly affronted to be called anything by this white boy, and certainly not "my man." A medium reaction shot of Riegert follows and at last shows him uncomfortable in this situation.

As in some of the best scenes in *Porky's*, the double perspective here takes the comedy in the direction of nightmare, directly playing on our own unwitting involvement in the attitudes of the characters. It's as if we find ourselves on a stage we don't want to be on, destined to play out roles we don't know how to play. What finally emerges from this double perspective is a well-articulated sense of black-white relations in which the white's adulation of primitiveness devalues at the same time that it honors. Riegert's ecstatic anticipation of Otis's joy in seeing the white boys finally makes sense as an unconscious acknowledgment of the actual subservient position of black culture. The music is important not as a thing in itself but only insofar as white boys are willing to take it up.

For all the acuteness in sending up conflicting views of black culture, the film itself moves in a wildly different direction by the way it views blacks in the rest of the scene. For all the initial satire against the whites, it can finally never move beyond the closeness the camera establishes with them. Shortly after "Frank" and Shelly leave the restaurant so that she can "comfort" him alone in the car, three black men—identified in the final credits as "Mean Dude," "Meaner Dude," and "Meanest Dude"— surround the table, and one, presumably "Meanest Dude," asks Riegert, "Do you mind if we dance with your dates?" In an extreme low-angle two-shot that makes him look like a dwarf next to "Meanest Dude," Riegert anxiously replies, "Why, no, go right ahead." Riegert is all obsequious politeness, which the audience can laugh at sympathetically because the image has made us accept the implicit threat of violence as something real. There follows an actual act of violence: Meanest Dude tears out the table that had been bolted to the floor to let the girls stand up.

The action is comic in its grotesque exaggeration. But where comedy was initially directed against white fears, here it reinforces them by further actualizing the physical prowess of the blacks. Immediately after this act of violence against an object, there follows a medium shot of one girl looking up apprehensively as we see a large black hand enter the image, dominating the center of the shot. She places her small white hand in the engulfing black hand. By this point in the scene we have moved from social satire on race relations to a nightmarish image of white femininity threatened by engulfing black sexuality that can find parallels all the way back to the sexual and racial hysteria of D. W. Griffith's *Birth of a Nation* (1915).

"Hip" is a word that has entered American speech from black culture, and it does imply an attitude that this film frequently seeks to emulate. But how hip is this film in its view of race? By the conclusion of this scene, it is really the white boys who have become hip. When another black advises Riegert, "If I were in your shoes, I'd be, uh . . . ," Riegert is able to complete the sentence himself: ". . . leaving. What a good idea!" Leaving the girls to their new dancing partners, the three guys scramble out of the club, pile in the car (which sends Matheson's now half-naked consort away screaming), and peel out of the parking lot in a slapstick getaway that has them bash into four other cars in the lot. The violence of their getaway echoes the violence of the uprooted table in the club. When the boys at last reach the open road, exhilarated by their escape, they howl with delight, and the film reassuringly returns to its celebratory mode.

If the blacks had initially been seen as some kind of ally for the more liberated and egalitarian whites, why then does the film evoke an almost nightmarish anxiety about escaping, why the sheer physical destructiveness of the escape itself, where the bashing of the black patrons' cars is presented as a source of delight for the audience, and why the exhilarating sense of triumph in an escape that leaves their girls behind when the original aim of the episode was to bed down those very girls? The movie partly covers over these questions by abandoning the distancing device of satire that initially colored the scene to opt for a direct involvement in the slapstick excitement of the boys' escape. Most of all it conceals with a striking ellipsis that moves us directly from the boys' escape to the girls' return to campus. As often happens in nightmare, however, a departure can return you to the point you were trying to leave. The ellipsis effectively encapsulates the more disturbing aspects of these questions in one final question: what happened to the girls after the boys abandoned them?

We never see any of this. Instead, from a medium shot of the boys in the car howling with delight, there is a dissolve to a medium shot (or rather what I think must be called a medium shot) of girls' legs. Normally, the term designates a person seen from the waist up, while here we are looking from the waist down. The legs are walking, so the odd camera position emphasizes that the girls had to walk back to campus after the boys drove away. But since we see more than their feet, the shot also serves to emphasize their lower bodies. After the camera tracks for a brief while with these legs so that we can fully absorb the meaning of what we are seeing, it pulls back to show us a full shot of the girls as they walk. In spite of the fact that the last image we had of these girls was the small white hand in the large black hand, and in spite of the fact that they were forced to "dance" with partners they were terrified of, when we finally see them again the characters themselves abet the narrative's ellipsis by saying nothing of their black partners and their subsequent experience in the club. Instead, they are complaining about the *white guys*: "Boys like that! . . . They reminded me of animals!" When Shelly objects that "Frank was kind of cute," the others respond with something that sounds like "Eeeeyuuuuooow!" to end the scene with a howl of disgust that neatly echoes and parallels the boys' howl of delight.

The film is particularly devious in how it finally works through the issues of this scene, but as it approaches nightmare it has to be devious to maintain its comic equilibrium, much as dreams themselves have to be devious to maintain mental equilibrium. In fact, the film hits on a familiar strategy from dreams: a displacement that transfers the girls' disgust from the blacks to the white boys. Up until the quick exit, the boys' behavior to the girls was politeness itself, contrasted to the aggressive blacks who apparently raped them. Yet it is the boys who are dubbed "animals," while the blacks go unmentioned. In this way, the film conceals the image of black-as-animal it had already created. Instead, by inviting the audience to direct its derisive laughter toward the girls' response, the film effectively congratulates the boys for an animalness they nowhere demonstrate. The concealment through displacement is important here because, unlike the parallel nightmare sequence in *Porky's*, the central issue in *Animal House* is not so much sex as it is power.

Actually playing this scene out—to confront what had happened without the displacement—would uncover all the contradictory attitudes that in fact underlie the narrative. The whole sequence had begun, remember, by invoking death as a stimulus to sex: Shelly's willingness to "comfort" "Frank" in his apparent bereavement is immediately given a sexual coloration in the performance. Much as the mourners' behavior immediately becomes sexual, sex here is directly tied to power. Shelly's sexuality is stimulated by the power that compassion grants her over the seemingly distraught "Frank," at the same time that "Frank" has power over her by virtue of his ruse. The notion of death as a stimulus to sexual excitement is continued in the black club when "Frank" pronounces himself and all his fellow whites "dead." Again, the underlying issue is power. "Dead" means the white boys no longer have the upper hand as they did at the beginning of the sequence in the manipulative power they have over the girls.

The animals in this film are most of all *political* animals for the film always sees sex in terms of power. Why should the black "dudes" want to dance with the white guys' "dates"? They aren't exactly the most attractive women in the club, In fact, one of them is named "Prunella" and looks as if she had just stepped out of a Charles Addams cartoon, the name and look suggesting that she is both dried up and ghoulish at the same time. Hardly desirable, then, yet the blacks want her, and in this regard the film is simply supporting stereotypes that the beginning of the scene would seem to deny. As in the Cherry Forever sequence from *Porky's*, these blacks are nightmare figures, threatening and rapacious. The real nightmare in this scene from *Animal House* is that white boys have found themselves in a place where blacks are in power. Regardless of what the white girls look like, the blacks *have* to want to dance with them as an assertion of their power over the whites.

The slapstick device of crashing into cars provides a displacement from sex to violence, but much as violence *can* displace sex in this film, the two are really connected. The slapstick comes as the boys' unconscious answer to the blacks' threat of violence. It is a reassertion of power by the white boys after a confrontation with their own powerlessness. There is one other point about the slapstick here that is relevant to the political issues of the scene. The car the boys are driving is a new Lincoln Continental on loan from Stephen Furst's older, successful brother. Because Furst's near hysterical concern about possible damage to the car had already been a source of comedy in the sequence, there is a double whammy to the comic punch here as the smashing of the blacks' cars also leads to the crunching of the Continental. The upper-class-status image of the Continental leads the boys' assault in two directions—against both the lower and upper classes—and reinforces the supremacy of middle-class power. There is, then, a fairly conservative view underlying all this raucousness. In this light, the satire at the beginning of the scene might in retrospect make most sense as an attack on Riegert's liberal Jewish assumptions of brotherhood. The film itself sticks to a sense of immutable hierarchy that Riegert doesn't understand.

The image of white female hand in black male hand moves off in similarly contradictory directions. If it effectively conveys white fears of black sexuality, the image is also intended comically. We had already learned that Dickinson College girls are interested in civil rights, so the satirical testing of Riegert's liberal views that began the scene are reinvoked here. Now, however, the context is specifically sexual, as we are clearly asked to laugh at the frail and frightened girl helplessly acquiescing to Meanest Dude's invitation to dance. By extension, the film is also asking us to laugh at rape, but it cannot do that directly. The ambivalent position that blacks occupy in this scene comes about because they end up doing what the white boys wanted to do all along. The white boys are called animals at the end of the scene because the blacks are seen as an extension of them. What the film finally does is to find good reasons for keeping the blacks separate by another means of displacement. The blacks carry out the white boys' actions while the white boys carry out merely a "harmless" prank. Blacks are granted power within their limited confines, but whites, even animals like these white boys, end up in power on the outside.

Mel Brooks's *Blazing Saddles*, made four years before *Animal House*, offers a good point of comparison with the later film because it does place a black in a position of power by making him the sheriff of a white town, much to the horror of his white constituency. That this can happen at all is partly a matter of mode: *Blazing Saddles* is burlesque parody, taking an already existing genre as its reference to reality, while *Animal House*, for all its farcicality, claims greater connection to the real world. Still, Brooks's film is more straightforward in confronting black-white relations (although not without its own confusions). Politics might come first here in that the black-man-as-sheriff motif serves as a premise for the rest of the plot, but this inevitably leads—inevitably for American culture at least—to sex.

Villain Harvey Korman dispatches his secret weapon, Lili von Stüpp (Madeline Kahn's lisping Marlene Dietrich imitation), to dispatch black Sheriff Cleavon Little. After her song-and-dance number in a saloon, Kahn invites Little back to her dressing room where she changes into "something more comfortable." The change hardly looks more comfortable, but it does spectacularly show off her body. The aim of the spectacle might be seduction, but Kahn immediately blocks our view. She walks around the room turning off the lights, until the entire Panavision image is in near total darkness. On the right is a patch of light from a window, while Kahn and Little are on the left of the image where they cannot be seen. The sudden discretion is much like the unexpected discretion in *Porky's*. Totally out of keeping with the blatant vulgarity of the rest of the film, it nevertheless presents the film with a necessary concealment. On the soundtrack we hear Kahn ask Little if it is true what they say about his people. Rather than an answer from him, we hear a loud unzip, followed by Kahn's ecstatic, "Oh, yes! It is twue! It is twue!" From this there is a direct cut to a brightly lit breakfast scene in which Kahn is feeding Little giant wursts.

Why the sudden discretion? Unlike John Landis's more devious approach in *Animal House*, Mel Brooks is willing to confront the unthinkable. In order to do so, however, he must make it invisible. This is not a necessary discretion in dealing with sexually graphic material. The giant penis gag could still be handled indirectly, but the point here is that we never see Little and Kahn so much as kiss or embrace. The necessary conclusion is that even such modest actions would go as far beyond the bounds of then currently acceptable taste as *showing* the white woman admiring the black man's penis. The subsequent breakfast scene offers an odd displacement of all this material. It is now Kahn who is wielding the giant phalluses and, as a grotesquely dominating and solicitous mother, forcing Little to consume his bigness.

Blazing Saddles might bracingly confront and send up what white American culture has traditionally found acceptable, but it also confirms the fears at the root of white hostility. Black males are as potent as we've always dreaded, but a sexually ravenous and powerful white woman can make them consume their own potency. When Little finally returns to his job at the jail from his lovemaking night and wurst-eating morning, he is totally exhausted and for reasons the film seems to regard as self-evident. Sexually satisfying a beautiful white woman, even for a black man with the requisite big dick, is harder work than keeping a hostile white town peaceable.

Much as both *Blazing Saddles* and *Animal House* end up reinvoking older American attitudes toward blacks that they initially seem to be sending up, I don't want to sound overly critical in pointing out these confusions. There is also clearly something different from earlier films taking place here. The fact that black man–white woman sexuality could be brought up at all in a comic framework and in a way that at least partly satirizes white fears of black sexuality indicates the terms of the discourse on white-black relations is changing, moving toward something more open. And, to their credit, both *Blazing Saddles* and *Animal House* demonstrate that attitudes on sexuality necessarily connect to issues of power.

The brief epilogue at the end of *Animal House* make clear that power is the key issue in that film, especially when tied to sexual matters. The epilogue might be intended comically, but it is also fitting for the political confusions implicit in the film that John Belushi, seemingly the most anarchic character, should end up as a U.S. senator. At this point Belushi is also granted his only sexual contact in the film as we learn that he marries one of the Wasp sorority girls. Ascension to power is inevitably connected to sex in this film, so what might be regarded as an anarchic force in fact reinforces the power structure. Matheson's future sees him becoming a gynecologist in Beverly Hills, while "Greg Marmalard" (James Daughton), the only Wasp brother to make it in the power structure, has an equally sexual but less successful future: "Nixon White House Aide / Raped in Prison 1974." This of course is not the only time that rape is considered funny in this film.[13] The very smuttiness of these last two items from the epilogue presents a kind of humor unthinkable in *Porky's*, where sex is almost always good clean fun. But while sex might always equal power in *Animal House* and a sexual act may be a fitting act of revenge, the sense of power that finally emerges in *Animal House* does in fact parallel the sense of sex that emerges in *Porky's*. The liberations engineered by the power reversals in *Animal House* carry with them their own chains, and the apparently revolutionary impulses remain calls to the status quo.

Chapter 8 *Outer Limits of the Inner City*

Cooley High (1975), *Car Wash* (1976), and *The Bingo Long Traveling All-Stars and Motor Kings* (1976)

Of all the sociological improbabilities in *Animal House*, with its fraternal mix of Jewish, Irish, and assorted subordinate ethnics, most preposterous of all is the location of the Dexter Lake Club. This enclave of black musicians and black power is apparently located somewhere in the wilds of rural New England. The fantastic location is appropriate enough to the nightmare the scene eventually becomes, but it implicitly denies blacks a power they might have had in reality if the club were located in the inner city of practically any American metropolis. In earlier periods, white people might have gone up to Harlem to listen to the music. But after a decade of legislative maneuvers toward integration, Harlem through the 1960s oddly seemed to be moving in the direction of a no-white-man's land. Increasingly, whites began to think of Harlem as a fairly dangerous place to go, as dangerous as the Dexter Lake Club turns out to be in *Animal House.*

Animal House (1978) signaled changes in the white culture's attitude toward blacks that in many ways provide a reflection on what had happened to the image of blacks in movies of the early 1970s. The first half of the 1970s saw the emergence of a substantial number of movies about blacks that, for the first time in Hollywood history, tried to give a sense of inner-city life.[1] One of the earliest of these films, *Cotton Comes to Harlem* (1970), presented fairly familiar genre material made unfamiliar by cast and setting: a detective movie in which black actors played the two lead detectives investigating a robbery that involved a fraudulent back-to-Africa movement. Even more unfamiliar was the setting: it was the first time that Harlem had been explored to such a great extent by a Hollywood film.

There were quite a few films made subsequently that had predominantly, if not entirely, black casts and often involved black screenwriters and directors. There was a fairly strong reaction against these films at the time.[2] They were lumped together as "blaxploitation" movies, a term that automatically derides the status of the films. The neat elision of black and exploitation suggests that films aimed at a black audience necessarily invoked exploitation fare. Designed for a target audience and intended for quick playoff, these films clearly deserved the exploitation epithet. But the term also suggests something of a double standard since the films appeared precisely in a period when exploitation genres aimed at white audiences lost their exploitation attributes by virtue of higher budgets. Violent *policiers* and horror films might have been cheapjack exploitation movies in the 1950s, but *Dirty Harry* (1971) and *The Exorcist* (1973) granted them a patina of respectability that established the two as key genres for the 1970s.

If innumerable cop movies following in the wake of *Dirty Harry* were not necessarily exploitation fare, why should a movie with a black cop be specifically tagged as "blaxploitation"? There is perhaps a condescending suggestion in this that black audiences were being exploited in a way that white audiences were not, that in some way they were being tricked out of their ready cash by being offered white genres in blackface (which was in fact the opinion of a number of black critics). Whatever the critical opinion at the time or since, the blaxploitation films were certainly popular with their target audience. Noting this necessarily raises the question whether giving an audience what it wants to see is a form of exploiting them. This is a question I had asked concerning gross-out comedies and gross-out horror films in the first part of this book, but asking it about blaxploitation (and it was a question most insistently asked by blacks)[3] necessarily raises political issues that don't come into play when a similar kind of genre film is geared to a white audience.

I can clarify these issues by noting that the most startling aspect of the black films was a simple novelty. They were really the first films finding wide commercial release through major studios that gave any accurate indication of the realities of black life in inner-city America, however stylized they might be by genre conventions. It was almost as if the genre conventions didn't detract from the realism of the films, but instead, by putting blacks in filmic environments normally occupied by whites, they created a greater sense of reality. The concomitant usurpation of familiar territory probably accounts for all the head-shaking in print that greeted these films in the white press. Locating white genres in a black context can never be simply a matter of playing them in blackface. There are ways in which a black cast changes the genre, and often in striking fashion. Exploitation is not so much the issue here as appropriation, a borrowing of existing forms for idiosyncratic purposes.

Partly because of content, partly because of unruly audiences, questions were frequently raised when these films first appeared if they would encourage rebellion. I suspect that this response in part derives from an actual rebellion that was taking place—but on the aesthetic rather than the political or social playing field. Appropriating white genres is itself something of a political act since it is laying claim to material that has belonged solely to white society, material that in the past could at best acknowledge black characters solely in inferior positions. As a consequence, even the schlockiest films generally demonstrated more of a political awareness than their white counterparts because they were effectively born in a political context.

This is truly an act of appropriation because recasting white genres for black audiences necessarily transforms the way we understand the conventions of the original genres. Starting with *Cotton Comes to Harlem*, one of the most insistent attitudes that emerges from blaxploitation films is that white men should stay out of black men's business, and black men will do all right if left to their own devices. In a sense, this becomes a statement about the genres themselves. Left alone to the devices of genres inherited from dominant white society, the black creators can create new meanings for old devices by the simple device of a radically altered context. Consider, for example, the familiar convention of the detective genre that the detective is always more competent than the police if he's a private detective or more competent than his superiors if he's a police detective. The latter applies in *Cotton Comes to Harlem* with the important difference from earlier detective films that the detectives are black while the superiors are white. The general inability of whites to accomplish much of anything in this film reverses most thoughts about racial superiority lurking in white America's collective unconscious.

The opening of *Blacula* (1972), a blaxploitation reworking of the vampire film, ups the ante by recasting conventional terms of European self-identity. Europe itself gives birth to monstrosity because the film presents the genre's progenitor, Count Dracula, as a key representative of European culture. It is 1790; somewhere in Transylvania an African prince named Mamawaldi is supping with Count Dracula on a mission to elicit his help in stopping the slave trade. The date of his visit seems particularly calculated since Mamawaldi, as a spokesman for the rights of the individual, is an Enlightenment figure. The "enlightenment" here will end with an act of rapaciousness, but one instigated by the representative of what is claimed to be the more refined culture. Count Dracula acts the gracious host, cordially welcoming the African to his table. But after dessert, he has the African as a cordial, thus reversing myths of civilized European gentility and savage African cannibalism.

The rest of the film, which advances in time to "mod" Los Angeles, doesn't live up to the premise of this contrast, but it does provide a framing motivation for the vampirized African's behavior. From the original Bram Stoker novel on, the Dracula myth generally connects vampirism to sexual desire. In *Blacula*, however, the key driving force for the character is more an anger at his condition, a rage at the transformation European culture has worked on his identity. This is the only vampire film I know of in which the central vampire brings the narrative to an end by killing himself. The rage that he feels over his condition is necessarily turned inward by the constraints of the society he must inhabit.

Anger, then, is a key emotion in this film, much as anger played a large role in many blaxploitation films. Complementing their distinctiveness in exploring the life of the inner city, these films were unique in Hollywood history for their forthright and casual presentation of racial anger, and racial anger from a decidedly black perspective. The anger of blacks toward whites in blaxploitation is unusually open for an American film, although understanding it often involves an understanding of the generic context from which these films spring. Early on in *Shaft* (1971), for example, the eponymous private dick, as elegantly turned out as a high-fashion model in turtleneck sweater and leather topcoat, has trouble getting a yellow cab to stop for him. This is enough reason to get angry, of course, but the genre itself serves to intensify the emotion by contextualizing it with an implicit reference to dozens of other private-eye films in which the dick hero seems to magically summon up a cab by a mere wave of his hand to carry him on his next adventure. The private eye might operate on the margins of society, but he generally has resources like the ability to command cabs that give him a certain power over that society. The black private eye is doubly marginalized, and his opposition to the power structure is consequently politicized in terms of racial anger.

The very aggressive quality of blaxploitation films echoes the aggression the films performed on other films. To say that a film is ripping off a previous film, as it was claimed (accurately) that *Cooley High* (1975) ripped off *American Graffiti* (1973), would normally be to condemn the new film, but blaxploitation managed to transform ripping off into a positive act. Possession is said to be nine-tenths of the law, and the thefts that *Cooley High* and *Car Wash* (1976), both directed by Michael Schultz, perform on *American Graffiti* and *M*A*S*H* (1970), respectively, are acts of taking aesthetic possession, borrowing formal strategies and content from earlier films to create new works that effectively undermine the premises of their models. I am interested in *Cooley High* and *Car Wash* in particular precisely because they display such a tight relationship to the earlier films. By looking at these relationships, I can map out an alternate route of development on the road to Animal Comedy at the end of the decade. Along the way I will note markedly different inflections given to some of the implicit political concerns that turn up in the later gross-out films.

For all the cruising around and feeling of open space on an endless road in *American Graffiti*, the film nonetheless takes place in something of a hermetically sealed universe. Although people keep talking about going "back East," there is very little sense of a world outside the specific world of teenagers the film moves in. There is a gang of toughs that Richard Dreyfuss gets involved with, but oddly there is little sense of class distinction in the film: indeed, by the end of his encounter with the toughs, Dreyfuss has become an honorary member of their gang, effectively erasing social differences. Further, this is a world in which there are no blacks, although black music is of central importance for it.

Because the characters in this film are all people who have unlimited freedom of movement, any sense of a larger social structure may be conveniently omitted. These are people who *know* from their own experience that society is fluid because the world they live in is defined by a constant flow. This quality of flow is at the root of the film's lyricism, so that the modal method of the film ends up reinforcing the attitudes of the characters, a certitude that all is fluid in this free and open world. On the surface, the film seems to have a fairly broad social focus, to the extent that it has a very large cast of characters. At the same time it is actually fairly myopic.

Blaxploitation films could be accused of a similar myopia in their insistence that whites stay out of black life and their generally antiwhite attitudes. Nonetheless, it was a myopia based on the incontrovertible knowledge of a world that extended far beyond this particular social and racial group. Blacks in these films are defined socially as well as racially, as the social inevitably connects to the racial for African-Americans. These films were not about a black middle class that could seem more acceptable to a white audience (as "The Cosby Show" was on television by in effect stripping racial differences of any political content and suggesting that we are all just members of one great middle class). The lower-class focus of these films, itself fairly unusual in American movies, made them seem especially dangerous to critics who thought the overt airing of racial hatred could stir up class hatred and prompt, if not revolution, at least riots.

Much as *Animal House* wants to honor black culture, the black films themselves are more explicitly concerned with power than *Animal House*, which instead constantly seeks to deny what it embraces. The black films are more explicit about power because they are about people who are conscious of not having power. And while *Animal House* can put forward animals as positive characters, the black films feature characters rejected by white society precisely because they are seen as animal. Realistically, there is no sense in the black films that an ascendancy of the characters on the outs could transform society, as happens in *Animal House*, quite simply because possibilities for such a rise to power always remain fairly limited in real life. The black culture that Animal Comedy often embraces inevitably views questions of sexual and social liberation in very different terms because of a difference in social perspective.

Cooley High invokes *American Graffiti* in so many specific ways that it finally seems an inner-city gloss on the suburban culture of the earlier film. A grittiness with roots in economic necessity replaces the distinctive lyricism of *American Graffiti*, much as Chicago's El train replaces the individual automobile that gives the original its lyricism. The constraints placed on the kids' lives in *Cooley High* are both more real and more apparent than in the earlier film. When the mother of "Preach" (Glynn Turman), one of the leading boys, returns home to discover that he has been out most of the evening trying to have a good time instead of staying at home to look after his sisters, she complains she has to be able to depend on him because she has to hold down three jobs to make ends meet. Obviously, with that kind of necessity these kids have very little option about what they can actually do with their lives.

With such economic demands, how can anyone enjoy the adolescent freedom the teenagers in *American Graffiti* take for granted? That does not mean the kids of Cooley High have any less desire for the kind of carefree behavior that typifies *American Graffiti*'s kids, who can move about at will. In fact, given the restrictions of their world, the desire for freedom becomes more of an imperative. But the sowing-wild-oats aspect of later teenage comedies that *American Graffiti* set the pattern for takes an odd turn in *Cooley High* precisely because these kids have a more predictable future than the characters in the other films: as we learn from the first shot of the school building, Cooley High is specifically "Edwin G. Cooley Vocational High School." With a vocational high school at the center of ghetto life, future options are mostly closed off right from the get-go.

Like later teen comedy, *Cooley High* honors its characters' tremendous sense of vitality, but it does so in a way that factors in the economic limitations placed on their lives. Behavior that will define characters in later Animal Comedy as animal—like breaking rules and reckless daring—becomes in part a response to economic restrictions here. There is a funny moment in which a character places his own aspirations for something better in the context of the actual limitations of his life. Preach is trying to pick up a girl, Brenda (Cynthia Davis), who has no desire to be an ordinary pickup. He discovers her at a party sitting in a room by herself reading a book of poetry. To her surprise, Preach shares the girl's interest in poetry, in fact has some ambition to be a poet himself. Reading and writing poetry, then, becomes a way of making more of yourself, setting yourself apart from other people in your aspirations to some kind of better life. As if to validate himself to Brenda, Preach lets her know that *he* knows the poetry she's reading. Then, to show how really knowledgeable he is, he recommends a different poet from whom he quotes a few lines by heart. All of this is by way of demonstrating that he has the same kind of upward aspirations as Brenda, but in his romantic enthusiasm he concludes by saying, "I'm gonna give you that . . . as soon as I steal a copy." For these characters, simply to have any aspirations is itself like breaking the rules.

American Graffiti celebrates a freedom that is specifically a freedom of mobility. Later Animal Comedy picks this up and translates it into a freedom to do practically anything, although as I have noted with both

Animal House and *Porky's*, this apparent freedom constantly creates its own constraints. The constraints are always externally applied in *Cooley High*, and the contrast emerges most clearly on this issue of mobility. The kids in this film do not have the privilege of cruising around in their own cars at night. The only actual escape they can find comes by playing hooky and cadging a free ride on the back of a bus, a brief sequence that carries with it more of a genuine sense of exhilaration than all the endless driving in *American Graffiti*. Escape is a key issue in both *American Graffiti* and *Cooley High*, but in *Cooley High* the boys want to break away from their environment first of all and only by implication from their adolescence, while *American Graffiti* reverses the priorities and views them ambivalently.

The two main characters in *Cooley High* are Preach and his close friend, nicknamed "Cochise" (Lawrence Hilton-Jacobs). Cochise expects to escape through the traditional route for blacks of sports by winning a basketball scholarship that will enable him to go to college. Preach is taking a more unexpected direction in his aspiration to be a writer. As in *American Graffiti*, the boy who will become a writer also has a dream-girl, the albinolike features of the blonde in the white T-bird from the earlier film here transformed into what the film itself calls a "high yella bitch." Unlike her model in *American Graffiti* who remains at the end of that film an elusive fantasy figure, the "high yella" Brenda has a flesh-and-blood reality, and Preach does eventually get involved with her. This is to say that dreams can be realized in this world, but what they realize is itself limited. In *American Graffiti*, where there is no economic necessity, ideals are never deflated, and it becomes preferable that a dream remains a dream even at film's end. The necessary limitation of the ideal in *Cooley High* is given its most disturbing force by the "high yella bitch" epithet that attaches itself to Brenda, hardly a fitting name for a romanticized ideal, yet appropriate enough to the environment the film creates. The very hostility of the language suggests the extent to which the dream is despised as much as it is also sought after.

A very common element of the blaxploitation films is the use of the word "nigger" as the ultimate slur against anyone, at the same time it's a word the characters recognize applies to all of them anyway. Early on in *Cooley High* there is a compelling scene when Preach and Cochise are with their cronies, one of whom has found some of Preach's poetry. The kid reads a poem out loud (some pretty purple stuff about "throbbing manhood"), and the reading is clearly intended to wound Preach for the ambition that is implied in his writing poetry at all. The stung Preach responds with a counterattack, snatching back the poetry and angrily accusing the whole group, "You guys think it's funny because I want to be something besides a factory worker or a football player. Well, that's because you're all a bunch of stupid niggers that don't know shit!" There follows a reaction shot of the others, who remain in startled silence at first, then recover their wits and respond with laughter that must seem defensive after the silence.

Preach has raised very realistic pictures of their future for them, the only two choices they have: the factory workers that most will become, or the sports player Cochise hopes to become. The pain of Preach's attack lies in the truth of its inescapable double bind. To have any kind of aspirations to move beyond this environment necessarily implies a rejection of all the people they know, and by extension a rejection of a part of themselves. At the same time, the attempt to reject being a "nigger" is confounded by the fact that the larger society will continue to see the person moving up in precisely those terms. The boys in *American Graffiti* have the luxury of toying with choice, but the boys in *Cooley High* in effect have no choice at all, much as they can try acting as if they did. To move up in the world, the blacks must create a radical break in their lives, find a way of denying their past selves. In *American Graffiti* adolescence is treated more nostalgically, a blessed period from which all the characters are eventually exiled (with Richard Dreyfuss ending up in literal exile in Canada according to the epilogue at the end).

Cooley High ends with a funeral for Cochise, who is killed in a street fight. *American Graffiti* also courts death at its conclusion with the penultimate sequence of the race in which John Milner (Paul Le Mat) is almost killed, but it leaves the actual event for the epilogue, where we learn that he was later killed in a car crash. Apparently, projecting his death into the future has the effect of fixing the nostalgic glow in which the whole film is bathed. Death must be delayed until the magic moment of adolescence is (literally) *past* and the dreariness of adulthood has set in. *Cooley High*, on the other hand, takes death as all the more reason to escape from this world. Cochise, the character most likely to break out of his environment because of his skill as an athlete, turns out to be the character most fully trapped in it.

After the funeral, Preach, standing alone by the graveside, delivers a eulogy that is meant as much for himself as it is for Cochise. At one point he assures the dead Cochise, "Don't worry, man, I'm gonna make it. I can steal and lie too good not to survive." Preach's vitality is precisely located in his ability to go against the standards of his society, and yet he puts this rebellion forward as a way of making it in this society. Throughout the eulogy, the phrase "I'm gonna make it" keeps getting repeated, almost in incantatory fashion, almost as if this character has to convince himself he can survive in order to survive. The whole speech seems to be very future-oriented, yet peculiarly it ends by Preach announcing, "We live for today . . ." The inevitable restrictions society places on Preach's life necessitates this irreconcilable opposition between living for the future and living for the moment. The film ends appropriately with a freeze frame that arrests Preach's movement precisely at the moment that he runs forward. Lying and stealing well is the most this character can hope for, much as the film itself succeeds by ripping off *American Graffiti.*

A year later Michael Schultz made *Car Wash* (1976). The film appeared a couple of years before *Animal House*, but it anticipates Animal Comedy in a number of striking ways: it has a large cast, raunchy humor (which emphasizes the grossness of its characters), and an impulse toward egalitarian utopianism; moreover, there is a marked randomness and a seemingly improvised quality to its narrative. As with the later Animal Comedies, *M*A*S*H* again seems to be a prime earlier model, with low-angle shots of a speaker horn—here broadcasting a local radio station—similarly used to punctuate and structure the narrative (and also to deliver the final credits). Although it appeared earlier than *Animal House, Car Wash* takes all these qualities and drives them to a far greater extreme than that film or really any subsequent Animal Comedy. Commensurately, it takes the implications of form and content in a far more consequential and radical direction than any of the later films.

Consider the opening—right from the very credits in fact. The film begins with the word "Starring," followed by a list of twenty-nine names (virtually the entire cast), before it finally presents the main title: "in *Car Wash.*"[4] There are a number of deliberate reversals engineered by presenting the credits this way. The whole star system, which of course antedates the movies, implies a hierarchy of character importance that is in place even before the dramatic work starts. Furthermore, Hollywood convention acknowledges that performers whose names appear before the main title have more power than those whose names appear after.[5] Finally, in the film's opening credits the whole list is alphabetical, so that to some degree its application here is a sendup of that convention—a strategy normally reserved for movies with a lot of big stars in them. There aren't really twenty-nine big stars here, of course, so the alphabetical listing is partly an inside joke making fun of the film's very apparent low budget. Nonetheless, the alphabetizing does prevent a hierarchy based on familiarity—so that someone named Franklyn Ajaye appears well ahead of Garrett Morris and Richard Pryor, better-known performers of the time.

All this takes place before the film proper has even begun. So right from the beginning, by systematically overturning all normal markers of status in conventional Hollywood movies, the film points to an egalitarian impulse that is both more conscious and perhaps more radical than later Animal Comedy. This overturning of hierarchies is a point that is supported by the style. After the credit sequence, the film proper begins with Lonnie (Ivan Dixon), a man we will later find out is entrusted with the responsibility of opening and closing the car wash. He gets off a bus, and the camera pans to the left with him as he walks toward the car wash office and starts to take his keys out. At this point the camera stops to let him go out of the image as "Hippo" (James Spinks), a very fat man riding a motorbike appears in the background moving to the right. As the camera lets Lonnie go out of the left of the image, it reverses direction to pick up Hippo on the motorbike and pan right with him as he comes around the corner, onto the lot, again reversing direction to pan left with him as he drives onto the lot and reaches Lonnie, who is now opening the door to the office. The point of the style is to undermine our sense of certainty about conventional hierarchies in the image where the foreground performer becomes the central focus and the background remains precisely that, a setting for the foreground. Here the background supersedes and takes over the camera movement, turning it into a foreground, but the reversal of hierarchy doesn't create a new hierarchy in turn because it doesn't supplant the initial point of interest. Rather, it joins up with it.

This visual strategy of shifting back and forth between points of interest as a way of undermining any hierarchical sense of interest is a consistent method of the film's narrative as well. Until the final sequence when it deliberately reverses its method, the film rarely spends more than a few minutes with any one character or plot line. There is one scene in the film that could function as a star turn for Richard Pryor, accompanied as he is by the Pointer Sisters. In this sequence, the star voltage of the film suddenly jumps a few megawatts by bringing together some of the best-known people in its cast. But then virtually the whole cast appears in this scene, and Pryor is not made the primary focus. For one thing, his presence is competing with that of the Pointer Sisters, who soon launch into a musical number that brings the scene to a close. For another, there is a minor character here whom the camera keeps singling out as equally important.

Pryor plays a venal minister named Daddy Rich, who lives up to his name by preaching the value of "that effing green," which he hopes everyone will give to him. As Daddy Rich is playing to his crowd, the camera looks at a Black Muslim named Abdullah, formerly Dwayne (Bill Duke), who is disgusted by Daddy Rich's spectacle. There is no easy way of attitudinizing about the characters' responses to the extent that the camera does, by paying full and delighted attention to the vital venality of Daddy Rich and his strutting cohorts at the same time that it honors the disgusted response of Abdullah to the musical number by intercutting reaction shots of him. The intercutting in effect undercuts the star turn by putting it in a critical perspective. At the same time, the film doesn't fully embrace the criticism because it also takes pleasure in the performance of the stars.

The extent to which the egalitarianism of this film differs from later Animal Comedies can best be seen in the treatment of one of the workers, Vendy, a male homosexual who enjoys "flaming" and playing the queen. He is the third character that we meet, connected to the first two by means of a radio broadcast. The radio news broadcast already heard in the shot of Lonnie and the fat man seems to be the focal point as a cut takes us to a shot of a loudspeaker, from which there is then a tilt down to Vendy looking in a mirror and trying to fix a very elaborate hairdo. He shakes his head, mutters "This will never do," and walks out the door as the radio announcer is heard on the soundtrack reading a news story about congressmen hiring male aides in exchange for sexual favors. As Vendy walks outside and then into another room, the announcer continues, "A Southern senior committee member replied that he had no objection to homosexuals as long as they stayed in their place." At precisely this point, Vendy, having walked into another room, slams the door shut and the camera zooms in on a "Ladies" sign. The juxtaposition of soundtrack and image makes clear that this is a character who triumphantly is *not* going to stay in his (or her) place.

The confusions that Vendy embraces are played to the hilt in a later scene with Abdullah, who is disgusted by him and calls him a "sorry-looking faggot." This prompts the following exchange:

VENDY: Who you calling sorry-looking? (*the workers laugh*)
ABDULLAH: Can't you all see that "*she*" ain't funny? She's just another poor example of how the system has of destroying our men.
VENDY: Honey, I am more man than you'll ever be and more woman than you'll ever get. (*snaps fingers and saunters off*)

By this point in the dialogue, all categories are so confused that any judgment of exactly who this person is and exactly what his/her place should be are rendered impossible. The strength of the character is precisely in the self-respect that he/she demonstrates here, and that is what makes him equal to all others. Much as the later comedies seem on the surface to be embracing a wide variety of experience, Vendy is not someone they'd likely accept.[6]

That the film can accept a character as deviant as a flaming queen signals the utopian impulses behind its egalitarian vision. Nonetheless, the film does not operate within a utopian world. It never minimizes the demeaning work in the car wash. And the work itself signals the characters' equality: they are all at the bottom of the social structure where they can operate as checks on each others' aspirations. When a foreman (Leonard Jackson) who delights in ordering others around answers the question, "What makes you think you're so special?" by saying " 'Cause I'm the one nigger here who doesn't get wet around here," he invokes that odd inversion that I noted with the use of "nigger" in *Cooley High*. By calling himself a nigger, he unconsciously allies himself with the others at the very moment that he's claiming to set himself apart. While trying to claim higher status, he ends up lowering himself. By the end of the film his claim for elevation will find its answer in a dog turd that his fellow workers have neatly placed on the hood of his otherwise spotless car.

Underlying the film's egalitarianism is a sense that the characters have to accept the limited aspirations of their lowly place in society. Most of the film does not address this issue directly until the one extended dramatic sequence that brings it to a close, a sequence granted power both by its placement and stylistic difference. It concerns Abdullah's attempt to rob the car wash in response to his having been fired earlier in the day. He is talked out of it by Lonnie, an ex-con who tells him this robbery won't enable him to buy a revolution. Convinced by this argument, Abdullah breaks down and starts to cry, "I don't know, man, I don't know. I know I'm not crazy, but every day I have to come here and watch this clown show, man. And sometimes I just can't take it." Abdullah is right that the workers put on a clown show. Yet it is precisely the clown show that makes this life and this working situation endurable. There is a striking moment early on in the film before the workers start washing the first car: someone tosses out a tennis ball and they all get into an impromptu volleyball-type game. For a moment, demeaning work is turned into liberating play; the enjoyment of messing around together makes this work something more, something that belongs to them. If they are the clowns that Abdullah dismisses, being a clown clearly has value at this level of society (much as being an animal will have value in the later films). *Car Wash* occasionally falters in its inventiveness, and its humor is at times crude without being funny. Yet in its repeated moments of clowning, the film honors an irrepressibility in its characters that grants them distinction.

The film's utopianism is different from most later Animal Comedies because it is bought at the price of accepting the inevitability of the hierarchical nature of the larger society. These men can all be equal simply because they are all on the bottom rung of the social ladder. How radically different this is from later films might be seen by comparing it to *D.C. Cab* (1983), written and directed by Joel Schumacher, who was the screenwriter of *Car Wash*. Centered around a run-down taxi company, *D.C. Cab* strives for a mood similar to *Car Wash* with its episodic structure and large cast, but inflected in a way that shows the subsequent influence of *Animal House*. Like the ethnic mixture of the animal fraternity, there is more of a racial mixture in the group of workers at the cab company than there was at the car wash. Paralleling the hierarchy of casting in *Animal House*, *D.C. Cab* establishes a clearly defined central character in Adam Baldwin, who is white.[7] Although he starts out as a coworker, he ends up managing the company. His assumption of power echoes the move into the seats of power of the animals from *Animal House*, but it is a destiny not imaginable for any of the black workers, who remain in the lower ranks. His rise to power does not signal a new social order since the order remains pretty much the same. Unlike *Car Wash* (but like much Animal Comedy), the film implicitly endorses the hierarchy of society by establishing a hierarchy of character interest.

The Bingo Long Traveling All-Stars and Motor Kings (1976) is a fascinating film for its period because it has a more overtly political subject than any of the other black films of its time. The film is about a group of players from the Negro National League, a separate and parallel league of baseball teams organized in the 1930s because the major leagues were not yet open to blacks. The action that sets the plot in motion has a political motivation. A number of players, headed by Bingo Long (Billy Dee Williams), feeling that they are being exploited by the league's owners (wealthy blacks), break away from the league to form their own team. They barnstorm across the country giving exhibition games, initially against other black teams. Not only is this excellent film one about blacks, it is one of the few Hollywood films that is genuinely about a labor movement. The players are in effect battling two forces—the power of the bosses as well as the power of cultural prejudice—and the film remarkably conveys the difficulty of this struggle without ever taking on an over-bearing paranoid tone. In fact, it manages to be one of the most good-natured and charming black films from this period without ever losing a sense of commitment to the most serious concerns of its narrative.

Appearing the same year as *Car Wash* and two years before *Animal House*, this film shares a number of traits with later Animal Comedy. Yet it does not really belong to the genre because the lead characters in it could never be regarded as animals (in the way that the characters in *Car Wash* might well be). Unlike the laborers in either *Car Wash* or *D.C. Cab*, *Bingo Long*'s skilled ball players derive a strong sense of dignity from their abilities and profession. Nonetheless, there is one scene in which the black players at least approach the clownishness of some of the characters in Animal Comedy. It also serves as an acute analysis of why the players in effect have to become animals in the context of white society.

Bingo Long's All-Stars have been shut out of playing other black teams by a conspiracy of the owners. In a last desperate attempt to survive on their own, the players decide to play a local white team they can easily beat. Initially, the game goes very badly because the black players are obviously better athletes than their white counterparts. This display of superior prowess causes the entire white crowd in the stands to become increasingly hostile. To defuse the building tension and forestall a very real possibility of violence, Bingo Long, the head of the team, begins acting in the deliberately clownish manner of the shuffling Negro, and most other members of the team soon follow suit. With this peace offering, the crowd calms down to enjoy antics that reduce the status of the black players without denying their athletic skills.

The laughter the black players invoke to defuse the animosity is not a good-natured response signaling blissful social harmony. There is a sig-nificantly sharper edge to it here since it is clearly self-deprecatory from the players' point of view and moderately derisive on the part of the spectators. In order that their athletic skills be accepted and appreciated by white society, the blacks have to denigrate themselves in ways that will offer a necessary balance to their prowess. They have to portray them-selves as the animals the rest of society thinks they are in order to dem-onstrate the power they actually possess. There is a deep ambivalence about blacks in American society since we seem willing to grant them, within limits, physical prowess and honor them for athletic skills, at the same time that we want to restrict the areas in which that prowess can be demonstrated. These are, of course, issues we have tried to address through legislation and social action over the past several decades. While the film is set in the past, how much the actual situation has changed is open to question; at the least, the film itself stands as a witness to changing awareness, especially because of the audience it was aimed at.

Although it has a predominantly black cast, *Bingo Long* was intended as a "crossover" film, one that would appeal to white audiences as well as black. Like *Lady Sings the Blues* (1972), it had a higher budget than most other black films at the time, which enabled a meticulous period re-creation. But *Lady Sings the Blues* could work for a larger audience, as *Bingo Long* did not, because its subject was music and it had a big-name star (Diana Ross made her screen debut in this softened and fictionalized biography of Billie Holiday). And although blacks have been accepted by the larger culture as major figures in sports, a drama about black athletes was not as likely to have the same kind of acceptance. Moreover, part of the problem the film had in reaching a wider audience might in fact con-firm what the film itself implies: the characters simply have too much dignity. There were a number of other films about sports teams in this period (mentioned in chapter 6 as a precursor of Animal Comedy), and in all of them the players, mostly white, are generally scruffier and often more foulmouthed than Bingo Long's crew.

This initial efflorescence of black filmmaking grew dim by the end of the 1970s and early 1980s, with only a small number of movies still being made for black audiences with predominantly black casts (and these gen-erally had some basis in music).[8] Michael Schultz, who had directed some of the most interesting of these films in the 1970s, would in 1985 find himself directing *Krush Groove*, a musical about breakdancing. By the end of the 1980s, however, a new black cinema began to emerge, garnering a lot of attention in the national press and once again raising questions about crossover potential. Unlike earlier blaxploitation, the new black cinema is less overtly a genre cinema, and, on the surface at least, owes little to the white cinema it departs from. The generally more naturalistic approach of these films has helped them attract the kind of favorable critical commentary rarely accorded blaxploitation.[9] I have tried to suggest here, however, that there is much of interest in blaxploitation precisely because of genre conventions. In particular, I have sought to locate blax-ploitation as a low-class genre that parallels the low-class genre of Animal Comedy and even (in the case of *Blacula*) of gross-out horror. One key difference—and a key source of interest—is that blaxploitation never succeeded beyond its low-class origins as mainstream gross-out films would.

What happened in the intervening period between blaxploitation and the new black cinema, a period when black audiences were becoming increasingly important to the box office, was a kind of containment.[10] Billy Dee Williams, a talented actor with matinee idol looks, might have had the male lead in *Lady Sings the Blues* and *Bingo Long*, but by 1980 he was playing third-string behind Mark Hamill and Harrison Ford in *The Empire Strikes Back*. Except for comedians, black actors generally receive supporting parts to dominant white actors in genres that normally appeal to black audiences, and they have a very clearly defined place that generally keeps them out of any romantic plot. Even with the comedians, the plots (as noted earlier) usually find strategies for containing their sexual energy. Animal Comedy might invoke the hipness of black culture, but because they operated from the lowest positions of society, the black films of the 1970s were too aware of the power of the larger order to embrace the peculiar conflict between anarchy and conservatism that typifies the later comedies.

Chapter 9 **Bill Murray,
Anarchic Conservative**

Caddyshack (1980), *Stripes* (1981), *Ghostbusters* (1984),
and *Scrooged* (1988)

Values rejected become the values espoused as values espoused are finally rejected. The paradoxes of Animal Comedy are most fully expressed
in the figure of Bill Murray. As an actor whose screen persona is balanced
between proletarian slob and egalitarian snob, he has become something
of an icon of the genre. Murray's first big success came when he succeeded
Chevy Chase in the second year of broadcast on "Saturday Night Live"
after Chase left to make feature films.[1] When Murray himself moved into
feature films a year later with *Meatballs* (1979), a *Time* reviewer complained that the film demanded John Belushi-type antics from Murray
while Murray was really more suited to a romantic comedy like *Foul Play*
(1978), Chevy Chase's first film.[2] At about the same time, a *Rolling Stone*
reporter in an extended profile on Murray attacked Chevy Chase for thinking comedy was nothing but sex.[3] Murray was above this, and although

the article doesn't say it explicitly, the style implies that Murray was better than Chase because he focused on power rather than sex. It is a fair indication of the contradictions in Murray's persona that he could be compared to both Belushi and Chase—which should be reason enough why he had difficulty in playing romantic comedy. He has become sufficiently distinctive that he is finally like neither, but the points of similarity effectively set off the differences.

When Murray first came on to "Saturday Night Live," Jane Curtin had taken over Chase's role as anchorman on "Weekend Update," a mock newscast, but eventually Murray moved into this role, appropriately enough because he could convey some of Chase's silly suavity. There was one piece of familiar business for Chase, however, that Murray did not take over. After a commercial break, the camera would always discover an unaware Chase in a suggestive phone conversation with an unidentified woman. Chase, realizing he was being observed, would quickly hang up and attempt to recover from his apparent embarrassment. The trick of the routine is that the embarrassment itself is a put-on, a fluster that actually congratulates itself for parading a sexuality the character would like to pretend is discreet. A lot of the comedy in Chase's performances comes from his own conception of himself as suave and debonair while events around him conspire to puncture holes in that image. Ultimately, though, the image proves real. Starting with the second broadcast, practically every "SNL" show in the first season began with Chase taking a pratfall, from which he would then rise after initial befuddlement and announce with a sense of triumph, "It's Saturday Night!" If the pratfall undermines the cool image, the subsequent triumphal rebound reinforces it by announcing that this is all play anyway. Chase is a schlemiel Cary Grant.

Murray is more genuine schlemiel, a character who lets it all hang out, which is why he became king of Animal Comedy. Still, he is a schlemiel who has sufficient shrewdness and aggression to turn his weaknesses into strengths. There is no real inner strength, as with Chase. Rather, his is a strength that grows out of weakness and seems to supplant the original weakness. But, paralleling my suggestion about *Porky's* that liberation built on denial is not real liberation, Murray's strength built on weakness is not a real strength. In his earliest appearances on "Saturday Night Live," he played straight man to all the other comics, a kind of pallid Chevy Chase, until a skit written by Murray and Gilda Radner gave him his comic launching pad on the show. Murray is in a shower holding a bar of soap shaped like a microphone when wife Gilda Radner steps in. In a joking manner that Radner would like to ignore, Murray conducts a mock TV show with her, something halfway between Johnny Carson and *This Is*

Your Life. Try as she might, Radner can't ignore this because Murray, as always, has the forceful insistence of an ignored child. Just when the joke is starting to wear thin, the following ensues:

BILL: [*to camera*] Well, you know, folks out there, what my wife doesn't know is that I know she's been cheating on me for the last couple of years and . . . we've got behind the curtain a surprise guest, the man she's been seeing behind my back for the last two years. Here he is— Richard Cularsky! Come on in, Richard, good to have you aboard!

[*Buck Henry enters in coat and tie, shakes hands and stands between them under the shower.*]

GILDA: What are *you* doing here?

BILL: Yes, I brought him all the way from his home in the city to be with us here today. Isn't that terrific? . . .

Well . . . honey, you've been confronted with this thing now. Are you gonna break it off with him for the good of your marriage, or are you just gonna continue to stick the knife in and twist it and twist it, huh? Ha, ha.

GILDA: Ah, ha, yes, Richard, that's exactly what we're gonna do, ha, ha.

BILL: [*laughing*] Wow, that hurts. Ah ha ha ha. *Okay,* you'll have to excuse me, but I'm an emotional guy. I really hate to get bad news. I'm sorry, but that's the way I'm built, *okay.* Gee, I'm afraid that's all the time I've got today—thanks, kids, for dropping by. . . . Thanks for stopping by— Mrs. Richard Herkiman and the guy she's been messing around with. Woo! [*audience applauds*] Thank you everyone.[4]

What's so funny about this scene? It's mock melodrama, the confrontation of a man with his unfaithful wife warped by surface absurdity: the naked couple and the fully dressed lover who has been magically summoned up, the imitation TV show that becomes real because it is in fact part of a real TV show. But why should people think Murray so funny as the injured party? How did this scene unleash his comic talents?

Anyone who has ever seen Murray perform should be able to imagine his delivery in this scene, the almost whiny lingering over some words, deriding the feelings at the same time it invokes them, then the sudden abrupt halt with one exclamatory word as if this has all been too much to listen to anyway. The dismissal of feelings at the same time that they're invoked is the important thing here because it points to Murray's absolute need to gain control over everything, including his own vulnerability. Much as he has inverted ordinary expectations of weakness and strength, Murray has taken on a stock role of the cuckolded husband, an object of scorn in conventional comedy, and turned it into a hero. There is no doubt that Murray is the dominant character here, the dynamo that drives the comic engine of the scene, and it is his dominance that inverts the usual expectations of this material and makes the other characters look ridiculous. Murray might talk of pain, but in a way that makes pain a source of pleasure: "Wow, that hurts. Ah ha ha ha." Most of all Murray's pain leads to pleasure because it enables him to bring to the surface what others would like to keep concealed. Where *he* should be embarrassed, he makes his wife and her lover embarrassed by engineering an unexpected and undesired confrontation. The embarrassment is all theirs finally because Murray is simply too much in control. Weakness is his source of strength.

When Chevy Chase did the "Weekend Update" on "SNL," his indiscreet phone conversations foregrounded an attitude that made his delivery of the news funny. He didn't really want to be there when there were much better things to do, so his response to the news was always an ironic detachment from the absurdity of it all. Murray could be equally ironic, more often sardonic, but he *did* want to be there because he approached the news on a level of attack that was beyond Chase. Both could give the appearance of being laid-back, but with Chase it's the real thing, while for Murray it's a shrewd disguise to cover the high level of aggression in his comedy. Chase is cool, but Murray is hip.

Chase and Murray are both in *Caddyshack* (1980), but they only have one scene together, a scene that works a striking contrast of their respective styles: low-key suave versus aggressive slob. Murray, living in a fantasy world in which he is a great golfer, tells Chase that his golf stroke is off and proceeds to show him how to correct it. The comic premise of the scene rests on the absurdity of Murray presuming to teach Chase anything, yet Murray does end up taking charge here in his own distinctive way. Earlier in the film Chase himself had given his caddy a golf lesson, and in typical Chase fashion: first bumbling, then deft. As he tries to remove his driving club from the bag, he inadvertently lifts out the whole group of clubs and scatters them. This clumsiness incredibly leads to his making a hole-in-one while blindfolded! Chase's ineptness is, as always, a momentary and disarming diversion from his real ability. Murray's ability never *has* to be real because the fantasy image he has of himself—a product of the omnipotent ego—supplants the reality, and in total take-over fashion. The punch line to the joke of Murray giving lessons to Chase is that he is so narrowly focused on the fantasy of his accomplishments that he doesn't see he is hitting ball after ball into a group of other players. Chase can be literally blind while playing golf and still succeed. Murray, on the other hand, is figuratively blind, and the blindness allows aggressive action that has him take over the whole field of play.

Because he is so focused on himself, Murray can be sexual without ever being romantic. In *Ghostbusters* (1984), when Murray drugs the possessed and sexually inviting Sigourney Weaver, he immediately considers taking advantage of her. Weaver's "possession" makes her dangerous because as the film works out the metaphor possession becomes a sign of her autonomous sexuality. In her drugged state she is more available to Murray (and for reasons that turn up in other Animal Comedies). Now that her own sexuality has been neutralized, she can be possessed, not by devils but by Murray himself. Sexual aggression is a kind of power, which makes it the appropriate mode of heterosexual activity for Murray, while romance depends on the greater sense of mutuality that Chase can convey. Audiences clearly understood this difference through the late 1970s and early 1980s. Articles on Chase appeared in *Ladies Home Journal*, *Redbook*, and *Mademoiselle*, while Murray was profiled only in *Rolling Stone*, a magazine that values the aggression and energy of rock music. If Murray in the early 1980s enjoyed a greater success in films than Chase, it was largely because Animal Comedy was ascendant, romantic comedy descendant.

In a minor part, as in *Caddyshack*, Murray can be purely an anarchic spirit, operating in a world of his own that is constantly threatening to destroy the real world. But for all the aggression he projects, Murray is not really a comic anarchist. In fact, in his first film role, in *Meatballs* (1979), he heads a summer camp and does the job effectively enough to turn a shy and weak boy with whom he sentimentally identifies into a gregarious and successful athlete. As always with Murray, there is an unresolved confusion between strength and weakness. Murray is a bully who allies himself with weaklings.

In starring roles, Murray's character is inevitably fleshed out in contradictory ways. In *Stripes* (1981), his most commercially successful film until *Ghostbusters*, he plays a cab driver whose life falls apart: in short order he loses his job, his girlfriend, his dry cleaning, and his pizza for supper. Actually, he quit the job in a fit of temper, so his anarchic impulses are initially set up as self-destructive. It is for this reason that he tells his friend Harold Ramis that he must join the Army: "I gotta get in shape. I gotta dry out before I'm thirty. The army's my only chance." But the film never fully accepts its own unlikely premise that this apparently antiauthoritarian and cynical character would ever submit to the discipline of the army. Rather, it keeps working riffs on the apparent contradictions implicit in the plot.

"You could join a monastery," Ramis suggests to Murray, rather than the army, and the following exchange ensues:

MURRAY: Did you ever see a monk get wildly fucked by some teenage girls?

RAMIS: Never.

MURRAY: So much for a monastery.

Murray, then, is not looking for order, but rather for a place from which he can pursue his wildly anarchic interests. But if this is the case, why does he need the army at all? The strange thing about this dialogue is it presumes some kind of choice, but it is a choice between two impossible options. The comedy is occasioned by a necessary evasion to cover the lack of any real motivating force in the plot. Murray is not suited to be either monk or soldier. But an inner emptiness of Murray's persona makes this plot trickery possible.

Although he joined the army to put his life in order, Murray's prime purpose seems to subvert the order of the army—at times, anyway. At other times, his character moves in opposite directions. When it looks like his troop will not be able to pass inspection, Murray conducts an all-night drill and whips them into shape with a bizarre speech that approaches a split personality in its blend of mockery and patriotism: "We're Americans. You know what that means. That means that our forefathers were kicked out of every decent country in the world. We are the wretched refuse . . . the underdog. . . . We're mutts—no animal could be more faithful." The self-mocking disparagement that starts this speech suddenly turns into a virtue, and Murray keeps shifting back and forth between these opposing modes until his peroration when he becomes as militantly jingoistic as any top brass would ever want a good soldier to be: "But we're *American* soldiers. We've been kicking ass for two hundred years. . . . We're ten and one!"

Murray's football metaphor that places his troop in a precarious position shows a way out of potential defeat by turning negatives into positives and weaknesses into strengths. At this point in the speech, there's a reaction shot of pride from Harold Ramis, which carries a double meaning—one for the character within the film, the other congratulating himself (the actor who is also the screenwriter) on the apparently inspired rhetoric. Murray concludes, "All we have to do is be the great American fighting *soldier* that is inside each one of us!" All irony has fled: when he says "American" and "soldier" toward the end of this speech, he drags both words out, in familiar Murray fashion, almost chanting them as if they possess magic power. And the power apparently works since the troop puts on the best show at the review the next day, and Murray accedes not only to power but, by the end of the film, even the heroic rescue of a squadron that has accidentally wandered into Czechoslovakia. Murray apparently has "the force" with him.[5]

Murray has some affinities with comic American anarchists of the past, most especially Groucho Marx. In his television quiz show Groucho was literally in the power position, which enabled him to direct comic barbs against his guests (although the sting of power was shrewdly deflected by a shared authority with his announcer). In feature films, Groucho was often given roles of power, as he was also the dominant brother in the trio or quartet. But when Groucho has power, he inevitably uses it to destroy the power structure—much as he frequently undermined all civil conventions of the quiz show on TV. *Duck Soup* (1933) ends with the world literally in ruins, with all four Marx Brothers continuing to mock heroic attitudes as they strike patriotic poses amid the rubble. The comic resiliency in all this destruction lies in the fact that the brothers can maintain the integrity of their individual characters even as the world falls to pieces. Bill Murray, on the other hand, depends on the outside world for a sense of inner self. If the outside world were to fall apart, so would he.

Where Bob Hope and especially Groucho maintain a consistency in their mockery that sets them decisively apart from the values of the dominant world in their films, Murray inevitably and unironically moves into the power position in his movies, much as the animals in *Animal House* (1978) move into the power structure of the dominant society in the epilogue. For all the comedy at the end of *Ghostbusters*, the three lead characters do in fact act like heroes (and are even attended by a black servant). What's more, they *expect* to be treated like heroes, surrounded as they are by the teeming crowd that cheers them on to their inevitable success. Something of a tongue-in-cheek quality may be read into the excessiveness of the adulation, but the tone is really not all that different from the slightly tongue-in-cheek quality of the *Superman* movies (1978–87) that coincided with the Animal Comedy cycle. It's as if we can only accept heroism in the post-Vietnam era if there is some ironic distance incorporated into our underlying belief: we now know that belief in heroes is childish, but along with George Lucas, Stephen Spielberg, and a kind of infantilization that took hold of American movies (starting with *Star Wars* and *Close Encounters of the Third Kind* in 1977), we would like to believe in that belief.[6]

Infantalism is hardly foreign to comedy since the form often glories in an at least temporary throwing off of all civilized restraints to arrive at a state much like childhood in its irresponsibility. I have already noted the eternal adolescence of Sutherland and Gould in *M*A*S*H* and opposed this to an underlying concern with maturation in Animal Comedy, much as the movement into adulthood may be regarded ambivalently at times. The revels of *Animal House* invoke childish irresponsibility, especially as they are opposed to the parent-authority figures of the administration and the Wasp fraternity, but they are also preparation for taking over the reins of authority. Sowing wild oats turns out good power figures, while the repressiveness of the Wasp fraternity turns out staff members for the Nixon White House and Watergate shenanigans. Much as Murray's first film, *Meatballs*, invoked *M*A*S*H*, Murray is closer to the animals of *Animal House* than he is to Gould and Sutherland in that he is always aiming toward taking over power.

In one of the oldest of Animal Comedies, Aristophanes' *The Birds*, Pisthetairos lands in Cloudcuckooland where he organizes the birds to form a barrier between the gods above and humankind below, thus enabling Pisthetairos to become more powerful than Zeus himself. Pisthetairos is as much out for himself as any of the animals in Hollywood Animal Comedy. He even manages to steal a woman from Zeus for a wife, much as Tim Matheson steals away the dean's wife in *Animal House*.[7] But Pisthetairos' seizing of power also involves a radical reorganization of the world of a kind that never happens in Animal Comedy.[8] Murray might be as aggressive and egocentric as Pisthetairos, but he moves to the top of an *existing* social order and, in effect, validates the order, much as he finds the order a means to validate his self.

One of the oddest aspects of the invasion of Czechoslovakia at the end of *Stripes* (in itself a fairly odd event for a comedy) is that Murray and his cohorts move into the then-Communist country in a souped-up van that is specifically identified as an experimental model of an "urban assault vehicle" under development by the army. The vehicle proves to be as ingenious as any of the fanciful gadgets in a James Bond movie, and it passes its unscheduled test with flying colors. At the least, this whole episode could be taken as a paean to American technology since a lot of the fun in the sequence lies in discovering the great capabilities this vehicle has for bashing Commies. But since it looks like an innocuous van, I don't think we can ever quite forget the "urban assault" designation: what's good for bashing Commies can also be good for bashing blacks and any other disruptive urban minorities. Pisthetairos, operating from a strong sense of self that is seen as insatiable, offers us a radical rearrangement of the world; for all his seemingly anarchic impulses, Bill Murray in his other-directed need of affirmation from the crowd presents a conservative reaffirmation of the existing order. The laid-back slob is a necessary disguise for Murray because it conceals the impulses that animate his personality. Power in his films is invoked and celebrated at the same time that it is denied.

Genres, like cultures, may be defined by their contradictions. The rise of women's liberation in the late 1960s and the concomitant rejection of sexual stereotyping and objectification also saw the rise of women's skirts to an unheard of height and the concomitant objectification of women. And blacks, who occupy contradictory roles in Animal Comedy (both honored and second-class at the same time), have a peculiarly contradictory role in American culture. Their subservience to the dominant white culture, their perceived less-than-humanness, is most clearly seen in the outmoded American view of miscegenation: blacks with a bit of white blood remain blacks, but whites with a bit of black blood become blacks.[9] If the ability of black blood to contaminate is a sign of its inferior quality, it also becomes a sign of its potency. White blood is such a fragile thing that only a drop or two of black blood is enough to change its color. Attitudes on sex and minorities possibly reveal a good deal about any culture, but they are especially important to me here because the contradictions they point to in American culture are contradictions that are central to Animal Comedy as well.

The contradictions of Animal Comedy might be seen as responses to the changes in American values and mores since the 1960s. The anything-goes attitude of sexual liberation also brought with it a heightened awareness of sexual crimes and abuses as more prevalent than we would have thought in more repressed times. The absence of pain in contemporary attitudes toward sex has made us look more closely at the pain in sex. And the ambivalences about power and heroism in these films are appropriate for a post-Vietnam post-Watergate society. Americans came to like the affably stolid image of power that Ronald Reagan projected, but the repeated rejection of his actual policies makes me wonder if there isn't a trace of unconscious mockery in all this that parallels the confusions projected by Bill Murray. Reagan was in many ways the Bill Murray of politics: he has a strong propensity for mock aggression (bombing the Soviet Union in sixty seconds), mock diplomacy (export the farmers and keep the grain), and, most Murray-like of all, mock self-mockery (seeing a therapist because of his problem with pressing buttons). "Now there you go again!"

is a bullying attack that would work comfortably as dialogue for almost any Murray screen character.

In the cases of both Reagan and Murray the mockery seems a necessary defense against a nihilism so deep that neither can afford to confront it directly. It is not simply ironic that a president so given to mockery, the most thoroughly derisive of comic modes, should also constantly be professing to profess beliefs. Rather, the beliefs contain their own contradiction, and the resulting sense of hollowness is really beyond the reaches of irony.[10] Writing toward the end of the first Reagan administration, Robert G. Kaiser, borrowing a phrase from one of House Speaker "Tip" O'Neill's aides, described Reagan as "the nation's host," comparing him to Ed Sullivan, who always promised "a *really big show* . . . however dreary or distinguished the performers." The "hucksterism" that Kaiser finds in Reagan's public pronouncements is a kind of sincere version of the mockery in Reagan's humor. "But what does Reagan himself really believe?" Kaiser is moved to ask, and can only answer, "That is mysterious."[11]

It is equally difficult to tell what Murray's character in *Stripes* really believes about the sentiments in his exhortatory speech. It is consonant with his mocking humor that the rhetoric can seemingly become an end in itself. "Where's the rest of me?" (the famous line from Reagan's 1941 movie *King's Row*) is an all-too-fitting title for Reagan's autobiography, but it is a phrase that applies to Murray as well because the real center of self is located in the adulation of crowds. And this decisively sets Murray apart from an earlier mocker like Groucho Marx.

One of the *Rolling Stone* profiles of Murray tells how he turned up at the opening day game of the Utica Blue Sox to sing "The Star Spangled Banner":

> Thousands cheer as Murray arrives. "Come on," he shouts. "You all know the words!"
>
> He sings the song. *Plays it straight.*
>
> "I sang like a bird," he later reminisces. "They just went crazy."
>
> Well, not completely straight. He does a little reprise of the last lines. Nicks it. *The la-and of the free-hee-heee And the home . . . of the . . . Utica Blue So-hoxxxx!*
>
> Then Murray runs down on the field and taunts the Little Falls Mets. "You guys are nothing!" he yells.
>
> The crowd goes wild.
>
> The Sox win going away.[12]

At first the reporter appears a little surprised that Murray plays this scene "straight." It is with some satisfaction that he can recognize the return of the old mocker, however benign the mockery might be in this case, and his subsequent derisive aggression. Can an audience finally believe that Murray believes in anything other than adulation?

After *Ghostbusters* Murray's career took an odd turn, caught up in the contradictions inherent in his own mocking stance. *The Razor's Edge* (1984) was Murray's first attempt to break away from low comedy into drama, a failure that kept him away from starring parts until *Scrooged!* in 1988.[13] Audiences just couldn't believe a Murray who was playing it straight, much as the reporter for the *Rolling Stone* article couldn't believe Murray would sing "The Star Spangled Banner" straight. The choice of *The Razor's Edge* (a remake of the 1946 film based on Somerset Maugham's novel) seems especially revealing because it is the story of a character looking for faith, and the screenplay (coauthored by Murray) does have him find something—but it is hard to tell what. Murray's performance is quite strange: surrounded by a very competent cast that has no trouble externalizing feelings, he himself seems uncertainly tentative and even suspicious about what exactly these other actors are doing and how he might manage to do it as well. Stripped of his defensive aggression, Murray goes dead on the screen.

There *is* a startling moment where some of the old mockery returns, but the context makes comprehension impossible. An old girlfriend from America visits him in his Paris flat. There she is surprised by a wall piled high with books. "Did you read all these books?" she asks. Murray, standing behind her, puts his hands on his hips, nonchalantly tilts his head to one side, clears his throat and replies, "I skim them." This is actually one on the most detailed moments in his performance, an elaborate setup for the letdown of the actual statement. Still, it remains unclear why he can't answer her directly at this point: Maybe he *has* only skimmed them, maybe he's read them and is angry she has to ask, maybe they came with the apartment. The only thing Murray believes in is a will to power that he can never look at directly. To do so would undermine his defensive stance, so he wraps desire in mockery. Caught up in the rhetoric of mockery, he can move toward apparent belief as he does with his cracked patriotic speech in *Stripes.* But the mockery masks a hollowness that moves to center stage when the mockery itself is unmasked.

There are interesting psychological implications to this that surfaced in Murray's only major public performance between the disaster of *The Razor's Edge* and the comeback of *Scrooged!* He appeared as the host on the occasion of the five hundredth broadcast of "Saturday Night Live" in 1987. The comic premise for the show was the supposed discovery that Murray had given only 109 performances of the 110 for which he had a contractual obligation to NBC. The show opens with an argument between Murray and his lawyers on one side and producer Lorne Michaels and the NBC lawyers on the other side. After much wheedling to get out of the obligation, Murray finally agrees on the following terms.

MURRAY: "One o'clock I'm out of here, and I'm gone with you people. I never have to come back in here again. Promise, huh?"

MICHAELS: "Unless, of course, they pick up your option."

NBC LAWYER: "That is—"

MURRAY: "Option?"

NBC LAWYER: "A ten-year option."

MURRAY: "Hold on a second here, man, you can't tie me up here for ten years. I mean, I've got some hungry lawyers here. Besides, I'm no good anyway. I'm burned out. [*almost crying*] I'm damaged goods. You don't want me here, not for ten years, [*whining*] please. Hey, listen, man, this isn't Eddie Murphy you're dealing with. C'mon! I'm not some punk from Chicago. You know! Like Mike Singleterry. Al Capone. You know what I'm saying."

There's a lot of aggression in this speech, but it keeps changing direction, moving outward, inward, outward, shifting between polarities of sadism and masochism. As always, it's difficult to locate the real Murray in this. Does he really believe he's burned out? If so, why is he doing the show? If not, why had he stayed away from performance for so long?

He did offer a personal explanation for his absence in the show's opening, but the explanation turned to the outside world to involve him in patriotic rhetoric similar to his speech in *Stripes*. He noted he took time off to be with friends and family, and somehow "three years are gone. But I'm just too fat and old to know the difference." This attack on himself comes in the middle of an attack directed outward, as Murray avers he had to come back

because I love this country. . . . And something happened this year that just drove a dagger right through my ticker. For the first time in the nation's history, a film comedy from another country was the number one hit. This country didn't make *Crocodile Dundee*. We should have. We didn't. We got a little cocky, I think, and they kicked our comic butts, those people down under. . . . [*here he talks of his absence*] But

I'm gonna try to help . . . this country regain her natural, genetic racial comic supremacy. Are you with me? [*cheers from the audience*] . . . Will you promise to laugh even if it's not funny?

We're still trying to recover from past defeats, and Murray, once burnt out, now taking charge, is trying to overcome the cultural equivalent of Vietnam and the Japanese economic invasion in the form of a successful film comedy from abroad. Can we take any of this seriously? As always, the excessive rhetoric signals the mockery, but there remain the questions of what exactly is being mocked and why.

I can get at this by noting one other contradiction that marked the 1970s, the period of Murray's rise to prominence and the advent of Animal Comedy. The decade came to be frequently tagged in the popular press with phrases from two different writers: "the Me Decade" from Tom Wolfe and "the culture of narcissism" from Christopher Lasch. At first blush, the phrases sound similar, and they were generally used in the popular press as if interchangeable, but in fact they point in opposite directions. For Wolfe, "the Me Decade" signals an expansive self grasped through "the Third Great Awakening" that is a consequence of "this unexpected post–World War II American luxury: the luxury enjoyed by so many millions of middling folk, of dwelling upon the self." Wolfe doesn't view this development without irony. However, he also sympathetically sets it against theories of mass culture by noting how the common man did not behave the way intellectual theories assumed he would in mass society: "once the dreary little bastards started getting money in the 1940's, they did an astonishing thing—they took their money and ran! They did something only aristocrats (and intellectuals and artists) were supposed to do—they discovered and started doting on *Me*!"[14] All this assumes there really is a "me" there to be indulged and expanded.

In naming this decade Wolfe might have been aiming for linguistic euphony, but his choice of words is revealing: why "the Me Decade" rather than "the I decade"? Why dwell upon the self as object rather than subject? The answer is implied in the phrase itself: this is object without subject. Translated into psychoanalytic terms, the self so totally indulged sets loose the function of the ego as the guardian watchdog of instinctual life. In becoming the primary site of satisfaction, the ego begins to evaporate. In other words, "I" becomes divorced from "me" so that personality in the "Me Decade" loses any sense of a centered self.

Christopher Lasch makes precisely this kind of psychoanalytic turn, which leads him to quite a different conclusion from Wolfe. The "culture of narcissism" signals a deep and disturbing absence of self. Lasch quotes from Wolfe's article, but points out that Wolfe's own observations "call into question his characterization of the new narcissism as a third great awakening."[15] Lasch sees more of a deadening than an awakening brought on by the triumph of an individualistic ethos that denies the interdependencies of individuals in a complex society. Possibly because of the common misunderstanding of what he intended by "narcissism," which he used more in its clinical rather than popular sense, Lasch very emphatically distinguished between narcissism and egoism in his next book: "As the Greek legend reminds us, it is this confusion of the self and the not-self—not 'egoism'—that distinguished the plight of Narcissus. The minimal or narcissistic self is, above all, a self uncertain of its own outlines, longing either to remake the world in its own image or to merge into its environment in blissful union."[16] Writing on the 1970s, Lasch notes, "We are fast losing the sense of historical continuity, the sense of belonging to a succession of generations originating in the past and stretching into the future."[17] In losing that sense of belonging, we are losing our sense of self, and hedonism becomes a doomed pursuit to find what isn't there.

In 1985, *Habits of the Heart*, a serious sociological study published by a university press, became a bestseller by detailing for Americans how the traditional ethos of individualism conflicts with a healthy society's need for commitment from its members: the Me Decade was preparing to look beyond self-indulgence as an ultimate good. And as Hollywood moves further and further away from the ruggedly indulgent world of Animal Comedy, Murray's return to the big screen with a starring part in *Scrooged!* staked out a new direction for himself, reaching out for a thousand points of light and oddly echoing calls heard in a different venue for a kinder, gentler nation. Unusually, Murray starts off in this film in a very powerful position: as president of a major network, someone who has apparently risen so high so early by his fine sense of whose throat to cut and when to cut it. From the outset, then, this plot is necessarily different from that of the earlier films: rather than moving progressively into a position of power where he can most fully indulge himself, Murray must now be chastised for the power he already has and must learn in the process that there are other values in life.

At the beginning, Murray is all sadistic aggression, but (strikingly, in light of the earlier films) the sadism here is given a pronounced narcissistic turn. Just as he is about to berate subordinates to the point of humiliating them, he pulls open a drawer as if to check for something. An overhead shot reveals him looking into a mirror to make sure that his expression is appropriately ferocious. Murray still needs outside confirmation of his claims to strength, but the narcissism has never before been so explicitly addressed. As it openly points to a vulnerability in the character, an uncertainty of any real strength, the narcissism paves the way for a series of punishments that only the Marquis de Sade might have devised. But these punishments are narcissistic in one other regard: they are projections of Murray's own imagination, as is emphatically made clear by the fact that no one else sees them. Inside the sadist a willing masochist has always lurked. To my knowledge, Murray made only two major public appearances before *Scrooged!*: the hosting of "Saturday Night Live" and his cameo role in *Little Shop of Horrors* (1986) as the lunatic patient who enjoys submitting to a sadistic dentist (Steve Martin). It is perhaps no accident that both parts cast him in a masochistic relationship to other people.

The ending of *Scrooged!* finds a thoroughly battered Murray pleading for a nation of goodwill and traditional family values, and even though Murray has apparently changed his message from self-indulgence to reaching out, he once again has the force with him. A series of cutaways to people watching their TV sets show all of them powerfully influenced by his message: they all end up doing exactly what he urges them to do. There is a very high pitch to the rhetoric in all of this, not just in Murray's speech but in the sequence itself since the insistent cutaways try to convince us by actions much as Murray is trying to convince by words. The rhetorical strategy is necessary not just for the movie to try to convince us of its sincerity, but to cover over a key problem with the plot at this point. Why should Murray find the chief means of showing his redemption by *preaching* to others? As the film presents it, he is just about the only character who *doesn't* understand the spirit of Christmas, so no one else but him really needs such preaching. Murray can signal his conversion solely by trying to impose his will on others, and in this regard the film has arrived at a fairly familiar strategy for Murray's persona.

If Murray can be redeemed from his sadism only by a retreat into masochism, there must be some question of how much goodwill may finally prevail. Murray's name in this film, Frank Cross, is evocative: the given name points to his unpleasantly direct manner with others, while his surname suggests the high level of anger in all his actions and pronouncements. Furthermore, "Cross" evokes a burden, which is precisely what the anger becomes for Frank when it is directed inward. But if masochism becomes his overt position at the end, its component instinct of sadism can never be far behind—and it is in fact there in the bullying rhetoric of

Cross's final exhortation and the demanding aggressiveness with which he browbeats a nation of television viewers within the film and a nation of movie viewers in the theaters. Once more Murray is rendered heroic by the end of the film. Again he is able to transform the rest of the world into an image designed to confirm a sense of self that must perversely always remain uncertain to itself.[18]

In *Scrooged!*, the belief-seeking Murray of *The Razor's Edge* has been married to the power-hungry Murray of the comedies. Sincerity is intended to be the keynote here, although an earlier version of the *Scrooged!* screenplay that I have seen (designated a "Fifth Draft") had a more mocking conclusion. At one point one of the cutaways during Frank's final speech took us to a "biker bar" where Frank's message of goodwill converts a group of Hell's Angels menacing a lone Yuppie. The film was to have ended with a shot of the Hell's Angels singing "Angels We Have Heard On High." This odd confluence of two very different kinds of angels would have undercut the film's apparent message in a way that might have been more congruent with anarchic moments of Murray's earlier films. But even at his most seemingly anarchic, Murray has had a strongly conservative streak: he has never "threaten[ed] to smash the prevailing social order to smithereens" in the way that Old Comedy does.[19] Murray has a strong need for the prevailing social order as a confirmation of self.

By the end of *Scrooged!* anything that might cast doubt on the sincerity of Murray's position must be erased precisely because the sincerity itself is so tentative. For all that the movie occasionally seems a send-up of the Charles Dickens novel (and all the other movie and television adaptations of it), by the end of this version there is an attempt to believe deeply and fully in the message of the original work—but the message has been turned into pure rhetoric by which the messenger himself is made more important than the message. The rhetoric is necessary to mask the inner hollowness that must never be allowed to surface in an era of image-making where one is what one appears to be, where belief can be achieved by enunciation. For Murray, if the rhetoric is strong enough to create belief in others—if it is presented in a sufficiently insistent way with all the puling aggressiveness he can muster (which is considerable)—then perhaps belief in the outside world can create a sense of belief in the inner world of self.

When Bill Murray's aggression is directed outward, it usually focuses on a desire to "remake the world in its own image" (in Lasch's words). As Lasch finds a diminished "sense of historical continuity" in 1980s America, the attempt to make 1950s mores more congruent with 1980s behavior (which I noted about *Porky's*) might reflect a similar attempt at remaking the world. Murray's aggression often focuses on a comparable rewriting of history, whether it is to turn a group of incompetent soldiers into the best fighting machine the world has seen or to regain the crown of comedy for America. Yet Murray's aggression can also turn inward, the masochist in the shower with wife and lover who seemed to glory in his own pain. The element of mockery in all this is there to smooth over the confusions, confusions that parallel the very different ways Wolfe and Lasch viewed the 1970s.

Murray is a "me" person, driven by the demands of an infinitely expanding self that tries to gain control over every circumstance. At the same time, the incessantly mocking tone by which he gains control points to an inner emptiness, an inability to convey belief and a sense of commitment. Murray's connection to others is defined in narcissistic terms: the adulation they can grant provides a way of defining self. There is a real sense of pain in all this that occasionally surfaces in the masochism and the whiny tone in his delivery, but it is always quickly camouflaged by mockery. There is also, I think, an analogous pain at the center of the contradictions in Animal Comedy, but one that the films are also wont to cover over so as not to distract from their seemingly carefree hedonistic pursuits. This results in the contradictory attitudes I have noted in the last few chapters.

A whole genre may be built on these kinds of contradictions: the western constantly shifts between the poles of lawlessness and law-and-order, and the average western often does so in fairly confused fashion[20]—but the result can be richly evocative. When this confusion is confronted by a major artist who understands the nature of the confusion (as director John Ford with his extraordinarily dialectical mind understood the western), the result can be a legacy of classic films. Possibly for this same reason, the films that fully confront the pain in sex and social relations, that in effect make overt the contradictions inherent in their material, these films are the most fully realized and articulated works of the Animal Comedy genre: *Fast Times at Ridgemont High* (1982), *Revenge of the Nerds* (1984), and *Heaven Help Us* (1985).

It is easy enough to ignore entire genres that may somehow seem like lesser creations than art that presumably creates itself anew each time. But to do so is to overlook a vital part of our culture that in fact offers fertile territory from which major works can grow. For example, *Time* magazine rejected the body of what it calls "teenpix" by claiming "The glandular convulsions of adolescence are just not interesting or complex enough to sustain the plots of half a hundred Hollywood films each year."[21] The premise of this objection is itself questionable, and in any case this is hardly the first time that Hollywood has turned out lots of films focused on the young. The genre has effectively created a language we can use to talk to each other about key concerns of our culture: about conflicts between liberation and repression; about the demands of individual desire against the demands of society; about what it means to become adult in a world permeated by a "youth culture."

A good number of the Animal Comedies I've seen, and certainly all the best ones, focus on kids at the borderline between adolescence and adulthood, kids moving from the protective cocoon of a home environment to a world where they are compelled to take responsibility for their fate. Animal Comedy is not necessarily about adolescents. *Bachelor Party* (1984), *Police Academy* (1984), and *Moving Violations* (1985) all feature adults, even though the last two do send the adults to school. In a sense the project of these films is always educational. So, if they frequently focus on teenagers, it is for two reasons. As noted earlier, adolescence is a period in which we freely grant people license to behave like animals, but it is also a period in which they learn to grow into adults. Many of these films express a real ambivalence about this double function, often finding themselves stuck in a period they are trying to move beyond.

Becoming adult should mean learning to move beyond a kind of infantile demand for the gratification of one individual's desires to an understanding of the connections of self to society. In this regard, it might seem contradictory for the films to use sexual initiation—an act of gratifying individual desire—as the benchmark for maturity. But this is also an act that specifically defines connection to another person. The double meaning in the act itself, then, parallels a conflict at the center of these films in their double focus on both group membership and libidinal drives as means of defining character. So many of these films pivot on first-time sexual experiences because the first time is really the last act of our adolescence, the last moment at which we can define ourselves solely by our individual needs—because the great divide between the world of childish things and adulthood is irrevocably crossed. How many events in our lives ever remain so indelibly fixed in memory? The success of the genre lies in the potency of its central material, focusing as it does on one of the most dramatic, memorable, and decisive moments in our lives. The majority of these films might be undistinguished, yet they clearly touch a nerve close to the heart of American culture. The most fascinating for me are *Fast Times at Ridgemont High*, *Revenge of the Nerds*, and *Heaven Help Us*, in part because they contain none of the strategies of denial familiar from other Animal Comedies. Instead, they convey a concomitantly real sense of pain unusual in these films. All present, through the discourse they engage in with Animal Comedy, the fullest and most intelligent articulations of the conflicting impulses at the heart of the genre.

Growing Pains

"*I found it was all too easy to recapture one's adolescence. The hard part was growing up again.*"

—*Cameron Crowe*

Chapter 10 Sexual Politics

Fast Times at Ridgemont High (1982)

Fast Times at Ridgemont High appeared as a book in 1981. Its author, Cameron Crowe, was a *Rolling Stone* reporter who, in 1979 and only five years out of high school himself, realized that "the kids" he and his colleagues were constantly writing about had become an indefinite abstraction. He decided to return to high school and learn firsthand what "the kids" were *really* like. The result of his senior-year regression was a book billed on its title page as "A True Story." In the preface Crowe reasserts the essential truthfulness of his enterprise: "I have tried to capture the flow of day-to-day life, as well as the life that begins as soon as the last bell rings. It was my intention to write of the entire business—from academic competition to sexual blunders—of teenage adulthood."[1]

I doubt if any book, even this one, could ever present "the entire business" of anything, and Crowe's brief indication of what the entire business consists of shows how circumscribed his approach is. Animal Comedy has generally been overtly circumscribed in the way it presents its characters in at least one important regard: from *American Graffiti* onward, these kids seem to live in a world without parents.[2] Although he could claim to write from actual experience of the "real world," Crowe himself seems to have followed the patterns of Animal Comedy by paying no attention to relationships between his "fellow" teenagers and their parents. This can make sense to the extent that adolescence represents a final pulling away from parents to establish autonomy, but how very strange the absence of parents is might be seen by comparing this book or any of these films to the contemporaneous Peter Yates–Steve Tesich film *Breaking Away* (1979), where the son's growing autonomy is dramatically tied to his relationship with his parents.

In the past it had been a routine matter to see children's problems *in relation to* their parents. Even in films that dealt explicitly with rebellion—for example, the first two James Dean films, *East of Eden* and *Rebel Without a Cause* (both 1955)—parents were an important part of the drama, and the films moved toward some sense of ameliorative accommodation between parents and children. But since *Summer of '42* (1971) and *American Graffiti* two years later, it has become standard dramatic strategy to leave the parents out altogether or, at most (as in *Summer of '42*), present as only an offscreen voice. In the rare film in which parents and family do appear—*Sixteen Candles* (1984), for example—the parents are broadly caricatured.[3] *Sixteen Candles* is especially striking in this regard because the father is played by Paul Dooley (who had played the father in *Breaking Away*), and toward the end of the film he has one sweetly tempered scene of genuine communication with daughter Molly Ringwald. But the scene feels distinctly out-of-place because the rest of the film has mercilessly mocked the entire family. In any case, the full-bodied and sympathetic treatment of the parents in *Breaking Away* had become unusual enough by 1979 to cause critical comment.[4]

The insistence on caricature whenever parents and family are present has created an odd problem in teen comedies: how did these children ever result from these parents? This is not exactly an unfamiliar problem in Hollywood comedies of the past: after all, we might very well wonder how Carole Lombard in *My Man Godfrey* (1936) and Henry Fonda in *The Lady Eve* (1941), could spring from father Eugene Pallette, how two of the most beautiful performers in movies could find their paternity in a comic grotesque. The opposition is one familiar to New Comedy: Pallette is a *senex*, grown fat and past sexual prime, while the beauty of the younger generation promises regeneration. Within this scheme, the parent may be physically grotesque but still capable of an underlying sympathy for his children. Furthermore, the children themselves never see the parents as grotesque, so while they might look different, they never feel as if they were operating in a different world. New Comedy in its insistent movement toward a new conjugal union that is opposed by the parents implies a renewal that links what is declining to what is being born.[5] In Animal Comedy, however, sex is a kind of sport, an activity that is an end in itself with no consequence beyond the immediate action. Procreation is never an issue in these films, while it is always at least implied in New Comedy.

The opposition between generations in Animal Comedy, then, is always starker because it is a comedy that insistently denies continuity. Parents, when present in Animal Comedy, are caricatured as a way of establishing how they are viewed by their children.[6] Parents must be either scarce or ridiculous in these films in the way that all foreigners were generally scarce or ridiculous in American comedy of the past: the parents are foreigners in the world these films create. No doubt there is a good deal less discontinuity in real life than these films see, but the fact of a separate "youth culture" points to a greater disjuncture between adolescence and adulthood than in the past.

This difference can be seen in an earlier teenage exploitation film, *Beach Party* (1963), an American-International quickie that was successful enough to spawn a string of beach movies. The parent figure in this film, Robert Cummings, is an anthropologist who sets out to study teenage mores much as he has studied "primitive" tribes, and he initially finds a great deal in common between them. In this regard, the film seems to support the notion of a *cultural* difference in adolescence, but it turns out this is merely a delusion of the adult. The real problem is one in his psychological development. It seems Cummings had to grow up too fast in his pursuit of academic success so he missed out on the adolescence his subjects are now enjoying. He can understand this by the end of the film because the teenagers help him to regain an adolescence he never had. Adolescence is to be celebrated not as a separate stage of life but rather as part of the continuity of life. In the 1970s, as a more definite sense of a youth culture emerged and films treated adolescence as something apart from the rest of life, the notion of an "extended adolescence" in American life became a cliché in popular journalism. But even as adolescence extended, it did become a separate period, to the extent that Cameron Crowe, writing for *Rolling Stone*, itself an emblem of youth culture, felt he had to go back to high school to get in touch with "the kids."

Animal Comedy has established a way of thinking about adolescence, and Crowe's book, for all that it purports to be a "true story," takes its frame of reference as much from the movies as from reality itself. There is one episode in the book about the destruction of a car that seems lifted directly from *Animal House*. This is not to say that the episode itself did not happen (I am quite willing to accept the *factuality* of Crowe's report), but the *way* events are reported in the book often seems colored by filmic counterparts. The nature of the object observed is transformed by the ways we choose to observe it. While no way is truer than any other, we can at least question those attitudes that have been brought to bear on the object under observation. Nowhere are Crowe's attitudes to his material clearer than in the book's treatment of its girl students, who are as much creatures of untroubled and compliant sexuality as their sisters in the male wish-fulfillment world of Animal Comedy.

Wish-fulfillment for male adolescents might well be nightmare for adults, and the book of *Fast Times* is well aware of the double-edged sword it wields both in its title and its brief and punchy opening paragraph:

> Stacy Hamilton lay under the covers, still fully dressed, and stared at the ceiling. Somewhere in the course of the long and uneventful summer she had come to an important decision. There was no way she was going to start senior high school still a virgin.

As opening paragraphs go, this one's a real grabber. Horny teenage boys with short attention spans do not have to look very far for the salacious parts: here's something like a neon sign pointing to a whopper right on the first page. And parents who might fear the worst from the book's title are granted immediate if distressing satisfaction. From the very start, purported objectivity is a neat dodge for rambunctious sensationalism. What the book finally lacks is not so much the "truth" but any sense of authenticity.

The film version of *Fast Times* was scripted by Crowe but directed by a woman (Amy Heckerling). Taking most of its events directly from the book, it achieves the kind of authenticity so lacking there—especially in regard to its female characters—by investigating the characters' emotions in a way that transcends the book's sensationalism. By honoring at least the potential for emotional complexity in all its characters, the film offers something of a corrective both to its source material and to the genre to which it nonetheless belongs.

The book of *Fast Times* came out just before *Porky's* (1982), with the film version of *Fast Times* appearing later in 1982, so it is unlikely there is any direct influence of the porcine pic on either book or film.[7] In any event, the opening of *Porky's* (which begins with a character in bed, worrying about his sex life and determined to lose his virginity) is quite a bit like the opening of *Fast Times* the book. The ardent desire to lose one's virginity is, as has been noted, one of the key motifs in these films, but the twist in *Fast Times* was to make the sexually avid character a fifteen-year-old girl. The film of *Fast Times* might be something of a feminist *Porky's*, but the book is more pseudofeminist in that it defines its liberation by appropriating a male approach to sex for its female characters.

The sexual initiation of fifteen-year-old Stacy Hamilton appears in both book and film, but with a marked difference of treatment that is indicative of the way the film treats both its source material and its source genre. In the book, the sex is mostly fun and games in a manner typical of Animal Comedy:

"You look nice tonight," said the Vet.

"You do, too."

Silence. Stacy rearranged her hands in her lap.

"It's pretty warm out tonight."

"It is. It's real warm. I wonder how long it will last."

The Vet leaned over and kissed Stacy on the cheek. *Was that the first move?* She sat quietly for a moment, her hands folded in her lap. *It had to be the first move.* She waited another moment. *When I'm eighteen it won't matter either way.*

She lunged for the Vet and kissed him squarely on the mouth. At first surprised, he held her there and kissed her even more deeply. She began to run her fingers through his blow-dry haircut.

It was The Vet who spoke first. "Are you really nineteen?"

"Yes," said Stacy. "I am *really* nineteen."

She kissed him again.

"I'd better take you home," he said.

"What about those other guys you live with?"

"I mean back to *your* home."

But they made no moves in any directions. A few seconds later, The Vet had apparently resolved his inner conflict. He began tugging lightly at Stacy's red corduroy pants. She looked down at his hand on the snap.

This was it, Stacy thought. The Real Thing. A thousand schoolyard conversations and tips from Linda Barrett jumbled in her head. Would it hurt? Would it be messy? Would she get pregnant? Would they fall in love?

"Do you really want to do this?" Stacy heard herself ask. "I mean, it's your final decision."

"I think we both want to."

Slowly, awkwardly, Stacy reached down to help him. She unsnapped her pants, and suddenly the Vet needed no more reassurance. He tilted her backward onto the concrete dugout bench. They continued kissing, feverishly, his hand slipping up into her blouse. He massaged her breasts. Then he pulled off her shoes. Then her pants. Then his own pants. Ron "The Vet" Johnson was different from the other boys she'd made out with. He had Technique.

"Is this your first time?" he whispered.

"Yesssssssss . . ."

As she held onto The Vet's shoulders and felt a man enter her for the first time, Stacy looked up at the top of the Ridgemont dugout. She would always remember reading the graffiti above her:

Heroin in the neck

Lincoln was here — Sieg Heil

Led Zeppelin

Day y Roberto (Disco Fags)

Stacy Hamilton, fifteen, slipped back into her room at three that morning. Already her room felt different to her. Those frilly pillowcases, those Scholastic Book Services paper-backs she'd ordered in junior high school, that bubblegum chain on the dresser . . . they all seemed out of place to her now.

She was giddy, wide awake. She sat on the edge of her bed and examined herself in the mirror—no difference. Somehow it was just like Linda Barrett had explained it to her. Her first feeling would be one of relief, the second, that she would want to go out and sleep with all the cute guys in the world because it was *so much fun.*

The passage seems to be focused on the girl: we are privileged to her thoughts throughout the scene (with one important ellipsis I will come back to shortly). She is even partly the aggressor here: in response to his rather chaste kiss on the cheek, she doesn't just kiss him back—she actually *lunges* for him. And although we are subsequently told the man has "technique," and he is made into something of a skilled sexual machine that even the book itself seems to admire, she does help him with her own undressing. Oddly enough, however, the adverb "awkwardly" gets attached to her action rather than his, even though she has to help him unsnap her pants. The awkwardness, of course, serves to remind us of her inexperience, and that in itself becomes a kind of titillation here: Stacy practically hisses with pleasure when Ron asks if it is her first time.

So enthralled is this passage with the deft mechanics of the two participants—for all the momentary awkwardness, they both seem like old hands at the routine—that it never really confronts the dichotomy between action and experience that the language nonetheless suggests. The breach could be vividly realized through the graffiti that Stacy reads at the moment of coitus (and as it actually is presented in the film), but Crowe, who is practically garrulous about her feelings throughout the rest of the scene, suddenly goes mute on us at this point. Having raised the curtain (so to speak) on this momentous event, he suddenly changes the scene to Stacy's bedroom, never giving us a moment to reflect on what we've just read other than to experience its sensationalistic impact. When we are no longer caught up in the act itself, Crowe lets us know that Stacy had a terrific time and, as a result, now wants to "sleep with all the cute guys in the world." What was that graffiti doing there then if Stacy was so engaged in the action? As soon as she reports the great news to Linda Barrett, she calls up a local radio station and asks them to play a Led Zeppelin record! So it turns out that, in the book, the graffiti, instead of distancing Stacy from the experience, is in fact to be regarded as part of the romantic atmosphere that she enjoyed.

If the book asks us to take any kind of ironic stance toward action and character in this passage, it is irony of a fairly benign kind, one that laughs at the romanticizing nature of the character. Still, it fully accepts the "truth" of how much fun the experience was because that's presumably what the principal participant reported to Crowe. However, the chapter does end with a peculiarly inflected irony:

> Stacy's clock radio clicked back on. She lay in her bed, face pressed into the pillow. It was 6:45 A.M.
> "Get up, Stacy honey," came her mother's voice through the door. "These are the best years of your life!"

The passage plays on a shock of misrecognition. The adult reader likely startled by this fifteen-year-old's sexual adventurism can see a grim irony in the mother's declaration, but the underlying irony is directed both against the mother and the parent-reader. Crowe *himself* sees this as the best years of life, just not in the same way the mother does. Like the characters in *American Graffiti*, Crowe finds growing up hard to accept because of all the good things you have to leave behind. In *Fast Times* the film, growing up is hard because it involves pain *along the way*. If anything, the film is clearer than the book in showing that the uncertainties and ignorances of adolescence are something worth growing beyond (while at the same time, it honors the still-childlike qualities in its too rapidly maturing teens). The film understands the odd demands for maturity placed on teenagers more fully than the book and more fully than other Animal Comedies.

I can most accurately convey the film's achievement (both in its departures from the book and from other Animal Comedies) by looking at how the same events presented in the book are depicted in the film. Immediately to be considered, of course, is the difference in the amount of detail and kind of information that can be given in each medium—which must reflect in part the difference between words and images—even though the event in book and film is identical; yet it takes many more words to describe what is going on in the film. The sequence in the film is quite brief, lasting only about a minute, but the still photographs that follow should give some sense of the psychological richness the film achieves in this scene. Also, the breakdown of the action shot by shot should give some indication of Amy Heckerling's editing style and how she deftly manipulates point of view.

As in the book, the scene is the dugout of the Ridgemont High baseball field at night in early fall. Crowe offers little description of the scene and virtually nothing on the dugout itself other than to note that it is illuminated by "a single light bulb." Unlike prose, film can never *describe*; it must always *show*. What might be deliberately vague in the book must necessarily be pinned down in the film. That "single light bulb" can have quite a different impact on the way we experience the scene, depending on whether the light is shaded or bare, glaring or diffuse, gloomily stark or romantically shadowy. In the film the lighting for this scene suggests a darkly desolate mood that does have an impact on the way we view and experience what happens, so much so that the culminating long shot exposing the full expanse of the setting acts as an inevitable comment on the psychological issues the scene dramatizes.

Although specific events are pretty much the same in the two versions, there are some immediate differences that have nothing to do with the differences between word and image. In the book, Ron "the Vet" is a veterinarian whose profession seems little more than an excuse for a nickname endowed with sexual resonances. In the film, Ron (D. W. Brown) works as a stereo salesman at the mall where Stacy (Jennifer Jason Leigh) is a waitress. The point that he is a part of her world is not unimportant,

Stacy: "That's a really nice jacket."

Ron: "Thanks a lot. *(he carefully folds it and puts it next to him to his left. He continues to look to the left and he straightens his sleeves, then looks back to her)* It's warm."

Stacy *(pushes her hands into her sweater pockets as if she were cold as he rubs his leg)*: "Yeah, it's really warm. I wonder long it will last." *(she looks down to the right)*

Ron: "So..."

Ron: "...am I gonna get to first base?" *(Stacy laughs nervously)*

(Ron leans over, takes Stacy's head in his hands and kisses her, sticking his tongue out first)

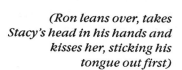

(Ron finishes kissing her, breaks off from her but leaves his right hand on her face. She looks at him almost with curiosity. He takes his hand from her face and moves back from her)

Ron: "Are you really nineteen?"

Stacy: "Yeah, yeah, I am... *(she puts her right hand on his shoulder)* I'm really nineteen." *(Ron caresses her face again, and the o.s. music* ["She's got to be somebody's baby tonight..."] *starts. Ron moves in and kisses her again)*

(Holding onto her right thigh and continuing to kiss her, Ron pushes Stacy down against the bench, moving his whole body on top of her)

(Stacy moves her head to kiss Ron on the mouth, at the same time that his hand moves down her body)

(Ron's hand starts to unbutton Stacy's sweater)

(Stacy tucks her head down a bit as if embarrassed)

(Ron finishes unbuttoning her sweater and then un- buttons her blouse and exposes one breast)

(From kissing the hollow of her neck, Ron breaks off from her and pulls back)

(Ron unsnaps his shirt to bare his chest although he leaves the shirt on)

(Ron moves back to Stacy and kisses her. As she puts her left hand on his shoulder, he moves his body up against her, which causes her to wince twice. She looks away from him)

A point-of-view shot shows what Stacy sees: "Disco Sucks."

(Ron moves back from Stacy)

(Ron raises himself up and throws his head back)

(As Ron moves back in on Stacy, she raises her eyes up as if to look behind her)

A point-of-view shot with a slight tilt up to suggest the movement of Stacy's glance and show what she sees: "SURF NAZIS."

(Ron moves up again, leaving Stacy with look of confusion, possibly even devastation)

In the one bright spot of the dugout, we can make out Ron's body moving.

as her best friend Linda Barrett (Phoebe Cates) later makes clear when she consoles Stacy after Ron's departure by pointing out that she shouldn't want to spend the rest of her life with a stereo salesman. Linda's comment implicitly indicates the film's unusual sensitivity to the relationship between class issues and sexuality; at the same time, the comment also points to the centrality of the mall to the film and its contradictory status as a place of dream fulfillment but also a place of severely limiting restrictions.

Whether "Ron" or "the Vet," the character is not given much identity in either film or book. He is generally more hesitant in his actions with Stacy in the book, although the reasons for his behavior are never indicated. In the film, Ron's hesitancy is limited to the question of Stacy's age, and it comes up only after she responds to his kiss with a look of curiosity. The question of her age makes sense in the film as a response to her less-than-engaged way of regarding his kiss. The look of curiosity does establish her as girlish—a child looking at adult behavior and wondering what it is about at the same time she is taking part in it. In the book Stacy's youth becomes part of the salacious appeal of the scene. In the film Stacy's youth becomes a singular source of discomfort, both in its casting of little-girlish Jennifer Jason Leigh and in the way her performance is directed, which constantly remind us that this is a girl who has not yet quite put away childish things.[8] These reminders create a tension in the way sexual desire is defined in the film: for Stacy especially it is clear that sexual desire has become confused with some kind of emotional need that can never really be met by sexual contact.

The imbalance in the way the characters look at sex and affection is an undercurrent throughout Stacy's first sexual experience in the film. Ron is more the aggressor here than he is in the book, and he has a more single-minded interest in sex. He is the one who suggests they drive to "the Point," and he is the one who initiates the sexual activity with an inspired improvisation taken from their dugout setting: "So, am I gonna get to first base?" Sex is a sport, a game in which the guy wants to score. The guy may hit a home run (as Ron eventually does here), but what does the girl get out of it? If the terminology suggests a gain for the guy, a loss for the girl is implied, and sexual contact is immediately established as something unequal.

Given the sports metaphor, Stacy's look of curiosity in response to the kiss establishes her as more spectator than participant, which means that she is in part divorced from the experience of her own body. The somewhat hallucinatory, almost nightmarish quality of the sequence derives from a split between observing and experiencing—a necessary split for the girl since she has complied in establishing herself the loser. Better to be a spectator in such circumstances and deny any involvement with the actions you are participating in. By defining a very precise way of looking that colors our perception of the rest of the scene, Heckerling's high-cut, high-point style incisively insists on the split by separating heads from bodies (shots 8 through 14), separating expressions that register the feelings from the flesh that stimulates them.

The split between observer and participant suggests another metaphor that is important for the scene in the film: if Ron has a sense of sport in the activity, Stacy necessarily has a sense of performance. Her initial curiosity is a near mistake since it signals more observer than participant, and she tries to correct this subsequently in attempting to disguise the awkwardness of the experience with a look of pleasure (shot 8). When Ron begins to unbutton her blouse, she has to hide her reaction to perpetuate the performance: the embarrassment over exposing her breasts leads her to conceal her face by tucking her head down (shot 10). The gesture is a defensive one, as if she were seeking to protect herself from a blow, and in a sense she is since the moment of penetration seems felt as an invasion, making her wince twice (shot 14). At this point Stacy abandons the performance entirely, both as participant and observer, to look at the graffiti above the dugout (Crowe also leaves the scene at this point in the book, but never fully accounts for why Stacy should look away at the height of what is later described as being "so much fun"). Heckerling does not avert her eyes, so neither can we, and at this point the scene really gathers its fullest power.

There is a seemingly minor yet important change in the graffiti that Stacy first sees: "Disco Sucks" (presumably a reworking of "Disco Fags" in the book). At first glance this might seem to some extent a less sexual expression than an overt reference to music. Dismissing something by saying it sucks retains a vulgar force through its coarseness that does not immediately call up a specific sexual image. But the context of the scene necessarily resexualizes the phrase. A sexual expletive used as an oath is ordinarily "positive" in its active form and "negative" in the passive: the aggressor in sexual terms (the one who "screws" or "fucks") is ordinarily triumphant, while the passive recipient (the one who "gets screwed" or "was fucked") is a loser. Fellatio strikingly reverses these polarities: the person performing fellatio might in fact be the aggressor, but in the terminology of the oath the active position becomes negative. The debasement of the one who sucks assumes the sexual pleasure is one-sided but also implies infantilization in conjuring up the image of an infant sucking at the mother's breast. Such an image has specifically been invoked in the scene: when the lovemaking begins in earnest with Stacy's assurance that she is in fact nineteen (shot 6), the film offers an ironic underscoring of her fib with a song on the soundtrack that assures *us,* "She's got to be somebody's baby tonight . . ."

Fellatio is not what takes place here, of course, but Heckerling has worked in a variety of ways to reinforce the childlike image of Stacy that makes the scene so disturbing. The only thing we have heard previous to this scene about Stacy's interest in sex comes from her questioning Linda Barrett about fellatio during a lunch recess and then receiving some instruction from knowledgeable Linda via imagined practice with a carrot.[9] The resonant use of food as the practice object sets up the quest for sex as a quest for nurturance: Stacy *must* be somebody's baby. The sense of tremulousness and uncertainty that Stacy projects in her sexual initiation is not just a matter of embarking on an unknown physical activity. The physical vulnerability translates into an emotional vulnerability at expressing a need that might not be fulfilled. As she literally opens herself up to a man, there remains the danger she will not receive what she is asking for. It is from this sense of need that the inequality of the sex act in the film derives: the person fucking aggressively satisfies his needs, the person getting fucked has her needs denied. Even as Stacy wills it, the sex act must then be seen as a violation because it is so devoid of emotional connection, so little focused on her needs.

What the act means for Stacy then must ultimately depend on what it means for the man. This sense of an exchange of meanings is made most forcefully in an extraordinary juxtaposition of shots (17–18) where Ron's movement away from and back toward Stacy is answered by her own movement away from him. Shot 17 is particularly striking (possibly because I have never seen anything quite like it in any attempt at showing sex on the screen). Sex scenes even of the artiest ambitions inevitably have a voyeuristic quality that directly involves the characters in a kind of *display* that exists apart from any emotional interaction of the characters. Normally it is the woman's body on display. There is actually little nudity in the *Fast Times* scene, and the greatest expanse of flesh, which comes from a gesture immediately preceding the moment of coitus, is of the man's body: Ron raises himself up to open his shirt and bare his chest (shot 13).

Ron's action is presumably made for the sensual contact of the two bodies, yet there is an element of display that is defined by the way we view him at this moment: he turns his body away from Stacy and toward *us* as he fully exposes his chest. The voyeuristic appeal is thus shifted to the male body, not only for the audience's delectation but also as a way of defining the character's relationship to the experience. Ron's gesture of pulling himself up to remove his shirt is echoed in shot 17 when he again pulls himself up and arches his back. This gesture immediately follows the initiation of coitus, yet it is not connected to sexual thrusting. Rather, it has a meaning of its own, which, by echoing the first pull back, is clearly tied to display. This is not a point-of-view shot, but the low angle nonetheless allies us with Stacy's position to underscore the meaning of the gesture by placing Ron in a superior position. As he penetrates her, he exults in taking possession. Rather than any real *emotional* connection here, there is in fact a kind of pulling away that makes the real focus of the sexual activity himself, as he puts himself on display.

In shot 18, he moves back in on Stacy, but his movement away and back (a physical motion that denies emotion) causes her to move her eyes up to an area behind her, as if she now wanted to disengage herself spiritually from an activity she is physically bound to. The graffiti she encounters (shot 19), "Surf Nazis," offers no escape, but rather, in its invocation of an athletically aggressive masculine mystique, reinforces the meaning of Ron's gesture. As if to confirm this, Ron again moves away from her in the next shot (20), and she now looks as if there is no place left even to look for escape. There is in fact no escape as the final devastating shot with its great expanse of blackness makes clear.

Heckerling's style is always sensitive to the expressive potential of cutting as a way to underscore or modify our response to the previous shot. The blackness of this final shot is answered by the brightness of the next shot: Linda and Stacy in a well-lit school corridor against a row of bright yellow lockers, the daylight intensity of the scene retroactively casting the previous nighttime scene as anxiety dream, the dream of sexual fulfillment proving both more and less than Stacy hoped for. The conversation is about the night before:

LINDA: "So tell me, do you like Ron?"
STACY: "I like Ron."
LINDA: "You do?"
STACY: "But it hurt so bad . . ." (*laughs*)
LINDA: "Well, don't worry. Keep doing it, it gets a lot better, I swear."
STACY (*as if she had some doubts*): "Better? . . ."

Hardly the enthusiastic Stacy of the book, this Stacy expresses affection for Ron in such a noncommittal way that Linda has to question the statement itself. Stacy's qualifying remark about pain, offered with a defensive laugh, is a kind of displacement, for the previous scene has already made clear that the pain is not merely physical.

If that were the case, the power of the scene would be delimited by physiological idiosyncrasies. For some an initial sexual experience might be painful, for others it might not. Heckerling is after something more here: the emotional pain that her style defines gives Stacy good reason for questioning if it will ever get better. Generally the only emotional content granted sex in other Animal Comedies is its meaning for the male psyche, and most especially its bolstering a sense of masculinity. Ron is like a male from the other films, but for once we are looking at the female. Granting sex an emotional content for the girl opens this film up to a kind of pain that is absent from other Animal Comedies.

I have spent some time on this scene, even though it is brief, because I think it is worth looking at in detail for a number of reasons. For all their carryings on about sex, none of the other films is willing to look at an actual sexual experience this closely. When they get to the real thing, the camera either becomes unexpectedly discreet or fairly distanced in its view of the event. The psychological density of this scene from *Fast Times*, the detail in the characters' responses and interaction, sets the film starkly apart from its fellow comedies, which treat the sex drive as a fairly simple thing, capable of a dangerously complicated response only when it is threatened with frustration (and then only in the male). By making sex a thing unto itself, a whole field of experience that is nevertheless self-contained, *Porky's* in effect limits the power of sex, detaching it from the rest of life much as penises are constantly threatened with detachment from bodies throughout the film. What emerges is the notion that sex can in fact be compartmentalized from the rest of life, even as the film almost single-mindedly focuses on it.

True to its Animal Comedy origins, *Fast Times* is as focused on sex as *Porky's*, but with an important difference. In *Fast Times* sex is like a magnet that in exerting its power pulls in a range of other emotions with it. The vulnerability of Stacy's adolescence is felt most strongly in her confusion of desires and a resultant inability to read her own or others' responses. The sheer force of the sexual drive that the film sees as central to adolescent experience is itself troubling in the way it inevitably confuses any coherent sense of self. With this kind of confusion in her own desires, the men Stacy becomes involved with must inevitably disappoint, and this is in fact what happens to her throughout the film.

The sense of devastation in Stacy's sexual initiation is a daring dramatic strategy in a film that has such a jokey surface, as if the pain that lurks behind all the jokes were suddenly let loose and allowed to dominate the proceedings, however briefly. In no film have I ever seen a sexual scene not specifically a rape which presented such an overwhelming sense of violation. Recognizing this power, I find it extraordinary that the film never looses its equilibrium. By its almost narrow-minded focus on adolescent sexuality, it stays firmly within its genre, yet the power of this particular scene lingers over the rest of the film and finds echoes in other scenes. Even when the film is exposing male sexual interest in "scoring," it never attitudinizes against men. In fact, it grants the boys their own pain, which it explores with as much psychological perception as it does the pain of the girls.

A parallel plot line to Stacy's sexual disappointments follows her older brother Brad (Judge Reinhold) and his progressive decline in job status. Brad has been working after school as the chief cook at the "All American Burger," a position that grants him a great sense of pride and self-worth. When he finds himself fired because he stood up to a rude and demanding customer, he winds up with a job as a counterman in a seafood restaurant where he is saddled with a ridiculous pirate costume. As often happens in this film, the pain of the characters finds its fullest definition in their sexual experiences. When Brad considers himself at the height of his powers frying burgers, he thinks about dumping his constant girlfriend of the past year to play the field. He is fired before he can make this power play, and only later when he has a new job of less status does he discover that the girlfriend has had similar thoughts of freedom. The loss of the job brings with it a commensurate lowered sense of self-worth that is compounded by the loss of a girlfriend. This combination of pain across social and sexual lines leads to an insightful scene that plays on a notion of sex as domination in much the same way that the earlier scene with Stacy does, but from a different perspective and with a different location for the pain.

The scene centers on a masturbation fantasy Brad has after a day at the new job. Stacy and Linda have been joined at the pool in Stacy's backyard by Mark and Mike, the former would-be and future lovers of Stacy. As they are all splashing around in the pool very much like little kids, Brad walks into the backyard in his pirate costume, looks disgusted at all the people there, complains about the mess Stacy is making with her friends, and walks into the house. Heckerling's camera stays on Stacy and Linda alone briefly where they talk about how Brad hates wearing the pirate uniform. The attention paid to age is important here. If we are made to see the playful swimmers as kids before Brad's entrance, then Brad in his pirate costume looks like a little kid returning from a Halloween party. This kind of infantilization is precisely the point since Brad is trying to escape from his childhood and assume the responsibilities of adult power. The costume as a sign of his powerlessness is also a sign of his adolescence.

In a world that offers adolescents no orderly progression toward the power of adulthood, the kids have to create their own rituals of authority. Brad's depression over the bondage of his adolescence, the pirate costume that he is not allowed to take off even when making a delivery, leads to its own compensating mechanisms. From a bathroom window inside the house, Brad watches Linda in her bikini and begins masturbating while having a fantasy about her that we see through the romanticizing clichés of 1970s films: slow motion, telephoto lens, star filters, and even a slight echo chamber on Linda's voice as she speaks. In the fantasy, Linda comes out of the pool, the water dripping off her body with a slow sensuousness, and walks directly toward the camera (that is, toward Brad), at the same time opening the halter to expose her breasts and telling him that she is his. Throughout this scene, Heckerling intercuts shots of the real Linda—without the romantic accoutrements—coming out of the pool and asking Stacy if she has any Q-tips to get the water out of her ears. Stacy sends her up to the bathroom, which she enters abruptly to find the masturbating Brad. Doing this, she inadvertently demolishes Brad's submissive fantasy figure of her with the more mundane and less compliant real thing. After Linda mumbles an excuse and quickly leaves, Brad plaintively wails, "Doesn't anybody fucking knock anymore?"

The scene could be merely jokey, playing on familiar humiliations of teenage sexuality. But point of view and context are important here. Why should we want to witness Brad's humiliation and where do we stand in relation to it? Is it a source of delectation or are we in any way implicated in it? As I have suggested in my description, the context does provide a kind of critical distance on the fantasy to the extent that it makes Brad's domination over Linda in the dream a compensation for the lowly status of his job. But in a way we are also implicated in the fantasy by the romanticizing style that should be familiar to us as moviegoers. In the utopian world of romance, all desires are met, all participants are compliant (which is, of course, what happens in other Animal Comedies).

The way the fantasy is designed in *Fast Times* plays on another sexual confusion that is important to the film: as the fantasy Linda tells Brad she is all his, she undoes her halter and exposes her breasts, walking straight toward the camera, as if offering her breasts to the audience as well as to

Brad. Brad, not just fully clothed but dressed in a dark blue suit, walks into the image from the left, as if from in front of the screen, and kisses the near naked Linda. The breasts remain untouched, which means they remain exposed, the key object of attraction, what pulls Brad out of the real world into the fantasy of the image. But the opposition between his being overdressed and her being nude keeps them in separate worlds: they might kiss, but in a sense there is no physical contact. Rather, it is nurturance and support that are central to the character's sexual desire here, and Brad's domination of Linda as compensation for his demeaning job conversely becomes his submission to her. Brad reasserts a positive sense of self by creating a fantasy of control, but the fantasy in turn controls him. Linda's breasts draw him into the image, much as they attract the spectator's eyes, and a fantasy of possession turns into a fantasy of being possessed.

One other male-oriented fantasy sequence in the film also makes a connection between women and status. In a dream the drugged-out surfer Jeff Spicoli (Sean Penn) surfs a wave so gigantic that he gains adulatory public recognition in the form of a TV interview. As in the fantasy sequence with Brad, the interview (staged against a back-projected ocean to indicate that this is not reality) invokes the familiar language of film fantasy, but not romanticized here. A fully dressed sports announcer interviews a swim-suited Spicoli, who has two smiling Playboy-bunnyish girls in bikinis leaning against either shoulder, apparently entranced by everything he says. In a sense women come with the turf of the surf—part of the spoils of victory, a possession that Spicoli gains along with his surfing trophy. But if women in male fantasies are again initially seen as submissive possessions, Heckerling undercuts this interpretation through her mise-en-scène: both girls might be leaning on Jeff, but they are in fact taller than him, so that the leaning itself becomes a kind of domination. The boy might be central to the grouping, but the appeal of the fantasy derives from placing himself in the midst of dominant women.

It is part of the film's generosity that it insists on similar treatment for the boys and girls. Just as Stacy has to be somebody's baby, just as she is looking for a kind of nurturance in her sexual relations, so too are the boys. The chief difference for Heckerling is that the boys are more concerned with defining themselves as independent, so they rebel against their needs and confuse them with issues of domination. That this can become hardened into a search solely for domination has been made clear by the earlier scene between Stacy and Ron. But the fact that Ron pulled himself back to show his dominance at the same time that he thrust himself forward makes the desire for domination and independence always an ambivalent act for men. Independence can't be won through domination, because domination implies a dependency on the necessarily submissive person. Heckerling's camera can take a critical stance toward all her characters, male and female, but its analytical power also points to a deep sympathy.

Like most Animal Comedies, *Fast Times* is resolutely white middle-class in its atmosphere and outlook. There is no poverty, only a couple of black characters (one of whom drives the most expensive car in the film) and a general matter-of-fact acceptance of the material comfort of these characters' lives. The pain they feel has nothing to do with material deprivation, yet there is also a sensitivity to issues of status that gives the film a class dimension unusual for the genre (and exceeded only by *Revenge of the Nerds*). I have mentioned work as a source of status in writing about Brad, and jobs are important for most of the characters in the film as a way of gaining a sense of self. Like *American Graffiti*, *Fast Times* establishes two main settings as places the characters inevitably return to and are in part defined by: in *American Graffiti* the high school and Mel's diner, in *Fast Times* the high school and Ridgemont Mall. Although what we see of the mall is largely a fast-food hangout (making it comparable to the diner in *American Graffiti*), there is an important difference in the way the two films use their eateries. In *Fast Times* it is chiefly a place of work, while in *American Graffiti* it is a resting place for kids in their endless peregrinations through the night.

While *Fast Times* establishes a real contrast between school and mall, *American Graffiti* gives short shrift to the school setting. All we see of school life is a freshman dance that the superannuated seniors decide to crash, but this is mainly to give the film its continuing sense of a nonstop party. The streets are where all the real action takes place, but even this has the feeling of a party on wheels. Every now and then the kids have to stop to "refuel" (the diner) or to reminisce over the past (the high school dance). But all in all, adolescence in *American Graffiti* seems mainly to be a giant party—which is why these kids find growing up as hard to do as Cameron Crowe did when he returned to high school in his twenties. The emphasis on work in the film of *Fast Times* and its implications of self-reliance show how much the kids here are in fact trying to grow up. And the film is also concerned with establishing a real opposition between the high school and the mall as a way of defining the dimensions of their lives.

In the high school, we get to know only two teachers and see only two classes: history, taught by Mr. Hand (Ray Walston); and biology, taught by Mr. Vargas (Vincent Schiavelli). These two classes define the school as a place of tradition and connection—through learning one finds connections with the outside world, to one's historical past as well as to one's biological destiny. In theory, at least. For although the teachers in *Fast Times* are not as reductively caricatured as most adults and authority figures are in these films, they nevertheless seem to be living in another universe, one that leaves them largely insensitive to the problems of their charges. Mr. Hand assumes that most of his students are on drugs and begins his class with a set of rules, the most important of which is that students not waste his time.

Education, which at best should offer an intellectual and emotional exchange, becomes an entirely one-sided affair.[10] While history and biology represent the overt subject matter here, power is the subtext; what the students are really learning about is hierarchical structures. The extent to which Mr. Hand enjoys wielding his power over students is clear enough in the pleasure of his attacks on their intelligence and derelictions, but the abusiveness potentially inherent in the teacher's role reaches its subtlest and most disturbing resonances with Mr. Vargas. The distinction the film makes here is indeed relevant. These kids do seem cut off from history, as they are repeatedly thrown back on themselves; but as far as biology goes, they are all busy exploring that out of the classroom.

Biology, the study of life, is peculiarly introduced in the film with a close-up of a jar containing the body of a dead animal. This biology class, it turns out, will be more concerned with death and a sense of the limiting factors of one's mortality than with the study of life. The class's field trip to a hospital begins with Mr. Vargas's assurance that the students will learn everything about "how doctors take care of us . . . in life, and in death." The hospital sequence then moves from a close-up of a squealing baby to a visit with a corpse in the morgue. The positioning of this sequence and its point of view are central to the way we experience it, for it immediately follows a scene about Stacy's abortion, and Stacy remains a central figure throughout. A nurse carries the squealing baby to a window directly in front of Stacy; and later, when Stacy gets sick after viewing the corpse and runs out of the room, the camera leaves with her.

Exactly what has caused Stacy to leave is the abusive act I am interested in here. As Mr. Vargas and the morgue attendant stand over the male cadaver, its chest cut open to expose its organs, Mr. Vargas puts on rubber gloves and exchanges a knowing smirk with the attendant. Talking about the organs all the while, he reaches into the chest of the corpse and pulls out the man's heart, then holds it up in the air as if displaying some prized object. The level of grossness is probably more extreme than in most biology classes, approaching as it does some of the gross-out of the horror film—but high school biology, with its emphasis on dissection, *is* concerned with bringing the inside outside. The film does not portray knowledge itself as bad, but rather the way it is presented. Vargas and his assistant obviously take sadistic delight in their power to terrorize and shock the students, all in the name of instruction.

The awful irony here, of course, is that Stacy has just confronted her own insides in a dreadful way through her abortion. This is why the camera singles out Stacy's reaction to Vargas's casual sadism. Another irony achieved here comes through the casting: Vargas has a gaunt face, sallow skin, and dark circles under his eyes so that he himself has something of a cadaverous appearance. The man embraces death at the same time that he seems to deny it by foisting the terror off onto his students. The whole scene has the quality of an initiation rite and makes clear that the point of such rites is to establish the power of the initiators over the initiates.

If the school is primarily concerned with the past and death, then the mall is its exact opposite. A self-enclosed environment, brightly lit with artificial light, shiny and plastic, it is perpetually new. With its emphasis on fast foods, it exists in an ever-consuming but ever self-renewing present. A temple of consumption (the mall cinema is showing *The Best Little Whorehouse in Texas*), it is the place where Stacy first meets Ron and hears him ask for her phone number as part of his order for hamburgers, french fries, and milk shake. In its sense of being cut off from the world at large, the mall emerges in the film as a kind of fantasy world for teenagers, the place where they can most fully define themselves. Adults might impinge on their lives at school, but it is in the mall that they really live. Much as the mall is a fantasy world, it is also an opportunity for the characters to confront the real world through working.

The fact that these characters work sets them apart from their colleagues in other Animal Comedies. For the most part, they can no longer afford the kind of childlike irresponsibility, the one last fling before adulthood, that other films seem to embrace. I have already suggested that work can carry a great deal of meaning for these kids by the kind of status that Brad finds in his job, and while these typical teenage jobs are pretty low on the totem pole of larger society, they carry a meaning that is felt everywhere through the film (although it is never specifically articulated): they become an entry into the world of adulthood through the independence and responsibility they signify. Maturity itself becomes a kind of status. As Linda Barrett always likes to point out to an impressionable Stacy, her college-age boyfriend Doug is "no high school boy."

Linda Barrett presents herself as the most self-assured among the major characters, the most self-consciously mature and the most aware of status issues. When Stacy complains that Ron seems to have abandoned her, Linda offers her reassurance: "Stacy, what does it matter? . . . . He's a stereo salesman." After Stacy's failed attempt to seduce Mark Ratner (Brian Backer), Linda offers comfort with the reminder, "He's an usher." In both cases the assertion of low status is compensatory, a way of bolstering the rejected self by demeaning the rejector. Linda's sense of maturity is illusory because it is dependent upon outside confirmation for its existence. Much as she offers Stacy status as a defense, the illusion of being grown up becomes a defense against her own adolescent helplessness. Her college boyfriend Doug is talked about throughout the film, but never seen. He remains a fantasy figure, a projection of her own illusions about herself. But, in the one major narrative departure from the book, Linda is dumped by Doug.[11] In tears, she reads Stacy a letter she has written Doug in response: "You're the one being childish," she asserts, saving her maturity at the same time that she is losing the external sign of it.

It is on the issue of maturity that the film makes most sense regarding the absence of parents. In real life, the parents might not be physically absent, but the film suggests an emotional absence. The problem confronting most of the major characters is that they are trying to grow up in a world lacking in connections, a world as hermetically sealed off from the larger world as the self-enclosed mall is. These kids have few guidelines and no external confirmations to indicate that they are in fact getting anywhere in their efforts to enter the adult world. As they constantly test the parameters of their lives, the film carries them through a series of disillusionments that threaten the developing sense of an adult self. By the end, Stacy is able to make sense of her pain by gaining knowledge of her needs. "I don't want sex," she tells Linda, "Anyone can have sex. . . . I want a relationship. I want romance." Linda is sweetly indulgent: "You want romance? In Ridgemont? We can't even get cable TV here—you want romance." In a sense Linda's irony turns against herself: she is continuing her position of worldly wisdom, maintaining her position of maturity. And yet it is Stacy who has confronted the pain of her adolescence and has gained the most from it by acknowledging it. Linda is more like the characters in other Animal Comedies.

At first blush, the jokey surface of *Fast Times* might seem to have little to do with the characters' pain, but it is in fact central to the experience of the movie and not simply a matter of slavishly adhering to formulas dictated by genre. Rather, the jokiness gives the film a vitality that allies itself spiritually with the vitality of its adolescent characters. The vitality of adolescence is evoked and celebrated since it grants the ability to live through pain and emerge into some understanding of one's own life, one's own needs. Considering this the central element in this film, I want to look at Jeff Spicoli because he is the one character in the film who is purely comic and the one character who seems destined never to grow up.

Between them, Heckerling and actor Sean Penn have turned this spaced-out surfer into the most original comic creation of the entire genre. He is related to characters in other films, and yet he is taken to an extreme that makes him operate simultaneously as a celebration and a criticism. When Spicoli is first introduced in the film, we hear a boy whisper to Stacy, "This guy's been stoned since the third grade." In a sense, Spicoli has never quite left the third grade: he retains the innocent trust of a child and can never understand why his teachers don't have the same faith in him that he has in himself. In a perverse way, the character embodies a distinctively American notion of self-fulfillment that is entirely focused on self. Self-realization is the prime goal, and anything that might get in its way, like reality, is simply not to be countenanced.

Spicoli is graced by never having to face the kind of disillusionment that all the other leading characters confront in the course of the film. Similarly, he is graced by never having to experience pain. In part that's because he's too drugged to feel pain, but Heckerling never allows any indication that drugs are for him an escape from pain. That would indicate too easy a formula for what is going on here. Toward the end of the film, he calls up a friend he prepares for the graduation dance by getting stoned and tries to convince the friend that he's really smashed by hitting his head with a sneaker, then announcing with delight, "That was my skull!" The moment is hilariously funny and appalling at the same time. On the one hand, the film has sketched in enough of Spicoli's response to his family to suggest real pain here. On the other hand, there is simply too much vitality in the performance to suggest a deadening of experience. Rather, the character seems to embrace everything that comes his way, even numbness, with the greatest delight. The celebratory quality of this film does not deny a character's pain. Rather, in acknowledging the pain, the film more fully venerates the sheer vitality of its characters than do most other Animal Comedies.

Part of Spicoli got left behind in the third grade because he has never

had to take any responsibility for his actions. He is destined for the prolonged adolescence that became central to American culture in the late
1960s and early 1970s. He is an eighteen-year-old baby who looks at life
as a movie that's playing especially for him. And life conveniently obliges
at the end of the film with an impromptu staging of a scene from Fritz
Lang's *The Big Heat* (1953). Brad has gotten a job as the night manager
of Mi T Mart. Spicoli comes in for a snack, and Brad suggests to him that
he get a job. Spicoli thinks this is foolish and goes in back to use a rest
room. In the meantime, a robber enters and demands all the money from
the safe. Brad, flustered, fumbles with the combination. The robber, with
the handgun trained on Brad, becomes more and more insistent. Brad, in
exasperation, screams at him to get off his case. At this point, Spicoli
reenters the store, distracting the robber briefly but enough time for Brad
to fling the hot contents of a coffee pot in the robber's face and take
control of the gun.[12] A delighted Spicoli responds, "Awesome! Totally
awesome!"

Spicoli's delight is, of course, allied to our own experience of the film;
much as his passive enjoyment of life is set against the more active pursuits
of the other characters, it finds its own celebration here in that it reflects
our moviegoing enjoyment. The last shot of the film provides the appropriate frame for this: the young waitresses of Perry's Pizza, where Stacy
and Linda work, pull down a metal gate that works much like a curtain
descending on the film itself. The demand for activity, for maturity, is
countered by the infantilizing wish that dominates the other comedies.
Fast Times at Ridgemont High both understands the appeal of regression
at the same time it looks to the comparable demands of maturity.

Chapter 11 **Politics of the Image**

*You expect fried rice with your Chinese dinner, and you expect certain things, like a belching scene, in your teenage comedy.... They're basically about guys trying to get laid. When I became involved with **Nerds,** the script already had a party scene, a peekaboo scene, a panty raid, a food fight, a beer-guzzling contest. The studio's instruction to me was, 'Give us **Animal House.'** I gave it to them but tried to layer it with some humanity and real characters. I didn't think anything was tasteless as long as it was funny.*

—Jeff Kanew[1]

Revenge of the Nerds (1984) and *Back to the Future* (1985)

Toward the beginning of Jeff Kanew's *Revenge of the Nerds* there's a raucous riot of a fraternity party that seems to have started sometime in the early morning: crowds dense enough to make walking through a room a source of sensual pleasure, impressive beer-guzzling topped by beer spitting and beer showers, open sexuality, and "stairdiving" (leaping from the top of a stairway into a child's wading pool filled with beer). At one point in the middle of all this furious fun, an inventively incendiary frat brother demonstrates to one and all the discovery of the "fireball." He takes a slug of 188 proof liquor, holds it in his mouth, sends up a flame from a cigarette lighter, and spits the booze into it, turning himself into a human blow torch. The first demonstration produces such an enthusiastic response that he outdoes himself with a second try, going beyond everyone's wildest expectations. This time his tongue of flame reaches to the opposite wall and immediately sets fire to the drapes, leading to a conflagration that will end up burning down the entire fraternity house. In the farcical world of Bacchanalian revels, consumption and destruction are intimately linked, so no one is much put out by the house in ashes. As they stand around the smoldering remains, the delighted partygoers improvise a saturnalian chant: "Our house . . . Our house . . . Our house is burning down!"

Animal House redux? The party would hardly have been out of place in that 1978 film, and the frat members seem to be at least as much wise-acres as their brothers from Delta House. As the fire starts dying down, a character named Ogre (a combination of Bluto and Nidermeyer from *Animal House*) and two girls that both appear to be his dates make use of the remaining flames to roast some marshmallows. Comedy loves opportunists: much like the boys from Delta House, the guys from Alpha Beta, a somewhat more primitive fraternity, know how to turn every setback into an advantage. A good deal of the comedy in this opening sequence comes from slapstick victories they gain over their adversities. Needing a new residence, they take over the freshman dorm in a scene that is staged and shot to the rhythms of a conventional slapstick piece: half-asleep freshmen, some nearly undressed, are driven from their beds or thrown through dorm windows along with their suitcases and belongings, and everyone is made to look ridiculous and defenseless against these conquering animals. Nonetheless, these comic conquerors are also the film's villains.

Revenge of the Nerds moves through as many comic contests as *Animal House* and it ends up with a sporting event like *M*A*S*H*, but the lines of sympathy and antipathy are not so easily drawn as in the earlier films because the nerds themselves initially appear—as their name dictates they must—as figures of fun. That the audience is mostly with them by the end of the film indicates the extent to which *Animal House* is being turned inside out here, but some qualifications are introduced from the very beginning. Alpha Beta man Stan Gable (Ted McGinley) in *Nerds* is parallel to the Matheson-Riegert characters in *Animal House*. Better-looking than his frat brothers, the most openly sexual, and the only one with a romantic attachment, he seems to be the unofficial head of the fraternity, its spokesman and prime mover. But as far as looks go, he is also fairly close to

Greg Marmalard, the head of the Wasp fraternity in *Animal House*—and the Alpha Beta fraternity here seems as much a bastion of the Wasp power structure as the Wasp fraternity in the earlier film. They are also powerful for one other reason—they're all jocks. So the opposition is worked out as much in physical as behavioral terms. At its simplest, the opposition should be between body-dominant and mind-dominant characters, but to his credit Kanew's camera doesn't like simple oppositions, and the film ends up qualifying almost every comic opposition it sets up, much as it immediately qualifies the animal house fraternity.

To an American ear, the very sound of the word "nerd" is funny, but why exactly do we want to laugh at them? Comedy often encourages us to laugh at what is strange and different. In films of the early 1930s, foreign accents in themselves often seemed to be a source of great hilarity, and in the first couple of years of the sound film in particular there was a much greater sense of delight in the variety of American speech patterns than would turn up in later films. Henri Bergson has suggested that laughter is a "social gesture," a corrective device operating on behalf of society that restrains differences and aims toward uniformity of behavior.[2] The American delight in ethnic humor is both a way then of acknowledging cultural differences and attempting to homogenize them. The acceptability of ethnic humor really depends on a belief in the melting pot: laughter is there to correct the foreignness of foreign behavior and to turn us, one and all, into true-blue Americans.

American attitudes on ethnic humor began to change a good deal in the 1960s and 1970s when the melting pot ideal was supplanted by idealized lineages and the search for roots. If society in fact values the ethnic differences of its members, the differences can no longer seem funny.[3] It is not that such jokes are nowhere to be heard anymore. If you move in the right circles you can still hear plenty of anti-Semitic, antiblack, or antihomosexual jokes, but even if the tenor of the joke is indulgently benign, most of this material is now considered taboo in public discourse. Much as Animal Comedy is concerned with extending the bounds of what may acceptably be presented in public, these categories are mostly closed off to it. Comedy is often rude and offensive, but the targets for offense have become increasingly limited. Nerds, however, are still fair game because they represent one of those categories that none of us likes to think we belong to. It is always the *other* fellow, and we don't mind laughing at him.

Revenge of the Nerds plays on this sense of strangeness, of being the outsider, and it has a fair degree of irony about the strategies we use to distance ourselves from qualities we would rather fob off onto other people. Although it moves in more of a fantasy world than *Fast Times at Ridgemont High* and its manner is more openly farcical, by the time it ends *Revenge of the Nerds* will make connections to real questions of political organization through the simple device of connecting minorities, finding fraternal power in nerds and American blacks. Initially, however, the nerds are chiefly a distinctively American addition to the venerable caravan of traditional comic characters: simpletons, braggarts, hypocrites, ironists, lechers, cuckolds, plain dealers, misers, cunning servants, ad infinitum ad gloriam. Traditionally comic characters are often defined by a "comic vice," a delimiting and frequently compulsive quirk of character that needs the corrective therapy of laughter. The level of savagery in the attack depends on how serious and damaging we perceive the vice to be. Nerds are to be laughed at solely because we do not want to regard ourselves as nerds, but they are also to be laughed at because they embody traits that we at least have the potentiality for.

The opening of the film sets up the characters as a source of humor in a very specific way. Lewis (Robert Carradine) and his father drive up to Gilbert's house to pick Gilbert (Anthony Edwards) up for the trip to college. As they honk the horn to announce their arrival, we see Gilbert still in bed with the comforter pulled up to his chin, creating something of a womblike enclosure around him. His concerned mother enters to find out why he isn't ready, and the following dialogue ensues:

MOTHER: Gilbert, you better get up. They're here.

GILBERT: I'm up.

MOTHER: You okay?

GILBERT (*noncommittally*): Yeah.

MOTHER: You sure?

GILBERT: Sure I'm sure. (*she gives him an indulgent and questioning look*) Mom, do you remember the first time you left home?

MOTHER: Yes, and I was just as scared as you are. (*sits on his bed close to him*)

GILBERT (*looking very intently at her with a concentration that continues throughout*): Oh, I'm not scared really. I just don't like the idea of leaving you here all alone.

MOTHER: Oh, I'll be fine. I was fine when you went away to computer camp.

GILBERT (*smiles, then ruefully*): Mom, that was just for two weeks.

MOTHER (*caressing him on the back of his neck and cheek*): I can take care of myself. I'm much more worried about you.

GILBERT: I going to be just fine. Anyways, I'm not going to be alone. I've
got Lewis. (*he smiles; she laughs lightly and strokes his forehead*)

At this point Lewis himself arrives, surprised to find Gilbert still in bed
because they're all ready to leave. He pulls back the comforter from the
bed to reveal a fully clothed Gilbert, who even has his shoes on. Gilbert's
mother expresses surprise, Lewis laughs for the first time in his distinctive
braying way, and Gilbert keeps tapping his toes together in a fit of obvious
pleasure at having successfully pulled off his little ruse.

There's an intricacy to the humor here that I want to explore because
it distinguishes the film from other Animal Comedies. The sequence starts
out with an image of regression: faced with his first departure out into the
"real world," Gilbert has not just returned momentarily to the womblike
security of his bed, he's pulled the covers up to just under his chin. The
gesture as it turns out is necessary to conceal his clothing, so ultimately it
means something quite different. Initially, however, it seems an expression of terror, a powerful defense against any incursion of reality. The
ludicrousness of the image lies in the full-grown boy taking the defensive
position of a child, seeing bed as the one safe place of comfort, so that at
first we are encouraged to laugh at this character for his retreat to childhood. And at first the dialogue works pretty much in the same way as the
image: the child talking about leaving home for the first time, the concerned and sweetly indulgent mother. The roles are soon reversed, by
Gilbert himself, as he moves to his position of concern about his mother.
From this point (and not entirely the object of fun), he points out the
absurdity of his mother using computer camp as something parallel to his
leaving for college.

So far we have managed to laugh at both characters, although in the
last case we are at least partly allied with Gilbert in rejecting his mother's
statement. Of course, any discussion may be made to appear silly in a
comedy since it is in the nature of comedy that everything is at least
potentially funny. Nonetheless, what I find particularly striking about this
scene is the underlying assumption that a contemporary audience—and,
I imagine, specifically a teenage audience—would find this particular discussion funny. In the last half of this century, going away to college has
become practically the only ritual the United States has for marking the
transition from adolescence to adulthood—and like some rites of passage
in more primitive cultures, the means are radical: a new home, a different
environment, and a whole new group of people to live with. What makes
it especially fitting as the first step toward maturity is that students have

to accept, for the first time, full responsibility for *their* actions. This point has been reinforced in the last twenty years or so by the strong rejection of the in loco parentis role once routinely granted colleges in the past. We now see the break between college and family much more sharply than in the past. Since college is the beginning of the end of family life as the student has known it for about seventeen or eighteen years, there is in fact plenty of cause for anxiety in both parents and children. There are few events in our lives which so clearly say, life will never be quite the same again.

Why, then, is this leave-taking between mother—a *widowed* mother no less—and her only son fit subject for comedy? As the focus of Animal Comedy is generally male, these films offer by virtue of their characters' behavior our culture's definition of maleness. Independence, irresponsibility, and sexual adventurousness are the qualities that appear over and over again in these films, perhaps supplanting past "male" values like loyalty, bravery, and nobility. Past generations might have seen rescuing the damsel in distress as a particularly stirring definition of masculine strength. In Animal Comedy, masculinity is more likely to be defined by men leaving the damsel in distress or even creating the distress themselves. They insistently maintain their independence from women, even to the point of finding triumph in cowardliness (as the frat brothers in *Animal House* do when they leave their dates behind to be raped at a black nightclub). If American children define their maturity by an abrupt departure from their families, American men in particular define their maleness by a resolute independence from their mothers.[4] The caricaturing of parents in some Animal Comedy creates a kind of emotional absence that parallels the physical absence of the parents in others. These are parents the child is made independent of by the suggestion that he (rarely, she) never could have come from them in the first place. The parents in these films were *never* young; rather, they were born middle-aged, pompous, and asexual. To indicate any real adolescence for the parents as well would be to grant them a commonality with their children that these films always insistently deny.

The opening scene of *Revenge of the Nerds* reverses this pattern to establish a commonality that acknowledges mutual concerns. If Gilbert graphically announces his dependency by appearing wrapped up in bed, he also acknowledges a dependency in his mother as he makes himself, in effect, the "man of the family" and expresses worry about how she will function alone. The humor underlying Gilbert's objection to his mother's example of a previous separation plays on audience assumptions about possessive parents and dependent children, but there is in fact nothing in the mother's performance that suggests an enforcing dependency. Exactly where our laughter is directed here is an intriguing matter. The mother is astonished that Gilbert has been pretending all the time, but Lewis immediately sees the whole thing as a joke and laughs accordingly. Is this, then, a joke that only a nerd could love? If so, then the joke is at least partly on us since we have been laughing at Gilbert's apparent dependency on his mother, and it turns out that the dependency has been an act. On the other hand, the gesture Gilbert uses to express delight at the success of his ruse—tapping his toes together—has a distinctly childlike quality to it. By the end, then, we are encouraged at the least to smile benignly at his trick.

If the playfulness is childlike, it is also a playfulness that should belong to adults because it offers a way of accepting the seriousness of the emotions involved and yet working them through at the same time. This is to say that there is an acknowledgment of dependency here in a way that the other films are unwilling to accept, but presented in such a hyperbolic form that the feeling, by being taken to its most extreme representation, seems to offer its own resolution. The emotional dependency between parents and children is first taken to an extreme of emotional dependency so that both parent and child can reject it at the same time that they maintain a commonality. They are now united in their desire to extricate the child from his cocoon. The advantage of play is that it offers a chance to acknowledge feelings that must be denied in reality. On the whole, then, the character is very much in control of a situation in which we initially perceive him as passive.

What is being presented here very clearly, and what is central to the humor, are the contradictions that are implicit in the whole notion of the "nerd." On the one hand, they are boys who are still children. Still dependent on parents, they suggest creatures unformed and possibly even asexual. On the other hand, they are boys who have matured too quickly, reaching a stage of single-mindedness and the kind of fierce dedication to a pursuit that is more often associated with adults. They have leapt from childhood to adulthood without having sown their wild oats or enjoyed the bacchic revels that Animal Comedy insistently celebrates. Yet, as was suggested earlier, characters in Animal Comedy often find themselves locked in their own adolescence at the same time that they seem to be moving into adulthood. Adolescence in these films is often seen as the main event, while the rest of life is merely an epilogue. Nerds are oriented toward the future, while the animals of Animal Comedy have trouble seeing beyond the present. Much as liberation for the animals becomes a kind of bondage, adolescence becomes an end in itself rather than a transitional stage. In a sense, the whole advent of youth culture in American society is dependent on the notion of adolescence as a separate period of existence that is somehow set outside the rest of life.

The commonality between parents and children in *Revenge of the Nerds* is partly achieved by recognizing the adults as people who were once children and people who can still understand the feelings of children. On the drive to college, when Lewis makes a joke of the number of "boobs" he and Gilbert will find on the campus, the father responds by saying, "Ah you college guys are all alike—all you really care about is getting laid." Lewis and Gilbert look at him abruptly, clearly startled, until he adds, "I wish I was going with you." They both laugh at first, but then Lewis protests, "Dad . . ." as if to remind his father that adults shouldn't talk like that. In a sense, this brief exchange works as a commentary on the earlier films in that it recognizes the children's desire to separate themselves from adults precisely on the issue of sexuality, which will signal their passage into adulthood. The other films, then, play into the desire of their teenage audiences by denying feelings to the adults that the children wish to make their exclusive property. While the child might wish to separate himself from the father in this instance, we as the audience can lump them together since they are both clearly "nerds."

Because we are allowed at this point in the film to regard ourselves as superior "non-nerds," our laughter is exclusionary, directed against the presumption to sexual desire from these three ineffectual characters. This talk of sexual potency immediately follows the father's announcement that he has the "cruise control" of his car set at thirty-five on the thruway. All the other cars constantly pass his tortoiselike pace, honking in irritation at him. The theme of sexual presumption is immediately elaborated when the father has a private talk with Lewis after they arrive at campus.

DAD: Lewis, c'mere . . . sit down. I envy you, Lewis. This is one of the finest institutions in the country. You're gonna do fantastic here. Try not to break too many hearts, Lewis.

LEWIS: That hasn't been a real problem yet, Dad.

DAD: Oh, c'mon, you're gonna make some lucky girl very happy. You're smart, easy-going. You got your father's good looks. (*Both Lewis and his father start to laugh in their distinctive braying way; then the father puts his arm around Lewis's shoulder*) And you got a great sense of humor. . . And I believe in you, son.

LEWIS: Thanks, Dad, I won't let you down.

DAD (*taps him on the shoulder, then quietly, almost inaudibly*): I know.

There is again a real intricacy to the humor that distinguishes this film. We are seemingly made to laugh *at* the characters at the same time that the laughter doubles back on itself in that it is more knowingly produced by the characters than might seem the case at first. Laughter might correct, as Bergson asserts, but the only thing finally rejected here is our insistence on seeing the image of nerds as nerdy.

First of all, there would be no comedy if the characters were in fact good-looking. Change the way they look and you have something close to an archetypal scene of father sending son off on a task to demonstrate his independence (like Judge Hardy, in an earlier time, exhorting Andy to do the right thing). It's the assertion of good looks against the egregiously visible evidence to the contrary that makes the scene something less than archetypal. Yet how the father sees the son, and how the son in turn sees himself, is a key point to the rest of the film.

A year later another popular movie featured a nerd who gets his revenge. In *Back to the Future* Michael J. Fox's father (Crispin Glover) takes nerddom to a far greater extreme than any character in *Revenge of the Nerds*. Cruelly oppressed by his bully of a boss at work, set upon by his family at home, the only respite this poor schlemiel of a human being can find is total absorption in endless television reruns of *The Honeymooners*. Fox, a high school student, is troubled by his parents, and his father in particular. For reasons the character can never fully articulate, his nerdy father makes him particularly anxious about a weekend trip he (Fox) is going to take with his girlfriend, during which time, it is implied, they will make love for the first time. Although the character doesn't understand his anxiety, the point is clear that his father's lack of aggression and his mother's extreme prudishness about sexuality have given him doubts about his own self. His salvation comes by a trip to the past that enables him to see his own parents as teenagers and in the process to understand how they became the adults they are. To the extent that the film grants the parents an adolescence and tries to make the son understand them in terms of their own youth, *Back to the Future* seems to be setting itself apart from other teen comedies as much as *Revenge of the Nerds* does. But there is a catch here: Fox can find himself only by teaching his father to stand up to a bully, thereby redeeming the father from his seemingly ineluctable nerdiness. Accepting the father finally depends on recasting him in the image of the son.

There is a psychological reality underlying this fantasy in that the undesirable parents may be seen as projections from the son that reflect his own desire to separate from them. In this regard the film is much like other Animal Comedies: independence is signaled by the extent to which the child is different from the parents. And it is exactly when Fox is about to assert his move into adulthood by losing his sexual innocence that his parents seem most foreign to him. But his detour into the past doesn't so much let Fox discover a continuity that moves from parent to child as to create a new one that moves from child to parent. In this new continuity, Garry Wills has seen an "anti-myth to the Fall" in which parents are "not outmoded but still young": "Parents redeemed erase the sins of the past and become Paradise regained. . . . At the final eucharistic table of the free lunch, Ronald Reagan is the rehabilitated parent par excellence, the faded idol as reachable ideal."[5] As much as there is clearly paradox here, we can only believe the rehabilitation if we suppress the knowledge that we the children have given birth to the parent. There is an irony in the inversion, but an unconscious one.

As its title suggests, everything in *Back to the Future* happens backward. Oedipal themes are made explicit enough that virtually every reviewer noted them, yet the film finally turns all Oedipal conflict on end and ultimately dismisses it. When the mother (Lea Thompson), as a teenager lusting after her teenage son from the future, kisses him, she's disappointed to discover a lack of erotic feeling. It's rather like kissing her brother, she observes. The son himself harbors quite the opposite of incestuous and patricidal feelings. All the while he is fleeing his mother's advances, he scores the double success of turning his actual father into a real man and saving from death his surrogate father (Christopher Lloyd), who had accidentally sent him into the past. The father at the end of the film, then, is acceptable inasmuch as he reflects the son, and maturity for this film represents a movement toward being able to see yourself in your father, rather than your father in yourself. This is not a trivial difference because it suggests another kind of bondage in an apparent liberation because the projection of self into parent becomes necessary for definition of self. It is not incidental that Fox sees his parents in a new light before his sexual initiation, before his own movement into adulthood, for he narcissistically requires finding himself in the other in order to accept himself.

The conventional chronology between parent and child in *Revenge of the Nerds* creates a more fully developed sense of self that grows out of psychological dependence. Strikingly, Kanew shoots most of the final dialogue between Lewis and his father (quoted above) on angles, a fairly conventional way of handling two-shots, with the camera angled more toward one character or the other. Cutting to reverse angles underscores the emotional dominants of the scene. But precisely at the moment that the father enumerates his son's positive qualities, in response to Lewis's slight embarrassment over the possibility of getting a girlfriend, Kanew breaks this pattern and shifts his camera to a perpendicular that places the characters on the same plane in the image, creating a mirrorlike effect as the two face each other. What is taking place here is a genuine mirroring, in the psychological sense of the word: Lewis is building a self-image on the foundation of a self that his father reflects back to him. Unlike *Back to the Future*, the parents in *Revenge of the Nerds* can disappear from the rest of the film because the children have achieved a real sense of self from them. Unlike other Animal Comedies, however, the independence is seen as a consequence of continuity rather than in opposition to it.

If we then have presented here a generous and sweet-natured view of a father-son relationship, why is there laughter at all? Certainly we laugh when Lewis's dad assures him he'll do okay with women because he has his father's good looks. If not good looks, he at least has the same looks as the mirroring profiles with their oversize noses emphasize, which would seem to be the derisive comic point here. But then the characters themselves start to laugh, so that their visual mirror gives way to aural echoing as each brays in exactly the same way. Lewis's laugh has already been established as a source of comedy in the film. Lewis surprisingly doubled here is almost doubly funny in the quality of replicating absurdities.

That is, all this might apply until we stop to listen to our own laughter, as we might very well with the very next line from Dad: "And you've got a great sense of humor." What, then, have the two of them been laughing at? Presumably at the assertion of their "good looks," so that in fact their laughter is joined to ours as the characters display more a sense of self-awareness than might at first be apparent. At the same time, our own laughter has to double back on itself to move from a laughter of rejection to one that is sympathetically bound to the characters. It is at this point that Kanew allows the strongest expression of feeling between the two characters to emerge. To Lewis's intense assurance that he will live up to his father's expectations, Dad makes his first physical gesture to his son and speaks with a sudden quietness unlike any other moment in the actor's performance. By this point, the whole tenor of the scene has shifted to something that almost seems to celebrate the high spirits and exaggerated facial features of these two characters, because the physical element that we have so far regarded as comic is now connected to the emotional empathy that we have been made to share.

Although the film operates in a mostly realistic framework, the characters do have ties to the grotesque tradition from earlier drama and literature where comic figures were often defined as comic by taking on aberrant forms and shapes (as with hunchbacks or cripples). Something of the sense of the grotesque that Mikhail Bakhtin analyzed in Rabelais may be found here as well, where the exaggerations and deformities actually take on a kind of celebratory quality, defining an excess of feeling that is always seen as positive. Here the excess of feeling is located in the character's nose, which, as Bakhtin notes, always signifies the phallus in grotesque imagery: Lewis's sexuality lives up to the promise of his nose and proves to have irresistible power to move the immovable object of his affections. As his face seems to be all nose, his mind is all sex. In other Animal Comedies, sexuality is generally marked off from the grotesque. The sexuality of the specifically grotesque characters in *Animal House*, for example, is either denied (as in the case of D-Day), or infantilized (as in the case of Bluto). It is only the conventionally handsome men who are allowed real sexual power. One of the most striking aspect of *Nerds*, then, is the way in which the grotesque becomes specifically tied to the sexual, thoroughly undermining conventional movie typology.

Comic characters *are* often sexual, but their sexuality is usually hemmed in by force of circumstances or conventions. In the Marx Brothers movies, Harpo and Groucho may chase after pretty extras. Still, the only involvement with a leading lady is likely to be with Margaret Dumont, herself a grotesque whose greater size indicates a sexual imbalance the grotesque brothers try to right by their various attacks on her social standing. There is even a suggestion of impotence in Harpo: he might be the most satyrlike of the brothers (with his ever-ready phallic horn), but he never seems to use it for anything other than honking. In the early films, actual "love interest" was reserved for Zeppo, the most "normal" looking of the brothers, while the later films provided conventional leading men to take up the romantic slack. Almost inadvertently, the grotesque becomes tied to a sexual desire that is destined not to be fulfilled, a point explicitly picked up by Woody Allen in his early films.

If the grotesque in earlier American comedy seems a sign of sexual powerlessness, then it is in the horror film where the grotesque becomes specifically tied to sexual prowess. Films about vampires and werewolves generally carry at least a subtext that equates the strange state with sexual power. And most strikingly for these later films, the violence of the grotesques in *The Texas Chainsaw Massacre* (1975) generally has at the least sexual overtones (and often something more explicit than that).

As noted in an earlier chapter, Bakhtin thought the post-Renaissance West saw the grotesque as primarily satiric. There are ways in which *Revenge of the Nerds* seems to invoke the grotesque as satire. In fact, what is possibly most distinctive about the film is the way it plays between celebratory and satiric modes in its use of the grotesque. Here I am specifically concerned with comedy that rejects (since that is how Animal Comedy most often uses the grotesque), but more particularly with the distinctive ways *Revenge of the Nerds* has of inflecting ridiculing laughter. Consider, for example, the scene in which the female counterparts of the nerds are introduced. This comes at a point when the major plot line of the movie has been set in motion: the nerds' attempt to affiliate themselves with a national fraternity in order to gain a measure of power for themselves on campus. It is worth keeping in mind in any consideration of plot developments that power is a key goal for the characters in all their activities. In *Revenge of the Nerds* this overt task makes explicit what is only implicit in *Animal House*, where sexuality is used as a kind of displacement from the central issues of power.

The nerds understand that gaining access to power comes in part from being able to manipulate the images of power. For this reason, they assume the way to win acceptance into the national fraternity is by throwing a party that will establish them as socially adept in conventional terms. To ensure success, Lewis has the temerity to invite beautiful Betty (Julie Montgomery) and her Wasp sorority sisters of Delta Pi as their dates at the party, convinced this will make them look good by extension. Insulted, Betty plans a revenge (together with the brothers of Alpha Beta) that involves promising the nerds their dates, then standing them up. The party is going very badly because only two guys have dates—Gilbert, who met bespectacled, studious Judy (Michelle Meyrinck) over a computer terminal; and gay Lamar (Larry B. Scott), who is wildly boogying with another guy. The representatives of the national fraternity are unimpressed. To save the day, Gilbert's date Judy suggests they invite over her sorority sisters of Omega Mu, whom she characterizes as very "spontaneous." At her suggestion, Booger (Curtis Armstrong) cries out, "Oh, no, not the Mu's—they're a bunch of pigs." As he says this, he picks his nose.

If this scene offers a grotesque nosepicker commenting on grotesques, the film finally defines *all* of its characters as grotesques, a point made clearest by the names given the sororities and fraternities. The nerds eventually become members of "Lambda Lambda Lambda," a triple invocation of their apparently meek and mild existence (as well as a reminder of an early humiliating encounter with a sheep foisted on Lewis and Gilbert by the jock fraternity). "Alpha Beta" suggest the primary and primitive qualities of the jock fraternity that can't get beyond the first two letters of the alphabet. The *pi* of "Delta Pi" is expressly connected to a piece of pie, which itself echoes all the longing references to "hair pie" earlier in the film (as well as quite explicitly evoking the delta of Venus). Finally, the "Omega Mu" girls complement their lambent boys in two ways: not only are they cows ("moo") to the Lambda's sheep, but their initials ("OM") also suggest another sound that turns them into stragglers from a Hari Krishna convention, much as their initial contribution to the party will be to turn it into a leftover from the earnestly committed late 1960s. As the names suggest, no character can really be more debased than any other, yet those in power nonetheless insist on a hierarchy that they perceive as defined by grotesquerie. The point of having Booger live up to his name by picking his nose just after he describes the Mu's as "a bunch of pigs" is to stress the displacement between the way the characters view others and themselves.

In a sense, the movie effectively forces the same kind of displacement on us. When the Mu's arrive at the party, we see them—in a medium shot—parade by the camera, each one funnier-looking than the previous one, and everyone in her distinctive fashion. But the shot is set up so that Booger, in the background, registers their looks at the same time we do. As a result of this mise-en-scène, our reaction to this parade, prompted by an invitation to laugh at new grotesqueries, is necessarily conditioned by the reactions of a character we have already laughed at for his own grotesqueness. The film constantly encourages, then undermines, our derisive laughter. As it keeps shifting back and forth between the ways we view what makes the lowly characters lowly, it both invokes and undercuts the hierarchies I noted in *Animal House*, hierarchies that are important for Animal Comedy in general.

How different this is may be seen through another comparison with *Back to the Future*, again appropriate because that film presents us with a clearly defined nerd character in the protagonist's father. If the project of that film is a Reaganite rebuilding of the father, the successful transformation of the father into a Yuppie finds a parallel transformation in the father's former antagonist, the town bully. As the present is rewritten by the trip to the past, the bully becomes the lowly nerd the father once was (in fact, something close to a slave as he servilely washes and waxes the family car). Not only that, where he previously had tried to rape the son's mother, he now seems to have become homosexual in the process of his transformation to nerd (a suggestion, in the terms the film sets up, of his total lack of power).[6] The film, then, is not content simply to redeem the father from his nerddom. In its efforts to punish the original tormentors, it ends up insisting that there must always be a nerd underclass. If *Revenge of the Nerds* finally assures the audience that most of us are nerds, then *Back to the Future* offers the assurance that there will always be nerds— but they won't be us.

What is happening in both these films, nonetheless, is the association of an image with a social status, a fairly common way of treating the grotesque characters in Animal Comedy in general. But as Animal Comedy is distinctively American, it often invokes a sense of fluidity in its view of society.[7] The emphasis on groups, albeit most often groups of boys, in these films serves to celebrate a kind of pluralism. Yet, as was noted earlier, issues of power and powerlessness are often central to the plot lines of these films, so that very definite hierarchies emerge even within the seemingly pluralistic groups. There are often class issues *implicit* in these oppositions, and yet the films generally remain fairly indirect in confronting them.[8] Ethnic issues are more explicit, however, with Wasps generally emerging as the bad guys because they are inevitably tied to the power structure. Oppositions are worked out more along lines of racial rather than economic identity. In this regard, there is a concern for how you appear to the world that is important in *Revenge of the Nerds*.

Part of the pain of growing up in the fluidly stratified society of the United States is the extent to which our society depends upon external markers as a way of determining class.[9] As I have defined it, being a nerd is more a state of mind than anything else, an introversion and social maladroitness. Yet strikingly, Lewis and Gilbert are initially recognized as nerds by sight alone, an event that establishes a connection of power to sight and that is crucial to the film itself. Appropriately, the first revenge the nerds seek from their good-looking tormentors is to place themselves in a superior position of *seeing*.

Living up to their reputation as whiz kids, the nerds stage a kind of technological panty raid on the Delta Pi sorority house, the underlying purpose of which is to wire it with remote control television cameras in such strategic places as bedrooms and bathrooms. They then return home to watch their favorite coeds not only in various stages of undress but in a wide variety of mundane activities. A dissolve to the next morning indicates that the boys have been glued to their private TV show all night and begins with one of them saying, "I'm tired of watching them brush their teeth" (implying that, initially at least, watching them brush their teeth had held some fascination for him). The pleasure for these voyeurs is not just in seeing the objects of their desire naked but in seeing them engaged in activities not normally seen, an invasion of privacy that seems to penetrate essence by appropriating appearance.

This generically motivated sequence has clear enough parallels in other Animal Comedies (Bluto in *Animal House*, standing on a ladder and peering into sorority bedrooms; the three boys in *Porky's* who find the three peepholes into the girl's shower). These are among the most interesting scenes in Animal Comedy because they all, in varying degrees, promote a self-consciousness of the voyeurism at the center of the scene. In *Animal House* the voyeuristic character acknowledges the audience's complicit voyeurism whereas *Porky's* revels in its mutual display of boys and girls playing doctor, then seems to undercut the voyeuristic impulse with fears of castration. Of these films, only *Revenge of the Nerds* makes a connection between voyeurism and power. After all, the voyeuristic act here is undertaken for revenge, and yet the results are very different from the revenge in *M*A*S*H* that exposes Hot Lips naked to the entire camp. In *M*A*S*H* the display of male power is used as a counter to Hot Lips' inadvertent display of female flesh: it is important that she *see* her audience. In *Revenge of the Nerds* the audience remains invisible to their unwitting performers, but the invisibility is central to the notion of power as it is to the voyeuristic impulse.

In both cases, the impetus for the action is an attempt to right a perceived injustice (although in *M*A*S*H* that perception might itself be questioned). *Revenge of the Nerds* departs from *M*A*S*H* to the extent that in *M*A*S*H* the desire to right an injustice is complemented by an equal desire to inflict pain on the character regarded as the source of the injustice. And if you look at *Revenge of the Nerds* with the expectations of the genre (as the film certainly encourages you to do), you realize that this vindictive course of action is indeed a possibility when Lewis finally makes love to his wetdream Betty Child by disguising himself as her actual lover Stan. This turns out to be actually a double disguise (a device long familiar in comedy). At a fairground where various fraternities have set up booths to benefit charities, Stan turns up dressed as Darth Vader. Excited Betty invites him for some fast action in the fun house, but Stan goes to work at the Alpha Beta booth instead. Lewis, spotting all this, picks up Stan's discarded mask and follows amorous Betty into the fun house, locating her in a "moon room" complete with wall murals of a moon landscape and funny creatures peeking out from behind hills. In this setting, Lewis makes love to Betty (who of course thinks he is Stan because he has kept his mask on, a gesture Betty delightedly calls "kinky"). When Lewis finally unmasks after the lovemaking, one might expect—from seeing other films in the genre—that Betty would shriek in horror at the sight of him (much as she had done earlier when he had merely asked her out on a date). Lewis could then have his triumph by leaving her, satisfied at having gotten the revenge promised in the film's title. Instead, Betty falls in love with Lewis—quite unrealistically of course, but with a sweet consequentiality that is typical of the film's generous spirit and a full embrace of the grotesque tradition in which the lower body reigns supreme. She in effect accepts the fact that having experienced him without seeing him has led to a new vision of him.

The way the scene is filmed makes it almost single-mindedly concerned with issues of *voyeurism*. As Lewis (still in his Darth Vader mask) begins to make love to Betty, the camera tilts up, moving Betty and Lewis out of the frame, to the wall mural where we see a little moon creature peering over the rock, seeming to look at the action the camera has just discreetly left behind. His gaze is also directed toward the camera (which is to say, at us), so it serves to remind us of our complicity as viewers of the film. This seems an odd moment to do so, however, since the camera, by its tilt, has just denied us a view of the chief activity in the scene. At this key voyeuristic moment, our sight is effectively disenfranchised.

Metaphorically, however, our sight is satisfied. From the little moon creature looking at what we can't see, there is a direct cut to the Lambda Lambda Lambda charity booth, which is having an enormous success with its cream pie sale. The sign exhorts the viewer to "Eat a Pie for Charity" and shows a cartoon drawing, in a grotesque style reminiscent of R. Crumb, of a man with an enormously elongated tongue lasciviously wrapped around a piece of pie. The camera might become suddenly discreet in not looking at Lewis and Betty, but the subsequent content of the image makes clear enough what activity is *not* being shown. This crude joke (quite commensurate with the genre and here effectively complemented by the obliqueness and apparent discretion of a presentation that compels us to substitute the metaphorical for the actual) suggests there is a limitation on what we can be shown.

Oblique as the presentation may be, one is hardly likely to confuse it with, say, the metaphorically indirect style of Ernst Lubitsch. For the cutaway from the lovemaking has led us into a series of fairly explicit images:

from the lasciviously elongated tongue to the actual "pie" being sold for charity (a plateful of whipped cream that, once licked away by lusting tongues, reveals a photograph of naked Betty). The contrast between the explicit and the implicit is important for the way we understand the presentation of images here: In the cutaway episode we see an image of Betty (previously appropriated from the "panty raid"), now being possessed as guys lick the cream off the plate to uncover her image—which they then continue to lick. The image is being consumed in the most primal fashion, and yet it finally remains unaffected. The power of the image is that it simply stays there for what it is. Lick it as much as you like, it does not yield, it does not respond, it stays immutable. On the other hand, the licking we have not been allowed to witness has apparently produced radical changes that take the characters beyond the discriminations of vision. Betty, deprived of the power of sight, discovers a kind of liberation—which will lead her later to realize, "My God, I'm in love with a nerd!" The ironic ambivalence in that statement fully expresses the dichotomy between vision and feeling that is central to the film. Inner sight is the liberation of not seeing.

The power of sight is the power to discriminate, which overpowers other senses and other understandings. In this regard, the presence of blacks in the film and the peculiar alliance set up between them and the nerds establishes another major thematic element. The blacks make their entrance into the film because of an issue of sight. The nerds, attempting to gain some power on campus, are trying to affiliate themselves with a national fraternity. Unfortunately, they have been rejected by almost everyone because of the photograph of themselves they included along with each application. The one exception, the one fraternity that expresses interest in them (Lambda Lambda Lambda), is the one fraternity they forgot to send a photo to. Appropriately, Tri-Lam is an all-black fraternity (appropriately because the form of discrimination used against the nerds here parallels historical discrimination that kept blacks out of American colleges and universities). When the nerds show up at national headquarters where they can be seen, the head of the fraternity initially rejects their application—not because of skin color but because, as he puts it, "After all, you're nerds" (a determination he is able to make merely by looking at them).

The film can be quite funny on its connection between nerds and blacks, but it is never frivolous. This is not the kind of wished-for affinity hip whites would like to think they feel for blacks and black culture that is common in other Animal Comedies (and often sentimentalizes an empathy that goes untested). If anything, the film sometimes defines nerd "culture" and black culture as being antithetical. Nevertheless, nerds and blacks share a viable bond between them in regard to discrimination based on sight: blacks know what it means to be people whose place in society is defined by how they look. However, fitting in with its grotesque nature, the film is not at all afraid to trade on stereotypical characteristics: not only are the members of Lambda Lambda Lambda all black, they all look like big football players as well—a fact that should make them feel antipathy toward the nerds and, conversely, sympathy toward the Alpha Betas, an all-jock fraternity. Yet the blacks remain ostracized like nerds.

Lamar, the lone black member of the nerd fraternity, represents the one salient exception to the oppositions the film sets up (and may be the only time in Animal Comedy when the central group is sufficiently pluralistic to accommodate other races). But Lamar is not exactly the football type: not only is he black, he's homosexual—and not just homosexual but wildly and flamboyantly so, in the kind of floridly exaggerated limp-wristed manner that befits the style of a film full of purposeful grotesqueries. To complete the stereotype, he's also a dancer. The film's emphasis on how you look as defining who you are in society finds a special inflection in Lamar. The problematic position of blacks in American society derives precisely from the fact that they cannot change how they look. As has been suggested before, in a fluid society how you look—an *apparent* marker—is transformed into something *essential*. How you look becomes a revelation of essence rather than a possible confusion of the essential. Since blacks are defined solely by how they look, and nothing else, how they look determines their position in the social structure.

Because of this connection between the apparent and the essential, American culture is particularly concerned with the issue of passing when the apparent marker deviates sufficiently to indicate a different essential.[10] Because of its concern with language as a class marker, George Bernard Shaw's *Pygmalion* should be the quintessential "passing" drama, yet oddly enough Eliza Doolittle's transformation into a lady is more complete for an English audience than it would be for an American one,[11] which must suspect an indelible essence underlying the original appearance. "Passing" is never presented in American culture as a matter for comedy. Rather, there always remains something of a tortured quality as the inner blackness is concealed for the sake of the apparent whiteness.[12]

Lamar is a key character here, with good reason: for while he could never pass for white, he *could* pass as a heterosexual—and chooses not to. He makes his homosexuality as apparent as his blackness. When Lewis explains to the head of the national fraternity that the nerds should be allowed to affiliate because they don't discriminate against any creed or color, Lamar delightedly adds, to the discomfort of the fraternity officers, "or sexual preference." What is distinctive about the film is the way in which it allows grotesque stereotypes to discover their own power through extreme exaggeration. Lamar may be limp-wristed to a fault, but he is able to win the javelin throw because one of his fellow nerds (with a good knowledge of aerodynamics) has designed for him a wobbly javelin that gains special power by being thrown with a limp wrist. There is something ineffably funny in the spectacle of Lamar's limp-wristed javelin throw as it contradicts all our notions of athletic prowess. This is almost primal comedy, some of the earliest laughter we erupt in as we discover mastery over our bodies, however various they may be. Lamar may look funny as he unintentionally parodies every accomplished athlete, but he also triumphs in his contest, so the comedy of the scene exults in the freshly discovered power of an identity the rest of society would like to reject.

Although the film explores ways in which appearance and essence diverge, it remains centrally concerned with the power of appearance—the power of the image. When an entire squad of well-muscled blacks from Tri-Lam national headquarters turns up at the end of the film, they are there to put on a show of strength to back up the nerds in their final contest with the Alpha Betas. Because the nerds have neither real power nor even the appearance of power, it is important to note this *show* of power especially since white society always defines blacks by their appearance anyway, and usually in a negative fashion.[13] When the nerds achieve a fair victory over the Alpha Betas at the charity games, and gain control of the fraternity council, the Alpha Betas resort to their one superior attribute over the nerds—their sheer physical strength. Earlier, like the Ku Klux Klan, they had burned a cross on the front lawn of the nerds frat house as a warning of their power. Now that the social order has proved useless in stopping the advance of the nerds, they simply trash the frat house. As Alpha Betas prepare to attack the nerds themselves, the blacks from the national fraternity arrive and surround a bandstand where the Alpha Betas have gathered. Just by crossing their brawny arms across their expansive chests, they are able to cow the Alpha Betas with this display of force; it is enough because it operates on a level of image-making that the Alpha Betas understand.

Nonetheless, the film does point to a hopeful utopian vision of a more fully equitable and harmonized society than the one from which it departs.

It suggests a radical inversion of the social structure to the extent that it ends by having the lambs (or at any rate, the Tri-Lams) inherit the earth. The final nighttime rally has a certain evangelical quality to it as members of the crowd are asked to come forward and proclaim themselves nerds. Acting from the passionate acceptance of their own identity forced on them by the Alpha Beta's violence, Gilbert and Lewis inadvertently become proselytizers at what turns out to be a kind of revival meeting for nerds:

GILBERT: I just want to say that I'm a nerd. And I'm here tonight to stand up for the rights of other nerds. I mean, uh, all our lives we've been laughed at, and made to feel inferior, and tonight . . . those bastards trashed our house. Why? Because we're smart? We're different? Well, we're not. I'm a nerd, and I'm pretty proud of it.

LEWIS: We have news for the beautiful people: there's more of us than there are of you. . . I know there's alumni here tonight. When you went to Adams, you might have been called a spaz or a dork or a geek. Any of you that have ever felt stepped on, left out, picked on, put down, whether you think you're a nerd or not, why don't you just come down here and join us, okay?

GILBERT: Just join us cause no one's really gonna be free until nerd persecution ends!

The various alumni and other gathered guests respond to the pleas of Gilbert and Lewis by coming forward, ready to acknowledge the pervasiveness of nerddom. All come forward—everyone, that is, except the Alpha Betas, who necessarily remain stranded behind.

As the above quoted material makes clear, the tone of the scene is complex in that it honors the feelings of the characters (we have been made to share the anguish of their rejection and their powerlessness), yet it also functions as parody. The scene's double-edged quality is typical of the undercutting method of the film as a whole, but it is particularly relevant here because it serves to distance the film from the very utopian vision it has projected. Besides the revival-meeting quality parodically invoked here, the scene also has distinct echoes of other films—in particular the "we-are-the-people" endings of Frank Capra's social comedies. If the film invokes the world of Capra, it does so to explore the problem of presenting an egalitarian vision within a comedy framework.

There is always a problem of presenting a democratic vision in comic form to the extent that comedy, in advancing the cause of one person or group of people, inevitably seems to put down others. If egalitarian views seek to embrace all humanity, the movement of comedy is often from one exclusionary state to another—one that we might perceive as a more just ordering of society, but one that continues to be exclusionary nonetheless. In a sense, much of Animal Comedy plays on these contradictory anarchic and conservative poles of comedy: it often moves through a freely enjoyed anarchic stage to end up with a new order that is no less rigid than the order in force at the beginning of the film.[14] As noted in an earlier chapter, *Animal House* ends up with the same power structure with which it began, only with different characters in charge (ethnics rather the Wasps).

As *Revenge of the Nerds* takes its narrative point of departure from an inversion of *Animal House*, it partly inverts the inversion of the power structure it shares with that film. Because comedy is exclusionary, we initially laugh at the nerds, separating them from any connection with ourselves or the dominant society; similarly, by the end of the film, when we have joined ranks with them, we now exclude the people who were originally at the top of the social hierarchy. In this regard, comedy is elitist; but it can also often be utopian: in this case, for example, by dealing in idealizations that the film itself heralds. There is a problem in form here that the film signals its awareness of in a compelling way. When Lewis proclaims, "We have news for the beautiful people: there's more of us than there are of you," director Kanew cuts first to a medium reaction shot of Ogre (looking very puzzled by this claim), then to a close-up reaction shot of Stan, whose eyes begin to move about wildly. The first shot provides the ironic undercutting typical of Kanew's style since Ogre hardly seems to fit the "beautiful people" category (even though he is one of the most vicious oppressors). The shot of Stan functions somewhat differently—both because he *does* belong to the "beautiful people" category and because there is a direct and dramatic quality in Ted McGinley's acting at this point (signaled by his eye movements) that is unlike any other performance in the film. There is an unexpected urgency in this shot that seems to go against the comic grain of the rest of the scene.

Eric Bentley has written the following on the appeal of the theater: "The art of the theater starts in the simple sensuousness of direct physical attraction. . . . The public's love of matinee idols, insofar as it is founded in the good looks of the stars, is basic and sound. The theater, if it does nothing else, should exhibit fine male and female specimens, so that the spectacle may, at the very least, be a sort of human equivalent of a horse or dog show."[15] This raises an interesting question about the film: do we finally go to the movies to see Robert Carradine, Anthony Edwards, and

Michelle Meyrinck in the leading roles?[16] In asking this, we have to accept a need for idealizations of the human form that the theater and film in part satisfy. There is a kind of power we grant to beauty that these characters do not have. By making these characters the leads, the film recognizes its own unique role in using as leads actors who are probably more destined to play character parts in their careers; the film therefore inverts the hierarchy of beauty by making the beautiful characters (actors) the ones we exclude. But it does this with an awareness of exactly what is being excluded, which is precisely the point of the strikingly dramatic cutaway to Stan just when all the other characters are joining happily together in their utopian future. A resonant sense of what it means to appear different, based on how one *looks* (and here accorded to a character who had not been previously excluded) has the effect of balancing the idealization of society the film points toward. By this balance *Revenge of the Nerds* more fully achieves the egalitarian promise of Animal Comedy than other films in the genre.[17]

Chapter 12 **Power**

Without Politics

Heaven Help Us (1985)

CAESAR: I will appeal to him as one human being to another. I'll reason
   with him.
ROONEY: Oh, sure, you're going to reason with a grown man in a dress.

It is the evening of a dance hosted by the boys of St. Basil's parochial high
school for the girls of the Virgin Martyr. To kick off the dance, Father
Abruzzi (Wallace Shawn) of St. Basil's delivers a lecture aimed at keeping
the virginal girls from becoming martyrs. He tells his wide-eyed listeners
all about lust with a passionate intensity appropriate to the topic. Typical
of the boys in Animal Comedy, class bully and cutup Rooney (Kevin Dillon) knows that his only interest in virginity is in losing his. Rather than
heeding any of Father Abruzzi's explosive exhortations, Rooney has every
intention of persuading Jeanine (Dana Barron), a comely blonde virgin,

to her own martyrdom in an evening of joyriding with him in his father's
new car, which Rooney claims boasts "electric leather seats." Attracted by
the car, adventurous but still cautious Jeanine agrees, but only on condition that Rooney arrange a date for her girlfriend, the plain but brainy
Cathleen (Yeardley Smith), with Caesar (Malcolm Danare), the chubby
class egghead who up to this point has set himself apart from his fellow
animals by displaying absolutely no interest in girls (although he is fascinated by Freud). Through a neat plot twist that has granted him almost
unlimited power over Caesar, Rooney brings the whole thing off in spite
of the fact that he's not yet old enough to have a license and, even if he
were, his father would never let him take the new car out for an evening
of joyriding. How does he get the car? It seems his father is off in Chicago
on a business trip, and there is apparently no one else at home to prevent
Rooney from his evening's adventure.

You need not have seen very many of these films to know in advance
that by the time the evening is over this new car won't look very new.
This is a generically motivated scene: the joyride in a new car that belongs
to someone else. The film fulfills a number of the perks of the genre in
the way it presents the scene. The car inevitably belongs to a close relative,
generally a parent,[1] and it's always driven without the permission or
knowledge of that relative. The joyride is inevitably tied to a bid for liberation in two ways. First, it offers an escape from adult authority (here
doubled by escape from both the actual father, who would deny access
to the car, and Father Abruzzi, who would deny access to sex). Second,
the joyride gives the film a kind of dramatic liberation that takes the characters beyond the confines of the film's setting up to that point.

There are limits to the freedom the car signifies, however, as there are
constraints put on every movement toward liberation in these films. And
the constraint is built into the means of liberation itself—since the joyride
inevitably leads to the car's destruction. Joyriding, then, has a particular
meaning in these films precisely because the scenes are generic. We know
in advance that the liberation will lead to some kind of destruction, so
any sense of exhilaration we might share with the joyriders is in part
undercut by our sense of where this must inevitably end. In fact, anticipation of the destruction perversely becomes part of the scene's pleasure.

Although generically motivated, the scene can never be entirely predictable because genre usually works on a play between the familiar and
the unfamiliar. This is to say that we know *where* we're going to end up
in this episode—a totaled car—but each film takes as its specific task the
discovery of a different and unique way of arriving at this end (a kind of
variations-on-a-theme creative approach that carries across the whole

genre). The appeal of the scene, then (if it is appealing), is not so much in the event as the invention—the unexpected route it will take to arrive at the expected destination.

The variations that *Heaven Help Us* provides are striking in a number of ways. Joyriding is normally seen in the other films as a male activity, although women might be the ultimate goal. Here the car is clearly regarded as a vehicle for seduction, an attraction for girls that carries its sexiness over to the boy driving. As the adventure of the open road invokes sexual adventure, the inevitable destruction of the car parallels the failure of the seduction. Rooney has brought along some liquor with which he plies Jeanine until the two of them end up downing the entire bottle. Taking a momentary pause in the joyride (for which they have been joined by Caesar and Cathleen), Rooney has parked the car on a bridge over a canal so he and Jeanine can go off to a more private spot under the bridge. Judging her to be properly primed for his attack, Rooney lunges at Jeanine's blouse and starts to unbutton it. But Jeanine is more than primed: woozy as well as boozy, she throws up on the back of Rooney's neck just as he's about to caress her breasts. A little later in the scene (after the destruction of the car), Jeanine will heave once more, this time in Rooney's lap, the grossest moment in the film.

The other wrinkle the film works on this familiar scene lies in Rooney's attitude toward the destruction of the car, and the way that destruction is brought about. In the other films (*Animal House*, for example), the car is banged up as a direct result of the characters' own actions during the joyride—which in effect defines a complicity in the destruction that is congruent with the ways these films qualify their liberations. Here, however, the destruction of the car is largely a matter of circumstance. While Rooney and Jeanine go off for their anticlimactic rendezvous, Caesar and Cathleen have been left behind to guard the car because they are presumably less interested in the kind of activity Rooney has planned. But they prove to be a surprising couple. Being intellectual, they soon move from a discussion of Freud and Jung (apparently headier stuff than booze) into a more direct experiment with the real thing.

When Rooney and Jeanine return to the car, the discomfited couple discover the bridge is starting to open to let a tugboat pass. Caesar and Cathleen don't notice this because they have slipped below the seat and apparently take the moving earth as a matter of course. After much ado about getting the car door open, a frantic Rooney gets into the car, as Jeanine gets in on the passenger side. The bridgekeeper, previously distracted by a movie on television, suddenly spots the impending catastrophe and brings the bridge to a halt. This leaves the front axle and bumper suspended between the crack of the bridge, but the kids are at least safe from drowning. Rooney, powerless to affect what happens to the car, responds to this apparently benign intervention by saying, "Oh, thank you, God. I'll never forget you for this, God." At this point the bridgekeeper starts to close the bridge again to insure the kids' safety, but the meeting ends crush the car's entire front axle and a good deal of the rest of the car with it. Bewildered by this sudden change in fortune, Rooney cries out, "Oh, God, what are you doing?" It is at this point that Jeanine heaves into Rooney's lap.

Rooney has a very personalized view of religion. He seems to think that all of this is happening specifically at the behest of a higher authority, that God is taking a direct hand in these actions. If things are in fact as Rooney sees them, then this must be a very cruel God, taunting us with the hope of salvation, then paying those hopes off with an irretrievable damnation. The film offers some support for Rooney's view, but without the cosmic framework. The person with direct control over what's happening, the bridgekeeper, certainly seems to be operating beyond the pale of ordinary human understanding. He has not noticed the car on the bridge because he is inexplicably convulsed with laughter as he watches the ending of *Gunga Din* on television (which portrays the very serious death of Gunga Din himself). A streak of cruelty is thus invoked in the scene although the actual destruction of the car is in fact an accident. But such circumstances make it easy to understand Rooney's notion that some kind of intentionality must drive the divine plan behind it all. Accidents must happen for a reason in a world where there is a disjunction between cause and effect, where even innocuously spontaneous behavior can bring down the wrath of God.

I will return to these issues later because they invoke notions of hierarchy and authority central to the film. For now the main point I wish to make about this scene, the thing that really sets it apart from its counterparts in other Animal Comedies, is its sense of consequentiality. This time the destruction remains immutable, and it leads to an unpleasant result for Rooney. In all the other films in which a car has been destroyed, either the car is restored—as in *Risky Business* (1983) or *Weird Science* (1985)— or there is no noticeable personal consequence for those involved in the destruction. In *Heaven Help Us* the consequences are spelled out in the very next scene, glancingly, but clear enough for even the least attentive audience. In fact, the understatement itself serves as something of a commentary on the nature of the consequences. The next scene will show Rooney with two black eyes, lightly presented as the inevitable result of his father's return from Chicago. This retroactively helps to explain Rooney's sense of something both very cruel and inescapable in authority.

While Rooney's punishment establishes a consequentiality unusual in the world of Animal Comedy, the matter-of-fact, understated way it is presented could make the event seem inconsequential. The scene after the destruction of the car takes place at a Fifth Avenue parade in Manhattan to honor Pope Paul VI, the first Pope to visit America. Rooney, still in pursuit of Jeanine, has managed to locate the Virgin Martyr girls, and the camera picks him up as he moves through the crowd toward her. She notices the black eyes and asks what happened to him. "Oh," he responds casually, "my father returned from Chicago." Then, as if he had just commented on nothing more serious than the weather, he launches into his latest proposition to her. The power of the understatement lies in the fact that the character himself makes the consequentiality inconsequential. The comedy becomes both dark and absurdist with this consequence, almost as if the sequence of events could in themselves provide the disturbing answer to Rooney's plaintive cries: Why is God doing this to him? So that his father can come home and beat him up.

In this deeply unsettling comic style, the film continues to explore (albeit from a secularized and more psychological perspective) issues of power and authority through an odd juxtaposition of scenes that peculiarly reinvokes and reinforces the religious connotations that Rooney had originally read into the events on the bridge. The film engineers the juxtaposition through an ellipsis that takes us directly from the destruction of the car to the Fifth Avenue parade for the Pope. The last thing we heard in the earlier scene was Rooney crying out, "Oh, God, what are you doing?" For someone seeking to find some kind of grand design in everything (as Rooney seems to do here), then it might be possible to regard Jeanine's heaving into Rooney's lap as God's answer to what He's doing. From this gross action there is a direct cut to the parade honoring the Pope, almost as if this scene functioned as a reinforcing second answer to Rooney's question. If the earlier scene is presented, in Rooney's terms, as an invocation of God's authority, we then move from God's authority to a scene honoring Papal authority. Further, the ellipsis whose action is implied by Rooney's blackened eyes invokes parental authority, allying it to both the metaphysical authority of God and the worldly authority of the Pope.

Inevitable connections are thus set up here by the juxtaposition of scenes and events. Placing an event familiar to us from other Animal Comedies in this unexpectedly religious context makes both the original event and religion strange, almost foreign in that the event must inevitably look very different to us by being interpreted religiously, while religion, by being tied up to this event, is suddenly given a distinctive coloration of its own. In this sequence of events, religion in effect becomes an environment that reinforces the notion of hierarchical authority. At the Fifth Avenue parade Rooney himself specifically appeals to Papal authority (but in a way that none of his teachers at St. Basil's would approve). After dismissing Jeanine's question about his black eyes, he tries to convince her they can have sex without sin—just as good as if they were married—if they can get the Pope to wave at the two of them standing together. This is certainly conferring quite a bit of power on the Pope, which is precisely the point. In such a repressive atmosphere as the parochial school of this film, Rooney's understanding of religious authority has been made into a very personal thing because he has been inculcated with an exacting sense of his own position in the hierarchy of authority. The hierarchy is incontrovertible, so the only actual option in dealing with it is to try to use it against itself, in this instance by getting the Pope to bless a union he would otherwise reject.

Students like Rooney might still implicitly be fighting this image of authority by trying to find ways of turning it to their own ends, but otherwise the scene presents us with a quite literal image of patriarchal authority to which the adults in the scene are more than willing to submit— in fact, they express their submission with a feeling akin to ecstasy. The adults who take pleasure in exercising their authority take a comparable pleasure in their adulatory submissiveness to a higher authority. As masochism complements sadism, submissiveness in this case complements power: by expressing their ecstatic submissiveness, the brothers of St. Basil's reinforce their power in an inevitable and immutable hierarchy that guarantees their position of power by making them submissive to another power.

All this probably makes *Heaven Help Us* sound fairly grim (and the film does become darker as it goes along). Nonetheless, we are still in the world of Animal Comedy, even on so unlikely an issue as power and religious authority (as implicitly defined in comic terms by Rooney's sense of a very personal God). The soundtrack itself insists that we view the Pope's visit in comic terms: the whole parade scene is accompanied by Figaro's first aria ("Largo al factotum.") from Rossini's *The Barber of Seville*. Initially, this recalls and reinforces an Irish grandmother's dismissal (heard earlier in the film) of the "Italian invasion," by reducing it to the buffooneries of Italian comic opera. But even more to the point, the music is simply all wrong for the reverential expressions we see on the adoring faces of the brothers. It's too sprightly, too lighthearted, too . . . well, too *Italian.* Moreover, the words to the aria provide an amusing counterpoint to what we actually see on the screen. "Make way for the factotum!" Figaro sings, and expounds on how his services as a barber make him constantly in demand, at the beck and call of all the people in the city. Ironically, his position as a servant establishes him as one of the most important people in Seville, perhaps even one worth honoring with a parade. The Pope is "the servant of the servants of God," but Figaro is the servant wily enough to outwit his masters. Appropriately, the scene ends with the five boys from St. Basil's outwitting their teachers by slipping off to the local theater to take in an Elvis Presley movie.

The emphasis on the institutionalization of authority in *Heaven Help Us* ties into something already discussed in regard to other Animal Comedies (but inflected here in a distinctive and intriguing way). In chapter 7, I wrote about the general antiauthoritarian strain running through Animal Comedy, but I have also noted a peculiar ambivalence about this that finds different and often devious forms of expression in the various films and gives rise at times to very contradictory attitudes. Usually in these films it is simply a matter of kicking out the haves and moving the have-nots into the positions of power (the approach used in *Animal House* but more incisively explored and reexamined in *Revenge of the Nerds*). Yet the antiauthoritarian strain of these films usually has a prominent corollary: the presence of a central institution that defines, at least in part, the identity of all the characters in the film. Even if all the characters are brimming with antiauthoritarian impulses, the institutions themselves are almost never questioned in these films, no matter how trivial or inconsequential the "institution" may be (whether a country club or a driving school for people with traffic violations).[2] The institution is thus a given of the film, but one that frequently takes on a near-monolithic inevitability.

In this respect, then, *Heaven Help Us* represents a somewhat radical departure for the genre in that it does question its central institution—St. Basil's parochial high school—and in the process it questions the authority of authority. Because this aspect does receive a fuller treatment in this film than in other films of the genre, it may prove useful to consider the ways the institution is defined here.

If one were to judge American educational institutions as normally presented in Hollywood movies of the past, one would have to conclude that football was their primary pursuit. Animal Comedy has changed all that: sex has replaced football (which is, I suppose, something of an improvement over football in that sex, in these films at least, represents a kind of educational experience). *Heaven Help Us* is unusual in Animal Comedy in that it spends a fair amount of time in the classroom, although it does make clear that the real education going on is not in the intellectual subject matter. Rather than sex (this is a parochial school, after all), this institution provides the education of socialization—an education determined to reinforce one's position, and especially one's submissive position, within the hierarchy that the school so insistently presents.

The way the film shows this is to use the strategies of an initiation drama. We are slowly brought into the rigidly stratified world of St. Basil's through the experiences of a newcomer, Michael Dunne (Andrew McCarthy), who has recently moved from Boston to Brooklyn, where he and his younger sister live with their grandparents (apparently the parents have died). There are a couple of scenes with him in dealing with the principal and one of the teachers before we move into the first classroom scene. Michael will remain central to the film's narrative, but, typical of Animal Comedy, he is soon paired off with another leading male, Rooney, his opposite in intelligence and sensitivity. The focus will eventually broaden out to encompass a group of five boys, but because Michael is established first he initially provides our point of entry into this world. His reactions will become the key to defining how we are to respond to this world.

In the first classroom scene we naturally gravitate to Michael because, like him, we are experiencing a St. Basil's class for the first time. The scene is written in a way to make it point toward his response, yet, oddly, director Michael Dinner does something a little different. Since Michael has not yet acquired the school regulation dress, he tends to stand out, even when out-of-focus and in the background. Throughout the first part of this scene, Michael is in fact shown out-of-focus and in the background much of the time, so that while we are always aware of him, we cannot read his expression. We are left pretty much on our own in responding to the scene, and this sudden lack of certainty (since we cannot gauge Michael's responses) conditions everything that follows.

Dramatically the scene has a double purpose: to introduce us to the classroom experience at St. Basil's (an attempt to discuss the Holy Trinity, in this first instance), and also to define the three characters who will become the dominant trio of the film (a kind of Unholy Trinity in counterpoint to the subject matter being discussed). Michael is the appropriate person to lead us into this classroom because he is clearly a sensitive type, someone who might write poetry, or the quiet one who will help us to understand what is going on. This is also our first meeting with Rooney, clearly defined in this scene as an unstoppable, brash, willing-to-try-anything personality. Finally, there is Caesar, the overweight class intellectual who likes demonstrating his putative superiority by occasionally talking about himself in the third person.

The personalities of these characters are initially defined in relation to the power structure, not in the more intimate context of home or friends. This fact will color our impression of them throughout the rest of the film, with the resultant sense that personality is rooted in the institution. The institution helps to define character here because character, as the film defines it, does not exist apart from the social world, something the other films ignore since the institutions there serve as mere background. If the institution itself is presented and accepted as a mere given, its authority is never questioned, and the relationship of character to institution can never really be probed.

The scene begins as comedy, a kind of one-upsmanship founded on attempts to subvert authority. Brother Constance (Jay Patterson) is giving a lesson on the nature of the Holy Trinity. He calls on Rooney for a definition. Rooney stands up, takes a sheet of paper (blank as it turns out), and pretends to read from it: "The Holy Trinity is total mystery; therefore it cannot be understood"—a nifty definition that begs the question. While all the other students laugh, Caesar (sitting behind Rooney), waves his hand wildly, anxious to demonstrate his knowledge. The students are laughing at Rooney for the blatancy of his response, a convoluted admission that he knows nothing by saying something. In part, the laughter denotes delight in Rooney's momentary victory over Constance, and his ingenuity in expressing his ignorance. Constance recognizes the ingenuity as well but is less appreciative: "Brilliant! But I wanted the definition that's in the book." Rooney, thrown a bit by this, gives it a few seconds thought, then answers, "Oh, right, the book! The Holy Trinity is, was, and always will be Total Mystery that can't, never could, and never will be understood," giving a nice indication of what the reading assignment might have sounded like to him had he in fact done it.

As the scene goes on it isn't clear that Constance does in fact want the right answer to the question he poses, or if he's posing another kind of question altogether. It is clear enough from Caesar's handwaving (which becomes more insistent in its frustration after Rooney's second and more ingenious try), that Caesar has the right answer. It's even possible that other students might also. But instead of calling on any of these other candidates, Constance calls on Michael, the "new boy," as he addresses him, to provide a definition from a book he is not yet likely to have read. Michael stands up and simply admits his ignorance, an admission that functions as an excuse solely because he is in class for the first time. Nonetheless, Constance reminds him, "There will be no excuses tomorrow," and that lesson seems to have been the sole point of calling on Michael.

It is only after he has made Michael look bad that Constance finally calls on Caesar for the apparent certainty of a right answer. But even then the definition is never spoken, so that a pattern of comic frustration continues as the original direction of the action is constantly deflected. With almost a tone of disgust in his voice, almost as if he had to resign himself to getting the proper answer, Constance, without even looking at Caesar, simply says, as if this is enough to prompt a response, "Alright, Caesar." In his typically pompous manner, Caesar stands up and says he would like to make a few prefatory remarks before offering his definition. But for all his apparent attempts at showmanship and rhetorical suasion, he has made one fatal flaw in his performance: he is chewing gum. Constance, apparently so bored with the certainty of Caesar's definition that he is now bent over his desk and writing something on a sheet of paper, says to Caesar, without looking at him, "What are you chewing?" Rather than letting him continue with his definition, he tells Caesar (who has just admitted the gum), "Stick it on the end of your nose, please" (this last phrase of politeness giving a nice sense that Constance, in requesting this humiliation, is just asking for a favor).

What happens at this point is striking for the way the editing inflects the comedy. When Caesar puts the gum on the end of his nose, there's some laughter (presumably from the same students who laughed at Rooney's devious definition). Then Dinner immediately cuts to a reaction shot of Rooney, still standing and still subject to further humiliation himself. Rooney nonetheless laughs at the gum incident as well. Constance has turned Caesar into the clown that the class already perceives him to be. He has created a kind of theater of comic cruelty that clearly plays to the class, and it elicits a positive response in the form of laughter, even from Rooney. The "educational" aspect of this lesson, then, is that it establishes a complicity between teacher and students when the teacher humiliates individual students: the students are encouraged to assume the attitudes that engender the humiliation.

There is subsequently an escalation of brutality when Rooney is once again made part of the spectacle he had only moments before been laughing at. Constance calls Rooney to the front of the class and asks to see his homework assignment. On receiving the blank sheet of paper, he addresses the class as much as Rooney, saying, "Your homework seems to have disappeared, mister." Clearly playing to the other students, Constance makes a mildly sacrilegious joke. "I realize this was a religion assignment," he says (holding the blank sheet up for the class), "but I hardly expected you to perform a miracle." Dinner once again cuts to a shot of the students registering their amusement (most strikingly Rooney's friend Corbett, strategically placed in the center of the frame to attract our attention, who is laughing along with the rest of the class). Constance is entirely successful in his attempts to play to the audience and to bring the students over to his side by gaining their complicity through laughter, by making them share in the pleasure of witnessing Rooney's humiliation.

I want to look at the rest of this scene very closely with reference to specific shots because there is a very powerful attempt here to relate these little humiliations to the hierarchical and religious setting. From the shot of the students laughing, Dinner cuts to a medium two-shot of Constance on the left with his back to the camera and Rooney on the right facing Constance (and the camera) as they continue talking about his homework assignment. Strategically placed between them on the wall hangs a large crucifix with the body of a suffering Christ twisted along its bars. As they stand with this image of torture looming in the background, Constance demands of Rooney, "You were trying to deceive me, weren't you?" Rooney says nothing. Constance pulls him by the ear past the crucifix, making him writhe much like the Christ, to the blackboard, where he demands, "The truth, mister!" Confession is what's needed, and Rooney does finally confess. Even this is not enough for Constance, whose Christian sensibility demands that repentance follow confession.

There's a good deal of torture here in the name of truth, but not much in the way of forgiveness. Rooney has to go beyond confession to further humiliation. Constance demands, "And now you're sorry, aren't you?" Rooney has plenty to be sorry about by this point, so he immediately replies, "Yes, brother," but even this is not enough to placate the morally offended Constance, who feels a more direct admission is needed. "Well, then, say it," Constance demands. "Say, 'I'm — sorry, — brother,' " and on each word he bangs Rooney's head against the wall.

At this point there is a cut to a reaction shot of Michael, who up to now has been largely absent from the scene, but is now restored as a focus for our own response: he winces. Constance keeps repeating the "I'm — sorry — brother" and head-banging routine until Rooney is finally able to say that he is sorry. There's a point to keeping these reactions separate. Michael never laughs at any of the earlier humiliations visited on either Caesar and Rooney before this escalation into outright violence. We have nonetheless seen Rooney laugh at what happens to Caesar, so to some degree he becomes implicated in his own torture. On the other hand, we never see any of the other students react in the way Michael does (probably because they've seen too much of this already). Acceptance of the humiliation through laughter is a way to become inured to the inevitable brutality.

There is, of course, the problem of how far to go along with Constance's theater piece and of how implicated one feels in it as it has progressed from its earlier comic tone. Constance now maneuvers a return to the comic tone with one further escalation, this time into an absurdist universe. He makes Rooney stand directly in front of his fellow students and orders him to eat the blank sheet of paper, which is a reestablishment of Constance's cruelly comic theater: not only must Rooney endure the humiliation of having to eat the sheet of paper, he must do so in front of his classmates.

With the escalation from comedy to horror throughout the scene, Dinner can now play the two contradictory responses off each other. From the shot of Rooney beginning to eat the paper, Dinner cuts to a reaction shot of the still-shocked Michael. This is followed by a reverse angle of Caesar, a wondrously composed shot with a dexterous mise-en-scène that unifies all the complex and divergent elements of the entire sequence: from a space just to the left of Michael (who is not in the shot) we see Caesar in the foreground turning around to face Michael, while farther in the background behind Caesar and over the heads of the other students we can see Rooney and Constance as Rooney embarks on his pulpy snack. Facing the camera as well as Michael, so the statement seems addressed to us as much as to Dunne, Caesar says with as much irony as he can muster, "Welcome to St. Basil's," smirking as he finishes saying this. As if in answer Caesar's all-knowing smirk, there is a cut to a medium single shot of Rooney, who takes another bite from the sheet of paper and begins to chew, an ambivalent expression starting to form on his face (almost as if he thinks he ought to like what he's eating).[3] With this shot, the scene ends.

There is clearly some kind of comedy intended in Caesar's remark, as if he were welcoming us to a wild and wonderful place, however ironically the remark is intended. In some ways the initiation aspects of this scene parallel the opening scenes of *Animal House* (where we first visit the Animal House fraternity and see it chiefly through the eyes of two freshmen, potential pledges to the fraternity who have a wide-eyed response to all the unexpected and wild goings-on they witness). And in some ways Constance's actions are a bit like hazing, an initiation rite intended to establish lines of authority. But the early scenes in *Animal House* always stay within the domains of raucous comedy. In this classroom scene from *Heaven Help Us*, however, the shifting in and out of a comic mode (typical of the rest of the film) is not unlike *Fast Times at Ridgemont High*, especially in its vivid presentation of a teenager's pain. But the pain here is often as physical as it is psychological, and it is given the full support of an institution. As a consequence, the return to the comic mode becomes a difficult and more complex matter. There is little that can counter the pain (as there is in *Fast Times*) because everything in this world seems designed to maintain the lines of brutality. The return to comedy always takes on a kind of ambivalence: it is necessary as a mark of sanity, the only sane way to deal with an insane situation, both by providing distance as well as celebrating individual resiliency.[4] Yet at the same time that laughter betokens sanity, it also signals accepting the insanity of this world. Given this kind of double bind, only two responses are really available: laughing or screaming.

In writing this, I am putting forward the film as the logical meeting place of this book's two genres, which accounts for the central position I've accorded it. If you were to look at *Heaven Help Us* as a kind of horror film, it is in fact fairly easy to see the teachers as monstrous, as monsters who threaten the autonomy and sexual identity of these teenagers. A real horror film would probably stylize this material a bit by making all the brothers vampires—a defensive measure that would only mitigate some of the horror of the actual situation by moving it into fantasy. In a sense, though, the horror of the teachers' brutality is akin to a horror film in that it is accepted as a given of the film's setting. Although finally subject to an astute but covert analysis, the brutality is never seen as anything other than inevitable in this setting, much as the horror of horror films is always inescapable.

The film, nonetheless, does remain pretty much within the bounds of Animal Comedy, strongly drawing, as we have seen, on the hallmarks of the genre. But I am also looking at this film last (before moving on to the horror film per se) precisely because I want to separate it from its genre counterparts. Much as it is not fantastic in the manner of horror films, it also strives for a more seamless, realistic style than most other Animal Comedies. Generally the stylizations in these films are those of farce, but even *Fast Times*, which is less farcical than the other films, has a stylized quality in its mosaiclike interlacing of episodes. *Heaven Help Us* is the only one of these films that might garner praise for its screenplay, for its ability to capture the feel of a particular time and place, the way people talk, indeed its entire milieu.[5] So vivid is its sense of accurately observed reality that the film carries with it a strong impression of autobiography.[6]

Because of the more realistic style of this film, there is a crucial difference in the way we understand the struggle against authority and the dominant social institution. In other Animal Comedies, the opposition against which our heroes are struggling is always caricatured or made grotesque.[7] In the other films, the opposition might be in control of society at the beginning of the film, but because they are so grotesque their inevitable defeat becomes an inescapable triumph for the "normal" (and normal is most frequently defined in these films as an unbridled and "healthy" sexual appetite). The caricature of the antagonists sets them up for defeat from the very beginning of the film, and in this regard these films draw on some of the hoariest traditions of comedy. What these characters really represent are comic "vices," characters who, as Northrop Frye has it, are in bondage to certain traits that must inevitably be purged.[8] *Revenge of the Nerds* radically reworks this ancient strategy by creating a genuine consistency in characterization in which *everyone* becomes a grotesque. *Heaven Help Us* moves in the opposite direction to provide a more realistic portrayal of all its characters, even the most monstrous and hateful. This establishes more of a balance between the opposing forces, so it becomes far more difficult to define the putative norm, which the other films seem to take as their incumbent task.

By reworking the power struggle in this manner, *Heaven Help Us* makes clear that the meaning of an event lies not just in how you look at it, but rather in the power you have to enforce your interpretation. The grotesqueness of the opposition in the other films always ensures that we will accept the protagonists' understanding of events as a truth that the world at large will eventually acknowledge (even if the antagonists are in the position of power). The idea of an easily perceived unitary truth is one kind of utopian fantasy that *Heaven Help Us* will not accept. Because the style of the film makes no distinctions in characterizations between protagonists and antagonists, the antagonists here are given an advantage in their ability to define themselves as "normal."

Shortly after Brother Timothy (John Heard) has witnessed a class given by Brother Constance (a later class which is in fact more brutal than the one described above), he has a conversation with the principal, Brother Thadeus (Donald Sutherland), that effectively identifies the power of power to define itself as normal. The conversation is worth quoting in its entirety because it lays out the issues of the film so clearly. Before I do, I want to note that among the brothers Timothy operates as something of a parallel figure to Michael Dunne in that he is also a newcomer to St. Basil's; thus, at times the film functions as a kind of initiation drama for him. As a newcomer, he becomes a focus for our responses much as Michael has been in other scenes. The dramatic strategy of this particular scene is to play our responses (as embodied in Timothy) off against the more entrenched position of Thadeus. Timothy and Thadeus stroll through the school courtyard as Timothy tries to articulate his feelings about Constance's class.

TIMOTHY: I thought I was going to learn something about running a class, but instead I was offered a demonstration of brutality. The man seemed to be enjoying himself, brother.

THADEUS: A rather slanderous thought, brother, and one that really ought to be kept to oneself. Brother Constance is an effective teacher, one of the best we have.

TIMOTHY: Yeah, I hear you, brother, but—

THADEUS: But what? . . . We all come to the order full of ideas. After a while we often find that we have much to learn ourselves. In any event, authority must never be undermined by the spirit of dissension among the faculty . . . for the student's sake, you understand.

TIMOTHY: No, [*laughingly*] I don't understand.

THADEUS: Then you should try to restrain yourself [*quietly threatening*] until you do.

At the end of this scene Timothy is in effect barred from any further comment on Constance's teaching methods until he learns the proper way of understanding them. He must see, as Thadeus implicitly suggests, that there is an intimate connection between teaching and inculcating a sense of authority, a point that Thadeus himself is clearly trying to teach Timothy in this exchange.

This is to say that the meaning of the classroom lies not in the event itself but rather in Thadeus's interpretation of the event, the interpretation that will eventually become the event. In other Animal Comedies, "normal" in a familiar American fashion becomes allied to the natural, a state or condition that is constantly threatened by rigid social structures: it is normal to let things hang loose and give full vent to natural drives. Anything that represses the natural is inherently threatening and deserves attack. In *Heaven Help Us*, the dialogue takes over the same terms, but inflects them in a strikingly different manner. Normal is what the status quo, the power structure, defines it to be, even if that involves systematized forms of brutalization.[9] In the film's climactic scene, Brother Constance is about to administer corporal punishment to all five of the boys we have followed through the film. The normally goody-goody Caesar, who has been subject to various humiliations from Constance but has otherwise escaped any physical retribution, objects to the corporal punishment as "barbaric." In response an outraged Constance demands, "Who are you calling barbaric!" From Constance's perspective the beating he's about to administer represents the height of civilization, while Caesar's instinctive cowering from pain, a perfectly "natural" response, is made to seem strange.

Brutality, then, serves to support normality in that it establishes lines of authority, hierarchies that must be made to seem natural. The existence of the hierarchy enables the hierarchy to define itself as the natural and inevitable state of things. One of the most disturbing aspects of *Heaven Help Us* that lingers long after the final scene, and that is clear from the first classroom scene on, is that no one in the film ever really questions the *authority* of the authorities. What finally emerges in this film is a world that doesn't even offer the possibility of political redress. Submission to power is the only option offered to these kids, who find themselves trapped in a world of power without politics.

This is why there is always a residual feeling of uneasiness and disquiet when the film moves from its scenes of brutality back into comedy. Comic equilibrium can never be fully regained because the social order is never really assailable to comic attack as it is in the other films. *Heaven Help Us* is more or less engaged in a dialogue with other Animal Comedies (since it uses most of the same terms of discourse), but it inflects them differently in that it begins to question its own status as comedy. When laughter in comedy basically extols the potential power of the protagonists, the ironic quality in Caesar's "Welcome to St. Basil's" becomes a tacit admission of powerlessness since irony in effect betrays the inability of the character to address any of the social inequities he is confronting.

Rooney, the character most sensitive to the power of authority to establish itself as natural and inevitable, is also (not coincidentally) the most brutalized character in the film. He is the first character to receive corporal punishment (in the head-banging incident); he is also, we learn, abused at home as well as at school. He therefore has the most incisive sense of power hierarchies, and this sense is reflected both in his responses to his teachers as well as in his interactions with his fellow students. In a kind of vicious circle of abuse, he has to assert his own power in his first meeting with Michael. On the way to school, he calls Michael over to him and kicks the books out of Michael's hand. When Michael doesn't respond in kind, he smears him as the "St. Mary's Fairy," referring to Michael's previous school in Boston. The slur speaks in the power terms that Rooney best understands: he denies Michael the power of his own masculinity (which the film finally makes the ultimate power for these characters).

Like Constance, Rooney is strongly aware of an element of show in maintaining his own position of power. Provoked by Rooney's incessant taunting, Michael finally moves to Rooney's level and attacks him physically, fittingly enough right in Brother Constance's classroom. Once they are separated and equally punished, Rooney proposes friendship, a move he sees as necessary in order to maintain appearances: "Hey, look, Dunne, you jumped me in front of everybody, made me look pretty stupid. I gotta save face. If I don't make you my friend, that means I gotta kick your ass every time I see you. Now, nobody wants that to happen, right? So, what d'ya say, let's give it a try. [*putting his hand on Michael's shoulder*] C'mon."

Now there is a kind of crazy logic here, to be sure: if I'm not your friend, I have to be your enemy, and not only that, I have to give regular demonstrations of my enmity. In any case, it is logical in this context, in the world of power and position in the parochial school. Thus, while his actual grades may be low, Rooney has become an expert student of the education this school has to offer; his understanding in fact parallels what Thadeus says to Timothy on the subject of Constance's classroom.

The dramatic arc of the film follows the escalation of the violence. Much as Constance's second class is more brutal than the first, much as Rooney's taunting will move Michael to take action, the whole plot moves toward the moment when Michael will violently react against Constance's beating of five boys by slugging Constance in front of the entire school (assembled for a platitudinous address by Brother Thadeus). The knockout brings the hundreds of boys in the auditorium to their feet cheering, but the film is not aiming for the charged response of the victories in any of the *Rocky* films (1976–90) or *The Karate Kid* (1984). Rather, the film presents Michael's reversal and "victory" as an ambivalent thing since it has in effect moved him from his stance of turning the other cheek (in his early encounter with Rooney) and has put him on the same level with Constance and Rooney. It is impossible to be Christian in this Christian environment with its covertly encoded patterns of violence. Violence is a potentiality that is inevitably brought out by a rigid social structure that in fact seeks to suppress aggressive impulses.

Rooney has been more clearly formed by this environment. He combines an adolescent irrepressibility that is attractive in itself with a sullen suspiciousness. Heavy browed, he often keeps his head down and looks up at people as if he expects to be hit quite a lot of the time. The suspiciousness does approach paranoia in his constantly seeing "faggots" everywhere, a word so liberally employed in his speech that it quickly takes on a fairly general quality, acting like a lodestone for everything negative he sees in the world. As one who has so often been on the receiving end of masculine power, he is almost obsessively concerned with possibilities of emasculation and the need to display his own power for the sake of his masculine identity. When he and his cohorts sneak off from the celebration of patriarchy in the papal parade to an Elvis Presley movie (trading in a prince of the church for the King of Rock), they find Elvis covered with flowers and crooning his way through a Technicolor pretty lagoon in a syrupy confection called *Blue Hawaii*. Seeing this prettified and anodyne Elvis, Rooney calls out: "What did they do to Elvis, cut off his balls or something?" The brief glimpse from *Blue Hawaii* (1961) that *Heaven Help Us* offers us seems to support Rooney's complaint: this person who had stood for an unleashed masculine sexuality suddenly seems feminized, perfumed, contained. There is nonetheless a kind of confusion inherent in this response because the film doesn't offer any real outlet for the masculine aggression that the institution seeks to contain. All aggressive feeling must necessarily be checked except by those in power.

The "natural" order of things that the parochial world tries to construct where everything becomes defined by power inevitably has to call for a constant fear of and vigilance against the unnatural. This, of course, is Rooney's position because he is a part of this world. The film itself sees things a bit differently: it both inhabits this world but also stands outside of it by working inversions that in effect turn the natural and the unnatural upside down. In the piece of dialogue I have used as the epigraph for this chapter, Rooney points out to Caesar that they're dealing with a grown man in a dress. This exchange takes place shortly before Constance is to administer his most brutal act in the film. What Rooney does not point out is that this most vicious of all male characters in the film, the most aggressively masculine, also has a woman's name. So the character who is most concerned with making a show of his physical power over these kids is given a couple of features the film specifically identifies as feminine.

The film offers an intriguing and counterbalancing inversion to Constance in the person of Michael's girlfriend Danni (Mary Stuart Masterson). She is the closest thing to a romantic lead in the film, yet, as a complement to the brutal brother's feminized moniker, she has a boy's name, she always dresses in jeans and sweatshirt (appropriate enough for her boyish-looking body) and she's aggressively independent. The independence has in part been forced upon her because she lives in a household where the mother has deserted and the father has been incapacitated by bouts of melancholia. There is an edginess in Mary Stuart Masterson's performance that suggests an anger underlying the independence, resentment at the abandonment that has forced her to be self-reliant, and yet the ability to take care of herself and stand up to others is presented as one of her most attractive traits. She is, in effect, the head of a household: she runs the house where her father sits in desperate silence day in and day out, and she earns their keep by running the soda shop attached to the house (which serves as a local hangout for the St. Basil's boys and Virgin Martyr girls). Necessity has made her a power in a world in which male power has deserted.

She is also important because she is the one character who exists entirely apart from the parochial world, the one connection the film offers to the world at large. From her constant interaction with it, she nonetheless understands the rules of the parochial world, so that her interactions serve as an additional running commentary on it. She is witness to the first confrontation between Rooney and Michael (Rooney's kicking the books out of Michael's hand), which takes place in front of her soda shop. Rooney has been talking to Danni, when he spots Michael across the street and calls him over. Michael compliantly crosses the street and passively receives Rooney's hazing. After Rooney leaves, Danni says to Michael matter-of-factly, "You should have kicked him in the balls—that's what I would have done." Much as she is a power in her own right, she clearly understands the world of sexual identity and power the film inhabits.

On the other hand, she is also outside this world in that she is a power within her own limited universe, and this fact in itself must make her antagonistic to the brothers of St. Basil's. Much as her name suggests the inversion of sexual status, her independence from the brothers and her occasional direct opposition threatens the dominance of their hierarchical power. Her power is contained, however, almost tolerated, so long as it doesn't claim anything for itself beyond its immediate jurisdiction. When she seeks to go beyond this, she finds out precisely how limited her world is. Late in the film, when the brothers stage one of their periodic raids on her shop, Danni (now romantically involved with Dunne) decides not to allow this: she locks the shop, lowers the blinds to protect her charges within from being recognized by the authorities, and bars the brothers' entry. In retaliation, the brothers are able to appeal to a higher authority, albeit secular: they have the shop closed down by the state, the father hospitalized, and Danni sent to a home for orphaned children. The fact that the brothers are able to effect this points to a larger social structure that makes the power inversions the other films glory in ultimately impossible.

As the film strives for greater realism than other Animal Comedies, as it strives to connect the world of its narrative to an order that lies beyond the immediate institution, it is also the most genuinely historical of any of these films. *Animal House* might be set in 1962, *Porky's* in the mid-1950s, yet the fictive dates of these films are more or less excuses to justify the kinds of behavior we witness (although often behavior not entirely faithful to the mores of the periods in which they are set). *Heaven Help Us* takes place in 1965, and the date is fairly important: the film in fact has a very precise sense of its time and is far more faithful to period mores than any other of these films. This is not just a matter of fidelity to period detail. The historical framework itself has significance for the film's central concerns. While there is no portentous invoking of Vietnam here as in *M*A*S*H* or *American Graffiti*, there is some hint of major social changes when Woodstock is mentioned later in the spoken epilogue. More to the point is the way the film locates itself in history by including one important historical event as part of its narrative: the first visit by a Pope to the United States.

The visit implicitly invokes the Second Vatican Council (1962–65) and, by extension, the changes that would soon be taking place in parochial schools. As much as the film takes this as a central event, however, it does not also take it as a possible excuse for its analysis of hierarchical power structures. There are some problems with the ending of the film, but oddly they come about because the film chooses not to take the out that history offers. At the end of the film, after the public exposure of Brother Constance's extreme brutality has forced Michael's equally brutal response, Brother Thadeus does a complete about-face from the character we have seen in the rest of the film. He tells Constance he is not only transferring him from St. Basil's, he is going to keep him from teaching so that he will never go near children again. It is not unusual in American art to cap a fairly incisive social analysis with blame suddenly shifted from the institution to one individual. There is certainly a local failure here: the film inevitably seems to be pulling back from its analysis by engineering an unbelievable reversal in a character, a reversal it cares so little about that it does not in any way try to prepare for it. In fact, Thadeus ends up contradicting much of what he had said to Timothy in the conversation quoted above.

This is clearly a serious flaw, and I am not excusing it, but I am fascinated that the film is willing to shift everything onto individuals rather than look for an institutional justification that will right the wrongs it has been detailing when history does in fact offer just such a justification. The film could more explicitly focus on Vatican II rather than indirectly invoke it, which would put all these events in a nostalgic past, making it clear that we are looking at horrors and excesses no longer present because parochial schools have greatly changed since this period, that the majority of teaching is now done by lay teachers and so on, that none of this applies anymore and it's a wonderful thing that we have gotten beyond it. But the film itself is apparently not looking for this kind of conclusion.

The pain this film invokes as part of adolescence is more inescapable than in any other Animal Comedy. Like *Fast Times* the film does honor the vitality of the kids, but unlike *Fast Times* it offers no real hope of any outlet for that vitality. Charles Dickens's *David Copperfield* is brought up a number of times in the film—kids are reading it for class and writing reports about it—but there is an underlying futility and sense of waste in this film that is closer to the later Dickens, especially *Great Expectations.* About to enter the brutal world, these kids necessarily have to scale down what they can expect to get out of it. Throughout the film Caesar constantly talks about going to Harvard, always expressing dread that some misstep in a world that is like a minefield will end up sending him to Queen's College. As we learn from the epilogue, that's exactly where he goes.

In many ways the fate of these kids is more limited and even more desperate than that of the kids in *American Graffiti* (Ron Howard might stay behind, confining himself in his small town mentality, but this is treated as a matter of choice). The epilogue in *Heaven Help Us*, on the other hand, suggests that the choices are already made for the kids, who really have very little control over their destinies. In *American Graffiti* the dark cloud of Vietnam seems to hang over everyone's lives, yet the boys in this film mostly exist outside of the flow of history; it's the flow of cruising in an automobile that provides the real context for their lives. *Heaven Help Us* nods toward future historical change (implicitly invoking Vietnam and mentioning Woodstock), but the film itself establishes a more genuine historical sensibility by making clear that the world these people inhabit already directs their futures and limits their expectations.

Fittingly, it is Rooney who delivers the epilogue—fittingly because, of the three central characters, he is the one least able to comprehend the processes he is caught up in (although, paradoxically, he most fully articulates the implicit values of this world):

> In 1966 everybody graduated from St. Basil's . . . except me. Caesar went on to graduate with honors from *Queen's* College, and he became a podomatrist, or psychiatrist, or some fag job like that. Williams got a job as a projectionist at the Peekaboo Theater in Times Square. Corbett married Jeanine . . . imagine, a turd like him. They have six kids. I heard Dunne and Danni ran into each other at Woodstock at Max What's-His-Face's farm where half a million faggots stood in the rain for three days with no clothes on. Me? I went through beautician school, where everybody graduated . . . except me. But I got a job as a shampoo boy at Marissa's House of Hair in Bensonhurst. The hours suck, the pay sucks, I'm surrounded by funny guys. But the tips are great. Thank you, God.

Rooney manages to see "faggots" in the future of four of the six people he mentions here. The other two end up in a specifically heterosexual world, but at two extremes: in conventional Catholic marriage, where the goal of sex is reproduction, and in a sleazy porno theater, where sex is commodity. By reducing the "normal" world to these two extremes, each is made to operate as the mirror image of the other, the normal made to invoke the abnormal.

For a boy so concerned with promoting his masculine identity, Rooney has the strangest fate: he ends up surrounded by "funny guys," actual homosexuals presumably, but for once he doesn't call them faggots. Instead, his perception is displaced onto his description in the same sentence of his hours and wages, both of which "suck." Confronted with the real thing, he can't bring himself to recognize it, much as he can't recognize the actual desperation of his situation. Instead, he shows appreciation for the one positive thing he can get from his life, the economic benefit which he assumes accrues to him by the intercession of a benevolent authority.

It is especially striking that the last words of the film are "Thank you, God," because they exist as a counterpoint to the image. For the prank that led to Constance's beatings and dismissal, the five boys have been suspended from school for two weeks. At first uncertain how to handle this, they suddenly realize the punishment offers an unexpected blessing: they will be away from St. Basil's for two weeks! At the moment that all their faces light up with elation and Rooney raises his fist in a victory salute, Dinner freezes the frame. Then, as Rooney begins his epilogue in voice-over, the image turns from color to black-and-white. There is a kind of exultation in Rooney's voice as he thanks God, but of course the surge of vitality in the expression is itself undercut by the image drained of color. Because the character's vitality expresses itself by obeisance to a higher authority, the full expression of vitality is necessarily undercut. Instead, it becomes frozen in past time.

Most Animal Comedies, for all their apparent anarchism, accept the institutions that serve to define their characters without questioning their validity. While *Heaven Help Us* does accept the inevitability of a power structure, it departs from other Animal Comedies in that it questions the institution and questions it in a fairly far-reaching way. As a consequence, it ends up offering less hope than the other films because, once it has dared to question, it can find nothing to put in the institution's place. In this regard, Danni's plight is of particular importance because, as noted earlier, she takes us outside the defined setting of the parochial school. Even beyond this limited arena, however, she finds herself trapped by the larger society. This is one way in which the film extends *itself* beyond the world it is centrally concerned with.

In the world of the parochial school we are concerned with issues of *male* power and *male* brutality, but this specific concern is extended in Danni's last appearance in the film. The closing of Danni's shop and her being sent away are actions that have of course been initiated by the brothers, but there is one striking detail in the scene of her departure that is worth noting. Forcibly separated from her father, whom she has taken care of throughout the film, she is led away to a different car by a kindly *female* social worker who speaks to her in a soft and soothing voice. This is unexpected and maybe even a little startling because the film has accustomed us to thinking of the exercise of power in male terms. The point here is that the oppressiveness of these power plays comes in many different disguises, but they always claim to be "for your own good."[10] Yet there is a clear enough sense from what we have seen of them throughout the film that both father and daughter will be worse off for this separation, that neither will receive the kind of care they receive living together, that they will be denied a contact which has a meaning for them that transcends specific physical conditions of living. The point is that they have been living a little too independently of the rest of the world—Danni cannot remember the last time she went to school—and the world seeks to correct the transgression of independence. This kind of thing is not merely a male prerogative, but rather the prerogative of all power structures.

Imagery of escape attaches itself to Danni throughout the film. As the romance with Michael develops, she offers to teach him how to dance. She takes him to a place in Coney Island, almost empty now because it's early in the season, where they can dance to a song from a jukebox ("I've Been Loving You Too Long"). There follows an extended lyrical montage sequence, with the song overlapped throughout. It starts with them dancing and ends with them under a pier, sheltered from the rain, where they kiss for the first time. In between there are images of openness unlike anything else offered in the rest of the film. Michael and Danni stroll along the ocean, just at the edge of the waves, a vastness stretching out behind them. In a film that is so insistently verbal, we are suddenly given only snatches of dialogue, and that turns out to be about talking: Michael tells Danni she is the only person he has ever been able to talk to about himself. The openness of space, then, is neatly scaled down to an intimacy of feeling. The style here, in its lyricism and spaciousness, is quite different from anything else in the film (necessarily, because the release the characters find in this setting and in each other is itself limited). The real world is still waiting for them, and it is not something subject to their interference.

Comedy is often utopian, and most of all Animal Comedy because it always posits a liberation, specifically sexual but also social in that it seeks to establish some kind of egalitarian society. As noted throughout this section of the book, these films often get caught in contradictions raised by their own utopianism, but this should in no way deny the utopian aspirations. *Heaven Help Us*, as much as it draws on the earlier films, is clearly set apart from them in that the only kind of liberation it can posit is of a necessarily limited nature (like the trip Danni and Michael make to Coney Island).[11] By its insistence on recognizing the power structures of the real world and the repressions inherent in them, the film constantly denies the utopian strivings of the genre and hems in the vitality of its adolescent characters. But while always remaining a comedy by at least honoring these aspirations to vitality, *Heaven Help Us* radically departs from other comedies in the genre by approaching dystopia, the kind of world that will be the subject of the next section of this book.

The Case for Child Abuse

The history of childhood is a nightmare from which we have only recently begun to awaken.

—*Lloyd de Mause,* The History of Childhood

Chapter 13 *Abusing Children*

Victims and Villains

Bram Stoker's Dracula (1897) and *The Birds* (1963)

Playgirl practical joker Melanie Daniels (Tippi Hedren) suddenly finds herself on the defensive in her conversation with lawyer Mitch Daniels (Rod Taylor). Mitch has begun to ask her about her childhood and her mother, who, it turns out, had "ditched" her and her father when she was eleven. Melanie is full of sarcastic bravado in talking of her mother, but Mitch effectively shifts the emotional terms by asking if Melanie knows where her mother is. Throughout much of this conversation, Melanie has repeatedly turned away from Mitch as if trying to protect herself against his inquisitiveness. Now, on the question of her mother's whereabouts, she turns away decisively, and says, with her voice breaking, "I don't know where she is." Recovering her poise, she turns back to him and says, "Maybe I ought to join the other children." The others are children who have just begun a game of blind man's bluff as part of celebrating the birthday of Cathy (Veronica Cartwright), Mitch's twelve-year-old sister.

It is at this point, about a third of the way through Alfred Hitchcock's *The Birds* (1963), that the first full-scale attack by the eponymous villains takes place. Previously, there had been some indication of peculiar behavior by birds: a seemingly unmotivated gull who abruptly swoops down at Melanie, pecks at her head, and just as abruptly flies off; another gull who, on a moon-bright night, crashes into the front door of a house where Melanie is staying. But now the birds—and birds of different feathers flocked together—have revealed their capacity for evil, and it is especially evil because it is directed toward children. The context of the scene seems to suggest it is not just actual children that are objects of the attack but the child that continues to reside in even the well-composed adult: it is precisely when Melanie rejoins "the other children" that the birds join the party.

The scene ends with a shot of three children looking up at the skies, uncomprehending, after the departure of the birds. This final shot by its very placement establishes the children's responses as a keynote for the scene in both psychological and physical dimensions. Psychologically, they are uncomprehending: what sense can they make of it when a familiar aspect of their universe is suddenly rendered unfamiliar in the most brutal fashion? Physically, the children are simply more vulnerable than the adults, as they are clearly dependent on the adults in this scene for their rescue. In a horror film, the victim in part determines the characterization of the villain, so *The Birds* chooses to make its villains especially loathsome by making their first victims children. There is nothing more nefarious than taking advantage of a child because a child presents a kind of double vulnerability. Not only are children less capable of defending against assault. Lacking more fully developed powers of ratiocination, they are less able to explore and determine possible reasons for the seemingly unmotivated assault, reasons that might offer a way of dealing with it.

Whether or not we can determine why the birds choose children as their prey or why the birds are attacking at all, these are questions I must leave for a later chapter. What I want to look at now is the victim-villain dyad that is so important for the horror film—because victims are often overlooked in favor of villains. As the advertisements for many later films would acknowledge, *Psycho* (1960) was a primary influence on later horror films (many of which will be discussed in the following chapters). But in many ways *The Birds* is of even greater importance, which is why I have chosen it to begin this discussion of the gross-out horror films. Nevertheless, for all that *The Birds* looks ahead to the future, in this one instance of the choice of victim it is very much working within past traditions.

If villains can do nothing worse than attack children, then the most horrible monsters in horror fiction and film may do precisely that, with every subsequent transgression tainted by this original sin. Consider how this works in one of the major literary sources for horror films, Bram Stoker's *Dracula*.[1] Professor von Helsing is trying to convince a group of men that recently deceased Lucy is not in fact dead but one of the undead. The dreadful events have been recorded from a doubly amorous point of view: written in the diary of Dr. Seward, who was once in love with Lucy, they had been witnessed with him by Arthur, Lucy's fiancé in life.

> [Van Helsing] pointed; and far down the avenue of yews we saw a white figure advance—a dim white figure, which held something dark at its breast. The figure stopped, and at the moment a ray of moonlight fell between the masses of driving clouds and showed in startling prominence a dark-haired woman, which held something dark at its breast. . . . We could not see the face, for it was bent down over what we saw to be a fair-haired child. There was a pause of a sharp little cry, such as a child gives in sleep, or a dog as it lies before the fire and dreams. . . .
>
> It was now near enough for us to see clearly, and the moonlight still held. My own heart grew cold as ice, and I could hear the gasp of Arthur as we recognized the features of Lucy Westenra. Lucy Westenra, but yet how changed. The sweetness was turned to adamantine, heartless cruelty, and the purity to voluptuous wantonness. . . . [B]y the concentrated light that fell on Lucy's face we could see that the lips were crimson with fresh blood, and that the stream had trickled over her chin and stained the purity of her lawn death-robe. . . .
>
> . . . Lucy's eyes in form and colour; but Lucy's eyes unclean and full of hell-fire, instead of the pure, gentle orbs we knew. At that moment the remnant of my love passed into hate and loathing; had she then to be killed, I could have done it with savage delight. . . . With a careless motion, she flung to the ground callous as a devil, the child that up to now she had clutched strenuously to her breast, growling over it as a dog growls over a bone. The child gave a sharp cry, and lay there moaning.[2]

Since the primary aim of their expedition is to find and destroy the dreaded thing that is abducting and biting children, these vampire hunters must find sufficient provocation to move them to murder, and murder of a particularly vicious sort. Not only must they drive a stake through the villain's heart and let it remain there for all eternity, they must also cut off her head and stuff her mouth full of garlic. To themselves these characters can only justify this excessive violation of Lucy's body in death by the excessiveness of her own violations in life. The rhetorical task of the narrative in this description is twofold: not simply to prepare the reader for the extraordinary violence that will be done to Lucy's body, but to make the reader desire such violence as well.

The description here is pervasively sexual and predicated on distressing inversions. The pure Lucy has been replaced by another Lucy the men just as soon not look at: "She seemed like a nightmare of Lucy as she lay there [in her coffin]; the pointed teeth, the bloodstained, voluptuous mouth—which it made one shudder to see—the whole carnal and unspiritual appearance, seeming like a devilish mockery of Lucy's sweet purity."

I think it is not claiming too much to see this passage as detailing a male anxiety about female sexuality, which disturbs by being both "bloodstained" and "voluptuous."[3] For this reason, translated into the positive explanation of restoring purity, her fiancé Arthur must be the one to drive the stake through her: "the infinite kindness which suggested that his should be the hand which would restore Lucy to us as a holy, and not an unholy, memory." What Lucy inspires in these men, two of whom had been sexually attracted to her, is a fear so powerful it can only be allayed by an act of literal dismemberment.

The inversion of body and spirit that I wrote about in regard to Animal Comedy is here rendered right side up in its more familiar Western dialectic. If Animal Comedy can challenge this dialectic by elevating the lower body, *Dracula* can assume we will accept the dismemberment, however gruesome it might be, because the lower body is always literally lower in our estimations. Severing the head, the home of the spirit, from the body, the repository of impure desire, will ensure a resurrection of purity. The beatific expression that returns to Lucy's spiritually cleansed face after her staking will remain there forever. *Dracula* posits that a head permanently detached from the disturbing nether regions of the body may remain free from the contamination of the body for all eternity. These men who were once sexually attracted to Lucy can only regard her as beautiful again by literally cutting her off from her sexuality.

So far the sexual imagery in the descriptions of the corrupted Lucy should seem familiar to anyone versed in other renderings of the vampire

Getting shafted by an erect sword (*City Lights*, 1931).

Charlie helps with his accidental unraveling (Virginia Cherrill and Charlie Chaplin, *City Lights*, 1931).

An unconscious act of anal revenge (*City Lights*, 1931).

The power of the gaze in a dangerous environment (*City Lights*, 1931).

Charlie asserts his power (*City Lights*, 1931).

Charlie loses power (*City Lights*, 1931).

Charlie defensively covers the bottom of his face (*City Lights*, 1931).

The jump-cut; Charlie fully exposes his face (Charlie
Chaplin and Virginia Cherrill, *City Lights*, 1931).

Elliott Gould as the pivotal figure in a confrontation between Bud Cort (*left*) and Robert Duvall (*right*). (*M★A★S★H*, 1970)

Bud Cort's uncertain response to his friend's desire to see the giant penis "angry" as the line of soldiers behind them take their turn peeping into the shower tent (*M★A★S★H*, 1970).

A surprising amount of male nudity (*Porky's*, 1982).

Cherry (Susan Clark) expresses mock astonishment as she inspects "Meat" (*Porky's* 1982).

Sexual arousal conjuring up the nightmare image of the threatening black male (*Porky's* 1982).

The risks of being uninhibited: the castrating Miss Balbricker moves in on her prey (*Porky's*, 1982).

Feeling right at home, Boone (Peter Riegert) calls out, "Otis, my man!" (*Animal House* 1978)

The low angle suggests Boone's inevitable reaction to Meanest Dude's request to dance with his date (*Animal House*, 1978).

A scary invitation to the dance (*Animal House*, 1978).

A reaction shot shows Otis affronted to be called anything by this white boy (*Animal House*, 1978).

A dissolve from the boys cheering in triumph as they drive away from danger to the girls they left behind (*Animal House*, 1978).

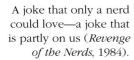

An image of regression: Gilbert (Anthony Edwards), in his womb-like enclosure, receives comfort from his mother (*Revenge of the Nerds*, 1984).

A joke that only a nerd could love—a joke that is partly on us (*Revenge of the Nerds*, 1984).

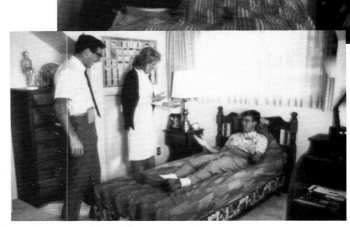

Mirroring profiles with oversize noses: Lewis (Robert Carradine, *left*) and his father enjoy their "good looks" (*Revenge of the Nerds*, 1984).

Primal comedy in the limp-wristed javelin throw that contradicts all notions of athletic prowess (*Revenge of the Nerds*, 1984)

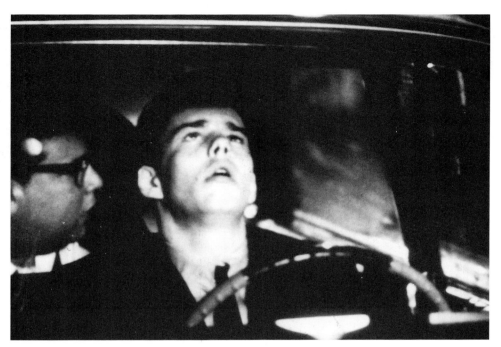

Rooney (Kevin Dillon): "Oh, thank you, God. I'll never forget you for this, God." (*Heaven Help Us*, 1985).

But "God" in the figure of the bridgekeeper destroys the car anyway (*Heaven Help Us*, 1985).

A strategically placed crucifix provides the background for this lesson in humility (*Heaven Help Us*, 1985).

A reaction shot of Michael (Andrew Mc Carthy) establishes him as the focus for our response (*Heaven Help Us*, 1985).

A wondrously composed shot with a dexterous mise-en-scène that unifies the complex and divergent elements of the entire scene: Caesar (Malcolm Danare) welcomes Michael to St. Basil's (*Heaven Help Us*, 1985).

With a smile of complacency, Damien (Jason Miller) challenges the devil to tell him his mother's maiden name (*The Exorcist*, 1973).

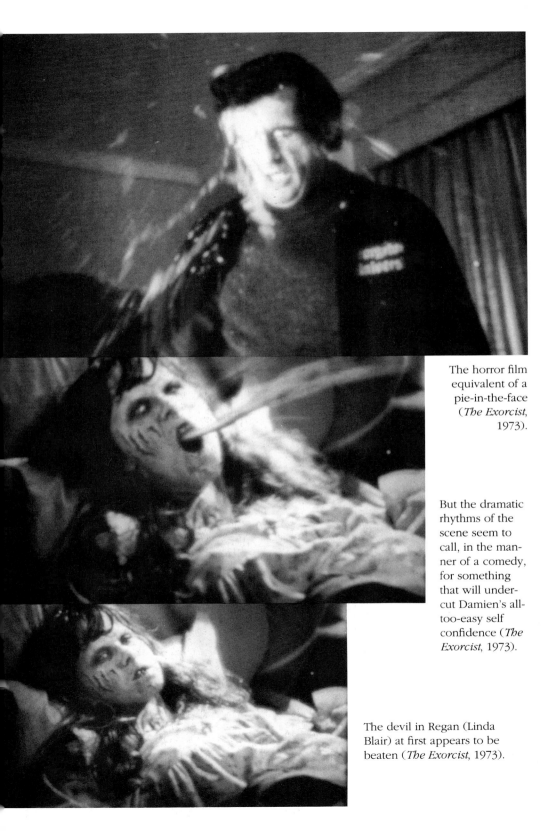

The horror film equivalent of a pie-in-the-face (*The Exorcist*, 1973).

But the dramatic rhythms of the scene seem to call, in the manner of a comedy, for something that will undercut Damien's all-too-easy self confidence (*The Exorcist*, 1973).

The devil in Regan (Linda Blair) at first appears to be beaten (*The Exorcist*, 1973).

Having beaten the devil out of Regan, the now possessed
Damien harbors newly violent feelings toward the young girl
(*The Exorcist*, 1973).

A point-of-view shot as Damien moves in on Regan: the style grants us complete identification with a character at the moment when he is drawn to and repelled by his own
murderous impulses (*The Exorcist*, 1973).

Ways of seeing: Danny (Danny Lloyd) is rendered immobile by a vision that mysteriously appears in the real world (*The Shining*, 1980).

Ways of seeing : Jack (Jack Nicholson)' *overlooks* the model of the Overlook maze: beholding a spectacular view, supervising, and not noticing (*The Shining*, 1980).

Danny caught between two images of Jack—Jack in the real world and Jack in the mirror world, an internal space that in effect can only reflect itself (*The Shining*, 1980).

Jack Nicholson's mercurial performance: an expression of genuine concern at the beginning of the scene (*The Shining*, 1980).

Jacks speaks to Danny in the overly emphatic mode that adults reserve for children: "I love you more than anything else in the *whole* world" (*The Shining*, 1980).

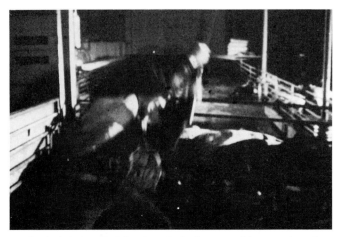

Billy (John Travolta) lands a sledgehammer blow against the pig Chris has asked him to kill (*Carrie*, 1976).

A shock cut to Chris (Nancy Allen) reacting with an erotic pleasure at the attack on the pig (*Carrie*, 1976).

Carrie (Sissy Spacek) views herself in a mirror as it breaks into shards, suggesting that Carrie's image of herself is destroyed (*Carrie*, 1976).

After saying goodnight to her mother, Carrie looks back up at the mirror (*Carrie*, 1976).

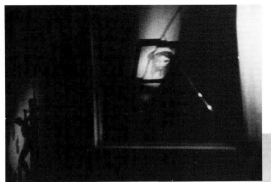

The camera pans up to the mirror magically restored, with only two cracks in it, signifying a fragmented self (*Carrie*, 1976).

Miss Collins trying to restore Carrie's self-image by itemizing her most attractive features (*Carrie,* 1976).

The zoom in on the mirror that seems intended to single out Carrie's pretty features actually ends on a close-up of Miss Collins with a distinctly troubled expression on her face (*Carrie,* 1976).

After Carrie has endured her mother's punishment, the mother (Piper Laurie) tells her to go to bed without looking at her (*Carrie*, 1976).

An echoing mise-en-scène as the good maternal figure of Miss Collins punishes her girls without looking at them (*Carrie*, 1976).

Nola (Samantha Egger) raises the curtain on her wandering womb, daring her estranged husband Frank to look and admire (*The Brood*, 1979)

Frank (Art Hindle) proves that he cannot play his part well by showing his disgust, thus ruining Dr. Raglan's plan to save Frank's daughter (*The Brood*, 1979).

Rather than rejecting what her body is doing, Nola embraces the fruit of it, biting into the placenta like an animal to give birth to her baby (*The Brood*, 1979).

The alien finally reveals himself but in the process reinscribes confusion: what appears to be the head of a penis is in fact the bottom of the alien's head (*Alien*, 1979).

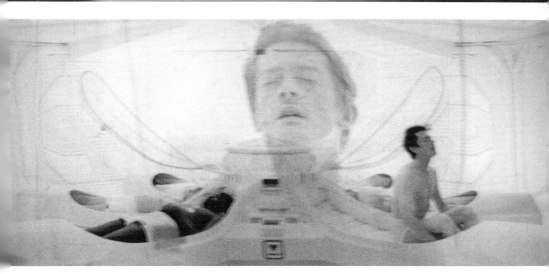

Obliterating boundaries with a dissolve: the crew of the *Nostromo* wakes up (*Alien*, 1979).

Dawn of the Dead (1979), like *Alien* and *Videodrome* (1983), begins with a character about to wake up, seemingly one of the most repeated openings for a horror film in this period.

As if inside a body, she wakes from her nightmare to a reality that is as much as a nightmare (*Dawn of the Dead*, 1979).

The necessity of an added end title to let audiences know the film was in fact over (*The Birds*, 1963)

myth. The seductiveness of the vampire, the vampire as a figure of sexual transgression, these are key attributes of the genre. Relating this transgressive aspect to my discussion of Animal Comedy, I would say the most disturbing aspect of the vampire is the extent to which he or she may challenge prevailing Western valuations of the mind and body. The vampire is an animal from Animal Comedy turned into a figure of terror. But in *Dracula*, Lucy as vampire represents another inversion. This moves beyond the specifically sexual to define why it is particularly vile for the vampire to choose a child as victim.

When the vampire hunters first see Lucy, she is holding the child to her breast, a wolf clothed in Madonna iconography. There is also something wrong with this image, which is why it is initially presented as so indistinct. Our vision is deliberately obscured because this is not something we can look at easily. As Stoker contrives to bring more light on the scene, it is the final detail of the child's fresh blood on Lucy's chin that prompts Seward to note, "We shuddered with horror." There is a deliberate culmination of details here, a mounting sense of just how terrible the terrible may be, finally enough to prompt Seward to claim he could kill Lucy "with savage delight." The truly terrible thing here is a vision of the world turned upside down: the child who should be nurtured has become prey; the maternal figure who should be nurturing is herself feasting on the child. Being sexual in itself might make Lucy an animal, but it is not sufficient to make her unnatural, which is precisely what she is here. She is unnatural because she challenges what we take to be a natural order, in which the mother nurtures and the child suckles. Feeding on the child makes her supremely monstrous.

The Birds operates within the *Dracula* tradition in that oral aggression—the birds are fearsome chiefly because of their pecking beaks—is turned against creatures who are orally dependent.[4] In this way, tales of horror from *Dracula* through *The Birds* become artistic recreations of familiar childhood nightmares dominated by images of biting animals.[5] These nightmares effectively deal with the anxiety of dependency, the fear that the subject's hunger (which creates dependency on others) also makes the subject vulnerable to the hunger of other beings. This kind of nightmare imagery generally recedes in adulthood because it belongs to a period of life in which oral concerns dominate. Yet the history of horror demonstrates that there remains a residual power in this imagery. The connection of Melanie to the children in *The Birds* points to a dependent child that continues to exist even in adults, a child who metaphorically still has oral needs and might seemingly be punished for them. Horror has traditionally played on that sense of dependency and anxiety about punishment.

Victim into Villain

Night of the Living Dead (1968)

Night of the Living Dead first appeared five years after *The Birds*, and it was strongly influenced by it. In fact, it is practically a remake and elaboration on the final third of the earlier film in which four characters find themselves trapped inside a house they have barricaded in an attempt, ultimately futile, to stave off invasion from marauding monsters on the outside.[6] In both films, the denouement is marked by an invasion into a remote but seemingly protected space: in *The Birds*, the pecking villains break through the roof to an attic bedroom, where they manage to terrorize into catatonia the childlike Melanie; in *Night of the Living Dead*, a child in the basement has turned into one of the living dead and proceeds to eat her parents. After this devotedly filial repast, she survives to join the throng of living dead outside.

The ongoing drama of both *The Birds* and *Night of the Living Dead* focuses on the tensions among the central defending group, but with differences that anticipate the striking differences in their conclusions. In *The Birds* newcomer Melanie is unabashedly welcomed by the young Cathy but greeted with hostility by Lydia (Jessica Tandy), Mitch's mother, while Mitch occupies something of an ambivalent middle-ground. By the end of the film, hostile responses have for the most part been tamed to unite these four people in a common cause. For all the uncertainty and possible bleakness of its conclusion, *The Birds* nonetheless manages to move toward the formation of a more tightly knit group in a newly constituted family.

It is precisely within the family, however, that the most threatening danger proves to be lurking in *Night of the Living Dead*. The core group here is more disparate, more at each other's throats, almost from the moment they come together; and even the family within the group, the people who seem most dedicated to their mutual dependency, display internal tensions. By the end of this film, all the members of the defending group are either dead or living dead, so there is not even the possibility of redemption here as there is in *The Birds*. There is a literal sickness at the core of both the family and society.

While the use of the child as the ultimate monster may be consonant with the unrelentingly dark tone of *Night of the Living Dead*, we might still question why specifically the child becomes emblematic of the tensions that exist within this group, why the dramatic expectations the film raises should be answered by the child as the ultimate horror. To get at this, to determine how this helpless child, sick and ailing throughout the film, how this perfect image of a victim may finally appear as the film's ultimate villain, we need to consider the way the child is shown in the film. In particular, I want to draw attention to a number of seeming gaffes in narrative logic and visual continuity that crop up around the child.

Throughout the film, the child is presented as an image of absolute dependency, someone who must be constantly cared for and fretted over by her distraught parents. Karen Cooper (Kyra Schon) is sick, although the specific nature of the sickness is not revealed to us or other members of the group until a key dramatic moment: from her first appearance in the film onward, she is lying in the cellar in a semiconscious state, where her parents Harry (Karl Hardman) and Helen (Marilyn Eastman) tend to her. Although they are frequently a source of divisiveness within the group, Harry and Helen are generally motivated by concern for their daughter. The two opposing aspects that define these characters—hostility and empathy, really—create an ambivalent perspective on them for the audience. Harry's grandstanding desire to take over, and particularly to take command away from Ben (Duane Jones), a black man whom the audience is led to regard as the most sensible character in the house, frequently makes Harry seem to be acting out of some desire to assert a shaky sense of masculinity. But much as this makes him unsympathetic, the portrait is balanced by his constant concern for his daughter.

The shifting sympathies and perspectives become the most intricate in a final confrontation between Harry and Ben. It is only at this point, close to the end of the film, that we learn the actual cause of Karen's illness: she has been bitten by one of the living dead. And it is only at this point that we are allowed to question the wisdom of keeping Karen with them as Ben suggests she might be harboring some disease from the bite. There follows a struggle between Harry and Ben for control of the gun, which leads to Ben's shooting Harry, an action that prompts an ambivalent response in the audience. We are likely to feel the need to get rid of Harry (the most argumentative and disruptive character in the group); but at the same time, this shooting represents the only instance of Ben, the most rational of the characters, losing control.

Even if we take full satisfaction in the fatal wounding of Harry, the film seeks to undercut that satisfaction somewhat by Harry's final gesture: he retreats to the cellar where he struggles to approach his daughter, solely thinking of her as he himself is dying. His emotional state at this moment is given a direct expression rare in this film: a couple of hand-held point-of-view shots (one going blurry as he looks at Karen, the other tilting back and forth as he staggers toward her) make palpable for the audience his difficulty in trying to make contact with her. He dies reaching out to her, as if still trying to comfort her. All this reasserts paternal concern as a prime motivating force and makes it difficult for the audience to hold on to the simple pleasure of just desserts.

The frenzy of responses encouraged by this scene is a setup for the final and strongest challenge the film will offer to our sympathies: when we next see dead Harry with his dying daughter, the seemingly restored-to-health Karen is kneeling over her father's body (which now has a sev-ered off stump of arm hanging from the shoulder). Karen is hungrily munching on a shank of her father's arm. The image startles because of its plot twist, but most of all it is intended to be revolting—in fact the climax of a series of gross images that showed other zombies biting into real flesh (actual meat, including entrails, for the film was supplied by a meat market).[7] The physical violation of the victim, increasingly a concern of Hollywood movies in the late 1960s,[8] had rarely been presented with such graphic vividness in earlier horror films.

Since all the actual flesh-eating in this movie helped to raise the level of grossness in the horror film, we might fairly ask (as I did with the comedies) what value this grossness has, what its underlying appeal might be. This scene (and the murder of the mother that immediately follows) represents a culmination of the film's violence, but it is violence that goes beyond the physical to an intense psychological violation. The cannibal-ism we've seen so far, already revolting, is made worse by being made familial—cannibalism conjugated by incestuous desire. To underscore the incestuous element, the film quickly brings on the return of its first mor-tality, Johnny (Russell Steiner), to reclaim his sister Barbara (Judith O'Dea), who, shocked to see him, puts up resistance that turns into an embrace as Johnny drags her off.

The grossness, then, explicitly relates to some sense of taboo, and the pleasure in horror that these events occasion derives from a desire to see the taboo broken at the same time that we feel the terror of the violation. In a book on violence in art, John Fraser has described *Night of the Living Dead* as "so refreshing a change from the normal run of beleaguered-fortress movies" because the victims are "people whom one normally doesn't expect to become victims at all, and hence a number of violences that are likely to seem eminently unnatural."[9] There is some sense in which we enjoy having our values attacked. To see why this might be true, let's look more closely at what is being violated here. The exact nature of the violation (and one of particular importance for later horror) is made evident by two striking departures from the rest of the film—one a shift in narrative logic, the other a break in visual continuity.

Much as monsters in horror movies might seem to challenge conventional behavior, they are nonetheless generally bound by fairly well-defined rules that audiences quickly learn. We know that vampires normally operate only at night, for example, while werewolves are subject to phases of the moon. Because his living dead represented a new kind of monster, director George Romero was free to devise new rules for their behavior. A new kind of monster provides a source for dramatic interest as we try to figure out the parameters of its behavior at the same time that it retains the possibility of surprising us. Romero's living dead are not entirely nontraditional, in that they seem a rough combination of zombie, werewolf, and vampire: they exist in a nether world between life and death like zombies, they devour like werewolves, and they communicate their "disease" by biting like vampires. But we can never be entirely sure precisely how much like their forebears they will behave.

Only one thing seems certain: the living dead kill their victims by eating them alive. Once this is said, however, one striking exception turns up in the course of the film. After eating her father, Karen kills her mother by stabbing her in the breast with a gardening spade. Since the mother will later, briefly, return as one of the living dead before she is quickly dispatched to eternal death by Ben's rifle, we may also conclude that the daughter has bitten her. But we see none of this. Rather, we have an elaborately edited sequence (one that stylistically replays *Psycho*'s shower murder in miniature) of the garden spade slashing again and again at the mother. Why does the film contradict one of the few rules of living dead behavior that it has managed to set up?

The simplest answer is dramatic variety. As we have already seen Karen as a nasty biter, something is needed to raise the ante, to give the scene a sense of dramatic escalation that can top the outrageous act of eating one's father. Moreover, because the audience by this point in the film believes it understands the standard operating procedure of the living dead, a sudden shift in that procedure heightens the feeling of violation. Finally, this shift lends an unexpectedly premeditated quality to the murderous action. Previously, we would have said the living dead are driven chiefly by hunger. Here, because a violent attack uniquely precedes satisfaction of the hunger, some other need must claim primary satisfaction, a need that apparently finds pleasure in the violence itself. The source of that pleasure may be found in the specific site of the attack.

When we first see daughter feasting on father, there is a powerful visual echo of the last time we saw the two of them. The edible arm is precisely the arm with which Harry had been reaching out to Karen as he died; the arm that signified compassion, concern, and parental nurturance becomes the object the child attacks. In this light, the location of the attack on the mother must seem ominously significant: Karen stabs her in the breast as if attacking what might offer her comfort. This, then, is why the film contrives the shift from biting to stabbing. Actually eating the breast would still carry a sense of violation, but it would only be a violation of degree: nursing notched up to actual cannibalism. All we could conclude from that is the girl should have been weaned quite a bit earlier, and the fault for the attack would lie with the mother. The stabbing, however, establishes that the evil exists in the child herself because she is declaring that nurturance will be taken only on her own terms. It is not the mother's to offer.

How we look at children, how we regard their own neediness, provides the foundation on which the horror of this scene builds. The fact that we generally look at children in a special way leads to the one other point of departure I mentioned above—the break in visual continuity. After consuming both her parents, Karen ascends to the first floor where Ben is trying to fend off the living dead who have begun to break through the barricade. Initially, Ben has a rifle in one hand, but as Karen tries to take a chomp from his free arm, he doesn't use the rifle to defend himself. In fact, the rifle disappears! In long shots, Ben has the rifle, but in closer shots both his hands are free to deposit Karen in a chair. When Romero cuts back to longer distance and Ben begins his retreat to the cellar, the magic of editing has returned the rifle to its rightful place in Ben's left hand. In just a minute or so, that very same rifle will be used to dispatch Karen's parents when they return to life as the living dead.

Ben doesn't hesitate to shoot the parents, but he literally loses his most powerful weapon when confronting Karen. Monsterdom ought to make all ages equal, but it is age that makes the difference here and accounts for the abrupt visual discontinuity. Even the nastiest children should be dealt with by putting them in their place (as Ben does here), not by shooting them. Ben has to "lose" his gun because the child as monster makes him impotent. The psychological boundaries being crossed here are simply too awful to take in, and yet the movie encourages us to take pleasure in contemplating them. Furthermore, the whole thrust of the sequence has been to create a desire in us to see Ben use his rifle on this evil little creature and then to frustrate that desire.

The perverse wish that the scene gives rise to is actually a consequence of the mother's confrontation with her daughter. Particularly strange is the mother's behavior on sighting Karen, with bloody mouth, over her father's body. Even though it is her daughter, a cry of horror would not be inappropriate. But the mother is peculiarly quiet, seemingly more concerned about Karen's unfortunate state than about her mangled husband (who begins to function almost as a prop in this scene). She calls out to her quietly, "Karen . . . Karen . . . , " then adds with a very sympathetic tone of voice, "Poor baby." Karen is prepubescent and hardly a baby, and in this context there is something more than a little perverse about the mother's sympathy. She herself seems to realize this when Karen starts to approach her with outstretched hands. The gesture could appear that of a dependent child reaching out for a parent, but both mother and daughter seem to understand it as threatening (possibly because it looks like something from a cheap horror movie). At this point the mother's tone changes from sympathetic to placating, and she utters one more, "Baby . . ." Although insisting this creature is still her baby, she is sufficiently wary of her now to be backing away from her approach.

The film deftly toys with its audience here by allying us with the mother in feeling the daughter's threat at the same time we are distanced from her by her imperceptive response. Individually, the living dead are pretty easy to kill, and the incommensurateness of the battle is made almost ridiculous by using a child as a villain (a problem that many of the films to be discussed later have to deal with.) There is such a grotesque difference in physical size and power between adults and children that we have to ask the question, how could we ever be afraid of the child as monster? The mother's slow backing away from the daughter who seems to be playing a Halloween ghoul builds in us a drama of frustration. It is ridiculous to be so passive, so helpless, when confronting a monster that can easily be destroyed. As in the subsequent scene with Ben, there is real frustration here, originating from our desire to see Helen bash the brains out of this little demon. Because Helen is the agent of that frustration, our anger must inevitably turn against her. By refusing to give Karen what she deserves, Helen deserves what she gets.

There is, then, peculiarly for a horror movie, a mobilization of conflicting antipathies set up in the audience—one that is conventionally felt against the monster, but also, in an anti-genre move typical of Romero, one that is unconventionally felt against a victim who has otherwise engaged audience sympathies up to this point.[10] There could be a suggestion here that all-forgiving, unquestioning mother love is more monstrous than the monster it creates. The mother is simply abdicating her *authority as parent* in trying to placate this thing she still insists is her "baby." It might be better were the mother to attack the daughter, and in this context the resultant violence would probably be as satisfying for the audience. The film posits the horror of hierarchy run amok. It is the loss of authority that is the terrible thing to contemplate.

In a world as we used to know it, a world before anyone began to talk about children's rights, parents ruled over children and children saw their proper subservience to parents. It is easy enough to see this as a natural order since parents possess so many more powers, both physical and mental, than children. And children, of course, are well aware of this difference. This is why monsters in fairy tales are inevitably adults, never children. In the adult world of the horror film, the very obvious mismatch must make any abuse of power seem more monstrous when directed toward children. While monsters in horror films, and especially in earlier horror films, occasionally appear sympathetic, they risk sympathy if they make children their prey.[11] But if all this is so, how did children, once the ultimate victims of horror fiction, become the ultimate monsters? And how did parents in turn become such defenseless victims, unable to cope with their progeny's predations?

The change is striking, and it's pervasive.[12] Just how pervasive is unwittingly pointed out by Stephen King when he nominated the three most influential novels of modern horror: *Rosemary's Baby*, *The Exorcist*, and *The Other*, all of which were made into movies.[13] Although his own work often deals with themes of child abuse and childhood trauma, both covertly and overtly, King does not intend a point about monster children with this list.[14] Nonetheless, the child as monster distinguishes all three novels. And this change extended beyond the horror film in ways of particular concern to me here. *Teen Wolf* (1985), more Animal Comedy than horror film, definitely established the connection between the two genres. Much as gross-out horror anticipated gross-out comedy, the child as monster anticipates the teenager as animal. If modern horror has asked us to think about children differently, then Animal Comedy offers a changed perspective on their older selves as well.

In noting these parallel inversions, I do not want to claim them solely as an aesthetic development any more than I see the changes of Animal

Comedy purely in aesthetic terms. The very different view of children that these films posit points to a changing cultural context worth interrogating. I am necessarily dealing with historical issues in looking at aesthetic changes because these are changes predicated on new perceptions of ourselves and our families. To answer the question of how the child-as-victim metamorphosed into the child-as-monster—a transformation I consider the central defining feature for horror films of the 1970s and 1980s— I will have to look further back than I did in tracing the roots of Animal Comedy. While gross-out horror parallels Animal Comedy in many respects, it differs in having grown out of a continuous tradition, that of horror fiction/film. In trying to determine the genesis of the child as monster, nevertheless, I will have to look at a work not generally seen as part of the horror tradition.

Postwar Malaise and the Ontogeny of Evil Children

The Bad Seed (1956) and *Village of the Damned* (1960)

The Bad Seed was a striking multimedia success in the 1950s. As germinated through best-selling novel (1954), Broadway hit play (1954), and sensationalistic Hollywood film (1956), it proved to be the seminal work for the child's rebirth as monster. Three decades later Warner Brothers recognized its centrality via a 1985 made-for-TV movie advertised as *both* the precursor and, thanks to the remake, the obvious successor to *The Exorcist* (1973) and *The Omen* (1976). This location within a horror tradition is appropriate, at least after the fact, because of what the horror film became in the 1970s, yet it is not one that is often made. Stephen King does cite *The Bad Seed* on a list of the twenty scariest movies of all time, yet he also includes such obvious nonhorror items as *Looking for Mr. Goodbar* (1977), *Midnight Express* (1978), *The Night of the Hunter* (1955), and *Deliverance* (1972).[15] The film and its sources remain unmentioned in other histories of horror, and I think it would have surprised contemporary audiences that the original merits the designation of "horror" as in "horror film," although the word cropped up in other contexts.[16]

This is not a minor question of determining genre; rather, I think the way in which *The Bad Seed* relates to horror fiction, yet stands apart from it, is of real importance for later horror films. The work challenges how we evaluate art in ways not unlike the provocations we saw with Animal Comedy, and which will be found again in the big-budget horror films produced by major studios in the 1970s and 1980s. *The Bad Seed* is really a work of exploitation art (in that it has one sensationalistic element as its primary appeal), and yet it found ways to sell itself as something more.

This is not to suggest that critics at the time didn't see something horrible in Rhoda, the murderous child of this fable. The word "horror" was used variously to describe novel, play, and film, while the word "monster" turned up with some frequency as an epithet for the murderous moppet in reviews of all three versions.[17] The horror appellation might be appropriate as a way of defining audience experience, but it did not signify the same thing as the more common 1950s use of "horror" for works that featured a creature from the black lagoon or monstrous mutations created by nuclear testing fallout. More ominously, Rhoda was a monster created by the nuclear family.

It would have been difficult for critics of the period to see any continuity between her and the giant ants in *Them!* (1954), for example, because of the seemingly different generic worlds they inhabited.[18] Mutant monsters marauded through the cheapjack world of the B movies, while monstrous Rhoda purveyed her evil in a novel the *New Yorker* appraised as "Undoubtedly one of the year's best."[19] And on Broadway she terrified audiences in a Tony award-winning play written by an author with the ambition to produce modern tragedies in blank verse. Clearly, Rhoda kept better artistic company than giant ants and black lagoon creatures.

Even though the respective authors on page and stage could be dismissive of their own work on *The Bad Seed*, their names insured a serious reception for the work.[20] For William March, who previously had attracted some attention for his realistic fiction, the move into melodrama with this novel presented an unexpected turn, but one that critics and more especially the public were willing to take with him. Similarly, melodramatic horror is an alien element in the artistically ambitious plays of Maxwell Anderson, who adapted the novel for the stage. The stature of these two writers affected the critical reception of novel and play in a particularly striking way. The work was treated seriously in its first two incarnations, even though its generic cousins at that time generally earned a great deal less respect.

Horror films of the 1950s might take place in a world that has some connection to our own, but they were also more formulaic and more overtly marked as fantasies. Their clear unreality probably played against any serious accord as achieved works of art, but they could be treated seriously as cultural artifact, subject to sociological analysis on American anxieties about "the bomb" or Communist paranoia. At first glance, *The Bad Seed* might seem to be set in a more prosaic and commonplace world, but it slowly moves in a very different direction as it seeks to reveal the meaning of its title. My concern here is not to demonstrate that the central conceit of *The Bad Seed*—that evil may be a genetically inherited trait— is equally fantastic. Let it suffice to note that a substantial number of critics reviewing the work in its various incarnations, even those who greatly admired it, were careful to point out that the genetic theory was absolute nonsense.[21] *In other words, the book/play/movie was as much a fantasy as any contemporary horror film.* And yet *The Bad Seed* could still be taken as something more than artifact, as a work dealing seriously with the nature of evil in the contemporary world.

How could critics embrace novel and play, while rejecting an idea that is foregrounded by the very title of the work and made central to its dramatic structure? This seeming contradiction is not an idle peculiarity of the work's reception in its first two forms, but is central to the issues of both novel and play because it indicates something glossed over—an acceptance of fantasy for its value in avoiding reality. Recognizing the value of the fantasy in this work is of some consequence for later works that feature child monsters. Did the identification of Satan as the source of trouble from *Rosemary's Baby* (1968) on indicate an increasing literal belief in Satan? There were some attempts to claim this (as there were claims of an increase in devil worship), but the numbers could not justify these kinds of sociological allegations. The devil simply could not count as many followers in a social movement as *The Exorcist* could count in audience. The fantasy of the "bad seed" argument in *The Bad Seed* film is as much a fantasy as the devil in the later films. Our concern here must be the value of the fantasy, what it accomplishes by deflecting our considerations of reality.

Effectively, the novel and play versions of *The Bad Seed* end up denying any source for evil, while the form in which evil is embodied offers a kind of titillation. Presumably, the "bad seed" argument could just as well be put forth using an adult who begins a series of murders (even if some validity could be claimed for the genetic argument of the work, there is no genetic reason why the murderous mayhem should begin at such an early age). But it is precisely the age of the murderess that was clearly the kick in this work, the thing that attracted audiences to it in its three incarnations. And if we view her age as an *attraction*, we should also keep in mind that audiences must find some pleasure in imagining an eight-year-old girl capable of murder. There are presumably few things more terrifying to contemplate than an eight-year-old murderess, yet we willingly contemplate such abominations.

Horror always invokes this kind of ambivalent response, showing us what we presumably don't want to see—except of course we do and are even willing to pay for the pleasure. If we can admit to enjoying a good fright, we don't have to examine the source of the pleasure any more than we have to do so with a good laugh. Screaming seems as self-explanatory as laughing. The form of expression is so much an end in itself that we don't have to examine its content. *The Bad Seed* insistently plays on our desire to see and not to see, without encouraging us to reflect on these contradictory impulses. While this is a strategy central to the horror genre,[22] *The Bad Seed* employs it in a way that was fairly unusual for 1950s horror (which is perhaps why it was seen as something different). In the past, horror was most frequently represented as something exotic, something foreign to everyday experience. The double impulse of attraction and repulsion lay precisely in the foreignness: the lure of the unknown complemented by the desire to stay within the security of the known. With *The Bad Seed* the distance of the foreign disappeared and with it a good deal of the security and comfort familiar surroundings offered as a counter.

The Bad Seed effectively brought horror home, domesticating it by locating what is most horrible *within* the family. If critics have not generally perceived it as a horror film, this is nonetheless its greatest importance for the horror genre in the 1970s and 1980s. Never before had middle-class homelife been the primary locus for horror; by the late 1970s it began to seem the only place.[23] This might be a function of the more realistic mode *The Bad Seed* employs in contrast to 1950s horror films: the work aims not to let us distance ourselves from its horror as conventional horror films did. If the monster is no longer a fantastic creation (even though the idea behind it *is* a fantasy), but rather a member of a seemingly ordinary middle-class family, then we are directly implicated in the creation of the monster. This monster could be a part of our family as well.

As much as it anticipates the family horror of the 1970s and 1980s, *The Bad Seed* at first glance must seem very different from the gross-out mode of the later films. Put simply, there is no blood and no visible violence—even though two murders take place in the course of the narrative while a third from the past is uncovered and a fourth is promised for the imminent future. Still, the basic fable embodied in novel, play, and film constituted what the Warner Brothers advertising department insistently proclaimed a "shocker," and the audience's desire for shock is at least analogous to the desire for gross-out. What is shocking in this material, the thing that both attracts and repels us, what is finally *gross* for a 1950s audience, is the figure of a predatory preadolescent.

Why should a character chiefly compounded of rage and greed have the power to disturb us? In an adult, Rhoda's behavior would probably be considered pathological, and it might even have some dramatic interest. But such behavior would also not result in a particularly unsettling villain, hardly one worthy of the name monster or "Gorgon," as a number of reviewers dubbed Rhoda. More specifically they called her a "baby Gorgon," and in that adjectival addition lies all the difference.[24] If the child is the parent of the adult, the creature from whom the adult is born, why should we be shaken to find traits in a child that would seem less startling in an adult?

All three versions of *The Bad Seed* try to shake us by pointing to the mother's suspicions that something is not quite right with her daughter. But the film version is the most effective in making the audience itself perceive the daughter as strange early in the narrative and independently of any predatory behavior. It can do this because it has the power of the image to work alongside the narrative and make us see an apparently ordinary little girl as disturbing in and of herself. One shot in particular effectively encapsulates the creepiness of this character, and, significantly, comes well before any of the narrative events that dramatize her monstrousness. We sense that Rhoda is a monster by her *nature*, because the camera can create something very odd about the way she appears to us.

As Rhoda's mother Christine (Nancy Kelly) says goodbye to her husband, who is taking a temporary but extended assignment in Washington, their upstairs neighbor Monica (Evelyn Varden), a garrulous matron with a passion for Freud and psychoanalysis, is presenting Rhoda (Patty McCormack) with a pair of rhinestone-studded sunglasses. Up to this point, Rhoda has seemed a pretty, polite, and cheerful eight-year-old. She is perhaps overly coquettish with her father (at the same time, she seems oddly unperturbed by his imminent departure for several months), but the film provides no way of placing these behaviors as negative. We simply don't know enough about the character yet. The gift of the glasses, however, does manage to provide a couple of unsettling moments.

As Rhoda tries on the glasses, director Mervyn LeRoy shoots the scene in the following manner: the camera, angled over Rhoda's left shoulder, looks at her reflection in a wall mirror as she looks at herself; over her right shoulder in the mirror appears the reflection of Monica, who stands behind looking on fondly at Rhoda. With looking and reflection the key issues of this shot, the positioning of the camera and the reflected gaze of Monica both ask us to focus on how Rhoda appears to herself in the mirror. Yet there is a disturbing break in the chain of communication here, something muddied by the presence of the dark glasses. Since we cannot see her eyes, we cannot in fact see how she is reacting to what she sees. Rhoda is a character who seems to see out of two vacant areas, black spaces that have taken over her eyes. She is blind and seeing at the same time.

Appearance is as much an issue as seeing here because there is another character watching Rhoda looking at herself. We see Monica looking fondly at Rhoda, but we also see Monica as a reflection in the mirror, a reflection looking at another reflection. Much as this image seems to interrogate its own status as reflection, Monica unwittingly turns appearance into interrogation by using a question to praise the way the sunglasses affect Rhoda's appearance. "Who," she asks, "is this glamorous Hollywood actress?" Who indeed? As written, the scene provides an answer intended to make us understand a more general motivation for Rhoda's behavior. Where we might expect a thank-you or some girlish effusiveness directed toward Monica, Rhoda's voice instead takes on a suddenly hard tone as she asks Monica for the case to go with the glasses. At this point there is a reaction shot of the recently returned Christine. The suddenly grim expression on her face keys the audience on how to respond to Rhoda's request: Rhoda is clearly asking for too much.

This is the first sign of the greed that will seem to drive all of Rhoda's murderous behavior through the rest of the film, and greed is the global explanation for what is wrong with her in the novel, the play, and at least the screenplay for the movie. But Mervyn LeRoy's direction of this scene almost ends up making the greed a side issue. In the movie, the greed is not an inner secret of her character, momentarily glimpsed, so much as one manifestation of something already deeply troubled. As the creepy appearance precedes and paves the way for the expression of greed, the way the child looks to us becomes more disquieting than any behavioral abnormality. Because this is finally just an eight-year-old wearing sunglasses, our reluctance in accepting the way this child appears in the mirror suggests the disturbance is more in us.

In my discussion of the comedies in the first half of this book, I had written of the grotesque as a combination of animal and human. As we see Rhoda in this shot, there is something commensurably grotesque about this child murderess, but the confounded categories differ. Monica's comparison to a movie star suggests what the image spells out. These rhinestone-studded glasses are simply too grown-up for an eight-year-old, but they do in fact make her face appear older. The perplexity here lies in the transportation of the eroticized glamour of a movie star to a prepubescent child. Is this innocence corrupted or corruption made innocent?

This uncertainty complements the uncertainty of seeing through blank eyes. Rhoda is grotesque because she forces a combination of opposing categories: adult and child, experienced and innocent, sighted and blind. In this combination that transcends our ordinary understanding, she must appear monstrous.[25]

As a child, Rhoda seems a strange kind of monster. She is monstrous not because she embodies a demented exaggeration of childish traits, which was the case with the zombie daughter in *Night of the Living Dead.* Rather, she threatens because she seems an adult in a child's body. Not only is she independent and self-sufficient, with defenses so strong she seems to lack any emotional vulnerability; not only does she lack traits we would normally regard as inevitable components of childhood, but she treats her parents with an indulgent and sophisticated talent for manipulation derived from an awareness of how adults expect a child to behave. At times her attitude toward her mother's ministrations is outright contemptuous, as if it were impossible for her to have any regard for a woman who is so easy to control.

Since we are generally willing to believe that children are in fact childlike, the movie *must* find a way of letting us in on Rhoda's secret. Otherwise we might be fooled by her consummate ability to play a child. Even more disturbing than her duplicity would be our inability to spot it (as none of the characters in the movie is able to do). The film plays on a certain unknowability that we must find in all children, and makes their motivational opacity an area of monstrosity. In its exposition, the film allows one moment when Rhoda reveals her hand solely to us: the camera allows us to see an expression of disgust on her face when she submits to Monica's hugs in exchange for the gifts. The shot helps explain Rhoda's motivation, pointing to a duplicity in the way she uses her childish effusiveness with adults, but, still, there is something odd here. Why should this child who so craves the material generosity of these adults be disgusted by their emotional generosity? Rhoda, in fact, displays the distaste of an adult cynic viewing the gushy behavior of adults toward children, and the object of her scorn is a garrulous old woman whom the film sets up as a target for laughs in other instances. It is peculiarly easy for us to share in her reaction toward Monica!

Rhoda's monstrous adulthood is a thematic strategy in novel, play, and film because it facilitates a critique of adult society. If we experience discomfort in seeing Rhoda as an adult, it is because her precocity serves to mock our own behavior, behavior that we would be more inclined to regard as normal in adult society. In fact, Rhoda both embodies and satirizes post–World War II consumerism, a frequent target in American art in the 1950s (here made ridiculous by its reduction to childish greediness). As a child, Rhoda can easily represent ungovernable hunger, and, as such, she is clearly a relative of her cannibalistic descendent in *Night of the Living Dead.* But the elevation of hunger into an insatiable desire for things, however, moves her into adult society. Since she comes from a comfortable middle-class home with loving parents, we have no way of finding a realistic motivation for her greed. We cannot see it as a compensating desire to make up for what is wanting in her life. Rather, it is simply something that belongs to her culture.

But here *The Bad Seed* runs into a confusion that parallels its confusions about adult and juvenile traits. If Rhoda is seemingly too adult in her frequent displays of precocious control and discipline, how can we see her as representing uncontrollable desire? Early on in the film there is a revealing conversation between Christine and Miss Fern, the headmistress of the girl's private school, over Rhoda's behavior. Christine wants to know how Rhoda is doing in school, specifically because of a problem that she and her husband have noticed: "I . . . I . . . I don't quite know how to say it, but there's a mature quality about her that's disturbing in a child, and my husband and I thought that a school like yours where you believe in, oh, discipline and the old-fashioned virtues might, well, perhaps teach her to be more of a child." The notion that an educator keen on discipline might want to teach a child to be less mature involves a strange kind of reasoning, yet Miss Fern replies as if this were all perfectly clear, "Yes, yes, I know what you mean." Both characters effectively pinpoint the monstrousness that the mirror image had revealed to us in the previous scene: this is an adult in a child's body.

The connection of education to discipline that both Christine and Miss Fern make is based on an assumption that children do not possess self-control, that they need outside restraint in order to mature. But why send Rhoda to a school known for its discipline if she is in fact always well behaved? What is disturbing about her to adults is that she seems to have taught herself self-control, that she really has no need of them. The confusion in Christine's remarks points to a confusion of desires, that she wants the child to have the qualities of children that we then seek to deny by the use of discipline. Rhoda does not provide adults with the satisfaction of offering opportunities for punishment. *The Bad Seed* frequently plays on a sense of frustration around this character because it assumes we accept punishment as a normal part of a child's upbringing, making the ungovernable governable.

Punishment, specifically the desire to inflict physical harm for the child's own good, is in fact the key issue here, as it will be for later horror films.[26] Many of these films build their dramatic impetus around a frustrated desire to see a child punished, much as we experience a sense of frustration in *Night of the Living Dead* when the mother seeks to placate her zombified daughter. I can get at how powerfully we feel this frustration when there is no punishment by looking at the problems that faced the film version of *The Bad Seed* in dealing with the self-inflicted censorship of the period. I have one other reason for looking at attempts to bring this property to the screen since it represents an early challenge to the very restrictive Production Code adhered to by the major studios. I have written that *The Bad Seed* is not exactly gross-out, yet it did represent a kind of similar transgression by daring to show what could not have been seen on the screen before, by extending the boundaries of public discourse beyond the rigid confines of screen censorship in the 1950s.[27] As such, it was a work that extended the realm of permissible public discourse in the postwar period.

The play was enough of a sensation on Broadway to garner the interest of at least three studios—20th Century-Fox, MGM, and Warner Brothers—who made inquiries to the Production Code Administration (PCA) about the possibilities of bringing this material to the screen. An MGM executive, anticipating possible objections, wrote to the PCA, "We would not for a moment consider the possibility of showing the murders on the screen."[28] Perhaps this was an issue that was necessary to raise because movies often did show things that were kept offstage in plays, generally because of differences in resources. But oddly enough, the murders were never shown in any of this work's three versions as novel, play, or film.[29] It seems to me that actually showing Rhoda in the act of murder would reveal the ludicrousness of the conceit, but this indirection in the 1950s seems more overtly motivated by the sense that there is in fact something too horrible to be shown here, something we would rather avert our eyes from. This apparent discretion will carry over into later films even when grossly detailed violence is more explicit. There are, for example, two possible murders in *The Exorcist*, but even though we are able to see the young girl herself battered and bloodied, the deaths of the two older men who are possibly her victims take place offscreen.

In spite of the various arguments the three studios put up, the PCA responded by sending the same letter to all three, categorically denying the possibility of ever making a suitable film from this play:

It seems to be especially in violation of Section 12 of the Special Regulations on crime, reading:

> "Pictures dealing with criminal activities, in which minors partic-
> ipate, shall not be approved if they incite demoralizing imitation on
> the part of youth."

> In addition to this specific objection, it seems to us that this type of
> material would be enormously dangerous as a basis for a motion picture
> to be played before mass audiences generally. The portrayal of an eight
> year old murderess with no conception whatever of right and wrong
> and who in the course of the story, would be shown successfully and
> with impunity first drowning one of her classmates and later burning a
> man to death, could hardly escape having a very powerful effect on
> impressionable children who might see it.

> Furthermore, we cannot envision any treatment of this story which
> would make it acceptable under the Code. It seems to us impossible to
> remove the pervasively evil flavor of the play, and it would be difficult
> if not impossible to think up any punishment for an eight year old mur-
> deress that would adequately counteract the obnoxious influence of the
> story on susceptible children.[30]

Initially, then, the problem seems to center on how children would respond to this film. An MGM executive tried to deal with the problem of
identification by writing the PCA, "Rhoda is obviously a monster, not a
character for whom audience sympathy is created."[31] The argument is not
exactly specious—as the film presents her Rhoda is very much an object
of hatred. But the executive does ignore how much in the past monsters
might in fact appear sympathetic to audiences. It is perhaps the context
of 1950s horror films that facilitates this claim. Giant insects inevitably rule
out the kind of empathic response that, say, Frankenstein's monster makes
possible. Perhaps only in this context might a monstrous little girl seem
solely an object of loathing.

I want to linger over this point because the extent to which we regard
the child as object does really determine what we make of her as monster.
This is precisely the kind of reasoning that affected the PCA's judgment
of the project: in some ways Rhoda was not sufficiently a monster for
them. An interoffice memo from the PCA files was fairly explicit on what
is dangerous in Rhoda:

> I think the "Bad Seed" is unacceptable on the grounds that it is subject
> matter which can do younger people in our audience harm. The iden-
> tification of youngsters with Rhoda, the eight-year-old, will be very com-
> plete. They will understand her *effective* killing of three persons who
> stood in her way, which, at the same time, since Rhoda is a poised,

charming child, they will *completely* miss her psychotic and tragic nature. To my mind, this is a very dangerous combination.[32]

Much as the work in its three incarnations insisted Rhoda did not behave like other children, there seems a real anxiety here that the film version might teach other children to behave like her. Underlying this, then, is an attitude that children are not simply dangerous but possess a power that is threatening to adults.

When the play finally won approval from the PCA and the film was released, the effect of the film on children did become something of a public policy issue. Warner Brothers had tried to forestall any censorship by creating an advertising campaign that promoted the film as for adults only, although the policy was made optional and left up to individual theaters.[33] This is to say that children might be admitted if an individual theater thought it could make money by doing so without raising much protest. The Chicago censors board made national news by closing off this option and declaring all Chicago theaters showing *The Bad Seed* off-limits for children.[34] Nevertheless (as later producers of gross-out would recognize with their insistent R ratings), banning children could work as an economic strategy in itself: at least one key industry executive saw the "adult material" this project represented as a way of attracting dwindling audiences back into theaters.[35]

The great irony of *The Bad Seed* on film, of course, was that it featured a child in a leading role but was specifically outlawed to children. No one seems to have questioned the impact of playing this part on child-actress Patty McCormack (although precisely such a concern sparked a controversy over Linda Blair's role in *The Exorcist* seventeen years later).[36] This omission is striking and throws into question, I think, any real concern about the impact of the film on children as children. Rather, with the greatest anxiety occasioned by *The Bad Seed* residing in the extent to which children in the audience might identify with the child on the screen, the issue became not so much protecting the children from what they might see as protecting the parents from what their children might become.[37]

I have mentioned punishment as the key issue in bringing *The Bad Seed* to the screen. The film had to find some way to punish Rhoda sufficient enough to reassure nervous adults and to frighten any children who managed to evade the ban. The right kind of punishment would insure good behavior by intimidation and provide a bad end for the bad seed so spectacular that even the most dull-witted child would find no good in emulating Rhoda.[38] The new ending for the film version became a means of publicity as well as an object of ridicule. It was kept secret even from the cast members and locked away in a studio vault; reviewers were exhorted not to reveal it to their readers; and an end title asked audiences for this "movie which dared to be different" to keep it to themselves. I can't document how silent audiences were, but reviewers not only revealed everything but generally derided what Hollywood had once again done to an award-winning play. In fact, the ending is not so much a betrayal of the play as the fullest realization of something inherent in it.

Both novel and play move toward a deliberately scandalous denouement topped by an ironic twist: the mother's attempted murder of her daughter and subsequent suicide followed by a coda that allows for the surprising "resurrection" of the indefatigable child. Part of the trick of the novel and play is to move the reader/viewer into the state of understanding that necessity is literally the mother of invention when it comes to murdering a daughter: the mother plans to kill the daughter in order to save her. If the mother doesn't take action, then the authorities will; so she spoils the child in order to spare her, forestalling the emotional pain of publicity and legal action. To insure a painless death, she gives her an overdose of sleeping pills. For herself, as if in unconscious recognition of her own need for punishment, she has something more painful in mind: a handgun to her head (the handgun is also a plot necessity because it conveniently alerts the neighbors to something funny going on). As a result of the big bang, the kindly busybodies are able to save poor little Rhoda even though Christine's suicide is successful.

This twist is clearly the final shocker both play and novel have to offer, as if the survival of Rhoda is something we should view with pleasurable dread. It is kept secret until the final scene when the father, absent from the entire narrative, returns home to bury his wife and reclaim his daughter. The play in particular creates an effective frisson over this surprise: as the father and the neighbors talk about poor Christine's strange behavior, the familiar sound of Rhoda playing "Au Claire de la Lune" is heard offstage before we actually know that Rhoda is still alive. Then the little monster appears onstage, ready to dupe over and over again the all-too-gullible adults.

With this ending the play and novel depart from the horror fiction of their period but oddly anticipate the lack of closure that becomes one of the striking features of gross-out horror films in the 1970s and 1980s. A film for the 1950s audience needed a more definite sense of closure, but also (thanks to the PCA) a neater moral balance sheet. In a morally tidy universe there might in fact be two issues that needed straightening out here since the mother's suicide is itself a transgression. So the film makes her botch just about everything in the name of a higher justice: not only does Rhoda survive the mother's murder attempt; Christine survives her own suicide attempt! This makes possible a scene of confession to her husband in which she acknowledges all her wrong-doing: "And—and I committed a dreadful sin—and I've got to pay in some way for that, too, I know . . ." This sounds like an obligatory Code line, assuring us that the woman awaits the appropriate punishment in the future (although this seems excessive even for the Code). Surely her own painful death is sufficient acknowledgment of her moral culpability. Given the difficulty of getting this property accepted by the PCA at all, the filmmakers might have been hedging their bets to guarantee that no stone of moral just desserts was left unturned, but under the Code a painful death for a murderess might well have been sufficient punishment. In any case, the mother's fate is perhaps better clarified by the more startling fate the film had in store for Rhoda.

Compulsively driven by greed, Rhoda returns to the scene of her original crime in order to retrieve the object for which she had committed murder. In the words of the script:

> In the far b.g., we see the little figure of Rhoda leaning over the end of the pier. Suddenly, there is the double SNAP! SNAP! of two bolts of lightning. The screen is filled with a brilliant, blinding light as they strike. The thunder is on top of us. When our eyes become adjusted to what is on the screen again, the figure of Rhoda has disappeared. Only the smashed end of the newly-rended timbers showing at the end of the pier. Rhoda's childish methodical piano notes of "Au Clair de la Lune" come mounting terrifically and then peacefully on the soundtrack. A prayer has been answered.[39]

Apparently, only total annihilation was good enough for Rhoda. The script avers "A prayer has been answered," but doesn't exactly specify *whose* prayer. It must have been a very influential supplicant because this is the only time I can recall that Hollywood required such a blatant and direct intervention of divine authority outside of Biblical epics. Yet it was precisely this "treatment" that enabled *The Bad Seed* to be brought to the screen.[40] Something else is being threatened here that needed straightening out.

One of the most striking features of *The Bad Seed* in all its incarnations is the absence of the father, a theme that will turn up in a number of later horror films which feature powerful and threatening female children. In all three versions of *The Bad Seed* we are clearly meant to feel the anguish of the mother who has to confront a very difficult situation without the aid of her man. In the novel, the husband Kenneth, who works for a shipping company, is away on business in South America. He remains absent until the last few pages, when he returns to retrieve his dead wife and still-living daughter. In adapting the novel for the stage, Maxwell Anderson made a couple of changes that carried over into the movie and helped establish the father as a stronger presence.

First, the play begins with Kenneth (who now has the more timely occupation of military man during the Cold War) as he gets ready to leave for his extended assignment in Washington to help keep the Cold War cold. Thus, he is both closer geographically to his family during its own cold war as well as tied to an organization concerned with enforcing a peaceful order on the world (even if by violent means). He hovers over the play, then, as a resource the foolish wife never turns to. Second, Christine's father (deceased in the novel) makes an appearance at a climactic moment in the play in order to reveal Christine's actual heritage and the source of the "bad seed" she carries within her. This is again someone Christine could turn to, but she chooses to keep Rhoda's rotten behavior to herself.

It is an important dramatic strategy of *The Bad Seed* in all three incarnations to arrive at a key moment when the reader/viewer has been eagerly primed to expect Christine at last to strike or punish her daughter. In all three versions, Christine always disappoints. The consequent frustration is similar to what we experience with the mother in *Night of the Living Dead*, but unlike this later, more consciously challenging work, *The Bad Seed* always insists on our allegiance with Christine.[41]

Director Mervyn LeRoy forcefully and perhaps unknowingly articulated the perversity of this by a statement he made at the time of the film's release: "It's a great love story—the greatest I ever made. . . . It's the love of a mother for a daughter she knows is a sadistic killer. It tears your heart out to see what the mother goes through when she finds out that her only child is a killer—a child she can't stop loving no matter what."[42] What is peculiar in LeRoy's description of the film as a love story is that the love is entirely one-sided, since there is never any question of what the daughter might feel for the mother. That is of no interest whatsoever. Rather, the daughter is merely an object on which the mother gets to cathect all her feelings, ranging from love to anguish to murderous impulse. Throughout, though, we are also made aware that as a mother she is necessarily incapable of dealing with something that requires more potent action. In both play and film, actress Nancy Kelly as Christine was directed to strike at her womb as she begins to realize the full horror of her daughter's monstrosity. The implication is clear: as a woman, she cannot have the full dispassionate power to act against this daughter-monster because any action against her is also an action against herself. Hence, her own suicide must accompany the attempt to murder the daughter.

Changing Kenneth's occupation to the military in the play enabled Maxwell Anderson to invoke male authority (and specifically the compromised and delicately balanced male authority of the Cold War period, which could be available to Christine if she were only weak enough to call upon it). The much-ridiculed ending of the film, then, is not so much a betrayal of the play and novel, but more a realization of something always implicit in the material. When the daddies were away, the girls did play, but at the end, God, the ultimate patriarch, makes an appearance and, boy, is he angry! The very excessiveness of the movie's determination to visit yet a second punishment on Christine—this time at the hands of the authorities—underscores this reassertion of male authority. None of the women in this movie will be allowed to get away with anything.

The film makes clear an anxiety about female power that underlies all three versions of the work. Although the source of evil is assigned to a seed, evil is specifically matrilineal here: Rhoda has inherited her evil genius from her grandmother's genes (thus, *The Rotten Egg* might have been a more appropriate title). But the granting of a seed to women plays into confusions of masculine power with female reproduction, which is precisely what makes women threatening to male authority. Christine must attack her own womb in realizing the power she has released into the world. Much as *The Bad Seed* anticipates *The Exorcist* in its vision of an evil child, it also anticipates another key work of modern horror, *Rosemary's Baby*, in its vision of female reproduction as a source of terror. Children are objects of dread and loathing because they emerge from the woman's body.

As fantastic as the genetics in *The Bad Seed* may be, the story still attempts to be grounded in a scientific explanation. Things moved more fully into the fantasy mode with *Village of the Damned*, a 1960 British film backed by MGM and successful in the United States. An adaptation of John Wyndham's science-fiction horror novel *The Midwich Cuckoos*, it proposed the possibility of an intergalactic seed invading England to produce a new race of children. Much as the overt fantasy seems to bring the film closer to the realm of the later "evil children" films, it nonetheless shares a few traits with *The Bad Seed* that would be subsequently abandoned. Most particularly, it sees the problem with children as their being too adult. The children in this film mature more quickly than normal chil-

dren, they are extremely disciplined, and they possess an uncanny ability
to read adult minds. Perhaps underlying the anxiety of too-adult children
in both films is the increasing sense in the postwar period of childhood
as distinctly separate from adult life rather than part of a continuum (as
was most evident in the advent of youth culture). Parents were losing
control not just of their children but of their ability to define the culture
these children lived in.

To allay anxiety over the loss of control, both films offer the satisfaction
of adults attempting to murder their children. As the narratives evolve,
this is a gratification that doesn't come easily since killing children is inevitably killing a part of oneself. It is perhaps for this reason that both *The
Bad Seed* and *Village of the Damned* propose that adults must sacrifice
themselves in trying to destroy the evil their children represent. But *Village
of the Damned* does go farther than *The Bad Seed* by having George
Sanders not only more successful at his own suicide but also actually
managing to destroy a whole schoolroom full of kids in his desire to make
the future safe for adults from adultlike children. The fantasy shifts the
terms somewhat from *The Bad Seed*, however, in order to mitigate guilt
over these murders. There remains the comfort that the murdered children
are not in fact our children but children from outer space, as alien to us
as the real-life teenagers then defining their own separate culture. This
sense of absolute separateness created by fantasy will pervade the later
films, where the children are more likely to best their parents. In these
films, the children turn on their violent parents and reassert their own
right to violence. Evidence of youth culture's triumph lay in the children's
greater proficiency at murder and mayhem than their parents.

Child abuse became one of the most pervasive themes of modern horror, and in such an ambivalent fashion that many of the films seem to be
offering a justification for abusing children. While it has never entered the
canon of Hollywood horror, by its creation of the evil child *The Bad Seed*
nonetheless established a number of key elements that are picked up by
later horror films. These are:

- *The equation of the child with absolute malignancy.* With this
  might come the view of the child as a repository for all that is
  negative in the culture (much as Rhoda could serve as a vehicle
  to condemn the consumerism of the postwar period). As we shall
  see, *The Exorcist* will place its young rebel in the context of the
  late 1960s student rebellions, while subsequent films will generally locate something in the nature of prepubescence or adolescence as the source of evil.

- *A disturbing combination of precociousness and regression in the child.* While *The Bad Seed* is distinctive in making Rhoda seemingly adult in her control and calculation, she is also driven by almost infantile greed. While later films (beginning with *The Exorcist*) make the childish nature of children specifically evil, there frequently remains confusion over issues of juvenile and adult behavior that surface chiefly around the problem of sexuality, with children expressing a seemingly precocious sexuality.
- *The age of the evil child is generally prepubescent or just pubescent.* The age helps to tie the monstrousness to sexuality. Make the characters a little older and you end up with *Halloween, Friday the 13th* and its clones, plus the *Nightmare on Elm Street* movies, where the theme of child abuse is specifically invoked. In shifting the age upward, I am not trying to collapse both kinds of films into one pattern. I merely want to point out the contiguity and close connection of films that at first might seem disparate.
- *A desire to see the child punished.* As we shall see, *The Bad Seed* is the one film to address this in a very direct way by moving outside its narrative, but a key dramatic strategy in most of the other films is to foment a desire in the audience to see the child physically attacked and then, in most cases, to deliver on this.
- *A dramatic strategy of slow revelation that makes us both anxious and pleased at discovering evil in children.* This plays on our fears, but importantly it is a source of pleasure as well: we gain something by acknowledging the evil in children.
- *Indirectness.* Murders are almost inevitably kept out of view, or, at the least, the direct involvement of the child is usually obfuscated. Somewhat problematical for all these films is the question of how to show a small child terrorizing a mature adult so that the result is not ludicrous. This points to a central consideration that must always be kept in mind: if we cannot make sense of the terror in purely physical terms, what psychological sense can we make of it?
- *The absent parent.* Family life is generally presented as being disrupted or disturbed in some way, with an absent parent the clearest source of difficulty. If the offending child is a girl, the absent parent is most likely to be a father, and the film is concerned with female power as a problem.

All these elements from *The Bad Seed* add up to a new way of thinking about children that came to dominate horror films of the 1970s and 1980s. A comprehensive study on children in literature noted that the "sweetly vicious protagonist [of *The Bad Seed*] is an original contribution to the literature dealing with a very specific type of menacing child, the cursed youngster who by the fact of his childhood is by definition evil."[43] This indeed remains one of the most compelling aspects of the work: this child is evil simply by virtue of being a child. Another important aspect of the work is its insistently antipsychiatric stance (with psychiatry presented as a kind of comic relief in the form of the busybody neighbor who has been analyzed by Freud and a disciple). Psychoanalysis cannot provide us with an understanding of evil, *The Bad Seed* seems to say—and not just because the neighbor is so ridiculous. In all other respects save Rhoda's pernicious character, this appears to be a perfectly happy family. These are, we are assured in a variety of ways, perfectly normal parents who are perfect in every respect. The work then runs into a problem that confronts later "evil children" films as well: how could such perfect parents possibly produce these predatory progeny?

I will deal with this question shortly, but for the moment I would like to consider why it should come up at all. The child who is evil because she is a child *is* "an original contribution," but one tied to a specific historical period. This work's success in all three incarnations as a novel, play, and film took place in the postwar years, years dominated by a marked determination to return to normal family life. Of particular concern to me here is the baby boom, the sudden surge in the birthrate that effectively celebrated both the end of the war and the end of the Depression. People now had enough disposable income to indulge in large families (much as they had disposable income to spur consumer culture). In a sense, *The Bad Seed* might be seen as the dark side of the baby boom: even though this is a one-child family, this one child would be too much for most parents. As we shall see, baby boomers as a source of disturbance will also figure in *The Exorcist*.

There is one other previously noted concern of the postwar period that surfaces here: the sense that parents were becoming overly permissive and indulgent. Concerns about juvenile delinquency were often accompanied by complaints about new child-rearing practices, parental indulgence, and specifically the perception that Dr. Spock's prescriptions against physical punishment were responsible for the increasingly undisciplined behavior of our children.[44] I have also noted some confusions about these issues in *The Bad Seed* (e.g., the mother's feeling that her daughter might become more of a child if subject to more discipline).

Both the play and film were more overt than the novel in establishing the need for punishment, by moving outside the diegesis itself to hit home a point that clearly needed hitting.

As little Rhoda goes up in a ball of smoke and "The End" appears across the screen, Mervyn LeRoy exhorts the audience to stay in their seats and see the "distinguished cast." Part of the reason for doing this was the unusual situation for Hollywood of using most of the original cast from the Broadway production. But I suspect there was a more particular reason, namely to give the audience a satisfaction the narrative of the film did not provide: after little Patty McCormack and big Nancy Kelly have taken their bows, Kelly beckons to McCormack and says, "As for you . . ." She then takes an apparently compliant McCormack across her knees and begins to spank her as McCormack playfully kicks her legs back and forth almost in pleasure, with a smile spread across her face. As bizarre as this moment might seem now, I find it even more bizarre to realize that it was repeated night after night as the curtain call for the play.[45] This is punishment as ritual, and we need ritual to assuage all the anxieties the play/film has given rise to.

The spanking functions as an end to all the frustration we have felt throughout: the assertion of parental power over the child; the final willingness of the bigger and stronger to act on their size and strength over the weak and apparently compliant. This is an acknowledgment that we all must finally reject the mother of the play and return to the proper order: the "bad seed" argument as the source of evil is made the nonsense we all ought to recognize by the simple means of a good spanking. There is, then, a pleasure in acknowledging our power over children, and it is apparently a pleasure the children share: Patty smiles and kicks her legs playfully. If this coda effectively demolishes the "bad seed" argument, it also suggests that parents have no one to blame but themselves for evil children. Children not only need physical discipline, they enjoy it. Being too good to your children is doing no good: kindness is the cause of juvenile delinquency.

That the evil in children can be controlled, at best, only through powerful adult supervision became an increasingly common view in popular culture of the 1960s, when the lack of constraint in child-rearing practices seemed to have found its apotheosis in sex, drugs, and rock 'n' roll. First published in 1954, William Golding's *Lord of the Flies* became very popular with the baby boom generation in the 1960s and was made into a film in 1963.[46] Although not specifically horror fiction, the work shares enough in common with modern horror for the videotape packaging of the 1963 film to suggest a horror film (a remake appeared in 1990, at the end of the gross-out horror cycle). In all three versions, the children serve to some degree as a metaphor for all human evil: evil is simply part of the nature of humankind, and under the right circumstances children will revert to their terrible natures. The point of this fable ought to work equally well with adults, but, as in *The Bad Seed*, the use of children has a kind of shock value because they conventionally stand for innocence. This inversion became increasingly common in the period as a response both to the apparent unruliness of America's children and the escalating violence of the Vietnam War. When *The Wild Bunch* appeared in 1969, critical opinion conjoined the two by viewing its opening sequence of children playfully burning a scorpion as revealing the violence inherent in human nature, much as the film itself was taken as a metaphorical explanation for why we were in Vietnam.[47]

Still, *Lord of the Flies* leaves open the possibility, perhaps not intentionally, that the children revert to evil ways because of the absence of adults. Adults, or at least some kind of outside authority, are still necessary as a restraining force.[48] And if adults are there and essentially good people, and the children turn out badly anyway, then evil must be laid to some other cause. This remained a problem for a number of the "evil children" films: what kind of motivation could be found for evil in children if all adults were good? *The Bad Seed* had its phony genetic argument, while *Village of the Damned* literally traveled to outer space for its solution. *Rosemary's Baby* had the genius to opt for Satan as an answer. By bringing on Satan, *Rosemary's Baby* also managed a peculiar restoration of the father (albeit a father whose fantastic existence permitted our not recognizing him as a father). With Satan as the most satisfying solution to the problem of causality, *The Exorcist* created the most disgusting of evil children and, in the process, became the most phenomenal success in horror film history.

Chapter 14 *Possession, Regression, Rebellion*

The Exorcist (1973)

It is impossible to exaggerate the phenomenon of *The Exorcist*, the film version of William Peter Blatty's sensational bestseller. People either hated it or loved it—sometimes loving it *and* hating it—and all were very vocal in their opinions. Initially embraced by the Roman Catholic church, it featured three Jesuit advisers, two of whom actually appeared in it. After the film's release an excommunication of embarrassment followed in its wake. A psychoanalyst condemned it as "a menace to the mental health of our community," and told stories of two distinguished persons driven by the film's terrors into psychotherapy where they became "seemingly much improved," although "still undergoing treatment."[1] These two were well off compared to the unfortunate six who, according to news stories from Chicago, were possibly driven insane by the film.[2] Less extreme but nonetheless bizarre behavior appeared in frequent stories of patrons fainting or vomiting during and after performances of the film.

Much as it elicited very powerful responses, *The Exorcist* served as a lightning rod for the entire culture, attracting commentary from virtually every possible source. It became a cover story in *Newsweek*, while a *Village Voice* columnist complained that it "seems to be taking steady place money to Watergate in the news."[3] Three separate books detailing its production history were published.[4] And it became a frequent subject for cartoon comment. More journalists pondered its meanings, more newspaper articles revealed secrets of its production, more clergy wrote opinions on it, just more sheer print appeared on this film than any other in the last several decades.

I am clearly writing about a cultural phenomenon as much as an individual film. But I would like to approach this phenomenon in a different way from contemporary commentary (which was necessarily more concerned about the sudden rise in sympathy for the Devil). With twenty-twenty hindsight, it is easy to find a fairly simple reason for *The Exorcist*'s importance to film history: it spawned a host of imitations, both in real life with reports of possessions and exorcisms, and in movie life, where satanic violations became box-office sensations. Demotic critical opinion thought the film a worthy work of art: it made the "Ten Best" lists of mass-market critics and even collected a slew of Academy Award nominations.[5] More elite critics generally despised it, often in a high dudgeon of offended sensibility.[6] Whatever the critics thought, however, the extraordinary box office was bound to make the film a prototype, both a model for future productions and an achievement that begged to be bettered.

Twenty-twenty hindsight also makes inescapable something understood at the time by only one reviewer, notably a reviewer with a particular interest in horror film. The review in *Cinefantastique*, a magazine specializing in fantasy film, put it boldly: "**THE EXORCIST** has done for the horror film what **2001** did for science fiction: legitimized it in the eyes of thousands who previously considered horror movies nothing more than a giggle."[7] It isn't just that no horror film ever before had qualities that could snag an Academy Award for Best Screenplay Adaptation, as *The Exorcist* did. It's hard to imagine horror films even being nominated for major categories, as *The Exorcist* was. Although the seriousness with which *The Exorcist* was greeted in some quarters is as remarkable as all the hysteria, it is even more remarkable for another reason: it is the film that really established gross-out as a mode of expression for mainstream cinema. The Devil be damned! It was the gross-out that brought audiences in.

But the acceptance of gross-out did not occur without contention, as the frequent responses of moral outrage indicate. A number of critics saw a connection between *The Exorcist* and cheapjack horror films ("[It is a] costlier cousin of those ghoulish cheapies released to drive-ins and fleapits almost weekly in major American cities"),[8] and that connection was a large part of the problem in the very ambivalent reception that greeted the film. A fair number of reviews also mentioned the budget and high production values as something to hold against the film—perhaps because these things confused traditional critical values in a way that has been an ongoing concern in this book.[9]

All the external markings said very strongly, this film is not a ghoulish cheapie.[10] In his first film since winning the Oscar for *The French Connection* (1971), William Friedkin directed an award-winning actress (Ellen Burstyn), an award-winning playwright (Jason Miller), and to insure the high level of seriousness, a tormented Bergmanian performer (Max von Sydow), who in previous screen incarnations had wrestled with God and the Devil, as well as played chess with Death. It featured a score made up of music by some of the most difficult and advanced of contemporary "serious" composers. It had a dream sequence that was surreal to the point of incomprehensibility (not a familiar strategy of simple-minded genre movies). And its screenplay bandied about a fair amount of dialogue torturing over faith and the existence of God. Complementing all this signposting of a kind of high seriousness, the ad campaign established a decorousness atypical for a horror film: no screaming faces or bloody bodies, not even a minimal indication of heart-gripping action—just a graphically elegant design, dominated by black tones, of a man's figure with black bag standing in silhouette at the foot of a stairway and large white letters against a black relief announcing the film's title.

The film had gone way over budget, making it one of the most expensive ever produced by Warner Brothers, and the studio was clearly handling it as their classiest production of the year. They had secured a New York premiere at the East Side Cinema One, the prime art-house booking in New York, which would occasionally feature exclusive runs of distinguished Hollywood product[11] (its previous booking, *Mean Streets*, straight from its showing at the New York Film Festival, was more typical of the kind of film it played). Within a week of its run, an unprecedented audience had flooded the theater—unprecedented not just in numbers but in composition: joining the large numbers of educated white middle-class adults that usually frequented the theater were large numbers of teenagers and lower-class blacks. Recognizing their mistake, Warners wanted to open the film in other theaters, but the Cinema One always had a policy of exclusivity, which the theater management immediately invoked. Warners threatened to yank the film entirely, especially since a big Broadway theater would have been a more appropriate venue for the hot film it turned out they had. Not wanting to lose the cinematic golden goose of the decade, the theater chain that owned Cinema One relented by offering Warners three of its other theaters, creating a mini–mass booking for a film that initially had been handled like art product.

I have detailed the New York booking because it best encapsulates something that was happening within the film industry and to audience taste at the time. It is possible to say that Warners had miscalculated on their booking strategy throughout the country. At the least, they also had to add a theater in Los Angeles.[12] And in general they had taken the track of exclusivity for a film that turned out to be the ultimate mass-market product.[13] Within two years, *Jaws* (1975), the next big-budget horror sensation, would open simultaneously at five hundred urban and suburban theaters. But at the time of *The Exorcist*, this kind of booking was still considered an exhibition strategy chiefly for exploitation product.

What this points to is a confusion of categories. In the past, horror films had mostly been exploitation product and had been treated accordingly.[14] Because of their big-name director, both *Psycho* (1960) and *The Birds* (1963) had offered a challenge to this kind of categorization.[15] And the big-budget *Rosemary's Baby* (1968) had helped move the horror film in the direction of respectability both by its stylistic restraint and European art director, Roman Polanski. For all that it might relate to the horror film and be of great importance to subsequent horror with its invocation of Satanism, *Rosemary's Baby* was neither graphic nor even violent; its classy status lay in its rendering of horror as a psychological experience.[16] By comparison, *The Exorcist* was insistently physical, tracing its origins as much to Grand Guignol as to Bergmanesque dramas on religious faith, with clear cinematic kinship to low-budget blasts like *A Bucket of Blood* (1959).

By Hollywood's way of measuring things, the budget alone should have moved *The Exorcist* out of the exploitation category, but this transformation was more than a matter of budget. As a film, *The Exorcist* does have an air of seriousness about it and a deliberateness of pacing that is more like an art film than standard horror, so that it does effectively conflate horror with more ambitious filmmaking. It was precisely this conflation that most upset critics. In a Sunday *New York Times* think piece on the film's success with audiences, Vincent Canby was explicit about this:

> What makes "The Exorcist" such an affront (and, I suspect, contributes to its huge popularity) is its cruelties and big-budget piety with which they are presented. . . .

"The Exorcist" is about demonic possession, which, presumably because the film has been made with the technical advice of three Roman
Catholic priests (two of whom play roles in the film), allows the movie
to exploit cruelties, and our fascination with them, in ways that would
surely have had the police (and the church) down on a more skeptical
film.[17]

Canby implicitly sees a strategy of denial at work in this film: the film is
able to pander to our basest instincts by pretending it isn't pandering. A
rhetoric of denial is in fact central to this film's method, as we shall see,
although it is not solely to facilitate transgression.

If the seriousness managed to let the film get away with the cruelties
that Canby saw, I might also say that past exploitation films managed to
exploit their cruelties by virtue of their marginality. *The Exorcist* made
cruelty respectable, as it made exploitation respectable. By the end of the
decade, the exploitation booking strategy of opening films simultaneously
in hundreds to thousands of theaters became standard industry practice.
By effectively forcing Warner Brothers to change its original exhibition
plans, *The Exorcist* was one of the films that helped establish the new
standard. These changes, which subsequently became institutionalized in
the new booking practices, forcefully signal the changes in public discourse that I wrote about in the first section of this book. Gross-out had
entered the mainstream.

I do not want to ignore the markers of respectability that made gross-
out acceptable for an audience. The film spends too much time on religious matters to dismiss them entirely, and in my opinion one of the truly
radical aspects of *The Exorcist* lies in its connecting gross-out specifically
to religion. But for now I want to move away from the religious aspects
by posing a simple question: do you look at this movie to witness the
agonies of a priest who is losing his faith or do you look at it to see him
get splattered with thick green slime spewed from the mouth of a prepubescent girl? In asking this question, I am necessarily raising the issue
of why we are attracted to gross-out at all (something I have dealt with in
the comedies). The horror films complement that discussion, accounting
for the dystopic side of the gross-out aesthetic.

Why we should be attracted to gross-out became a common question
because of *The Exorcist*. The film marked a sufficient departure from conventional taste to occasion concern over how audiences could enjoy such
disgusting material. A *New York Times* article implied this by its title: "They
Wait Hours—to Be Shocked."[18] The focus of the article was entirely on

the audience: for four days the shocked reporter stood in line at the Cinema One trying to figure out why so many people would be willing to wait so long for such a dubious experience.[19] Only toward the end of the article does she have anything to say about the film itself, and then it is to worry a bit about the graphicness of it. The shifting of concerns away from the film, which is readily dismissed, to the audience was a very common response to the film at the time.

In fact, to my knowledge, there is no film that ever attracted so much commentary on the audience itself. One can gain some sense of how extensive this was by a cartoon that appeared on the Associated Press wire service: as a couple stands at a box office to buy tickets to *The Exorcist*, the cashier tells them, "Sorry, the seats are all taken, but we're selling tickets to the lobby to watch the audience."[20] The audience had become a spectacle equal to the film. There were frequent reports of fainting, nausea, throwing up, and possibly even a heart attack or two. The *Cinefantastique* reviewer described his visit to the restroom as the "vomit spattered bathroom after the show (you couldn't get near the sink)."[21] Warner Brothers disputed most of these reports, and at least the claims of heart attacks probably were hyperbolic. But there were too many articles interviewing theater managers who reported vomiting to discount these entirely.[22] The vomiting is especially striking because vomit provides the film with one of its greatest moments of gross-out. Perhaps the audience was vomiting as much in an act of identification as it was in response to the vomit on the screen.

Rather than ignore the very apparent seriousness of the film, I would say it largely conditions the way we experience the disgust. If *The Exorcist* were in fact a comedy, a priest getting hit by flying pea soup might well provoke comments of "gross" among all the laughter, but it would seem to have nothing to do with the feeling of horror this film wants to inculcate. A sense of the disgusting was a key element in the comedies that I wrote about in the first half of this book, but now disgust seems to be moving in another direction. If disgust inevitably involves an ambivalence, a simultaneous attraction and repulsion, then the comedies play to the positive pole of disgust, the horror films to the negative.[23] In *The Exorcist* the religious framework ensures that we understand disgust in negative terms because religion assures us of the elevation of the spirit over the flesh, an attitude foreign to gross-out as celebration.

Contemporary reaction to the film focused on disgust as a way of trying to understand audience response. Another cartoon comment pointed this out. A "Peanuts" comic strip that appeared a couple of months into the run of the film had Sally Brown and Linus standing in line at a movie theater as Sally waxes dubious about what they might be seeing: "Is there a lot of throwing up in this movie? I'm not going to pay some good money just to watch some stupid actor throw up! If I want to watch someone throw up, I can watch the kid who lives next door to us . . . He has the flu!" A thoroughly sickened Linus turns to leave, "I'm going home. All your talk is making me sick." But Sally importunes, "Don't go! Maybe there won't be any throwing up . . . Maybe there'll just be killing!!"[24] The film isn't specified, but by this point in time it needn't be: *The Exorcist* had become famous for its green vomit.

The joke in the last panel lies in its ironic inversion, a surprising reduction of the significance of violent death. If Sally Brown was more open to killing than barfing, it was because the post-*Psycho* explosion of increasingly graphic violence had prepared audiences for the worst until *The Exorcist* definitively upped the ante. The apotheosis of screen violence up until that time had already come in the previous six years before *The Exorcist*, especially via the spurting blood capsules in *Bonnie and Clyde* (1967) and in Sam Peckinpah's films. Still, the violence in these films could be viewed in a socially redeeming way, as they were often open to allegorical interpretations that explained why we were in Vietnam. Cinematic killing could be acceptable because it carried with it an extra social meaning that enabled us to pretend at least that the pleasure in the spectacle was not in the bloodletting itself. The violence in these films was entirely a consequence of a violent age.

The Exorcist was something else again. If killing offered ample opportunities for exegetes, what could they make of green vomit? The *New York Times* review did in fact complain that the film was "about nothing else but what it says, demonic possession and exorcism."[25] This is to acknowledge that the spectacle of what happens to the child's body in the course of the film, the various disgusting transformations it undergoes in being possessed and then exorcised, these transformations are themselves the primary appeal of the film. Watching violent killing, we can allow ourselves to believe that our revulsion has a purpose, usually a point of view that is ultimately opposed to violence. But because the appalling transformations of the young girl's body in *The Exorcist* are presented as a spectacle in themselves, because they cannot allow interpretative meanings that could make them seem socially redeemable, they must be more revolting than mere killing.

This, of course, is precisely the point of gross-out aesthetics: a strategy of working against meaning in favor of spectacle, the ascendancy of the physical over the conceptual. The physical was certainly there in all the killing in violent movies before *The Exorcist*, but it could be justified by the conceptual. With *The Exorcist*, the physical became dominant. What makes the gory spectacle in *The Exorcist* seem gross is the fact that it's gratuitous, but gross-out actually depends on a sense of the gratuitous. One could find similar unwarranted grue in cheapjack horror movies before *The Exorcist*, but the film's high budget and apparent seriousness provided by its religious framework (i.e., the whiff of something conceptual) enabled *The Exorcist* to distance itself from its bloody ancestors.

Gratuitousness was not necessarily a conscious aim of either screenwriter William Peter Blatty or director Friedkin. There is in fact a passage in the novel, transported verbatim into the screenplay (but cut from the final film), that attempted to deal with the question of the spectacle's meaning, an explanation that could provide us with a possible rationalization. This passage seems to be pointing toward a higher motive for our looking at such gross things, a motive that finds something spiritual in all the physicality. When the exorcism finally gets under way toward the end of the narrative, the young tormented priest, Father Damien Karras, asks the old, experienced exorcist, Father Merrin, why God allows possessions to take place.

> "Then what would be the *purpose* of possession?" Karras said, frowning. "What's the point?"
>
> "Who can know?" answered Merrin. "Who can really hope to know?" He thought for a moment. And then probingly continued: "Yet I think the demon's target is not the possessed; it is us . . . the observers . . . every person in this house. And I think—I think the point is to make us despair; to reject our own humanity, Damien: to see ourselves as ultimately bestial; as ultimately vile and putrescent; without dignity; ugly; unworthy."[26]

This explanation does double duty, providing not just a purpose for the young girl's possession but also a purpose for wanting to witness it that the audience for this narrative might well offer itself. We look as a form of temptation, to see a part of ourselves that we must reject if we don't also want to reject our humanity. And our humanity is specifically defined in opposition to the "bestial."

When I wrote about Animal Comedy in the first half of this book, I noted that this comedy opposed conventional Western hierarchies by celebrating, however ambivalently, the physical over the spiritual. Father

Merrin is making the more familiar case for the spiritual over the physical, which is very forcibly condemned as "without dignity; ugly; unworthy." No doubt this is an argument a man who has chosen a celibate life must make to himself with regard to the physical, but we might at least question why the "ugly" should necessarily be attached to the "bestial." And we might further question what meaning such a distinction might have for those of us who continue to lead a life of the flesh. At the least, the conjunction of ugly and bestial would signal an enforced ambivalence toward the body, an attraction complemented by a revulsion that arises from our sense that the body is low. But since Father Merrin's explanation aligns our bodies with those of animals, he effectively authorizes our voyeurism. He offers an excuse for our taking pleasure in the spectacle of degradation as a way of reminding us that the flesh which attracts is also the repository for ugly things.

Still, Father Merrin's answer effectively begs the question since it never really acknowledges that there is something attractive in what is bestial, that we might find delight in that side of our nature that ties us to the animal world. To do so would be to acknowledge that we might in fact be positively attracted by this spectacle of grossness that the film in particular has to offer us. By its insistent and graphic presentation of its gross details, by elevating its grossness to a grand spectacle, *The Exorcist* plays on some kind of awareness, perhaps unconscious, of this attraction. After all, the film in its final form was quite willing to dispense with the spiritual explanation that provided the novel with its apparent raison d'être, and with good reason. By the time the film reaches the actual exorcism, only a priest might buy a spiritual explanation. The film has already offered too many thrills around all the awful things that could happen to this prepubescent girl's body.

But if the film foregoes a theological explanation, that does not mean we should entirely ignore the insistent recourse to religion here as an aspect of the film's appeal. After all, Regan could have been possessed by invaders from outer space (and if this were a film of the 1950s, she probably would have been). Possession by the Devil necessarily moves us into the realm of theology, yet the presentation of religion defines that theology in peculiar terms. The whole prologue in which Father Merrin (Max von Sydow) confronts some kind of devil in the deserts of Iraq would seem to establish the central theological conflict, yet the sequence is virtually unintelligible to anyone who has not read the novel.[27] Further, it establishes as central a character who then disappears from the narrative until the final twenty-eight minutes of a 121-minute film. With his return, we might say that religion has become a marker for the return of the repressed in this film. But religion itself also specifically represses here because it is chiefly allied with obfuscation; religion provides us with a means of denial, a way of not looking at what might attract us here. Religion, as the film presents it, simply stands for all that is unknowable.

Religion allows evasion of one other key question that might occur to us if we were to interrogate the purpose of possession. A good many contemporary reviewers (no doubt alerted by Warners' press releases for the film) commented on the fact that the story was based on an actual exorcism that had taken place in Pennsylvania in 1949. Most also noted that the twelve-year-old exorcisee was in real life a boy. Blatty claims he made the sex change in order to protect the person's identity, but this seems an ingenuous explanation at best. Since he happily offered specifics of time and place in interviews, he hardly provided his real-life subject such thoroughgoing anonymity. In fact, one industrious journalist was able to locate the priest who had performed the original exorcism.[28] The decision to change the boy to a girl is in fact crucial for our experience of this narrative, but in neither its literary nor filmic forms does anyone question why the Devil has specifically chosen a young girl as his intended victim. By extension, we in the audience may ignore why we should want to see this happen to a girl rather than a young boy (even though this had been the case in real life). From a religious point of view, the possession itself is the key fact, not the identity of the possessed.

It would hardly be an unusual thing in Western culture to say that a boy has a bit of the Devil in him, and we would probably say that with a degree of admiration. A girl with a bit of the Devil in her is another matter entirely. We might infer from this distinction that the specific grossness in *The Exorcist*—everything that is clearly intended to attract, excite, and disturb an audience—centers on the body of a prepubescent girl. In the course of the film this body will lose motor control, extrude foul ooze, be covered with welts and encrustation, develop yellow eyes, become contorted in impossible ways, and exhibit superhuman strength. The kind of body I am describing here is the concern of a significant group of horror films that follow in the wake of *The Exorcist*; this is a body we regard as revolting precisely because it revolts and begins to act autonomously. I will discuss these films in part five. but for now I want to consider the very specific ways in which the gross body is defined in this film in order to understand why this grossness specifically attaches itself to the body of a young girl.

The first sign of grossness, one that appears well before any of the more extreme manifestations of possession, is fairly mundane. This simple beginning is part of a shrewd dramatic strategy of escalation, setting up an ambivalence of anxiety and expectation in the audience about how far things will go. Each gross event is meant to lead to something even grosser, which we both want to see and can't possibly imagine seeing. "Astonish us!" is the call the drama prompts from us, and the film will eventually satisfy this wish in a spectacularly bloody fashion. But considering how far things will be taken, it is crucial that the film initially establish grossness in mundane terms: what is gross must be first identified as something familiar, not something we can easily distance ourselves from via fantasy like demonic possession. Put simply, the first gross act is an act we ourselves have all performed.

Toward the end of a dinner party given by Regan's mother Chris (Ellen Burstyn), Regan (Linda Blair), who had been asleep, suddenly appears in a doorway, trancelike, seemingly still asleep but with eyes wide open. After mysteriously and unemphatically telling an astronaut, "You're going to die up there," she begins to urinate on the floor.[29] While emissions of the body may conventionally have a gross quality, their grossness is necessarily tied to circumstances. Urination may serve to remind us of our physical and animal state (key traits in defining what is gross), but urination itself is not automatically a sign of grossness. A stream of urine splashing against a toilet bowl would not necessarily prompt an audience to exclaim, "Gross!" but a stream of urine splashing against an exquisite Oriental rug will, especially when we get to see it in close-up via an insert shot that Friedkin emphatically provides.

What makes the act of urination gross here is clearly its indecorum: the artful object being degraded, the inappropriate public display of a normally private act (and at a posh party yet), and the very apparent lack of control displayed by Regan. An action once involuntary that we learned to make voluntary has become involuntary again. Small children might behave this way (and we all have at some point in our lives), but a prepubescent girl should not. What we are dealing with here, then, is a kind of regression, the retreat of a girl about to enter puberty, the period in which she will become an adult, to a stage of early childhood she should have left definitively behind. "Regression" is, in fact, a particularly apt way to define many of the activities that signify Regan's "possession." Much of what she does in the film would be familiar behavior in a child, if not particularly desirable: she can't control her bladder, she says words she isn't supposed to, she spits up her food, and she sticks objects in her vagina. If the girl in *The Bad Seed* disturbs because she is too old for her years, Regan transgresses by being too young. *The Exorcist* propounds a bathroom metaphysics: Regan seems possessed because her toilet training has failed.

Since we've all had to endure the rigors of toilet training, we might reasonably question the connection of Regan's momentary lapse to a sense of evil foreboding, but the film contrives a very particular way for us to view this moment of maladroit micturition. A precise sequencing of events makes it seem more ominous and laden with meaning than it might under ordinary circumstances. Much of the first half of the film works through a series of brief scenes that either do not seem to reach their dramatic denouement or else have their specific dramatic content obscured. This is the section of the film in which the audience has to work hardest to try to make sense out of the mosaic of scenes the film presents. By the time of *The Exorcist*, this kind of pointillist narrative structure had become fairly popular, so it set the audience a task familiar from other films. I might even say that it made the task more rigorous than usual since a number of critics complained that the film was difficult to follow without knowledge of the novel.

One broad strategy in particular necessitates a certain amount of construction on the part of the audience: the establishment of a narrative line that seems to be cut off before it is fully worked out. As a result, each individual segment of narrative operates much like a suspension in music by hovering over the next segment that is introduced, thus setting up an expectation of resolution in the audience. The first instance of this is the nearly impenetrable prologue featuring Father Merrin, who then disappears for about the next hour of the film. The prologue is given too much weight both by its mysteriousness and its length not to have some consequence for the rest of the film. We can see the unfolding narrative with some assurance that this plot will require the return of this character at some point in the future. After the prologue, the film continues this method of suspension on a smaller scale by roughly alternating scenes that center on Damien (Jason Miller) with scenes that center on Chris and Regan. A few points of distant contact—Chris sees Damien in the neighborhood, Damien sees Chris making a film—place them in proximity but don't provide a clue to a future connection. At the simplest level, the alternation between the two prompts the audience to speculate how these narratives strands will eventually be woven together (but given the title of the film and a likely advance knowledge of the content, the most probable audience speculation—not difficult to arrive at—will see Chris's eventual need for Damien as a representative of the Church).

So far, then, the audience's work is child's play. But there is more going on in this alternation of scenes since the scenes often break off abruptly, often as if they had not reached a point of resolution. As a consequence, subsequent scenes operate as a temporary resolution of what precedes, forging a kind of connection by contamination well before the narrative lines actually converge.[30] I am particularly interested in this contamination because it necessarily affects the way we understand Regan's regression: the dramatic structure makes her peeing on the rug seem a dramatic climax to the previous scenes, yet they are scenes as much about Damien as they are about her. By a simple listing of the scenes that lead up to the soiling of the rug (starting about a quarter of the way into the narrative), I can get at how this alternation affects our understanding of the climactic action.

1. A goodnight scene in which Regan tells Chris she's heard rumors about Chris's romantic involvement with Burke Dennings (Jack MacGowran), the director of the film she's acting in. Regan avers it's okay with her, although her manner possibly suggests the opposite. Chris assures Regan she still loves Howard, Regan's father, even though he has gone off to London with another woman.

2. Over a nightcap of beers, Damien complains to Tom, another priest, that he is not a good son because he has left his mother alone. He also feels inadequate as a father (i.e., priest), unable to help his parishioners because he thinks he has lost his faith.

3. A telephone scene in which an exasperated Chris tries to reach Regan's father in London because he seems to have forgotten his daughter's birthday. As her anger increases and her language becomes more foul because she cannot get through to him, the camera tracks back to reveal Regan overhearing this conversation down the hall and out of her mother's sight.

4. Chris is awakened at very early morning with script changes for the day's shooting. As she gets up, the camera pulls back to reveal that Regan has been sleeping beside her, something Chris did not know. Regan complains, "My bed was shaking. I can't get to sleep." Mysterious noises from overhead draw Chris up to the attic to explore. No source is located.

5. A priest walks into his church to discover that a statue of the Virgin Mary has been defaced with the addition of blood red breasts and a blood red phallus.

6. Damien visits his mother (Vasiliki Maliaros) in the mental ward of a hospital where she has been taken because of an edema which

"affected her brain." Damien's uncle (Titos Vandis) tells him, "You know, it's funny. If you wasn't a priest, you'd be famous psychiatrist now, Park Avenue. Your mother, she'd be living in a penthouse instead of here." As if this didn't offer occasion enough for guilt, the mother, on seeing Damien, has only one thing to say: "Dimmy, why did you do this to me, Dimmy? Why?"

7. Damien uses a punching bag to work out his frustrations over not having enough money to send his mother to a better hospital.

8. Chris's party, which will end with Regan's urination. The party is seen through a series of brief vignettes. Chris asks a priest (Rev. William O'Malley, S.J.) about another priest, one she frequently sees in the neighborhood. He is identified as Damien Karras, whose mother passed away the previous night. Burke Dennings, the man Regan thinks her mother is involved with, becomes increasingly drunk and increasingly loud and abusive with Chris's butler. He finally has to be sent home in a near stupor. The priest who told Chris about Damien plays the piano and talks about becoming a headliner in heaven. At this point, Regan appears in her trancelike state. Strikingly, we see her in a way that invokes the scene where her mother was trying to reach the absent father in London and the subsequent scene that showed Regan in bed with her mother: the camera slowly moves back from the priest and partygoers at the piano to reveal Regan entering the room initially unnoticed by them.

Throughout this outlined sequence there is clearly a thematic element about parents and children: Chris's relationship with Regan is contrasted with Damien's relationship with his mother, and with both there is a concern about distance and absence. The first two scenes are specifically about a child's connection to the mother, and each involves some anxiety over losing that connection. Regan is suspicious of her mother's involvement with Burke, a man who already limits Chris's time with Regan since she works for him. This possible anticipation of loss because of work finds an echo in Damien's complaint that his involvement in the Mother Church (his work) keeps him from his actual mother.

The scene centered on Damien provides a transition from mother to father that will lead back to Regan and Chris. When Damien notes that he cannot be a good father because he has lost his faith, he says in effect he has lost contact with his heavenly father. His biological father is equally absent in the movie and is never mentioned. At the time of the film's release, Jason Miller took note of this fact and related it to his character's religious agony: "Although we call it Mother Church, to Karras it's Father Church. Most of the older Jesuits he talked to when he said, 'I've lost my faith,' he's really giving confession to his father. You'll notice that there's a complete absence or no mention of his father—not even a picture."[31]

As Miller's remarks suggest, the film points to a parallel between the loss of father and the loss of faith. This is something the sequencing of events encourages us to consider since Damien's declaration is immediately followed by a straight cut to a shot of Chris on the phone trying to make contact with Regan's father. This more mundane father remains an invisible presence throughout the film, much like God himself. Damien's loss of faith, then, is paired with Regan's loss of her father. Scenes 3 and 4 detail the emotional meaning of the loss for Regan, ending with a seemingly compensatory attempt to draw even closer to the mother. Her disturbed sleep, which we necessarily see as a consequence of the father's absence, leads her to her mother's bed.

The fifth scene offers the one real break in the pattern of comparing Damien's family constellation with Regan's. But it does connect thematically to these other scenes about mothers and fathers since it takes an iconographic mother figure and turns her into a father by granting her a phallus. The resulting icon is sacrilegious, of course, but the form of the sacrilege is of consequence here: one of the key figures for the Church representing chastity and purity becomes aggressively sexual, and in a particularly disturbing way. The resulting figure is not simply male: it is also given overly emphatic breasts, seemingly tipped with blood. This finally becomes a complete inversion of what Mary conventionally stands for. She is no longer the asexual mother, the figure who enables us to reject our animal side, who renders what we have most in common with animals—our most animal physical activity—into something spiritual. Rather, the desecrated statue transforms her into the ultimate figure of transgression, with all the boundaries of Western tradition forcefully erased: spiritual and physical, male and female, are now all combined into one. Mary has become the ultimate vision of the grotesque.

Scene 5 is anomalous to the extent that it breaks into the developing family dramas that structure the sequence, yet in watching any drama we inevitably seek to regulate such anomalies by finding causal connections.[32] The film prompts us to think that the defacement of the statue grows out of the family dramas. We are prepared for this by the reports of Regan's shaking bed and the subsequent mysterious sounds emanating from the attic, which seem to follow directly from the abandonment of the father. Much as the film segues from a realistic presentation of a child's anguish over an uncaring parent into fantasy, the fantastic occurrences seem to be an outgrowth of the child's feelings. At the least, the film allows us to link the child's pain and the disfigurement of the Virgin Mary. Further, if we see that a parallel has been established between Regan and Damien, the priest himself becomes implicated in the sacrilege. The film supports this with a subsequent narrative development: when police detective Lt. Kinderman (Lee J. Cobb) first visits Damien to make inquiries about the death of Dennings and the concurrent disfigurement of the statue, he supposes it might be the work of a crazed priest (and there is a whisper of suggestion here that Damien could be that priest).

If we see some connection between Regan, Damien, and the Virgin Mary, we may still question why events in the lives of a prepubescent girl and a tormented priest should lead to this sacrilege against the icon. Placement of this shot of the statue in the outlined sequence determines how we answer this. There has been a steady increase in dramatic tension throughout the sequence. The first two scenes are naturalistic and understated to the point that the audience has to strain a bit to understand all the dialogue. The dramatic tension increases with Chris's outburst against Regan's father in the third scene, although the naturalistic style continues. Then, in the fourth scene, the naturalism gives way a bit with the mysterious knockings that lead to the extended suspense sequence exploring the attic. Scene 4 ends with a jump-out-of-your-seat shock that possibly signals a move into fantasy: with no apparent explanation, the candle that Chris has been holding to light her way suddenly flares up and goes out.

At the center of a rising curve, the appearance of the statue seems to operate as a turning point, moving events into a more explicit and intensified direction. In scene 2 Damien had only worried about leaving his mother alone, but in scene 6 both she and his uncle now directly attack him for his abandonment, leading directly to the brief shot of him boxing—and once again we are left to make the causal connection without aid of dialogue.[33] Clearly Damien is working out emotions pent up from the previous scene in which he was attacked from all sides. His response is to strike back as well, but against an inanimate object. This signals rage, but a rage that cannot be vented against its actual object, his mother. Thus, even if we cannot articulate it directly, the context necessarily makes us feel the disfigurement of the statue as an expression of rage against the mother, a figure made grotesque by its aggressively protruding body parts.

As the culmination of all this, Regan's defilement of the rug must seem an expression of rage. The party scene itself encapsulates the dramatic escalation of the sequence as Dennings, Regan's possible rival, becomes

progressively drunker and more hostile, finally erupting in an open physical attack on Chris's butler. And when Regan appears here, she continues
the notion of striking back by predicting the death of a man we may have
trouble identifying (but someone paternal-looking and clearly old enough
to be her father). Furthermore, the repeated camera movement that reveals Regan's presence echoes the two earlier scenes where the camera
has served literally to foreground the emotional meaning of the absent
father for Regan. Finally, as with Damien, despair caused by the absent
father seems to lead to an attack against the mother as indirectly expressed
against an inanimate object: for Damien, his punching bag; for Regan, her
mother's carpet.

The unexpected pairing of a prepubescent girl and a tortured priest
establishes a parallel between this young girl on the verge of sexuality
and a man who has forsaken his own sexuality. Damien's boxing could
make him seem aggressively masculine (in the sense of turning this twentieth-century Jesuit into a nineteenth-century American Protestant's fantasy of the fighting Jesus, both tough and tender at the same time), but
the scene that proceeds his violent assault against the punching bag emphasizes his sense of impotence as both father and son. Boxing is compensatory, a way for Damien to reassert a masculinity that is constantly
denied. The only other time in the movie that Damien flaunts his pugilistic
skills, we shall see, is also an expression of helplessness. He inhabits a
world that seems to undermine masculine strength.

Like the defiled statue, both Damien and Regan are liminal characters.
Damien is secular and religious, a trained psychiatrist and a priest, powerful and impotent, capable of masculine aggression and female compassion. The sense of regression in Regan's character helps make her seem
equally liminal: on the verge of adult sexuality she remains a child as well.
She is both sexual and presexual. But much as she regresses, she does so
in a way that transgresses: she pees standing up. On the verge of sexuality,
she regresses with an aggressive presentation of herself in masculine
terms. Much of the way we understand this has to do with conventional
understanding of sexual roles, which makes the Devil in a girl seem a
presumption to masculine prerogative.

As the Devil enters this seemingly innocent girl, Regan becomes more
male in at least two regards: her voice changes, shifting down to an aggressive and growling bass, and she develops physical powers more appropriate to an adult male.[34] But as she becomes more male, she also
becomes increasingly liminal, crossing categories and confounding any
understanding of gender lines. In one instance she uses her masculine

power to further the kind of transgression of sexual categories initially invoked here: at her most possessed she uses sheer muscle to push her mother down toward her crotch in an attempt to force Chris to perform cunnilingus on her. This is the grossest inversion the film can muster, an attempt by the child to suckle the mother, rather than the mother the child, and in an overtly sexual manner. The possessed Regan is dangerous because she operates without any sense of boundaries.

This perverse expression of Regan's sexuality invokes regression because it suggests the polymorphous perversity of childhood, both attractive in its sense of liberation but repellent in its refusal to recognize boundaries that are set by the time we reach adulthood. To recognize any of this is to recognize infantile sexuality, something we generally tend to repress in favor of viewing childhood as a time of "innocence." Of course, depending on how progressive and Freudian we want to be, we might consider the possibility of an innocent sexuality in childhood, but the film hardly allows us to view things in this light since the sexual expression in it is generally made into something disgusting. The emphasis in the film is more on the perversity than the polymorphousness: this is a horror film simply because we are meant to be horrified by such occurrences.

The forced cunnilingus is a clear enough example of something we are meant to look at in repelled fascination, something we want both to watch and turn away from at the same time. Even more extreme, and more revelatory, is the action that immediately precedes this, the most notorious of the film's events and the one that attracted the greatest comment when the film came out: Regan's inventive play with a crucifix. According to theater managers and contemporary observers, this scene caused the most physical reactions (swoons, fainting, and vomiting), with a couple of people noting that men reacted more violently than women.[35]

I have intentionally left my description of the action in this scene imprecise because there was real disagreement among contemporary viewers over what exactly was going on here, whether Regan was masturbating with the crucifix or mutilating herself. The novel is completely unambiguous about this:

> Then abruptly the demonic face once more possessed her, now filled her, the room choking suddenly with a stench in the nostrils, with an icy cold that seeped from the walls as the rappings ended and Regan's piercing cry of terror turned to a guttural, yelping laugh of malevolent spite and rage triumphant while she thrust down the crucifix into her vagina and began to masturbate ferociously, roaring in that deep, coarse,

deafening voice, "Now you're *mine*, now you're *mine*, you stinking cow! You bitch! Let Jesus *fuck* you, *fuck* you!" Chris stood rooted to the ground in horror, frozen, her hands pressing tight against her cheeks as again the demonic, loud laugh cackled joyously, as Regan's vagina gushed blood onto sheets with her hymen, the tissues ripped. (p. 190)

There is blood in the novel, but it is chiefly a consequence of the sexual activity, occasioned by the torn hymen. The film also brings together crucifix, vagina, and blood, but the sexual connotation is at the very least undercut by the violence of the presentation. Blood dominates the film.

In the film, Chris is dramatically summoned to her daughter's room by antiphonal voices, a young girl's cries for help played against growling, guttural curses, "No! Please don't!" alternating with "You bitch!" Although Chris is responding to Regan's calls, and Regan is in her usual place in bed, Chris seems to have trouble locating her at first. Two point-of-view shots sandwiched between reaction shots show us what Chris sees: objects flying wildly about the room. Layered into one of the reaction shots, a voice-over of the possessed Regan seems to enable Chris to find her daughter: "Let Jesus . . . [the voice growls; the sentence is overlapped to the next shot, an insert shot of Regan's already bloodied hand aloft and tightly clutching a crucifix as it begins a downward thrust] . . . fuck you." As the hand descends, there is an abrupt cut to another insert shot, a close-up of Regan's crotch partially covered by a blood-drenched nightshirt as the hand enters the frame and jabs at the vagina with the crucifix. It is only after this shot that we finally see Regan's face in an overhead medium shot as she holds the crucifix directly in front of her face and repeats in her newly deepened voice, "Let Jesus fuck you!" The emphasis is clearly on sensation: through the insert shots and the cut on the thrusting action, the style abstracts the actual girl and highlights the violence, giving us both the thrill and the shock of all the taboos that are being violated here.[36]

Perhaps critics who described this as "masturbation" did so because they had read the book, but I doubt if anyone would be inclined to say Regan is playing with herself here. "Self-abuse" in its most literal meaning would be more like it, with the instrument of punishment—the crucifix—itself a symbol of punishment. "Let Jesus fuck you!" makes the action seem sexual, but if there is sexuality here, it is of a purely masochistic variety. As the already bloodied thighs suggest, sexual desire is wounding desire. If reports that men reacted more strongly against this scene than women were accurate, it is probably because the resulting imagery suggests castration, a lacerating punishment invoked by the onset of sexual feeling.

By extension, the girl's sexual organs are themselves an object of terror because they explicitly suggest a wound. Sexuality is itself a kind of punishment.

Mixed in with these conflicted sexual desires is the sacrilegious element of the crucifix and Regan's exhortation to Jesus. The crucifix had possibly been placed in Regan's bed to protect her from Satan, so the force of the sacrilege in making it a symbol of self-abuse lies in the apparent inversion of Jesus as the good shepherd.[37] The cross which signifies Jesus becomes an instrument of the Devil, but the film also suggests a perverse way in which its application here maintains a connection to the Church. If the Church stands for the triumph of spirit over flesh, and if Jesus Himself embodies chastity, it is a logical extension to make the crucifix an instrument of self-mutilation by a form of sexual activity that denies sexuality. Self-abuse might be the work of the Devil, but Christ's crucifix is the instrument by which the girl's sexuality is denied. The Church embraces this denial in its valorizing virginity, while the Devil ought to be allied with the girl's sexuality, but cosmology becomes irrevocably confused in this scene. Sexual arousal leads as surely to sexual punishment and images of castration here as we saw occur in *Porky's*. The important difference (perhaps because this is a horror film) is that sexual arousal is in itself never seen as something positive. It only has the power to punish.

A punitive spirit dominates *The Exorcist*, and it is set up in a commonplace and unobtrusive way early on in the film. In their first scene together, Regan tells Chris about seeing a horse and wanting one of her own. The horse is specifically identified as a gelding, which must seem a piece of loaded information in light of the later castration imagery. Regan pleads in a slightly whiny way for a horse, which Chris indicates probably won't be possible. At this point Regan gives in to another hunger and steals a cookie from a cookie jar. Chris runs after her into a darkened hallway, wrestles her to the ground, and tries to takes away the cookie, saying, "You'll be sorry!" All this might seem incidental, a way of defining a charming give-and-take between mother and daughter. But as they wrestle, the camera, viewing the activity at a fair distance, mysteriously tracks in on Chris and Regan. The movement seems mysterious because it has no specific functional motivation, neither bringing us significantly closer to the action nor revealing an unseen object or character to us. As if to compound the stylistic mystery, a shock cut to a subway train speeding toward the camera interrupts the movement and leaves the action unresolved.

Chris's final utterance in this scene is right to the extent that Regan certainly has a lot to be sorry for as the film unfolds, but can we possibly take the rest of this narrative as a punishment for the theft of a cookie? That must seem extreme, yet the unexplained camera movement, the shadowy lighting, and the shock cut to the hurtling subway endow the scene of wrestling with an ominous quality. It is as if we are meant to register some meaning, however uncertain, that goes beyond anything apparent from the events themselves. Precisely because we cannot identify that meaning, this perfectly ordinary occurrence becomes somewhat creepy, literally so if we choose to be literal about the camera movement.

I have wanted to look at this one brief moment closely merely to suggest that the film sets up an atmosphere in which punishment is anticipated. One of the contemporary reviewers did in fact see the possession as a punishment for Regan's daring to play with the Ouija board.[38] This seems about as far-fetched an explanatory motivation as the cookie theft, yet I don't want to dismiss it entirely because I think the film creates an atmosphere that allows such speculation. Wrestling her to the ground is fun, with both mother and child giggling through this activity much as mother and child laugh through the spanking at the end of *The Bad Seed*. There is pleasure in seeing Regan put down and controlled, pleasure in seeing impulse repressed and hunger punished. Eventually, Regan will become a literal object of loathing and dread that must be tied down and punished. Initially, then, and for the most part, we are encouraged to take pleasure in the punishments inflicted against Regan, and this (more than anything sacrilegious) is probably responsible for the vehement responses to the film. The film makes a powerful case for the value of child abuse.

The clearest evidence for this may be found in a scene that attracted much comment at the time, the arteriogram performed on Regan to discover if she has a lesion in the brain. This is a straightforward piece of medical pornography, with needles-in-the-neck and spurting blood all shown in gruesome close-up. Audiences at the time found the scene repellent, and rightly so, yet it is also one of the film's featured attractions, almost like a song-and-dance number in a musical. If we are revolted here, it is because of the invasive procedures being worked on this young girl's body; yet as the insistently close-up style of the film makes clear at this point, we are also drawn to looking at it, taking some pleasure in seeing this invasion. The revulsion operates as a safe cover for the fascination, a reassurance that we don't want to look at precisely that which keeps our eyes riveted in place.

Strikingly, this is the one disgusting thing in the film that operates outside the fantastic realm: it is very much something we could see in reality, and the film attempts to provide the audience with as realistic a presentation of the medical procedure as possible. What is less realistic lies in the narrative's inability to work out any kind of believable motivation for why the procedure should be required in the first place. The pointilillistic narrative structure allows a striking omission in the presentation of Regan's possession. Up to the point when she has to undergo the grisly medical procedure, the worst things Regan has done is pee on the floor, spit at a doctor, and say a few obscene words. In fact, the movie is extremely elliptical about the onset of her illness.

In most of her early scenes, she seems a perfectly normal twelve-year-old, unhappy about the decampment of her father but otherwise well-adjusted. After she pees on the floor, her mother is suddenly talking about Regan's nerves and what the doctors said, even though we have seen no evidence of doctors.[39] In this context, the arteriogram must seem an excessive response, and that's precisely the point. The scene reinforces the punitive aspect of the film in the most excessive way: even minor infractions warrant major castigation. Well before Regan's body has been invaded by a foreign spirit, it is subject to an extremely invasive medical procedure.

Much like *The Bad Seed*, the narrative of *The Exorcist* is contrived to prompt our desire to see Regan punished, but it delivers on this desire in more spectacular fashion and within the diegesis. After a pause in the exorcism, Damien returns to Regan's bedroom to discover that his senior coexorcist, Father Merrin, has had a heart attack and died. Damien's futile attempt to revive him elicits sarcastic laughter from the demonized Regan. Although Damien has been characterized by a measured and controlled response to events throughout the movie, the death of Merrin is finally too much even for him. In retaliation for the death, Damien flings himself toward Regan, knocks her to the floor, and begins pummeling her. The moment doesn't make any narrative sense because up to this point the demonized Regan has been endowed with superhuman strength. This strength apparently abandons her, however, when finally confronted with a muscular male who seeks not a feminized compassionate cure, but rather the emotional satisfaction of a good battering.[40] The audience cheers.[41]

This is a startling moment, and not just because it contradicts the film's narrative logic. Forget about the whole theological framework for a few moments and contemplate what we are to make of a movie that offers us the satisfaction of a grown man (in fact a trained boxer) landing a punch square in the face of a twelve-year-old girl. The film *does* become oddly discreet at this moment—Karras's back more or less blocks the action from our direct view—but this is perhaps to block the ludicrous inequality of the physical stature, to maintain the illusion of Regan's power or perhaps even make us forget about it. This blocking also prevents us from seeing Damien's face, so that we may fill in with our own satisfied response while maintaining the purity of Damien's motivation. But if Damien operates in part as the agent of our desire, then blocking a view of his face at this moment effectively keeps our own motivation at a distance. We only see Damien's face again when he realizes in horror exactly what he is doing to this little girl. This is to say, we see it when we can return to an expression of empathy, but only after we have registered the pleasure of the beating. This is guiltless sadism: we are granted both the satisfaction of violence and the satisfaction of regret.

The violation of narrative logic necessitated by Damien's violation of the girl led to much uncertainty about the film's ending among contemporary viewers. People variously saw evil triumphant or, conversely, the reassertion of good in Damien's ultimate self-sacrifice after he realizes the horror of his actions. Reports even circulated that Blatty and Friedkin were going to film a new ending that would make the triumph of good clear.[42] Things are simpler in the novel where there is no beating: out of pity for the girl, Damien calls for the demon to enter him, whereupon he hurls himself out the window. In the movie, he calls for the Devil to enter him as he strikes Regan. When the Devil complies, something very odd happens: Damien possessed by the Devil again wants to attack Regan, which is precisely what Damien had been doing when not possessed. What's the difference?

One clear difference is the way in which this latter sequence is shot. This time we get close up to the action, seeing it from a striking point-of-view shot in which the possessed Damien's hands move toward Regan's throat. Damien wrestles with the Devil inside him to pull away from the girl, but only by destroying himself. Our identification with him when he tries to attack her is complemented by a series of point-of-view shots when he leaps through window. The style grants us complete identification with a character at the moment when he is drawn to and repelled by his own murderous impulses. For once in the film, the camera explicitly acknowledges a conflict in the audience: the desire to see the child brutalized, the wish to pull back from that desire.

Wherein lies that desire? I have already suggested some psychological grounding for this in the way the film approaches sexuality, an anxiety about gender definition as well as a generalized disgust about carnal desire. But the film points to a social dimension as well, one that would be particularly resonant for an audience at the time. Chris is an actress, currently living in Georgetown because she is making a movie she tartly describes as "the Walt Disney version of the Ho Chi Mihn story." Shortly after Chris's first appearance in the main narrative, we see a brief scene of her being filmed for a scene of student protest on the Georgetown campus. This is a craftily constructed sequence because it begins with two questions that effectively prime the audience to consider its significance. As director Burke Dennings sets up a shot, a man, apparently a producer (played by William Peter Blatty, the actual producer as well as the screenwriter of *The Exorcist*), asks pleadingly, "Is the scene really essential, Burke? Would you just consider it, whether or not we could do without it?" Not even attempting an answer, and acting as if he weren't even listening, Burke walks over to his star Chris, who has been calling him. She also has a question: "Well, why are they tearing the building down?"

The first question serves as a way of alerting the audience to the significance of this scene. In one respect, producer Blatty is right: the actual scene is not "essential" because it contains no information to forward the narrative of the film that *we* are watching. It may be significant in that it is the one time in the film we see Chris plying her profession, but that significance would in turn depend upon how important we think Chris's acting is for this tale of possession. It is also the scene that introduces Father Karras, who is among a crowd of onlookers. We first see him in a reaction shot laughing in appreciation as Burke Dennings provides the answer to Chris's question about student motivation.

The answer to Blatty's initial question about the necessity of this scene, then, lies in Chris's question and Dennings's subsequent answer. If producer Blatty thinks the scene could be cut, screenwriter Blatty (who has invented the protesting students) knows the scene is necessary as a way of guiding us to an understanding of behavioral motivation. Should we even think about the film within the film? Should we consider what we are to make of protesting students who want to tear down a building? We should because Blatty's question leads to Chris's question which in turns leads to more questions. Dennings answers Chris by asking, "Shall we summon the writer? He's in Paris, I believe." Chris comes up with yet another question, "Hiding?" The implication to all these questions is that there are no answers, just as there seem to be no clearly understood reasons for the student behavior.

In deflecting any possible answer, the scene was not at all ambiguous for a contemporary audience. Rather, it provided a very definite way of looking at the students within the film. Dennings can only answer Chris with a question because there is no motivation for these students. They might threaten to tear down a building, but for no good reason. They are demonstrating merely to demonstrate, much as they are taking power for the sake of showing their power. This was not an uncommon perception of student revolts of the time, which saw students acting up to no good purpose, as if students were necessarily driven more by passion than intellect. If you take away any meaningful content to the protest, the protest is effectively diminished to the level of student prank, but rendered malignant because it is far more destructive. All this is presented in the context of acting, which further undercuts any meaningfulness to the activity. Not coincidentally, the possessed Regan will show an uncanny acting talent, capable of very precise impersonations of other characters in the film. The demonstration demonstrates the ascension of children to power, and, like Regan's body, the students are revolting precisely because they revolt. In their attempt to display their own power, they establish themselves as objects of revulsion, something that must be squelched. They act like children who have not learned to restrain themselves.

This brief invocation of the student demonstrations of the late 1960s and early 1970s points to a possible explanation for the shift from the horror of an overly grown-up child in *The Bad Seed* to the terror of the child who regresses in *The Exorcist*. As a work of the period right after World War II, *The Bad Seed* features the arrival of the nuclear family with a vengeance. If a return to normalcy was defined at the time in part by a return to conventional roles for women as wife and mother, then the novel/play/film works on two anxieties associated with that role. The first is simply the terrible aloneness of the woman in the family who discovers that she must rely solely on her own resources to try to work out the problems of her peculiar progeny. Second is the terrible child herself who is most terrible because she apparently has no need of a mother. By the time of *The Exorcist*, the mother may now be a working woman. Furthermore, she's a working mom who finds she has to devote more and more of herself to the needs of her child.[43] After the scene of the revolting students, we learn nothing more about Chris's work. The terror of the regressing child is that she completely takes over her mother's life.

A psychiatrist writing in *Saturday Review* implicitly raised a connection between revolting students and Regan by regarding the film as the product of an age of permissiveness.[44] Given the film's generally harsh treatment of Regan, it might seem especially odd that anyone could condemn the film for letting her get away with murder, yet this one viewer at least felt

she hadn't been punished enough. Such an attitude might be a consequence of the film's generally punitive attitude, but I want to consider
here that it might suggest another dimension to the film that my discussion
has overlooked, a dimension important for any work of gross-out. I have
stressed throughout this book that gross-out always implies an ambivalence because it is founded on an attraction to that which repulses, or
more precisely it inverts normal values to acknowledge an attraction in
revulsion. So far in my discussion of *The Exorcist* I seem to have found
more revulsion in the film than attraction, or at least a revulsion that does
not openly admit to attraction.

In a number of fantasy sequences, however, the ambivalence of gross-
out moves in another direction, one that actually allies us with Regan. The
potential for this alliance, more than anything else, must be what disturbed
the psychiatrist who felt Regan had not been punished enough. This is
set up in a naturalistic way on her first visit to the doctor when she receives
a injection. To fight off the needle, she spits in the doctor's face, a foreshadowing of her more luxurious expectoration later in the film. Even if
we think the response is overstated because the narrative has not sufficiently prepared us for the doctor's visit, we can understand the motivation for Regan's behavior as we will not be able to when she becomes
"possessed." For this reason, this scene at least grants a potential for allying ourselves with her, while the generally punitive quality of the film
often moves in the other direction.

If we can find any kind of alliance with Regan, we can also start to see
some of the grossness as hideous slapstick comedy, a view possibly taken
by audiences at the time. A number of writers reported that at least
younger members of the audience were laughing during the grossest
scenes.[45] I imagine it is possible to see this laughter as primarily defensive,
and perhaps for some of the audience it was, but the film actually sets up
its most famous gross scene in a way that utilizes the dramatic methodology of comedy. The comedy is as much in the film's approach to its
material as in the eyes of some of its beholders.

Damien's first visit to the possessed Regan quickly becomes a contest
of wills, with the scene building on little escalations of charge-counter-
charge (an *agon* of sorts that is not all that different from the battles of
comedy). As the Devil Regan repeatedly shows its demonic powers by
telling Damien things it should not know, and Damien responds with
challenges of his own, we are clearly meant to take pleasure in this game
of one-upmanship, seeing who can best whom. Finally, after the Devil
has mentioned Damien's mother, Damien challenges the Devil Regan to

tell him his mother's maiden name if he/she is so smart. At first Regan doesn't reply at all, simply staring at Damien in a resistant way, and we are left a moment to speculate on whether or not the Devil has been bested. But then Damien, seen in tight close-up, moves in on Regan, a smug little smile playing across his face, and he repeats the question. If this were a comedy, this is precisely the moment that Damien would be answered with a pie-in-the-face.

Horror films generally undermine complacency in the dramatic turns of events they place in their characters' way. But comedy even more specifically abhors smugness, and Damien is looking very smug indeed as he issues this final challenge to Devil Regan. Even though this is a horror film, the dramatic rhythms of the scene seem to call, in the manner of a comedy, for something that will undercut Damien's all-too-easy self-confidence. Since he/she has already done things that defy logical explanation, the possessed Regan could simply provide the mother's name, furthering evidence of the Devil's existence. And while that would certainly best Damien, it wouldn't provide the kind of comeuppance that comedy usually calls for. So, instead of saying anything, the little devil spits, and spits with the force of a seltzer bottle aimed directly into Damien's face at full throttle.

I do not want to claim that the comedy is quite as clear-cut as my description is intended to make it. I have loaded this a bit to make clear that there *is* some kind of comedy here. But viscous, slimy green vomit is a very different thing from a creamy pie or a seltzer spurt, and in this difference lies the difference in attitudes we necessarily take toward the slapstick. The projectile here is gross, which is to say it attracts and repels at the same time. If we are at all allied with Regan here, the pleasure we must share in her besting Damien lies in the pleasure of making a mess, and the messier the better since this offers something Damien could not possibly top. But taking pleasure in being disgusting is to acknowledge disgust in itself. Perhaps all the people who covered the theater bathrooms with vomit after the show were empathically responding to Regan's plight.

In a telling article, Yippie Jerry Rubin seemed to acknowledge this by forging a complete identity with Regan precisely on the issue of vomit: "People flock to the movie because it is a therapeutic experience. We are all possessed—by our addictions, our loves, our attachments, our social roles—and they talk through us. We vomit out our bullshit. We all want to be exorcised. . . . 'The Exorcist' is not an escapist movie. It is a mirror. To live in the perfection of the present we must vomit up the demanding past."[46] Rubin is allegorizing the movie for his own ends, of course, but the fact is that the film allows this kind of interpretation. There is a kind of defiant pleasure in regression, in wallowing in dirt as a way of rejecting social constraints. We take a fierce pride in our body's ability to produce disgusting emissions, finding pleasure in them precisely because they are disgusting.

There is only one scene, however, in which an identification with Regan is not only possible but explicitly acknowledged by the camera. This scene articulates the confrontation between an adult authority figure and the rebellious prepubescent in a way that invokes the sexual themes I have discussed earlier in this chapter. The scene occurs about halfway through the film when Regan is still being examined by medical experts seeking a rational explanation for the strange things that are happening to her. A psychiatrist has hypnotized Regan and asks to talk to the unknown person inside her. The scene is staged in the following manner: the entranced Regan is sitting in a chaise lounge, her right arm balanced on the side of the chair, with her hand turned around and pointing outward (palm down) as the psychiatrist asks her questions. The hand will figure prominently in the mise-en-scène as a visual indication of Regan's trance, but also as a sign of her submission to the hypnotist's will, his authority and power over her.

The viewer's alliance with Regan is there at the outset: the scene begins in darkness as we hear the psychiatrist's voice putting Regan into a trance. When he commands her to open her eyes, we in effect open our eyes by means of a fade-in to see the image of Regan herself in close-up. Initially, the psychiatrist is sitting facing Regan and asking her about the person inside her. When she refuses to let him speak to that person, the psychiatrist asserts the power of his authority by standing up and issuing something like a command: "I'm speaking to the person inside of Regan now. If you are there, you too are hypnotized and must answer all my questions." The contest of wills and the issue of complacency are present here as they will be again in the later scene with Damien (as described above): the psychiatrist is confident that he can command the entranced Regan. And the complacency sets him up for a fall.

Initially, he seems successful—almost too successful: Regan's skin seems to change to a greenish tint and she begins to growl. When the increasingly less certain psychiatrist asks, "Who are you?" Regan at first looks up at him challengingly, much as she will later look at Damien before spewing out her vomit. Regan's response in this scene more thoroughly fells the complacency of her male challenger. With the very hand that indicated her apparent surrender to him, she grabs him in the groin with such a powerful grasp that she is able to force him down to the floor with this single hold.[47] We see this last action in a close-up shot that tracks in on the terrified psychiatrist as he is forced to the ground, so that the camera effectively places us in the position of aggression against him.[48] No wonder the psychiatrist writing in *Saturday Review* thought she should have been punished more!

This is the only scene where the camera seems to forge a real alliance with Regan, and it is an alliance against a smug male authority figure who has not only his authority but also his sexuality threatened in a very powerful way. This is the film's first suggestion of castration (in the second instance, Regan will turn against herself with the crucifix). Here, she specifically attacks male power by turning on someone who is trying to assert power over her. The importance of the absent father in this film (as well as in many of the films about evil children) has already been noted. The absent father is possibly invoked in this scene in the figure of "Captain Howdy," the person inside of Regan, whose name echoes that of Regan's father, Howard.[49] Psychologically, her reaction to the psychiatrist might seem an expression of rage over the father's absence. Without dismissing this, I think it is more in keeping with the film's terms to see the absence of the father—the ultimate male authority—as the condition that makes it possible for Regan to usurp authority.

Once we recognize the significance of the absent father, we might note how many male authority figures dominate this film: doctors, psychiatrists, a police detective, and, most importantly, priests. The missing father returns in the figures of two exorcising *fathers*, Damien and Merrin. In my discussion of the outlined sequence leading up to Regan's first minor rebellion, I noted the way in which Damien and Regan are paired on the issue of rage at the mother. Also unifying them, however, is a sense of feeling abandoned by the father, with Damien worrying about his own ability to act as a father because he feels lost as a son. It is in this context of parents and children that the religious dimension of the film makes sense.

Regan's possession signals the return of the father not just in the figure of the priests who will exorcise her but also in the figure who possesses— a bad father to set against the good fathers who rescue her. In a case study of demonic possession, Sigmund Freud explicitly proposed "The Devil as a Father Substitute"—but as a bad father because he is an introjection of the son's ambivalence.[50] If we accept Freud's analysis, we could say that the bad father-devil who possesses Regan does so because of her anger at her absent father. We are never meant to question the goodness of the good fathers' intentions in *The Exorcist,* yet we may still probe their motivations. If Regan may renew contact with the absent father by introjecting his bad imago, Damien may do the same thing. For all his show of compassion in dealing with Regan, then, Damien is motivated by self-interest since he is a man who has lost his faith, lost contact with his God. In his confrontation with the Devil, he finds faith and a renewed connection to his Father. Damien and the Devil have already united in using Regan's body as a site to contest each other's authority. Father Merrin has a comparably strong personal interest in the exorcism because it signifies another round of a lifelong battle with his nemesis.

Neither Damien nor Father Merrin is disinterested; both work from a motivation that seeks to reestablish a threatened authority, a hierarchy that has turned upside down. As men, they assert power over a young girl; as celibates, they put down the sexual autonomy of a budding teenager. This is an insistently religious view precisely because it sees the hierarchy and communal life within that hierarchy as more important than the life of the individual. Regan is merely a vehicle for an expression of the need for this hierarchy. All that has happened to her can finally mean nothing to her: once exorcised, she will have no memory of these experiences. In effect, Damien, in exorcising Regan, returns her to the amnesia stage of prepuberty. Still, as the film has it, his victory is ambiguous, which is perhaps why there was debate over how positive the ending of the film was. If we allow, as the film does on brief occasions, that there is anything positive in Regan's rebellion, then the authority of authority is undermined.

Because of its adamantly ambiguous style, *The Exorcist* allows a variety of responses to its cruelties (including the laughing teenagers noted earlier). No two people ever experience any work of art in the same way, but it finally seems unnecessary to have to segment the audience to understand the powerful appeal of this film. Gross-out art always works on ambivalence and contradiction, and the rhetoric of this film manages to work on many levels, which is probably why is was so successful in establishing gross-out as a respectable means of expression for classy movie product. The dominant tone of the film is punitive, derived from its overpowering sense of disgust at the body; but there are moments, however fleeting, in which we are allied with precisely those elements that give rise to this sense of disgust. Later films, as we shall see, will handle this ambivalence differently. And as with the comedies, the most artistically successful of these films are those that most fully realize the contradictions inherent in this ambivalence. For all its failings as a coherent work, *The Exorcist* established this push-pull aspect of disgust as mass entertainment for a large audience.[51]

The Exorcist is the key work for horror films of the 1970s and the 1980s because it established both a mode of expression and two concerns that would dominate later films. The two concerns are a natural outgrowth of the gross-out mode. The first is more sociological, a link between monstrosity and rebelliousness. Rebels are not unfamiliar figures in early horror, but they tended to be the creators of monsters, not the monsters themselves. With *The Exorcist*, rebellion began to define the monstrous. The connection also established an attitude toward rebellion that grows out of generic convention: rebelliousness was invoked as something threatening, as something to be put down. The gross-out element in this lies in two areas: an extreme ambivalence that wavers between a disgust at the rebellion and a celebration of it, and an uncertainty about what is more monstrous, a little girl spewing vomit or an adult male beating her up. The second concern has to do with the way we view the body, and here there is a comparable ambivalence, moving between a celebration of the physical over the spiritual to a revulsion at the very nature of the body itself.

While modern horror films probably contain more direct references to *Psycho* than any other predecessor, *The Exorcist* remains the most decisive influence, and not just in mode. *The Exorcist* also established the child with special powers, the child who needs to be punished as the central character in horror films. Make the child younger than Regan and you end up with a gaggle of magical moppets: *The Omen, It's Alive, It Lives Again, Firestarter, Children of the Corn, Halloween, The Brood, The Shining*, and so on. Make the child a teenager and the films reach floodgate proportions: *Carrie, The Fury, Halloween*, the *Nightmare on Elm Street* series, the *Friday the 13th* series, *The Lost Boys, An American Werewolf in London*, and so on. In many of these films, the special power of the teenagers might simply be their budding sexuality—which in *The Exorcist* strips the fantasy metaphor of its figurative cover. If Regan is poised between her childhood and her adolescence, between the amnesia period and the period of sexual development, the former group of films tend to emphasize generalized magical powers of the children that in some way threaten the family, while the latter group emphasizes sexuality as a power in itself. In some films, sexuality might be allied with a fantasy power (although in the *Nightmare on Elm Street* series that power is something the teens wish they did not have). As in *The Exorcist*, self-abuse is made literal in these films as magical dreams seemingly triggered by active libidos lead to self-destruction. In all these films, the need to punish these children is a dominant motif, although the attitude toward these punitive impulses varies widely with individual works.

Chapter 15 *The Revenge*
of Oedipus

The Child as Metaphor

Halloween (1978), *The Omen* (1976), *It's Alive* (1974)

John Carpenter's *Halloween* has such a striking opening that it has prompted quite a bit of analysis. In a single four-minute take, a Stedicam-mounted camera shows us someone's point-of-view movements around and into an average-looking suburban neighborhood house—someone who will commit a murder. That this person will commit a murder is not at all clear from the beginning of the shot, which sees a teenage boy and girl initially through the open front door and then the living room window as they embrace and kiss. Just as the camera moves up to peer through the window, the boy asks the girl if anyone is around. She says, indifferently, "Michael's around someplace."

After the couple decides to go upstairs to make love, the camera observes lights being turned off in an upstairs bedroom, then moves around to the back of the house. Here it enters the kitchen where we see a hand from behind the camera pick up a large carving knife and hold it in a menacing position. Moving toward the front hall stairway, the camera waits expectantly, although it doesn't have to wait very long. In a little over a minute since we first saw the lights go out, we hear the boyfriend offscreen saying, "Look, Judy, it's really late. I gotta go." When she asks if he'll call her tomorrow, we see him appear on the stairway putting on his shirt and answering, "Yeah, sure." "Promise?" Judy calls out again, and, descending, he replies, "Yeah," but when he reaches the landing he looks back up with an expression that seems to say, "Are you crazy?"

With the boyfriend departed, the camera begins to move upstairs, stopping along the way to pick up a Halloween mask the boyfriend had worn, so that the resulting image we see is partially obscured, now only visible through the two eye holes in the mask. Through this we see the girl, who addresses the camera with a slight annoyance as "Michael?" In response, a hand from behind the camera brings the knife forward and stabs the girl to death, striking principally at her breasts. It is her breasts that she chiefly tries to protect, and it is her breasts that are most covered with blood as her body slumps to the floor. It is only when the camera abruptly descends the stairs and moves outside that the take finally ends and we get a cut to a reverse-angle shot that reveals the identity of the killer.

Halloween does not belong to the "evil children" cycle, but the power of its opening is not merely a matter of bravura filmmaking; it clearly depends on the shock in its revelation of the killer's identity as a six-year-old boy. Although the film was greeted for its originality and is seen as the primary influence on subsequent "slice-and-dice" movies like the *Friday the 13th* series, much of it follows a pattern established three years earlier by *Black Christmas* (1975; aka *Silent Night, Evil Night* and *Stranger in the House*), directed by Bob Clark (auteur of *Porky's*). That film also shows a prowling killer whose presence is always indicated by a moving subjective camera (but with no reverse-angle shot to identify him) as he goes about murdering a series of girls in a sorority. John Carpenter extends the moving camera into a more extraordinary elaboration and provides the reverse angle immediately after the first murder. The initial withholding of six-year-old Michael's identity is partly a matter of practical necessity (of a kind noted in regard to *The Bad Seed*). If we were actually to see Michael right away, we would very likely find the murder ludicrous at best, and probably unbelievable, as we would wonder why the sister, who appears to be a full-grown woman, doesn't simply grab hold of his little six-year-old arm and wrest the knife from him?

By concealing the killer's identity until after the murder, the film clearly intends the revelation of the reverse-angle shot to register as a startling surprise. A large, hulking adult male would have rendered this sequence more routine and made the withholding of the killer's identity seem overly elaborated. We can, of course, dismiss the revelation as mere shock value, and we also may fairly ask why the audience doesn't simply laugh in disbelief when the killer is revealed. The line between comedy and horror is often very thin, and part of the shock here derives from the fact that it is not fully a surprise; we can accept the murderer's identity because the cultural context of other films has prepared us for it. Still, we may question why we find this revelation such a satisfyingly disturbing conclusion to this scene.

Surely part of the shock is to undermine our certainty about what the attack may *mean*. The child disturbs because he undercuts any coherent motivation that we may have originally attributed to the point-of-view shot—especially any sexual motivation.[1] After the revelation, we should not be able to look at the sequence of events in quite the same way again. This very brutal murderer is clearly a cousin of Rhoda from *The Bad Seed*, albeit offered to us without benefit of genetic argument. As the rest of the movie will insist, he is evil incarnate, pure and simple. As if to confirm this, he himself seems to be in some kind of stupor: he literally does not seem to know what he has done or is doing. The shock that comes from the reverse-angle shot is to make us feel a frisson of ignorance, a sense that why he does this is ultimately unknowable. The scene is a necessary prologue for the rest of the film (when Michael is an adult) to define just how evil this killer in fact is—so evil that his predations extend back to early childhood. This is evil so great that, by the end, we will have to acknowledge it as supernatural.

But if the murderer is an adult through the rest of the film, we cannot fully lose the sense of childhood because the film takes place on a festive holiday we associate mostly with children. A number of things come into play here. Centering the film on Halloween does give it a peculiar nature of festivity, something that is central to gross-out as I have defined it so far. The specific nature of this festival thus presents a way of looking at murderous children. However much it may have been denatured in the modern world, Halloween is a time when children confront the terror of supernature (at least, the festival suggests that a sense of evil and dread is not entirely foreign to children). Further, Halloween is a time when children may play with identity, learning that they can use the mask as the facade of an alternate self, which is how it is used here: six year-old Michael puts on the mask before he murders his sister.

This is the same mask the sister's boyfriend had put on as a prelude to sex, which suggests another transgression: that their furtive sexual act had to be hidden from others. It also happens with truly exceptional rapidity (although none of the commentary I've encountered on the film thinks this worth noting); yet it seems to me the speed is of special consequence here. Of course, this is partly dramatic necessity: one may make the audience wait just so long before the murder takes place. Carpenter doesn't attempt to conceal this dramatic problem. Instead, he reinforces the sense of brevity by showing the boyfriend's hurried desire to get out of the house. This lad has shared barely a minute of intimacy with his girlfriend, but he's already responding as if she were a nagging wife. There's both a trick and a treat here, a hostility that is somehow connected to the pleasure.

As a festival of license for children, Halloween also connects hostility to pleasure, defining a time in which children can vent their own hostile impulses. "Trick or treat" carries with it a threat: we'll punish you if you don't give us what we want. Treats in this instance usually mean candy or something sweet, so underlying this opposition is an anxiety over the greed of children—what they might do to us in our neglect if granted license. All these issues are played out in the interaction between the two teenagers, with the young girl cast in the role of the child. When the roles are reversed, when she becomes the abandoning figure to Michael, the site of attack—the young woman's breasts—becomes as pertinent as it was in *Night of the Living Dead*: Michael attacks the very source of nurturance of a woman who was supposed to be taking care of him but did not. As presented in the film, revenge is certainly a key motive here: the lack of treat in the form of caretaking brings about a terrible trick. Michael's deadly mischief may begin in the spirit of the holiday (after all, he puts on a mask), but he goes too far. But then, going too far is central to the gross-out aesthetic.

A number of commentators have seen a specifically sexual motivation in the film's prologue, especially the playing out of an Oedipal drama. This kind of interpretation seems problematic to me: is latent sexual desire really that motivating? At best, such an interpretation must be based on a strange assumption of what the needs of a six-year-old might be, but then analysis of this film has made little of the fact that this is indeed a very young child committing *murder*. One might have expected at least *some* consideration of how murder by a six-year-old defines the act as truly horrible for us. The fact that this does not happen might be worth considering in itself as a commentary on the context in which this film has been viewed—the expectations that audiences already had about the evil capacities of young children. For my own part, I would like to make some attempt here to reinstate the *child* into these child murderers, to see what we might make of them if we see them as children rather than as monsters in the form of children.

As the little drama between the two teenagers indicates, the theme of abandonment is the key issue here, and it is something that comes up over and over again in these films. This is effectively an extension of the absent father in *The Bad Seed* and *The Exorcist* as well as a parallel to the absent parents that were noted in many of the comedies. *The Bad Seed* keeps this issue in the background by making Rhoda completely self-sufficient, but we normally see children—and certainly children as young as the murderer in *Halloween*'s prologue—as dependent. Abandonment is of central importance to young children, and abandoned children are significantly present in films of this period—as they would be about a decade later but transmuted into the comic form of *Problem Child* and *Home Alone* (both 1990) as a way of rendering the theme harmless.

As critics commented at the time, the virgin is the only main character who remains alive at the end of *Halloween* (as if that were a sign that she should be saved from Michael's predations). But she is also the only babysitter in the film who actually does her job, who stays focused on the children and who knows how to talk to them. And it is only the children that she cares for who can see the murderous Michael most clearly. Something like this will turn up in the original *Friday the 13th* (1980): again, the sexual activity that seems the primary cause for the violence has an underlying trigger. The murderer is avenging her son's death; he was neglected by the very people who were supposed to take care of him because they were selfishly engaged in sexual activity. Keeping all this in mind, we might pay a little more attention to what else is going on in *Halloween*'s opening tracking shot.

In very insistent fashion it defines a character on the outside looking in. Our not knowing who the character is reinforces this sense of separation; he himself seems to occupy an empty space. The whole sequence establishes one element that will remain constant throughout the film— the sense of terror in isolation, a key motif. This film is very much about the terror of suburban life, its isolation and lack of community. Strikingly, although the film takes place on Halloween night, there is no air of festivity. And although we hear a chorus of chanting children overlapped into the first shot, we never actually see any kids out trick or treating! There was in fact an increased anxiety about Halloween in this period, but it centered on the terrible things that some adults did to children (like putting razor blades in apples). This, perhaps more than anything else from the time, signaled a breakdown of the sense of community in American life. Appropriately, the streets and sidewalks of this typical American suburb appear to be completely deserted on a night that usually sees many boisterous groups of kids walking around. Instead, the opening shot evokes a powerful sense of being stranded and alone, a feeling that will dominate the rest of the film.

Children in the horror films that center on demon children seem to use them to define conflicts and contradictions at the center of family life. It might be reading too much into the opening of *Halloween* to make that claim here since the film doesn't grant us enough information about this family or Michael's position in it to attribute any actual psychological motivation to his actions. What we can finally conclude from this is some sense of the child as an agent of vengeance. There is indeed something punitive in the way sexual activity throughout the movie is viewed; nevertheless, the vindictiveness is not solely about sexuality but rather the ways the characters react to issues of self-indulgence and caring.

By the time *Halloween* appeared, there no longer appeared to be any need to explain how a child could turn out to be like Michael. It was enough to assume that children could be guilty of the most outrageous, most incredibly evil behavior. Prior to this film, however, films generally did seek to trace an etiology for the sources of behavior. *The Omen* (1976) went the satanic route with a child that was the spawn of the Devil and possessed by the Devil's magical powers, enabling him to harm others. *It's Alive* (1974) echoed the ending of *Invasion of the Body Snatchers* (1956) combined with an intimation of *Village of the Damned* (1960) to suggest a possible invasion by creatures from other worlds. In all cases, there was a sense of the child as being alien to the family. But if the child as alien is a fantasy that conceals the actual etiology of the evil child within the family, it also serves to define how families in this period could look at their children as strange and foreign, an intrusion on their existence. Both *The Omen* and *It's Alive* raise the issue of abortion, giving rise to the specter of children as disposable objects and establishing how fully alien these children are—they are not quite human.[2]

Combining *The Bad Seed, Rosemary's Baby*, and *The Exorcist, The Omen* featured lavish production values, big-name stars, a brief scene with its own exorcist, and an end credit for the "Religious Advisers to the Producers."[3] In its aspirations to class and a kind of seriousness, it was following the lead of *The Exorcist* since it is also clearly a work of gross-out, distinguishing itself with the spectacular decapitation of one of its lead players (in slow motion and covered by nine shots to make sure we see it in all its gruesome detail).[4] Like *The Bad Seed*, the film presents us, on the surface, with a "perfectly perfect family" (as the wife describes herself and her husband, at a moment when things are far from perfect). Toward the beginning of the film, Robert (Gregory Peck) is appointed ambassador to England, with headquarters in London, and is even in line for the presidency of the United States. His wife Cathy (Lee Remick) is beautiful, gracious, and devoted.

Although *The Omen* is more overtly a fantasy than *The Bad Seed*, it nonetheless seeks a more realistic foundation for its problem with the family's child and provides a motivation of a kind *The Bad Seed* did not consider necessary. About halfway through the film, the wife's psychiatrist confides to the husband that she thinks the child is evil and not hers. Under ordinary circumstances such thoughts ought to indicate a delusional person. The problem in the film, however, is that the wife is right and that her husband is in on at least part of the story. Unbeknownst to her, Cathy's baby died at birth. Hoping to spare her pain over this loss, Robert has approved substituting as their own a child whose mother had reportedly died in childbirth. Alas, this child actually turns out to be the Devil's spawn.

If our acceptance of the fantasy helps to implicate us in the wife's delusions, the fantasy also partly operates to divert us from what's actually going on in the family. Consider, for example, the first scene in which we are made aware there may be something disturbingly special about Damien, Cathy and Robert's (adopted) son. At a birthday party for five-year-old Damien, Cathy is constantly losing track of him. She finally finds him with his governess, who is being asked by a society photographer to have their picture taken. Clearly annoyed, Cathy goes up to the governess and asks her to give Damien over to her, presumably so that she can now be photographed with him as his rightful mother. Shortly after this, the governess hangs herself, apparently as a consequence of some mysterious power that hovers over Damien. That's the fantasy; but the death of the governess also comes after a moment when the wife had clearly felt jealous of her.

As a consequence, the fantasy conceit of the Devil posits one possible motivation for the governess's death, while the underlying psychological drama posits another, a dichotomy the film does in fact continue to utilize over much of its length—for example, in the way it uses photography. Taking the family's picture becomes a running motif in the film, a natural occurrence because Robert is a man of public renown. But it also has a larger meaning for the film because establishing how this family appears is a key concern. Together Robert and Cathy represent an eminent and successful couple, people who have almost everything; but a child is necessary to complete this picture. Most of the time, these well-to-do parents freely give their child up to others for caregiving, but Cathy has a finely tuned sense of what a family should look like. So at Damien's birthday party, she makes herself a mother for the photographer.

The movie does not fully articulate this, but it gives the impression that the father wants the son more than the mother. The father is the central character in the birth scene (not the mother), and it is the father who effectively gives birth to the child by arranging for the secret adoption of another newborn. Although the fantasy conceit of the Devil's child may make covert the mother's actual psychological motivation, her suspicions that the child is evil and not hers occur before he has done anything that might remotely be described as bad behavior, let alone evil. This mother does not really want her own child: even his happy shouting in routine child's play drives her up the wall. In hiring a woman who literally turns out to be the governess from hell, Cathy and Robert add to their household someone who can facilitate Damien's evil. That's on the surface of the fantasy, but underlying this is a sense that they would welcome anyone into the household who could engage in the actual quotidian tasks of child-rearing. The governess immediately becomes closer to Damien than either of his parents precisely because neither parent wishes to be especially close to him.

The Omen confirms a sense of the child as being actually alien to its family. This is something that is in fact always true to the extent that the configuration of the couple as a family is never the same after a child arrives. Yet this truth seemed to have particular resonance for this period. Children do disrupt norms and necessarily create new modes of behavior. For this reason the family may finally seek to destroy the child before the child apparently destroys them. Throughout, the film keeps playing on an alternating vision of the child as seemingly helpless or powerfully manipulative. Moreover, the child is manipulative in his apparent helplessness by making demands on his parents that only they can meet (precisely because the child cannot take care of himself). The exasperated parents want to punish the child for his very helplessness, an attitude the movie makes safe through a fantasy that renders the child all-powerful and the parents seemingly helpless. Indeed, the parents cannot do anything about the child because he is a child, after all, and so helpless.

These conflicting attitudes about children culminate in the climactic scene when Robert tries to carry through the ritual sacrifice of his own son (doubtless an allusion to Abraham's attempt to slay his son Isaac, since this is done ultimately at the behest of God). In the dramatic tension that it sets up, *The Omen* follows *The Bad Seed* in contriving a moment in which the audience is rooting for a parent (in this case the father) to kill his own child, and we are meant to understand the necessity of this action, especially because the child is apparently responsible for the mother's death. Also like *The Bad Seed* in its original book and play versions, the parent is killed while a coda tells us of the child's survival.[5] But there is a striking difference here typical of the period and important in defining the work as gross-out. Whether or not Robert has successfully killed his son is withheld from us until the funeral, where we discover that the child is alive, seen from the back, standing between a man and a woman and holding onto their hands. As the funeral comes to an end, we learn that the man and woman are the President of the United States and his wife, and they vow to raise the child. At this moment when we realize that Damien has acceded to a position of potentially great power, he turns around and smiles directly at us as if to acknowledge our own complicity in his achievement.

It is not just that Damien has gotten within reach of the position of power predicted for him (a position from which, we are told, he will ultimately rule the world). There is the even more immediate satisfaction of revenge against a father willing to slaughter him. Here is where this film truly departs from *The Bad Seed*, which asks us to see Rhoda's survival as a terrible catastrophe. If the Most Exalted Patriarchal Authority has to intervene in the film version of *The Bad Seed* to set things right, the exalted patriarchal authority of the President in *The Omen* titillatingly becomes potential prey for the satanic son. Damien's smiling acknowledgment of us as he looks directly at the camera points to our involvement in his actions, some sense that we have in fact shared in his anger and his revenge against his parents.

Ascribing vengeance to the child—even taking pleasure in such a direct acknowledgment of that vengeance—is something of an anxiety projection. Because we harbor murderous feelings toward the child (which, after all, is part of the titillation of this film), the child must harbor murderous feelings toward us. The fantasy conceit has helped to disguise the murderous feelings we—and the parents in the film—might have. But at least in this one instance in which Damien recognizes *us*, the ambivalence breaks through the protective cover of the fantasy. It is terrible fun to see him triumph not just over his dad, but (for the time being, at least) over the Ultimate Patriarch.

It's Alive escalates the premises of the "evil children" films by presenting a monstrous and physically deformed baby, a demon from birth. The film is basically a feature-length variation on the final scene of *Rosemary's Baby* in that the parent who initially rejects the lineage of the infant (in this case the father) finally comes around to acknowledge that he is in fact its parent. Robin Wood has effectively argued that the monstrous child is in fact a result of disturbances in the family that are evocatively expressed before the child is born.[6] Still, I don't think this interpretation fully addresses why the birth of a marauding child is the most effective metaphor for expressing family tensions. In *The Omen*, the attitude of the mother in particular opens the film up to a psychological interpretation early on that sees potential problems in the child as a reflection of problems in the parents (especially since the child has apparently done no wrong, at least up to a certain point early in the narrative). Although the fantasy conceit allows for a different interpretation, the increasingly bad qualities associated with Damien are initially a matter of how the mother looks at him. In *It's Alive*, however, we can't entirely blame the parents for their response to their own progeny since the monster baby does, after all, inspire anxiety and disgust in the audience as well. Nonetheless, much as we may be repelled, the film seeks to define something about how we look at children in general, not just how we react to a father's ambivalence toward his own child.

At the least we can pinpoint a kind of generalizing anxiety here, as in *Rosemary's Baby*, about reproduction and birth defects, reflecting a contemporary increase in diagnostic testing and public awareness of genetic abnormalities. But *It's Alive* goes farther than its predecessor in this regard, as it goes farther than any film about evil children in decreasing the age of the child (an infant!) while increasing the child's capacity for violence. In doing this, the film makes explicit something previously noted as implicit in the other "evil children" films: an underlying anxiety over a child's helplessness. As *It's Alive* effectively dramatizes it, this aspect of human life is truly a source of terror. The prolonged period of dependency which ties the parents to the child is a unique human trait. Horror films about evil children allay the anxiety by making the child all-powerful (rather than helpless), which enables us to give full vent to our own murderous impulses. Put simply, if we don't get him, he'll get us. This is potentially a constant source of parental ambivalence toward children but, strikingly, one that became more and more a concern in a period that saw a great increase in public interest over the abuse of helpless children. We were ready to become aware of this abuse in actuality perhaps because we had never before been so ready to see it imaginatively. Ambivalence over that helplessness became indirectly articulated in the fantasy conceits of the "evil children" films.

In *It's Alive*, however, the articulation is less indirect. In this film, the chief feature of this monstrous baby's grotesqueness is his teeth, in particular his canine incisors, which he immediately uses at birth, attacking virtually everyone but his mother in the delivery room. Ordinarily his mother would be the aim of his oral aggression, but the film initially conceals the goal of his rapaciousness by exempting her from the attack. This is perhaps a devious strategy, but it serves to define the creature as alien for us as well as for the parents. This is an attitude we must progressively adjust as it slowly emerges that hunger is the chief motivation of his attacks. Like any other hungry baby, he is a creature of appetite who literally devours everything in his path. His hunger dominates to the point that the film can even turn it into a joke. In one scene the father finally realizes the presence of unwanted demon child (who had escaped from the hospital and instinctually found his way home) by coming upon the suddenly empty freezer (once full of meat) and the pillaged refrigerator (once full of milk). This creature literally threatens to eat his parents out of house and home.

The overwhelming dominance of the demanding impulse, and the extent to which hunger defines his or her existence, makes any infant monstrous from an adult's point of view. We might gain a measure of independence as we grow up by learning to control our impulses, but as we become parents we become tied to our children who live under the reign of their impulses. Even as we have partially renounced our impulses, the fact that we must attend to theirs (and in fairly prompt fashion as their maddening crying demands) finally engenders our ambivalence toward children. Every child is an alien to the extent that his or her behavior is alien to the way we must behave as adults—and in that regard every child is a monster. But this was an insight that was really only salient in a period that could in fact countenance the monstrosity of children. *It's Alive* is distinctive in the way it asks us to confront and accept the child-monster as a kind of normality.

The demonic children in the "evil children" films discussed up to this point have no real identity of their own. None of the films seeks to explore any actual psychology for the children. Rather, the children are symptomatic of something else, either a problem in the family locally, or more globally a problem in society at large. Still, as has been suggested, we can try to determine not so much the validity of using the child as metaphor as the reasons why children should present themselves so readily in this period for such metaphorical purposes. That they could suggests how distinctively this period looked at children.

Aside from the emphasis on hunger, there is one other aspect of the monstrous baby in *It's Alive* that marks it as a child. Following the common method of horror films from this period as noted at the beginning of this chapter, there are camera shots from the child-monster's point of view, shots that often show him moving in on what may be a potential victim. These shots are of a peculiar nature, however: a double image that looks something like a 3-D movie seen without the glasses. This might be simply an attempt to reflect on the fact that a newborn does not yet possess binocular vision. But if we can interpret the monstrous baby metaphorically, then it makes sense to see something metaphorical in this kind of presentation. At the least, this metaphor ascribes a different way of viewing to children, one that cannot see the world with the more experienced and precise understanding of an adult, but rather, in this case, one in which the vision is entirely driven by hunger.

A small number of the "evil children" films did indeed focus more on the different ways in which demonic children necessarily see the world in reality—and not just through the lens of the subjective camera. As a consequence, they focused more on the children themselves. These films—Mark Lester's *Firestarter*, Robert Mulligan's *The Other*, and Stanley Kubrick's *The Shining*—are concerned with exploring the particular psychology of the child, especially as a reflection on and response to the psychology of the parent(s). In regard to the Mulligan and Kubrick works, this more balanced approach to the monster child produced two of the most original horror films to come from the 1970s and 1980s. A distinguishing characteristic of all three films is that the children in them possess some kind of magical power.[7] This might suggest a metaphorical dimension because it moves the children into the realm of fantasy. And by a strict definition of the term they must in fact be considered monsters since they possess characteristics that make them something other than human. But the monstrosity here is used to define a particular aspect of childhood, a distinctive way of *seeing* that belongs to children alone. In the Mulligan and Kubrick films particularly, this monstrous dimension is a striking consequence of the child's interactions with the parent(s). In all other respects, these children are far more human—and poignant—than their demonic counterparts in the other films.

The Child as Visionary

Firestarter (1984), *The Other* (1972), *The Shining* (1980)

In *Firestarter* the power of young Charley (Drew Barrymore) is exactly what the title succinctly suggests: the ability to set things on fire. But she is no simple pyromaniac, and the fact that she can do it by thought (pyrokinesis) suggests a psychological dimension that the film fully dramatizes: whenever she is angry, Charley makes the object of her anger burst into flames. Sometimes she does this intentionally, but more often than not it is something that happens in response to her emotional state. It is not an ability she can control, any more than a child can easily control hunger. The fantasy here, then, is not unlike that of *It's Alive*, suggesting a developmental drama about a child learning to control her urges. In outline, the focus is more on Charley herself than was the case with the monstrous baby in *It's Alive*, but what is potentially most interesting here is shunted aside for a good father/bad father melodrama that sends the ultimate bad father—a nasty government intelligence agent—against Charley and her real father. This good father (David Keith) possesses magical powers himself, but beyond these he is an uninteresting character who is defined chiefly by his own devotion to Charley.

If the Devil often gets the best parts, the more potentially interesting character here is the bad father. Rainbird (George C. Scott) is a character built on contradictions since he is both Native American and a government agent. The Indian background perhaps alludes to magical powers he might have in his own right, which could point to an alliance with Charley, but the plot mostly moves him into the routine position of villain as he falsely befriends Charley, hoping to get close enough to kill her. In his murderous motivation for becoming her friend, the film might suggest a metaphoric split, an ambivalence of father to child of a kind we've seen in other "evil children" films. But *Firestarter* draws no real connection between the two fathers and offers no possibility that the bad father might in fact be a reflection of the good. Further, the film has trouble dramatizing exactly why the bad father wants to kill young Charley so much.

My chief reason for paying more than cursory attention here is that *Firestarter* is so naked in stating the bad father's murderous desire, even as it finds no way of exploring it dramatically. At the very end, when Rainbird successfully kills Charley's father and attempts to kill her as well, he yells out a declaration of love to her. Raising at least the possibility of an incestuous wish, the film implies an Oedipal drama, but with the focus unusually shifted to the father's desires. Still, this sudden intrusion of incest and pederasty has the dramatic quality of an afterthought, a startling surprise to give added spice to a routine action. The character of Rainbird has been too mysterious, too unexplored, to give this declaration any meaning for the audience. And we are in no way implicated in his desire to kill the monster child as we are in many of the films in which the child's chief function is metaphorical. *The Other* and *The Shining* remain unique in the extent to which they characterize both parents and children, seeing the desires of the parents as a key component in the identities of the children.

Firestarter has the ambition of moving its monster child out of the realm of monstrosity, but there is finally a problem with the way the girl herself is dramatized. This is not merely a matter of ineptitude (as so much else in this film is). Rather, it is a problem that stems from the source novel. Stephen King declared that he thought the film worked a fine invention with the scene in which Charley's parents try to teach her to control her urges by training them on toasting bread.[8] The scene stands out in the context of the rest of the narrative since it is the only time her magical power is used in a positive way (albeit with an element of silliness since I find it difficult to see the metaphoric value of a mind making toast to evoke a child's special relationship to reality). Other than this one positive instance, Charley's special power is always dramatized as something negative: its value lies in its ability to destroy other people. She ends up destroying so many in the film's climactic scene that the film defines its chief pleasure in its elaborate special effects of destruction. We are asked to see Charley as a vengeful creature, plain and simple, and to approve her revenge against the bad father. As a consequence, her magical power finally suggests nothing more than the uncontrollable impulses of childhood (perhaps even raising the possibility that the government forces were right in wanting her destroyed).

J. P. Telotte has suggested that the horror film is dominated by a childlike perspective, but nowhere is this as true as it is for *The Other* and *The Shining.*[9] In plot outline, *The Other* is something of a post-Code remake of *The Bad Seed.* A young child (eleven in this instance), driven by greed for an object, commits a murder, which, in turn, leads to other murders, all committed during the father's absence. A maternal figure (in this instance the child's grandmother) slowly comes to realize that the child is responsible for all the murders. As a consequence, she is moved to murder and suicide as a solution, although the maternal figure here does acknowledge some complicity in the child's evil doings. As in the source novel and play adaptation of *The Bad Seed,* the maternal figure is successful in her suicide and the murderous child survives.

But there are striking differences between the two works as well. The central conceit of the film (and its source novel) more or less demands a psychoanalytic interpretation because the murderous child is in fact one of two children—twin brothers, Holland and Niles Perry. And there is another important difference, particularly in regard to motivation. Whereas *The Bad Seed* stridently denies any psychological motivation in favor of its cockeyed genetic argument, *The Other* gives the murderous child's actions a distinctly psychoanalytic cast by the fact that the first murder (shown elliptically in flashback) is of the boy's own father. The boy appears to have killed the father to gain possession of the father's ring, suggesting that he is motivated by a desire for the authority the ring confers. The closest the film comes to indicating supernatural sources is in one line of dialogue that attributes a special power to the ring, as if the ring itself were somehow dictating the evil actions. But such a supernatural explanation is given little force in this film. Rather, the moody and evocative style of the film underscores a more fully realized psychological dimension. Further amplifying this quality is the fact that the boy carries around the father's severed finger as well, suggesting that a castration anxiety has been projected outward and enacted on the castrating figure himself.[10] What the film dramatizes, then, is a bizarre and troubling realization of an Oedipal fantasy.

The psychoanalytic interpretation is further emphasized because, in the manner of older movies about twins, the two brothers separately represent good and bad impulses in one personality. The fable of the novel/film further complicates this with the surprise revelation that the evil brother Holland has in fact died by the time of the narrative events we witness. He continues to live solely in the imagination of his brother (which the film externalizes for us as actual images). As indicated in the directness of its title, the movie is quite explicitly about otherness, those bad parts of ourselves that we repress and project onto others. Ever since Robin Wood's influential writings on horror films, otherness has been widely regarded as one of the major concerns of horror fiction.[11] In the scheme of the film, the bad Holland—a fantasy projection of the good Niles—acts out the impulses that Niles suppresses.

The psychological scheme allows for attributing all responsibility for the evil actions to the child himself (Niles/Holland), but the film actually realizes this in somewhat different terms because it refuses to create an identity for the child that is entirely separate from the child's family. The child here is less opaque than Rhoda in *The Bad Seed* because this film has a far more interior quality, one dominated by Niles's point of view.[12] Since so much of the film is concerned with exploring his psychology, there is more elaboration on motivation. A key consideration is the nature of the household itself: the boy's nuclear family no longer exists and now he is part of two families living together with the grandmother, who dominates everyone. This world appears to be matriarchal: the men are nondescript, uncharacterized, and generally remain in the background of both the image and the narrative. But if the household seems dominated by women, it is owing to the film's interior quality, which presents its world to us through the boy's point of view. In his imagination, women appear as both givers of life and takers of life. It is finally in the child's relation to women that the film moves beyond a purely Oedipal fantasy.

The Other, released a year before *The Exorcist*, eschews the kind of physical grossness that would become mandatory for horror films after the success of *The Exorcist*. Yet the potential for gross-out is there, as the source novel makes clear: it begins with the description of a child hanging a cat and goes on to describe a killing with a pitchfork as well as the severing of a finger from a corpse with garden shears. But all the violence in the film is shown in an indirect and evocative rather than explicit fashion, with not one drop of blood spilled on-screen.[13] My main interest here is to show how it relates to the "evil children" cycle, yet the film does suggest gross-out in at least one respect.

Even if it does not show the killing explicitly, a film that features the murder of a newborn infant moves into the realm of the gross already held by the contemporaneous "dead baby" joke cycle. In the relatively quiet context of this film, the crown of an infant's head surfacing in a wine keg is a vision as disturbing as the gorier sights in other gross-out. Encapsulated in this image of the dead infant is an overriding anxiety about birth and death that similarly surfaces in dead baby jokes as well as subsequent gross-out horror films. By focusing on the subjectivity of its now twelve-year-old boy, *The Other* transforms this concern about the troubling limitations of physical existence into an ambivalent form of play that moves between accepting those limitations and attempting to transcend them. The centrality of a child's vision to this film has to do with the growing discovery of the meaning of his own physical existence (a discovery we all must make in childhood) and the necessary anxiety that must result from this awareness. Like other gross-out, this film is very much oriented toward the flesh, but in a way that attempts to confront a world of spirit.

Niles (Chris Udvarnoky) and Holland (Martin Udvarnoky) both play "the great game," a game of the imagination taught to them by their very spiritual Russian grandmother Ada (Uta Hagen) as a means of confronting the disturbing limitations of our physical lives. In a kind of living metempsychosis she teaches the boys to experience the world as experienced by another human being or animal or object. That this is specifically connected to anxiety over death is made clear by a plot revelation, about two-thirds of the way through, that Holland is dead, that he has continued to exist solely through Niles, who conjures his spirit back into corporeal existence by playing "the great game." But if Holland offers a kind of comfort to Niles, he also brings with him disturbances as he externalizes dreadful desires.

The film's first presentation of the game comes when Ada and Niles are talking about loss, explicitly Ada's loss of her Russian homeland, but implicitly, as we will later understand, the loss of Holland. In its ability to define the ambivalent forces pulling at Niles, it is one of the most impressive sequences in the film. Ada has Niles focus on a crow. As the bird takes off from its perch, so does the camera, transcending in soaring flight the oppressive languor of rural summer life. Throughout the sequence, Mulligan's aerial shots are all centered on specific objects on the ground, at first trees, then a river, then houses, barns, and finally a farmer haying. These specific points of reference on the ground orient us in space so that we never lose a sense of exactly what we're getting away from, and the shots become simultaneously exhilarating and vertiginous. There are, then, opposing emotions evoked by this sequence, which might at first appear to be all release. There are two reasons for this.

First, for all the good that Ada does in giving Niles a sense of spiritual transcendence, there is a potentially destructive element in their relationship. Ada may help to develop Niles's emotions, but she also comes close to dominating them—a point strongly underlined by Uta Hagen's grandly theatrical performance as Ada. Grandmother Ada's dream of transcendence, which she gives to Holland as a way of dealing with death, becomes grandson Niles's nightmare as transcendence increasingly means denying Holland's death by becoming him. As the child begins to lose control over his own identity through his play of imagination, his sense of self is gradually destroyed.

Second, as this first sequence of "the great game" makes clear, once the imagination is let loose, it might go anywhere. The vertigo that arises from the exhilaration signals a sense of losing control. Toward the end of the sequence, Mulligan begins intercutting static shots centered on a pitchfork concealed in the hay, much as the soaring shots are centered on a specific object. The contrast here is clear: if the dynamically soaring shots express a transcendental quality, these static shots abruptly bring us down to earth. But both are the work of the imagination.[14] The shots of the pitchfork reveal an object concealed by "Holland" to get revenge against an obnoxious cousin, but of course Holland is actually Niles acting out as Holland. As Niles begins to see shots of the pitchfork that "Holland" has planted, he also begins to "feel" the sharp prongs of the pitchfork. This "game" that allows a free play of the imagination thus indiscriminately unleashes evil as well as good impulses. As Niles imaginatively feels the prongs of the pitchfork intended for his cousin, Niles as Holland effectively turns against himself.

Because the grandmother is the source of the game, Niles receives a kind of spiritual life from her as well as his actual physical existence. There is an ambivalence inherent in these gifts, however, since birth brings with it the promise of death. The spiritual gift may transcend physical existence through imagination, but Niles's imagination also identifies Ada with death. In a scene in a church, Ada tries to soothe Niles's worries about death by pointing to an angel on a stained glass window—an angel of death whom Ada calls the "angel of the brighter day" because she promises delivery from death. But Ada will subsequently attempt to murder Niles, at which point a dissolve to the angel of the brighter day shows that Niles sees the angel in Ada. Much as the gifts she offers Niles move ambivalently between life and death, in the liberation Ada offers him there is also domination. In a sense, he seeks a vengeance that will grant him freedom from her domination to control how he lives his imaginative life. Once she has given him the power of the game, it is not within her power to withdraw it.

As with *The Bad Seed* and *The Omen*, *The Other* ends with the surprise reappearance of a child we thought had been killed. And, as with *The Omen*, the child stares directly at the camera. But there is no smile here, no sense of triumph that the audience can take a kind of evil pleasure in. Rather, as the camera tracks in toward a window of the house, we can begin to make out Niles's face looking out the window. Moving into medium shot, we see that his expression is blank, merely staring straight ahead through the reflection of sky we see on the window. The frame freezes at this moment, freezing Niles forever behind that window, looking out. The film frustrates any easy satisfactions familiar from other "evil children" films, either in our sense of pleasure in the demonic child's destruction or in our complicity with his vengeance. By film's end Niles has escaped his grandmother's deadly embrace, but he remains trapped in the world of his own imagination. The influence of *Psycho* (where Norman Bates will always be trapped as his mother in his imagination) is clearly felt here: both films end in a kind of terrible stasis achieved by submerging one identity in another. What makes the stasis all the more terrible in *The Other* is that Niles is so young. He may have escaped from his grandmother's domination, but Niles has a lifetime ahead of him—a lifetime dominated by his dead twin.

A similar devolution of a character—again in an adult—occurs in *The Shining* (1980), Of all the horror films discussed in this book, *The Shining* comes closest to the world of fairy tales and, in doing so, most fully invokes a child's perspective of the world. The film contains specific references to "Hansel and Gretel" and "The Three Little Pigs" as well as to the familiar fairy-tale prohibition against entering a locked room. Even adult characters invoke these tales and figure prominently as characters in a fairy-tale-like plot centering on the escape from an evil parent. Furthermore, there are a number of references to "Road Runner" cartoons and various cartoon animals that populate a child's universe in the United States.

While working on the screenplay, Stanley Kubrick and his coscreenwriter Diane Johnson read psychiatrist Bruno Bettelheim's book on the value of fairy tales for children, *The Uses of Enchantment*, published four years before *The Shining* was released.[15] In this book Bettelheim raises a point about the nature of fantasy in the fairy tale that is worth considering here: "The fairy tale is the primer from which the child learns to read his mind in the language of images, the only language which permits understanding before intellectual maturity has been achieved. The child needs to be exposed to this language, and must learn to be responsive to it, if he is to become master of his soul."[16]

Bettelheim argues a defense of fairy tales in their original and often violent forms against those who advocate bowdlerizing more offensive materials to make them safe for children. Although Bettelheim might well have disapproved of many films I am writing about in this book, I think his argument has a valid application for them. Like the fairy tale, with which it does share affinities, the horror film is especially appropriate for dealing with "primitive" feelings, feelings that arise during the earliest periods of our lives. It is perhaps for this reason that every horror film involves a kind of regression, a return to an earlier form of thinking and a short-circuiting of the rational understanding of life we develop as we mature.

Perhaps because it is centrally concerned with thought and knowledge, *The Shining* more fully explores this kind of thinking implicit in all horror films than any of the other films discussed here. It is not just that young Danny's mental landscape is dominated by magical thinking and animism

(ways of thinking that belong distinctly to childhood). The film more particularly dramatizes his mental life by the special power it grants him,
powers that are specifically assigned to seeing. Danny (Danny Lloyd) has
an imaginary friend Tony who "lives in his mouth." Through Tony, Danny
is able to see things removed from him in time and space. As his mother
Wendy (Shelley Duvall) recalls it, Tony first appeared to Danny when he
was three after an "accident" in which his alcoholic father Jack (Jack Nicholson) broke his arm. As Tony's existence was brought on by tensions in
the family (caused particularly by the violence of the father), his chief
function is to provide Danny with visions that express these tensions.
Danny is able to understand through visions, the "language of images,"
familial tensions that he cannot fully express through words.

If "the child learns to read his mind in the language of images," as
Bettelheim has it, seeing is the key to understanding. The film foregrounds
seeing as a form of understanding by an extraordinary invention it works
on the original novel. In both novel and film, the father Jack takes a job
as winter caretaker for a once famous Rocky Mountain resort, the Overlook Hotel. He moves there with his wife and son at the end of the summer
season, planning to use his winter of isolation as an opportunity to finish
a book that he expects will bring him great success. As the winter progresses and snow accumulates, cutting the family off entirely from the
outside world, Jack increasingly descends into a madness that eventually
convinces him he must kill his wife and son. Adjoining the hotel in Stephen King's *The Shining* is a large and wondrous topiary that Danny's
animistic thinking eventually endows with life. In Kubrick's version the
topiary is replaced by an enormous hedge maze which Danny learns to
navigate with his mother.

The maze might be taken as a metaphor for the mind itself, but more
specifically (especially as the film realizes it), it is a puzzle connecting
sight—and particularly acute powers of vision—to knowledge.[17] The notion of the maze dominates the film not just in the hedge creation beside
the hotel, but in the way the camera treats the interior of the hotel itself.
In no other film is Kubrick's penchant for long tracking shots as richly
expressive as it is here, for in no other film is the connection between
forward movement and knowledge made so powerfully direct. Throughout the first half of the film, Danny relentlessly explores the seemingly
endless corridors of the hotel, the camera tracking along just behind him
so that we see the space unfolding, mazelike, as he moves through it.
Danny's movement is always purposeful, although he doesn't necessarily
know where he is going. This is exploration, and space explored becomes

space known. Danny is learning something about his position in the real world through his explorations, but in doing so he is also constructing an internal world. By the end of the film, he has the best knowledge of the hotel as well as the maze, a knowledge that will save his life.

The point where Danny constructs an internal reality from what he sees in external reality is made dramatically clear by a vision that one of his corridor travels leads him to. He suddenly stops before two young girls who beckon him to play with them.[18] We will eventually learn that these girls were killed by their father Grady, a previous winter caretaker who was driven by cabin fever to take an ax to his entire family. As the fantasy conceit of the film has the spirit of Grady taking possession of Jack, Danny's vision here signals an understanding through the "language of images." How this is staged and shot is of particular importance to our understanding of this moment, our perception of what the acquisition of knowledge means to Danny, and, ultimately, to us.

The ambivalence about sight noted earlier as a central element in the horror film—the desire to see conflicting with an anxiety over what may be seen—is most frequently realized in a trope similar to what I have been discussing here: a character moving through an ill-defined space with an open framing that we, the audience, know can be broken through at any time. By priming us to be surprised by an unexpected element, something we are aware must lie just beyond the frame line, this movement through space plays on our desire to receive a pleasurable jolt to our nervous system by suddenly expanding our knowledge of what waits in the world beyond our immediate apperception. What we might see plays with our expectations: It could be something completely innocent (like a screeching cat). Or we might suddenly confront the monster and expect to see disposable characters disposed of or our heroic characters emerge victorious. In any case, a kind of suspended knowledge is made safe and certain.

Kubrick plays with this convention in a number of ways. First of all, he keeps the framing so loose and expansive through all his tracking shots that he plays down the inherent suspense. We can see far enough around Danny to know precisely how distanced will be any threat that may arise. Second, when Danny finally does confront his startling apparition in the corridor, Kubrick simply cancels the confrontation by cutting to the next scene, leaving Danny suspended in the corridor with his hands over his eyes as the only defense against the ghostly pair. Danny, who is characterized by movement, is rendered immobile by the first vision, leading to a central paradox in the film: forward movement (a necessary part of growing up in the film's terms) must lead you to disturbing sights that will make you want to regress. You will see things you might want to turn away from, yet you must also look at them because they represent an acquisition of knowledge that you need to live your life. There is something more here, however: once you have committed yourself to that forward movement, there is no turning back. Or, as the film has it, once you have begun to explore the mazelike world of the intellect, you cannot retreat to an ignorance-is-bliss state.

Fairy tales themselves often imply a mental journey by an actual journey, which leads me to a fairy tale that the film itself evokes. While Danny's father Jack explicitly compares himself to the Big Bad Wolf, Wendy more pointedly invokes "Hansel and Gretel" when she suggests leaving a trail of bread crumbs to find her way back from the kitchen. Indeed, the best fairy-tale model for this film is probably "Hansel and Gretel," where children sent out into the wilderness come upon a strange house and discover an evil adult who wants to eat them. Toward the end of the film the demented Jack will pursue his son with an ax, but the specter of cannibalism is raised early during the initial drive to the secluded Overlook Hotel. At one point, Danny's mother Wendy asks if they aren't near the Donner Pass, whereupon Jack brings up the issue of cannibalism and asks Danny if he knows what that means.

DANNY: Y'mean they eat each other up.
JACK: They had to, in order to survive.
WENDY (*wanting to end the conversation*): Jack . . .
DANNY: Don't worry, Mom. I know all about cannibalism. I saw it on TV.
JACK (*sardonically*): See. It's okay. He saw it on the television.

Jack takes obvious sadistic delight in telling his son about the cannibalistic activities that once took place there. But this dialogue is situated in a context that directly relates it to the child's hunger. Danny had just told his father that he was hungry, prompting an annoyed response from Jack, "Well you should've eaten your breakfast." At this point, the conversation turns to the Donner Pass.

Bettelheim sees "Hansel and Gretel" as a work dealing with a child's oral greediness.[19] In offering a world of oral plenitude to the children, the gingerbread house represents a kind of regression for them. The punitive terror of the witch, as Bettelheim sees it, defines a common strategy in fairy tales that should be familiar from horror films as well. She represents the child's repressed feelings projected outward onto a character perceived as threatening and evil. The guilty child's oral greediness finds a punishment in an oral aggression perceived in the outside world. The conversation that segues from Danny's hunger to the topic of cannibalism replicates the answering of oral need with oral aggression that Bettelheim sees in "Hansel and Gretel."

There is an important difference here, however, in that Jack is not simply Danny's projection. He is his father with his own wants and needs, many of which are clearly in conflict with Danny's. While the witch has no definable character outside of what the children project onto her, the film grants Jack's annoyed response to Danny's hunger a realistic psychological motivation. Rather than seeing all its adult characters merely as projections of the child in the manner of fairy tales, *The Shining* redresses this balance by suggesting something more mutual. As Kubrick himself described it, this film is "just the story of one man's family going insane together."[20] No character has an internal life that belongs to him/herself alone. Danny's fantasies are necessarily conditioned by his father's response. The drama of Danny's development defined by his literal progression through the world finds an inverse parallel in the drama of Jack's metaphoric regression, his retreat into the world of his mind.

To get at these double parallels in the narrative, let's turn to another psychiatrist and another tale to understand a truly radical aspect of this work. Clearly, this film is centrally concerned with the family, and as such it yields to a Freudian interpretation of Oedipal conflicts. More specifically, the film is about the "nuclear family," a phrase heard with much frequency in the popular press during the period when the film was made.[21] The nuclear family should allow for Freud's family romance in its most rarefied form, and, indeed, this family seems completely turned in on itself. The central conceit of the narrative facilitates an isolation that goes beyond anything an actual nuclear family might achieve, yet it was this isolation from the larger society that gave the term its generally negative connotation—an isolation that escalated with the development of suburban life in the 1950s and the increasing flight from the cities in the 1960s. Criticism of the nuclear family and a strong rejection of its isolation was particularly associated with young people in the late 1960s and early 1970s since many had moved out into communes to regain a sense of community. That this retreat from communal life could occasion horror was noted earlier in this chapter in the case of *Halloween*.

The Shining dramatizes isolation within the family itself even before they begin their winter retreat, suggesting that the retreat is merely an extension of something that already exists. Rather than defining the family as a single unified entity, the film sets up an opposition in the way we first see them. Jack is introduced separately when applying for a job, while mother and son are introduced as a unit, sitting at the kitchen table having lunch. In this way the film inscribes a typical problem of the nuclear family, where the father's devotion to work makes him an absent presence. *Kramer vs. Kramer* (1979), one of biggest hits the year before *The Shining*, presented a similarly absent man, but with a less compliant wife. In this film the wife, stultified by the demands of her family, leaves to become her own person. Forced to become the primary caregiver for his young son, the father learns the joys of fatherhood—joys that, as the film has it, are normally denied fathers in our society. At the time, a number of critics saw *The Shining* as the dark underside of *Kramer vs. Kramer*.[22] In *The Shining*, the father clearly feels stultified, blames it on the family, and seeks his independence. But seeing the film in these terms simply shows how *Kramer vs. Kramer* appropriates a pop feminism by assigning to a woman qualities not unusual for a man in American culture. What is darkest about *The Shining* is not the return of those qualities to a male,[23] but rather the way the film turns what Freud called "family romances" inside out.

Five-year-old Danny is about to embark on the "latency period," the period in which the sexual feelings of childhood are temporarily repressed until they return under the hormonal urgings of adolescence. What precedes and leads into the latency period for Freud is an Oedipal conflict. There is an almost naked Oedipal pattern outlined in Kubrick's film (albeit not with the proper resolution for Freud): the father is killed, and the child goes off with the mother. For Freud, the passing of the Oedipus complex paves the way for the latency period because the child finally renounces romantic fantasies of union with the mother. This happens for two reasons: the child's fear of castration by the father and, ultimately, the child's identification with the same sex (father) figure. The father, then, always occupies something of an ambivalent role in the life of the son, but in the Freudian scheme this ambivalence is created entirely in the son's fantasy life. The father does not actually wish to castrate his child; this is merely an outward projection of the son's anxiety. A strict Freudian interpretation of this movie would therefore have to see it as pure wish-fulfillment (and regressive for that reason). But such an interpretation plays against the whole tenor of the ending, which grants a real achievement to Danny, much in the manner of fairy tales.[24]

In suggesting that there is perhaps another way of looking at this, I do not intend to rewrite Freudian psychology since I am not trying to further psychoanalytic thought. But I want to stress a cultural context for the film that was becoming increasingly concerned with recasting the Oedipal drama. Much as Freudian thought was enjoying a resurgence in literary academia, it was subject to attack in more popular intellectual forums. In 1973, the same year as *The Exorcist*, Morton Schatzman published *Soul Murder: Persecution in the Family*, in which he looked at the father's persecutorial behavior toward his son Dr. Schreber, one of Freud's most famous paranoids.[25] After this followed numerous feminist writings on incest, in addition to the popular books by Swiss psychiatrist Alice Miller that quite consciously sought to reinstate the "seduction theory" Freud first proposed in "The Aetiology of Hysteria" in 1895 (and later supplanted with drive theory, which placed the focus more firmly on a person's fantasy life as opposed to events that might or might not have happened).[26] The most notorious attack on Freud to gain widespread attention was Jeffrey Masson's *The Assault on Truth*, successfully promoted as an exposé because of the book's claim that Freud had made a cowardly retreat from his original formulations.[27] All were connected by a common thread rejecting the Freudian model of fantasy projections in order to look at the consequences of actual parental abuse.[28]

In an anthology of psychohistorical pieces on several centuries' worth of child-rearing practices published in 1974, editor Lloyd de Mause wrote, "The history of childhood is a nightmare from which we have only recently begun to awaken."[29] In this chapter I have tried to suggest that such a nightmare turns up in the "evil children" films as an early manifestation of a cultural dialogue that would become increasingly vocal throughout the 1980s on the position of children within the family. Through their fantasies, these films implicitly acknowledge the hostility of the parents, but do so by projecting it onto demonic children. The ambivalence in these works, the shifting and conflicting sympathies between apparently good parents and terrible children, results from the fantasy's attempts at concealing what it everywhere points to—the parents' hostility.

The Shining recast the terms of the debate by stating the matter directly: What if the father is in fact murderous? What if his violent impulses to maim and dismember (explicitly invoked in this film by the father's ax) are real and not merely a projection of a guilty son's anxiety? In asking these questions, the film redirects Freud's Oedipal drama to the original myth. While Freud picks up Oedipus at the crossroads where he kills his father Laius, the story of Oedipus himself actually begins with his parents' abandonment, an abandonment that is inscribed in his name (Oedipus means "Swollen Foot": to signify the moment that Laius put the infant

Oedipus out in the wilderness, piercing his ankles and binding his feet together with a thong).[30] This engenders a very different kind of family drama than what Freud proposed since it focuses both on the father's fear of his own child and the child's absolute dependency on his parents/ caretakers. The parental abuse is more than an unfortunate accident in the child's personal history: by making it apparent even in Oedipus' name, the myth incorporates the abuse into Oedipus' very identity. We know him by the swollen foot, which signifies what his father did to him.

When we consider the entire myth, it might seem particularly odd that Freud would choose it to define the fantasy life of the child independent of the parents' desires. But we might follow the lead of Marie Balmary in applying a Freudian method to Freud himself to say that even as Freud conceals the abuse, the telling of the myth must inevitably reveal it. Picking up the tale of Oedipus at the crossroads, as Freud does, represents a kind of unconscious repression that, like all repressed material, will find another form of expression, in this case in Oedipus' very name.[31] I want to call attention to this repression here chiefly to observe that it connotes something we apparently have trouble looking at. What seems to me radical in *The Shining* is the way in which it effectively dramatizes something so insistently repressed in Western culture, the hostility of the father toward his own son.

The film places this issue in a very broad context by the music Kubrick uses for his title sequence, a twentieth-century version of the *Dies Irae* by Polish composer Krzysztof Penderecki. The words of this portion of the requiem mass in the standard liturgy tell of a terrible time to come ("Dies irae, dies illa/solvet saeclum in favilla . . ."): the Day of Wrath will come and reduce the world to ashes.[32] This quite specifically means that the wrath of God the Father will come, the final Judge of all our sins. But the "Recordare" section offers a prayer to an intercessor, this wrathful father's Son, to ask for forgiveness ("*Jesu pie*"). In the light of *The Exorcist* and *The Omen*, this musical invocation of religion is especially meaningful, a way of establishing a context to react against. In the earlier works, the children are the wrathful figures, while the murderous fathers act from compassion.

If *The Exorcist* seems to reverse the terms of the *Dies Irae*, there is nonetheless an important religious narrative it may descend from. Where *The Exorcist* visits a wide variety of terrible punishments on a young girl's body in order to restore a priest's lost faith, the Book of Job features a "son" subjected to gross punishments by his "father" in order to demonstrate the son's abiding faith in the father. *The Exorcist* might well be seen as part of a similar tradition: the Book of Job seems to me a fairly early work of gross-out in that the principal narrative drive of this tale comes from our anticipation of each increasingly gross indignity Job will submit himself to. As in any gross-out work, each new turn of events must top the previous one in disgust. The religious purpose may conceal this appeal by an apparent imputation of philosophical meaning (a consideration of humanity's relationship to God), but the narrative nonetheless achieves much of its momentum and ambivalent attraction from the accumulation of gross incidents that structure the tale.

Indeed, the underlying ambivalence here is not unlike what is found in the best moments of gross-out horror, as we are asked both to sympathize with Job and take pleasure in the spectacle of events the narrative offers. The sympathy is clearest in this passage, when Job addresses his heavenly father:

> I am blameless; I regard not myself; I loathe my life. It is all one; therefore I say, he destroys both the blameless and the wicked [9:21–22]. . . . Does it seem good to thee to oppress, to despise the work of thy hands and favor the designs of the wicked? Hast thou eyes of flesh? Dost thou see as a man sees? . . . Thy hands fashioned and made me; and now thou dost turn about and destroy me [10:3–8]. . . . Why didst thou bring me forth from the womb? Would that I had died before any eye had seen me, and were as though I had not been, carried from the womb to the grave [10:18–19].

God is quite willing to have his agent, the "Accuser," visit a wide variety of disgusting miseries on Job, and particularly on Job's body, to show that there is no other creature like him in his fear of God. Is Job merely an object to God, a creature whose very abjection better shows off God's glory? Why indeed should God turn on what He Himself has created? The passage I have cited are words that could easily be spoken, if not with quite so much eloquence, by an abused child. What is of particular interest here is the apparent unknowability of the father figure, a shadowy figure not subject to our powers of analysis. As with an abusing father, the child necessarily submits but cannot fathom motivation.

There remains something unknowable about the father in Western thought, and this unknowability seems especially tied to issues of cruelty. Even within the Freudian model, which in other instances attempts to look at religion from a clear-eyed and rational perspective, the father remains something of a shadowy figure. Freud may look at the ambivalence of the son toward the father in great detail, but the father himself is protected from any such ambivalence toward the son. In attempting to understand the father's view of the son, I have to turn to a son-disciple of father Freud. A conventional view of the Book of Job holds that "it does not aim to explain the mystery of suffering or to 'justify the ways of God with men.' It aims at probing the depths of faith in spite of suffering."[33] This claim neatly exonerates God since we no longer have to consider why He might actually do something like this; God's actions always remain beyond our understanding.

But Freud's disciple Carl Jung, in his brilliant *Answer to Job*, puts the focus back on God's motivation, and in a way that has relevance for my concerns here. As Jung has it, God is jealous of Job for his "keener consciousness based on self-reflection," a consciousness that grants Job "a superior knowledge of God which God himself did not possess."[34] Job sees through God's weakness, that He needs humanity's absolute devotion to complete the picture of His greatness. In punishing Job without apparent reason, God acts from an anxiety about his autonomy—or, conversely, an anxiety about His own power. Jung recuperates the tale of Job for Christianity by seeing an anticipation of Christ in Job's confronting God over His motivation. The division of God in Christian mythology is an attempt to address the imbalance inherent in the originating Jewish myth of the omnipotent and frequently cruel father by purging him of ambivalence, granting him a son who embodies mercy. Job's statement, "For I know that my Vindicator lives, and at last he will stand upon the earth" (Job 19:25) was taken by later centuries to foretell the coming of Christ. The cruelty of the father may still be there, as the liturgy of the *Dies Irae* suggests, but it finds a mediator in the son.

Much as *The Shining* attempts to overthrow traditional ways of looking at the wrathful father, its most brutal moment comes in how it deals with the intercessor figure. Dick Halloran (Scatman Crothers), a chef at the Overlook during the season, befriends Danny because he also has the "shining," the power to see beyond ordinary vision. It is to Halloran that Danny prays (or "shines" as the novel and film have it) when the wrathful father becomes murderous. Halloran the intercessor arrives to save Danny, but in the film's one real moment of bloody violence the wrathful father murders the intercessor with an ax. There is no intercessor in the world of this film; the child is thrown back on his own resources.[35] It is possible to read an ambivalence into the father in the Book of Job, as Jung does, a division that Christianity possibly attempts to purify by its division of God into separate parts. In this context, what remains most striking about *The Shining* is the extent to which it looks at the ambivalence of the father.[36] Perhaps especially within the context of Western thought, this must be seen as a matter for horror.[37]

This might also explain why much of the criticism of *The Shining* appears to treat Jack as the central character in the film, even though its fairy-tale atmosphere and childlike perspective would seem to shift the focus to Danny. I don't want to ignore this apparent distortion, however, because it does point to the contradictory ways in which the film treats the father's ambivalence. As Jack enters deeper and deeper into his own fantasy world, he becomes increasingly a bizarre figure of fun, consciously enacting a fairy tale by impersonating the Big Bad Wolf. He is a crazed prankster, or, to complement his own fantasies of omnipotence, a murderous Lord of Misrule. His sarcastic view of his family, barely held in check in the first half of the film, suddenly takes flight and grants him the funniest lines in the film's second half. A number of critics, used to a sense of Kubrick as satirist, moved this humor to center stage.[38] A wild ambivalence toward the monstrous is typical of gross-out horror, however, and there really is more of a balance among the principal characters here. As in *The Birds* (1963), *The Shining* presents an unexpected chamber drama amidst its spectacle of horror. What is distinctive in this film is not the ambivalent view of the father, but the full recognition of the father's ambivalence.

This ambivalence receives its greatest articulation and force by the way the film dramatizes issues around the power of sight. The hotel to which this tight nuclear family makes their winter retreat is called the "Overlook," a name with an easy capacity for multiple meanings in a film that centers on vision. In one brilliant sequence, Kubrick effectively gives dramatic shape to all three primary meanings of the word. The moment comes as a culmination to a crosscut sequence of a housebound Jack unsuccessfully trying to write as his wife and child explore the grounds. The crosscutting plays on a thematic issue I have already suggested: the increasing interiority of Jack and his withdrawal into himself, as Danny moves more and more out into the world. At one moment, Jack, wandering around his room aimlessly, looks at a model of the hedge maze Wendy and Danny have just wandered into. A high-angle shot approximates Jack's point of view as he looks down on the maze. The camera begins to zoom in and, as it does so, it picks up the figures of Wendy and Danny, seamlessly transforming the shot of the maze model into the real thing.

This one shot contains within it all three meanings for "overlook" in the film. First, it signifies a vantage point from which to behold a spectacular view (the most apparent meaning for the hotel itself). But this image earns it as well for it turns out to be even more spectacular than we imagine at first, as the model becomes reality, giving us the only overview of the maze in the entire film. Second, the word means to oversee, to direct, to supervise. As such, it signals a power in the person who is looking, a power defined by sight. This is how Jack sees himself in relation to the family: they are subservient to his vision, neatly contained within the confines of the maze. Finally, and contradictorily, "overlook" means not to notice. This simply signifies that Jack from his perspective cannot see what Wendy and Danny can from theirs, as the subsequent eye-level shot of Wendy and Danny in the maze makes clear. It is precisely what Jack overlooks in his overview and what Danny sees by his immersion that will enable Danny to successfully evade Jack in the film's final sequence. The word *overlook* as the movie realizes it actually contains opposing meanings that signal an ambivalence about the power of sight central to the way the film defines the father/son relationship.

To get at this, I want to look at a powerful sequence between Danny and Jack that comes almost halfway through the film. In many ways this is the film's central scene,—an intense moment in which they most directly confront each other. In analyzing this scene, I want to pay particular attention to its context, for in the sequencing of events leading up to and away from this scene, sight remains a central concern:

- In a sequence described above, Danny has the vision of the two Grady girls in the hallway. He covers his face but remains immobile, frozen in terror over what he has seen.
- Watching television with his mother, Danny goes to his room to get his fire engine. While there, he sees his father sitting on the bed and staring straight ahead. A conversation between the two ensues.
- Looking for his mother, Danny walks into Room 237, the door to which has been left invitingly ajar.
- Wendy is checking the dials on gauges in the basement of the hotel when she suddenly hears Jack scream.
- Wendy comes to Jack, who tells her of a nightmare he has just wakened from in which he has a *vision* of killing his wife and child. Danny appears covered with bruises, which makes Wendy think Jack has attacked him.
- A disgruntled Jack walks into the hotel bar where he conjures up an actual vision from the past in which he sees Lloyd the bartender, who serves him a drink.

From this point on, sight becomes increasingly confounded as we ourselves have difficulty in determining which vision is actuality and which is fantasy. When Jack, at Wendy's request, visits Room 237 (the room in which Danny had been attacked), what we see is possibly a vision for Dick Halloran, the hotel chef whom Danny is trying to reach by "shining." This ordering of scenes imbues a sense of confusion in the ways of seeing—in looking outward and looking inward. The central scene, the dialogue between Danny and Jack, begins with Jack apparently looking at nothing, then trying to connect with Danny, who is troubled by his father's appearance.

When Danny first walks into the room, we see him standing between two images of Jack: a reflection of Jack in a mirror on the left of the image and Jack in actuality on the bed on the right. There is a feeling here that Danny is caught between these two images of Jack; at the same time, the film marks precisely Jack's descent into a mirror world, an internal space that in effect can only reflect itself. Jack is becoming a figure of pure *stasis* and is, in effect, trying to make Danny into that as well; he tells him he wants to stay at this hotel "forever and ever and ever" (echoing exactly the words the murdered Grady girls had earlier uttered to Danny). Nicholson's performance is mercurial in the way it shifts between real love and real hatred in this scene. The tone at the beginning implies genuine concern, but by the end Jack is talking to Danny in the overly emphatic mode that adults reserve for children: "I love you more than anything else in the *whole* world" (a declaration of love that Nicholson makes sound like one of the most terrifying things any father could say to his son). The ambivalence of the father must create ambivalence in the son. What can he be without a father's love, yet what can he be with the love offered?

If we keep in mind the contrast between movement and stasis that is suggested here, the contrast between constant exploration of the outside world and withdrawal into some interior world, we can see that Jack's growing insanity is specifically tied to Danny's growth. Danny's exploration of the exterior world enriches his interior world, but Jack's withdrawal into his interior world cuts him off from the exterior world. Parallel regressions at the end of the film point to this difference. Danny learns to move backwards, literally, as a way of saving himself, learning that movement need not be in only one direction, that one may in fact move forward by retracing one's steps. The father figuratively moves backwards into a kind of eternal regression, achieving the independence of a static existence. The child's birth, then, commemorates the father's decline and death. Hence the father's ambivalence, which is perhaps the darkest underside of Western culture. Eschewing the diversionary device of the cruel stepfather, *The Shining* is one of the rare works that has looked directly at that nightmare.

At the time of the film's release, Kubrick said "ghost stories appeal to our craving for immortality."[39] This is a notion I have already dealt with in *The Other*, but in *The Shining* it receives a distinctly physical dimension. As a conventional matter, we can often say that our immortality resides in our children, but that offers little comfort to our own aging bodies. The inverse parallel of Danny's growth with Jack's decline and increasing sense of impotence finds a direct corollary in the fantasy Jack has in Room 237. When Jack enters the bathroom, a beautiful young woman rises naked from the tub and walks toward him. She embraces Jack, but as he kisses her he looks in a mirror where he sees himself holding the body of a diseased old crone. He breaks away as the old woman begins to laugh at him mercilessly, taunting the sense of immortality he seeks in fantasy with the reality of her withering body. In its graphicness this is a gross-out scene, one that directly connects it to contemporaneous horror films. A sense of the body as an object of revulsion (especially a woman's body) had become one of the most distinctive features of gross-out horror.

Revolting Bodies

The patient's abdomen was opened with an inverted Y-shaped incision that started just above the breast bone and ended above the navel. His skin was deeply yellow from the build-up of bile salts that his failing liver could no longer metabolize....

Soon after, the baboon liver arrived in the operating room and was placed in a metal bowl of crushed ice to preserve it.... The liver was smooth and healthy looking, less than half the size of the patient's shrunken liver.

If the new combination of drugs allows successful baboon liver transplants, surgeons will try it with other organs so that baboons could be raised for a dependable, ready supply of organs for humans.

—"Terminally Ill Man Gets Baboon Liver in Untried Operation," New York Times, *July 29, 1992* -

Chapter 16 *Menstruation, Monstrosity, and Mothers*

The most obvious interpretation of the [dead baby joke] cycle seems to be a protest against babies in general. The attempt to legalize abortion and the increased availability of improved contraceptives (e.g., the pill) have brought the debate about the purpose of sexual activity into the public arena, where even teenagers can participate. . . . But a price is paid for contraception and abortion. That price includes the guilt of preventing the creation of, or destroying, a potential human being. . . . It is possible that one way of fighting the fear or gilding the guilt is to tell gross dead baby jokes, as if to dehumanize babies and thus destroy them through modern technology (including contraception devices).[1]

—*Alan Dundes,* Cracking Jokes[1]

In this quote folklorist Alan Dundes deals with a form of gross-out that entered public discourse at roughly the same time as the films discussed in this book. As such, it seems probable the cycle addresses concerns that turn up in the films themselves. If these films are more likely to feature murderous babies rather than dead ones, they nonetheless contrive, as was noted earlier, to make us feel the necessity of punishing or even killing these babies. Dundes's explication of the dead baby jokes, however, points in another direction explicitly taken by a number of films. If abortion and subsequent debates over reproductive rights and screaming fetuses conditioned the way we look at babies, it also affected our view of bodies, particularly women's bodies. How the reproductive organs of a woman's body actually work became more of a topic of public discourse than ever before.

If *The Exorcist* established the body as a site of horror, the horror film through the 1970s became increasingly focused on the body, and specifically on two interconnected aspects of the body: its excretions (products of the body beyond our control), and as a corollary of this, lack of control (the autonomic responses of the body). In this chapter, I want to look at two important films—Brian De Palma's *Carrie* and David Cronenberg's *The Brood*—that elaborate on these concerns. *Carrie* is the more mainstream film, very much operating in a manner derived from *The Exorcist* but expanding it in ways that would in turn become influential.[2] *Carrie* does not wound the body of its eponymous heroine in the manner of *The Exorcist*; rather it sees her body as already wounded, with menstruation the key sign of gross-out. *The Brood* is more global, defining the image of the gross body by the entire female reproductive system. *The Brood* invokes concerns about the body that had become common in horror films of the time, but it also questions attitudes about the body that had become conventional with the genre.

In both films, the ambivalence of gross-out dominates the point of view to the extent that it influences the surface tone of these films more than any of the others yet considered. In *Carrie*, the ambivalence conditions the film's mode of address, leading to abrupt shifts between comedy and horror.[3] In particular, the ambivalence serves to make us question how we define monsters by setting up a pair of opposing monstrosities: throughout the film it is uncertain if the monstrous is allied with rebelliousness or with the forces of repression. The vision in *Carrie* is more social—the place of the body in society. In *The Brood*, the scope is more narrowly psychological, more on individual responses to the body. In *The Brood*, ambivalence is both mode and subject matter as the film self-consciously explores the ways in which our bodies may become divided against themselves. In both films, characters are both at home in their bodies and irrevocably alienated from them.

Carrie (1976)

Brian De Palma's early work as an independent filmmaker was in wild comedy, and his first major studio film was also a comedy (*Get to Know Your Rabbit*, 1972). *Carrie* is of particular importance, then, since much of it does work as a teenage comedy, a forerunner of some of the comedies discussed in the first half of the book. There is a good deal of comedy here, but it tends to move in a different direction from the later comedies, where laughter is generally celebratory, valorizing gross physicality. Gross physicality in *Carrie* is more openly a troubling matter, and as a consequence the laughter in this film is more derisive, often turning back on itself and to become a subject for horror.

Befitting the derisive mode, much of the comedy is satiric, with a pointed view of the social cliques that dominate American high school life (but which generally remain absent from the earlier surveyed high school films). Laughter itself becomes thematized in the course of the film so that this comedy metamorphoses itself into a horror film precisely by examining its status as a comedy. The movie begins with an extended scene of high school girls cruelly laughing at Carrie as she experiences her first menstrual period (in the girls' shower room after gym class) and moves toward its climactic scene of a blood-drenched Carrie hearing the entire school laughing at her. This is a comedy, but one turned inside out as it encourages us to laugh at its characters while at the same time questioning what it means to be laughed at.

The film's fluctuation between comedy and horror is in part a function of the presentation of its central character. Carrie (Sissy Spacek) has a superhuman power (telekinesis), which she uses to kill a gymnasium full of people, and at the end of the film, she rises up from hell. And yet, when I've asked some fairly large lecture classes how many people think she's a monster, very few hands go up. It is possible that older audiences may see the monstrosity more clearly, that college students are still too close to the pain of high school social experiences not to identify with Carrie's situation. The source novel by Stephen King, however, does make the monstrosity clearer with its initial description of Carrie:

> Girls stretched and writhed under the hot water, squalling, flicking water, squirting white bars of soap from hand to hand. Carrie stood among them stolidly, a frog among swans. She was a chunky girl with pimples on her neck and back and buttocks, her wet hair completely without color. It rested against her face with dispirited sogginess and she simply

stood, head slightly bent, letting the water splat against her flesh and roll off. She looked the part of the sacrificial goat, the constant butt, believer in left-handed monkey wrenches, perpetual foul-up, and she was.[4]

The Carrie of the novel is specifically defined as a scapegoat, and she is presented as someone easy enough to distance ourselves from since she is made a physical grotesque from the outset: plump and nondescript to the point of colorlessness except for the bright red splotches evoked by the pimples covering her back. She is, the voice of the author assures us, exactly what she looks like, so that the psychological grotesquerie necessarily complements her physical appearance.

Since movies are much more an art form of appearances, it is unlikely the film could have cast someone that looked like King's description and held onto an audience.[5] The casting of Sissy Spacek is something else again because she is clearly, as a kindly gym teacher will tell her, a very pretty girl. The association of seductive beauty with evil in Western culture has found expression in earlier horror films with women who are both beautiful and monstrous (such as female vampires). Their beauty, however, is generally of a more openly sexual kind than that of Spacek, who is waiflike, ethereal, and physically underdeveloped. Her pleasant looks and slightness of stature signal goodness, and yet the film also insists on seeing her as monstrous. There is an underlying ambivalence in the way the film presents Carrie that centers on the presentation of her body.

What, then, is monstrous in Carrie? The first two scenes of the movie (both played under the titles) provide us with two possible ways of approaching Carrie—one in social terms, the other in more personal, and specifically physical, terms. The first scene shows Carrie playing volleyball with a group of girls, and playing badly. A long crane shot slowly moves in on Carrie toward the back of the court as if singling her out, but also reinforcing a mise-en-scène that has already separated her from the other girls: in contrast to them she is defined as weak, awkward, ungainly, and isolated. As the camera reaches her, a ball hits her head, causing her side to lose and turning all the girls against her. She is quite literally a loser, someone who necessarily provokes hostility because no one wants to see themselves like her.

Ever since the cogent and persuasive writings of Robin Wood, the monster in the horror film has been generally seen as embodying the "Other," that part of ourselves that we repress and banish from our conscious mind but then project onto other people.[6] Carrie is certainly "the other" here, but not in a way that is really threatening to anyone. For this reason, the camera can encourage an empathic response to this otherness: when Carrie has been fully isolated by the camera movement, after she has missed the ball, a red hat surprisingly enters the image from the right to hit her across the head. Because it is unexpected, the hat produces something of a physiological jolt for us that allies us with her by establishing a similar vulnerability. Otherness here is entirely a social issue that reinforces the film's status as a kind of teen comedy. The full range of Carrie's monstrousness, however, will play itself out in a more physical arena, where the film makes empathic identification more difficult to sustain.

The scene immediately following the volleyball game is built on a contrast in its differing views of a woman's body, moving from a lyricism that prettifies to the horror of bloody excretion. The scene is shot entirely in slow motion until the horror intrudes. By rendering all movement graceful the slow motion beautifies the presentation of the girls' bodies. Because the elaborate camera movement past all the lockers with the naked and dressing girls is seemingly set in motion by a girl brushing her hair, the cause for the lyricism lies in how the girls present themselves to the camera. While it might be more accurate to see the scene as a male fantasy of a girls' locker room, the audience, both male and female, is being set up to appreciate something here that will be destroyed. Indirectly, we come to regard this retrospectively as Carrie's first act of destruction.

When the camera singles out Carrie, isolated in the shower, the film directly inverts the method of the book. Far from presenting her body as a gross object in itself, the camera beautifies it, anatomizing it to let different parts of the body dominate the image. As if in recognition of the sexual aspect of this beauty, the montage conveys a sense of autoeroticism as shots of Carrie's hands caressing breasts and thighs with soap are crosscut with close-ups of her face showing signs of dreamy pleasure. A number of critics have seen an invocation of *Psycho* here, but I suspect that's solely because De Palma has primed his critics to be on the lookout for Hitchcock references. It is more accurate to say the sequence invokes a soap commercial, with the same erotic lyricism these commercials grant to the act of washing. Beads of water on flesh enhance the sensual beauty of the image and alludes to a real pleasure in cleanliness, or in making something clean. The connection of washing to eros is given a purgative psychological dimension as well: isolated in the steam, taking pleasure in her own body, Carrie finds a kind of compensation in autoeroticism for the vicious rejection in the previous scene.

The lyrical mode is abandoned with the onset of Carrie's period, and it will condition the way we view menstruation. By virtue of a context in which making something clean is defined as a specifically erotic activity, the sudden intrusion of menstrual blood must seem dirty. The subsequent sequencing of shots and a significant change in the soundtrack underscore the sense of pollution. The flow of menstrual blood starts immediately after an insert shot, still in slow motion, of the bar of soap slipping out of Carrie's hand. It is as if in losing the soap she loses the power to keep herself clean, and the defilement of menstrual blood ensues. At this point the lush music playing under the titles ceases, and live sound is heard for the first time; the slow-motion photography is abandoned. In short, everything that has made this sequence lyrical abruptly gives way to a more prosaic rendering. In dropping the soap, in breaking off the lyricism of the soap commercial, Carrie herself has destroyed a pretty picture.[7]

Menstruation is specifically tied to monstrosity in that we are made to feel the grossness of the flow of blood. The pretty has been made ugly, the attractive made repulsive. And the sequencing of shots specifically makes Carrie responsible for this terrible transformation since the editing implies that her dropping the soap has invoked the flow of blood. Carrie is a monster because she cannot keep herself clean, she cannot maintain the unspoiled image of beauty that first appears to us. This places Carrie's monstrosity in a peculiar light. She is an object of attraction and sympathy for the audience; but because she also destroys the prettiness, because she turns it into something the film makes us see as gross and disgusting, the film provides a rationale for seeing the later punitiveness directed against her as being justified.

Carrie's own reaction to her first period mirrors ours: she is horrified. Her terrified screams attract the attention of other girls in the locker room, who present an alternative response: they laugh at her derisively. The laughter might seem a way for the girls to distance themselves from Carrie, a way of keeping her and her experiences other. But in both cases it is a *female* response to the menstruation that the film highlights. Much of the film is in fact structured around female responses to Carrie. Men don't seem to notice her at all unless their attention is directed to her by women. Precisely because the film insists on the centrality of female responses, it defines Carrie's monstrosity as a universalized problem of femininity.

The women in the film present two sets of opposing views—one from girls who are Carrie's age, the other from two maternal figures—that parallel the social-sexual opposition by which the film defines Carrie. The difference in her classmates' responses provides the starkest contrast. The popular, sweet-natured, and rather proper Sue (Amy Irving), who ordinarily would be crowned prom queen, sees Carrie primarily in social terms: as an outcast whose plight prompts a sympathy so extreme it leads Sue to send her boyfriend to Carrie as a prom date. For sweet and simple Sue, the solution to Carrie's problem is comparably simple: social integration achieved by the attentions of a good-looking boy who also happens to be the school's star athlete. The implication is that even the most outcast of women will feel more whole, more fully herself if connected to a man. The more sexual and vulgar Chris (Nancy Allen) openly hates Carrie, specifically focusing on an area less amenable to alteration: Carrie's bloodiness.

By having Chris's anger center on Carrie's sexuality, the film directly connects Chris to the object of her animus. Chris's personal involvement with Carrie is signaled by the fact that the planned revenge against Carrie seems overly elaborate for the actual impetus. Chris wants to embarrass Carrie at the prom because she herself is not able to go; but in order to do this she has to have her boyfriend Billy (John Travolta) kill a pig, collect its blood, set into motion a complicated scheme that will get Carrie elected prom queen, and then rig up a device that will pour the pig's blood all over Carrie just at the moment of crowning. The narrative events are already excessive in their own right, but the way they are presented to us grants the excessiveness a specific meaning: the film emphasizes in clear erotic terms the pleasure Chris feels in venting her anger against Carrie.

De Palma's overblown style signals the excess at two key moments: the killing of the pig and the suspense sequence leading up to the bucket of blood being dumped on Carrie. In the first scene, every time Billy lands a blow with his sledgehammer against the pig's head, De Palma provides a shock cut to Chris reacting with pleasure to each blow. The erotic quality of Chris's reaction is clearly delineated by Nancy Allen's performance, but the rocking rhythm established by the editing effectively eroticizes the violence for the audience as well: to some degree, we are asked to share in Chris's response. Chris's pleasure in the killing is clearly sexual, but is it really enough to note this?

Our understanding of Chris's pleasure in the killing is partly determined by some dialogue just before the killing takes place. As Chris and her male minions steal into the stockyard, one of the boys talks about a girl he knows whom he keeps describing as a "real pig." If "girl" equals "pig" and Billy's beating blows produce an ecstatic response in Chris, the film suggests a connection between her and the pig. Chris's implicit identification with the pig implies a masochistic pleasure in the violence. Violence is inherently a part of sexual feeling for her since her relationship with Billy throughout the film is shown to be combative. But in her combat with Billy she is also extremely manipulative, to the degree that she is always able to win her position. Here, however, she seems to have manipulated Billy into an act of violence that she experiences as both sexual and directed against herself. She identifies in a sexual way with the victim of her "prank."

This eroticized pleasure of revenge motivated by an implied identification with the victim finds its climax in Chris's humiliation of Carrie. This brings us to the other instance of stylistic excess: as Chris amusedly waits for just the right moment to overturn the bucket of blood, De Palma cuts to an extreme close-up of her lips, the tightest shot in the movie, as her tongue slowly moves across them, exhibiting a pleasure in anticipation so delicious she can taste it. Again, there is an unexpected eroticization here, and, again, one the audience is invited to share in by virtue of the style, an image that is all lubricious flesh. But this is also specifically an autoerotic expression—Chris's tongue stroking her lips—that effectively returns us to the beginning of the film and the scene in the shower.

There is commensurately a structural parallel here: if the opening scene moves toward the climax of a bloodied Carrie, here the climax is Carrie drenched with blood from Chris's prank. The blood from the pig (which has been equated with woman) is menstrual blood, and the ultimate humiliation of Carrie is the exposure of her menstruating self that lies behind the glamorous facade of prom queen. She is not really beautiful after all, but a bloodied grotesque. Chris's sexual pleasure in all this is built on an ambivalence: a simultaneous identification with the victim and a denial of that identification. Chris's excessive need to scapegoat Carrie by projecting a grossness onto her is a defense against the grossness in Chris herself. In this respect Carrie truly is other, so that it is Chris's conception of Carrie that defines her monstrousness.

Much as the film forges audience sympathy for Carrie, it does so ambivalently because it also offers support for Chris's view, which is to say that it alternates between its vision of Carrie as defined by Chris and Sue. Carrie is either all waiflike innocent, which is the way Sue sees her, or she is all menstruating grotesque, which is what Chris sees. It is at the point when Carrie is drenched in blood that she becomes most fully monstrous, destroying a school full of people and murdering Chris, Billy, and, ultimately, even her mother (Piper Laurie). As De Palma reworks it through the casting of Sissy Spacek, Stephen King's narrative becomes a variant on the ugly duckling story in which the duckling becomes a beautiful swan only to revert to ugly duckling status again. The film's Manichaean approach to beauty—King's Carrie could never be a swan—suggests that beauty itself is a lie, the menstruating monster the reality. In this way, the film seems to support the view of the most monstrous character in the film, Carrie's mother.

As the film has it, the monstrosity of the parent becomes the key to understanding the monstrosity of the child. When Carrie responds to Chris's practical joke with her fullest fury, she hears three voices in obsessive ostinato repeating things said to her earlier in the film: that of two parental figures (the principal and the gym teacher) as well as the voice of her actual mother. The principal is the only male in this group, and as such in the film's scheme has the weakest voice: he is heard inappropriately addressing Carrie as "Cassie." As this scene presents the most powerful demonstration of Carrie's telekinetic powers, the voice-over appropriately refers the audience back to the first scene that clearly indicated those powers.

The kind gym teacher Miss Collins has brought Carrie to the principal's office after the menstruation melee in the shower. The two adults talk about Carrie as if she wasn't there, although she is sitting by a window just outside the office and can hear every word they utter. When the principal finally talks to her directly, he always addresses her as "Cassie." Carrie quietly corrects him but is clearly upset by his mistake. Her increasing anguish, which she cannot show directly, is finally expressed by her causing an ashtray to jump off the principal's desk and smash to the floor. The scene sketches out in miniature what will be played out in full at the film's climax: Carrie's telekinesis operates as revenge for misrecognition. And it is the monstrousness of misrecognition that finally turns her into a monster.

The film's major themes are played here in miniature because the scene involves a male parent, and men are not particularly important in this film. The motif of the absent father common to the child abuse films is thematized in a distinctive way here. The actual father is absent, as usual, but there is another absence here as well since all the other male characters are distinguished by their apparent weakness. While Miss Collins paces back and forth through his office trying to explain how she understood the scapegoating reaction of the other girls toward Carrie, the principal sits uncomfortably at his desk, very apparently made nervous by all this talk of menstruation. Yet his nervousness is clearly based on a kind of ambivalent response to Miss Collins herself at this moment. He is fully dressed in a brown business suit, while she, coming directly from the gym, is still in shorts, and fairly snug ones at that. The difference in dress, one concealing, one revealing, establishes a voyeuristic theme here that the camera then articulates in a distinctive way.

There is a striking shot that for want of a better term must be called a two-shot. Two-shots are a familiar figure in conventional films for dialogue, but they normally involve medium to close shots of two heads talking. This two-shot, however, presents the viewer with a medium view of the principal (upper torso and head, on the left back of the image), paired with Miss Collins's lower torso on the right front. Her bright white scanty shorts stand out, distinguished by a few faint smears of blood, presumably from Carrie's menstrual flow. As the offscreen voice of Miss Collins tries to explain her own responses to the principal, he alternates his gaze, looking to the right and down at her pubic area, not up at her face; then, as if embarrassed, away from her and to the left.

This complexly detailed response might seem odd, to the extent that Carrie's troubles are the apparent concern of the scene. Why does the camera pay so much attention to a man's response at this moment, especially a man who is of so little consequence for the narrative? I think this is because of an underlying sense in this film that women for men represent an ambivalent object. Much as the principal is drawn by the attraction of Miss Collins's thighs, he is also repelled by what he sees and, as such, remains helpless and passive with this direct confrontation of female sexuality. Male weakness, then, is specifically defined as a consequence of female sexual allure. The two other key male characters in the film, Tommy (William Katt) and Billy are both almost slavishly subservient to their woman, and both are easily manipulated. Woman for the male audience, by extension, has the ambivalence of an object of horror, one that fascinates and repulses at the same time.

Although it might well dominate the film's point of view implicitly, the way men look at women seems a minor concern for the film. Rather, it is displaced for a more explicit focus on the way the women characters view each other—and especially on how daughters take their identity from the ways their mothers look at them. Two women operating in different realms of home and school dominate the film much as they dominate

Carrie herself to establish a bad mother–good mother polarity: Carrie's actual mother, who is a powerful repressive force in her life, and the benign Miss Collins, who seeks to help Carrie develop a more positive view of herself. A mirror motif establishes the connection of identity to a mother's recognition/misrecognition.[8] A mirror figures prominently in two scenes, in both instances its appearance triggered by a mother-daughter interaction.

Alone in her room and rejected by her mother, Carrie looks in a mirror that begins to warp back and forth as a literal mirror of her anguish. Finally it breaks into an infinite number of shards, suggesting that Carrie's image of herself is destroyed. There is an unexpected sleight of hand in the way the film presents this scene to us, perhaps the only instance in the film in which we are meant to question the veracity of the image. Although we had previously seen the mirror completely destroyed, the next time we see it, the mirror has only two cracks in it. The point of this discontinuity is to force us to interpret the mirror metaphorically, to see its breakage not as a reality but rather as a reflection of Carrie's state of mind.

The mother who constantly tells Carrie she is sinful and bad metaphorically holds a negating mirror up to Carrie and shows her an image of herself that she would like to reject but never can entirely. As the film presents it, the child experiences the mother's negative mirroring as literally shattering. The negation of self that comes with the bad image makes Carrie feel obliterated. Hence, the apparent destruction of the mirror at the very moment when Carrie looks at herself. Yet even with the experience of this devastation, the child continues to exist, so that the mirror must continue to exist. Rather than destroy her entirely, the negative mirroring merely leaves her cracked like the mirror, divided into an ambivalent and literally fragmented self.

The mirror that figures in the scene between good mother Miss Collins and Carrie points toward another view of Carrie, one that suggests a wholeness that Carrie herself has trouble seeing because of bad mirroring from the bad mother. Unbeknownst to Carrie, Sue, feeling guilty over the scapegoating of Carrie, seeks to make amends by having her boyfriend invite Carrie to the senior prom. Carrie confesses her despair over this invitation to Miss Collins by saying she feels it is another attempt to trick her. Miss Collins responds by saying, "Carrie, I want to talk to you. It's about this attitude you have about yourself." Miss Collins apparently regards the restoration of the self as her key task: as a way of trying to convince Carrie that an invitation to the prom is something she ought to expect, Miss Collins leads Carrie up to a mirror and itemizes her most attractive features for her. As she does so, the camera begins to zoom in on the mirror as if to call both Carrie's and our attention to these features. Carrie's reflection smiles back at her in acknowledgment of her capacity to see herself as Miss Collins tells her to.

The film seems to set up a simple dialectic between these two maternal figures that is echoed by the two lines heard from them in voice-over as Carrie begins her mad rampage near the end of the film: her mother's "They'll laugh at you" is set against the counterpoint of Miss Collins's "You can trust me." But much as there is a third voice heard in the climactic sequence—that of the principal misnaming Carrie—the opposition between the two mothers is in fact not so simple. The zoom in on the mirror that seems intended to single out Carrie's pretty features actually ends on a close-up of Miss Collins. Furthermore, Miss Collins raises two fingers to her lips as if to hold back something and displays a distinctly troubled expression on her face. To underscore this, her angry offscreen voice uttering a peremptory "Well?" is layered over the image of the mirror.

That angry voice pinpoints the source of disturbance for us: it is the first line of dialogue from the next scene, one in which Miss Collins confronts Sue and her boyfriend Tommy over why he has invited Carrie to the prom. While Miss Collins may tell Carrie she is sufficiently pretty for Tommy to proffer an invitation, Miss Collins apparently doesn't really think so. As it turns out, she even aligns her understanding with Carrie's in confronting Sue: "C'mon, Sue, we're not that stupid. Neither is Carrie." But if Carrie isn't, should we see Miss Collins's attempt to convince her of her beauty as an attempt to render her stupid? Does Miss Collins not in fact believe what she tries to convince Carrie of? By cutting directly from Miss Collins assuring Carrie to her interrogating Sue, the film effectively undermines the credibility of Miss Collins. But it does something else as well by extending the anger she directs at Sue and Tommy back into the scene with Carrie: Carrie is in fact the source of Miss Collins's anger.

Even at the moment when Miss Collins asks Carrie to accept her vision of her, she effectively compromises that vision. Carrie's trust must necessarily be tenuous since accepting Miss Collins's word at this point would require that she reject an earlier overheard conversation. After the scene in the shower, when Miss Collins is trying to describe events to the principal, the scene is set up with Carrie sitting just outside a window looking into the principal's office. As the soundtrack makes clear, the scene offers her the further humiliation of overhearing the discussion of her humiliating experience. At one point in this discussion, Miss Collins tells the principal that she understands why the girls humiliated Carrie in the locker room. In fact, she admits to similar sadistic feelings toward her: "But, see, the thing is, Morty, that, um, I know how they felt. See, the whole thing just made me want to take her and shake her, too."

This confession is delivered over the business discussed earlier of the principal averting his eyes from Miss Collins's shorts. This juxtaposition of dialogue and action conjoins Miss Collins's anger with male attraction-repulsion. As a consequence, the anger itself begins to slide into a kind of disgust. The girls humiliate Carrie for being frightened by a natural function of her own body, yet they themselves are implicated in Carrie's response. As suggested earlier, their aggressive humiliation of Carrie involves a form of denial in that they resolutely distance themselves from her, as if she could not possibly have anything in common with them. If Miss Collins shares in the girls' feelings, then, her very ambivalence makes it impossible to offer the fully positive mirroring to Carrie that she evidently wants to.

As a conscious matter, sympathy overrides sadism: Miss Collins will not allow herself to express her sadistic feelings toward Carrie. Yet her sadism finds another outlet. Much as the narrative seems to set up an opposition between Miss Collins and the actual mother, the revelation of Miss Collins's sadism points to a strong parallel between her and the mother, a parallel the film establishes visually. Sometime after the mother has banished Carrie to her "prayer closet" as punishment for her menstruation, the chastised Carrie emerges. A shot shows the mother at a medium distance on the right at her sewing machine with Carrie in long shot on the left. The mother can't quite bring herself to look at Carrie as she speaks, "You can go to bed now." About ten minutes later in the film Miss Collins is punishing the girls who made fun of Carrie by having them stay after school to perform rigorous calisthenics. A repeated shot in this sequence directly echoes the earlier shot of Carrie and her mother: Miss Collins stands in close-up on the right of the image as the group of aerobic girls appears in long shot on the left. Miss Collins also can't quite look at the background figures as she calls out orders to them. The point of the parallel is to establish a similarity between the two maternal figures precisely on the issue of punitiveness and a refusal to make contact.

The motivation for the mother's antipathy is presumably her disgust at sexuality in general. Miss Collins's antagonism would appear to be in contrast since it is consciously motivated by her sympathy for Carrie and a desire to make the other girls see that their behavior toward Carrie was wrong. Yet at the time she does this we know Miss Collins has also allied herself with the girls' responses. What at first appears opposite is in fact similar, as the similar mise-en-scène points out. Miss Collins's motivation is finally identical to that of the mother, with both experiencing a deep and divided response to their own sexuality. There are ultimately no good mothers in this film because there is effectively no goodness. An underlying sadism derived from an ambivalent sense of one's own body makes impossible any attempt at a truly empathic response to another person. In the world of this film, empathy in fact is closer to a defense mechanism, a surface manifestation that conceals and possibly denies powerful sadistic impulses.

Horror films generally operate in a Manichaean universe to the extent that the monstrous and the human inscribe a world of polar opposites. *Carrie* seems to take over the Manichaeanism of the horror film, but it ultimately challenges it as well. Everywhere the film seems to point toward dualities. High- and low-angle shots contrast the hell of Carrie's prayer closet with the somewhat parodied heaven of the school prom and its "Love Among the Stars" theme. Two couples flank Carrie—one upper class, Waspy, and virginally romantic; the other lower class, ethnic, and crudely sexual. Finally, Carrie herself will eventually appear drenched in blood as a challenge to her mother, the pure Mrs. White. Yet the film sets up these schemes only to collapse them, much as it collapses the good mother–bad mother opposition.

Part of the charge of any horror film lies in the implicit connection of the monstrous to the human (a connection the contemporary horror film has generally made more explicit). But because the horror film depends on a sense of the monstrous as something different from the human, the genre still enables us to distinguish between the two and preserve some sense of an area in which humanity seems precious, even if more fragile and possibly more endangered than in earlier works of horror. *Carrie* offers a radical shift by invoking this familiar opposition in order to collapse it. The human and the monstrous are not polar states in this film precisely because the human *is* the monstrous.

This sudden shift in the familiar terms of the horror film between the monstrous and the human is, I think, the reason for our uncertainty over who exactly is the monster in this film, whether it is Carrie or her mother. If we have an apparent monster, the horror film has conditioned us to look for the opposing human character. In the manner of the post-*Psycho* horror film, the mother is the more overtly monstrous because she is the more obviously deranged.[9] On the other hand, Carrie is monstrous because she possesses inhuman powers, powers that necessarily make her other. We may sympathize with Carrie as the eternal outsider and even take some pleasure in the exercise of her powers, but the mere fact that she has superhuman powers is disturbing enough to prevent us from seeing her as the opposing human character. Further, we cannot ignore that she always uses her powers for negative purposes, always to get back at someone. There is nothing creative or affirmative in precisely that area that makes Carrie special.

The seeming opposition between Carrie and mother as monsters has its roots in other horror films. Robin Wood has proposed a way of schematizing the monster that is useful here. For Wood, the monster may represent the "return of the repressed" or it may be the repressive figure itself. Wood sees horror films as progressive or regressive, depending upon how they treat the monster. If the monster signifies the repressed, the film is progressive because the monster offers a possibility for liberation by releasing the forces of the unconscious; if the monster signifies the repressor, the film is regressive because the monster has allied itself with the punitive forces of the super-ego.[10] Borrowing this scheme, we might say the difficulty of determining who's a monster in *Carrie* lies in the fact that there are two kinds of monsters: Carrie's mother is the repressing kind, while Carrie herself is literally what gets repressed. This opposition would account for the greater amount of sympathy Carrie earns, a sympathy that seems to confuse our willingness to designate her as monstrous. Yet since the film does finally insist on her monstrousness, it invokes a scheme of opposing monsters only to collapse it much as it collapses its other oppositions.

The ending is the place in which all oppositions are finally made one— and with such a shock that one's synapses are still tingling after the lights have come back up. In a sequence that turns out to be a dream, Sue approaches the charred ruins of Carrie's house. In the center of the ashes stands a "For Sale" sign in the shape of an enormous cross; on this someone has scrawled, "Carrie White burns in Hell." When Sue bends down to place a bouquet of flowers on this impromptu grave, a bloodied hand suddenly shoots up through the ashes and grabs hold of Sue's hand. A simple technical device here returns us to the opening of the film: the entire sequence up to the moment where the grasping hand appears is shot in slow motion. The lyricism of the opening sequence is further echoed by the lyrical flute melody that plays through both scenes. Once again, the lyrical mode is interrupted by a shock, a shock that returns us to a brutal reality.

The reality that undercuts the lyricism in the opening is the menstruating body. The final sequence reveals the lyricism as a dream that turns into a nightmare. It is uncertain, however, how much ease the return to reality brings. As Sue struggles to break free from the grasping hand, there is a surprise cut to Sue's bedroom where Sue's mother is trying to comfort a hysterical Sue who has just awakened from a nightmare. In my experience, most viewers, even those reluctant to see Carrie as monstrous, assume that the hand belongs to Carrie, and I do as well, but I would at least like to question this assumption.[11] If we associate the mother with all that is repressive and punitive, shouldn't a terrible grasp that extends beyond the grave properly belong to her? Since this is, after all, a nightmare, such confusions about whose hand it is are permissible. Further, we may subsequently understand the grasping hand as Sue's projection, a guilty anxiety over Carrie's bloodied humiliation. And if we think back to the lyrical mode of the opening, we may conclude that once again Carrie is destroying a pretty picture.

Yet the transition to waking reality actually forges an alliance with the maternal. As Sue comes out of her nightmare, we see that the hand of her mother is holding on to her arm, attempting to restrain her, much as Carrie's hand had held on. To underscore this connection between hands, the camera moves into a close-up of the hand grasping Sue's arm. The grasp of the mother, apparently attempting comfort, is experienced as something very different. "It's all right, I'm here," the mother keeps saying over and over again, to a Sue who remains hysterical. The continuing hysteria is appropriate, apparently, since "I'm here" is not comforting news. An ability to comfort has not defined this mother's personality since she has chiefly been characterized by the twin addictions of television soap operas and afternoon drinking. But even when the mother is emotionally distanced, the maternal grasp is the grasp that never lets go. This is perhaps the ultimate terror for the film.[12] If the human is the monstrous, as the collapsing Manichaeanism of this film suggests, most monstrous of all is the bond between mother and child.

The Brood (1979)

David Cronenberg's *The Brood* takes the mother as monster to the furthest extreme by making the maternal body itself an object of revulsion. This might seem to be merely fulfilling a tendency I have already noted in the mainstream horror film, yet the film operates somewhat outside the mainstream by its overt self-consciousness. The film is replete with some of the most disgusting imagery the horror film has offered us, but it is also a film about the nature of disgust. This self-reflexiveness makes Cronenberg's status as a genre director somewhat odd. While Cronenberg may have shifted into horror film after his first two features, which were frankly experimental (*Stereo*, 1969, and *Crimes of the Future*, 1970), the art sensibility never fully left his work. His works foreground their meaningfulness in a way that is unusual for the horror film.

In any case, the horror film is not entirely foreign to the experimental film or the art film: two of the earliest works in the horror canon, F. W. Murnau's *Nosferatu* (1922) and Carl Theodore Dreyer's *Vampyr* (1932), both come out of the art film. The horror film can dovetail with the experimental and the art film because the genre itself allows for a free play of fantasy that grants unlimited opportunity for outrageous metaphors and images perhaps not otherwise acceptable to mainstream audiences. In the course of his career, Cronenberg has moved more into the mainstream to the extent that his films began to get major studio distribution, but that is largely because the horror film began to move more into the mainstream, as it shifted from the kind of low-budget, minimal production values that Cronenberg began with to the high-budget, special-effects driven films that followed in the wake of *The Exorcist*. The horror film may share affinities with art and experimental films, but it reaches a broader audience by disguising its issues through fantasy. It is generally the disguise that allows the issues to be explored. Cronenberg is unusual to the degree that he insists on tearing away the mask from his metaphors.

Monstrousness is, of course, the disguise the horror film most frequently draws on. The mother in *Carrie* is a monster because of the repressive power she wields against her own child. In *The Brood* the mother is a monster because she creates offspring that carry out her own repressed wishes. In both cases, the horror plot serves to play out an underlying psychological drama. But there is also a marked difference between the approach of the two films. As close as it may come to the surface, the terror of the female body remains something of a subtext in *Carrie*, submerged in the fantasy of telekinetic prowess. In *The Brood*, the mother is literally made a monster by a monstrous physical deformity that is *physiologically* tied to what makes her a mother. In moving beyond the psychological to the physical, the film also threatens to transcend the metaphorical into something more explicit. The grossness in this film lies solely and overtly in our responses to the disturbing potential of the human body.

Cronenberg's films have been attacked for their disgusting qualities. Robin Wood finds them generally unredeeming in that they suggest that the very condition of being human is itself revolting.[13] Wood's criticism parallels my claim that *Carrie* promotes an equation between the human and the monstrous. Nevertheless, I would argue that something very different is taking place in Cronenberg's films. Specifically in *The Brood*, Cronenberg probes the question why we ever find the human body disgusting. Gross-out might celebrate the disgusting, but that celebration is rooted in ambivalence. By creating a horror fantasy around truly bizarre psychosomatic disorders, *The Brood* focuses on that ambivalence in overt fashion.

As Cronenberg has it, we actually desire a split between *psyche* and *soma* because it is *psyche* that makes us distinctly human, while *soma* ties us to the animal world and makes us gross. By acknowledging the desire for this split, Cronenberg pushes things further then most horror films, to the point that the ambivalence inherent in gross-out is much more apparent in his work than anywhere else. I suspect there would be general agreement on the extent to which the images in *The Brood* make us uncomfortable (unlike *The Exorcist*, where it would be easier to claim gross-out is fun). As noted in my discussion of the earlier film, it was precisely the response of teenagers who found the film fun that disturbed older critics. I suspect that young and old might be more united in their response to the Cronenberg film. *The Brood* makes us uncomfortable precisely because it makes us confront why we experience disgust in looking at the body. For this reason, a consideration of disgust is the best place to begin a discussion of this film.

If I were to ask, what specifically is disgusting in this film, anyone who has seen *The Brood* would most likely conjure up the image of the woman with the external womb. This is certainly the most disturbing image the film has to offer, which is precisely why I want to consider this film in the context of mothers as monsters. But this image comes at the climax of the film, and it exists as the culmination of a gross-out progression not directly concerned with the maternal body. Although the mother as monster is central to the film, the monstrosity itself is contexualized within a succession of other monstrosities. Like other horror films, *The Brood* initially keeps the monstrous partially at bay and hidden from our view, only gradually revealing it until we are given the dubious pleasure of full disclosure.

In other horror films, this visual reticence is often necessary as a way of keeping the horrible in the horror. Full vision of the monster is often anticlimactic to the extent that the horrible requires obliqueness in order to defy our powers of conceptualization. The moment we can see it, we begin to find ways of categorizing it and, in doing so, render it an anodyne for anxiety. "Oh, that's a giant ant," or "Oh, that's a man with very long incisors." As we shall see in the next chapter, *Alien* (1979) represents the most extreme version of this method since its monster keeps changing with every partial view we have of it, finally becoming both smaller and more humanoid as we achieve unobstructed vision. In all, a rhetoric of digression is a fairly common method in the genre because it serves to delay full view of the monstrous. *The Brood* is markedly different from other horror films to the extent that the full vision of the monstrosity brings with it the film's greatest moment of disquiet, not a sudden sense that things aren't quite as bad as we imagined. The dramatic escalation in this film finds its clear payoff with a sight that goes well beyond our worst imaginings.

If *The Brood* borrows a familiar dramatic strategy in order to rework it, the film has a similar purpose in taking over the hoary horror plot formula of the mad doctor. This is not apparent at first because the mad doctor has been displaced from central position in favor of his chief antagonist, the architect Frank (Art Hindle), who wants to keep his young daughter from his estranged and seriously disturbed wife Nola (Samantha Eggar). She is being seen by mad Dr. Raglan (Oliver Reed), who has pioneered a new form of psychiatric treatment which involves transforming re-pressed feelings into physical expression. Initially, Frank is concerned that his wife is physically abusing their daughter, but as the film progresses, and both of Nola's parents are killed by mutant moppets, it becomes ap-parent that something much stranger is going on with Nola. Nola is in fact exhibit A for Dr. Raglan's "psychoplasmic" treatment, the person who has demonstrated the most extreme ability to transform her inner rage into physical manifestation.

In his overweening ambition to explore the depths of human existence, Dr. Raglan invokes both the mad doctors of *Dr. Jekyll and Mr. Hyde* and *Frankenstein*.[14] His project, like that of Dr. Jekyll, is to release that which is hidden, the dark underside of human emotion. And like Dr. Jekyll, in releasing that hidden underside, he releases more than he can control. Unlike Dr. Jekyll, but like Dr. Frankenstein, Dr. Raglan does not experi-ment on himself. Rather, like Dr. Frankenstein, he is seeking to create a more perfect human being, in this particular case one who more effec-tively connects mind and body. In the process, like Dr. Frankenstein, he ends up inadvertently creating something that is decidedly inferior and monstrous, a creature in which the body is so transformed by the mind that the body begins to operate as if it had a mind of its own.

The ironic name Cronenberg gives Dr. Raglan's workplace, the "Somafree Institute of Psychoplasmics," is enough to indicate wherein lies the doctor's madness since it points to the contradictory nature of his project. While the first of the two neologisms implies a liberation from the body, the second ties the mind directly to the physical basis of life, making clear that liberation from the body is impossible. The film initially establishes Raglan as a powerful man, one who exercises total control over his patients much as he exhorts them to discover a new kind of control over their bodies. Because Raglan himself seems to be all control, it is as if he wants to deny that he might have any of the inner demons that seemingly drive most of the other characters in this film. Yet we are allowed increasing glimpses of cracks in this facade as the narrative develops. While Raglan's project might be mad from the outset, he doesn't so much descend into madness as progressively lose all control over events.

The film is structured around three interlocking progressions: the slow revelation of what the monstrous children look like; an escalation in the kinds of physical deformities we see as a consequence of Raglan's treatment; and Raglan's own disintegration. Each of these progressions represents a different narrative line that will eventually converge on one consummate horror at the end of the film. Since each narrative line is constructed around a mystery, we necessarily correct our understanding of what is taking place as the narrative develops and we get more information about events and characters. But as Cronenberg cuts from one narrative to the other, our understanding of each narrative line is further conditioned by what is happening in the other. Ultimately, these three developing progressions create a very complex context through which we view the grotesque body at the end of the film. It is only by looking at the full complexity of this context that we can understand how the film finally views the grossness in human existence.

The first narrative line focuses on our developing understanding of Raglan's treatment and its consequences. The film begins with a demonstration of the mad doctor's new method of doctoring, but it does so in a deceptive way, one that does not allow us to understand precisely what we are seeing by concealing that we are watching a kind of medical experiment. Rather, the film sets up its opening scene so that we question what we are seeing, then leads us to a false conclusion that affects how we understand the rest of the film. The film begins with a simple over-the-shoulder two-shot of two men in off-white robes seen against a black background; we look toward Raglan as he says to the man he's facing, "You're not looking at me, Mike. [*long pause*] You're not looking at me in the eyes." Mike's head is indeed tilted downward, so the film immediately establishes a connection between looking and feeling, that look-ing—and specifically an inability to look—is directly connected to feeling.

There is enough that is mysterious here to make us at least ponder possibilities. A reverse-angle shot shows us a bearded balding man (Gary McKeehan), who addresses a not much older Raglan as "Daddy." Cross-cutting between the two shots continues as Raglan begins to berate the man, accusing him of weakness, yet the two continue to sit calmly, facing each other. Finally, a high-angle long shot over the heads of an audience shows us that the two are on a stage bathed in a single spotlight; a reverse angle shows us a section of the audience as Frank arrives and sits next to another man immersed in the drama onstage. The inexplicable exchange is now given a context that seemingly explains it: we are watching some kind of experimental theater, a kind of psychodrama, one that will come complete with a spectacular special effect when Mike, in response to Rag-lan's ragging, reveals that his body has broken out in welts. It is only after the lights have gone out on this little sketch that we learn we were actually watching a session between Dr. Raglan and his patient, but the deception of the scene is important because it introduces a note of theatricality and display into the way we will regard the grotesque body. The two subse-quent appearances of monstrous bodies—a man with gills on his neck and Nola's external reproductive organs—are both presented to us in very dramatic, even theatrical fashion, as a kind of unveiling.

Theatricality here serves one powerful function in establishing our re-sponse to the disgusting transformation of the man's body. A scene that is all talking heads, however engrossing and mysterious, must call forth a desire for something more spectacular. As Raglan's taunting of Mike mounts, we must not only expect but actually hope for some kind of eruption, some movement into action that will cut through the tension of the dialogue. In a sense, then, our own desire for spectacle implicates us in the eruptions of Mike's body. Much as we might find the welt-covered body gross, Mike's performance (especially if we regard it as a perform-ance) is something we may take pleasure in because it resolves the an-guish of the interaction between the two men. And we can take pleasure in the fact that Mike comes back at his tormentor Dr. Raglan in such an unexpected way. There is a real sense of satisfaction in this. And yet, of course, there must remain a disturbance as well, one that becomes even stronger when we realize that Mike's performance is more actuality than performance.

What, then, is specifically disturbing here? For one thing, the body seems to have taken on some kind of awful life of its own in response to the individual's emotional turmoil. Our initial shock must stem from our sense of the body's simultaneous interdependence with and independence from mental life. The film plays on our reluctance to think of the body as expressing a mental state in such a direct and automatic way. Yet later in the film, a police psychologist will remind us that ulcers may occur even in young children. Cronenberg wants us to accept that the body connects to the mind in ways we normally don't think about. If Mike were simply blushing or getting red in the face as response to Raglan's taunting, the transformation would not make us consider connections between mind and body. There is something gross in Mike's eruptions because they transgress conventional boundaries. As most commonly used, the word "psychosomatic" suggests not so much a connection between *psyche* and *soma* as an opposition, a precise boundary between the two. The film's grossness lies in its rejection of such boundaries. Psychosomatic illness in this film is disgusting because it is real.

A further source of disturbance in this opening sequence lies in the fact that Mike, the man/boy, seems to take some kind of pleasure in all this; he seems to enjoy the wounding of his own body. Because of this, the scene possibly works both on our fascination and our difficulty in watching a masochist. We do not necessarily want to be cast in the role of sadist, yet we may remain fascinated by how far Mike can go in inflicting wounds on himself. As Mike's pleasure puts us into a somewhat uncomfortable position, there is necessarily a psychological factor in how we perceive the grossness. Gross-out may be in part determined by the way a person responds to his/her own physical state. A Mike who was horrified by what was happening to his body would prompt a very different response from the Mike that we do see, with compassion comfortably superseding our disgust. What disturbs us here is the acknowledgment of some kind of pleasure we take in disgust. It is for this reason that each of the two subsequent revelations of a gross deformity in the film are accompanied by a display of pleasure on the part of the person showing the deformity.

Jan Hartog (Robert Silverman), the man with gills on his neck, is a less willing participant in the eruptions of his body. The man had summoned Frank by offering to help him get at Raglan because he himself has been a victim of Raglan's treatment. As he tells Frank, "Raglan encouraged my body to revolt against me, and it did. Now I have a small revolution on my hands, and I'm not putting it down very successfully." In saying this, the man suggests a connection between revolt and revulsion: we are revolted by those activities of the body over which we cannot exercise control. With this man, we are still apparently operating in the realm of realistic possibility to the extent that his condition is given a seemingly realistic medical explanation ("lymphosarcoma"). And yet this revolt is also connected to an individual's emotional life, as if the person is *still* in some way responsible for the illness without even willing it. This represents an escalating challenge to the breakdown in boundaries the film engineers: *psyche* and *soma* connect, but not necessarily as equal partners for *soma* may take on a life of its own. Our mental apparatus, the pride of our humanity, is merely one component of our physical existence.

Even if we see the strange growth on the man's neck as within the realm of medical possibility, a medical explanation does not mean we want to look at the manifestation of the illness any more directly. We may still regard the man as disgustingly monstrous. One of the gravest emotional problems facing cancer patients is coping with family members who turn away from them. Why is it so difficult for us to look at illness? There is possibly some anxiety of contamination: we want to keep ourselves separate, to deny that we have anything in common with the sick person because to acknowledge this opens us up to similar disease. But *The Brood* makes it difficult for us to see the man with the cancerous growth as a monster. He might have an odd manner, but he does genuinely want to help Frank, and his anger at Raglan is well earned. By granting him these sympathetic elements, the film denies us an easy separation between the monstrous and the human. For this reason, as the film progresses through its escalating gross-out, "gross" begins to move into an area that is difficult to define as either exclusively negative or exclusively positive.

Before looking at the culmination of this progression (the unveiling of Nola's body), I want to consider the presentation of the murderous infants. As the offspring of Nola, their appearance necessarily affects the way we finally look at her body. In the traditional manner of horror films, we see the monster in progressively revealing stages. During the first murder our view is almost completely blocked: we catch glimpses of it, enough to tell us that the murderer is the size of a small child and apparently wearing children's clothing, but that is all. At the second murder, the view is slowly fleshed out: first we see an insert shot of small but withered hands; then we have a clearer view of the clothing to see that it resembles the snowsuit of Frank's daughter; finally, we see the creature from a full frontal view that shows us a deformed and withered face on a child's body.

Much as our vision is blocked, the creatures are indeterminate. They seem to be children, yet they appear very old as well. As such, they challenge our ability to categorize. A subsequent autopsy of the creature who commits the first two murders extends this transgression of categories: it possesses neither genitalia nor navel. It is a creature both of indeterminate gender as well as indeterminate birth. Like the psychosomatic disorders, then, the small monster has the ability to disturb by confounding conventional categories. But there is something more. The doctor performing the autopsy draws particular attention to the absence of the navel as the most striking feature of this creature. In having him do this, the film establishes the creature's origin as the most disturbing aspect of its existence. In a sense, the rest of the film becomes a kind of quest to define the origin of this very particular life—and possibly of life in general. The scene revealing Nola's body to us, the culmination of the deformity theme, also works as the culmination of the creature motif since it provides us with the final answer about their origins.

The third line of progression uses the unveiling of Nola's body as a climax in the downward trajectory of Dr. Raglan. Although the film also draws on the terrifying power of the mother, it works in stark contrast to *Carrie* where virtually all the women are strong and all the men are weak. In *The Brood* there are two strong men who at least appear to be the driving forces of the plot. Raglan is clearly the more powerful of the two: while the plot may center on Frank's quest to preserve the safety of his daughter, Dr. Raglan is the force behind everything, the man who successfully encourages his patients' bodies to revolt. His power abates only as we begin to approach a view of Nola's body, that body that he set in revolt against itself. Like other mad scientists, his creation ultimately goes beyond what he intended to the point of becoming dangerous to himself, but the undercutting of his power is specifically tied to the power of the maternal body.

Unlike his generic forebears Drs. Jekyll and Frankenstein, scientists driven by passions, Dr. Raglan is the most dispassionate of scientists and, perhaps as such, more a late twentieth-century creation, something of an engineer of the body. On the wall in Nola's flat, where she lives after the breakup of her marriage to Frank, are side-by-side photos of Raglan and Sigmund Freud. Clearly, Freud hovers over much of this film in that it is centrally concerned with conversion reactions, ways in which repressed emotions may resurface in physical expression. But in a context that defines him as a predecessor of Raglan, Freud's presence and his "science" signal the dispassionate side of Raglan as a man who tames the raging unconscious (that over which we have no control) by making it known to the conscious mind, our agent of control. But Raglan himself might also be a subject for Freudian analysis as he goes beyond Freud to a point of denial: he is all control. He is a too-perfect father, one who fully conceals any of the inner demons that drive most of the other characters in this film.

If Raglan seems like a candidate for psychoanalysis himself, it is because the film shows cracks in Dr. Raglan's facade as the narrative progresses. In a key session with Nola, when she complains that her father did not protect her from her mother's attacks, the camera focuses on *Raglan's* responses, so that we see him struggling as he loses control over the direction of the exchange. The ability to drive events is an important motivating factor for this character. The issue of theatricality that characterizes the beginning of the film is quite specifically tied to questions of power, a power the film keeps assigning to the father that Dr. Raglan sets himself up to be from the opening scene on. The "curtain speech" after our first view of Raglan at work points to him as the power behind all the drama: he is not only performer but also director and author, a kind of psychological prime mover. As with *The Exorcist*, we are again dealing with the power of the father, but in a much more ambivalent and disturbing fashion, in large part because the father is no longer a fantasy figure but is in fact present in the film as a fully realized character.

If Nola is the mother of the murderous moppets, then Raglan is certainly their father. But Raglan's role as father is rooted in ambivalence, much as his understanding of his own ideas involves denial. Raglan urges his patients to bring all their buried feelings to the surface where *he* will control them. At the same time, he keeps his own feelings fully suppressed. Ambivalently, he functions as both an agent of unleashed desire and an agent of control. As such, the conflicts in Raglan foreground a cultural conflict that culminated in the conservative backlash of the late 1970s and early 1980s against the predations of the 1960s. "Let it all hang out," a familiar phrase in the 1960s and 1970s, might seem a fitting slogan for Raglan's form of psychotherapy. It is certainly a phrase appropriate to the world of gross-out. But much as *The Brood* operates as a work of gross-out, the film also interrogates its very mode. The desire to bring everything to the light of reason has a darker side to it, as the controlling scientist ends up unleashing forces he cannot control.

The film is primarily concerned with the problems of "letting it all hang out" most literally in the case of Nola, since her very body is turned inside out. The literal does not obscure the metaphorical, however; rather, it gives rise to a very precise question that plays on both levels. What does it mean to unleash the powers of the unconscious mind, to bring to the surface all that has been repressed? Nola appears as the answer to this question, much as she appears at the convergence of these three plot progressions—as the final and fantastic stage of bodily eruptions that began within the realistic realm of medical possibility; as the explanation to the puzzle of the creatures' identity; and as the powerful figure who definitively signifies Dr. Raglan's loss of power. Where these narrative lines intersect, the unveiling of Nola's body is the most dramatically charged moment in the film, and certainly its most unforgettable moment. But how we experience this revelation has much to do with its dramatic context. The final presentation of this deformed body occurs in a situation that forces us to question our own reactions to it.

Dramatically, the scene is the climax of the film in that its two main antagonists, Frank and Dr. Raglan, must finally work together in order to rescue Frank's daughter. Alone, neither could counter Nola's power. Raglan, who knows that the creatures are the product of Nola's rage, tells Frank that he must placate Nola while he, Raglan, attempts to rescue the daughter from the brood. For Raglan's plan to work, it is essential that Frank convince Nola he also wants her back, even as her body has been remade. He can only do this by not showing any sign of disgust as Nola reveals her startling transformation to him. She does this in a nearly defiant way that seems intended to challenge him, a way that asks him if he can in fact accept the spectacle of her new body: she slowly raises her clean white robes over the womb that extends to the outside of her body. This raising of the curtain on a truly spectacular performance takes place just as she is about to produce a new creature.

The moment is a complex one for the audience because it necessarily involves two simultaneous and contradictory reactions. We know through crosscutting that any sign of disgust from Frank will alienate Nola and provoke the brood, thereby endangering his daughter's life. Yet Frank does precisely that! And this is where our contradictory response comes in. Because we also experience the sight as disgusting, Frank's reaction must seem justified. But even as we might share his reaction, we must turn against him somewhat for upsetting Raglan's plan, for not being able to play his part well. The scene, then, is artfully contrived to mitigate against any easy pleasure we might take in this gross-out display, as we generally take in other gross-out films. Gross-out asks for a pleasurable expression of disgust, but the drama makes any appearance of disgust in response to Nola's body here dangerous.

What, then, is disgusting about Nola's body? Like the creatures who have no determined sexuality, Nola's body offends our sense of proper boundaries between the sexes by making the inside outside. Robin Wood has suggested that this externalized womb looks like a giant penis, but I don't think we need to go this far to note simply that the female reproductive organs are here presented as being external like a male's.

In fact, I think it is important to insist that these are specifically *female* organs—not female organs that ape male organs (although they might well mock them). What we see here is a very literal form of hysteria, a term that originally designated a wandering womb as an explanation for female madness. Nola's womb has wandered so far as to emerge from the confines of her body.

This womb therefore prompts a response of disgust because of both expectation and propriety. When we look at a woman's naked body, we simply do not expect to see her reproductive organs as we would with a man. But although we do not expect to see this, we also probably do not want to do so. Because it conceals that which most directly ties us to animal life, a woman's body may be cosmeticized as a man's cannot. We might prefer the demurely airbrushed, decorative nudes of *Playboy*. But the rise of gross-out coincides with the rise of *Hustler* to challenge *Playboy* with its more explicitly posed models and bluntly spread legs that sought to expose more. While *Playboy* became somewhat more explicit in response, it has remained fairly prettified and continues to dominate its market. The appeal of uncovering a woman's body might seem a fairly uncomplicated thing in most conventional films—so long as they deliver the cosmeticized bodies of a *Playboy* feature. *Hustler* possibly took away some customers by defying the limits of what could be shown, but *The Brood*'s fantasy considerably upped the ante by making the internal external. In doing so, it introduced a certain anxiety into disrobing by effectively revealing everything, even that which the body itself normally conceals.

By extension, an issue of propriety is involved here. It is not just that a woman's body does not allow for such display (the unconscious after all is not so concerned with physical impossibilities). The psychological aspect is the key to the way we experience the physical. As the scene presents it, Nola takes some pleasure in showing off her wandering womb, much as Jan Hartog had taken pleasure in showing off his gills. But with Hartog, the pleasure still had a consciously perverse quality to it. This is not the case with Nola. As a consequence, our disgust is in part triggered by her willfulness. A Nola who is herself horrified by her body would prompt a very different response from us, much as Carrie, horrified at her menstruating body, engenders a measure of sympathy. If Nola's response to her own body seems wrong, the feeling emerges from the scene that, physiological possibility or not, a woman *shouldn't* bare reproductive organs in this way. There is something decidedly alarming about such behavior, a challenge to all that we understand as feminine (both as a physical state but also as something more metaphorical having to do with what we understand as a mental and spiritual condition).

Disgust, then, is not solely located in the actual physical deformity of the character but also in her behavior. She does not have the good sense to be disgusted by something that Frank and we in the audience see as disgusting. And she compounds this with her actions immediately follow-ing the birth. Rather than rejecting what her body is doing, she embraces the fruit of it, embracing the bloody fetus in the most direct way: she bites into the placenta and begins to lick the blood off the baby. It is easy enough to want to reject this vision, as Frank does, but what she does here is not all that different from how an animal gives birth (and even for humans giving birth is a pretty messy activity anyway). If we find any disgust in this, does that necessarily mean we find disgust in the general human condition?

That we do find disgust perhaps suggests some difficulty in looking at the origins of human life in a clear-eyed way. As the movie has it, Nola's very fertility sets her up as an object of disgust. In her hyperreproductivity, she is simply too powerful—the omnipotent mother who can control an entire brood, and a counter to the super-rational father who finally con-trols nothing. The sense of disgust in this scene, then, partly echoes the disgust that Dundes found in dead baby jokes ("a protest against babies in general"). But disgust in this film moves from the babies to their point of origin. Here the disgust arises from a world that makes the internal external.

Because of its reproductive capacity, the female body itself provides the end point for each of the three progressions that structure this film: the body that deforms itself; the body that produces new life; the body that challenges the assumptions of male power. More than anything else, it is the revolting body that distinguishes gross-out horror. But it is not just *any* body: a forerunner of gross-out horror, *Rosemary's Baby* centers on the mother's body, and it is often the mother's body that underlies our sense of the body as an object of revulsion. If we find a disgust in the mother's body, we must also find a sense of disgust in the origins of life itself. Cronenberg's distinctive achievement in this film is to prompt our sense of disgust at the same time that he challenges it.

Chapter 17 *Alien Bodies*

Lost Boundaries

Dracula (1979), *An American Werewolf in London* (1981),
The Hunger (1983)

One of the most striking features of the post-*Exorcist* horror film is a
changing sense of the body. Put most simply, the body became much
more gross than in previous horror. To make it a little less simple, the
body became gross in a very particular way. *The Exorcist* (1973) initiated
an extraordinary metamorphosis of the makeup artist that *Variety* took
note of in 1981: "Among its varied impacts, it focused attention on the
makeup specialist, a member of the production team who was to achieve
virtual star status by the end of the 1970s."[1] The makeup man became a
special-effects wizard, someone who didn't just make up the actors but a
perverse alchemist who mutated the body in amazing and generally disgusting ways. For *The Exorcist* Dick Smith had simply been the man who
did the makeup. By the time of *The Hunger*, he and Carl Fullerton received
credit for "Make-Up Illusions," while *An American Werewolf in London*

explicitly conflated makeup with special effects by a credit that boasted "Special Make-Up Effects Designed and Created by Rick Baker." There is a keen reversal here: the men once responsible for making people in movies look better than in real life (the kind of thing that Hollywood had been attacked for in the past), these very men were now doing the reverse—making the body look so bad that the grossness itself became an attraction.

This meaningful change signaled a new way of looking at the body that found its fullest expression in the horror films of the period. The significance of the change is most evident in new shapes given to older forms. The extraordinary success of *The Exorcist, The Omen* and *Carrie,* all class A productions released by major companies, established new subgenres of horror, but soon older subgenres returned in new packages. The year 1981, for example, proved to be the year of the werewolf, with *An American Werewolf in London, The Howling,* and *Wolfen.* Old low-budget horror movies were remade with high budgets and grosser effects. As werewolves returned, so did vampires, but with A-list performers now instigating the iniquities amidst the lavish production values made possible by the bigger budgets.

Following his stage success, Frank Langella appeared in a new film version of *Dracula* in 1979. The play, a 1920s adaptation of the Bram Stoker novel, served as the primary source for Tod Browning's original 1931 film (starring Bela Lugosi), but by the 1970s it was bit creaky for contemporary audiences. What made it a success on stage was Langella's grandly romantic performance and the lavish Edward Gorey set designs. The film version replaced Gorey's stylizations but kept the lavish production values and added a big-name cast of serious actors (headed by Laurence Olivier as Van Helsing) to signal its serious pretensions. Although adapted from both the play and the original novel, this new film *Dracula,* written by W. R. Richter and directed by John Badham in the revisionist spirit of the post-*Exorcist* horror film, took the source material in a direction that undermined most of the premises of the vampire myth, making this Dracula heroic.[2] Among its changes, the most obvious is a type of graphicness that new makeup technology made possible (something missing on the stage as well as in earlier film adaptations). In the film, even before we see Dracula himself, we see his hand breaking through the top of his coffin to rip open the neck of a sailor, explicitly pulling his flesh away to expose the bloody interior of his throat.

Close-ups of Dracula's hand—used metonymically throughout the film to signal the Count's particular power—are of some importance for this new sense of the body. Initially defined by its ability to make the internal external, it carries that threat with it throughout the rest of the film. In the last chapter I had noted this ability as an explicit concern of *The Brood*, but it is in fact fairly widespread throughout this period. *The Brood* is more distinctive in the way it ties this concern specifically to female reproductive organs. But even though there are plenty of men eviscerated in post-*Exorcist* horror films, the female body often seems central to them.[3] There are a number of possible reasons for this that I will return to shortly. For now, I merely want to note the importance of *Rosemary's Baby* (1968) in the way it anticipates this change and particularly ties it to a woman's body. As Andrew Sarris wrote in a review at the time, beneath its horror fantasy the film dealt with the anxiety of pregnancy, particularly the fear over the well-being of the child growing inside the mother.[4] The anxiety follows from our inability to know exactly what is taking place inside the mother's body. We can never be assured of baby's health until what is inside comes outside, until the internal becomes the external. *Rosemary's Baby* anticipates later horror films by focusing on the interior of the body.

If the new graphicness about the body made violence more explicit and detailed in these films, it also brought sexuality more to the surface in horror films than it ever had been in the past. The final scene in *An American Werewolf in London* takes place in a porno theater that promises a "non-stop orgy" on its advertising posters. In the context of the film, the phrase carries a double meaning since we see it toward the end of the most extended violent sequence in the film, a nonstop orgy of killing, but it most obviously refers to what is playing inside the cinema.[5] It is one thing to claim that horror films deal with the return of the repressed, as Robin Wood has, and generally find the repressed to signify sexual material. Still, we may consider just *how* the horror film deals with this. In the past, there was something of a repressed quality even in the presentation of the repressed material itself that kept it implicit and metaphorical in most films. Of course, it does not take too much effort to see underlying sexual meanings in the vampire and werewolf films, but these were meanings that nonetheless remained beneath the surface. As *The Exorcist* introduced a level of explicitness about sexuality unseen in any Hollywood film, let alone the horror film, it led in particular to a greater explicitness in the horror film itself.

The 1979 *Dracula* foregrounded this new direction by casting a much younger and more dreamily romantic actor in the part of the Count than had any previous film version. Furthermore, it has an elaborate and delirious lovemaking scene that is the film's most elaborate set piece (dominated by orgasmic imagery of a blood-red, pulsating sun). This film most fully sets itself apart from previous vampire movies by foregrounding sexuality at the same time that it moves biting into the background. In fact, fangs are all too rarely in evidence in this version, presumably because they might interfere with the Count's noble looks. Made four years later, *The Hunger* shows a similar reluctance to disturb Catherine Deneuve's beauty with a direct view of her fangs, but it can be explicit in other matters that point up its comparable contrast with the past. While there might be lesbian overtones in *Dracula's Daughter* (1936), *The Hunger* features a scene of lesbian lovemaking that is as much its set piece as the heterosexual coupling in the 1979 *Dracula*. These changes are not simply a matter of manner that has no meaning. Rather, they are congruent with a period in which the hidden had to be exposed, or, to use my formulation about the body, the internal had to be made external.

I can get at this difference more precisely by comparing the transformation scenes in *The Wolf Man* (1941) with *An American Werewolf in London*. In the earlier film, change is signaled by a gradual (but discontinuous) metamorphosis in the extremities: overlapping shots of increasingly hirsute hands and feet with claws and a comparably hairy face. This werewolf walks upright like a man and keeps his clothes on like a gentleman. The handling of the transformation makes it easy enough to see the underlying allegory about the beast in man since this beast still appears to be a man. He never loses contact with his human side. The metamorphosis of David (David Naughton), the American werewolf, into beast is far more complete—at once terrifying and thrilling. First off, its onset is signaled by a desire to rip off clothes, bringing what ought to be hidden in polite society into full view, although the film is a bit coy about male genitalia.[6] After the clothes are removed, David's body undergoes progressive and complete transformation into an animal.

Of equal importance to the thoroughness of the body's revolution here is the way it happens: as suggested above, it seems to take place from the inside out. Some of this is accomplished through erupting sound effects that accompany the change, but it is particularly striking in one shot of David's backbone, which bursts from its indented normal position to form a kind of arch, as if trying to rip itself free from its human body. Something similar may be seen in *The Company of Wolves* (1985), where a wolf's head emerges painfully out of a character's mouth. As these brief descriptions indicate, the body in both these films revolts much more thoroughly and violently than in earlier return-of-the-repressed films. Werewolves in earlier films were often ambivalent about their transformations. What is unusual in *An American Werewolf in London* is the way the film creates an ambivalence in the audience as well. There may be disgust over what is happening, but at the same time there is fascination and pleasure in watching this reversal of inside and outside.[7] These films are no longer dealing in purely metaphorical terms as earlier horror films generally did. Rather, the physical reality of the body is of paramount importance. Why should this be the case?

I think there are a number of different reasons to account for why we have changed in the way we look at the body, although they all connect. We have seen (in chapter 15) abortion raised as an issue in a couple of films: *It's Alive* indicates that its central couple considered aborting what turns into the monster baby, while a good deal of *The Omen* centers on the wife's desire for an abortion. As was noted at the beginning of the last chapter, the widespread availability of abortion as well as oral contraceptives had something to do with this changing sense of the body (as the contemporaneous dead baby joke cycle indicates). But abortion also finds an inverse parallel in other medical technologies by raising the question of when, exactly, life begins, and in doing this it made more difficult our ability to draw boundaries.

Throughout this period developments in medicine demonstrated an increasing ability to interfere with the automatic processes of the body, especially those involving reproduction. *Roe v. Wade* (a Court decision announced the same year *The Exorcist* appeared) offered one solution for dealing with the possibility of an alien life form that might take over one's body. But *The Exorcist* revealed an additional terror that was also centered on the body. In chapter 14, I noted that contemporary audiences responded to the scene of Regan's arteriogram as one of the grisliest in the film. An actual medical procedure, then, could explicitly become vehicle for horror—and for good reason.

The Exorcist appeared during a period that saw extraordinary growth in a medical technology involving ever more invasive and manipulative procedures. Reaction to this was sufficiently pervasive to find expression outside the horror film: *Fantastic Voyage* (1966), for example, presented a fantasy based on our increasingly precise ability to see the inside the body via microscopic photography, while *Doctors' Wives* (1971) supplemented its melodramatic plot with documentary footage of an actual open-heart operation. But it was in the horror film that a new sense of the body conditioned by new technologies found its most extensive exploration because the fantasy conceits of the horror film were already oriented toward the body.

Some of this could be fairly explicit. For example, Dr. Christiaan Barnard performed the first successful heart transplant—perhaps the central event in new medical procedures—in 1967. *The Thing With Two Heads*, a film explicitly about transplant technology and its ability to create monsters, appeared in 1972. The fact that transplant technology peculiarly began with the most difficult organ to transplant, the heart, had to have a powerful impact on way we look at ourselves because the heart is the central organ, the one in Western culture most subject to metaphorical interpretation. If an organ that defines an aspect of our individuality could be transplanted, it became inescapable that we must be made up of interchangeable parts. As the heart is more than just a physical organ for us, this new procedure had to make us question who are we when we receive parts from someone else. This is, of course, the subject of the original *Frankenstein*, but that was clearly fantasy—not something that could happen to us. Accompanying the rise in gross-out horror, medical technology has regularly turned fantasy into reality. A man who receives a liver transplant from a baboon sounds like a pretty good premise for a horror movie, yet it became a reality in 1992.

We found that organ transplants and other invasive medical procedures could happen to us, and more and more they did. The consequent shift in our understanding could be seen in the way internal organs are put on display (in 3-D yet!) in *Andy Warhol's Frankenstein* (1974), a radical departure from the original film. As the 1974 film seems to suggest, cut us open and we all look like the meat counter in a supermarket. In earlier horror films, changes that manifested themselves in the body signaled something about libidinal drives. In gross-out horror, the emphasis is very much on the body itself: we are all just slabs of meat, with only the faintest suggestion (or none) of a spiritual dimension. If the body in gross-out horror threatens to break its conventional bounds by allowing the insides to take over and move outside, the body is also, conversely, more permeable, more open to the outside world, more capable of being invaded (as medical technology only too clearly demonstrated). Transplant technology made us question boundaries in one other regard: if abortion blurred notions about the beginnings of life, transplants in search of live organs blurred notions of death as an absolute boundary.

Finally, I would note something only indirectly related to medicine—the influence of the drug culture on our perception of our bodies. Mind-altering substances could turn up in earlier horror fiction (most obviously in *Dr. Jekyll and Mr. Hyde*). But as the drug culture became more pervasive, it could actually draw comment in horror films, as with *The Hun-*

ger, where even a prepubescent girl may be carrying Quaaludes around with her and an aging vampire may be dismissed as a "crazy fucking junkie." As hallucinogenic drugs became a fairly common experience for an entire generation and even psychology increasingly sought to find medicinal ways of treating mental illness, our conception of how our minds worked to connect us to reality necessarily had to change. If we are merely slabs of meat in *Andy Warhol's Frankenstein*, other films suggest we are merely a balance of chemicals that may become dangerously unbalanced. The drug culture's insistence on altering reality is of central consequence for gross-out horror because it points to how a physical element is translated into a perceptual element. Altering body chemistry may obliterate distinctions between internal and external, transforming the external by changing the internal. In all these cases, we may say that new perceptions of ourselves gained from interfering with reproductive anatomy, invasive medical procedures, and the drug culture overdetermine an annihilation of boundaries, erasing distinctions by which we have defined our individual bodies in the past.

Much as *Rosemary's Baby* looked ahead to later horror, there is one particular way in which it was rooted in an earlier sense of the body. If Rosemary's baby is presented as an alien she learns to accept as her own, the film implies a distinction between what is other and what belongs to the self. This distinction began to break down in gross-out horror. As the body in these films became more permeable, as the inside moved more and more to the outside, there was an increasing sense of the body losing its own boundaries, thus breaking down all distinction between self and other. This particular aspect might well explain the centrality of a woman's body to gross-out horror.[8] A woman's body is more open to the outside world, more subject to invasion by an alien, as *Rosemary's Baby* established; and, finally, in reproduction, it is the body that raises the question of where self leaves off and other begins. A woman's body invokes the mystery of life itself (or "the secret of life and death," as *The Hunger* has it, a film in which a man ages years in minutes while a woman remains eternally young).

The sense of life's mystery had often enough been the apparent subject matter of horror films in the past (most notably in *Frankenstein*). "Where do I myself begin if I began as part of another?" is not an unusual question in horror—but never before had it received such a strongly emphasized physical delineation. In *The Hunger* we watch a chimp decompose before our very eyes as a prelude to seeing something very similar happen to David Bowie, all in contrast to the seemingly austere eternal beauty of

Catherine Deneuve. Never before in the horror film had the physical basis of life seemed so pronounced, or so fragile. As a consequence, something implicit in both the vampire and werewolf myths that had not been given much emphasis in the past becomes foregrounded in gross-out horror: a loss of individual identity. As the victim is changed into a vampire or a werewolf, he/she loses a sense of self and becomes the very thing that had attacked him/her, obliterating any differences between them.

The 1979 *Dracula* established this distinction most fully because it is a revisionist version of a familiar tale. What is strikingly different here is not that women may succumb to the Count's power, but how they do so. Lucy (Kate Nelligan), called Mina in the original novel, in particular comes to Dracula of her own will. Consequently, this is the first version to restore the mutual drinking of blood fully and in graphic detail.[9] After Dracula has bitten Lucy on the neck, he creates a gash in his chest by his own hand (the very hand that had torn apart the sailor's neck) to allow Lucy to drink his blood. As he has addressed her at the beginning of this scene as "Flesh of my flesh, blood of my blood," the actual scene of lovemaking is filmed to suggest a sense of merger, an obliterating of boundaries.[10]

The Hunger takes this sense of merger to furthest extreme by creating deliberate confusions in its narrative structure. The opening of the film sets up parallel narratives in which we follow two different sets of characters: a stylish couple played by Deneuve and Bowie, who turn out to be murderous vampires, and a team of doctors, one of whom is played by Susan Sarandon, who are doing research on premature aging. Our genre knowledge of how old vampires may in fact be in spite of how they look might suggest some connection between these two parallel lines, but otherwise they remain quite distinct through the first section of the film. What connects them is a peculiar repetition of gestures across the parallel lines that breaks through conventional boundaries: as Sarandon runs a hand through her hair, there is a cut to Bowie making precisely the same gesture; when this scene ends with Bowie lighting a cigarette, the next scene begins with Sarandon lighting up as well. The repetitions are so fully inexplicable in terms of narrative coherence or apparent meaning that we in the audience have trouble making distinctions that we routinely make in watching any narrative. The film creates a confusion in how the audience perceives and understands the narrative that will parallel Sarandon's confusion about her own perceptions after she becomes involved with Deneuve. When Sarandon realizes she has been tainted with Deneuve's blood, Deneuve tells her, "You're part of me now, and I cannot let you go." By the end of the film, Sarandon apparently becomes Deneuve, or at least that's about as much sense as it is possible to make of this narrative.

Although the fantasy conceits of earlier horror films might have offered a metaphorical way of dealing with the demands of the body, the body itself was generally presented in fairly discreet ways, the very indirection pointing to metaphorical meanings. The explicitness of post-*Exorcist* films clearly changes that, emphasizing the body's physicality. This does not mean that the films lack a metaphorical dimension, but it is one that grows out of the explicitness concerning the body. Metaphor no longer points us toward the body; rather, the body itself becomes a metaphor by which we understand other phenomena. Consider, for example, something that appears to be a passing detail in the 1979 *Dracula*, a bit of local color that apparently adds no essential information to the narrative. Inserted between two scenes crucial to the narrative—Dracula extracting a loyalty oath from Renfield and Mina's gruesomely realized death—here is a brief scene of a cart emerging from a coal mine. Although a number of workers of all ages may be seen among the shadows of the mine from which they emerge, dominating the center of the image are a number of young boys, who look tired and dispirited.

The scene may be regarded as merely transitional, something to give us a sense of the period the film is set in. Even so, it is seemingly unrelated to anything else in the movie and has no apparent bearing on the narrative: we do not see any of these characters again nor do any of the leading characters have anything to do with the local coal industry. Indeed, with the notable exception of Renfield, all the active characters belong to the upper classes, and all the action takes place in this more refined world, where there is little sense of want or necessity. But even though the film offers little support for sustained social criticism, this does not mean that it eschews social commentary altogether.

This brief sequence does have important meaning for the movie, as is made evident when we learn that the mine facilitates Mina's nightly wanderings after she becomes a vampire. And coming as it does right after the scene showing Dracula's domination of Renfield, the scene of the coal mine offers a kind of echo, pointing up the subjection of the lower class. This is congruent with at least one other change worked on the source material. In my discussion of the original novel (chapter 13), I noted that the worst offense committed by Lucy (Mina in the film) is an attack on a young child. In the film, the first victim of Mina (Lucy from the novel) is a baby, one who is given a precise identity: she specifically belongs to the lower classes, the child of one of the inmates of the insane asylum.

Nonetheless, these unexpected nods to class cannot offer a coherent social critique because the film conflates class boundaries, much as body boundaries become obscured in the horror films discussed above. Dracula is the most aristocratic character in the film while at the same time he is the one most at home in the concealed world beneath the earth's surface. This concealed world has significance for the film in that it alludes to layers in the social order, layers that the coal mine serves to define in terms appropriate to the body. As with the individual body, the body of society is built upon inner and outer strata, the film creating a topology to contrast that which is visible with that which is concealed. Much as the horror plot requires the network of underground passages to provide the vampire's escape, it also serves to bring that which is concealed out into the open. This sense of an internal, concealed world that will erupt into the open turns up in many other horror films of this period as well, notably in *The Texas Chainsaw Massacre* (1975) and *Poltergeist* (1982). *Alien* offers the most detailed exploration of this metaphor, insistently connecting it to the physical body. In *Alien* what happens in the physical body parallels what happens in the body politic.

The Body Politic

Alien (1979) and *Dawn of the Dead* (1979)

On first consideration, *Alien* would seem to be the simplest of the horror films discussed here.[11] It certainly has the most bare-bones plot: a creature gets on board a spaceship and kills off the crew one by one. Moreover, the film offers minimal character development, and we don't even have to give much thought to the creature's meaning—or so it would seem. It is personified malignancy, pure and simple, with seemingly only one goal: to kill. The purity of the monster echoes this film's primal aim: to scare the living daylights out of us. What makes it important to this discussion is that the film accomplishes this by attacking our sense of bodily integrity. Indeed, the film's most notorious sequence—the one that took the gross-out repertoire into completely new and unexpected territory—shows an infant version of the monster ripping its way out of a man's stomach. This ghastly episode makes explicit what had only been implicit in other horror films of the time—the presentation, in horrific terms, of childbirth for a man. The scene obliterates all kinds of conventional boundaries: internal becomes external as male becomes female.

This horrendous image lingers heavily over the rest of the narrative, so it should be no surprise that the film yields easily to psychoanalytic interpretation.[12] In fact, it openly encourages psychoanalysis by providing a computer named "Mother," a monster that drips KY jelly, and doors in the spaceship modeled after the vagina.[13] The film seems designed to instill in the viewer an anxiety about the undifferentiated states of early infancy by creating a world in which the interior of the spaceship looks like the cavity of a body, a world that constantly thwarts our ability to make categorical distinctions we routinely make in everyday life. I can get at this quality most directly by attempting to answer what would seem to be a simple question. Except that "What does the monster look like?" turns out to be not so simple. This is partly because the camera denies us a full view of the monster until the very end. But more importantly, this turns out to be a young and growing monster, one that seems intent on following Freud's dictum that ontogeny recapitulates phylogeny by constantly changing shape: first it looks like an egg; then like some kind of internal organ; then like a crablike parasite—at which point it attaches itself to the face of Kane (John Hurt), one of the crew members; then it apparently becomes some kind of larva, until it bursts screaming from Kane's stomach in the famous scene described above.[14] Throughout the film the monster continues to change and grow, obliterating conventional taxonomies as it obliterates distinctions between life forms.

Krin and Glen Gabbard have explicitly allied the resulting confusions to a child's anxiety over the "phallic mother" (p. 237), and the film does offer some reason for such an interpretation. After the monster (at this point looking something like an erect eel with teeth) emerges from Kane's stomach and runs off screaming, it becomes increasingly indistinct for a while, but its image is dominated by mouth and teeth and is always dripping KY jelly. However, since this image of gaping maw and razor sharp teeth suggests the confusions implicit in the *vagina dentalis*, I think it is a mistake to see the monster as simply phallic. The sequel *Aliens* (1986) makes a comparable mistake that undercuts the unnerving quality of the original when it makes the monster specifically female.[15] Much as the scene of the terrible childbirth confuses male and female, the monster itself sustains this confusion through most of the original film.

This confusion would seem to cease only at the end when the alien finally takes on a specifically phallic appearance.[16] This new appearance may be to complement the more feminine appearance that Ripley (Sigourney Weaver) takes on as she sheds her concealing crew member suit.[17] As it/he becomes more precisely revealed, the alien also appears smaller, more humanoid, and less immediately bent on devastation. I do not think this distinction should be ignored in trying to understand both the effect and meaning of this film: as the alien can be perceived in its entirety, as he can be more easily identified, he can also be more easily dealt with. Not that this is easy, but Ripley can eject him and triumph over him as no other character did. With the polarities between male and female finally and firmly established, she can defeat the monster. As a consequence, what the film finally finds most terrifying is life without boundaries. Throughout, both in its style and in the narrative, the film plays on a tension between a sense of certainty in boundaries and a sudden undermining of that certainty.

If boundaries seem reinstated at the end, there is nevertheless one area of uncertainty that remains, and this uncertainty necessarily moves us beyond a purely psychoanalytic interpretation. The alien appears in fullest view when Ripley has escaped from the mother ship in a capsule she considers safe. As the alien slowly emerges from the wall where he has been hiding (seen through a strobing light that somewhat obfuscates our view), he reveals not just his most phallic appearance. He appears quite explicitly as the silhouette of a penis. There is no "phallic imagery" here, just a penis, plain and simple. This is nonetheless something easy to overlook, and not just because of the strobe light. Rather, we are not entirely prepared to see what we do see because of our own sense of a body's hierarchy. As the alien first emerges from the wall, he is upside down; the silhouette of the penis appears as he slowly rights himself to confront Ripley. Consequently, what appears to be the head of the penis is in fact the bottom of the alien's very elongated head, and, further, what appears to be the bottom is in fact the top. Even as the body seemingly becomes clear to us, the image reinscribes another kind of confusion, one in the conventional hierarchy of the body. If we can see this hierarchy metaphorically as a social hierarchy—and I think the film offers good reason for doing this—we can begin to make sense of long stretches of the narrative that have nothing to do with the psychoanalytic material I have been discussing.[18]

From the very opening of this film, the camera inscribes a sense of uncertainty in the way it explores space. We begin with what becomes a very typical way for this camera to move: seeming to have one thing as its aim, it will then move off in another direction. There is clearly a sense of a quest established at the beginning of the movie by the way the camera explores the seemingly empty spaceship as if looking for signs of life, but there is also a sense of uncertainty at the very heart of the quest. We do finally end up on space helmets, which are made to seem like a destination for the camera because they are seen at a close distance and the camera finally stops moving to yield to some crosscutting. It is typical of this movie that this isn't actually the final destination, but at least initially it may appear to be.

Throughout *Alien*, the film plays with our ability to make sense of what we see and frequently undermines it. This establishes a central idea that relates both to the physical body *and* the social body. Initially, the close-up of the helmets suggests that there is some life on ship. Up until this point the dark exterior and the empty interior have been the most striking features of the spaceship (especially since an opening title has led us to expect a crew). If the shot of the helmets finally seems to satisfy that expectation, the results are not entirely comforting. There is a disturbance here that comes in the reflected play of lights on helmet visors from a computer that has just turned itself on, signaling a coming to life that seems to point to death. The life is purely mechanical and existing solely outside the helmets. The boundaries between life/light and death/dark are made obscure. As a further disturbance, we've been led into close-ups of heads but cannot see faces. Rather, the exterior world is reflected back to us. Finally, under the helmets all the characters appear to be the same. Seeing the characters in this way, we cannot make the kinds of distinctions we would if we knew their actual position in the society of the ship. These are distinctions the film will articulate—and articulate clearly.

Much as the film draws on earlier science fiction and horror, there is one other generic source for this film that has much to do with its sense of social hierarchy. This element might not be readily obvious (although the sequel is in fact fairly explicit about it): the World War II combat film. In particular, the composition of the ship's crew in *Alien* suggests the war film in its mingling of types. The combat war film strove for geographic and ethnic distribution to convey the sense of a democratic nation. There was often one character named after a place, so sure enough in *Alien* there is a "Dallas" (Tom Skerritt). While the diverse members of the group in the combat war film learn how to make their diversity serve a common goal, how to be a truly cohesive group, *Alien* portrays a social microcosm that is in constant danger of pulling apart. This group does not function together well at all. Trouble begins right at the top. Both Dallas, the chief officer, and Ripley, his subordinate, believe they represent the interests of the "Company," the corporation that has sent them on this mission, yet Dallas does so cynically, Ripley idealistically. As a result, they constantly clash over decisions through the first half of the film.

The only characters that really work together, that suggest a potential for a group dynamic, are those on the lowest rung of the social ladder, Brett (Harry Dean Stanton) and Parker (Yaphet Kotto). Ripley, always the company person, seems particularly annoyed by them, and the film offers no good reason other than that she is their superior and apparently doesn't like their loyalty to each other: she makes sarcastic fun of Brett for always agreeing with Parker. When Parker makes a just complaint about wages to Ripley, she abruptly responds, "Why don't you just fuck off?" The film offers a critique of her attitude by having the camera remain with Parker and Brett after she leaves. This allows them a kind of power over her, especially when we are let in on the joke that Parker has been making speech difficult for Ripley by covertly manipulating a steam jet. As Ripley will subsequently learn, her own power is as subject to manipulation by the "Company," and the plot will lead to a critique of her attitude toward Brett and Parker by the fact that Parker will be the one to save her life in the attack by the android Ashe (Ian Holm). The casting of Yaphet Kotto is visually important in this regard because the black underclass has traditionally occupied the position of alien *within* American culture. As was noted in regard to both *Animal House* and *Porky's*, blacks possess an otherness in American culture that has made it easy for Americans to align them with the monstrous. *Alien*, then, presents a clear sense of class structure in this small social group, with class partly tagged by race and a real hostility between the classes.

The particular attention paid to the minority character here and the power granted him points to another revision on the combat war film. The narrative of the combat film derives its forward momentum from the progressive killing off of members of the group. Minorities occupy a very particular position in this progression, as Jeanine Basinger has noted: "After the loss of the leader, the minorities die first . . . for them are reserved the most brutish deaths."[19] Implicit in this ordering is the sense that the minorities are the most "expendable" members of the group (to borrow a word from *Alien*), the ones least necessary for the group's sense of itself. *Alien* reverses this progression by reducing its group to what conventionally would be the most expendable members: two women and a black man. Generic expectation is invoked and inverted to challenge conventional ways of thinking about hierarchy, much as the body of the alien challenges our sense of corporal hierarchy when finally viewed.

Conventional hierarchies that we ourselves bring to this film are undermined, and the kinds of social distinctions we routinely make are completely obliterated. In *Alien* the head is the first part of the crew's body to be cut off as they search for the alien presence. This film is very much the product of an age in which there is real anxiety about social hierarchies (but an anxiety that presents itself in adamantly corporal terms). The social structure in this film is based on something corrupt because corruption already exists at the top. After Watergate the loss of the head of state (with Nixon's resignation), and the greatly weakened presidency that followed it, provoked an anxiety about leadership that permeated the culture.[20] American society had become a social body without a head.

Because *Alien* takes place in the future, its paranoid fantasy about the terror of corporate power remains fairly generalized and nonspecific. George Romero's *Dawn of the Dead*, released the same year, is more directly about a contemporary social reality—urban decay and suburban flight. Here the body politic itself is in a state of chaos not unlike the uncontrollable body of the werewolf movies. The film begins as if it were inside a body, with one character waking from a nightmare into a reality that is a nightmare. A person next to her explicitly conflates waking and dreaming ("I'm still dreaming"). Further, the soundtrack reinforces the sense of still being inside a dream, of still inside your body, by having a bass play throughout the entire scene a two-beat phrase that exactly mimics a heartbeat. The irony of a reality that is a nightmare finds a complementary irony in the setting: the film begins in a television *control* room that is witness to absolute turmoil.

Dawn of the Dead takes place entirely in a world without governance, a society in which all order has broken down—in effect, a social body without a head. Heads seem the most vulnerable part of the anatomy in this film, and not just because the only way of killing the living dead is by shooting them in the head. The first murder we see is of a National Guardsman who is part of a force that seems to be employed in putting down an inner-city riot of Hispanics. He receives a bullet right in the middle of his forehead. The next murder—and the first instance of a real gross-out effect—has a soldier, presumably equipped with something that has the force of a bazooka, blowing off the entire head of a possibly innocent bystander, transforming the head into an exploding bloody pulp. This soldier is himself out of control, driven by rage against what he sees as privileged minorities, so that his destruction of the head becomes a projection of his own state. Everything about the opening aims to induce a feeling of hysteria in the viewer, to create the sensation that we, effectively deprived of our ability to understand exactly what is taking place in all this chaos, are also without governance.

The living dead in *Dawn of the Dead* are initially associated with inner-city minorities. While the confusion in the opening deprives us of any sense that there is any authority left in this world, we do see one possible authority figure, a black Hispanic priest whom two of the soldiers, Peter

(Ken Foree) and Roger (Scott Reiniger), meet in the cellar. Because these are two men who eventually form part of the central quartet we will follow as they flee the city for a safer environment, their encounter with this man lingers over the rest of the film, giving some kind of explanation for their flight. He tells them that he has given the last rites to people in a neighboring room, and the two soldiers can now do what they have to do to them. These are presumably the living dead, whom the priest is relinquishing to the soldiers for killing. But in turning these people over, the priest also offers the threat of further breakdown: "You are stronger than us, but soon, I think, they be stronger than you." In his confusion of adjectives, both distancing himself from the "living dead" ("they") as well as identifying with them ("us"), the priest points the way the film gives the living dead a specific social meaning, conflating them with the inner-city poor.

The subsequent flight to the countryside parallels a larger flight that took place in this country in the post–World War II years, a flight that escalated after the inner-city riots in the late 1960s. *Dawn of the Dead* is specifically concerned with the meaning of this move in itself. It defines the middle-class suburban exodus as an abandoning of the inner city to the poor to create a more perfect world whose perfection is defined by its separation from the world at large. As a stand-in for suburban life, the setting for the rest of the film is a large indoor shopping mall. In urban downtowns, stores are connected through exteriors that open them up to the rest of the world. By contrast, in the mall, which is at the center of suburban society, everything is self-enclosed. Most of the long middle section of this film is concerned with its central quartet's attempt to seal off the mall from the outside world, to restore it as an inviolable body over which our group of four has control. The film makes the work of sealing off the mall comparable to the flight from the city—a futile attempt to find a safe and private place, to construct a body that cannot be invaded. As the film has it, the inviolable body is always doomed because it is an isolated body.

The Mind-Body Problem

Videodrome (1983) and *A Nightmare on Elm Street* (1984)

This tension between the isolated private body and the body politic is also central to David Cronenberg's *Videodrome*. Where Romero focuses on the creation of a new reality in suburban culture, Cronenberg is concerned with ways in which the image in "image culture"—and, most of all, *video* image culture—acts as intermediary between external reality and internal perception. As an intermediate stage between external and internal, the image confuses our sense of boundaries between the two by offering a reproduction of external reality that implies a subjective reality. The film itself plays on our ability to make such distinctions between objective and subjective realities by a narrative that progressively blurs lines between external reality and internal fantasy.

Seeking near hard-core material for his pirate cable TV station, programmer Max Renn (James Woods) comes across "Videodrome," an illegal television transmission that features explicit sadistic material. Max is intrigued, initially because of how he thinks Videodrome will attract his customers, then because of his own fascination with it. He is drawn *into* his television set in what seems to become an increasingly literal way: by the end of the film either Videodrome has taken up residence in Max or Max has taken up residence in Videodrome. And we are either watching a fantasy about the power of television or witnessing the paranoid hallucination of one individual.

There is a kind of social satire at work in this film that correlates with the satire in *Dawn of the Dead.* Both films reveal a dark humor about their central conceits that distinguishes them from much of the other horror films of the period. What is unusual about *Videodrome* is how much it stakes concerns about the body that crop up in other horror films as the primary field for its satirical play. By utilizing an actual human body as its primary staging area, *Videodrome* takes on a psychological dimension that *Dawn of the Dead* does not possess. There is still the sense of a social body threatened with invasion from outside forces (paralleled by a very paranoid vision of society), but now we are also concerned with specific physical effects on a human body. Indeed, *Videodrome* demonstrates that your parents were right about what might happen to you if you watch too much TV! By being glued to the TV set, Max becomes an extension of it. If it is a primary dramatic strategy to make us question where Max leaves off and the TV image begins, by extension the film makes us consider the nature of subjectivity in a media-dominated culture.

Like *Alien* and *Dawn of the Dead* before it, *Videodrome* begins with a character waking up (seemingly one of the most often repeated gambits for horror films in this period).[21] As in the other films, the character wakes up to a reality that becomes more and more nightmarish. Here the nightmare is defined by Max's increasingly strange relationship to his TV set. The camera pans around a quiet room, coming to rest on a TV set that seems to turn itself on. As an announcer says "Civic TV, the TV you take to bed with you," a logo for "Civic TV" appears: a cartoon drawing of a man in bed with a television and a teddy bear, suggesting a regressive relationship to the TV. This is, then, a truly transitional object since it mediates between subjective reality as suggested by sleep and the external reality it (the TV set) apparently presents. Since we see an image within an image (a TV set seen on motion picture film), our relationship to it is equally problematized. The camera has chosen it for us to view, yet it appears to be addressing someone else.

Befitting its intermediary state, this is something like a TV version of a clock radio, but with added features. Because the image on the T turns out to be a wake-up call from Max's secretary: "Max, it's that time again, time to slowly, painfully ease yourself back into consciousness. No, I'm not a dream, although I've been told I'm a vision of loveliness." The secretary laughs and looks to her left (presumably in the direction of an offscreen voice and an offscreen laugh). There are problems in the way we understand this image in that we do not know to whom it is addressed. Further, we do not know who the offscreen person is or what he is saying. As the film camera resumes panning to the left, we come upon Max, whose head is turned away from the set. Although he now wakes up, we cannot say that he has actually seen the TV image. Does an image then exist as part of reality if there is no one to see it? An image assumes an origin and a point of address, but if neither can be precisely defined by us, then we must remain uncertain about the status of the image—what, exactly, its relation to reality is. As the image initially connects to a dream, by extension it evokes an opposition between consciousness and the unconscious, in some way mediating the two.

If the TV image suggests a kind of transitional world, an intermediary space between conscious and unconscious, between reality and fantasy, the film itself moves deeper and deeper into this transitional world. We don't move as fully into fantasy as in other horror films. Rather, the film establishes a slippery boundary between the real and the fantastic. By the end of the film, we seem to have entered fully into Max's paranoid fantasy (although it is difficult to say even that with absolute certainty). As an example of how the film achieves this kind of uncertainty about the status of the image for us, consider a moment when fantasy takes over in a way that is not clearly demarcated, but we nevertheless know that we are seeing a fantasy.

At this point in the film, Max has become the lover of sadomasochistic Nikki (Deborah Harry), an involvement that parallels his growing involvement with Videodrome. When Max's secretary Bridey brings him his wake-up cassette, Max becomes angry at her and apparently slaps her twice, but fantasizes that he is slapping Nikki. We see each slap with shots looking toward Max as he begins the slap into which are cut reverse-angle shots, the first time showing Nikki receiving the slap, the second time Bridey. Max assumes, as we do, that he has slapped Bridey, with the hallucination merely substituting one woman for the other. But as the subsequent dialogue makes clear, the entire event has *not* taken place at all. With this, a terrible gap opens up in the narrative: what has in fact taken place when we were watching the hallucination?

From this point on, we can never be certain about the reality of what we are seeing: could this all be the hallucination of a man who is going insane? And, perhaps even more important, we must question the reality the hallucination has prevented us from seeing, as if there were a reality we did not see. All we can say is, by the end the projected image becomes both a model for reality, literally, and the only reality we can possibly know as we look at this film. As "I see" in Western culture means "I understand," Cronenberg is concerned with the power of images in visual culture—or, perhaps more exactly, with the power of televisual culture to effect understanding. As the film sees it, the indeterminate status of the image as a mediator between us and reality grants it a religious dimension inasmuch as we may regard religion as a system that can shape our understanding of the world. Herein lies the meaning of the parody of a passage in the Gospel of John. When the inventor of Videodrome tells Max, "I am the video word made flesh," he means that the image (the "video word") has the power to concretize, to turn understanding into seeing.

These issues play themselves out directly on Max's body. Initially he sees himself as distinct from the rest of the world. He is a man who sells images—to be sure, degraded images to appeal to base instincts—but he sees himself as untouched by this, as if he has some kind of power over the image itself. What he cannot admit is that the image might in fact have some power over him, an ability to touch subconscious recesses that he might not be aware of, the area of hidden desires that we all normally repress. By the end of the film these hidden desires have been fully unleashed, and there is no distinction between the image and the reality, as there is finally no distinction between Max and the outside world. A vaginalike opening appears in Max's abdomen, into which a videocassette can be inserted.[22] With the cassette inside Max, the image becomes the only reality there is. The video word has indeed been made flesh

As the similar openings of *Dawn of the Dead, Alien,* and *Videodrome* suggest, a blurring between objective reality and subjective experience is not an uncommon strategy for horror films of the period. As such, they all offer a challenge to our understanding of such seemingly clear-cut divisions as that between dreaming and waking. For example, at the beginning of *Alien* we see the crew wake up through a series of unusual dissolves. In conventional film style, the dissolve is frequently used to indicate a passage of time, and at first glance that seems to be its intended purpose here. Yet each dissolve shows an exact overlap in action between its component shots so there is in fact no break in temporal continuity. Instead, by suggesting a passage of time, it does not actually show the dissolve is there to blur the boundary between sleeping and waking, internal and external, and, finally, objective and subjective. As the body became more permeable, as distinctions between internal and external broke down, there was a comparable breakdown in distinctions we routinely make in our perception of the world. Early in *An American Werewolf in London,* David, before he realizes he is a werewolf, has a dream in which he sees his family's idealized suburban home invaded by monsters who proceed to kill his parents and siblings. As one of them begins to cut David's throat, David wakes up, but he wakes up into what turns out to be another nightmare.

This is a curious dream because it is one of the indications that David is becoming a werewolf, and yet he appears in it as the victim of monsters. What is of most concern to me here, however, is the impact of the dream within the dream. It is rather similar to a sequence in Luis Buñuel's *The Discreet Charm of the Bourgeoisie* (1972) to the point that it might actually be quoting from it. I mention this because the Buñuel film is explicitly a surrealistic work. While there might be a kind of accidental surrealism in earlier horror films that is merely a consequence of their fantasy mode, surrealism explicitly entered the horror film in this period precisely because of the new orientation toward the body that I have been analyzing in this chapter.

One of the central tenets of surrealism, arrived at under the influence of Freudian psychoanalysis, is that the conscious and unconscious mind were no longer to be seen as distinct entities, each operating in a separate realm. Rather, what happened in the subconscious was a response to things happening to the conscious mind that would in turn find an outlet in the conscious mind. This blurring of boundaries between conscious and subconscious parallels the blurring of boundaries between internal and external. The kind of indeterminate territory that results is perfectly suited for film because of a dreamlike quality in its fantastic reality. It is an art form that is both substantial and yet insubstantial, creating a reality that appears to us in concrete detail and yet does not exist—a mere play of light and shadow. This is an issue made explicit in *A Nightmare on Elm Street Part IV: The Dream Master* (1988) with a quotation from a 1924 Buster Keaton film, *Sherlock Jr.*, in which a character walks into screen, blurring the boundaries between reality and fantasy. Keaton had been a key figure for the surrealists in the 1920s. With this direct quotation from him, the horror film for the first time directly acknowledged its surrealist intent.

The first *Nightmare on Elm Street* goes even further than the openings of *Dawn of the Dead, Alien,* and *Videodrome* by beginning in a nightmare. A nightmare will also end the film, so that this bookending of dreams effectively numbs our ability to make any clear-cut distinction between sleeping and waking states. Making it difficult for us to tell when waking stops and dreaming begins is this film's most characteristic feature. And beginning as a dream effectively blurs distinctions that we automatically make in looking at a film: we assume we are looking at a representation of reality unless otherwise informed. Because film has the facility to document any reality placed before it, it usually requires some elaborate optical cue to indicate that we have moved from one reality to another— whether fantasy or dream or everyday reality. By the time of *A Nightmare on Elm Street*, the omission of such clues had ceased to be much of a novelty in film (the nightmare from *An American Werewolf* cited above, for example, provides no indication that we are in a dream). Still, I can think of no film that so effectively blurs the boundaries between dreaming and waking reality as the original *Nightmare*, directed by Wes Craven.

Consider, for example, the transition between the first two scenes. We have just witnessed Tina's nightmare of Freddy (Robert Englund), and rips in Tina's nightgown has shown us that what happens in dreams might have consequences in reality, after which we see Tina (Amanda Wyss) grasping a crucifix and lying down to go back to sleep. At this point there is a sound overlap of girls singing a jump rope song ("One, two, Freddy's coming for you"), followed by a direct cut to a shot of four girls playing jump rope. The image is in slow motion and hazy because of an intense diffusion filter. While the song continues on the soundtrack, the girls themselves are not singing. The camera pans to the right past some trees to the street and a red convertible carrying three of the film's four central characters. As the camera reaches the end of the pan, stopping on the car, the diffusion filter disappears without interrupting the shot. The three get out of the car and, joined by the fourth, walk toward the camera, talking about Tina's terrifying dream from the night before. The camera rigidly holds the frame so that the left of the image cuts off our view of the area where the four girls were playing.

The image of Tina falling back toward her pillow, the sound overlap, the slow motion, the fogginess of the image, and the disjuncture between image and soundtrack all suggest we have returned to the dream world. And yet the single continuous camera movement makes it impossible for us to say if this is in fact a dream or reality. While dialogue among the principals is about the jump rope song we've just heard, the speakers themselves seem unaware of the girls, and the camera keeps the area the girls occupied cut off from our view. When we finally do see that area again—as background in a single shot of Tina—the girls are no longer there. All the film techniques point to a dream (the one time in the film in fact that a dream seems explicitly demarcated), yet the subsequent camera movement leads us back to a scene that we must accept as reality.

Much as *A Nightmare on Elm Street* is about four teenagers who are terrorized by their own dreams, the film constantly works on an anxiety about the reliability of our perceptual equipment, those nerve endings by which we know "reality." Is reality something inside of us or something outside? The terror over lack of boundaries is made fully a psychological problem with this film, with little attempt to connect this to the body politic that still lingers in *Videodrome*. In *Videodrome*, the terror resides in the outside world, in its capacity to invade and take over the individual body. In *A Nightmare on Elm Street*, the terror is more internal because we can never trust the senses by which we interpret the outside world. How can we ever determine if our understanding of the world is accurate, reliable?

Because the monster in this film can only attack people when they are asleep, there is implicitly a control issue here, a battle between different parts of the mind that gives the film its distinctive psychological feel. If we look at this psychoanalytically (which the film certainly encourages), we can determine that the problem in fact involves the two agencies in the mind that respond to external as well as internal stimuli—our subconscious and conscious minds. Since the conscious mind usually has control, entering a dream state means giving free reign to another area of the mind, one normally held in check. The film repeatedly plays on an anxiety about falling asleep since sleep always relinquishes control of the conscious mind. *Nightmare* emphasizes the terror of not being able to give in to a basic human need.

Another source of terror relates to the issue of control that obfuscates boundaries: the dreamer is the author of the monster's being. When Nancy

(Heather Langenkamp) begins to understand the reality of Freddy, she seeks to take control by arranging with her boyfriend Glen (Johnny Depp) to wake her at a crucial moment in her dream so she can defeat Freddy. As always in this film, we are tricked about the point of entry into the dream. We initially see Glen sitting in a chair by Nancy's bed, but when Nancy appears outside, we see Glen standing behind a tree and waving to her, which makes us think everything is still operating in "reality." We can only make sense of this when Nancy subsequently returns to the house and sees Glen asleep in the chair by her bed: he has never left the room. Nancy looks at herself in a mirror and repeats, as if in a mantra, "It's only a dream." But as Nancy looks at herself, Freddy's image begins to emerge from her reflection (suggesting that she is somehow bringing him into existence), and suddenly he bursts through the mirror and starts attacking her again.

Seeing is believing, but is it always reality? The opening credit sequence in *Nightmare* suggests another way of looking at the film's commingling of dream and reality. As the titles appear in a black area, a frame within a frame shows us images of Freddy manufacturing his bizarre murder weapon (the glove with finger knives). By echoing the rectangular shape of the movie screen, the internal frame makes us aware of the artificial nature of the image. We are distanced from the image here as we will not be at any other point in the film, yet this is our introduction to the film's terror. Further, as the images show us how something is constructed, by extension we are concerned with how we construct the image itself. The sequence is made up entirely of insert shots, which signals a fascination with procedure. However, the first full-screen image initially prompts more frustration than satisfaction since we can't locate ourselves in any identifiable space. It appears to be some kind of abstraction, a totality of the preceding construction. This is complemented by what might be a reverse-angle shot, a comparably abstract image of a teenage girl—Tina, against a seemingly blank background. As the sequence continues, we begin to fill in details, gradually making sense of what we've seen. At the end of the sequence the first full image is repeated, this time within a context that now grants it a meaning it did not have at first.

Much as the film probes the conflict between waking and dreaming as a psychoanalytic matter, it also sees a cognitive problem. Because of its ability to manipulate reality, to break it up into isolated details or to abstract it, the film image makes clear to us how much we are always trying to make sense of what we see. *Nightmare* pinpoints the way we look at its images and how we come to accept the reality of something that is not there. Seeing is believing, even when we know it isn't real. And therein lies the cognitive problem: how do we know this? There is a corollary to this: if we understand what we see by endowing it with meaning, then this grants a subjective dimension to sight that can in effect distort what we see.

Perhaps because director Wes Craven was an English teacher, he uses an English class to address this problem directly. The class comes right after the police capture Tina's boyfriend Rod (Nick Korri), in a trap set by Nancy's police captain father. Since Tina has previously been killed while in a bedroom with Rod, all appearances point to Rod as the murderer. Unbeknownst to Nancy, her father uses her to lead him to Rod. After Nancy criticizes him for this, the camera stays on the father as we hear a sound overlap from the following scene of the English teacher saying, "What is seen . . . [Craven then cuts to a medium shot of the teacher as she completes her sentence] is not always what is real." Initially this seems mainly to be a corrective to the father's way of seeing: he assumes Rod is the killer because that is the right conclusion given what was seen. But from our viewpoint there is also more here than meets the eye, as the teacher's next comment makes clear: "According to Shakespeare, there was something operating in nature, perhaps inside human nature itself, that was rotten."

There is in fact a dirty little secret at the heart of this film—dirty specifically because the upright parents we have seen are not the kind of people they appear to be. Out of this dark secret has come a very literal example of return of the repressed—because the parents have attempted to suppress all knowledge about the real Freddy. The English teacher discusses two of Shakespeare's plays, *Hamlet* and *Julius Caesar*. Both deal with regicide—the killing of a male authority figure—and suggest a general sense of the law's impotence, that there is a realm of human experience beyond the control of male authority. In other words, there *is* something rotten in this world, and it is powerless in the face of a character like Freddy: if a society cannot protect its children, what is the value of that society? We have arrived at another social body without a head. The children have inherited a world made corrupt by their parents, and they find themselves paying for their parents' sins.

So, what's wrong with the parents in this film?. They are mostly absent, as in earlier films, but here they are specifically tagged as being emotionally absent. As the children are the only ones who seem to know what is going on, the film works a kind of inversion on parents and children. In a key scene between Nancy and her mother, Nancy sits on her mother's bed facing her supine mother, assuring her that everything's okay, much like a parent comforting a sick child. The mother responds, "You face things. That's your nature. That's your gift. But sometimes you have to turn away too." The mother thinks that turning away can effectively change reality: what we don't see isn't there. But Nancy believes in what she sees and everything she says, she tries to make sense of it and to integrate it into her life. As such, she is the more mature person. Nancy is the parent here.

As was noted in the discussion of *Back to the Future* (chapter 11), resurrecting and redeeming the parent became a familiar feature of popular art in this period. In that film a tippling mother is made whole and healthy through the heroic efforts of her son. In *Nightmare* it becomes Nancy's task to restore her tippling mother as a good mother, but this film is much more pessimistic than *Back to the Future*. Nancy ultimately fails in her task because the inversion itself is an impossibility. It might be in her "nature" to face things, to see Freddy directly and to recognize the corruption at the foundation of society, but if the mother cannot see this as well, if the mother must look away, then the boundaries between waking and dreaming can never be fully reestablished. The reestablishment of the dreamworld at the end is appropriately signaled by Freddy's attack on the mother.

To let Nancy succeed would indicate a restoration of bodily integrity: she would drive Freddy out and reestablish herself as a whole person, separate and closed off. But then the film would lose the thrill of the final scream (de rigeur for horror films of the period after *Carrie*'s example). Furthermore, it would establish a sense of certainty by making clear demarcations between dreaming and waking. The whole film would turn out to be just a dream, returning to us the cast of characters who had been progressively killed off by Freddy throughout. Indeed, *A Nightmare on Elm Street* at first seems to do this at the end, but then suddenly Freddy reappears and attacks the mother, restoring the film's pervasive sense of uncertainty about boundaries. This abrupt about-face at film's end is not there for the sake of laying groundwork for a sequel. Rather, as the body lost its sense of boundaries in this period, so did the bodies of narrative. Where horror films once sought a definite sense of closure, there grew a need in this period for a final thrill that effectively undermined this. In its search for the final thrill, the horror film began to take on a kind of comic rhythm, moving toward a last scream that parallels the last laugh of comedy.

Laughing Screaming

You have to remember that Psycho *is a film made with quite a sense of amusement on my part. To me it's a* fun *picture. The processes through which we take the audience, you see, is rather like taking them through the haunted house at the fairground or the roller-coaster, you know.* —*Alfred Hitchcock*

Chapter 18 *The Comic Beat of Never-ending Terror*

The End of "The End"

Carrie (1976), *Psycho* (1960), *The Birds* (1963), *The Fearless Vampire Killers* (1967), *Poltergeist* (1982)

When I saw *Carrie* in a theater on its first release, the ending prompted a response from the audience almost unlike anything else I had ever experienced at a movie. Carrie's hand suddenly thrusting up through the charcoal, breaking Sue's reverie to grab her by the arm, produced the requisite scream. But there was something more, a buzz in the audience that continued even after the film had ended, the curtains had closed, and the houselights came up. It was as if the movie continued to have some hold on us (much as Sue's mom held onto Sue), exerting a control that reached us even in the cold reality of the illuminated auditorium.

How could we still respond to something no longer there? I think the strength of our reaction was partly a matter of context, the conditioning of our expectations by horror films of the past. The best of the earlier horror films usually found ingenious methods to dispatch a bothersome monster, but once it (or, frequently, he) was killed, it/he always had the good grace to stay dead. *Carrie* was one of the first films to let us know you can't keep a good monster down, even if that monster might only reappear in our dreams.[1] This was not an unwelcome discovery. Certainly the reaction of the audience was plain enough: there is pleasure in reasserting terror (sufficiently pleasurable to establish *Carrie*'s ending as a model for later films). As we walked out of the theater, the buzz initiated by the scream segued into laughter. We enjoyed seeing the lyrical mode of Sue's dream brutally trashed; we enjoyed being startled out of our expectation of an ending in which all the loose ends get neatly tied up.

Although there were certainly some precursors for this (especially in *Psycho* and *The Birds*), *Carrie*'s ending was the most direct assault yet on closure's dominance in Hollywood films. Attempts to define "Classical Hollywood Cinema" often feature closure as one of the key elements in Hollywood narrative codes, or what David Bordwell has called "the return of a stable narrative state."[2] *Carrie*'s ending, of course, destabilizes the narrative so that we lose any sense of a "stable narrative state." Clearly, the desire for closure says something about how we understand narrative, how we see it as something self-contained and cut off from the real world. Our satisfaction in a seeming resolution of all conflicts signals a pleasure we all too rarely find in reality. Closure in a fictional context such as a Hollywood film is not such a remarkable thing. Lack of closure is.

The horror film's decisive move away from closure after *Carrie* did not take place solely to pave the way for sequels. From the 1930s through the 1950s, Universal Pictures had no trouble revivifying its various vampires, werewolves, mummies, and assorted other monsters—even after they had been killed off in their respective films. But although horror films were often among the most emphatic in regard to closure (by definitely dispatching the monster one way or another in every picture), this did begin to change a bit in the 1950s when the horror film married science fiction to propagate new monsters. The resulting films often created a situation in which the requisite death of the monster did not offer the same fully reassuring resolution as in the past. At the end of *The Thing* (1951), for example, we are warned to be on our guard, to look to the skies—and with good reason. The caution here was not simply a reflection of anxiety over the Red menace (i.e., Communism), as it and similar films have been interpreted.[3] Rather, this cautionary signoff has something to do with the very origins of the monsters themselves.

Ending the narrative with a warning had not been uncommon in combat films made during World War II, so the Cold War context no doubt helped revive this practice. But the admonition to look to the skies had another and more connected meaning for the time: for certainly the most horrific things dropping from the skies during this period were the newly developed atom and hydrogen bombs. The consequences of smashing the atom were powerfully felt in the horror films of the 1950s, providing a prime cause for some of the era's most terrific monsters. Films that traced the etiology of the monster to atomic fallout necessarily opened up a fissure in closure. We might be able to get rid of the individual monster[s], especially if we allowed ourselves to work closely with the very scientists who had indirectly caused the monstrosity in the first place. But could we actually get rid of atomic testing itself? Not if we wanted to keep the country secure; so the search to keep the body of the nation inviolate, impenetrable, itself created new monsters.

The Thing might end with a warning, and *The Blob* (1958) could end with a question mark, but there is nonetheless an appearance of closure in these films. In effect, the 1950s saw an old form still trying to work for new content. Eventually something had to give, and, as I hope will become evident here, there are ways in which the form finally had to change to accommodate a postatomic world. The change can probably be seen most clearly in what happened to comedy in this period. In a 1956 essay, "The Meanings of Comedy," Wylie Sypher defined a "New Sense of the Comic" that he felt belonged to the post–World War II age: "Now that we have lived amid the 'dust and crashes' of the twentieth century [we] have learned how the direst calamities that befall man seem to prove that human life at its depths is inherently absurd. The comic and tragic views of life no longer exclude each other."[4] Sypher locates the change in the horrors of the twentieth century, but this seems insufficient to me. The twentieth century is not uniquely horrible. What *is* unique grows out of a necessary change in our understanding of what Sypher defines as the "entire ceremonial cycle" of comedy—"birth: struggle: death: resurrection." "Comedy," he notes, "is essentially a Carrying Away of Death, a triumph over mortality by some absurd faith in rebirth, restoration, and salvation" (p. 220). But what if circumstances conspire to undermine even that "absurd faith"?

Paralleling Sypher's ceremonial cycle is Northrop Frye's definition of comedy as the "mythos of spring," a promise of eternal return that has the certainty of the seasons.[5] But in a world after the atom bomb, the promise of spring gives way to the possibility of a nuclear winter. The atomic world has effectively destroyed the inherently cyclical nature of comedy, as the timely preference for absurdism, "black comedy" and "sick comedy" in the postwar world suggests. The closure of earlier horror films is not unlike the closure of romantic comedy: the return to spring that promises a future in the comic universe finds an echo in the return to normality that promises a nonthreatening future in the horror film. It isn't that there were no apocalyptic visions in the past, but for the first time the power of bringing on the apocalypse lay within our own hands. If we could now imagine a world with a definite end (one we could ourselves bring about through the splitting of the atom), we conversely had to reimagine what a narrative's resolution actually meant. As we experience it, conventional closure is as much a beginning as an ending in that clearly defined endings generally carry with them promises about the future. A refusal of closure perversely denies any certain future.

The first overt challenge to closure in Hollywood movies came with Alfred Hitchcock's *Psycho* (1960) and *The Birds* (1963), two films that strikingly conflate the horror film with comedy. Norman, the monstrous character in *Psycho*, is not so much gotten rid of as merely put away. Possessing the survival strategies of a comic hero, he transforms himself, creating a new identity that effectively puts him beyond the reach of a law that might otherwise seek his destruction. Further, the film has him become the dominating figure of its conclusion. In a close-up he stares directly at the camera (much like Niles/Holland in *The Other* and Damien in *The Omen*) as a voice-over makes us privy to his thoughts—his perhaps ironic claim to a gentleness that makes him spare a fly. A psychiatrist in the penultimate scene offers a rational explanation for his behavior, but the film nonetheless grants Norman the final word. Particularly powerful in Hitchcock's strategy against closure is the way he has Norman seem to address us directly, taking us into his confidence by smiling right at the camera (a smile that could readily be defined as knowing). By its direct appeal, the smile invites a sense of our complicity that the psychiatrist's explanation should have checked.

The Birds took the move against closure even further by ending *in the middle* of a suspense sequence, absolutely refusing to resolve the immediate concerns of the narrative—will this small family group escape from the next possible bird attack—or the tensions among its characters.[6] The screenwriter himself objected to Hitchcock ending the film in this manner, and audience reaction at early previews led to a "The End" title over the final shot (although Hitchcock had, reasonably, not planned to use one). People kept sitting in their seats, waiting for the next scene, assuming some projection problem had interrupted the narrative.[7] The ending is actually part of a piece with the entire film, since the film deliberately frustrates all attempts to make sense of the action. Coming after the mutant animal horror cycle had run its course, *The Birds* constantly encourages the audience to look for explanations about the strange behavior of the winged avengers, but never grants an explanation (like atomic testing), which would allow the illusion of a meaningful universe. *The Birds* has occasionally been described as "apocalyptic," but even this suggestion makes it too purposeful (we certainly never get anything close to a real apocalypse). Rather, the film is more accurately absurdist, built on a mounting frustration that makes the audience feel as stranded as its characters.

While *The Birds* was very influential on gross-out horror, no later film goes this far, so that even current audiences can be brought up short by its ending. Still, the desire to move away from closure that *The Birds* represents might finally have come more from audiences than filmmakers. As has been noted (in chapter 14), at the time of its release, the ending of *The Exorcist* generated a good deal of confusion, giving rise to reports that screenwriter William Peter Blatty and director Friedkin were contemplating a coda to make sure the ending was understood as they had intended it to be. The problem was, they saw a triumph of good in the film's conclusion, but audiences weren't convinced. Once the devil had been unleashed, they seemed ready to accept the possibility that he could not be put down again.

By the 1980s, the movement away from closure had become formulaic, something to be expected from a horror movie. The double ending of the Tobe Hooper/Steven Spielberg *Poltergeist* (1982), for example, provides a sharp point of comparison with the resolute ending of another ghost story, *The Uninvited* (1944). In the earlier film, when the lead characters successfully drive the bad ghost from the house, the audience knows the narrative is over. By contrast, *Poltergeist* also moves toward expulsion of a bad ghost—a domestic exorcism that would seem to be an appropriate ending to the film. And since the restoration of the family's five-year-old daughter, lost in the spirit world, has been the main quest of the narrative up to this point, her return (along with the bad ghost's expulsion), ought to signal a definite end to all the excitement—especially since her reappearance takes place amidst a satisfying show of special effects, sufficient to suggest a genuine climax. Yet the film has a good fifteen minutes of narrative left and even more spectacular special effects in store.

For anyone used to the conventions of earlier Hollywood films, the most startling aspect of the film's recharging its narrative battery is its absolute refusal to indicate it is doing so. On the contrary, there is every indication that things are winding down: we return to a new day, with the family getting ready to move away from this place of evil. This appears to be a convincing epilogue since a social theme on corporate greed here receives a definitive resolution: the real estate salesman father (Craig T. Nelson), discovering the impure foundation of his business, decides to quit his job and go with his family into a more decent future. A new day is dawning, brightness lies ahead—surely this should be sufficient to bring the narrative to a conclusive end. The film gives nary a clue that the exorcism of the ghost, the restoration of the daughter, and the father's moral resolve are still not enough—except that the film doesn't end. Yet even without the faintest suggestion of unresolved business, the film could assume that audiences would stay with it, that they somehow knew there was more and that the bastion of the family could not be so easily defended. And, indeed, the audience had the right expectations.

By the 1980s, Hollywood had conditioned its audience to expect a double ending. The pull against closure had moved far enough outside the precincts of the horror film that a new convention—the second ending—arose to restore a sense of closure.[8] In the romantic suspense thriller *Fatal Attraction* (1987), Glenn Close comes back to life after the hero apparently drowns her in a bathtub so that the heroine can get a whack at her as well. Perhaps even more extreme is the fate of one of the villains in the action film *Die Hard* (1988). Here hero Bruce Willis suspends villainous Alexander Godunov about twenty feet off the floor with an iron chain wrapped around his neck. Nevertheless, with no indication of the supernatural, Godunov turns up in the very next scene to continue his menacing ways before *really* being killed. Although the first "death" seemed entirely convincing to me, the film felt no need to explain how the dead has risen. Audience expectations conditioned by convention took care of that. In both these cases, what ought to be a supernatural event takes place in a world that otherwise disallows the fantastic.

Still, these films do move toward true closure. The second ending is there chiefly to secure it after a period in which closure has become greatly attenuated. For the most part, the truly open ending became the precinct of the horror film. Even the second ending of *Poltergeist* is not enough to allay an anxiety that the ghosts may still return. After the spectacular ghost jamboree that provides the real climax of the film, the family leaves their haunted house for good, retiring to a "Holiday Inn" for the night as the first stage of beginning a new life somewhere else. As they enter their hotel room, the camera remains outside, looking down the corridor of a balcony. After a beat, the room door opens and the father rolls out the TV set, banging it up against the railing of the balcony. He looks at the set for a second, as if with grim satisfaction, then blankly, straight ahead, a bit less certain. Finally, he moves back into the room and slams the door. This ending is effective because, throughout the film, television has served as the means of transmission to the world of ghosts: the young daughter first becomes aware of the ghostly beings via the television set, and once she disappears into the spirit world, the family keeps contact with her through the TV set. For an American family to renounce television as a way of defending itself against the world of monsters is about as effective as renouncing scientific discoveries in the mutant animal films of the 1950s. No wonder the father seems uncertain about this final act of exorcism!

Even as the narrative of *Poltergeist* appears to be closing, then, it suddenly opens up anew, which it does by shifting into a comic mode. The first image we had seen in the film was a montage of American monuments on a TV screen, accompanied by the "Star Spangled Banner." The point carries over to the ending: can an American family truly live without television? Television is not only its connection to superreality but to reality as well. And the film does make direct reference to a concern about the impact of television on children, for whom it increasingly defines the outside world. Early on, there is a brief scene after breakfast that shows the youngest daughter looking at a blank television screen (which the audience already knows is the ghost channel). The mother, passing by, notices this and comments "Oh, honey, you're going to ruin your eyes. This is no good for you." The mother then abruptly changes the channel but doesn't bother to look at what she's changed to, presuming that any actual image on TV is good for her daughter. Instead of the ghost channel, however, she's brought in a good dose of movie violence—killing, dying, and explosions. The film is clearly sketching out something satirical here, so that the opening shot coupled with subsequent references to television sets up the ending to register as a joke. The opening up of the narrative at the end directly connects to audience laughter. The final scream is also a final laugh.

I think this is worth remarking because the only experience I've had in a movie theater that was at all like the ending of *Carrie* was the ending of Billy Wilder's *Some Like It Hot* (1959). Much as with *Carrie*, the audience at *Some Like It Hot* was still reacting to Joe E. Brown's hilarious last line even after the house lights came up. That the *Carrie* experience should recall a comedy points to how I would like to think about the move away from closure. In chapter 16, I noted ways in which *Carrie* functions like a teen comedy that alternates and eventually merges with the horror film. The conflation of screaming and laughing at the conclusion is the satisfying culmination of a film that had occasionally seemed stranded between horror and comedy. Like the final laugh in comedy, the final scream is something we take pleasure in because it brings the work alive again just at the moment it seems to be ending.

The end of closure, then, suggests a resurgence of vitality we normally associate with comedy. In this respect, noting just how different *The Birds* is from later films helps to clarify the eventual alliance between comedy and horror film in opening up of the ending. *The Birds* provides none of the satisfaction that a good scream—or a good laugh—can offer since the ending leaves us completely suspended. While it may not have the finality of narrative closure, the sudden scare ending nonetheless offers a satisfaction that is akin to finality in the pleasantly surprising surge of our own feelings, our own vitality. In this one convention the gross-out horror film would seem to be taking over the rhythm of comedy. But this is in fact something more far-reaching, as can be seen in two other aspects of these films—one structural, the other modal.

In trying to define these structural aspects, I want to return to *The Birds* because it often served as a model for later films that depart from it. *The Birds* might fairly be described as a variation on what Northrop Frye has called the "green world comedy."[9] I hope this claim won't seem too much of a stretch since the film, until the first isolated attack by a seagull, initially plays like a straightforward, if somewhat brittle, romantic comedy. The conventions are very much that of a green world comedy, where the couple encounters obstacles in the city they will eventually overcome in the green world, the world of nature. The implication underlying this conventional plot structure is that nature, given free reign away from the constraints of society, will simply take its course. This seems to be precisely what is happening in *The Birds*—except that then nature itself goes crazy. The comedy segues into horror film.

But the comic structure does not leave the film entirely since the rest of *The Birds* builds on a kind of episodic escalation that recalls Old Comedy. In an otherwise rather loosely plotted narrative structure, the film achieves a sense of forward momentum by increasing the frequency and size of the attacks, and, in the process, creating a dramatic expectation that each attack must in some way top the preceding one. The result is a dramatic structure largely like the structure of broad comedy with its progressive building up of a gag always seeking its own topper. In this aspect, *The Birds* set a pattern for other films, from *Night of the Living Dead* and *The Texas Chainsaw Massacre* to most of the *Friday the 13th* series and their various clones: in all these films, people move out into the world of nature where things go progressively crazy, while the primary narrative drive comes in the form of an ever-increasing escalation.

This narrative structure parallels the distinctive structure of Animal Comedy described in part 2. Because the narrative in all these films is episodic, the forward drive comes primarily from topping a previous episode. The only suggestion of closure we get in these films, of any sense that we have reached the end of an otherwise contingent narrative, comes from what might be called the "big production number" toward which these films generally move. As noted earlier, these endings are often tied to some sporting event in order to emphasize the spectacle, but the sporting metaphor might have a broader significance for both the comedies and the horror films, suggesting an element of game playing in the way the narratives define themselves.[10]

In this sense of game playing—an infinitely repeated confrontation of obstacles to be overcome—I see an almost rarefied version of Suzanne Langer's biological view of comedy. Langer writes: "Destiny in the guise of Fortune is the fabric of comedy; it is developed by comic action, which is the upset and recovery of the protagonist's equilibrium, his contest with the world and his triumph by wit, luck, personal power, or even humorous, or ironical, or philosophical acceptance by mischance."[11] This sense of overcoming obstacles is clear enough in *The Birds*, where each successive attack by the birds moves the central characters to new measures by which they may survive. But *The Birds* is most odd in the way it refuses the final payoff. This is the case, however, only if we regard the birds as the main obstacle the central characters must overcome. Although the film itself does not entirely warrant this, we might arrive at something close to a model for the later films if we were to see a vital force in the birds themselves.

I can perhaps define more precisely what happens in the later films by looking at another forerunner, Roman Polanski's *The Fearless Vampire Killers* (1967). As Polanski's *Rosemary's Baby* anticipated the corporal concerns of the later films, *Vampire Killers* (made the year before *Rosemary's Baby*) anticipated their distinctive modal qualities, particularly in its treatment of the ending. The eponymous vampire killers, Alfred (Roman Polanski) and Professor Abronsius (Jack MacGowran), do not succeed in their primary ambition to eliminate the children of the night, but they do rescue the victim/prey Sarah (Sharon Tate) from an intended blood feast. As they evade their pursuer, however, even this rescue seems to fail when the enamored Alfred notices that Sarah's "tiny hand" is frozen. Alfred bewails his fate to the Professor, but he soon notices Sarah's eyes open again. Overjoyed, he focuses all his attention on her tiny hand, not noticing what we can see very clearly—that Sarah has grown the fangs of a vampire. As he rhapsodizes over her hand (". . . my little hand . . . my pretty hand . . . soon I will be sleeping the—"), she lunges at his neck with her open mouth and puts an abrupt end to his romantic prattle. A voice-over narration informs us, "That night, fleeing from Transylvania, Professor Abronsius never guessed he was carrying away with him the very evil he had wished to destroy. Thanks to him, this evil would at last be able to spread across the world."

The film takes a certain pleasure in confusing our expectations, much as it takes pleasure in making comedy out of the myopia of both men in this scene. Alfred unconsciously realizes a pun on the word "sleep," using it perhaps in one metaphorical manner to suggest sex, but suddenly realizing another metaphorical meaning in the eternal sleep that Sarah brings him. If comedy always moves toward a rebirth, there could be no more triumphantly comic happy ending than having an apparently dead character return to life. Yet the moribund Sarah confounds this plot pattern by returning to life as the living dead. As the resurgence of vitality here comes from a newly born vampire, it is the monsters in the later horror films who seem to stand for the vital principle, not only by overcoming all the obstacles placed in their path but also evading their destruction in the final scenes of the film, as we would normally expect. The transformation of the monster into a kind of comic character is most evident in films that spawned sequels. In the original *Nightmare on Elm Street* (1984), Freddy is primarily a figure of terror who avoids ultimate defeat. In all the sequels he became as much a comic character as a frightening one, with a sense of humor that seemed to become increasingly sardonic with each succeeding sequel.

In *The Fearless Vampire Killers*, the final laugh is quite specifically conflated with the final scream, something more tacit in later films where screaming may give way to laughing as the house lights come up. The implication of this is that we gain some satisfaction in the monster's return, in a resurgence of what we feared most throughout the narrative. Even when it is not as explicitly comic as it is in the *Nightmare on Elm Street* sequels, this sense of a vital resurgence of the monster remains one of the most distinctive qualities of gross-out horror. But how can we finally ally the monstrous with the vital? We can if we see in the monstrous an anarchic force that is worth celebrating as much as it is worth fearing, something we want to embrace and pull away from at the same time. The resistance to closure in these films keeps anarchy in a suspended state halfway between wish fulfillment and nightmare. If the comedies and the horror films should both conflate humor and terror, pleasure and anxiety, it is to produce an art of ambivalence and, with it, the promise of ceaseless festivity since ambivalence, by moving in two directions at once, always denies finality.

The Aesthetics of Gross-out

Gross-out, whether comedy or horror, is based on ambivalence because gross-out explicitly acknowledges the attractive in the repellent, the beautiful in the ugly. As it is a mode moving in two directions at once, the horror films may invoke comedy, while the comedies may take on suddenly nightmarish imagery (as we saw most clearly with *Animal House* and *Porky's*). Gross-out vacillates between extremes within each individual work, much as these two allied genres of horror and comedy travel in seemingly opposite directions. *Animal House* may be anarchic in its freewheeling challenges to authority at the same time it expresses a conservative bent by the way it transforms its anarchists into authority figures. Similarly, *The Exorcist* may be liberating in giving full vent to infantile rage at the same time that it is permeated by a sense of punitiveness toward that raging child.

There is a challenge in all this that I am trying to suggest merely by claiming an aesthetics of gross-out. Gross-out aesthetics must seem an oxymoron since *aesthetic* means the beautiful, implying a sense of decorum and proportion singularly absent from most of these films. This more usual definition was in fact a main ambition of earlier mainstream Hollywood films, which strove for middle-class respectability. This is not to claim that no films had ever tested these boundaries before. Certainly they had. But never before had an ambition to grossness *in itself* become such a prominent element in mainstream Hollywood production. Only in this way could new projects be given the formidable resources of A-picture budgets to reach new heights of excess. Clearly the movement of gross-out into the mainstream is a consequence of class change in American culture, the transformation of the proletariat into a genuine middle class of property owners, landed gentry who led the transformation into a suburban country. But this merely sets out conditions for why gross-out might have happened.

Something more was needed for it to flourish, and that something was more specifically connected with questions of value. Gross-out as a mainstream mode of discourse was born in a period of radical changes in social mores that challenged belief in traditional verities. Starting right at the top, the high became the low as the President of the United States engaged in petty crimes and spoke the language of the gutter. Gross-out continued to thrive through the early 1980s, a period of retrenchment that sought to reject the terms of a cultural debate set in motion by the student revolts of the late 1960s. Eventually, this would become a summons to "traditional values," a phrase that seeks to accrue all value to itself. Questioning what we mean by high and low—an insistent cultural concern throughout the period of gross-out—does not in itself deny value. Rather, precisely because it deals with value, and consequently evaluation, it necessarily moves us into the realm of the aesthetic.

Gross-out signifies an art of inversion. If traditional aesthetics values the beautiful, gross-out clearly poses the opposite; but its force is nonetheless based on a sense of traditional values—except they are inverted. The repellent becomes the attractive, or, perhaps more accurately, we must acknowledge that we find something attractive in the repellent. Things could not repel us if we were not initially attracted. In the confusing process of this push-pull aesthetic, we are forced to consider what we mean by both *repellent* and *attractive*. The ambition of trying to "go too far," which has been ascribed to the comedy of this period, is central to gross-out. As such, it must always imply a pull in an opposite direction because a "too far" would not exist without boundaries that aim at containment. One of the things these films must do is inscribe boundaries to challenge, then set new boundaries. As this ever-shifting concept keeps redefining itself, a rambunctious discourse emerges that is not univocal. Rather, it is a discourse of inversion, one that constantly changes its terms and parameters.

Inversion does not necessarily point to subversion. I mention this because some of these films, the horror films in particular, have been valued for their apparently subversive elements.[12] A good deal of academic criticism of the past decade or so has moved subversion into a privileged place as an evaluative norm for a work of art, pretty much replacing "self-reflexivity" as a measure of value. In both cases, these seem questionable standards of value to me. I wrote in chapter 1 that subversion may be one of the appeals of art, but an appeal is not the same as a value. We may be drawn to these works for their subversive elements, but we do not necessarily applaud them for this quality. Value must lie elsewhere. The valuing of subversion may well be traced to a Romantic view of the artist as set apart from bourgeois society. The way academic criticism has embraced this as a value is perhaps an expression of its own marginality. The central problem with subversion as a standard of evaluation may be seen with works that do not display the apparently requisite subversive elements: they become merely symptomatic of what is wrong in the culture in general. This essentially returns film and popular culture to a social utility that I wrote about and queried in the first part of this book.

I have had broad cultural/social concerns in this work, but I hope it is also clear from the discussions of individual films that I am concerned with aesthetics. I do not see how I can divorce the two if any individual work is an expression of its time. Collectively, these works define a discourse that reflects a period's concerns, a discourse that each individual work both contributes to and draws on. I have especially valued the best of these films for their forceful deployment of that discourse. Without debating the particulars of the aesthetic argument he propounds in *What Is Art?*, Leo Tolstoy's notion of art as the language of emotion is something I think we should still attend to, keeping in mind how the terms and syntax of that language can change with time as much as the subject matter of language changes. It is this concern for their emotional charge as a key to understanding that has prompted me to look so closely at how these films work on us. We have to pay attention not only to the surface meanings of the films, but how they articulate those concerns and how they affect us because it is in these articulations that their value is to be found.

In claiming an aesthetics of gross-out, I have tried to get beyond a teleology in discussions of art that perhaps begins with Aristotle's notion of the purgation of pity and terror. For Aristotle, the purgative aspects of tragedy help us get rid of undesirable feelings. Gross-out, on the other hand, does not seek purgation so much as *indulgence*. These works invite us to take pleasure in feelings that in their undesirability probably go beyond anything Aristotle imagined. Concern about an indulgence in the undesirable underlies the question frequently asked at the time of *The Exorcist*: why do they wait hours in line to be scared? To answer that it is fun may seem insufficient, yet fun might be an appropriate point of departure for any consideration of what these works actually do.

In chapter 5, I wrote about amusement park fun houses as places of letting go since I think that gross-out has a similar ambition. Keeping this in mind, I want to consider Alfred Hitchcock's description of *Psycho* as "a *fun* picture" and his comparison to a fairground "haunted house" because he specifically conflates comedy with terror in the context of this film.[13] Why should we see "fun" in a work that specifically aims to terrify us? It might seem less problematic to claim fright as an appealing element of the amusement park, where we quite consciously make a game out of our own feelings and in interaction with other people. It is *fun* to indulge in feelings that in the context of the real world would give us pause, to experience the surge of vitality that comes with the sudden onset of any strong feeling. Precisely because we do not take anything in the amusement park seriously, it is easy for us to see the emotions we indulge there as ends in themselves. Problems arise when we try to import a comparable value into a work of art, especially one with claims to artistic ambition, such as *The Exorcist.*

All too often, we make art serious and seemingly of value by downplaying *play*, by making art something other than fun. But like play, art may well be an end in itself, one of the ways we collectively define ourselves. As with play, we ought to value art precisely because it evades teleology. In his book-length study of play, Johan Huizinga specifically addresses this issue by noting the irreducible quality of play as a counter to definitions offered by psychology and physiology:

> All these hypotheses have one thing in common: they all start from the assumption that play must serve something which is *not* play, that it must have some kind of biological purpose. . . . They attack play directly with the quantitative methods of experimental science without first paying attention to its profoundly aesthetic quality. As a rule they leave the primary quality of play as such, virtually untouched. To each and every one of the above "explanations" it might well be objected: "So far so good, but what actually is the *fun* of playing? Why does the baby crow with pleasure? Why does the gambler lose himself in his passion? Why is a huge crowd roused to frenzy by a football match?" This intensity of, and absorption in, play finds no explanation in biological analysis. Yet in this intensity, this absorption, this power of maddening, lies the very essence, the primordial quality of play. . . . This last-named element, the *fun* of playing, resists all analysis, all logical interpretation. As a concept it cannot be reduced to any other mental category.[14]

Recent studies in animal behavior find a purpose in play as a preparation for actual behaviors, thus attributing a teleology to play.[15] But at some point the rehearsal becomes an end itself, the current reality that transcends future purpose. Young children laugh spontaneously for the sheer pleasure of laughing, and they scream with equally spontaneous delight. You can get lost in play, you can get lost in the rush of immediate experience, much as you can get lost in the world that any art work creates.

There are values in gross-out horror and comedy that have more to do with the immediacy of play than the delayed satisfaction of ultimate purpose. Even the ways in which these works pull against closure points to this. The final laugh of the Animal Comedy or the final scream of the gross-out horror film might be satisfying—and certainly more satisfying than the ending of *The Birds*—but we always have some sense in these films of its being arbitrary. As a number of prominent Animal Comedies signal their end with a sporting event or a festivity, these films often enough conclude much like the ending of a game: it can always start again, much as a monster suddenly reasserts his vitality.

It should be clear that what I value in these works at their best is their playfulness. Even *The Exorcist*, with its apparent cover of dour seriousness, has an underlying playfulness that can break through at unexpected moments and become a central appeal in our experience of the film. Is Father Karras perhaps a long lost fourth stooge? Certainly the shot of him getting hit by green goo would be completely at home in a "Three Stooges" short (though it wouldn't have quite the comic charge that the serious veneer of *The Exorcist* grants this moment). Like other gross-out films, *The Exorcist* has to establish boundaries in order to challenge them. In defining *Psycho*'s fun, Hitchcock also compared it to a roller coaster, which seems particularly apropos. As roller coasters make us both laugh and scream, these films present a constant shifting back and forth between extreme states and then mark their conclusion by ascending to the highest point and rushing into a vertiginous descent. Much as it is rooted in ambivalence, gross-out works by an ever-shifting concept as boundaries are drawn and redrawn. It may ultimately wear itself out as it begins to approach a sense of no boundaries—that truly anything is possible and all is permitted. But with no boundaries there is no ambivalence. If the aim of gross-out is to test boundaries, then the period in which art like this flourishes must necessarily be limited because, eventually, in its decadent phase, all boundaries will be overstepped.

Gross-out Fadeout

Problem Child (1990), *Home Alone* (1990), *The Silence of the Lambs* (1991)

When I first began thinking and writing about these films they were a contemporary phenomenon. Now they have clearly become historical. As gross-out comedy declined in popularity and production, romantic comedy returned in 1987 with the critical and popular successes of *Moonstruck* and *Broadcast News*. In the same period, the horror film pretty much retracted to its core audience, with the few successful horror films generally merging with other genres. *Aliens* (1986) most clearly demarcated the shift as it moved decisively toward the combat war film; *Predator* (1987) merged with the action-adventure film, *Child's Play* (1988) with the *policier*, and *They Live!* (1988) with the martial arts film. There are occasional gross-out moments in all these films, as well as in others. But gross-out is no longer the chief aim of the work.

Two successful comedies and a suspense thriller of the early 1990s help to clarify the differences being suggested here. *Problem Child* was a surprise hit in the summer of 1990. A modestly budgeted film, it told the tale of a child no one wanted. *Home Alone*, released in the fall of the same year, was a monster hit about a child whose parents inadvertently leave him behind when they take a trip to Paris. I might say it was also about an unwanted child, but the film works very hard to cover this, raising an issue that it constantly seeks to deny throughout the rest of its narrative. It is the way the film tries to camouflage this issue that moves it decisively away from gross-out.

Both films clearly descend from films of the period described in this book. *Problem Child* explicitly invokes *The Bad Seed*, *The Exorcist*, and *The Shining*. And the final sixteen minutes of *Home Alone* parallels the final fifteen minutes of *A Nightmare on Elm Street*. The extended sequence that provides a climax for both movies shows a resourceful child/adolescent boobytrapping his/her house to defend against a marauding intruder. And, by a coincidence that is perhaps less startling than at first appears, both *Problem Child* and *Home Alone* begin with shots of a full moon, as do *The Fearless Vampire Killers*, *An American Werewolf in London*, and *Wolfen* before them. What should we make of such a coincidence?

The iconography of the horror film has fully entered the world of comedy (albeit put to very different uses). In *Problem Child* the child is explicitly a descendent of the evil children of horror films, so the moon appears to be the sign under which he is born, much like a werewolf. But the source of his monstrosity, as this opening dramatizes, is the absolute rejection of the adults he is dependent on. In *Home Alone*, the family is more apparently caring, on the surface at least, so that the opening shot of clouds breaking apart to reveal a full moon (accompanied by mysterioso soundtrack music) serves to signify a magical world in which the inexplicable may happen and never needs explanation. How could loving parents possibly forget their child? Well, they can't, and the magic of the moon assures us that they don't really.

The film seems to attribute to the moon the premise that makes the plot possible, although there is a grounding for this in the fantasy desires of the characters. The opening shot is repeated at the start of a brief storm sequence that follows a tense scene between Kevin (Macaulay Culkin) and his mother (Catherine O'Hara). Exiled to the attic because he has been something of a nuisance during the hectic last-minute preparations for the family's vacation in Paris, Kevin complains to his mother:

KEVIN: Everyone in this family hates me.

MOTHER: Then maybe you should ask Santa for a new family.

KEVIN: I don't want a new family. I don't want any family. Families suck.

MOTHER: Just stay up there. I don't want to see you again for the rest of the night.

KEVIN: I don't want to see you again for the rest of my whole life. And I don't want to see anybody else, either.

MOTHER (*with a mildly threatening manner*): I hope you don't mean that. You'd be pretty sad if you woke up tomorrow morning and you didn't have a family.

KEVIN (*quietly, not so certain*): No, I wouldn't.

MOTHER (*almost taunting, with a bit of a nasty edge*): Then say it again. Maybe it'll happen.

KEVIN (*loudly, defiantly*): I hope I never see any of you again.

At this point Kevin goes upstairs, while a reverse-angle shot shows the mother closing the door, weary and exasperated. In the attic Kevin lies on his bed as we hear his thought in voice-over ("I wish they would all just disappear"). At this point, the opening shot of the moon repeats itself, complete with the mysterioso music.

The scene ends with Kevin's fantasy wish, which the subsequent sequence apparently fulfills: the brief storm signaled by the clouds moving away from the moon will lead to a power outage that will lead to an alarm clock not going off that will lead to a mad rush for the plane to Paris, that will lead to much confusion and a jumble of children—all in order to account for how one child gets left behind and the parents don't notice it. But if the moon operates as a magical sign of Kevin's desires, these desires do not arise on their own. In each instance, the mother provides the idea for the wish. Angrily ignoring his clear anxiety, she is the one who suggests Kevin ask for a new family, she is the first to say she doesn't want to see him, and she is the one who challenges him to experience life without a family. The dialogue articulates other fantasies, fantasies that belong to the mother, although the subsequent moon magic effectively denies what is revealed here.

The difference in the way the moon is used in *Problem Child* and *Home Alone* points to key differences in the two films. The final shot of *Problem Child* is a close-up of a hog's hindquarters, prominently featuring its testicles, just at the moment it is about to defecate. This film is still firmly rooted in the world of gross-out (which accounts for the generally harsh response of critics who objected to all the ca-ca and pee-pee jokes). *Home Alone*, on the other hand, seeks to deny this world. It raises the possibility of parental ambivalence in its exposition but spends much of its development trying to deny this, shifting its concern onto two other seemingly disparate but interconnected issues—the return of the family and the threat to the family's home by two comically bumbling criminals. Through much of the central section of the film the mother (implicitly punished for feelings that are never overtly recognized) has to cope with various inefficient forms of transportation at Christmastime to get back to her son, while the rest of the family arrives home at the same time on a comfortable nonstop flight. Meanwhile, the film centers its climactic scenes on the cartoonlike punishments of two comic criminal characters on whom the parental ambivalence has been displaced. Much as Kevin keeps his home inviolate from the would-be intruders, the family in *Home Alone* is kept safe from an ambivalence that is foregrounded throughout *Problem Child*.

Audience taste had clearly shifted.[16] The initial success of *Problem Child* was merely a prelude to *Home Alone*, which is what audiences were really waiting for. The dismal fate of *Problem Child 2* (1991) makes this evident. Apparently assuming that the gross-out elements were responsible for the original's success, its creators piled them up even more, determined to go farther than the original. And in doing so, they simply went too far for their audience. *Home Alone 2: Lost in New York* (1992), on the other hand, simply repeated the formula of the first, taking care once again to camouflage the fissures that its basic plot opens up. The distancing and fragmented families with their absent or hostile parents that I have noted as a striking feature of both the comedies and the horror films of the 1970s and 1980s faded in favor of celebrating the traditional joys of *Parenthood* (1989) and the apparently unified family with its submerged hostilities of *Home Alone*.

A similar kind of containment happens to gross-out horror as it is transformed in *The Silence of the Lambs* (1991). Not only is it easy to imagine just how much more graphic this film would have been had it been made seven or eight years earlier. It also ends with the apparent resurgence of the monster as demented psychiatrist Dr. Hannibal Lecter (Anthony Hopkins), newly escaped from jail, roams free in disgusting pursuit of a new cannibalistic repast. But compared to the monsters of gross-out horror, Hannibal turns out to be a relatively discreet monster. The most graphic display of his horror—the evisceration of a policeman—comes about half an hour before the end of the film, after which point he drops out of the narrative altogether (except for a brief phone conversation and the end sequence alluded to above). Unlike gross-out horror, which generally reserves its most terrifying sights for the climax, *The Silence of the Lambs* moves decisively away from spectacle toward psychology, which grants it a more award-winning appearance of serious purpose.

Even though Lecter's escape from jail means he is free to perpetrate ever more horrifying acts, the film can effectively remove him from the narrative proper for the final half hour because he is no real threat to anyone we care about. The film assures us we needn't think about him since he offers no harm to the film's heroine, FBI trainee Clarice Starling (Jodie Foster). Trying to determine the identity of a serial killer, Clarice has twice interviewed the jailed Lecter because of his brilliant understanding of a serial killer's psychology (since he is one himself). Although he has made Clarice uncomfortable during these interviews in the way he has probed into her feelings, she subsequently does not feel threatened by him when he escapes. As she explains to an FBI classmate, "He won't come after me . . . He won't. I can't explain it. He . . . he . . . he would consider that rude." Lecter might contain within him the most horrific of murderous impulses, yet he is polite in how he deploys them. He is contained.

As with gross-out, the sudden reappearance of Lecter at the end of *The Silence of the Lambs* gives us some terrible pleasure in contemplating his freedom to kill. But the pleasure lacks the ambivalence of the final scream in gross-out horror because Lecter intends a more limited and more directed kind of mayhem, with a very specific target in mind. Near the end of the film, he phones Clarice, providing us with further evidence that she is not in danger: "I have no plans to call on you, Clarice. The world's more interesting with you in it. . . . I do wish we could chat longer, but . . . I'm having an old friend for dinner." As Lecter says this last line, the camera shows people disembarking from an airplane. Among them is Dr. Frederick Chilton (Anthony Heald), Lecter's former jailer, whom Lecter eagerly follows through a crowd in what turns out to be the final shot of the film.

Revenge is a specific motive for this attack, but it is a fairly generalized revenge, one we can readily revel in, for Chilton is not only Lecter's nemesis. He has also sexually harassed Clarice and generally made things difficult for her throughout the film. Further, the film has consistently portrayed him as proud, smug, arrogant, and self-serving. We can therefore take a kind of delicious pleasure in Hannibal's designs on Chilton precisely because we think the man qualifies as a just dessert. The film in no way encourages us to contemplate the random violence that "Hannibal the Cannibal" will likely commit after this. Rather, by having us focus on the specific victim of Lecter's revenge, the film moves in a decidedly conservative direction. Lecter facilitates the splitting off of Clarice's anger at Chilton, so that she herself neither has to acknowledge it nor act on it. Further, he rids society of one of its undesirable members and forwards the good work of the FBI, which this man had unconscionably obstructed. Thus, the film might seem to open itself up in the manner of gross-out horror by a resurgence of the monster, yet there is still closure here, a satisfying sense of resolution promised by this final act that we do not see, and an odd reassurance that the safe social order we desire has been preserved. As in *Home Alone*, a fissure has been opened in order to be closed.

Gross-out, on the other hand, is an art form of fissures, of ambivalence. As such, it is an apt expression of a period defined by radical changes in both the structure and mores of American society. A culture concerned with expanding the boundaries of acceptable public discourse set it in motion, but it flourished through the early part of what is generally seen as the new conservatism of the so-called Reagan revolution. But if this "revolution" was conservative, it also represented a period of increasing greed and excess in its own right. In writing about the absent parents in these films (and particularly the absent father in the horror films), I referred to a perception of the restored father that the Reagan presidency embodied. But if gross-out continued to flourish early in the Reagan years, I think it is because the restoration of the father in this period was itself ambivalent—and at least partly ironic because it was chiefly iconic, as the cardboard cutouts of Reagan that began turning up in major cities suggests. Appearance might well camouflage striking contradictions. The tongue-in-cheek heroics of the *Superman* movies that were a prelude to the Reagan era would eventually lead to the gloomy depression of *Batman*, a campy figure in the 1960s but by 1989 transformed into a morbid and peculiarly depressed hero.

In chapter 9, I had noted that "the Me decade" and the "culture of narcissism," used as if identical to define a large part of the period I cover here, actually meant different things. I might posit an inverse corollary of this: namely, that the terms we have used to define opposing cultural phenomena may in fact conceal underlying similarities, that the conservatism of the Reagan years is not so much in opposition to the various liberation movements that began in an age of oppositional movements, yet it flourished in a period of excess. If the Reagan revolution was "conservative," it also represented a period that honored individual desire beyond the needs of the community.

To make sense of gross-out as a cultural phenomenon, I have to account for why an artistic mode that has its roots in the late 1960s might flourish during the Reagan revolution. The politics of selfhood, the liberation movements that seek to empower individuals previously marginalized in the social order, may actually have something in common with the 1980s politics of greed. At the very least, both rest on an unresolvable conflict between the demands of the individual and those of the social order, with a strong sense that the commonweal cannot find a common ground that will support all its individuals. We have moved from pluralism, which believes it may make one voice from many, to "multiculturalism," which is variously a struggle to find communal value in a culture of competing values or an acknowledgment that we cannot find any values in common. Gross-out is distinctive in that it seems to speak in a single voice, but, paradoxically, a single voice that is equivocal; it is the voice of ambivalence.

Every culture must experience some conflict between the individual and the community, but what is particularly striking about gross-out is the way in which it foregrounds this ambivalence as a key attribute of its cultural environment: defining characters in Animal Comedy by both their hedonistic pursuit of individual pleasure and their institutional allegiances; finding a vitality in the monstrous of the horror film that forges a distinctive alliance between monster and victim. If the slow fade-out of gross-out in the late 1980s signals a retreat from this ambivalent mode of address, perhaps it is either because we no longer believe in the possibility of a communal social order, or, conversely, we have had to see, as *Habits of the Heart* insists, the ever more urgent need for such an order. In confronting a kind of cultural Balkanization and economic hard times, we either have to try to fortify the inviolable body represented by the self-enclosed mall of *Dawn of the Dead* or move toward the uncomfortable acknowledgment that such a defense is no longer possible, that the suburbs that grew up to isolate the city are in fact connected to it.

Perhaps the gross-out mode is always doomed to burn itself out by its very excesses until we can no longer embrace the contradictions of its discourse but must confront in their stead either/or choices. If gross-out is based on an aesthetic of challenge, with each new work daring to see how much more it may dare, then the mode itself must ultimately be self-consuming, reaching a point (best exemplified by some of the late Tobe Hooper) in which its challenges are so excessive they become self-defeating. Gross-out began in an age of oppositional movements, but it flourished in a period of excess. As we pull back from it, perhaps we do so with a sense that we can no longer afford to indulge its excesses. A serious world cannot afford an art that mocks seriousness. Nonetheless, gross-out has left lasting traces and changed perceptions. Much as *Home Alone* covers over its fissures, the absent parents of that film are a clear echo of the absent parents in gross-out horror and comedy. And we can perhaps never look at our bodies in quite the same way again, although the consequences of the changed perception of the body wrought by gross-out might be most apparent by inversion. For example, the grotesque body evident in the extraordinary inflation of Sylvester Stallone's musculature through the five *Rocky* films and the ascent of Arnold Schwarzenegger as a major star suggest a defense against the permeable body of gross-out. These grotesque bodies covertly express an ambivalence that brings them close to gross-out; in all their appearance of power, they seem to be independent and self-sufficient; yet the very nature of their appearance demands display, making them dependent on our recognition for their existence.

As gross-out becomes more fully consigned to history, I value all the more what these films achieved. I value them for their spectacle, I value them for their rawness, I value them for their direct assault on our emotions. The less fully accomplished works have their brilliant moments—the roadside club in *Animal House*, the first confrontation between Karras and Regan in *The Exorcist*—but they seem to get caught up in the contradictions inherent in their mode. Since gross-out is based in ambivalence, the best works are those that most fully confront their contradictions: *Fast Times at Ridgemont High*, *Revenge of the Nerds*, and *Heaven Help Us* for the comedies; *The Other*, *The Shining*, *Alien*, and *The Brood* for the horror films. In confronting these contradictions, these films exemplify the most powerful expressions of a period that was itself defined by fissures and disruptions.

Notes

1. Rousing Rabble

1. Henry James Forman, *Our Movie Made Children* (New York: Macmillan, 1933), pp. 224, 232.

2. What Robin Wood has written of the horror film audience is of some relevance here: "The popularity [of the horror film] itself has a peculiar characteristic that sets it apart from other genres: it is restricted to aficionados and complemented by total rejection, people tending to go to horror films either obsessively or not at all. . . .Most horror films make money; the ones that don't are those with overt intellectual pretensions, obviously 'difficult' works. . . . Much the same might be said of the audience for gross-out comedy." Wood, "An Introduction to the American Horror Film," in Britton, Richard Lippe, Tony Williams, and Robin Wood, *The American Nightmare: Essays on the Horror Film* (Toronto: Festival of Festivals, 1979), p. 13; reprinted in Wood, *Hollywood from Vietnam to Reagan* (New York: Columbia University Press, 1986).

3. A comprehensive survey of responses to popular culture may be found in Patrick Brantlinger, *Bread and Circuses* (Ithaca: Cornell University Press, 1983). Brantlinger uses the term "negative classicism" to define the most common strain in these responses, which generally sees popular culture as evidence for the decline of civilization.

4. There are of course other art forms we can determine beginnings for and for which we can even find some kind of technological determinants (as Leslie Fiedler has

claimed the development of the novel depended on the invention of movable type). But this example is really a matter of a genre or mode within the already existing larger framework of literature, whose exact origins we cannot locate. And the novel itself has other, more ancient antecedents, such as the epic poems of Homer. See Fiedler, *What Was Literature?: Class Culture and Mass Society* (New York: Simon and Schuster, 1982).

5. It is likely that the close connections to so many other art forms led to one of the most insistent concerns of much early film theory: the desire to distinguish the essence of film from the other arts (especially from theater, almost perversely because it was clearly the art form that most resembled the movies). See theoretical writings by Vsevolod Pudovkin (*Film Technique and Film Acting* [rpt. New York: Grove, 1970]), Rudolf Arnheim (*Film as Art* [Berkeley: University of California Press, 1968]), and others.

6. This reproducible quality is what most interested Walter Benjamin because he saw in it the destruction of the "aura" of an original work of art that made him view the development of film ambivalently: "Their [i.e., "contemporary mass movements"] most powerful agent is film. Its social significance, particularly in its most positive form, is inconceivable without its destructive, cathartic aspect, that is, the liquidation of the traditional value of the cultural heritage." Benjamin, "The Work of Art in the Age of Mechanical Reproduction," in Hannah Arendt, ed., *Illuminations*, trans. Harry Zohn (New York: Schocken, 1969), p. 221.

Benjamin clearly saw a connection between this art of the masses and mass movements like fascism (a point of concern later in this chapter). There seems to me a problem with Benjamin's argument that centers on questions of tradition I am dealing with here: in distinguishing film as a mechanically reproducible art, he sets it in a tradition of the plastic arts. This works well enough for still film (e.g., photography), but movies are something else again since the key thing they are reproducing is a *performance*, which means at the least that they belong as much within a tradition of the performing arts, where Benjamin's concept of "aura" would simply not apply. Further, one might say the particular theatrical form of commedia dell'arte was in some ways anticipating mechanically reproducible arts by its concern for creating uniform and interchangeable parts—a way, in modern terms, of rationalizing theatrical production.

7. Even fairly difficult films—cerebral, private, allusive—will inevitably be seen by more people than the readership for comparable works in literature. More people have probably seen a Jean-Luc Godard movie than the number who have read a James Joyce novel.

8. This is, of course, not the first time audiences have been used to make judgments about works of art. The supposed inappropriateness of some of the comedy in Shakespeare's tragedies has often been dismissed as vulgar concessions to the rowdier members of the audience. Still, I believe film represents the first time an *entire* art form has so frequently and insistently been criticized with reference to its audience. And that fact reflects on the uniqueness of the audience itself.

9. Good surveys of early responses to movies and the attempts to control them may be found in Garth Jowett, *Film: The Democratic Art* (Boston: Little, Brown, 1976), and Larry May, *Screening Out the Past: The Birth of Mass Culture and the Motion Picture Industry* (New York: Oxford University Press, 1980).

10. All eleven volumes were published in 1933 by Macmillan (New York) and were later reissued in 1971 by the Arno Press (New York). The description of the authors is

from the twelfth volume by Forman (*Our Movie Made Children*, p. 4), which appeared first.

11. The issuance of the popularizing volume first seems an intentional ploy to maximize the more inflammatory aspects of the study, since Robert Sklar has effectively shown that William H. Short, director of the National Committee for Study of Social Values in Motion Pictures, initiated the project specifically to launch an attack on the movies. The monumental social sciences research project that grew out of Short's initiative was thus shaped from the beginning by his special needs and goals: to get the goods on the movies, to nail them to the wall. Sklar, *Movie-Made America: A Cultural History of American Movies* (New York: Vintage, 1976), p. 134.

12. *New York Times*, June 27, 1931, p. 16. The edition of *Our Movie Made Children* that served as my source is a fifth printing dated March 1934 (almost a year after original publication).

13. Mortimer Adler, *Art and Prudence* (New York: Longmans, Green, 1937).

14. Raymond Moley, *Are We Movie Made?* (New York: Macy-Masius, 1938). The quote describing the instigation of the project is from Moley himself (p. viii). The movie industry might have profited by following the strategy of the Payne Fund studies and published the popularization first. Still, the tenor of the period was simply not open to the Adler-Moley argument. This might be seen from the response of the *New York Times*: while it had favorably reviewed Forman's *Our Movie Made Children*, it never reviewed the Adler response; instead, it did carry a brief notice on the Moley endeavor a year later, but sarcastically dismissed it as "an abstract of a criticism of a popularization of a series of surveys" ("Miscellaneous Brief Reviews," *New York Times Book Review*, August 21, 1938, p. 12).

15. Robert Sklar has astutely observed that much of the early attempts to control the content of films were at heart issues of class control: "the real nature of their [the American elite classes] desire . . . was to control access to information so as to limit the ability of the lower classes to gain knowledge about the social system in which they lived. . . . The struggle over movies, in short, was an aspect of the struggle between the classes. . . . Since the enemies of movies could deal only indirectly or covertly with the issue of class conflict, they made their case on the ground of protecting the young" (Sklar, *Movie-Made America*, pp. 123–24).

16. It is also possible that concern in the 1930s was exacerbated by the Depression, with the movie industry's tougher enforcement of self-censorship in 1934 a reflection of the attitudes of the period; Molly Haskell has suggested that the Production Code itself provides a reflection of American values: "Far from being a straitjacket imposed from without, the Production Code expressed, and reinforced, the instincts latent in the American psyche at its most romantic, puritanical, immature, energetic, and self-deluding." Haskell, *From Reverence to Rape* (New York: Holt, Rinehart and Winston, 1974), p. 21.

The connection of self-censorship to the Depression is perhaps made clearest by one of the running themes in Forman's *Our Movie Made Children*: the danger of the temptations to a good life that the movies hold out to the poor, who have no *legal* way to gain access to this good life, which should thus make it a duty of those in control of the movies not to show such temptation.

17. Or perhaps the movie studios' self-regulation was part of the attempt that Robert Sklar has noted in another context of the desire to transform a lower-class art form into

one more acceptable to the broader middle class with its attendant concerns for respectability and decorous behavior (Sklar, *Movie-Made America*, pp. 41–47). In this regard, the transformation of the middle classes after World War II that I note in a later chapter is perhaps central to the changing concept of what was acceptable subject matter for movies in the 1970s.

18. A number of such films probably would have received an X, but usually chose to avoid the X rating altogether for economic reasons since it can place severe restrictions on distribution and publicity. George Romero, for example, released his *Dawn of the Dead* (1979) and *Day of the Dead* (1985) independently to avoid receiving what seemed like an inevitable X rating, but then Romero was not working for an MPAA (Motion Picture Association of America) member company to start off with. MPAA companies can adopt a similar strategy themselves: rather than release *The Evil Dead Part II* (1987), a certain X, DEG, the producing/releasing company, farmed it out to an independent releasing company to avoid having it rated at all.

19. French sociologist Pierre Bourdieu provides an exhaustive exploration of the cultural determinants of taste in his massive study *Distinction: A Social Critique of the Judgment of Taste*, trans. Richard Nia (Cambridge: Harvard University Press, 1984). Of particular concern for my later class analysis of film genres, Bourdieu defines the ways in which taste aligns with class. In an unusually aphoristic passage, he writes, "Taste classifies, and it classifies the classifier" (p. 6). I am cautious, however, in my application of Bourdieu to my discussion here for two reasons. Typical of contemporary French intellectual writing, Bourdieu's study occupies an entirely relativist view that aims to reject all essentialist thinking. I do not go along with this completely as my concern for the physiological aspects of taste should indicate. Gross-out would not be possible without our common understanding that there is aggression in bad taste. Second, there are very real differences between the French bourgeoisie and the American middle class. For example, Bourdieu cites *La Traviata* as an example of " 'popular' taste," something that would be impossible to claim in the United States. More relevant to my concern with gross-out as a distinctly American phenomenon is Lawrence Levine's exploration of the alignment of taste and class in *Highbrow/Lowbrow: The Emergence of Cultural Hierarchy in America* (Cambridge: Harvard University Press, 1988).

Finally, while I may call the concept of taste into question, I must stress that I am not rejecting all sense of aesthetic distinction. I do not think that any of us, whatever our class origins, can in fact operate without a sense of distinctions. Bourdieu himself, for example, uses his writing style as a way of distinguishing what he is doing: "Likewise, the style of this book, whose long, complex sentences may offend . . . stems partly from the endeavor to mobilize all the resources of the traditional modes of expression . . . to prevent the reading from slipping back into the simplicities of the smart essay or the political polemic" (p. xiii). This very sentence is an example of the kind of thing Bourdieu expects to be offensive, so I had to shorten it for the sake of intelligibility, but the point is clear enough: even in a book that seems to question cultural biases in taste, Bourdieu fully subscribes to them when it comes to establishing his own credentials as a serious thinker who does not deal in "simplicities." By implication we should not expect to find thinking as complex as Bourdieu's in more popular writing.

I question this assumption, much as I question the assumption that we cannot find complexity and profundity in works of popular culture. The mode of address does not automatically validate or denigrate the work at hand. We can still find a range of qualities even in popular forms of address. While I think all films are worth considering as the products of a culture, my discussion should make clear that I do make distinctions among them. I take the artistic ambitions of all these films seriously, even if their apparent motivations are crass, and I regard a number of them as truly exceptional works of art.

20. Forman, *Our Movie Made Children*, p. 50. Forman is citing a comment made by Edgar Dale in *The Content of Motion Pictures*, one of the volumes produced for the Payne Fund studies. Page numbers in parentheses follow subsequent citations from Forman.

21. Theatrical movies, of course, occupy a different position in our society because of the advent of television. As noted in the text, theaters have now become *allowed* areas of license, which have made the transgressions that take place on theater screens of lesser concern than they were in the early 1930s.

22. The actual provision reads, "Miscegenation (sex relationship between the white and black races) is forbidden." From *The Production Code of the Motion Picture Producers and Distributors of America, Inc.*, reprinted in Jowett, *Film: The Democratic Art*, pp. 468–72 (the quotation appears on p. 469).

23. A.D.S., "Two Thugs," *New York Times*, April 24, 1931, p. 27.

24. In *On the Art of Poetry* Aristotle feels he has to defend tragedy against those who prefer epic because "tragedy appeals to meaner minds." He does this by suggesting what is really being objected to is overacting, not tragedy in itself, and goes on to the incredible claim that "the effect is as vivid when a play is read as when it is acted." The logocentric bias in this serves to minimize the appeal of spectacle as a thing in itself, a not unfamiliar ploy of serious film criticism that values the literary aspects of the work over the spectacular. For Aristotle, spectacle is merely the icing on the cake that makes tragedy a richer dessert: "Tragedy has everything that epic has, and it can even use the epic measure; and as a not inconsiderable addition, it offers scenic effects and music, the source of a distinct feeling of pleasure." In effect, Aristotle ends up reinforcing the suspicions against spectacle by giving primary value to the points in common with the more literary form, and especially the language. *Classical Literary Criticism*, T. S. Dorsch, trans. (Harmondsworth: Penguin, 1965), pp. 74–75.

25. The suspiciousness toward spectacle, especially by those in power, can be most clearly seen from any history of the theater because (as in film) theater presents seemingly unmediated action that can be appealing even if officially regarded as immoral. "Theater is the most dangerous of all arts," Glynne Wickham baldly writes, and then goes on to list examples of bans and prohibitions placed on theater over the past two thousand years, concluding, "the theater has thus ever been a constant source of anxiety the world over to leaders of Church and State alike." Wickham, *A History of the Theater* (Cambridge: Cambridge University Press, 1985), p. 11.

26. One of the most frequent claims leveled against Hollywood movies—that they induce an unthinking passivity in the audience—has been brilliantly answered on aesthetic grounds by David Bordwell, who is concerned with "describing a set of operations the viewer is expected to perform." See "The Classical Hollywood Style: 1917–60," in Bordwell, Janet Staiger, and Kristin Thompson, *The Classical Hollywood Cinema* (New York: Columbia University Press, 1985), pp. 3–84 (the quote is from p. 8).

27. In *Studies in Entertainment*, editor Tania Modleski designates MacDonald a

"humanist" in contrast to "the Marxist theorists of the Frankfurt School—Adorno, Horkheimer, and Marcuse" (Modleski, "Introduction" to *Studies in Entertainment* [Bloomington: Indiana University Press, 1986], p. xix). Nonetheless, in "Masscult and Midcult," *Partisan Review* (Spring 1960), a greatly elaborated version of "A Theory of Mass Culture" (the article Modleski cites), MacDonald admiringly quotes an extended passage from Adorno's essay "On Popular Music" (MacDonald, "Masscult and Midcult," reprinted in *Against the American Grain* [New York: Random House, 1962], p. 5). And in *A Cycle of Outrage*, James Gilbert specifies MacDonald and David Riesman as American intellectuals greatly influenced by the Frankfurt School (Gilbert, *A Cycle of Outrage* [New York: Oxford University Press, 1986], pp. 119–24).

28. Dwight MacDonald, "A Theory of Mass Culture," *Diogenes* 3 (Summer 1953): 1–17, reprinted in Bernard Rosenberg and David Manning White, eds., *Mass Culture: The Popular Arts in America* (New York: Free Press, 1957), pp. 59–73.

29. For example, Warner Brothers released *The Beast from 20,000 Fathoms* (1953) in 1,422 theaters and *Them!* (1954) in 2,000 theaters (*Variety*, June 18, 1953, p. 3, and June 2, 1954, p. 5). It should be noted that these theaters were much larger than today's multiplexes, so the number of potential customers was in fact greater. Joseph E. Levine established himself as a force in the movie industry in 1959 with the exploitation release of a cheap, dubbed Italian pickup—*Hercules*. Thomas Doherty has convincingly documented the importance of the exploitation market to the later 1950s, most especially with films centered around teenage themes (a striking anticipation of the period I am writing about). See Doherty, *Teenagers and Teenpics, 1955–1960: The Juvenilization of American Movies* (Boston: Allen and Unwin, 1988).

There is one real exception to the releasing strategies and types of films in the past that is worth mentioning here because it makes explicit the class issues involved in film distribution. Sensing he did not have another *Gone With the Wind* on his hands, David O. Selznick decided on a "revolutionary . . . multiple-booking plan" for the release of *Duel in the Sun* (1946) that would involve "enormously and unprecedentedly heavy newspaper and radio advertising by territories." This was in effect an exploitation release for a high-budget film, the kind of thing that would become commonplace in film distribution of the 1970s, but was unheard of at the time. The strategy was successful for the business of the film, but strikingly Selznick later felt "there was a price, and a heavy one." Even during the campaign Selznick sensed, in a telegram to his advertising director, that things were getting out of hand: "I THINK NOW WE ARE IN DANGER OF GOING OVERBOARD, TURNING PEOPLE'S STOMACHS AND MAKING OURSELVES AND THE PICTURE RIDICULOUS, AS WELL AS ROBBING BOTH THE COMPANY AND THE PICTURE OF ANY STATURE." A few months later a more reflective Selznick expressed even deeper regrets, now clearly stating them in class terms, noting "the advertising and ballyhoo on *Duel* was damaging, and was a complete contradiction of our former 'Tiffany' standards." Precisely because he took pride in himself as a purveyor of high-class quality films, Selznick experienced an anguish over the exploitation of *Duel* he could only express in the most personal terms: "even if I am wrong in exaggerating the extent of the loss to my position, there is the matter of my family to think of." By the 1980s, this kind of exploitation release had become routine even for some of the most prestigious of Hollywood films. See Selznick, *Memo from David O. Selznick* (New York: Viking. 1972), pp. 356–59.

30. Change might be a bit more difficult in the future, however, since the advent of

the suburban mall multiplexes offers the perfect complement to exploitation booking patterns, so that exploitation release has, in effect, been institutionalized by theater architecture. But any informed history of film industry economics cautions against making predictions about the marketing and distribution of films in the future.

31. MacDonald, "A Theory of Mass Culture," in Rosenberg and White, *Mass Culture*. Page numbers in parentheses following quotations in the text by MacDonald refer to this book. The phrase "conspiracy theory" comes from David Riesman; Patrick Brantlinger also uses it in describing the most familiar theoretical positions on popular culture since the fall of Rome (Brantlinger, *Bread and Circuses*, pp. 22–23).

32. Quayle, however, is not unique in mounting such an attack on the mass media from the right. His most notorious predecessor is, of course, Joseph McCarthy. In both cases, ideological alliance to market forces necessitates constructing a conspiracy theory that leads the unknowing buyer to purchase something inimical to his or her own interests. What is different about Quayle's position, and what makes him particularly relevant to this discussion, is his attempt to bridge a conflict that did not concern McCarthy, a conflict between cultural and political values. It is perhaps precisely because there is such a conflict that the entertainment industry felt comfortable in striking back at Quayle as it never could with McCarthy. (See Bernard Weintraub, "Angry 'Cultural Elite' Jumping into the Battle," *New York Times*, September 1, 1992, pp. B1, 3.) The apparent political retrenchment that began with Reagan could not completely revoke the 1960s, as Interior Secretary James Watt discovered when he attempted to ban the Beach Boys from the Washington mall. By the end of the 1980s, abortion rights became a powerful area of contention precisely because it offered an opportunity for public policy to intersect with a lifestyle issue.

33. These include: Seth Cagin and Phillip Dray, *Hollywood Films of the Seventies* (New York: Harper and Row, 1984), pp. 66–74; Diane Jacobs, *Hollywood Renaissance* (New York: Delta, 1980), p. 2; Ann Lloyd, *Movies of the Seventies* (London: Orbis, 1984), pp. 9–10; Axel Madsen, *The New Hollywood* (New York: Thomas Y. Crowell, 1975), pp. 22–23; Mark Thomas McGee and P. J. Robertson, *The J.D. Films: Juvenile Delinquency in the Movies* (Jefferson, N.C.: McFarland, 1982), pp. 131–35.

34. The film was in fact intended for American-International. How it came to be distributed by Columbia is detailed in Cagin and Dray, *Hollywood Films of the Seventies*, p. 62.

35. Columbia was not all that different from the other Hollywood studios since it also went into the red the following year.

36. After the disasters of the 1970–71 season, the majors swore off big budgets and announced budget caps for all forthcoming productions. These limits were adhered to for a while, but the blockbuster successes of *The Godfather* (1972), *The Exorcist* (1973), *Star Wars* (1977), and *Close Encounters of the Third Kind* (1977) led to a gradual raising of budgets. The shift that took place in this period can be seen most clearly with the sequels to *The Godfather* and *Star Wars*, whose costs ran roughly twice those of the original films. Still, the exploitation market left its impact; by the 1980s Hollywood had discovered a new mode: low-class films with high-class budgets—exploitation with a sheen.

37. The clearest evidence of this was the rise in "pop art" itself, but important shifts can also be found in the criticism of the period: the willingness to regard older American movies as serious art (the one truly radical aspect of auteurism); the new honor ac-

corded pulp fiction with the elevation of Dashiell Hammett to the ranks of major author (by a Columbia University professor); and the serious critical recognition given to rock 'n' roll (particularly with the advent of the Beatles, whom Ned Rorem favorably compared to Monteverdi, Schumann, Poulenc, and Mozart in the highly respectable pages of the *New York Review of Books*). See Andrew Sarris, "Toward a Theory of Film History," in Sarris, *The American Cinema* (New York: E. P. Dutton, 1969; rpt., Chicago: University of Chicago Press, 1985), pp. 19–37; Steven Marcus, "Introduction," in Hammett, *The Continental Op* (New York: Random House, 1974), pp. ix–xxix; and Ned Rorem, "The Music of the Beatles," reprinted in Jonathan Eisen, ed., *The Age of Rock: Sounds of the American Cultural Revolution* (New York: Random House, 1969), pp. 149–59.

38. Lindsay, *The Art of the Moving Picture* (1915, rev. 1922; rpt., New York: Liveright, 1970), p. 225. Page numbers in parentheses following quotations in the text by Lindsay refer to this edition.

39. Of the top twenty-five films listed in *Variety*'s "All-Time Film Rental Champs," only four (*The Godfather*, *The Sound of Music*, *The Sting*, and *Gone With the Wind*) won Best Picture awards, and all of those also received generally very favorable criticism; any Oscars won by the remaining films were chiefly in minor categories (*Variety*, January 14, 1987, p. 30).

There is something of a schizoid quality here that is perhaps best evidenced by the special award given to Steven Spielberg in 1987, an acknowledgment of the impact he's had on the industry even without honoring any one of his films in particular. Still, it is unlikely that the Academy would have been so moved to honor Spielberg without his attempt the previous year at a "serious" film with *The Color Purple* (1985), which J. Hoberman cleverly termed Spielberg's "artistic bar mitzvah." Hoberman, *Village Voice*, December 24, 1985, p. 76.

40. A. D. Murphy in *Variety* has suggested ever-recurring cycles of invention and imitation as a way of explaining three-year cycles of economic depression he has noted in the film industry: "Recessions last approximately 18 months, because that's the time between authorizing a film project and its release. The cycle runs like this: a couple of relatively good years at the b.o. [box office] inevitably creates a climate in which (1) major studios each make a few extra films which they shouldn't, and (2) one or two newcomers to the business arrive with a splash but wind up filming the studio projects of the past decade. When this load of extra junk reaches the screen, customers turn off, the studios go back to basics, and 18 months or so later—like a clock—the next crop of better pics are released" ("Par at Top of '86 Rentals Mountain," *Variety*, January 14, 1987, pp. 9, 46).

The point of this is that the consumer can in fact use the marketplace as a way of determining the product. Again, any consideration of the actual economics of film production and distribution leads to more of a sense of give-and-take between consumer and producer than most conspiracy theories of popular culture allow.

41. The wariness with which the theoreticians of the Frankfurt School approached popular culture probably had much to do with having witnessed the uncontrolled passions released by the awesome spectacles of National Socialism. As Martin Jay makes clear, "The Frankfurt School critique of mass culture took up where their critique of Nazism left off" (Jay, *The Dialectical Imagination: A History of the Frankfurt School and the Institute of Social Research 1923–1950* [Boston: Little, Brown, 1973], p. 178).

Herbert Marcuse's notion of "institutionalized desublimation" is relevant in this context because it, in effect, questions the kinds of release totalitarian art offers its audience (Marcuse, *One-Dimensional Man* [Boston: Beacon Press, 1965], p. 74). Further, while Bertolt Brecht's early plays indicate enough emotional turmoil to make his response as fully idiosyncratic as it is socially determined, certainly his mistrust of the emotional power of theater is in part a response to the rise of Nazism in Germany. Brecht's theatrical theories, which had a strong impact on post–World War II stage productions, are of interest here since his anti-Aristotelian theater proposes "an audience that is relaxed and follows the action without strain," as Walter Benjamin describes it—quite the opposite of the audience I am positing here (Benjamin, "What is Epic Theater?" in *Illuminations*, p. 147).

42. Stuart Kaminsky has explained an audience's response to extreme violence, why they "howl and laugh and *encourage* the protagonist" in psychological terms: "Viewers cannot cope with the blatant statement of violence or deal with the stark horror of it, and so they distort what they see. According to Leon Festinger [in *A Theory of Cognitive Dissonance*], dissonance takes place and the viewers work to create resonance, but the picture—the image—won't let them; it makes them nervous, challenges them." I think this overlooks the pleasure audiences can take in violence on the screen, but it does serve to explain ambivalent responses. Kaminsky, *American Film Genres*, 2d ed. (Chicago: Nelson Hall, 1985), p. 109.

43. Sarris's discussion of this film answers criticism that sees it as conservative by setting it against other films of the time. Sarris, *The John Ford Movie Mystery* (Bloomington: Indiana University Press, 1975), p. 97.

44. John Steinbeck, *The Grapes of Wrath* (1939; rpt., New York: Viking, 1972). pp. 617–19.

45. Peter Roffman and Jim Purdy argue the opposite viewpoint in an extensive comparison of novel and film, but they never confront the dramatic impact the film is able to achieve by placing the "We the People" speech at the conclusion. Roffman and Purdy, *The Hollywood Social Problem Film* (Bloomington: Indiana University Press, 1981), pp. 125–32.

46. The Editors of *Cahiers du Cinema*, "Young Mr. Lincoln," reprinted in Bill Nichols, ed., *Movies and Methods*, 2 vols. (vol. 1: Berkeley: University of California Press, 1976; vol. 2: 1985), 1:493–529.

47. Effecting political action is possible, I imagine, since it has been claimed that *I Am a Fugitive from a Chain Gang* (1932) eventually led to a reform of southern prisons, but I do not see this as a specific aesthetic aim.

48. Advertisement in the *New York Times*, April 24, 1931, p. 27.

49. Henri Bergson, "Laughter," in Wylie Sypher, ed., *Comedy* (Garden City, N.Y.: Doubleday Anchor, 1956), p. 64.

2. A New Language

1. The term derives, of course, from the attempt to employ rationalized modes of production for a creative art. The industrial nature of Hollywood has been most fully explored and documented by David Bordwell, Janet Staiger, and Kristin Thompson, *The Classical Hollywood Cinema* (New York: Columbia University Press, 1985).

2. Samuel McKechnie, *Popular Entertainments Through the Ages* (London: Samp-

son Low, Marston, 1932), p. 33. This book discusses the other forms of popular entertainment I have listed. For a more detailed description of fairground theater and the
economic demands involved in it, see Sybil Rosenfeld, *The Theater of the London Fairs
in the 18th Century* (Cambridge: Cambridge University Press, 1960).

3. In *The Concise History of the Theatre* (New York: Harry N. Abrams: 1969), Phyllis
Hartnoll notes, "Throughout the history of the theatre there is nowhere to be found a
complete break in continuity of development. Between the decay of one theatrical
presentation and the rise of another, however different, there must always have been
some connection, some current flowing, however far underground, to convey the fun-
damentals of the art from one era to another" (p. 32).

Hartnoll makes clear that in those periods when the theater was not producing
drama the high culture could embrace, it remained a vital art for the masses: in the
dark days of "the later Roman theater . . . the humbler entertainers of the classical world
wandered across Europe, alone or in small troupes. Among them were acrobats, danc-
ers, mimics, animal-trainers with bears or monkeys, jugglers, wrestlers, ballad-singers,
story-tellers" (p. 32). Strikingly (and of some importance for my argument if cinema is
rightfully seen as the inheritor of the traditions these performers represent), "Their
existence is proved by the attacks made on them by the more austere Fathers of the
Church, attacks which contributed not a little to the decay of the classical tradition,
since from earliest times Christians were strictly forbidden to attend theatrical performances or to appear in them" (pp. 32–33).

4. Of particular interest in this regard is Rick Altman's unpublished paper on Sergei
Eisenstein's essay, "Dickens, Griffith and Film Theory Today," in *Film Form* (New York:
Harcourt, Brace, 1949). Altman revised Eisenstein's claim for Dickens's influence on
Griffith by demonstrating a more immediate source in the popular stage of the period,
and particularly in stage adaptations of popular novels. In a print culture, finding the
sources in the novel was easier for the simple reason that the novels remained available,
while the stage productions vanished. Also, for Eisenstein there might been polemical
value in the literary connection since it possibly helped put film on a footing with more
accepted art forms. Altman, "Dickens, Griffith, and Film Theory Today" (paper delivered at the Society of Cinema Studies Conference, Montreal, May 1987).

5. The evidence for this comes from McKechnie, who mentions "an apparently
gory production of *Judith and Holophernes*" (*Popular Entertainments Through the
Ages*, p. 44). A plate in this volume (opposite p. 49) shows the theater in which this
performance is playing with a poster out in front that depicts Judith with raised sword
in one hand, severed head in the other, standing above the decapitated body of Holophernes.

6. Margarete Bieber discusses this form and its differences from other classical
comedy in *The History of the Greek and Roman Theater* (Princeton: Princeton University Press, 1961), pp. 129–46.

7. The Feast of Fools and its relationship to clowning is discussed in John H.
Towsen, *Clowns* (New York: Hawthorn Books, 1976); Midsummer Eve is described in
C. L. Barber's *Shakespeare's Festive Comedy* (Princeton: Princeton University Press,
1959).

8. Feste successfully begs money by making witty remarks. This occurs twice in
the play, first with Viola (3.1; numbers refer to act and scene) and then with Orsino
(5.1).

9. Mikhail Bakhtin, *Rabelais and His World*, trans. Hélèna Iswolsky (Bloomington: Indiana University Press, 1984 [1965]). The second chapter is entitled "The Language of the Marketplace in Rabelais." Page numbers in parentheses following quotations by Bakhtin in the text refer to this edition.

10. However, it is possible that advertising is in fact intimately connected to theater (since McKechnie in one line of development sees the theater of the fairground as growing out of patternmen hawking their wares to a crowd and eventually building their patter performances into shows very similar to the traveling medicine shows in America that survived into the early part of this century).

McKechnie cites the firsthand description of a visitor to a fair in Venice in 1608 that is worth repeating here: "Also I have seen a Mountebank hackle and gash his naked arme with a knife most pitifully to beholde, so that the blood hath streamed out in great abundance, and by and by after he hath applied a certaine oyle unto it, wherewith he hath incontinent both stanched the blood and so thoroughly healed the woundes and gashes, that when he hath afterward shewed us his arme againe, we could not possibly perceive the least token of a gash" (*Popular Entertainments Through the Ages*, p. 57). This little piece of medical pornography with its copious blood-letting has its clear echoes three and a half centuries later in any number of gross-out horror films.

11. Garry Wills has written: "If it is strange to see capitalism posing as individualist, it is even odder for it to act as the voice of conservatism. Conservatism, in a minimal definition, wants to conserve; but capitalism is an instrument for change, for expansion, driven toward ever new resources, products, markets. It reorders life drastically." Wills, *Reagan's America: Innocents at Home* (Garden City, N.Y.: Doubleday, 1987), p. 381.

12. As I suggested in a review at the time, Hollywood did do precisely this by the fantasy destruction of Los Angeles in *Earthquake* (1974). The film spectacularly exploited each moment of destruction, ultimately turning the destruction itself into a source of pleasure not unlike the ending of *Zabriskie Point* (1970). See Paul, "The End of L.A., Hooray!" *Village Voice*, December 23, 1974, pp. 90–91.

13. The quote appears in Seth Cagin and Phillip Dray, *Hollywood Films of the Seventies* (New York: Harper and Row, 1984), pp. 127–28. Cagin and Dray detail some of the problems the film encountered during production. They also report that Aubrey in his new post was "charged with the task of putting the company on a businesslike footing and reorienting it to the youth market." This could account for his initial rapture over the film.

14. Cagin and Dray, *Hollywood Films of the Seventies*, find at least a position of revolt underlying many of the most significant films of the 1970s, among them *Little Big Man* (1970), *M*A*S*H* (1970), *A Clockwork Orange* (1971), *Klute* (1971), *Straw Dogs* (1971), *The Candidate* (1972), *Ulzana's Raid* (1972), *American Graffiti* (1973), *Chinatown* (1974), *The Conversation* (1974), *The Parallax View* (1974), *Shampoo* (1974), *Nashville* (1975), *One Flew Over the Cuckoo's Nest* (1975), *All the President's Men* (1976), and *Taxi Driver* (1976).

15. In a book on film censorship, Richard S. Randall writes that exhibitors who claimed they would play only films with a Production Code Seal of Approval were nonetheless willing to show *Room at the Top* (1959) and *Never on Sunday* (1960) when it became apparent they were big money-makers. He notes: "The general rule is that exhibitors will abandon an unsteady ship, but that few have reservations about sailing on a financially promising one of any flag; one more indication that in the film industry

the prospect of immediate profits is likely to be the ultimate persuasion, stilling fears and principles alike." Randall, *Censorship of the Movies: The Social and Political Control of a Mass Medium* (Madison: University of Wisconsin Press, 1970), p. 210.

16. Tri-Star released *Silent Night, Deadly Night* (1984), an independently produced gross-out horror film that had a maniacal killer who dressed as Santa Claus. The film produced an uproar of protests, which forced Tri-Star to pull it from distribution, or at least try to pull it from distribution. The distributor found itself in the peculiar position of having some theaters refuse to return the prints because they were doing pretty good business with it. The marketplace can often be a more potent force than the companies themselves would like. Tri-Star did eventually get all the prints back and returned the rights to the independent production company, which was not able to find another distributor, although the film did make it onto home-video release and actually managed two sequels.

17. Sometimes the product does make the studios so uncomfortable they will end up disassociating themselves from it (as Tri-Star had to do with *Silent Night, Deadly Night*). Perhaps the most extreme example of this occurred around "Faces of Death," a home-video series *Variety* described as "deathumentaries . . . assemblages of often graphic and gruesome footage of executions, autopsies and other deaths." Because of the substantial negative press coverage the three released tapes received, MPI Home Video decided to take them out of distribution along with a fourth about to be released. This will remove them from official connection to this company, but it does not necessarily mean they or their profits will entirely disappear: "MPI would consider offers from outsiders who may be interested in licensing the 'Faces' programs for future release" (*Variety*, "MPI Homevid Pulls 'Death' Tape Series; Too Much Attention," July 22, 1987, pp. 1, 80). This subreleasing strategy was a familiar ploy of Hollywood majors in the 1960s when they were attempting to break beyond the limitations of the Production Code. See Jack Vizzard, *See No Evil: Life Inside a Hollywood Censor* (New York: Simon and Schuster, 1970), chap. 21.

18. Leslie Fiedler, *What Was Literature?: Class Culture and Mass Society* (New York: Simon and Schuster, 1982), p. 80.

19. Fiedler is also close to Bakhtin in his notion of an inherent ambivalence in works of popular art. For Bakhtin, folk imagery is inherently ambivalent as it seeks to articulate a worldview that combines polarities of life and death. Fiedler sees this ambivalence in more psychological terms that are of some relevance here: "Such works of art are subversive of all unequivocal allegiances, all orthodoxies—being in essence equivocal, ambivalent. Like our personal dreams, myths or communal dreams tend to express the repressed: especially the dark side of our ambivalence toward what any status quo demands we believe, and more often than not, think we do" (*What Was Literature?* p. 41).

20. Andrew Sarris, *The American Cinema* (New York: E. P. Dutton, 1969; rpt, Chicago: University of Chicago Press, 1985), pp. 19–25.

21. I should note that the ideology of *Rambo: First Blood Part II* is not as monolithic as most journalistic accounts made it out to be. Thomas Doherty has argued this persuasively in a review of the film in *Film Quarterly* (Spring 1986), pp. 50–54. In the notion of mixed messages, at least, it might even be possible to trace a connection between *Rambo* and *Head Office* since the latter film does honor the heroic exploits of two *individuals* who go against the system, one of whom is clearly engaged in a

kind of Freudian rebellion against her father, who owns the conglomerate. Even within a left-wing ethos—in American culture at least—individual initiative continues to count for something.

22. The importance of the vernacular in transforming the literature of the time has been extensively analyzed in Bakhtin, *The Age of Rabelais*; the influence of festive art forms on Shakespeare's comedies is the subject of Barber, *Shakespeare's Festive Comedy*.

23. This is not the first use of folk material in "serious" music, but the elevated quality accorded simple forms seems new. The folk elements Mozart uses in *Die Zauberflöte*, for example, are there precisely to define the simplicity and earthiness of Papageno as opposed to the greater complexity and nobility of the leading characters, so that a high-low opposition is maintained with the high receiving the greater value.

24. A biographical note in an afterword to a paperback edition of Tieck's fairy tales contains a remark of some interest here: "The child was introduced at a very early age to the new literature of the Enlightenment and *Sturm und Drang* by his learned father, to the bible and hymn book and to the world of fairy tales by his mother" (Ludwig Tieck, *Der blonde Eckbert*, with an afterword by Konrad Nussbächer [Stuttgart: Philipp Reclam Jun., 1962], p. 79; my translation). *Literature*, then, belongs to the world of learning and reason embodied in masculine authority where a father can rate the valorizing adjective "learned," while things of the spirit—the neat coupling of religion and fairy tale!—belong to the maternal world, where the mother rates no adjective of any kind. This is not to say the Bible can't be read for its glorious poetry or that a tradition of learning could not grow up around it. But as the writer formulates this opposition, the gifts of the mother are clearly outside traditional literature, belonging more to the world of nature, and as such beyond social valuation.

It seems that whenever a critic sets up a category to define works of art, the category inevitably moves beyond description to evaluation. Something of a parallel may be found in American literature where works by and for a female audience have generally been devalued, as Leslie Fiedler has noted: "The struggle of High Art and Low has, moreover, been perceived as a battle of the sexes" (*What Was Literature?*, p. 29; see also Ann Douglas, *The Feminization of American Culture* (1977; rpt., New York: Avon, 1978).

25. In "The Me Decade and the Third Great Awakening," Tom Wolfe notes the extensiveness of this change in the mid-1970s: "In America truck drivers, mechanics, factory workers, policemen, firemen, and garbage men make so much money—$15,000 to $20,000 (or more) per year is not uncommon—that the word 'proletarian' can no longer be used in this country with a straight face. So one now says 'lower middle class.' One can't even call workingmen 'blue collar' any longer. They all have collars like Joe Namath's or Johnny Bench's or Walt Frazier's." Wolfe, *Mauve Gloves and Madmen, Clutter and Vine* (New York: Farrar, Straus and Giroux, 1976), p. 136.

26. One of the most influential was James S. Coleman, *The Adolescent Society: The Social Life of the Teenager and Its Impact on Education* (Glencoe, N.Y.: Free Press, 1961).

27. Grace and Fred M. Hechinger, *Teenage Tyranny* (New York: William Morrow, 1963). This book draws very heavily on Coleman, *The Adolescent Society*. Page numbers in parentheses follow quotations in the text.

28. I would also like to note the "serene pool" the Hechingers mention is no longer

there, having been replaced by a high-priced restaurant that presumably earns the Metropolitan Museum more money than the cafeteria that surrounded the pool. In this case, the more adult drive for money has prompted a far more lasting desecration than the teenage libidinal drives the Hechingers deplored.

29. By the mid-1970s the Hechingers' worst fears appear to have taken place. A Yankelovich study on the "New Morality" published in 1974 noted: "Increasingly, the older generation has begun to move toward the value structure of young people." Daniel Yankelovich, *The New Morality: A Profile of American Youth in the 70's* (New York: McGraw-Hill, 1974), p. 21.

30. Wallace Turner, *New York Times*, December 3, 1964, p. 50 (emphasis added).

31. Vizzard, *See No Evil*, p. 329.

32. The X rating itself was probably the clearest sign of this uncertainty since it was in effect a nonrating. It could be self-applied and did not guarantee legal defense by the Motion Picture Association of America (MPAA), for which reason Stephen Farber was especially critical of it (see note 35 below). Since the X could be self-applied, there was no legal way to stop exploitation artists from inventing the Triple X (which would herald hard-core pornography on big-city screens within a year of the advent of the Ratings System). See Farber, *The Movie Rating Game* (Washington, D.C.: Public Affairs Press, 1972); Garth Jowett, *Film: The Democratic Art* (Boston: Little, Brown, 1976); and Vizzard, *See No Evil*.

33. There was, of course, some concern for screen violence and crime in the early 1930s, as should be clear from chapter 1, but the strongest drive behind the tougher administration of the Code was clearly the way sex was being presented on the screen. American movies continued to be fairly violent even after 1934 (although never with the explicitness of the 1970s, of course). The reaction to screen violence in the late 1960s and early 1970s is discussed by Jowett, *Film: The Democratic Art*, pp. 450–52. Vizzard also discusses reactions against violence in the late 1960s and ties it specifically to the assassination of Robert Kennedy in 1968, while noting, however, that the violence did continue (Vizzard, *See No Evil*, pp. 346–47).

34. The description is from Farber's chronicle of his six months on the board (*The Movie Rating Game*, p. v), a prime example of "the generation gap." Throughout the book, Farber keeps stressing the ages of the regular members of the board, stating directly that he was more in touch with the audience that actually attends these films.

35. Stephen Farber, quoted in "Rating the Rating System," *Time*, May 31, 1971, p. 72. The article further noted that "not only Farber but other critics in and out of the industry are often mystified by the board's assessments of the relative immorality of sex and violence."

36. In his interview with François Truffaut, Alfred Hitchcock, responding to Truffaut's remark that *Foreign Correspondent* (1940), though very good, "definitely belongs in the 'B' category," explained: "the problem is casting. In Europe, you see, the thriller, the adventure story is not looked down upon. . . . When I had completed the script of *Foreign Correspondent*, I went to Gary Cooper with it, but because it was a thriller, he turned it down. The attitude was so commonplace when I started working in Hollywood that I always ended up working with the next best—in this instance, with Joel McCrea. Many years later Gary Cooper said to me, 'That was a mistake. I should have done it' " (Truffaut, *Hitchcock* [New York: Simon and Schuster, 1967], p. 96). Genres

themselves can negotiate upward mobility: by the 1960s the suspense film, probably largely owing to Hitchcock's success, had become a classy genre.

37. I observed earlier (note 25, above) that Eric Bentley, for all his praise of melodrama and farce, nonetheless retains a commitment to the hierarchical opposition of high and low, accepting the greater value of higher forms as indisputable. Even John G. Cawelti, who has written compelling analyses of popular, formulaic art and always speaks against the assignment of value to high and low, can nonetheless observe: "Though it is likely for a number of reasons that a work possessing more invention than formula will be a greater work, we should avoid this easy judgment in our study of popular culture." Cawelti, *The Six-Gun Mystique* (Bowling Green, Ohio: Bowling Green University Popular Press, n.d.), p. 29.

38. According to a case study on the making of *Psycho*, Hitchcock was consciously imitating the exploitation movies released by American-International. Stephen Rebello, *Alfred Hitchcock and the Making of "Psycho"* (New York: Dembner, 1990).

39. Marx would probably not have liked to see this dictum applied to such a specifically middle-class milieu (although how bourgeois the American middle classes are is another matter entirely), where he would have been more inclined to view the openness I describe as "repressive tolerance." But the kind of utopianism I present here has deliberate echoes of Herbert Marcuse, who had a vogue with college students in the late 1960s and 1970s; the comedies they would most often go to by the end of the decade reflect a utopian liberation in both social and sexual behavior that comes fairly close to Marcuse. See Marcuse, *Eros and Civilization* (Boston: Beacon Press, 1966 [1955]).

40. "Man in the News—A Rebel on Campus," *New York Times*, December 9, 1964, p. 32. George Paloczi-Horvath thought the experiences in the civil rights movement in the South was of key importance to the Berkeley revolt (Paloczi-Horvath, *Youth Up in Arms* [New York: David McKay, 1971], pp. 226–29). Kirkpatrick Sale stressed the relationship between the civil rights movement and the student revolts in general, noting "the sit-in tactic was successfully transferred from Southern lunchcounters and Northern businesses to the halls of ivy" (*SDS* [1973; rpt., New York: Vintage, 1974], p. 162).

41. Clarence Major writes about the prevalence of this kind of inversion, which he sees as coming specifically out of jazz: "The sinner-man-black musician, unwilling and possibly *un*able to attain salvation through or to make peace with the worship of a white god-image *had* (in order to achieve and maintain his own chosen style of sanity) to turn *bad* into *good* and begin to change the negative definition of blackness." Major, *Dictionary of Afro-American Slang* (New York: International Publishers, 1970), p. 14.

3. Dirty Discourse

1. Randall, *Censorship of the Movies: The Social and Political Control of a Mass Medium* (Madison: University of Wisconsin Press, 1970), p. vi. This comment appears in a "Note to the Second Printing," necessitated by the radical changes that had occurred since the first printing only two years before: "since the first edition of this book appeared, the crumbling inhibitions on cinematic content have fallen away at an ever quickening pace" (p. v).

2. Wallace Turner, "Kerr Is Resigning at U. of California; Aide Also Leaving," *New York Times*, March 10, 1965, p. 1.

3. In his biography of Lenny Bruce, Gary Carey reports an incident at Bruce's last obscenity trial that speaks to the issue of multiple discourses. The defense had elicited testimony from sociologist Herbert Gans who claimed the word "fuck" is "commonly heard in all circles of society—in Boston (his hometown) as well as in the armed forces." At this point the presiding judge interrupted the testimony:

> Judge Murtagh challenged Gans's testimony. "I was in the army for several years and never heard it."
> The other two judges turned to look at Murtagh in bewilderment. Spectators in the auditorium tittered in disbelief.

The reaction to the good judge's claim signifies a public recognition that we all know discourse is determined by context. Public-private is not the stark opposition of Code-restricted films, but more a matter of gradations, ever shifting. Carey, *Lenny, Janis and Jimi* (New York: Pocket Books, 1975), p. 93.

4. Lawrence E. Davis, "Kerr's Resignation at Berkeley Is Laid to Conflicts with Regents," *New York Times*, March 11, 1965, p. 17.

5. Ibid.

6. See Jack Vizzard, *See No Evil: Life Inside a Hollywood Censor* (New York: Simon and Schuster, 1970), pp. 309–10.

7. Daniel Yankelovich, *The New Morality: A Profile of American Youth in the 70's* (New York: McGraw-Hill, 1974), p. 55. Yankelovich does tie this to the emergence of new "lifestyles" that placed a premium on "the right to be 'yourself' and 'tell it like it is' " (p. 56). That last phrase, very common in the period, is important since it provides the rationale for obscenity.

8. All the quotations from Kerr are taken from Lawrence E. Davis, "Kerr's Resignation at Berkeley Is Laid to Conflicts with Regents," *New York Times*, March 11, 1965, p. 17.

9. The two cases that first enunciated this principle, *Roth v. U.S.* and *Alberts v. U.S.*, and their consequences for the film industry are discussed in Murray Schumach, *The Face on the Cutting Room Floor* (New York: William Morrow, 1964), pp. 193–95. The actual phrase in my text, with emphasis from the original decision, is taken from a later case, *A Book Named "John Cleland's Memoirs" v. Massachusetts*, cited in Randall, *Censorship of the Movies*, p. 56. Randall also provides discussion of other cases that attempted to clarify the "redeeming social value" standard.

10. This made the situation even more ironic since, according to Randall, by the mid-1960s a "hard-core pornography standard" had been advocated by a number of judges and observers as the place to draw the line on obscenity. It should be clear from this that the general approach to obscenity through the period was chiefly one of retreat. Randall, *Censorship of the Movies*, pp. 59–60.

11. Thomas Buckley, "Berkeley Youth Leader Warns of Protests at Other Campuses," *New York Times*, December 12, 1964, p. 22.

12. "Bruce Boomlet," *Time*, May 31, 1971, p. 73. *Time* identified the off-Broadway play as a "multimedia homage" by writer-director Fred Baker (who made a documentary about Bruce in 1975), and the on-Broadway play as Tom O'Horgan's *Lenny*, while the film was a low-budget rip-off entitled *Dirtymouth*.

13. Carey, *Lenny, Janis and Jimi*, p. 97.

14. The quotation is described as "according to one journalistic definition," but no other source is provided (Carey, *Lenny, Janis and Jimi* p. 34). For an analysis of the importance of the stand-up comic in American culture and an exploration of how these "sick" or "new wave" comics with their appeal to the "counterculture" differ from traditional comedians, see Lawrence E. Minz, "Standup Comedy as Social and Cultural Mediation," in Arthur Power Dudden, ed., *American Humor* (New York: Oxford University Press, 1987), pp. 85–96. Minz does note that not all these new comics were as politically oriented and satiric as Bruce, Sahl and Gregory.

15. Dundes does trace "sick joke" cycles in American humor back to the turn of the century, but the bulk of his examples comes from the 1960s and 1970s. Significantly, it is only in this period that the term "sick humor" came into common use. Alan Dundes, *Cracking Jokes: Studies in Sick Humor Cycles and Stereotypes* (Berkeley: Ten Speed Press, 1987). Page numbers in parentheses follow quotations in the text.

16. Stephen Farber, who served on the Ratings Board for six months as a student intern in 1970, cites an earlier film as an example of the board's members expressing values in their ratings. He wanted to give a GP rating to *Cotton Comes to Harlem* (1970), a film about black detectives aimed at the newly lucrative black audience, because it "was not much stronger than films about whites that *had* been approved for GP." The other board members, however, sided with their chief Eugene Dougherty who "kept reiterating that the 'unethical behavior of the police' would set a bad example for Negro children" (Farber, *The Movie Rating Game* [Washington, D.C.: Public Affairs Press, 1972], p. 43). As striking as this is, *Ryan's Daughter* (1970) is finally more important because the confusion over its rating made public the unequal fairness of the Ratings System.

17. The case is discussed in detail by Farber, *The Movie Rating Game*, pp. 76–78.

18. Carey, *Lenny, Janis and Jimi*, p. 78. Carey also notes "some club managers complained that Bruce directed his act toward the band instead of the customers" (p. 27).

19. In *Aristophanic Comedy*, K. J. Dover has located the problem as a matter of different context that makes it difficult for a current mass audience to understand what might have appealed to an earlier mass audience: "The trouble is that if a modern audience is told that a Greek play is funny they will count every painful minute of the intervals between laughs, whereas if they are told it is serious they may be somewhat more inclined to blame themselves than to blame the poet if the play does not hold their attention all the time" (Berkeley: University of California Press, 1972), pp. 154–55).

Pasolini's *Decameron* (1970) comes closest to being such a film, and as such it demonstrates the kinds of confusions being discussed here since it was directed by one of Italy's leading art film directors and, in this country at least, it received an art house distribution.

20. Mikhail Bakhtin, *Rabelais and His World*, trans. Hélèna Iswolsky (Bloomington: Indiana University Press, 1984 [1965]), pp. 101–102. Page numbers in parentheses following quotations by Bakhtin in the text refer to this edition.

21. In a psychological study of disgust, Rozin and Fallon propose that "animalness" is a central feature of the emotion: "all disgusts are of animal origin." They cite a couple of studies for an "explanation [that] assumes that humans see themselves as quite distinct from (and superior to) other animals and wish to avoid any ambiguity about their

status by accentuating the human-animal boundary." Paul Rozin and April E. Fallon, "A Perspective on Disgust," *Psychological Review* 94 (1987), no. 1: 28.

The gross-out comedy and horror films considered in this book very insistently emphasize the animal side of human existence. As such, they embrace disgust as something desirable and, in doing so, challenge conventional understanding of our noble humanity.

22. Presley had appeared earlier, in 1955, in full pelvic glory on "The Dorsey Brothers Show," but the appearance caused such an uproar that the strategic camera placement was dictated for the Sullivan show. Subsequently, Presley could be seen in full-body shots on television, but the gyrations were always more subdued than in his movies or public appearances. See Thomas Doherty, *Teenagers and Teenpics, 1955–1960: The Juvenilization of American Movies* (Boston: Allen and Unwin, 1988), p. 60 and chap. 4.

23. The chief source for what follows is Freud's *Civilization and Its Discontents.* His point of departure is significant for the comparison I make to Bakhtin. Freud begins by citing an exchange he had with Romain Rolland over *The Future of an Illusion:* "He entirely agreed with my judgment upon religion, but . . . he was sorry I had not properly appreciated the true source of religious sentiments. This, he says, consists in a peculiar feeling, which he himself is never without, which he finds confirmed by many others, and which he may suppose is present in millions of people. It is a feeling which he would like to call a sensation of 'eternity', a feeling as of something limitless, unbounded—as it were, 'oceanic.' " Freud admits he can't find this feeling in himself, so he sets out to find its sources through a psychoanalytic investigation. In the process, the ideal is made real, the high made low, and the spiritual turned into something more firmly entrenched in the material world. See Sigmund Freud, *Civilization and Its Discontents* (1927), vol. 21 (1961) in the *Standard Edition* (hereafter, *S.E.*), 24 vols. (London: Hogarth Press, 1953–1974), p. 64.

24. This sentence has received particular attention in the last decade or so because it is central to Jacques Lacan's reformulation of Freud. See Lacan, *Écrits* (New York: W. W. Norton, 1977), trans. Alan Sheridan, pp. 128–29; and Lacan, *The Four Fundamental Concepts of Psycho-Analysis* (1978; rpt., New York: W. W. Norton, 1981), ed. Jacques-Alain Miller, trans. Alan Sheridan, pp. 44–45. My use of Freud's statement here is probably closer to the ego psychology that Lacan set himself in opposition to.

25. Henri Bergson, "Laughter," in Wylie Sypher, ed., *Comedy* (Garden City, N.Y.: Doubleday Anchor, 1956); and Sigmund Freud, *Jokes and Their Relation to the Unconscious* (1905), in vol. 8 (1961), in *S.E.*, pp. 9–236.

4. The Greater Tradition

1. Dwight MacDonald, "Masscult and Midcult," *Partisan Review* (Spring 1960), reprinted in *Against the American Grain* (New York: Random House, 1962); quotation is from p. 7.

2. Jeffrey Henderson, *The Maculate Muse: Obscene Language in Attic Comedy* (New Haven: Yale University Press, 1975), p. ix. Page numbers in parentheses follow quotations in the text.

3. There is a book by Eric Partridge, *Shakespeare's Bawdy* (London: Routledge and Kegan Paul, 1955), on sexual and scatological language in Shakespeare. Its first edition

in 1947, "limited to 1000 copies," perhaps reflects on the expected reception. It was republished in a "New Popular Edition (revised)" in 1955 and finally in paperback in 1968. As with Henderson on Aristophanes, Partridge notes this is a subject virtually unnoticed previously, but his critical aims are clearly different from Henderson's in that he does not want to make obscenity central to Shakespeare's art.

The bulk of the book consists of a very useful glossary, but an introductory essay makes "a fine, yet aesthetically important distinction. Shakespeare may have had a dirty mind, yet he certainly had not a filthy mind" (p. 9). Further, in writing on flatulent humor, Partridge makes a class distinction of some interest here: "Flatulence was, in Shakespeare's day, the source and the target of humor and wit among all classes: now-adays, its popularity as a subject is, in the main, confined to the lower and lower-middle classes and to morons elsewhere" (p. 11). This is to say we have to accept the fun about farts because such was generally acceptable in the past; now, however, since we are not of the wrong class, which is equivalent to being morons, we know better.

4. K. J. Dover, the Aristophanic scholar who most openly embraces the scatological and sexual humor before Henderson, nonetheless seems to value it chiefly as a means for characters' aggressively asserting themselves since he sees self-assertion as the dominant motif in Aristophanes. Dover, *Aristophanic Comedy* (Berkeley: University of California Press, 1972), pp. 38ff.

This reading has much in common with Cedric H. Whitman's approach, which also accepts the obscenity at the same time that it displaces it from a central position: "Aristophanes' bawdry—or whatever it should be called—is not the essence of the matter; it serves merely to illustrate vividly the poet's devotion to the limitless, that kind of world view which . . . is almost the exact opposite of what we term morality" (Whitman, *Aristophanes and the Comic Hero* [Cambridge: Harvard University Press, 1964], p. 23). Henderson, on the other hand, while embracing much of Whitman's interpretation of the plays, is more specifically concerned with the scatological and sexual images in themselves.

5. In 1972 K. J. Dover saw the issue entirely in terms of sexual appeal: "*Lysistrata* is one of the Aristophanic plays most often staged or broadcast at the present time, partly because people who know nothing else about Aristophanes may have a vague recollection of seeing translations of *Lysistrata* in pornographic bookshops" (Dover, *Aristophanic Comedy*, p. 153).

6. Here's a sampling of some past opinions: "There is abundant evidence in these pieces—it is impressed upon the reader disagreeably in every one of them—that, willingly or unwillingly, the writer pandered to the vulgar taste, and degraded his Muse to the level of the streets in order to catch popular favor. . . . [Nonetheless, this writer moves to a reassuring position] But the coarseness of Aristophanes is not corrupting." Rev. W. Lucas Collins, *Aristophanes* (Edinburgh: William Blackwood, 1872), pp. 6, 12.

"The Greek Comedy is often broad and vulgar in the extreme. . . . There is much in the play [*Lysistrata*] to which a *modern* audience would object, but the keenness of its satire and the piquancy of its situations can not be denied." Louis E. Lord, *Aristophanes: His Plays and His Influence* (Boston: Marshall Jones, 1925), pp. 18, 52; emphasis added.

While the latter writer saw himself as modern for rejecting the obscenity in Aristophanes, it is more common since then for critics to adopt a kind of anthropological relativism that accepts without fully embracing Aristophanic explicitness: "To understand the Old Attic Comedy it is necessary to make some effort of the historical, and indeed of the anthropological, imagination. The wit, the refinement, the high literary culture of comedy, and still more the rare public spirit and courage with which Aristophanes pled for reasonableness and peace throughout a fierce and dangerous period of war fever, are hard to reconcile with the indecency of language and sometimes of incident in most of his plays, or with the occasional foulmouthed abuse of individuals." Gilbert Murray, *Aristophanes: A Study* (New York: Oxford University Press, 1933), p. 1.

"Aristophanes is not prurient because his comedy is a comedy of pure wit, which attacks the head and not the entrails. None of the characters engages the audience's sympathy as human beings; with none can the audience identify itself." Moses Hadas, *A History of Greek Literature* (New York: Columbia University Press, 1950), p. 100.

"Old Comedy dealt so freely with what we call obscenity, that one wonders why such antics do not strike us as simply jejune and immature. Part of the answer may be in the fact that there is never any question of 'daring,' that lurid word which today sells so many mildly suggestive novels and movies" (Whitman, *Aristophanes and the Comic Hero*, p. 209).

7. Dover, for example, notes: "Anyone who goes to the play in the expectation that continuous bawdy jokes will keep him laughing from the first line to the last is likely to find that the choral lyric, after the first vigorous encounter between the old men and the old women, fall rather flat" (*Aristophanic Comedy*, p. 153).

8. Leo Steinberg, *The Sexuality of Christ in Renaissance Art and in Modern Oblivion* (New York: Pantheon, 1983), p. 1.

9. Steinberg, *The Sexuality of Christ*, p. 107.

10. In "The Critical Fortune of a Realist Painter," Richard E. Spear recounts the critical reception and frequent dismissal of Caravaggio, with two eighteenth-century opinions worth repeating here: "In the 1760s, Anton Raphael Mengs decided that Caravaggio 'was thoroughly defective in disegno' and that his followers' pictures 'made a strong impression on the sense but nothing on the spirit; they leave it as they found it.' Even the astute Italian historian, Luigi Lanzi, wrote with scorn (1789) that the 'features [of Caravaggio's figures] are remarkable only for their vulgarity . . . his figures inhabit dungeons.' " Spear, in John P. O'Neill (Editor in Chief) and Ellen Schultz, ed., *The Age of Caravaggio* (New York: Metropolitan Museum of Art/Electa International, 1985), p. 23.

11. "The portrayal of a dramatic and violent event at its expressive and physical climax, already essayed in the *Boy Bitten by a Lizard* (cat. no. 70) has its roots in Northern Italy." This comparison to the earlier work, disturbing in its own right, but neither as bloody nor as violent, really minimizes the impact of the action in *Judith and Holofernes*. Mina Gregori (commentary), in O'Neill/Schultz, eds., *The Age of Caravaggio*, p. 256 (no. 72: *Judith and Holofernes*).

12. In reviewing Chaplin's notes for the film in its early stage of composition, David Robinson has located what seems to be the source for this scene: "This might be a complex variation on the shame gag-nightmares: Charlie could lose his trousers, but then realize that there is no cause for shame since the girl cannot see." Robinson, *Chaplin: His Life and Art* (New York: McGraw-Hill, 1985). p. 394.

13. The scene is so described by Gerald Mast: "Charlie holds up his hands to help her. She, however, mistakenly grabs a strand from Charlie's undershirt, not from the package of yarn she has just bought." Mast, *The Comic Mind* (Indianapolis: Bobbs-Merrill, 1973), p. 108.

14. In a book-length analysis of the film, Gerard Molyneaux, drawing strongly on

Bergson's theory of laughter, provides extended analyses of the opening scene that concentrate on the satire and "social comment." Molyneaux, *Charles Chaplin's "City Lights": Its Production and Dialectical Structure* (New York: Garland, 1983), pp. 124–38, 212–18.

15. David Robinson identifies the male figure on the right as peace, although there is nothing in the statue that specifically indicates this. It is perhaps the presumption of satiric intent here that leads Robinson to assume Chaplin wants the figure with the sword to represent peace. Robinson, *Chaplin: His Life and Art*, p. 400.

16. In "some notes on a recent viewing," Stanley Kauffmann observed "a surprising amount of homosexual joking" in the film, but more or less threw up his hands in the face of it: "I can't remember this element in another Chaplin picture. I can't explain it here, but the hints are inescapable." Kauffmann, *"City Lights," Film Comment* (September–October 1972): 18.

While Kauffmann at least raises the possibility of an interpretation, Gerald Weales mentions the homosexuality chiefly to deny it: "[Charlie's] flirtatious attempts to show how harmless he is, which his opponent (Hank Mann) takes as a homosexual advance, suggests nothing so much as the placating behavior with which animals assure the pack leader that they are not challenging his position" (Weales, *Canned Goods as Caviar* [Chicago: University of Chicago Press, 1985], p. 26). That Kauffmann and Weales feel the need to bring up the homosexuality at all—even though they clearly do not want to write about it—is perhaps a reflection of the changing public discourse of the 1960s and 1970s that I charted in chapter 3.

17. Although I will have reason to question this view in my discussion of *Fast Times at Ridgemont High*, the connection of sight with phallic aggression is congruent with Laura Mulvey's argument about the masculine gaze in "Visual Pleasure and the Narrative Cinema," *Screen* 16 (Autumn 1975), no. 3, reprinted in Bill Nichols, ed., *Movies and Methods*, 2 vols. (vol. 1: Berkeley: University of California Press, 1976; vol. 2: 1985), 2:305–15.

18. Julian Smith notes two "blind" statues, lumping the nude together with "Peace and Prosperity" and seeing both solely as foreshadowing (*Chaplin* [Boston: Twayne. 1984], p. 92). Weales also notes the statue's "blindness" and regards its purpose similarly (Weales, *Canned Goods as Caviar*, p. 17).

19. Weales raises this point as well (again to dismiss the sexual meaning): "We do not need to play sexual symbology with the poor man's walking stick to recognize in his pathetic figure a loss of manhood" (*Canned Goods as Caviar*, p. 27). The capacity for denial when dealing with the more vulgar aspects of Chaplin's art seems limitless.

20. Smith refers to this action as an "unveiling" to relate it to other scenes of exposure in the film, but he is curiously unconcerned with what is being unveiled (*Chaplin*, p. 94). This is to say, once again the sexual aspects of the action are ignored.

21. Walter Kerr terms the mismatched shots a fault, which expresses a narrow notion of film style (*The Silent Clowns* [New York: Knopf, 1979], p. 351). Given the amount of time Chaplin spent on production and the endless retakes he indulged in, it's unlikely the jump-cuts weren't intentional. Robinson provides some information on the shooting of this scene, which included seventeen retakes (Robinson, *Chaplin: His Life and Art*, pp. 409–10).

22. This is an issue I have explored more fully in an article on *The Gold Rush* (1925). See Paul, *"The Gold Rush," Film Comment* 8 (September–October 1972), no. 3: 16–18.

5. A Festive Art

1. C. L. Barber, *Shakespeare's Festive Comedy* (Princeton: Princeton University Press, 1959), pp. 3, 6–7.

2. Christian Metz opposes movies to theater precisely on this issue of festivity. He locates the chief difference in the physical presence of the actor: "when actor and spectator are in each other's presence, when the *playing* (of the actor and the audience) is also a distribution of roles (of 'character parts') in a game, [there is] an active complicity which works both ways, a ceremony which is always partly civic, involving more than the private individual: a festival." Metz, *The Imaginary Signifier* (Bloomington: Indiana University Press, 1982), p. 94.

The sense of communality is truest for Greek theater, where both audience and actors shared the *parados* as a way of getting to their respective positions in the theater, and the *orchestra*, the stage itself, was not raised, so that it seemed a continuous extension of the audience. But with the raising of the stage in Roman theater, there came an enforced distancing between viewer and performer that puts the performers in a more controlling position. The strong communal sense is still there unabated in the audience itself (and there is no reason why this should not be the same for movie audiences). But Metz proposes quite a different audience: "The feast . . . is not shared— it is a furtive feast and not a festive feast. . . . The institution of the cinema requires a silent, motionless spectator, a *vacant* spectator" (p. 96). There are possibly cultural differences here (note how different this is from Vachel Lindsay's description of the audience quoted in chapter 1, at note 38); perhaps French audiences really do fit Metz's description, but I have trouble believing any individual could feel so totally "alienated" while sitting in a full theater watching a raucous comedy.

3. Plot descriptions of one hundred Grand Guignol plays, as well as a history of its theater, may be found in Mel Gordon, *The Grand Guignol: Theatre of Fear and Terror,* (New York: Amok Press, 1988). Aside from the alternation from one play to the next, Eric Bentley has noted, "At the Grand Guignol one often wasn't sure which way to take a play: it could be Jacobean tragic horror, it could be farcical nonsense—the difference lies not in the materials themselves but only in interpretation." Bentley, *The Life of the Drama* (New York: Atheneum, 1964), p. 341.

4. Michael Blowen, "Screen Scene," *Boston Globe,* September 17, 1987, "Calendar" sec., p. 9.

5. I have borrowed this term from Robert Alter, who has in turn borrowed it from Homeric scholarship. For his purposes (somewhat different from classical scholarship but relevant here), he defines the type-scene as "a series of recurrent narrative episodes . . . dependent on the manipulation of a fixed constellation of predetermined motifs." Alter, *The Art of Biblical Narrative* (New York: Basic Books, 1981), p. 51.

Of all twentieth-century narrative arts, movies make fullest use of type-scenes. Appropriately, Alter's discussion of the importance of type-scenes in Biblical narrative begins with a consideration of the purpose of familiar motifs in Westerns (pp. 48–49).

6. One writer on farce defines the form in terms that suggest nightmare: "Farce deals with the unreal, with the worst one can dream or dread. Farce is cruel, often brutal, even murderous. . . . Farce flouts the bounds of reason, good taste, fairness, and what we commonly think of as sanity." Albert Bermel, *Farce* (New York: Touchstone, 1982), p. 21.

7. Mikhail Bakhtin, *Rabelais and His World*, trans. Hélèna Iswolsky (Bloomington: Indiana University Press, 1984 [1965]), pp. 37–38.

8. In his book on Aristophanes, Cedric H. Whitman is interested in the grotesque for ways in which it "may help to clarify the comic hero's ambiguities, his 'lowness' and his stature." His discussion of this ambiguity suggests a reason why the grotesque might be regarded as ambivalent: "In the late Roman *grottesche* [which refers to paintings found in grottoes toward the end of the fifteenth century "characterized throughout by a free mixture of representational forms: men with legs of animals or terminating in fronded branches, horses adorned with leaves and having the hind quarters of serpents, winged *putti*, beast-headed men . . ."] themselves the minglings of animal, vegetable, and human do not suggest so much neurotic fear of the demonic as participation in it. . . . In early times it would seem that the grotesque, or at least the minglings of forms, could express dangerous and incalculable forces, but it could also express a human kinship with the burgeoning abundance of the demonic world." Whitman, *Aristophanes and the Comic Hero* [Cambridge: Harvard University Press, 1964], pp. 42–44.

9. Individual gross-out horror films of the 1970s and 1980s have received far more exegetical analyses than gross-out comedies. As a general matter, there is far more writing on horror than comedy. The extended bibliography in *Film Genre Reader* contains almost twice the number of entries for horror films, even though the comedy list contains theoretical works that have nothing in particular to do with film. Conversely, there is more theoretical writing on comedy than horror, as if comedy were only worth contemplating as a general rather than specific matter. See Barry Keith Grant, ed., *Film Genre Reader* (Austin: University of Texas Press, 1986), pp. 373–75, 383–87.

10. Wayne C. Booth has pointed to a connection between irony and metaphor: "In reading any metaphor or simile, as in reading irony, the reader must reconstruct unspoken meanings through inferences about surface statements that for some reason cannot be accepted at face value." It is perhaps easier to accept the face value meanings of simple jokes, but this is not to deny that they are also meaningful. Booth, *The Rhetoric of Fiction* (Chicago: University of Chicago Press, 1961), p. 22.

11. Freud explicitly treats jokes as an activity analogous to the dreamwork in *Jokes and Their Relation to the Unconscious* (1905), in vol. 8 (1961), in *S.E.*, pp. 9–236.

12. Alan Dundes has suggested that jokes often conceal precisely what we would prefer not to look at. On a joke cycle about the handicapped, he has written: "The joke typically provides a socially sanctioned outlet for talking about what normally cannot be talked about." Dundes, *Cracking Jokes: Studies in Sick Humor Cycles and Stereotypes* (Berkeley: Ten Speed Press, 1987), p. 16.

13. Susan Sontag is the obvious point of reference here for her "Notes on Camp," in Sontag, *Against Interpretation* (New York: Farrar, Straus and Giroux, 1967), pp. 275–92. Michael Wood wants to take movies seriously as mirrors of society, but thinks their "excess of style" prevents serious consideration of them as art: "The good moments of many movies have the flavor of old jokes told a bit too broadly." Wood, *America in the Movies* (1975; rpt., New York: Delta, 1978), p. 6.

14. At end of "Against Interpretation," Sontag exultantly states her position against criticism bent on ferreting out subtexts: "In place of hermeneutics we need an erotics of art" (Sontag, *Against Interpretation*, p. 14). Yet in confronting the many Hollywood objects that might well fit in with this aesthetic position, like Busby Berkeley musicals, she relegates them to the lower realm of camp.

15. Bakhtin describes the "Renaissance conception of laughter" as follows: "Laughter has a deep philosophical meaning, it is one of the essential forms of the truth concerning the world as a whole, concerning history and man. It is a peculiar point of view relative to the world; the world is seen anew, no less (and perhaps more) profoundly than when seen from the serious standpoint. . . . Certain essential aspects of the world are accessible only to laughter" (*Rabelais and His World*, p. 66).

16. Richard Grenier, in *Commentary*, provided the one review that did mention the invasion of Czechoslovakia and even attempted some analysis of what that might signify. Grenier thought the invasion appropriate to the Reagan years, but did not want to read too much into a "lightweight" comedy ("Arms and the Movies," *Commentary*, October 1981, pp. 71–72). Perhaps Sylvester Stallone was needed to put Bill Murray into perspective: in an article discussing *Rambo: First Blood Part II*, Thomas Doherty mentions Murray's Czech invasion (*Film Quarterly* [Spring 1986], pp. 50–54).

17. Two critics did take note of this scene, although only one thought it of interest. In an otherwise favorable review, David Ansen noted, "Particularly sour is an attempt to wring laughs from a racial encounter in a black roadside nightclub" ("Gross Out," *Newsweek*, August 7, 1978, p. 85).

In a more mixed notice, Andrew Sarris singled out this scene for praise: "A more interesting example of the film's runaway non-conformism is its blatant acknowledgment of racism even among its supposedly sympathetic characters. . . . I have never seen a scene like this in an American movie, and would not expect to see one nowadays, when we are in the midst of the largely mythical racial brotherhood of the rock revival" ("Films in Focus," *Village Voice*, July 31, 1978, pp. 38, 40). Sarris is more sensitive to what is interesting about the scene's "offensiveness," but he also sees the scene chiefly for its satiric content. This, I think, undercuts the full complexity of the scene as I describe it in chapter 7.

18. The dangers of not listening—or viewing—closely are best exemplified by the procrustean work of Nora Sayre, *Running Time* (New York: Dial, 1982), and Peter Biskind, *Seeing Is Believing* (New York: Pantheon, 1984). How easily individual films may be distorted by this generalizing approach is evident in a book by Jon Lewis that deals with many of the films I survey here. Lewis, for example, tries to make a claim for a critique of teen romance in *Revenge of the Nerds* (1984) by quoting a line of dialogue from the film. The line he quotes bears a vague resemblance to the actual line in the film but also grossly distorts it, completely inverting its meaning (Lewis, *The Road to Ruin and Romance: Teen Films and Youth Culture* [New York: Routledge, 1992], p. 75). The only justification for such lack of attention to the text must be the conviction that the particularities of the text are not worth attending to. I hope my own close attention will convince the reader otherwise.

19. John Fiske, *Understanding Popular Culture* (Boston: Unwin Hyman, 1989), p. 15.

20. In writing this I am deliberately echoing David Bordwell whose work on narrative film derives from Russian formalist criticism. Bordwell is of particular value to me here because he is concerned with establishing the agency of the work and, in the process, demonstrating that an audience itself is always a thinking audience, even for Hollywood movies. See Bordwell, *Narration in the Fiction Film* (Madison: University of Wisconsin Press, 1985).

21. Noting that the film was based on an actual exorcism, Canby wrote: "Not five

out of 100 people seem to give a hang about the instruction being received. They're getting their kicks out of seeing a small girl being tortured and torn, quite literally. The audience watches as if attending a porno film, moving around in their seats, talking, smoking, staring at the ceiling, during the conventional exposition, and then paying attention only to the violence that has been sanctified." Canby, *New York Times*, January 13, 1974, sec. 2, p. 4.

22. At work here is the common assumption that works of popular art cannot offer a complex experience or, conversely, that a mass audience cannot be open to complex works. A noble work of art reaches that stage in our culture by establishing itself as an object that rewards contemplation. I think this a questionable standard since any object will reward contemplation if the contemplation is sufficiently rigorous. In writing this I do not want to beg the issue of complexity. Complexity and simplicity may both be *attributes* of an art work, but they do not automatically certify value. At times we might prize one over another, but in neither case is the attribute necessarily positive. The value of the complexity or simplicity *as the work deploys it* is something that every reader/viewer/listener must define and defend.

23. There is an underlying question here of how genre creates and is created, perhaps something of a chicken-egg conundrum that has concerned many writers on genre. See Jeanine Basinger, *The World War II Combat Film* (New York: Columbia University Press, 1986); Andrew Tudor, "Genre," in Grant, *Film Genre Reader*, pp. 3–10; and John G. Cawelti, *The Six-Gun Mystique* (Bowling Green, Ohio: Bowling Green University Popular Press, n.d.).

24. The ads ascribe this panegyric to Bob Lape, ABC-TV. The *New Dictionary of American Slang* dates "grossed out" as an adjective and "gross-out" as a noun or modifier to the 1960s, while "gross someone out" as a verb is peculiarly pushed off to the 1970s. All three terms are ascribed to teenagers and/or students. As an example of gross-out as a modifier, the dictionary cites an undated phrase from *New York* magazine: "The *Animal House* gross-out movies are all about groups." Oddly, all the definitions here stress the meaning of disgust, giving no indication of the important positive connotations. Robert L. Chapman, ed., *New Dictionary of American Slang* (New York: Harper and Row, 1986), pp. 183–84.

25. Peter Dunn, "Special Effects Make 'The Fly' Worth Seeing," *The Tech* (MIT), September 16, 1986, p. 9.

26. Walter Goodman, "Film: Dreyfuss in 'Stakeout,' " *New York Times*, August 5, 1987, p. C21.

27. Michael MacCambridge, " 'Stand' Leans on $137,000, Chi . . ." *Variety*, August 27, 1986, p. 12.

28. John Towsen has described the Feast of Fools as "a New Year's celebration during which the minor clergy were allowed to usurp the functions of their superiors and engage in a wide range of blasphemous yet officially approved clowning. The prevailing theme was the inversion of status." John H. Towsen, *Clowns* (New York: Hawthorn Books, 1976), p. 16.

29. Bentley's oppositional stance (in *The Life of the Drama*) is clearest when he praises the value of "having a good cry": "Attacks on false emotion often mask a fear of emotion as such. Ours is, after all, a thin-lipped, thin-blooded culture. Consider how, in the past half-century, the prestige of dry irony has risen, while that of surging emotion has fallen" (p. 198). Although they encompass a smaller time frame, Bentley's obser-

vations on the status of irony nicely parallel Bakhtin's claim about the post-Renaissance rise in "reduced forms of laughter."

30. Sigmund Freud, *Civilization and Its Discontents* (1927), vol. 21 (1961) in *S.E.*, 24 vols. (London: Hogarth Press, 1953–1974), p. 26. Unless otherwise indicated, page numbers in parentheses follow subsequent citations in the text from this work.

31. Freud himself might contradict the primacy of the pleasure principle in his elevation of tendentious wit over other forms of humor in *Jokes and Their Relation to the Unconscious*. In any case, the issue does become more complicated in Freud when he sets the death instinct alongside the pleasure principle.

32. After several pages, Freud suddenly gives up on the metaphor, noting "There is clearly no point in spinning our fantasy any further, for it leads to things that are unimaginable, and even absurd. . . . The fact remains that only in the mind is such a preservation of all the earlier stages alongside of the final form possible, and that we are not in a position to represent this phenomenon in pictorial terms." Perhaps it is the very difficulty of imagining this simultaneity of levels that leads us into constructing hierarchies of transcendence. Freud, *Civilization and Its Discontents*, pp. 70–71.

33. Andrew Sarris's objection was formal: "The narrative is completely incoherent and the 'satire' ultimately too exaggerated to take hold" ("Films in Focus," *Village Voice*, July 31, 1978, pp. 38, 40). Penelope Gilliat was more moralistic in her reminder of what a proper satire should have done with this material: "Some of us—a lot of us—were there at the time, and the pit of any good lampooning would surely lie in the showing the straits of a privileged class of young people with a feeling of thwarted morality" ("The Current Cinema," *The New Yorker*, August 14, 1978, p. 54). In a more favorable review, Janet Maslin accepted the whole as satire, but in a peculiar mode that both denied the satire as it put it forward: "At its best . . . the movie isn't strictly satirical, because it doesn't need to be. The film makers have simply supplied the appropriate panty-girdles, crew-neck sweaters, frat house initiation rites and rituals of the toga party, and let all that idiocy speak—very eloquently and with a lot of comic fervor—for itself" ("Screen: 'Animal House,' " *New York Times*, July 28, 1978, p. C7).

34. Mark Singer, "Remembrance of Things Beastly," *New York Times*, July 23, 1978, sec. 2, p. 13.

6. Animal Comedy

1. This simple solution to the problem of what was "acceptable" pornography almost makes this seem an innocent period. Within a few years the authorities would have to consider child pornography, pornography with graphic violence, and alleged "snuff" films (films in which it was claimed a woman was killed during a sexual act).

2. A key defining aspect of this comedy is summed up in the title of Tony Hendra's *Going Too Far*, a history of comedy in the 1960s and 1970s that concentrates chiefly on stand-up comedy, the *National Lampoon*, and "Saturday Night Live," all important precursors of Animal Comedy. Hendra, *Going Too Far* (New York: Doubleday, 1987).

3. Even in some of the most commercial comedies that might have been treated as romantic comedy in the past, the romantic half of the generic name became a secondary element. The difference between *Some Like It Hot* (1959) and *Tootsie* (1982) makes clear how different this situation is from the past. *Some Like It Hot* is romantic comedy, but in *Tootsie* the romance is relegated to a subplot as both Jessica Lange and

Teri Garr subordinate themselves to Dustin Hoffman's star turn (Hoffman is even listed twice, as his own costar in the end credits, ahead of both Lange and Garr). In 1984 *Splash* emerged as a romantic comedy reworking of *E.T. the Extra-Terrestrial* (1982) but with the fantasy given greater play than the romance.

4. Primary sources for my discussion of Old Comedy are Margarete Bieber, *The History of the Greek and Roman Theater* (Princeton: Princeton University Press, 1961); Francis MacDonald Cornford, *The Origin of Attic Comedy* (Garden City, N.Y.: Anchor, 1961); K. J. Dover, *Aristophanic Comedy* (Berkeley: University of California Press, 1972); Moses Hadas, *A History of Greek Literature* (New York: Columbia University Press, 1950); F. H. Sandbach, *The Comic Theater of Greece and Rome* (London: Chatto and Windus, 1977); Robert M. Torrance, *The Comic Hero* (Cambridge: Harvard University Press, 1978); and Cedric H. Whitman, *Aristophanes and the Comic Hero* (Cambridge: Harvard University Press, 1964).

5. There is also Middle Comedy, but the time period it occupies is relatively brief, the texts we have from it are few, and it is generally regarded as a transitional form.

6. Some writing on Old Comedy treats the *agon* as a specific movement within the play, but Whitman notes that the *agon* "in Aristophanes is often handled with great flexibility," sometimes continuing throughout the play (*Aristophanes and the Comic Hero*, p. 11). And Torrance writes, "the contest, or *agon*, lies at the heart of Attic Old Comedy" (*The Comic Hero*, p. 42). The same might well be said of Animal Comedy.

7. Whitman has written: "Old Comedy does not depend primarily upon satire, political or personal. . . . Satire, pure and simple, has no heroic dimension. It reduces its targets, but not by including them in a larger vision. The purely ludicrous, however, admits the possibility of heroic exaggeration, or boundless inflation of itself until it engulfs and transforms the world. . . . Selfhood, not principle, is asserted" (Whitman, *Aristophanes and the Comic Hero*, pp. 36, 9).

8. Northrop Frye, "The Argument of Comedy," in D. A. Robertson, Jr., ed., *English Institute Essays* (New York: Columbia University Press, 1949), p. 60.

9. It is very likely that Laurel and Hardy could never really move beyond B picture status in their features because their personae were simply too farcical, more at home in two-reelers. Romantic comedy plots were never grafted onto their films as they were with the Marx Brothers or even Abbott and Costello. A significant indication of changing audience tastes in comedy is the fact that *Duck Soup* (1933), the Marx Brothers' most thoroughly farcical comedy, was a flop at the time of its release, while today it has gained a critical reputation as their best work.

10. See, for example, James Agee, "Comedy's Greatest Era," reprinted in Agee, *Agee on Film: Reviews and Comments by James Agee* (Boston: Beacon Press, 1964), pp. 2–19.

11. The description is Hawks's own, from "Interview [with Howard Hawks]," Peter Bogdanovich, *Movie*, no. 5 (1962): 18.

12. "I think the average plot is pretty time-worn. Television has come in and they have used so many thousand of plots that people are getting tired of them. They're a little too inclined—if you lay a plot down—to say, 'Oh, I've seen this before.' But if you can keep them from knowing what the plot is you have a chance of holding their interest." Shortly before this remark, Hawks had also made the connection to earlier styles of filmmaking: "I just got to thinking of how we used to make pictures and how we were making them now, and I reviewed the making of a lot of pictures that I had liked. Today, they want you to stick to a script and the easiest, simplest way for the

physical facilities of a studio is the best way to do it. So I determined to go back and try to get a little of the spirit we used to make pictures with" (Bogdanovich, "Interview [with Howard Hawks]," p. 17).

13. Molly Haskell, *From Reverence to Rape* (New York: Holt, Rinehart and Winston, 1974), p. 187.

14. Dave Kehr, "Funny Peculiar," *Film Comment* (July 1982): 13. Kehr was writing at a time when he could not gauge the full influence of *Animal House,* but this piece is a comprehensive and astute survey of developments in Hollywood comedy of the previous decade. Kehr generally regrets what he sees, but I think his response is an indication of the comic traditions that set his own expectations, traditions that were being overturned at the time. He takes note, ruefully, of the great rise of aggression in these films, observing a shift in "the rhetoric of American comedy . . . from seduction to confrontation" complemented by a shift "from comic as victim (Chaplin, Keaton, Laurel and Hardy) to comic as aggressor (Mel Brooks, Steve Martin, John Belushi)" (p. 15).

I would be less likely to minimize the aggression of the silent comedians Kehr names. Rather, I think the elements of their personalities that mark them as "victims" for Kehr are there precisely to make their aggression more acceptable. What is different about the newer comics, then, is not their levels of aggression but the fact that they are so direct about it. This transformation in comic address is congruent with the change in public discourse that I charted in part one and its resultant confrontational style in openly addressing matters previously concealed. And, in fact, this confrontational style returns us to the roots of comedy.

In trying to define the "comic hero," Robert M. Torrance, *The Comic Hero* (Cambridge: Harvard University Press, 1978), finds that, in all the various manifestations of this character, "what is constant is the potential or actual antagonism between his ways and those of his world" (p. viii). These later screen comics still haven't equaled the levels of aggression in Aristophanes' characters. And in Aristophanes aggression always seems to bring its own rewards; as Torrance notes, "the hero of Aristophanic Old Comedy, however low a character in the eyes of later moralists and philosophers, normally transcended all obstacles in his path and came out king of the mountain" (p. 10).

15. Jeanine Basinger, *The World War II Combat Film* (New York: Columbia University Press, 1986), p. 37.

16. Writing on the increased levels of aggression in comedy of the 1970s, Dave Kehr noted "it is no accident that the Marx Brothers and the Three Stooges (to name the high and low poles of the same phenomenon) are the most reliable draws at the revival houses" ("Funny Peculiar," p. 15).

17. This is a feature that Robin Wood has remarked on as well. Wood, *Hollywood from Vietnam to Reagan* (New York: Columbia University Press, 1986), p. 219.

18. *Cooley High* (1975), which precedes later Animal Comedy but is directly influenced by *American Graffiti,* focuses chiefly on the men, but it does indicate what happened to the only woman who has a significant role in the film. I will write in more detail about this film in chapter 8.

19. Frye, "The Argument of Comedy," pp. 61–62 (emphasis added).

20. Pauline Kael, "The Current Cinema," *The New Yorker*, January 24, 1970, p. 74.

21. Drawing on Freud's discussion of the component instincts, some theoretical writings on voyeurism and film would deny this possibility because they explicitly tie the voyeuristic impulse to sadism. Freud himself does not make the connection so explicit. Rather, he establishes a *parallel* between scopophilia and sadism because he sees them both as active impulses that pair off with the passive ones of exhibitionism and masochism. Sigmund Freud, *Three Essays on the Theory of Sexuality* (1905), in vol. 7 (1953) in *S.E.*, 24 vols. (London: Hogarth Press, 1953–1974), pp. 123–243.

Writing specifically on film, Christian Metz carries this further to note a tie between scopophilia and sadism, although his assertion is fairly tentative: "Voyeurism which is not too sadistic (there is none which is not so at all) rests on a kind of *fiction* . . . that stipulates that the object 'agrees', that it is therefore exhibitionist" (Metz, *The Imaginary Signifier* [Bloomington: Indiana University Press, 1982], p. 62). In defining "visual pleasure," Laura Mulvey is more emphatic about the sadistic aspect: "pleasure lies in ascertaining guilt (immediately associated with castration), asserting control and subjecting the guilty person through punishment or forgiveness." Mulvey, "Visual Pleasure and the Narrative Cinema," *Screen* 16 (Autumn 1975), no. 3, reprinted in Bill Nichols, ed., *Movies and Methods*, 2 vols. (vol. 1: Berkeley: University of California Press, 1976; vol. 2: 1985), 2:311.

22. Laura Mulvey assumes that men relate to men on the screen as idealized projections of themselves. I think this stops short of probing the need for the idealization, which can ultimately lead to a very different understanding of the way men may view other men. Mulvey, "Visual Pleasure and the Narrative Cinema," 2:310.

23. Of relevance here is Gaylan Studlar's defining a masochistic aesthetic as the foundation of visual pleasure. Studlar, "Masochism and the Perverse Pleasures of the Cinema," in Nichols, *Movies and Methods*, 2:603–21.

24. I am not too far here from Mulvey's notion that connects the voyeuristic impulse to castration anxiety. But for Mulvey only the woman can be subject for the male gaze, and the anxiety that she stirs up, which must be mastered, is signified by what she lacks. In this instance from *M*A*S*H*, the object of the gaze is in fact bountiful and the lack is perceived in the subject himself. See Mulvey, "Visual Pleasure and the Narrative Cinema," 2:311–12.

25. At the time of the release of *Staying Alive* (1983), publicity releases insistently called attention to the fact that director Sylvester Stallone had "remade" John Travolta's body. And the film itself is concerned to present Travolta's body as an object worth gazing upon: toward the beginning of the final production number, Travolta literally throws his bitchy female dancing partner offstage so that he can continue the dance on his own, the sole erotic focus of the mise-en-scène. The extent to which the male body became increasingly objectified in the 1980s can be seen most clearly with Stallone himself and the noticeable changes in his physique from the original *Rocky* (1976) through to *Rocky V* (1990).

26. See in particular Sigmund Freud, "Analysis of a Phobia in a Five-Year-Old Boy" (1909), in vol. 10 (1955), in *S.E.*, pp. 1–149.

27. Freud, *Three Essays on the Theory of Sexuality.*

28. The last refers to *Not Quite Paradise* (1986), which is not quite an Animal Comedy—or, more accurately, it's an Animal Comedy that misguidedly tries to elevate the genre by substituting a terrorist attack for the final sporting event/prank.

29. In an article that explores the cultural significance of the James Bond films in the late 1960s and the 1970s, Lee Drummond, drawing on an analysis of William Arens, notes the ascendancy of professional football in this period, which he ties to "an emergent corporate culture in the postwar United States." Drummond, "The Story of Bond," in Hervé Varenne, ed., *Symbolizing America* (Lincoln: University of Nebraska Press, 1986), pp. 82–85.

I don't want to push the possible analogues to Animal Comedy too far, but this idea at least comes to mind because of the final football game in *M*A*S*H*, and it does at least suggest some of the ambivalences at the heart of Animal Comedy: the group in the comedies are dedicated to the indulgence of individual desire, yet the primacy of the group also suggests that individual desire must, as in a football game, be to some degree made subordinate to the demands of the group.

30. Thomas Schatz draws a comparable analogy between genre and language as structures that facilitate communication through expectation. Schatz, *Hollywood Genres* (New York: Random House, 1971), pp. 18–22.

31. In making these disclaimers, I am aware of what Andrew Tudor has aptly termed the "empiricist dilemma," which catches us "in a circle that first requires that the films be isolated, for which purposes a criterion is necessary, but the criterion is, in turn, meant to emerge from the empirically established common characteristics of the films." Tudor, *Theories of Film* (New York: Viking, 1973), p. 133.

How can I claim a genre when part of my definition consists of films that in some of their aspects are exceptional? I cannot fully address this kind of question here because my concerns in this book are not specifically with genre theory. Nonetheless, recognizing the problems confronted in defining any genre, I feel I should at least offer my grounds for determining the emergence of a new one. And my grounds are entirely empirical—the discovery of an active moviegoer that a sizable group of comedies had appeared which seemed to recall earlier successful comedies. By the time of *Revenge of the Nerds* (1984), at least, I found myself entering the theater with very definite expectations of what I would be seeing, and that kind of anticipation is a key to the experience of most genre films. It had become clear that the films in some way were addressing each other as well as the audience, establishing reference points that assumed audience familiarity. For a more thorough consideration of this problem, I refer the reader to Jeanine Basinger's discussion of the characteristics of the World War II combat film, which is particularly relevant to my concerns because she directly deals with the "empiricist dilemma" in trying to define an *emerging* genre (Basinger, *The World War II Combat Film*, pp. 15–82).

32. Rick Altman has determined an opposition between what he calls the "semantic" and "syntactic" elements of genre that can help clarify the distinction between Animal Comedy and teenpix. By semantic he means the "common traits, attitudes, characters, shots, locations, sets, and the like"; by syntax he intends something more concerned with structure, "certain constitutive relationships between undesignated and variable placeholders." Altman, "A Semantic/Syntactic Approach to Film Genre," in Barry Keith Grant, ed., *Film Genre Reader* (Austin: University of Texas Press, 1986), pp. 26–40.

With this distinction as a guide, I can say that Animal Comedy and teenpix may on occasion share semantic elements, but the syntax of Animal Comedy is distinctive, as I have tried to make clear in my discussion of its structural elements.

7. *Sex and Power*

1. For Braudy this indicates a "desexualized masculine image" that ultimately leads in a very different direction from Animal Comedy because the guns "don't *mean* penises, they *are* penises" (emphasis in original). Still, they do function symbolically to the extent that they are substitutes—something very different from what occurs in *Porky's*. Braudy, *The World in a Frame* (Garden City, N.Y.: Anchor/Doubleday, 1976), p. 178.

2. In *What Was Literature?* Leslie Fiedler provides an extended discussion of images of the "bad nigger" in American literature, images that *Porky's* is clearly drawing on at this point. See Fiedler, *What Was Literature?: Class Culture and Mass Society* (New York: Simon and Schuster, 1982), pp. 169–231.

3. In most of my descriptions in this book I accept that my "we," "us," and "our" has a male bias—since most of these films are indeed specifically geared toward a male audience. But *Porky's* is something of an exception in this regard, which probably accounts for its greater commercial success than many other films in the genre. At the time of its release, Stuart Byron predicted very high grosses for the film because of unexpected results from two test-market bookings of the film: "Like most people, I assumed it was just another *Animal House* ripoff made on a low budget ($4.5 million), which would be given a quick playoff on the teenage exploitation market with the thought that it could become profitable on the basis of very low returns. . . . But the word on the Hollywood grapevine said *Porky's* was unique: It was variously termed 'the raunchiest,' 'the grossest,' and even 'the most disgusting' movie any major studio had ever been involved with. . . . In fact, it's doing so well [in the test-market bookings] that it's clear the movie must have crossed over into groups other than its target audience of young males. When I saw *Porky's* last week, I saw why: Though as raunchy as its reputation indicated, it's also so tender and sweet in its attitude toward the sexual anxieties of its characters that it can be enjoyed by women. And, being set in the '50s, it has a nostalgia element which appeals to older folks. . . . 'What our research showed,' says [Irv] Ivers [20th Century-Fox's senior marketing executive], 'is that a raunchy, hard-R campaign appealed only to teenage boys. By stressing the charm as well as the sex in the movie, we got women and older people, too.' " Byron, "Rules of the Game," *Village Voice*, March 16, 1982, p. 50.

As the trim naked body is clearly established as an appealing aesthetic object (that includes boys/men as well as girls/women), the fat naked body is presented as an object of disgust; the appeal and the frustration felt in *Porky's* is clearly intended to be the same for both male and female audiences.

4. While the *Jaws* reference is clear, I should note that Clark himself actually utilized the subjective camera-equals-villain's-viewpoint in his own *Black Christmas* (1975; aka *Silent Night, Evil Night* and *Stranger in the House*), a film that eerily anticipates *Halloween* (1978) and *Friday the 13th* (1980).

5. A large part of the confusion of *Porky's* stems from the way in which sexual arousal repeatedly invokes castration throughout the film. For Freud the fear of castration is itself the motive for resolving the Oedipus complex, which "must come to an end because the time has come for its dissolution, just as the milk-teeth fall out when the permanent ones begin to press forward." See Freud, "The Dissolution of the Oed-

ipus Complex" (1924) in vol. 19 (1961) in *S.E.*, 24 vols. (London: Hogarth Press, 1953–1974), pp. 173–82.

In *Porky's* sexual arousal inevitably gives way to fear of castration, rather than moving beyond it, so however much sex acts as a dividing line between childhood and adulthood, sexual arousal inevitably arouses anxiety that returns the subject to the fears of childhood.

6. The confusion most often noted in the popular press in this period opposes concern over the rising rates of teenage pregnancy to a reluctance to provide birth control for teenagers. A sophisticated exploration of the ways in which contradiction is built into the discourses on romantic love and sexuality employed by teenage girls to define their own sexual experiences may be found in Joyce Canaan, "Why a 'Slut' Is a 'Slut': Cautionary Tales of Middle-Class Teenage Girls' Morality," in Hervé Varenne, ed., *Symbolizing America* (Lincoln: University of Nebraska Press, 1986), pp. 184–208.

7. Helen Lefkowitz Horowitz has shown that fraternities were formed in opposition to the power wielded by faculty and administration, so the opposition to the administration here is a familiar one. Of special interest here is their insistence on a kind of democratic spirit. As Horowitz notes, "College men placed a high value on mutuality, on the bonds that united them with each other against their faculty. They insisted they did not share the social prejudices of their era and boasted of their 'democracy.' While their words suggest a degree of egalitarianism, their social structure was intensely hierarchical. What collegiate democracy meant was that college men did not fully accept the status system of the broader society but created their own where athletic prowess, social grace, and a sense of fair play weighed significantly." Horowitz, *Campus Life: Undergraduate Cultures from the End of the Eighteenth Century to the Present* (New York: Knopf, 1987), p. 13.

The animals of *Animal House* take this opposition a step further by throwing out the values of "athletic prowess, social grace, and a sense of fair play."

8. In fact, what often takes place in this film is an inversion of traditional ethnic humor, with Wasps now occupying the position of the rejected group. Joseph Boskin and Joseph Dorinson's consideration of the value of ethnic humor in American culture is relevant here: "Ethnic humor in the United States originated as a function of social class feelings of superiority and white racial antagonisms, and expresses the continuing resistance of advantaged groups to unrestrained immigration and to emancipation's black subcitizens barred from opportunities for participation and productivity." Boskin and Dorinson, "Ethnic Humor: Subversion and Survival," in Arthur Power Dudden, ed., *American Humor* (New York: Oxford University Press, 1987), p. 97.

In itself this inversion of ethnic humor in *Animal House* may signal the ascension to power of immigrant groups and minorities once denied power. The screenwriters for the film seem to have been aware of the social transformation this inversion indicated. In an interview that all three gave the *New York Times* before the film premiered, one of them, Harold Ramis, noted: "What I think happened to make fraternities what they were was that, after the Second World War, the G.I. Bill sent millions of people to college, and a lot of them were older and their behavior was—well, you know, guys in the army probably learned a lot of animal behavior." Mark Singer, "Remembrance of Things Beastly," *New York Times*, July 23, 1978, sec. 2, p. 13.

The idea of learning animal behavior is oxymoronic, but clearly what Ramis had in mind here was the influx of whole classes of people into places of privilege where they were once denied entry. The implied shift in the power structure is made explicit in the film's epilogue, as I note later in this chapter.

9. Because of the strong connections, direct and indirect, between *Animal House* and "Saturday Night Live," I think it worth citing here the observation by a member of the production staff for "SNL": "Cherie Fortis, who was hired in the third year as an assistant to Lorne's [i.e., producer Lorne Michaels'] assistant, Kathy Minkowsky, was surprised that for a show that considered itself anarchistic, everyone seemed to be very concerned with hierarchy. Many times she was told that she was not to do something because it was somebody else's job to do, and she found that she was not to speak to the cast members directly—there were those whose job it was to relay messages to them." Doug Hill and Jeff Weingrad, *Saturday Night* (1986; rpt., New York: Vintage, 1987), p. 321.

10. I also suspect that part of Murphy's extraordinary appeal for white middle-class audiences derives from an awareness that he is in fact a middle-class black from Long Island *playing* at being a ghetto black. He is therefore finally more one of "us" than one of "them" (which is why his successful revolts against the powers of white culture offer a safe titillation for us). Richard Pryor is potentially more subversive than Murphy, although this is a side of Pryor that appears more in his concert films than in the narrative features, which usually find ways of hemming him in.

11. While American popular music for the last half of the twentieth century has been centrally influenced by black music, in 1978 (the year *Animal House* was released) Michael Moffatt surprisingly found music itself as a racial dividing line in a college dorm: "*The* salient life-style difference cited by whites with reference to blacks was musical taste." At a party held to provide some sense of unity between white and black living groups, whites danced only to music chosen by white organizers, blacks only to music chosen by black organizers. Much as *Animal House* uses music to signal an allegiance to black culture and values, Moffatt's report suggests that allegiance is based on a fantasy of unity. Moffatt, "The Discourse of the Dorm: Race, Friendship, and 'Culture' Among College Youth," in Varenne, *Symbolizing America*, pp. 169, 173.

12. In the *New York Times* interview previously mentioned, Chris Miller, another of the screenwriters, responds to the interviewer's request to "recite his college achieve-ments" by adopting something of the self-congratulatory tone Peter Riegert displays in his relation to the black band, although Miller quite specifically places his reply in a context of gross behavior: "I stayed drunk for 37 consecutive days, breaking the old record set by Goblin, Class of '55. I also brought the first black bands to Dartmouth—rhythm and blues, that is, Chuck Berry, in fact." Singer, "Remembrance of Things Beastly," *New York Times*, July 23, 1978, sec. 2, p. 13.

13. There is one other scene that plays around with rape. When Tom Hulce's high school date passes out at a party after drinking too much, a devil and an angel appear to him, one advising rape, the other advising chastity. As is often true in the Western tradition, the devil gets the best laugh lines.

8. Outer Limits of the Inner City

1. The development of these films is chronicled in Donald Bogle, *Toms, Coons, Mulattos, Mammies, and Bucks: An Interpretative History of Blacks in American Films* (New York: Viking, 1973); Thomas Cripps, *Black Film as Genre* (Bloomington: Indiana

University Press, 1979); and Daniel J. Leab, *From Sambo to Superspade: The Black Experience in Motion Pictures* (London: Secker and Warburg, 1975).

2. Writing in 1973, Bogle attacked these films for often unconsciously perpetuating stereotypes of a more overtly racist past. Because of his general dislike for these films, he offers a curious reason for the great success of *Cotton Comes to Harlem* among black audiences: "The great irony of *Cotton Comes to Harlem*, and part of the reason it proved mindlessly entertaining, was that its audiences, at least black ones, were a step ahead of the director and knew the stereotypes to be just that. After so many dreary television programs on the 'race problem' and after a flood of newly published pseudo-relevant black literature, black audiences were content to sit back and laugh for a change. And so the audience triumphed over the picture" (Bogle, *Toms, Coons, Mulattos, Mammies, and Bucks*, p. 231). For an overview of contemporary response, see Charles Michener, "Black Movies," *Newsweek*, October 23, 1972, pp. 74–82.

3. Leab deals with the generally negative reception of "black community leaders and critics," who "blasted these films. . . . In addition to condemning the industry for showing black women as persons of loose morals, they charged that these movies glorified drugs, imitated successful white stereotypes, set forth impossible and ultimately debilitating fantasies, developed a negative image of the American black man and woman, and took no real cognizance of black oppression in the United States, This criticism carried across political lines." Leab, *From Sambo to Superspade*, p . 258.

4. There are in fact other actors in the film (in bit parts) and supernumeraries who are listed in the end credits, but this beginning roster includes *all* the names that would normally appear in the opening credits.

5. The rise in popularity of major stars in the past could normally be traced by noting at what point in their career their names began to appear before the title.

6. Robin Wood has noted that teenage comedies are peculiarly lacking any indication of homosexual experience, although it is hardly unusual in adolescence. Wood, *Hollywood from Vietnam to Reagan* (New York: Columbia University Press, 1986), pp. 216–17.

7. Schumacher's two changes—the shift to a more racially diverse ensemble as well as positing a white central character—may well be a matter of commercial calculation, an attempt to make the film work more as a "crossover" film for white audiences, as *Car Wash* did not. Further, the film featured one black performer, Mr. T., already well known to white audiences from a television action series, "The 'A' Team."

8. The most obvious exception is Steven Spielberg's *The Color Purple*, which became one of the top-grossing films of 1985—and thus the highest-grossing film ever made having a predominantly black cast. While shrewd enough to cast in its lead role a woman previously more noted for her comedy talent (Whoopi Goldberg), I do not think that this alone is enough to account for the film's great success and its emergence as one of the few genuine crossover movies. It is possible that its appeal, as in "The Cosby Show," lay in casting blacks as staunch defenders of family feeling.

9. Given their penchant for realistic presentation that does not depend on genre conventions, these films might seem like more of a departure from past blaxploitation than they in fact are. Consider one of the most commercially successful, *Boyz N the Hood* (1991), written and directed by John Singleton. The film is about two boys, one with enough intellectual talent to get him to college, the other hoping to go to college on a sports scholarship. The latter boy does get a scholarship (after successfully studying for and passing the SAT requirements), but is killed in gang violence. This rough

plot outline foregrounds the similarities with *Cooley High*, but I do not want to minimize the differences. All I want to do is suggest ways in which we might see connections to the past to indicate that we might now see a tradition of *black* filmmaking establishing itself, with models taken from past black films.

10. It is now estimated that about 25 percent of the audience for theatrical films is black.

9. Bill Murray, Anarchic Conservative

1. Doug Hill and Jeff Weingrad report that there was some attempt to make it seem Murray was not in fact succeeding Chase: "[Producer] Lorne [Michaels] had kept Billy waiting in the wings to help him avoid as much as possible the onus of being Chevy Chase's replacement, but there was plenty of resistance anyway." Audiences at least perceived him as the substitute Chase, and it took some time through the first season for him to find his own voice. He eventually did become Chase's replacement on the "Weekend Update" segment, but that was only a couple of seasons later. See Hill and Weingrad, *Saturday Night* (1986; rpt., New York: Vintage, 1987), pp. 250–57.

2. *Time*, July 16, 1979, p. 60.

3. The attack was done in the style of a Bill Murray monologue, borrowing Murray's distinctive blend of envy, aggression, and deflection: "Hey, maniacs, isn't that the truth? Because let's face it, there's a lot of comedians out there who are so funny, they're not even funny. . . . And you, Chevy Chase, sure you're handsome, you're adorable, you're well built—you think comedy is sex? Why don't ya try some variations!" John Swenson, "Bill Murray: Maniac For All Seasons." *Rolling Stone*, April 20, 1978, p. 25.

4. Swenson, "Bill Murray," *Rolling Stone*, p. 25.

5. The "force" might well be American technology since an almost mystical power is granted machines in both *Stripes* and *Ghostbusters* (both films directed by Ivan Reitman and coscripted by Harold Ramis). This is not all that different from *Star Wars* itself, where all the gadgetry—including the gadgetry to create the gadgetry in the film's special effects—became one of the prime appeals of the movie.

6. The uncertain ground that we occupy with regard to belief is perhaps clearest in the Spielberg-Lucas *Indiana Jones* movies, which might be seen simultaneously as homage and satire. The films presuppose (dubiously, I think) that the conventions they draw on were once taken seriously. In this way, we can feel both our distance from the material and our conscious decision to believe its fantasies.

7. Cedric H. Whitman has defined an important aspect of Aristophanic comedy that is relevant here: "the modern Greek word *poneria* . . . best expresses what the heroes of Aristophanes are up to. *Poneria* in modern Greek indicates not wickedness, but the ability to get the advantage of somebody or some situation by virtue of an unscrupulous, but thoroughly enjoyable exercise of craft. Its aim is simple—to come out on top; its methods are devious, and the more intricate, but the more delightful." Whitman, *Aristophanes and the Comic Hero* (Cambridge: Harvard University Press, 1964), p. 30.

8. It has been argued that Aristophanes is in fact a very conservative playwright, and it is only the fantastic nature of the play that enables him to turn the world upside down without offering any apparent reversion to right-side-up at the end of the play. This is likely true since this play that unseats the gods was itself part of a religious festival. But it is still worth noting that the comic vision of this play understands a

necessity for a consequentiality in its premises. The play itself never gives any indication that its comic propositions are not to be taken seriously, so that by the end the vitality of Pisthetairos' aggression becomes reason enough for the play's sense of celebration. The unlimited and insatiable ego of man is given free rein to delight the audience. By contrast, Animal Comedy presents a more limiting sense to the extent that it insists on maintaining the social structure with which it began. K. J. Dover discusses the difficulty of defining Aristophanes politically in *Aristophanic Comedy* (Berkeley: University of California Press, 1972), pp. 33–36.

9. In *What Was Literature?* Leslie Fiedler cites a passage from a Thomas Dixon novel in which a white character says to a black, "One drop of your blood in my family could push it backward three thousand years in history." Fiedler comments: "It is not, of course, with 'fact' that we are dealing here (though many reputable anthropologists of that time would have insisted that Everett Lowell spoke 'scientific truth') but fantasy: a fantasy based on fear of 'racial mongrelization' resulting from Emancipation, which presumably freed black males not just from slavery but from restraints on their lust for white women." Fiedler, *What Was Literature?: Class Culture and Mass Society* (New York: Simon and Schuster, 1982), pp. 182–83.

10. In his biographical study of Reagan, Garry Wills constructs this point somewhat differently by noting Reagan's ability to believe things that he must have known at some point did not in fact happen, most egregiously his claims that he photographed Nazi death camps after the war. In discussing Reagan's veneration of "modern individualism" in the reality of a world that can only work by interdependencies, Wills writes, "Reagan makes this absurdity believable, partly by believing it so thoroughly himself." Wills, *Reagan's America: Innocents at Home* (Garden City, N.Y.: Doubleday, 1987), p. 381.

I think Wills's point accounts for why Reagan is better able than Murray to negotiate moves from mockery to sincerity, but in both there remains an inner emptiness—the mystery of belief that Kaiser notes (see text and following note)—which I find to be of particular importance for the period, as my subsequent discussion of Christopher Lasch should make clear.

11. Robert G. Kaiser, "Your Host of Hosts," *New York Review of Books*, November 28, 1984, pp. 38–41.

12. Lewis Grossberger, "Bill Murray—Making It Up As he Goes." *Rolling Stone*, August 20, 1981 (emphasis added). This article was part of the advance publicity for *Stripes.*

13. *Club Paradise* (1986), directed by Harold Ramis and written by Ramis and Murray's brother Brian Doyle-Murray was intended as a starring vehicle for Murray. His part was eventually taken by Robin Williams. Murray also had a cameo role in *Little Shop of Horrors* (1986).

14. Wolfe, "The Me Decade and the Third Great Awakening," in Wolfe, *Mauve Gloves and Madmen, Clutter and Vine* (New York: Farrar, Straus and Giroux, 1976), pp. 165, 167.

15. Christopher Lasch, *The Culture of Narcissism: American Life in an Age of Diminishing Expectations* (New York: W. W. Norton, 1978), p. 7.

16. Christopher Lasch, *The Minimal Self: Psychic Survival in Troubled Times* (New York: W. W. Norton, 1984), p. 19.

17. Lasch, *The Culture of Narcissism*, p. 5.

18. Murray's screen persona seems to have become increasingly trapped in this kind of plot pattern. A rare and charming attempt to do a romantic comedy crossed with a caper film, *Quick Change* (1990), failed commercially. His comeback film, *What About Bob?* (1991), restores the plot pattern with a vengeance so that it explicitly defines a genuine pathology.

Groundhog Day (1993) represents Murray's greatest success in a romantic comedy, although the romantic plot is arguably of secondary importance to the fantasy conceit of a man who must relive the same day over and over again. The effectiveness of this film may lay in the way the fantasy plays on the sadomasochistic aspects of Murray's persona I've outlined here: he is both helpless in his inability to escape the ever-re-peating day at the same time that the very repetition gives him an extraordinary power over events. This comic bind reaches its most poignant moment when Murray succeeds in making Andie MacDowell see him differently and perhaps more honestly. Murray remarks to himself ruefully that she will not be able to remember any of this the next day when the same day starts up again.

19. This description of Old Comedy is from Robert M. Torrance, *The Comic Hero* (Cambridge: Harvard University Press, 1978), p. 40.

20. Peter Wollen has described the western in terms of "shifting antinomies." See *Signs and Meaning in the Cinema* (Bloomington: Indiana University Press, 1969), pp. 94–102.

21. Richard Corliss, "Is There Life After Teenpix?" *Time*, February 18, 1985, p. 90.

10. Sexual Politics

1. Cameron Crowe, *Fast Times at Ridgemont High* (Garden City, N.Y.: Doubleday, 1981). Page numbers in parentheses following subsequent citations in the text are from this edition.

2. But not necessarily without adults so that Oedipal battles can still occur, although in a displaced fashion, as in the fights with the administration in *Animal House* or the whorehouse owner and his sheriff brother in *Porky's*.

3. Mike Nichols's *The Graduate* (1967) might provide the definitive forerunner of this and perhaps drives it to even greater extremes by casting which suggests that two empty-headed Wasp parents have sired a sensitive Jewish son. The film may embody the extreme sense of separation between parents and children I am concerned with here, but in most other ways it is very different from Animal Comedy and can't be seen exerting the influence of either *M*A*S*H* or *American Graffiti*. In particular, throughout *The Graduate* there is a nagging sense that sex is unpleasant, a constant revulsion, an attitude that sets it decisively apart from the later films.

4. Andrew Sarris, "Films In Focus," *Village Voice*, July 30, 1979, p. 43.

5. Northrop Frye has noted that it is one object of New Comedy to have the entire cast of characters on the stage at the end of the play, an important point for the sense of renewal and continuity inherent in New Comedy. For all that the future pulls away from the constrictions of the past, it is necessary to remind ourselves that the future also derives from the past so that all can be united in one celebratory vision at the end. Frye, "The Argument of Comedy," in D. A. Robertson, Jr., ed., *English Institute Essays* (New York: Columbia University Press, 1949), pp. 60–61.

6. This point is most clearly made in Paul Brickman's *Risky Business* (1983), per-

haps because the film seems willing to explore the meanings of its own conventions and devices. The appearance of Tom Cruise's parents is appropriately brief (mostly limited to the beginning and end of the film), and there is the usual problem of how such a sensitive boy could have such crass and insensitive parents. The film seems to suggest an answer with a very long and elaborate point-of-view tracking shot in which the camera impersonates Cruise seeing his parents off at the airport (and the parents appearing at their most fully grotesque). The device possibly derives from *The Graduate*, where Dustin Hoffman's father forces him to model for assembled guests a new scuba outfit the father has bought, and the camera takes Hoffman's embarrassed point of view by photographing the whole thing through a diving mask.

7. The film of *Fast Times* does, however, offer a direct invocation of *American Graffiti* by the jokey epilogue with which it concludes. It also has a little homage to Fritz Lang's *The Big Heat* (1953), but that's another matter entirely (see text at note 12, and note 12 below).

8. I am not sure of their respective ages, but Jennifer Jason Leigh in this film looks a good deal younger than Sue Lyon did in *Lolita* (1961). In fact, Leigh in many ways fulfills Nabokov's description of Lolita more than Lyon, and this film frequently captures some of the disturbing tone of that novel more successfully than the film version of *Lolita* itself.

9. The scene is transposed from the book where it occurs much later in the narrative and has both Linda and a by-now greatly experienced Stacy giving instruction to a newcomer. There is one interesting change from book to movie which I think shows the male bias of the book: in the book the carrot of the film is a banana that keeps getting marks left in it by the young girl who is still wearing braces. The central image in the scene, then, and certainly the one given the strongest emotional resonance, is a kind of mutilation and implied castration, so that finally the scene deals more with male fear than female curiosity.

10. I do not think the film intends any specific criticism of high school beyond a general questioning of its educational efficacy, but I should note that the emphasis on rules so common in high school is in effect a kind of distancing measure, a way of dealing with oversized classes that add to making personal exchange difficult. Rules also serve to keep students in their place and further emphasize the gulf between adolescence and adulthood as Edgar Z. Friedenberg has noted in *Coming of Age in America* (New York: Vintage, 1969).

11. The last we see of Linda in the book she is talking with Stacy about whether or not she should accept Doug's marriage proposal. There remains the possibility that she herself might break off with him because she wants to go to junior college.

12. The event does derive from the book, but the way the scene is shot and a minor change in the action (flinging the coffee in the man's face rather than pouring it on his hand) are enough to evoke the Lang film.

11. Politics of the Image

1. The fact that the director of this film could claim good taste gives some indication of precisely how elastic this standard of value may be. "And *Animal House* Begat . . . ," *Time*, April 15, 1985, p. 103.

2. Henri Bergson, "Laughter," in Wylie Sypher, ed., *Comedy* (Garden City, N.Y.: Doubleday Anchor, 1956), p. 87.

3. It was in this period that Italian-American organizations were able to force Paramount Pictures to omit the word "mafia" from the film version of *The Godfather* (1972).

4. The first film to keep parents insistently offscreen, *Summer of '42* (1971), explores the tie between rejecting parents and accepting maturity in a far more paradoxical way than any of the later films. The mother of fifteen-year-old Hermie (Gary Grimes) never appears in the film: her presence is indicated solely by offscreen requests to get something from the grocery store or commands to keep his room clean, and occasional snatches of soap operas she listens to coming from her kitchen, which we never actually enter. The film ties Hermie's sexual awakening to this rejection of his mother but in a symbolically inverted way: he becomes infatuated with Dorothy (Jennifer O'Neill), a lonely war bride of twenty-two (a critical seven-year gap at this juncture in their lives). His first conversation with her is in her kitchen, after he has helped her carry home groceries, while his next meeting, which he treats as something of a date, has him helping her tidy up her house by putting boxes away in an attic. In other words, he does precisely those things for her that he has done for his mother earlier in the film, which makes it fitting that Dorothy should take the lead in his sexual initiation as well. Maturity comes in sexual awakening and rejection of dependency on parents, but in the process new kinds of dependency are being embraced, if not always knowingly.

5. Garry Wills, *Reagan's America: Innocents at Home* (Garden City, N.Y.: Doubleday, 1987), p. 388.

6. Although *Back to the Future* seems determined to raise the specter of the Oedipus complex in order to dismiss it, here it seems to accept fully the Freudian notion of homosexuality deriving from a perceived lack of masculine prowess. But for all its emphasis on nerds and uncertain males, the film emerges as a more celebratory view of masculine power than even most Animal Comedies, where the power of female sexuality often remains (at least implicitly) a counterbalance, and often even a threat.

7. The transformation of the father in *Back to the Future* plays into an American notion of unlimited aspiration, not unlike the idea that any boy can grow up to be president. This point was made explicit when "Saturday Night Live" parodied the film with a skit that had Ron Reagan himself playing the Michael J. Fox role: in the skit, Ron traveled into the past and saved his bumpkinish father and near-alcoholic mother from their complementary afflictions so that they could eventually become President and First Lady.

8. It is not difficult to read a suggestion of class conflict into *Porky's*, for example, in that the whorehouse seems to belong to a different class of people from the neatly dressed high school students who want to gain access to it: the whorehouse is a privileged place that the more privileged are barred from, so the more privileged stage a neat little revolution in which they totally wipe out the place for those who actually do use it. This seems to be the only kind of revolution American culture seems willing to confront, one from the middle classes waged with the aim of maintaining their privileges. None of this is made overt, of course, although within the group of boys the film does work out a prejudicial issue somewhat in social terms. The one lad who resents the new Jewish boy is tagged as being lower class and under the undue influence of

his redneck father. The film then traces his regeneration as he rejects the brutalizing father and moves toward a middle-class norm of tolerance that extends to Jews but not necessarily to the lower classes.

9. Possibly no film has explored this with so much unnerving incisiveness as King Vidor's *Stella Dallas* (1937), where clothes are presented as the key class marker: Stella is inevitably tied to the lower classes simply by the way she dresses and the way her clothes are a vulgarized expression of her desire for class. In general, there seems to be a much stronger sense of social class in films of the 1930s than in subsequent periods when the middle class totally dominated films. This shift perhaps reflects the transformation of the American working classes into the middle class, with the change finding its most acute expression in clothing (especially in the transformation of working-class jeans into "designer" wear for mass consumption, thus leveling haute couture at the same time that it elevates lower-class clothing). Vidor's prescience in focusing on clothing derives from his acute sense of the need in American society to find outward signs of social class since there is nothing either innate or inevitable about class allegiances.

10. Translated into the film's terms, the result would have to be, say, a brainy football player who is good-looking, well-built, and at least as interested in computers as he is in football. The film of course doesn't even allow for this kind of possibility because its grotesque style necessarily deals with excessively exaggerated stereotypes, which themselves create the necessary polarities.

11. In this regard, the change in the ending from *Pygmalion* to *My Fair Lady* possibly makes the play more acceptable to an American audience—and not just by giving it a so-called happy ending. It might in fact be seriously questioned how happy a long life with Henry Higgins might actually be. Rather, Eliza's staying with Higgins in effect continues to tie her to her lowly origins, her "real" self, which has been so artfully obscured by Higgins's tutoring.

12. While gender studies has recently appropriated *passing* as a term for crossdressing, I am using it here in its original racial meaning.

13. The scene from *The Bingo Long Traveling All-Stars and Motor Kings* described in chapter 8 is relevant here in that it deals with ways in which blacks have to compromise any show of power they might make.

14. Sometimes in Animal Comedy, however, a film will end having precisely the same order with which it began, and with nothing changed in spite of all the anarchic experiences that intervened—as *Risky Business* (1983) most clearly exemplifies (and in the most ambivalent fashion).

15. Eric Bentley, *Theater of War* (Abridged ed., New York: Viking, 1973), pp. viii–ix. As often, Bentley seems to be consciously going against academic ways of looking at plays, emphasizing instead their nature as spectacle.

16. This is often a hard thing to admit, so I am not especially comfortable even in asking the question in these terms and feel I ought to offer praise for these performers in other films. Edwards did in fact play a leading role in Kanew's next film, *Gotcha!* (1985), so in *Revenge of the Nerds* it would seem most likely that *his* nerddom is conveyed more through clothing and posture than actual looks. Still, he doesn't really look the leading man type: *Gotcha!* was a box-office failure, while Edwards's next role, as Tom Cruise's best friend in *Top Gun*, found him in one of the highest-grossing films of 1986. In the old Hollywood, he probably would have been instantly typed as the leading man's best friend for the rest of his career.

17. If nerds have moved more to the center of this social order, our acceptance of this change perhaps reflects a change in society as well. If the film attempts a kind of rehabilitation for a group previously excluded through derisive laughter, the fact that this group has indeed achieved a degree of power facilitates that transformation. *Revenge of the Nerds* plays on a conventional opposition of brain and brawn that still has some cultural resonance for us, but we recognize that such a dichotomy is beside the point, a dead issue. The film ends with a radical redistribution of power that recognizes where the real seat of power is in an increasingly technological world. "Adams College," the site of the film, becomes known as the "Home of the Atoms." More specifically, the images of the film explicitly portray the panty raid in terms of modern technological warfare, as a kind of war sortie. In this context, it seems fitting that Lewis should seduce Betty while dressed as Darth Vader, an avatar for a movie that glories in technological excess. In effect, the rise of technology as a dominant force in our society is changing the ways in which we understand and recognize power, a point that *Revenge of the Nerds* at least implicitly acknowledges.

12. Power Without Politics

1. In *Animal House* the car belongs to an older brother, but we learn that he's a doctor to signify that he's already a responsible member of adult society; the destruction of his car, which happens incidentally in the escape from the black nightclub, becomes implicitly an attack on the values of adult society.

2. I am thinking particularly here of *Caddyshack* (1980) and *Moving Violations* (1985) because both films raise, at least implicitly, the possibility of revolt. Of the two, *Caddyshack*, with its country club setting, offers more room for social criticism of an exclusionary institution, yet it always seems to pull its punches and directs most of its barbs toward one individual (Ted Knight) rather than toward the institution itself. *Moving Violations* sets up the conditions for revolt (since most of the violators sent to the driving school feel themselves unfairly condemned), but then it finally ends up going nowhere. In neither film is the existence of the institution ever questioned or its power to define those who take part in it.

3. I wouldn't expect that either director Dinner or his actor Kevin Dillon actually had this in mind, but Rooney's expression in this shot remarkably echoes a moment in *Way Out West*, a Laurel and Hardy feature from 1939. For reasons too complicated to detail here, Ollie is forcing Stan to eat the brim of his famous bowler hat. Stan cries a bit before acceding to Ollie's demand, but when he finally does, he actually starts to enjoy his meal. There is a brief moment—when he is on the verge of discovering that he actually likes the brim—that strikingly anticipates Kevin Dillon's expression in *Heaven Help Us.*

4. Distance would have laughter here functioning solely in a defensive mode, but there is celebration as well. In this regard, Suzanne Langer discusses comedy and laughter in a way that is particularly useful for Animal Comedy: "Comedy is an art form that arises naturally whenever people are gathered to celebrate life, in spring festivals, triumphs, birthdays, weddings, or initiations. For it expresses the elementary strains and resolutions of animate nature, the animal drives that persists even in human nature, the delight man takes in his special mental gifts that make him the lord of creation; it is an image of human vitality holding its own in the world amid the surprises of unplanned

coincidence." Langer, *Feeling and Form: A Theory of Art* (New York: Scribners, 1953), p. 331.

The effect of laughter may have multiple causes. While there is clearly a distancing function here, the laughter may also celebrate the resiliency of the kids, their ability to deal with whatever comes their way. This sense of resiliency is a key attribute of the animals in Animal Comedy.

5. Because of this, the one real break in the film's style comes with the bridgeman who is laughing at the ending of *Gunga Din*. It is not that such a crazy response is not possible in the real world, but the film never offers any explanation for his bizarre behavior, which marks him as a zany who would be more at home in the world of out-and-out farce than in a film that generally finds more realistic motivations for character behavior.

6. If any of the film is autobiographical, I assume this comes from screenwriter Charles Purpura, particularly in its focus on the Michael Dunne character (who, as has been noted, shows the kind of sensitivity usually reserved for poets—or maybe for writers in movies). Whether Michael Dinner (whose name sounds like that of the protagonist) had a similar background, I do not know; but the direction shows an attention to realistic detail and an awareness of the period and its mores to convey a sense of firsthand experience. In one respect, however, the film does blur its possible autobiographical responses by splitting the focus among three central characters and giving the concluding narration to Rooney. If Michael is a focal point for our reactions through the early sections of the film, Rooney has the final word, so the film's point of view ultimately presents an unexpected combination of the self-aware and the unaware.

7. *Fast Times* is somewhat different in this regard in that it does not set up real antagonists to the kids (although the teachers do come pretty close to caricature and the parents are absent as always in these films). The absence of the parents dilutes the Oedipal conflicts usual in comedy and makes them an opposition easy to overcome.

8. Northrop Frye, "The Argument of Comedy," in D. A. Robertson, Jr., ed., *English Institute Essays* (New York: Columbia University Press, 1949), p. 61.

9. I wouldn't want to base an interpretation on the lazy and thick-tongued delivery typical of Donald Sutherland, but I am at least intrigued by the fact that it is very difficult to determine if he says "ideas" or "ideals" in his comment to John Heard cited above: "We all come to the order full of idea[l]s." It's as if the character himself cannot separate an idea from an ideal and must necessarily view all events in idealized terms, at the very moment he is telling Brother Timothy that reality forces you to give up your "idea[l]s."

10. I am here deliberately echoing the title of Alice Miller's book because I think her exploration of the sadistic impulses behind all pedagogy is especially relevant to this film. See Miller, *For Your Own Good: Hidden Cruelty in Child-rearing and the Roots of Violence* (New York: Farrar, Straus and Giroux, 1983).

11. There is an odd and, I would guess, unintentional echo of King Vidor's *The Crowd* (1928) here where Coney Island is supposed to fulfill the same function for its would-be lovers. The similarity is worth pointing out chiefly for its contrast: Vidor uses the circular motifs of the amusement park, its crowdedness and sense of hectic fun to inscribe a similarity between the everyday life of his city dwellers and the place of release they go to escape it: the irony is that they end up embracing precisely what they seek to escape. Dinner's Coney Island with its emptiness, slow movement, and

open space is a very different thing: it does offer the characters some escape, but one that can never extend very far.

13. Abusing Children

1. Stephen King cites this novel, along with Mary Shelley's *Frankenstein* (1818) and Robert Louis Stevenson's *Dr. Jekyll and Mr. Hyde* (1886), as the three formative works for contemporary horror fiction and film: "I believe it's impossible to discuss horror in the years 1950–80 with any real fullness of understanding unless we begin with these three books." King, *Danse Macabre* (New York: Everest House, 1981; rpt. New York: Berkley, 1983), p. 49.

2. All passages cited are from chapter 16 of Bram Stoker, *Dracula* (1897).

3. The most insistent exploration of sexual themes in vampire fiction may be found in David Pirie, *The Vampire Cinema* (London: Hamlyn, 1977).

4. I do not wish to claim that *Dracula* is the first work to do this. Stories aimed at children may demonstrate a similar way of defining the villain. To take one obvious fairy-tale example, the devouring witch of "Hansel and Gretel" is a projection of children's anxieties over their own oral aggressions, here transposed to a negative maternal imago. As Bruno Bettelheim has noted, "The witch, who is a personification of the destructive aspects of orality, is as bent on eating up the children as they are on demolishing her gingerbread house." Bettelheim, *The Uses of Enchantment: The Meaning and Importance of Fairy Tales* (New York: Knopf, 1976; rpt., New York: Vintage, 1977), p. 162.

5. Carl F. Wiedemann notes this when he suggests that nightmares may be "a survival mechanism of the species": "The fact that children so often dream of being attacked by animals may reflect ancient realities. Thus, nightmares which rouse the sleeper to a state of alertness may have originally had a protective function." Wiedemann, "REM and Non-REM Sleep and Its Relation to Nightmares and Night Terrors," in Henry Kellerman, ed., *The Nightmare* (New York: Columbia University Press, 1987), p. 92.

Judith Hanlon gives this a more psychoanalytic turn by citing a study that "has noted the prevalence in adults' and children's nightmares of oral themes, reflecting primitive forms of infantile rage and aggression. The nightmare frequently expresses anxiety derived from wishes to incorporate, devour, bite, or eat someone. [J.] Mack writes [in *Nightmares and Human Conflict*] that whatever developmental level the child or adult dreamer may have reached, conflicts tend to be represented in pregenital and especially oral terms; this he sees as an outgrowth of the overall regression characteristic of dreams." Hanlon, "The Nightmare and Intrapsychic Conflict," also in Kellerman, pp. 23–24.

6. In *The Dark Half* (1993), George Romero offers a more direct tribute to the influence of the Hitchcock film on his work by making flocks of birds the symbol of a force terrorizing his hero.

7. "The 'guts' used for the scene affectionately known as 'The Last Supper,' in which the zombies feast on the remains of Tom and Judy, were graciously provided by an investor who owned a chain of meat markets." Paul R. Gagne, *The Zombies That Ate Pittsburgh* (New York: Dodd, Mead, 1987), pp. 31–32.

8. Chronologically bookending *Night of the Living Dead* are *Bonnie and Clyde*

(1967) and *The Wild Bunch* (1969), both of which made extensive use of exploding blood-capsule technology and offer the prime examples of this new trend.

9. John Fraser, *Violence in the Arts* (Cambridge: Cambridge University Press, 1976), p. 73.

10. This is not to say that we don't ever feel some victims get what they deserve in horror films. This, in fact, may frequently be the case for victims in the earliest stages of the narrative since those who die off first are clearly disposable. Generally, the rhetoric of horror fiction requires some way of keeping us distanced from the victims, which may be accomplished by creating a sense of just desserts. Andrew Tudor has noted an ambivalent response toward mad scientists like Dr. Frankenstein in films of the early 1930s: we might value science, but since science may also go too far, we may feel a sense of justice in the scientist threatened by his own creation (Tudor, *Monsters and Mad Scientists: A Cultural History of the Horror Movie* [Oxford: Basil Blackwell, 1989], pp. 29–31). And Robin Wood sees in "teenie-kill" films like *Friday the 13th* (1980) a comparably divided response: "The satisfaction that youth audiences get from these films is presumably twofold: they identify both with the promiscuity and with the grisly and excessive punishment" (Wood, *Hollywood from Vietnam to Reagan* [New York: Columbia University Press, 1986], p. 196).

What is peculiar in *Night of the Living Dead* is the placement of the negative response at the end of the narrative toward a character who has gained a fair measure of audience sympathy as a mediator in disputes instigated by her bullying husband. The husband might be worth attacking, but the daughter disturbingly makes no distinction between father and mother.

11. The best evidence for this is the sequence eliminated from the original theatrical release of *Frankenstein* (1931) in which the monster drowned a little girl.

12. The rise of evil children was sufficiently prevalent to attract attention in a wide range of venues: James S. Gordon, "Demonic Children," *New York Times Book Review*, September 11, 1977, pp. 3, 52–53; Edgar Z. Friedenberg, "Children as Objects of Fear and Loathing," *Educational Studies* (Spring 1979), pp. 63–75; Ann Douglas, "The Dream of the Wise Child: Freud's 'Family Romance' Revisited in Contemporary Narratives of Horror," *Prospects* 9 (1984): 293–348; and Wheeler Dixon, "The Child as Demon in Films Since 1961," *Films in Review* (February 1988), pp. 78–83.

13. King, *Danse Macabre*, p. 253.

14. For a discussion of the role of childhood trauma in King's fiction, see Lenore C. Terr, M.D., "Terror Writing by the Formerly Terrified: A Look at Stephen King," *Psychoanalytic Study of the Child* 44 (1989): 369–90.

15. King, *Danse Macabre*, p. 181.

16. What constitutes the horror film can change over time, as Andrew Tudor's book (*Monsters and Mad Scientists*) demonstrates by tracing changing notions of horror. In my own experience, students today do not consider *King Kong* (1933) a horror film and are surprised to learn that contemporary audiences did. The remake of *The Bad Seed* might have established a connection of the subject matter to the horror film, but the indirect presentation made it more suitable as a TV movie. With the movie theater a place of license, the contemporary horror film contributed to the expanded form of expression by fully embracing gross-out. In consequence, the contemporary horror film began to seem qualitatively different from its predecessors.

17. See for example the various reviews in *Time* (April 12, 1954, p. 117; December

20, 1954, p. 59; September 17, 1956, p. 100); *Newsweek*, December 20, 1954, p. 57; *Life*, September 17, 1956, p. 141; *The New Yorker*, December 18, 1954, pp. 54–56; *America*, December 25, 1954, p. 346; and so on.

18. *Them!* in fact belongs to the older tradition of horror as I have defined it because our introduction to the giant ants in the film is seen through the eyes of a traumatized child who has watched her parents being devoured by these nuclear monsters.

19. "Books—Mystery and Crime," *The New Yorker*, April 10, 1954, p. 151.

20. A biography of William March notes: "There is a certain irony in the fact that March considered *The Bad Seed* the worst book he had ever written. To his brother Peter, he referred to it as being little more than a potboiler. His reaction to the book's success was one of incredulity. On one occasion he confided that he thought it an almost vulgar work, one which he regarded even with some embarrassment." Roy S. Simmonds, *The Two Worlds of William March* (University: University of Alabama Press, 1984), p. 302.

In a letter Maxwell Anderson wrote around the time of *The Bad Seed*, he also referred to the work as "a potboiler." Laurence G. Avery, ed., *Dramatist in America: Letters of Maxwell Anderson* (Chapel Hill: University of North Carolina Press, 1977).

21. See for example reviews in *Newsweek*, December 20, 1954, p. 57; *Time*, September 17, 1956; *The New Yorker*, December 18, 1954, pp. 54–56); *Saturday Review*, June 5, 1954, pp. 33–34; and *Commonweal*, September 28, 1956, p. 633.

22. Dennis Giles writes about the "pleasure of *not* seeing" as a distinctive feature of the horror movie. See Giles, "Conditions of Pleasure in Horror Cinema," in Barry Keith Grant, ed., *Planks of Reason: Essays on the Horror Film* (Metuchen, N.J.: Scarecrow Press, 1984), pp. 38–52.

23. This is the one element that really unites the three books King thinks inaugurates the modern horror novel, but it is also something that has been commented on by a number of writers on post-*Exorcist* horror films. See especially Robin Wood in *Hollywood from Vietnam to Reagan*. Tudor's comprehensive study of the history of horror films (*Monsters and Mad Scientists*) thoroughly documents this shift in the concerns of horror.

24. "Mr. March writes with fine, cold restraint, and his baby Gorgon might easily be the envy and despair of her rather less accomplished prototype in 'The Children's Hour.'" "Books—Mystery and Crime," *The New Yorker*, April 10, 1954, p. 151. See also Wolcott Gibb ("Rhoda Penmark, the baby Gorgon . . ."), "The Theatre—Naughty Girl," *The New Yorker*, December 18, 1954, p. 54.

25. Forsaking his previous psychoanalytic interpretation of the horror film, Noël Carroll has proposed a cognitive approach that has some relevance here: "Monsters are not physically threatening; they are cognitively threatening. They are threats to common knowledge" (Carroll, *The Philosophy of Horror or Paradoxes of the Heart* [New York: Routledge, 1990], p. 34). Carroll offers the following reason for claiming this: "Following [Mary] Douglas [in *Purity and Danger*], I initially speculate that an *object* or *being* is impure if it is categorically interstitial, categorically contradictory, incomplete, or formless" (p. 32). This is an attractive idea, although it does involve Carroll in a fairly tortured explanation of why *Psycho* should not be considered a horror film, which is precisely how many people regard it. Further, while this categorical impurity might help define one aspect of the monstrous, it does not fully account for the distinction of horror films since it could apply to all grotesque art. Both Animal Comedy

and gross-out horror draw heavily on the grotesque, yet they are clearly different genres. Carroll himself makes no mention of *The Bad Seed*. He also ignores *The Birds*, although it is a key work for modern horror. See also Carroll's earlier, psychoanalytic article, "Nightmare and the Horror Film: The Symbolic Biology of Fantastic Beings," *Film Quarterly* 34 (Spring 1981), no. 3: 16–25.

Finally, Paul Rozin and April E. Fallon, in a psychological study of disgust, effectively challenge what they term Mary Douglas's "anomaly theory": "The large number of disgusts based on acceptable objects in negative contexts . . . and the large number of disgusting but common animals such as insects cannot easily be explained as anomalies. The biggest limitation of Douglas's view as a complete explanation of disgusts is that it cannot account for the virtually exclusive focus on animals and their products in the face of many 'anomalies' in the plant and inorganic worlds." Rozin and Fallon, "A Perspective on Disgust," *Psychological Review* 94 (1987), no. 1: 29.

If, then, the feeling of disgust that is so central to horror films of the 1970s and 1980s is not simply a matter of categorization but actually depends upon the nature of the object, then the feeling is open to the kind of psychoanalytic interpretation Carroll wants to rule out.

26. As in my discussion of *Heaven Help Us*, I am deliberately echoing the title of Alice Miller's book here about what she calls "poisonous pedagogy" because the film presents physical punishment as something that has real education value. Miller, *For Your Own Good: Hidden Cruelty in Child-rearing and the Roots of Violence* (New York: Farrar, Straus and Giroux, 1983).

27. For reasons that should become clear, this was in general a period of testing screen censorship. Not until late into the next decade would it become as far-reaching as it was in the other arts, but the desire to break down the restrictiveness of the old Code clearly begins in the 1950s.

28. Robert M. W. Vogel, letter to Geoffrey Shurlock, January 1, 1955, PCA files, Margaret Herrick Library, Beverly Hills.

29. It was only with the 1985 television remake that something close to showing the murders took place, and this largely because of audience expectations about explicit violence by this period. But even here the presentation remains fairly indirect so that we never see Rhoda physically attack another character.

30. Geoffrey Shurlock letter to J. L. Warner, dated December 14, 1954; to Dore Schary at MGM, January 3, 1955; and to Frank McCarthy at 20th Century-Fox, January 12, 1955, PCA files, Margaret Herrick Library.

31. Vogel, letter to Shurlock, January 1, 1955.

32. Undated handwritten memo, "Murf." to Geoffrey Shurlock, PCA files, Margaret Herrick Library.

33. The ad campaign that Warners prepared, pointing to the quality of the work by stressing the "prize winning cast of the play," contained display advertising with the prominently featured tag line "Recommended for Adults Only!" There were, however, also ads without the warning, or the warning was positioned so that it could easily be cut from the ad. The advertising may be seen in the *Bad Seed* pressbook, the Warner Archive, University of Southern California.

34. "Together they [the actors] turned out such a chiller that Chicago theaters are urging children to stay at home." "A Lethal Little Lass—'Bad Seed' as Movie Is Shocking Chiller," *Life*, September 17, 1956, p. 141. See also, "Chicago Bars Children," *New York*

Times, July 24, 1956, p. 20, and "Banned to Kids in Chicago," *Daily Variety*, July 24, 1956.

35. In a letter to Jack Warner, Walter Wanger wrote: "Congratulations on your fine campaign on THE BAD SEED. I was very happy to see your reference to adult audiences. I will be most anxious to know what the results are, because I believe that appealing to adult audiences might be one of the solutions to our present box office anaemia." Dated August 27, 1956, the Warner Archive, USC.

36. Although she was playing an eight-year-old, by the time of the filming McCormack was actually twelve. The fact that she had already played the part on Broadway for over a year might also have mitigated any concern for what performing in the movie would do to her. Publicity releases on the film emphasized what a normal young girl she was.

37. A review in *Saturday Review* makes clear the threat parents felt by noting, "[It] will at the least put you off talking baby-talk to your children" (Henry Hewes, "Broadway Postscript: How Many Inches to the Heart of a Child?" *Saturday Review*, December 25, 1954, p. 22). The reviewer in *America* was even more anxious: "Mr. Anderson's little monster is the first killer that has ever followed him [the reviewer] home. All through the night his sleep was broken by dreams of the young lady trying to sever his jugular vein or push him off a cliff" (Theophile Lewis, "Theater," *America*, December 25, 1954, p. 346).

Another reviewer made this concern more global by suggesting a connection between *The Bad Seed* and juvenile delinquency, a major public concern in the 1950s: "This is a play so horrifying to witness and so harrowing to the emotions that the anxiety it arouses in the spectator lingers on for days afterwards, its reverberations echoing down the chambers of the mind, bringing back the shiver experienced in the theatre; and it is prodded back into awareness every time one reads a newspaper story about children who beat old men to death or push homeless drunks off a pier to drown in a river" (Maurice Zolotow, "The Season On and Off Broadway," *Theatre Arts*, February 1955, p. 20). The connection to juvenile delinquency was also made by Wolcott Gibb: "Even for a public familiar with the mounting record of senseless juvenile violence, as reported in the press, these horrors may appear a little excessive" (Gibb, "The Theatre—Naughty Girl," *The New Yorker*, December 18, 1954, p. 54).

38. The Production Code files on *The Bad Seed* reveal that a number of would-be producers were considering how to punish Rhoda. Truly, none came up with anything quite as devastating as what director Mervyn LeRoy and screenwriter John Lee Mahin contrived (as will be described later). PCA files, Margaret Herrick Library.

39. Screenplay in the Warner Archive, USC.

40. When *The Bad Seed* went to Warners (with Mervyn LeRoy to direct), there was an angry exchange between 20th Century-Fox production chief Buddy Adler and Geoffrey Shurlock of the PCA because Adler had wanted to buy the play for Fox. To Adler's indignant question of how it was possible that the PCA could grant Warners permission to film a play that the PCA itself had declared unfilmable, Shurlock replied, "This was a generalization, made in good faith, which we had to retract when Mervyn LeRoy came up with a treatment which seemed to do exactly what we had originally thought impossible. And so in justice we had to reverse ourselves." Letter dated October 21, 1955, PCA files, Margaret Herrick Library.

41. While many reviews did express a sympathy for the mother's plight, one re-

viewer of the film did get fed up in a way that anticipates *Night of the Living Dead* (although he did see this as an unintentional failing of the work and almost apologized for his reaction): "Nancy Kelly makes the mother of this child so saturnine and so foolishly fatalistic that her outbursts of frenzy toward the end, when the little darling coolly compounds her murders, deprive her of the sympathy she should have. This reviewer had the inhuman feeling that this poor woman oddly got what she deserved." Bosley Crowther, "Screen: 'The Bad Seed,' " *New York Times*, September 13, 1956, p. 39.

42. This quote is taken from an Associated Press story on the film by James Bacon dated August 22, 1956. The Warners ad campaign for the film also supported LeRoy's claim: "A hidden shame out in the open—and the most terrifying rock bottom a woman ever hit for love!" *The Bad Seed* pressbook, the Warner Archive, USC.

43. Reinhard Kuhn, *Corruption in Paradise* (Hanover, N.H.: University Press of New England, 1982), p. 40.

44. Philip Greven points out that Dr. Spock did not in fact completely reject physical punishment (this was a view he advocated much later). He simply called for restraint. That was enough, however, to create the popular view of him as someone advocating extreme permissiveness in the matter of childhood discipline. See Greven, *Spare the Child: The Religious Roots of Punishment and the Psychological Impact of Physical Abuse* (New York: Knopf, 1991).

45. "At the film's end, LeRoy makes his final obeisance to the stage: all the characters smilingly take their bows, and Nancy Kelly—as she did during curtain calls on Broadway—puts Patty across her knee and gives her a spanking" ("Cinema," *Time*, September 17, 1956, p. 100). Crowther also mentioned the ending, but to complain about it in a way that points up my interest in how the film defines the spanking as fun: "The attitude toward the whole thing is betrayed in a postscript, calling the actors on for bows. Miss Kelly spanks Miss McCormack for a gagged-up fadeout. Anything for a howl!" ("Screen: 'The Bad Seed,' " *New York Times*, September 13, 1956, p. 39).

46. Writing in 1963, Francis E. Kearns noted, "In bookstores and newsstands surrounding college campuses a prominent display place is consistently given to William Golding's *Lord of the Flies*. Probably no other post–World War II novel has so seriously threatened to dislodge J. D. Salinger's *Catcher in the Rye* as the most influential work in the literary initiation of the American undergraduate." Kearns, "Salinger and Golding: Conflict on Campus," *America*, January 26, 1963, p. 136.

Kearns was interested in the popularity of these two works and the possible shift in taste because they seem so opposed. This apparent shift from a view of the child as an innocent in a corrupt world to children themselves as the bearers of corruption parallels the changing view of children I see taking place in the films considered in this chapter.

47. Vincent Canby, for example, described the children in the following terms: "Down the street, a group of children giggle as they watch a scorpion being eaten alive by a colony of red ants. A moment later, the town literally explodes in the ambush that has been set for the outlaws. . . . The audience, which earlier was appalled at the cynical detachment with which the camera watched the death fight of the scorpion, is now in the position of the casually cruel children." Canby, "Violence and Beauty Mesh in 'Wild Bunch,' " *New York Times*, June 26, 1969, p. 47.

48. As Reinhard Kuhn notes, "The defining feature of their pristine world is a negative one that, because of the lack of a positive counterpart, will lead to its rapid

dismantlement. This quality is the absence of grown-ups and consequently of the arbitrary rules which they impose" (Kuhn, *Corruption in Paradise*, pp. 156–57).

Where *Lord of the Flies* clearly differs from the "evil children" films is in defining the adult world (here embroiled in a global war) as equally corrupt. *The Bad Seed*, on the other hand, generally set the pattern for the "evil children" films in defining the parents/adults as innocent.

14. Possession, Regression, Rebellion

1. As if to give proof of the film's damage, the psychiatrist identified the people by their professional accomplishments: "an intelligent, stable, young social worker" and "a brilliant young university professor." Ralph R. Greenson, M.D., "A Psychoanalyst's Indictment of 'The Exorcist,' " *Saturday Review*, June 15, 1974, pp. 41–43.

2. *Newsweek* reported, " 'There is no way you can sit through that film without receiving some lasting negative or disturbing effects,' warns Chicago psychiatrist Louis Schlan. In fact, Schlan had to place young patients 'under restraint' after they saw 'The Exorcist,' and four other moviegoers, he says, are now under treatment" (*Newsweek*, "The Exorcism Frenzy," February 11, 1974, p. 61). *Time*, citing the same psychiatrist, reported only two people who "required hospitalization" ("Exorcist Fever," February 11, 1974, p. 53).

3. *Newsweek*, "The Exorcism Frenzy"; Joe Flaherty, "Cult of the Occult," *Village Voice*, April 11, 1974.

4. Howard Newman, *The Exorcist: The Strange Story Behind the Film* (New York: Pinnacle, 1974); Peter Travers and Stephanie Reiff, *The Story Behind "The Exorcist"* (New York: Crown, 1974); and William Peter Blatty, *William Peter Blatty on "The Exorcist" from Novel to Film* (New York: Bantam, 1974).

5. *The Exorcist* garnered nominations in five of the six major categories—Best Picture, Best Director (William Friedkin), Best Actress (Ellen Burstyn), Best Supporting Actor (Jason Miller), Best Supporting Actress (Linda Blair)—and actually won two Oscars, for Best Sound and Best Screenplay Adaptation (William Peter Blatty, from his novel). Roy Pickard comments: "[*The Exorcist* is] the only horror film to be nominated as best picture of the year. . . . Rarely has a soundtrack Oscar been so well deserved." Pickard, *The Oscar Movies from A to Z* (New York: Taplinger, 1978), p. 47.

6. Pauline Kael came up with the most peculiar among the frequent moral objections to the film: "Somewhere in the publicity for the film there was an item about William Friedkin's having looked at five hundred little girls before he chose his Regan. . . . I wonder about those four hundred and ninety-nine mothers of the rejected little girls—or about the hundred and ninety-nine if that's a more reasonable figure. . . . When they see 'The Exorcist' and watch Linda Blair urinating on the fancy carpet and screaming and jabbing at herself with the crucifix, are they envious? Do they feel, 'That might have been my little Susie—famous forever'?"

Although Kael, as noted in chapter 6 (note 20), had praised *M*A*S*H* several years before for knowing how to talk dirty, she was particularly upset by the language in this film, as were a number of other critics as well: "The movie also has the most ferocious language yet heard in a picture that is rated R, and is thus open to children (to those whose parents are insane enough to take them, or are merely uninformed)." Kael, "The Current Cinema: Back to the Ouija Board," *The New Yorker*, January 7, 1974, pp. 62 and 59.

7. Harry Ringel, "*The Exorcist*," *Cinefantastique* 3 (Summer 1974), no. 2: 24.

8. Michael Dempsey, "*The Exorcist*," *Film Quarterly* 27 (Summer 1974), no. 4: 61. Reviews in *The New Yorker* and *Time* made a similar point.

9. See especially Vincent Canby, "Why the Devil Do They Dig 'The Exorcist'?" *New York Times*, January 13, 1974, sec. 2, pp. 1, 4.

10. According to an interviewer in *Cinefantastique*, "Friedkin calls his film a drama, *not* a horror film." Dale Winogura, "William Friedkin," *Cinefantastique* 3 (Winter 1974), no. 4: 15.

11. Writing about the reception of *The Exorcist*, Hollis Alpert noted: "The theaters first chosen to show the film were what are known as prestige houses, and they attracted a relatively polite patronage. Then the film caught on with young people. It moved into areas where the patrons were working-class people and ghetto residents." Alpert, "In Answer to Dr. Greenson," *Saturday Review*, June 15, 1974, p. 43.

12. This additional theater promoted a similar confusion over the film's status as art film or exploitation product: "In Los Angeles, the crowds were so huge that Warners had to find a second theater in a hurry; the only one available was an art theater in Beverly Hills that most often shows foreign films. Since the audience for THE EXORCIST is at least one-third black, and since the only blacks ordinarily seen in Beverly Hills are maids, this movie may have done more to integrate Beverly Hills than any civil rights action. The confrontation has been explosive." Stephen Farber, "A Freak Show?" *Film Comment* (May–June 1974), p. 32.

13. Throughout its run, according to *Variety*'s box-office charts, *The Exorcist* was always playing at about half as many theaters as *The Sting* (1973), something that indicates the artistic status the studio saw in the film. *The Exorcist* conformed to a pattern that was about to disappear: single openings in downtown theaters, that had an air of exclusivity.

14. See chapter 1, note 29, for an explanation of this releasing strategy.

15. Alfred Hitchcock's desire to emulate the success that American-International had had in the exploitation market (noted earlier: chapter 2, note 38) perplexed many of his closest collaborators, who wondered why the great Hitchcock should want to make some low-budget sleaze like *Psycho*. Stephen Rebello, *Alfred Hitchcock and the Making of "Psycho"* (New York: Dembner, 1990).

16. A similar strategy led to the only previous time horror films had been accorded much serious critical attention. In the 1940s, Val Lewton produced a series of B-budget horror films for RKO (such as *Cat People*, 1942) that managed to stand above the common run of exploitation film by their indirectness and psychological approach to horror.

17. Canby, "Why the Devil Do They Dig 'The Exorcist'?" p. 4.

18. Judy Klemesrud, "They Wait Hours—to Be Shocked," *New York Times*, January 27, 1974, sec. 2, pp. 1, 13.

19. The article, which consists of a series of interviews with expectant patrons, contains one passage worth saving from the dustbin of history: "Another day at The Line, I met Bill Hurt, 23, who talked like a sociologist rather than the drama student that he is when I asked him why he would stand in line for a movie, any movie. He smiled and said, 'It makes the movie better, right? The more you pay for something, the more it's worth. And it also has to do with telling your friends you've seen it.'" Klemesrud, "They Wait Hours—to Be Shocked," p. 13.

20. Cartoon ("by Dunagin"), "Tell It Like It Is," Associated Press, February 16, 1974.

21. Ringel, "*The Exorcist*, p. 40. Indicative of the dawn of the gross-out age, Ringel sees this as an entirely positive thing, since it is a vomit from all walks of life and ethnic backgrounds, "the closest the Melting Pot ever comes to blending literally."

22. A psychological study of disgust proposes that it be defined as a "food-related emotion": "Revulsion at the prospect of (oral) incorporation of an offensive object. The offensive objects are contaminants; that is, if they even briefly contact an acceptable food, they tend to render that food unacceptable." Paul Rozin and April E. Fallon, "A Perspective on Disgust," *Psychological Review* 94 (1987), no. 1: 28.

Defining disgust in this way clarifies its attraction-repulsion aspect: we must first experience hunger, a desire for "oral incorporation," in order to experience a reaction against the object.

23. Let two reports from theater personnel suffice:

" 'I've been in this business 47 years, and I've never seen anything like it,' asserted Los Angeles Theater Manager Harry Francis. He estimates that each performance exacts an audience toll of four blackouts, half-a-dozen bouts of vomiting and multiple spontaneous exits" (*Time*, "Exorcist Fever," p. 53).

"Thomas F. McMahon, director of operations for the Cinema 5 theaters, said he had no knowledge of heart attacks brought on by 'The Exorcist,' but does know of blackouts and vomiting" (Lawrence Van Gelder, " 'Exorcist' Casts Spell on Full Houses,' " *New York Times*, January 24, 1974, p. 46).

24. Charles Schulz, "Peanuts," United Features Syndicate, April 29, 1974.

25. Canby, "Why the Devil Do They Dig 'The Exorcist'?" p. 4.

26. Here I am quoting the appropriate passage from William Peter Blatty's book *The Exorcist* (New York: Harper and Row, 1971), p. 311, which made it into Blatty's first draft for the screenplay almost verbatim (subsequent page numbers in parentheses following quotations in the text refer to this edition). The final draft, which was filmed but subsequently cut by Friedkin, compressed this:

KARRAS: Father, what's going on in there? What is it? If that's the Devil, why this girl? It makes no sense.

MERRIN: I think the point is to make us despair, Damien; to see ourselves as animal and ugly—to reject our own humanity—to reject the possibility that God could ever love us.

Through all three versions Blatty held onto the equation of "animal" with "ugly" and something that makes us "reject" our humanity. Blatty revealed, perhaps unintentionally, a problem with this line of thinking when he wrote a defense of the novel and film for a Jesuit magazine in which he paraphrased Merrin's explanation of the possession. In working out the paraphrase, however, he got the issues confused: "It [the possession] is aimed at those *around* the little girl, the *observers* of the possession, and particularly Fr. Karras, who is far more vulnerable to attack. For Fr. Karras has rejected his own humanity: the animal side of his nature; the side that rends foods and chews and excretes; the side that kills over lust for a woman." Here Blatty seems to have connected humanity precisely to the animal side, a position more in keeping with a gross-out view of the world: how could Karras possibly reject the part of him that "chews and excretes"? Blatty, "There is Goodness in 'The Exorcist,' " *America*, February 23, 1974, p. 132. The citation from the final draft screenplay appears in Mark Kermode,

"The Mysteries of Faith: Misinformation and Missing Scenes in THE EXORCIST," *Video Watchdog* (July–August 1991), p. 45.

27. This was noted by a number of observers on the film's release. A more recent analysis of the film, noting that it is "a very nearly incoherent cinematic text," turns to the novel in order to smooth out the problems and arrive at a coherent interpretation of this incoherent work. Carol J. Clover, *Men, Women, and Chainsaws: Gender in the Modern Horror Film* (Princeton: Princeton University Press, 1992), p. 87.

As popular as the novel may have been, however, the majority of the audience for the film would not have read it. The very obfuscation, then, must be considered as part of the film's appeal, as Friedkin himself seemed to recognize in an entry he made in his diary before production about the prologue sequence: "I feel the film would be incomplete without it. In that, [it] sets up a kind of mystery and strangeness having nothing to do with the central plot. That prepares the audience for something. Prepares them for a mystical experience." Friedkin's diary is part of the William Friedkin Papers on deposit at the Margaret Herrick Library, Beverly Hills.

28. *Newsweek*, "The Exorcism Frenzy," p. 64.

29. My description probably sounds somewhat less mysterious than the scene appears to most audiences since the identity of the character Regan addresses has not been all that firmly established. Only the most attentive viewer (or someone who read the book or knew the screenplay) would know this man is an astronaut since the moment that gives us this information is passed over very quickly as party small talk. This could be sloppiness on Friedkin's part, something that got lost in trying to compress an overly long scene, but it is part and parcel of a narrative approach that leaves much of the meaning of events very difficult for an audience to follow. As the quotation from Friedkin's diary indicates (note 7 above), the level of mystification in this narrative appears to be deliberate. This seems an appropriate strategy for a man who had previously directed the film version of Harold Pinter's *The Birthday Party* (1968).

30. Of course, this kind of "work" (making thematic connections among parallel narrative lines) is a fairly familiar activity for movie audiences, one foregrounded since D. W. Griffith's *Intolerance* (1916). My notion of the audience's work as set in motion by the film's promptings is analogous to David Bordwell's notion of "the viewer's activity." I can't fully embrace Bordwell's later interrogation of interpretative criticism, however, because I think much of the viewer's activity does in fact have to do with constructing meaning. Bordwell has done much to attack the notion of the movie viewer's passivity, thus establishing a more intelligent viewer than most past mass-media theory and a good deal of contemporary film theory has allowed. I simply want to grant the viewer even more intelligence as someone who can do more than speculate on the mechanics of the narrative to think about the meaning of events. See David Bordwell, *Narration in the Fiction Film* (Madison: University of Wisconsin Press, 1985), and *Making Meaning: Inference and Rhetoric in the Interpretation of Cinema* (Cambridge: Harvard University Press, 1989).

31. Dale Winogura, "Jason Miller," *Cinefantastique* 3 (Winter 1974), no. 4: 14.

32. As David Bordwell notes: "When information is missing, perceivers infer it or make guesses about it. When events are arranged out of temporal order, perceivers try to put those events in sequence. And people seek causal connection among events, both in anticipation and in retrospect." Bordwell, *Narration in the Fiction Film*, p. 34.

33. At the time of the film's release, William Friedkin commented on his method in

The Exorcist: "I'm very conscious of making a movie that will enter the minds of those who see it, and that will grow in their minds and alter and affect them. One way to do this is to take out all overt meanings and explanations, and that's what I tried to do." Dale Winogura, "William Friedkin," p. 17.

In a later interview, responding to complaints from screenwriter Blatty about what had been cut from the final film, Friedkin noted: "Blatty's feeling was that he had to have his characters explain the picture to the audience. That's where he and I differ. I felt the audience should fill in everything for themselves; we shouldn't have to spell things out for them." Kermode, "The Mysteries of Faith," p. 46.

34. Regan's "possessed" voice caused some notoriety and controversy when the film first appeared. Linda Blair's distinctively low voice in these scenes actually belonged to well-known character actress Mercedes McCambridge, who was initially denied credit but was given it on rerelease of the film. See Charles Higham, "Will the Real Devil Speak Up? Yes!" *New York Times*, January 27, 1974, sec. 2, p. 13.

35. *Newsweek*, for example, quotes a theater manager who said: " 'We've had two to five people faint here every day since this picture opened. More men than women pass out, and it usually happens in the evening performance, after the crucifix scene involving masturbation' " ("The Exorcism Frenzy," p. 61).

36. The abstraction might have been occasioned by the use of a body double, perhaps a way of limiting Linda Blair's participation in the scene. This itself became the subject of a lawsuit.

37. This is one of the most notorious examples of the film's rendering as oblique and uncertain something that is perfectly straightforward in the novel, where we learn exactly how and why the crucifix ended up in Regan's bed.

38. "But Ouija boards aren't toys—and neither is Satan, Regan discovers, though her punishment far exceeds her crime." Ringel, "*The Exorcist.*" p. 40.

39. Friedkin's cutting script (part of the William Friedkin Papers on deposit in the Margaret Herrick Library) does in fact contain a breakdown of this scene, but it was subsequently cut for the final edit. It is of note that he was willing to lose this scene, of course, but even with the scene the onset of the illness remains elliptical. Blatty objected to this deletion, calling it one of the "amazing holes in the carpentry of the story." Kermode, "The Mysteries of Faith," p. 39.

40. Some confusion might arise because this is a reworking of the novel, where there is no such action by Damien. It could be that Blatty and Friedkin felt a more dramatic medium required a more dramatic action and so added the beating even though it contradicted narrative logic.

41. William S. Pechter's description is based on a viewing experience "with an audience which filled a large theater": "In an access of rage, the younger priest (who has been portrayed as an athletic, powerfully physical figure with an unrelieved intensity by Jason Miller) turns on the girl, and begins to pound her violently with his fists (an act which the audience greets with immense satisfaction, as the tensions which have been gathering find release)." Pechter, "Movies: 'The Exorcist' and Its Audience," *Commentary*, March 1974, pp. 73–74.

42. *Newsweek* reported on this confusion: "Blatty himself has become concerned about the way audiences interpret the movie's climactic scene. 'Fifty per cent of those who've seen the film think the demon is taking Karras out the window, and that it's a triumph of evil over good,' he told *Newsweek*'s Jerome Gram. 'But it's an act of love,

not one of despair. It's clearly a triumph for Karras.' To make that point clearer, Blatty and director Friedkin will soon shoot a short new scene to tack onto the end of the film" ("The Exorcism Frenzy," p. 66). Kermode reports that Friedkin subsequently denied this, but Blatty holds to the story (Kermode, "The Mysteries of Faith," p. 50).

43. A sociologist reviewing the film on its initial release noted this aspect of it: "The social cause of Regan's illness is her mother's life style. This is only hinted at in the film but is made explicit in the book when the demon screams at Chris, 'It is you who have done it [made Regan into a demon], yes you with your career before anything, your career before your husband, before her [Regan].' " Herbert J. Gans, "Gans on Film— 'The Exorcist': A Devilish Attack on Women," *Social Policy* (May–June 1974), p. 73.

As with so many things in the film, full explication of a point requires the novel. This should make us cautious how much we want to read into the film about a woman's place. My chief concern here is why the audience should understand an evil child in such different terms.

44. So concerned was he by what Regan apparently got away with that he was able to extend it very far afield to social and public policy issues: "What all this means in practical terms is that we must set limits to permissiveness and to 'social' explanations of personal misconduct. Further, we must all assume some responsibility for the horrors of our world today, from Bangladesh, Vietnam, Watergate, to the famine in India. . . . It is against this background that *The Exorcist* is a menace to the mental health of our community." Greenson, "A Psychoanalyst's Indictment." p. 43.

Others also made a connection between Regan and the young people of the time:

"Rabbi Julius G. Neumann (Chairman, Morality in Media): 'The movie is adding to the frustration and confusion of our youth claiming that whatever they do contrary to accepted religious and society's norm is not really of their own making, but that of the devil inside them.' " David Bartholomew, "*The Exorcist*," *Cinefantastique* 3 (Winter 1974), no. 4: 10.

"Young people, some of whom have experienced first-hand the 'altered consciousness' that comes with hallucinogenic drugs, can readily accept the movie's tale of demonic possession." *Newsweek*, "The Exorcism Frenzy," p. 60.

And finally, by the end of the decade a newspaper writer could employ 20–20 hindsight to claim: ' "The Exorcist' craze grew out of the late '60s, when parents thought their long-haired, foul-mouthed, dope-smoking kids acted as if they were possessed." Richard Rothstein, "After 'Carrie,'" *New York Sunday News*, September 23, 1979, p. 7.

45. A writer for *Cineaste* segmented the audience and found a variety of responses: "Others, especially rebellious young people, actually enjoy the film tremendously, and identify with the cursing, blasphemous and sarcastic vituperation of the Regan/demon character as she/he shocks and defies the concerned administrations of the authority figures/grown-ups—Mother, Science, the Church." One of the examples she cites of the young audience identifying with Regan is the moment when she "grabbed an officious psychiatrist by the balls and set him howling." As I explain in my text, however, you do not have to be a young person to perceive this identification: the film directly encourages it. But how either this writer or Vincent Canby, who also wrote about youngsters' response to the film ("Why the Devil Do They Dig 'The Exorcist'?" p. 1), knew the age of the laughers is something of a mystery. Ruth McCormick, "'The Devil Made Me Do It!' A Critique of THE EXORCIST," *Cineaste* 6 (1974), no. 3: 21.

The film critic for a Jesuit magazine, *America*, objected to claims about the film that Canby made on the basis of audience reaction: "Now it happens I saw the film in the same theatre under similar conditions and with the same sort of heterogeneous audience. . . . To me, while some of the audience reaction was obstreperous and insensitive—tempered somewhat by judicious 's-h-h-h-ing' from other segments—the overall response was within the normal range of reaction to a horror film." Walsh's article is really quite a sophisticated and astute exploration of the way audiences were responding to this film, one of the sharpest at the time, and one that would anticipate current trends in popular culture studies. Moira Walsh, "Skeptical and Ironic Detachment," *America*, February 2, 1974, p. 73.

46. Jerry Rubin, "I Am Regan, You Are Regan," *Village Voice*, May 2, 1974, p. 95.

47. A letter from the MPAA to Warner Brothers noted "two visual elements" in the script would "could result in the necessity of an X rating." The letter offered a caveat on the first: "The scene in which the girl attacks the psychiatrist should not be presented in a manner which explicitly indicates she is gripping him by the testicles." Nevertheless, this is precisely what the scene does, so that Friedkin was willing to risk the displeasure of the Ratings Board in order to maintain the threat of castration. The other scene the board was worried about—the crucifix/vagina scene—also invokes castration. The letter is in the William Friedkin Papers at the Margaret Herrick Library.

48. The shot provides a remarkable echo (remarkable enough to seem deliberate) of the murder of Arbogast in *Psycho*, in which the camera moves with him as he stumbles backward down a flight of stairs.

49. As often, the connection is made more explicit in the novel where Blatty has Chris muse over the similarity of names between her former husband Howard and the spirit commanding the Ouija board. In the film, the connection is left up to the audience to make on the basis of easily overlooked details.

50. Sigmund Freud, "A Seventeenth-Century Demonological Neurosis" (1923) in vol. 19 (1961) in *S.E.*, 24 vols. (London: Hogarth Press, 1953–1974), pp. 72–105.

51. It is this push-pull aspect that made the appeal of the film so difficult to understand for critics operating from a more conservative aesthetic view. Speculating on what appeal the audience could possibly find in this film, Stephen Farber wrote: "Watching TV interviews with people who had become sick during the film, I was interested to note that they were not angry at the film for upsetting them. Although their voices were shaking and many were close to hysteria, they wanted to go back and see more; they seemed to feel they deserved the flagellation." For Farber, the appeal can only be masochistic. He can make no allowance for either ambivalence or a selective identification here. Farber, "A Freak Show?" p. 34.

15. The Revenge of Oedipus

1. I should note, however, that commentary on the film does generally attribute a sexual motivation to this sequence. On the other hand, I have yet to read any commentary that is particularly concerned by the fact that the murderer is a six-year-old boy. Reading sexual desire into this without accounting for the age of the child seems to me only slightly less perverse than the sequence itself. See Vera Dika, *Games of Terror* (Rutherford, N.J.: Fairleigh Dickinson Press, 1990), pp. 37–43; and Carol J. Clover, *Men, Women, and Chainsaws: Gender in the Modern Horror Film* (Princeton: Princeton University Press, 1992), pp. 34, 186.

2. Abortion gets fuller dramatization in *The Omen* than in *It's Alive*, although Carol Clover puts quite a bit of weight on the one conversation in which abortion arises (in

the latter film), attributing the child's monstrosity to the fact that the parents had considered aborting the pregnancy. Because it is so briefly dealt with in the film and never really dramatized, I question making it so central to the film's meaning. See Clover, *Men, Women, and Chainsaws*, pp. 76–77 n22.

3. As in the case of *The Exorcist*, the Roman Catholic church was not happy about its apparent association with this film. In a report on a "B" rating from the U.S. Catholic Conference, *Variety* stated the "Conference . . . blasts the pic as 'one of the most distasteful ever put out by a major studio.' Catholics are particularly bothered by what they regard as the film's misrepresentation of 'scripture and its appalling ignorance of all that pertains to Catholicism.' " "Catholic B (As In Berate) To 'Omen' For Mishmash Dogma," *Variety*, July 7, 1976, p. 5.

Subsequently, Vatican Radio attacked both *The Exorcist* and *The Omen* for being films in which "Satan appears destined to become the star of the screen." For me, the most interesting point about the Catholic church's response is its sense that Satan is the real star in these films, which does pick up on ways in which the audience might find an alliance with the devilish characters, something the film's narratives seem to deny, at least on the surface. "Vatican Deplores Screen's Romance with the Devil," *Variety*, December 15, 1976, p. 1.

4. How much the film was following the lead of *The Exorcist* in being a classy horror film is clear from a number of prerelease articles in *Variety* dealing with the unusual marketing strategies 20th Century-Fox had put into place in order to build word-of-mouth on the film: " 'We know we have quality but the public may think it's just another horror picture,' explains Peter Myers, 20th's domestic sales veepee. . . . 'The Omen' . . . lacks the presold appeal of a film such as 'The Exorcist.' " Gregory Peck and Lee Remick are topbilled, and 20th hopes their names at least will assure the public of the film's "class" aura." "Fox Hopes 'The Omen' Is, After Recent Release Letdowns," *Variety*, June 2, 1976, p. 4.

5. Although *The Bad Seed* has generally been overlooked in histories of horror, one contemporary reviewer of *The Omen* did note the borrowing from the earlier film: "It is a slick, fairly well-made piece of commercialism, aimed at producing the kind of squeamishness that made ROSEMARY'S BABY and THE EXORCIST so popular (with a little bit of THE BAD SEED thrown in for a predictable surprise ending)." Kyle B. Counts, "*The Omen*," *Cinefantastique* 5 (Fall 1976), no. 2: 27.

6. Robin Wood, "An Introduction to the American Horror Film," in Britton, Richard Lippe, Tony Williams, and Robin Wood, *The American Nightmare: Essays on the Horror Film* (Toronto: Festival of Festivals, 1979); reprinted in *Hollywood from Vietnam to Reagan* (New York: Columbia University Press, 1986), pp. 99–101.

7. Since two of the three films are adaptations of novels by Stephen King, it is no coincidence to find here an emphasis on childhood trauma, a common feature of his work (see chapter 13, note 13). But as the presence of *The Other* makes clear, this theme is by no means exclusive with him.

8. Michael R. Collins, *The Films of Stephen King* (San Bernadino, Calif.: Borgo Press, 1987), p. 123.

9. J. P. Telotte, "Faith and Idolatry in the Horror Film," *Literature/Film Quarterly* 8 (1980), no. 3: 143–55; reprinted in Barry Keith Grant, ed., *Planks of Reason: Essays on the Horror Film* (Metuchen, N.J.: Scarecrow Press, 1984), p. 32.

10. There is in fact some question about whose finger this is. It appears to be an

adult's finger, yet we see Niles (again in flashback) cutting off the finger of the dead Holland to get possession of the ring. We may infer from this, however, that it represents an action that Holland had previously performed on his father, so that the finger, whether adult's or child's, does signify the father.

11. This topic is discussed specifically in Wood, "An Introduction to the American Horror Film," *Hollywood from Vietnam to Reagan,* pp. 73–80.

12. John Belton has effectively analyzed how point of view in this film works, especially how Mulligan achieves a balance between subjective and objective presentation. Belton, *Cinema Stylists* (Metuchen, N.J.: Scarecrow Press, 1983), pp. 96–98.

13. While *The Exorcist* made graphic detail mandatory for the horror film, explicit gore had become sufficiently commonplace in American movies since *Bonnie and Clyde* and *The Wild Bunch* to move the *Variety* reviewer to comment on the discretion of *The Other.* "Mulligan's outstanding discretion in depicting the frequent physical terror and violence does not eliminate the appropriate physical manifestation, but rather intensifies the effect. Filmmakers of a past era knew these artistic tricks, but today it is virtually an antique art. The film's domestic rating is PG, but it is very easy to imagine with a shudder how it could have been in other hands a crude R or cruder *X-ploitationer.*" "Murf.," "The Other," *Variety,* May 24, 1972, pp. 19, 24.

One other comment from this review is worth noting because it clearly places *The Other* ahead of the "evil children" cycle: "Films which depict children who are endowed or possessed with occult, supernatural or abnormal traits are relatively few in number, for the genre has challenged over the years the utmost subtleties of William Wyler, Mervyn LeRoy, and more recently, Jack Clayton" (p. 19).

14. This is very different from the novel where the placing of the pitchfork is kept completely separate from "the great game." Niles feels a sharp pain when he sees the pitchfork in a neutral context: a hired hand is haying with it. The pain he thus associates with the pitchfork effectively suggests to him how he may use it against his cousin Russell. In the film, however, Niles feels the pain at the moment Russell is impaled on the pitchfork (conveyed through the film's editing), which makes Niles the recipient of his own action. See Thomas Tryon, *The Other* (New York: Knopf, 1971), chap. 4.

15. An article on Stephen King and Stanley Kubrick just before the release of *The Shining* reported that Kubrick and Johnson had read the Bettelheim book (see next note) as well as Freud's essay, "The Uncanny" (William Wilson, "Riding the Crest of the Horror Craze," *New York Times,* May 11, 1980, sec. 6, p. 54). A fine article by Christopher Hoile explores complementary ways in which the influence of these two psychoanalytic works surface in the film of *The Shining.* Hoile, "The Uncanny and the Fairy Tale in Kubrick's *The Shining,*" *Literature/Film Quarterly* 12 (1984), no. 1: 5–12.

16. Bruno Bettelheim, *The Uses of Enchantment: The Meaning and Importance of Fairy Tales* (New York: Knopf, 1976; rpt., New York: Vintage, 1977), p. 161.

17. For somewhat different but complementary interpretations of the maze, see Hoile, "The Uncanny and the Fairy Tale," pp. 7–8; and Thomas Allen Nelson, *Kubrick: Inside a Film Artist's Maze* (Bloomington: Indiana University Press, 1982), pp. 205ff.

18. Much of the criticism of the film identifies them as twins, but in fact they are different ages, eight and ten respectively. One is clearly somewhat bigger than the other, but they look sufficiently alike to evoke the uncanny. Critical comment has normalized this by making them twins.

19. Bettelheim, *The Uses of Enchantment,* pp. 159–66.

20. John Hofsess, "*The Shining*," *Washington Post*, June 1, 1980, p. H11.

21. In the Sunday *New York Times Magazine* piece on King and Kubrick, for example, William Wilson compares *The Shining* to King's earlier novels and finds "King now substitutes geographical isolation, silence and nuclear-family-style claustrophobia. The substitution is an effective one: 'The Shining' is arguably the scariest book in the King canon." Wilson, "Riding the Crest of the Horror Craze," p. 48.

Greg Keeler evoked the properly critical tone in noting that "in the long run, it is the nuclear family that is attacked. After all, no matter how one views the differences between these films [*Kramer vs. Kramer* and *The Shining*], there is no doubt that the family has to disintegrate for the characters to survive, either physically or psychologically." Greg Keeler, " 'The Shining': Ted Kramer Has a Nightmare," *Journal of Popular Film and Television* 8 (Winter 1981), no. 4: 8.

22. See, for example, Jack Kroll, "Stanley Kubrick's Horror Show," *Newsweek*, May 26, 1980, p. 97; Paul Mayersberg, "The Overlook Hotel," *Sight and Sound* (Winter 1980–81), p. 57; and an extended exploration of the parallels between the two movies in Keeler, " 'The Shining': Ted Kramer Has a Nightmare," pp. 2–8.

23. In his discussion of *It's Alive*, Robin Wood notes how often these attributes do in fact crop up around the American male. Wood, *Hollywood from Vietnam to Reagan*, pp. 99–101.

24. Although Hoile attempts a synthesis between Bettelheim and Freud (which should be easy since Bettelheim himself is a Freudian), he inadvertently brings up a problem here that he cannot fully acknowledge. On the wish-fulfillment ending Hoile notes simply and without comment, "As Laius in the myth of Oedipus, a father feeling threatened by his son tries to kill him only to be killed at a crossroads as the prophecy is fulfilled and the son runs off with his mother." Hoile, "The Uncanny and the Fairy Tale," p. 11.

25. Morton Schatzman, *Soul Murder: Persecution in the Family* (London: Allen Lane, 1973). The original case study may be found in Freud, "Psycho-Analytic Notes on an Autobiographical Account of a Case of Paranoia (Dementia Paranoides)" (1911), in vol. 12 (1958) of *S.E.*, 24 vols. (London: Hogarth Press, 1953–1974), pp. 9–82.

26. Most prominent among the feminist books is Judith Herman, *Father-Daughter Incest* (Cambridge: Harvard University Press, 1981). Alice Miller's books include: *Prisoners of Childhood* (aka *The Drama of the Gifted Child*; New York: Basic Books, 1981); *For Your Own Good: Hidden Cruelty in Child-rearing and the Roots of Violence* (New York: Farrar, Straus and Giroux, 1983); and *Thou Shalt Not Be Aware: Society's Betrayal of the Child* (New York: Farrar, Straus and Giroux, 1984). By the end of the decade the number of books on child abuse and domestic violence had grown sufficiently large to warrant separate sections in some large bookstores.

27. Jeffrey Moussaieff Masson, *The Assault on Truth* (New York: Farrar, Straus and Giroux, 1984; rpt. (with additional materials), New York: Penguin, 1985).

28. How pervasive this had become might best be seen in a book by noted psychiatrist Peter Blos, in which Blos retains the Freudian model but insists on seeing pre-Oedipal relations between father and son as equally important. Peter Blos, *Son and Father* (New York: Free Press, 1985).

29. Lloyd de Mause, *The History of Childhood: The Untold Story of Child Abuse* (New York: Psychohistory Press, 1974; rpt., New York: Peter Bedrick, 1988), p. 1.

30. In a fascinating book that attempts to account for the reasons why Freud moved

beyond the seduction theory, Marie Balmary extends the myth even further back, to Laius' sin in seducing and kidnapping the young son of King Pelops. This is the source of the curse against Laius, a just retribution in that the son rises up against the father: "At the origin is the fault committed by Laius; the abduction and homosexual violation of the young son of his host and the suicide that follows constitute the mainspring of the Oedipean myth." On Oedipus' name, Balmary astutely notes that it "does not come from the treatment he has been subjected to—he is not called 'pierced feet'—but from his body's response to this treatment: its swelling." His name, then, reflects the consequences of the abuse.

Balmary's book, first published in France in 1979 and in a later English translation in 1982 (two years before *The Assault on Truth*), did not receive the critical attention granted the more sensationalistic Masson book, but it is both more sophisticated than the later book and more generous to Freud. Balmary, *Psychoanalyzing Psychoanalysis: Freud and the Hidden Fault of the Father* (Baltimore: Johns Hopkins University Press, 1982), pp. 8, 9.

31. In writing this, I am drawing on Balmary's "interrogation of psychoanalytic theory by psychoanalytic method." Balmary, *Psychoanalyzing Psychoanalysis*, pp. 26–27.

32. In Stephen King's novel, the Overlook Hotel does in fact burn to the ground, but Kubrick decided early on not to use this ending. While the *Dies Irae* might suggest this, the Father Himself is not consumed in flames. Kubrick invented a much colder fate for the father in his film.

33. Herbert G. May and Bruce M. Metzger, eds., *The New Oxford Annotated Bible with the Apocrypha* (New York: Oxford University Press, 1977), p. 613.

34. C. J. Jung, *Answer to Job* (Princeton: Princeton University Press, 1958; rpt., 1973), pp. 13, 15.

35. Although I am claiming this inversion as fairly wide-sweeping, it is specifically Kubrick's inversion of the King novel (where Halloran does in fact save Danny).

36. Not even the original novel is able to sustain this. Not only does Stephen King grant Danny a good father in the form of Halloran, he gives Jack a last-minute change of heart as he lays dying: " 'Doc,' [Danny's nickname] Jack Torrance said. 'Run away. Quick. And remember how much I love you' " (King, *The Shining* [New York: Doubleday, 1977], chap. 55). In saying this, Jack is trying to save Danny from the explosions from the boiler that are about to rock the Overlook. The conclusion in the novel is therefore much more comforting than in the film version—for not only does Danny's father declare that he truly loves him, but the evil place that had corrupted the father will burn to the ground. In the film, the hotel is left standing and Jack remains trapped in it for eternity, achieving a terrible immortality.

37. Even within a Christian mythology that posits a God of love and mercy, the Father maintains an aura of inexplicable cruelty. For if God the Father has sent his only begotten son down to earth to fulfill a destiny of crucifixion, the crucifixion itself ends up commemorating the cruelty of the father. Much as with Oedipus' name, the repressed cruelty returns in symbolic form.

38. Of Nicholson's performance, Kroll wrote, "his metamorphosis into evil has its comic sides as well—which makes us remember that the devil is the ultimate clown" (Kroll, "Stanley Kubrick's Horror Show," p. 97). Mayersberg claimed that "the humor of *The Shining* puts it close to *Lolita* and *Strangelove* in Kubrick's work. . . . There is an underlying crazy comedy that is also deadly serious" (Mayersberg, "The Overlook

Hotel," p. 57). In a more critical vein, Larry W. Caldwell saw the playfulness of the film as "undermin[ing] any 'serious' intent. Can Kubrick still take seriously his once trendy but now largely blasé Beatnik nihilism? We think not." Caldwell, " 'Come and Play with Us': The Play Metaphor in Kubrick's Shining," *Literature/Film Quarterly* 14 (1986), no. 2: 111.

39. Kroll, "Stanley Kubrick's Horror Show," p. 99.

16. Menstruation, Monstrosity, and Mothers

1. Alan Dundes, *Cracking Jokes: Studies of Sick Humor Cycles and Stereotypes* (Berkeley: Ten Speed Press, 1987).

2. According to Laurent Bouzereau, "De Palma had wished that *Carrie* would become a phenomenon, and inspire attention comparable to the controversy *The Exorcist* (1973) had created. For De Palma, *Carrie* was a serious movie, and he wanted mature audiences to see it—not only horror fans" (Bouzereau, *The De Palma Cut* [New York: Dembner, 1988], p. 45). De Palma's hope in this regard reflect the changing status of the horror film in this period.

3. These shifts offer one way of accounting for the wide range of divergent critical reaction to the film that has been extensively surveyed by Kenneth MacKinnon. See MacKinnon, *Misogyny in the Movies: The De Palma Question* (Cranbury, N.J.: Associated University Presses, 1990), pp. 121–28.

4. Stephen King, *Carrie* (New York: Doubleday, 1974; rpt., New York: Signet, 1975), p. 4.

5. This recalls Eric Bentley's remark as cited in chapter 11 (see text at note 14) on the theater as a place we go to see beautiful bodies. There is something in *Carrie* not unlike what we saw in *Revenge of the Nerds*—a title that could well apply to this film if changed to the singular. But *Carrie* plays it safer in casting Sissy Spacek to play the lead.

6. Robin Wood, "An Introduction to the American Horror Film," in *The American Nightmare: Essays on the Horror Film* (Toronto: Festival of Festivals, 1979), pp. 7–28; reprinted in *Hollywood from Vietnam to Reagan* (New York: Columbia University Press, 1986).

7. It is essential to recognize Carrie's action as causing the shift into a different mode of expression. MacKinnon, who wants to see in the film a Laura Mulvey–style interrogation of woman as object-to-be-looked-at, does not consider this important moment of transition. Moreover, while he has something to say about the cracked mirror (discussed later in this chapter), he ignores the discrepancy between the shattered and the cracked mirrors in order to pursue an interpretation that will continue to be congruent with Mulvey. MacKinnon, *Misogyny in the Movies*, pp. 128–38; see also Laura Mulvey, "Visual Pleasure and the Narrative Cinema," *Screen* 16 (Autumn 1975), no. 3, reprinted in Bill Nichols, ed., *Movies and Methods*, 2 vols. (vol. 1: Berkeley: University of California Press, 1976; vol. 2: 1985), 2:305–15.

8. Once again I should note that I am using a concept that might invoke Jacques Lacan for much contemporary academic film criticism, but I do not intend this in a Lacanian manner. For Lacan, all mirroring effectively involves misrecognition. There is none of the opposition that this film sketches.

9. In his statistical survey of the horror film, Andrew Tudor notes the increasing

alliance between madness and monsters in post-1960s horror. See Tudor, *Monsters and Mad Scientists: A Cultural History of the Horror Movie* (Oxford: Basil Blackwell, 1989), pp. 19ff.

10. This scheme is fairly persuasive, but I find the explicitly political nature of these terms somewhat problematic in that they do not allow for the ambivalence that I see as central to gross-out (see Wood, *Hollywood from Vietnam to Reagan*, pp. 189–94). For critiques of Wood on this point, see Andrew Britton, "The Devil, Probably: The Symbolism of Evil," in Britton, Richard Lippe, Tony Williams, and Robin Wood, *The American Nightmare: Essays on the Horror Film* (Toronto: Festival of Festivals, 1979), pp. 34–42; and Dana Polan, "Eros and Syphilization: The Contemporary Horror Film," *Tabloid: A Review of Mass Culture and Everyday Life* (Winter 1982), pp. 31–34, reprinted in Barry Keith Grant, ed., *Planks of Reason: Essays on the Horror Film* (Metuchen, N.J.: Scarecrow Press, 1984), pp. 201–11.

11. The commentary by Laurent Bouzereau on the laser disc release notes that is in fact Sissy Spacek's hand. *Carrie* (Santa Monica, Calif.: The Voyager Company, 1991).

12. In this context, it is worth noting that the students attend *Bates* High School. The obvious reference to *Psycho* invokes another mother whose reach extends beyond death.

13. Robin Wood, "Cronenberg: A Dissenting View," in Piers Handling, ed., *The Shape of Rage: The Films of David Cronenberg* (Toronto: General Publishing, 1983), pp. 115–35.

14. In his commentary on the film, William Beard does not make the generic connection, but he does note that "it is this wish to effect a liberation from normal restraint, repression or balance that constitutes the hubristic Cartesian error in the Cronenbergian world." Beard, "The Visceral Mind: The Major Films of David Cronenberg," in Handling, *The Shape of Rage*, p. 32.

17. Alien Bodies

1. Lawrence Cohn, "Gore Perpetual Fave of Young Film Fans," *Variety*, August 26, 1981, p. 42.

2. Gregory A. Waller provides the most extensive comparison of the various versions. As he notes about the 1979 *Dracula*: "Badham's *Dracula* seems to me to adopt a critical, revisionist stance towards its sources. . . . Through his treatment of generic conventions, Badham implicitly comments on, for example, [playwrights] Deane and Balderston's assumptions about madness, [director Tod] Browning's image of the sanitarium, and, most important, on the ending of all three earlier *Dracula*s. Such revisionism is a major characteristic of American genre films during the last fifteen years." Waller, *The Living and the Undead* (Urbana: University of Illinois Press, 1986), p. 95.

3. See Vera Dika, *Games of Terror* (Rutherford, N.J.: Fairleigh Dickinson Press, 1990), pp. 37–43; and Carol J. Clover, *Men, Women, and Chainsaws: Gender in the Modern Horror Film* (Princeton: Princeton University Press, 1992).

4. Andrew Sarris, *Confessions of a Cultist* (New York: Simon and Schuster, 1970), p. 375.

5. The first glimpse of this poster comes as a respectable Brit is chased by the American werewolf through tunnels of a London subway station in what turns out to be the second in the series of murders that concludes the film.

6. *Wolfen*, released the same year, is less coy about this, although it is surprisingly discreet on the transformations.

7. David Cronenberg's *The Fly* (1986) perhaps offers the climax of this trend by literally turning the body of a baboon inside out and showing the results of this unintentional experiment to the audience in full view.

8. In writing this, I recognize that my claim runs counter to much feminist writing on film, which ranges from seeing woman in these films as the object-to-be-looked-at to ambivalent figures of identification. I do not regard my analysis as mutually exclusive, however.

9. This is implied in the 1931 version (especially since it helps explain how Lucy knows Dracula's whereabouts), but the film tries to be fairly discreet about it. It also turns up in a 1973 television movie (*Dracula*, starring Jack Palance as the Count), albeit without the graphic detail.

10. Perhaps because of this, the film fully restores an element from the novel usually lost and pushes it even further: Lucy begins to act fully as Dracula's surrogate.

11. This apparent simplicity comes partly from its reversion to a 1950s science fiction/horror formula. Peter Fitting has noted, however, that the film combines the three waves of SF films that precede it. Fitting, "The Second Alien," in a special issue ("Symposium on *Alien*") of *Science-Fiction Studies* 7 (1980), no. 22: 285.

12. Krin Gabbard and Glen O. Gabbard offer a persuasive psychoanalytic reading of the film that draws on Melanie Klein in *Psychiatry and the Cinema* (Chicago: University of Chicago Press, 1987), pp. 226–39. Harvey Greenberg merges a psychological approach with cultural history in "The Fractures of Desire: Psychoanalytic Notes on *Alien* and the Contemporary 'Cruel' Horror Film," *Psychoanalytic Review* 70 (Summer 1983), no. 2: 241–67.

13. The intentionality of all this is evident from interviews with the film's creative personnel which appeared in a special issue on *Alien* in *Cinefantastique* 9 (Spring 1979), no. 1.

In an article that provocatively delineates an abortion motif in *Alien*, John L. Cobbs traces this aspect to art director and set designer H. R. Giger, a Swiss painter whose "particular specialty is genitalia, male and female, a subject he presents incessantly." Cobbs, "*Alien* as Abortion Parable," *Literature Film Quarterly* 18 (1990), no. 3: 199.

14. Jeff Gould traces a somewhat similar developmental progression in "The Destruction of the Social by the Organic in *Alien*," in the special issue ("Symposium on *Alien*") of *Science-Fiction Studies*, p. 284 .

15. Susan Jeffords elides the two films, insisting that the monster in *Alien* is female in order to argue that both films present "a 'feminism' that can succeed only by making women 'alien' to themselves." Jeffords, ' "The Fall of the Big Mamas': Feminism and the Alienation of Women," *Journal of American Culture* 10 (Fall 1987), no. 3: 73.

16. The Gabbards describe the monster as "strikingly phallic," but they are in fact describing only what we see in the final scene. They otherwise overlook the shape-changing aspect of the alien. Gabbard and Gabbard, *Psychiatry and the Cinema*, p. 237.

17. Greenberg writes: "No erotic intentions are manifested by the Alien until its lust erupts during the final showdown with Ripley. . . . The sight of her nearly nude body is highly arousing, in the context of the previous sexual neutrality, in the wake of the

relaxation that follows the *Nostromo*'s destruction and the creature's supposed death." Greenberg, "The Fractures of Desire," p. 256.

18. Greenberg, among others, does focus on the social issues the film raises, but he doesn't specifically connect it to the body (although he takes a strongly psychoanalytic approach).

19. Jeanine Basinger, *The World War II Combat Film* (New York: Columbia University Press, 1986), pp. 57–58.

20. As was noted in the discussion of *Animal House* (made the year before *Alien*), Nixon was specifically repudiated by the epilogue that aligned him with the film's most despised character.

21. The Gabbards do mention this for *Alien* (*Psychiatry and the Cinema*, p. 230), but as I note here, it was a fairly widespread device.

22. In his famous study of Dr. Schreber, Sigmund Freud analyzes paranoia as a defense against homosexual desire. The original case study may be found in Freud, "Psycho-Analytic Notes on an Autobiographical Account of a Case of Paranoia (Dementia Paranoides)" (1911), in vol. 12 (1958) of *S.E.*, 24 vols. (London: Hogarth Press, 1953–1974), pp. 9–82.

Whether consciously or not, *Videodrome* seems to support Freud's notion in the way that Max takes on a specific female characteristic in response to the omnipotent media mogul who owns Videodrome. Still, we may fairly ask, as I asked in the child abuse films, what if Max's paranoia is not solely a matter of projection; what if the father—the controlling figure—does in fact persecute the son?

18. The Comic Beat of Never-ending Terror

1. Gregory A. Waller writes about closed and open endings in vampire movies. While he observes that a movement away from closure is evident in films of the period under discussion in this book, he notes (correctly) that open endings can also be found in earlier horror films. As much as I agree with this, I think it minimizes what is really different in these later films. The apparent revitalization of the monster doesn't simply open up the ending; it directly challenges closure. Waller, *The Living and the Undead* (Urbana: University of Illinois Press, 1986) pp. 168–70.

2. David Bordwell, Janet Staiger, and Kristin Thompson, *The Classical Hollywood Cinema* (New York: Columbia University Press, 1985), p. 36. See also Bordwell, *Narration in the Fiction Film* (Madison: University of Wisconsin Press, 1985), pp. 157–59.

Writing specifically about Orson Welles's *Touch of Evil* (1958) but intending more general application, Stephen Heath writes, "The task of the narrative—the point of the transformation—is to resolve the violence, to replace it in a new homogeneity" (*Questions of Cinema* [Bloomington: Indiana University Press, 1981], p. 136). But gross-out horror leaves the violence unresolved by promising renewed violence.

3. For example, see Peter Biskind, *Seeing Is Believing* (New York: Pantheon, 1984), pp. 133–34.

4. Wylie Sypher, "The Meanings of Comedy," in Sypher, ed., *Comedy* (Garden City, N.Y.: Doubleday Anchor, 1956), p. 194. Page numbers in parentheses follow quotations in the text.

5. Northrop Frye, *Anatomy of Criticism* (Princeton: Princeton University Press, 1957; rpt, 1971), pp. 163–86.

6. In his essay on *The Birds*, Robin Wood details the manner in which "every action [of the ending] becomes ambiguous." Wood, *Hitchcock's Films* (London: Zwemmer, 1965), p. 152.

7. Kyle B. Counts, "The Making of Alfred Hitchcock's *The Birds*," *Cinefantastique* 10 (Spring 1987), no. 1: 34.

8. *Dirty Harry* (1971) is the most important forerunner for this and perhaps with specific reference to horror films since this is a police movie in which the villain starts to take on some of the quality of a horror film monster. The transformation of conventional Hollywood narrative structure may be seen clearly with *No Way Out* (1987) because it is a remake of a 1940s film noir, *The Big Clock* (1948). To the original ending *No Way Out* adds a surprise revelation of bisexuality, something that was only implicit in the original. But even this surprise is apparently not enough for contemporary audience expectations, so the film adds on another ending that startlingly reveals the leading man was not the man we thought he was throughout the film. Critical reaction, conservative as it always is, was negative, but the box office suggests the ending satisfied audiences at least.

9. Concerning *Two Gentlemen of Verona*, Frye observes: "The action of the comedy begins in a world represented as a normal world, moves into the green world, goes into a metamorphosis there in which the comic resolution is achieved, and returns to the normal world. The forest in this play is the embryonic form of the fairy world of *A Midsummer Night's Dream*, the Forest of Arden in *As You Like It*, Windsor Forest in *The Merry Wives of Windsor*, and the pastoral world of the mythical sea-coasted Bohemia in *The Winter's Tale*. In all these comedies there is the same rhythmic movement from normal world to green world and back again. . . . The green world charges the comedies with a symbolism in which the comic resolution contains a suggestion of the old ritual pattern of the victory of summer over winter." Frye, "The Argument of Comedy," in D. A. Robertson, Jr., ed., *English Institute Essays* (New York: Columbia University Press, 1949), p. 68.

Keeping this pattern in mind, I would say that the suspension on which *The Birds* ends is the suspension of seasons.

10. Vera Dika, *Games of Terror* (Rutherford, N.J.: Fairleigh Dickinson Press, 1990), explicitly equates the "slasher" films with games.

11. Suzanne Langer, *Feeling and Form: A Theory of Art* (New York: Scribners, 1953), p. 331.

12. This has certainly not been without contestation, as a number of articles have questioned seeing anything "progressive" in the horror film. See especially Dana Polan, "Eros and Syphilization: The Contemporary Horror Film," *Tabloid: A Review of Mass Culture and Everyday Life* (Winter 1982), pp. 31–34, reprinted in Barry Keith Grant, ed., *Planks of Reason: Essays on the Horror Film* (Metuchen, N.J.: Scarecrow Press, 1984), pp. 201–11; and Andrew Britton, "The Devil, Probably: The Symbolism of Evil," in Britton, Richard Lippe, Tony Williams, and Robin Wood, *The American Nightmare: Essays on the Horror Film* (Toronto: Festival of Festivals, 1979), pp. 34–42.

13. Ian Cameron, V. F. Perkins, "Hitchcock," *Movie*, no. 6 (1962): 5. It is worth noting as an aside that the one *actual* amusement park in a Hitchcock film—a setting for murder in *Strangers on a Train* (1951)—is specifically used for its class connotations.

A place of cheap thrills for the lower orders, it is contrasted with the refined world of the Washington elite that provides the other chief setting for the film. This was a connotation the amusement park would eventually lose (following a pattern of the low being made high that I have noted in post–World War II America). Disneyland granted the amusement park a well-scrubbed middle-class respectability that became a model as "theme parks" eventually replaced most amusement parks. Effectively restoring an environment that was lost with this transformation, gross-out films reestablished the sense of an alternative, a raw, deliberately offensive world of license—in short, everything neutralized by Disneyland's transformation of the amusement park into a safe place for the entire family.

14. Johan Huizinga, *Homo Ludens: The Play Element in Culture* (1950; rpt., Boston: Beacon Press, 1955), pp. 2–3.

15. Natalie Angier, "The Purpose of Playful Frolics: Training for Adulthood, *New York Times*, October 20, 1992, pp. C1, C8.

16. With regard to the horror film, the reception of Steven Spielberg's *Jurassic Park* in 1993 offered the most striking evidence of this shift in audience taste. Perhaps in a reaction against horror films of the previous decade, reviews and publicity stories noted a downplaying of gore in the film as if that were something to praise. The reviewer for *Time*, for example, invoked the hoary imagination-explicitness dichotomy to laud what the film did not do: "Most of the movie eschews overt violence for its much more satisfying alternative—the threat of violence. The guts and gore are seen mostly in the viewer's lurid imagination" (Richard Corliss, "Jaws II," *Time*, June 14, 1993, p. 70). In chapter 2, I noted a general critical preference for art that works by indirection. Similarly, the praise of the *Time* reviewer implicitly carries with it a charge against the horror films of the previous two decades that showed as much "guts and gore" as their creative make-up artists could manufacture. By claiming a preference for leaving things up to the imagination, something gross-out is never content to do, the critic rejects spectacle as an end in itself.

In a comparison of the source novel and the movie, which is generally less graphic, an *Entertainment Weekly* article noted the reason why the filmmakers decided not to use a baby-as-victim as the novel had: "To ensure a family-friendly PG-13 rating. Says [producer and longtime Spielberg associate Kathleen] Kennedy: 'Steven's got kids, and he's got a good instinctual sense of to what extent kids want to be scared and at what point you're doing stuff that's simply horrific' " ("A Tale of Two 'Jurassics,' " *Entertainment Weekly*, June 18, 1993, p. 20). In claiming this, Kennedy has oddly forgotten—as did the many articles that specifically mentioned the rating of *Jurassic Park*—something I discussed in chapter 3, namely that Spielberg's *Indiana Jones and the Temple of Doom* (1984) was largely responsible for the advent of the PG-13 rating because it made gross-out imagery available to very young children in the context of a PG movie. Both Spielberg and his audience have clearly changed a good deal in less than a decade's time.

All this is a matter of manner, and manner is always an important aspect of gross-out. But there is one striking thematic element in *Jurassic Park* that also looks back to gross-out, but in a way that ultimately rejects the distinctive push-pull of the gross-out mode. The absent father theme so central to the horror film of the 1970s–1980s is here reworked so that the father has to pay dearly for his desired absence. The absent father is a fairly insistent theme in Spielberg's films as well, but the different inflection it receives in *Jurassic Park* seems to me very much a consequence of its period. Sam

Neill is a paleontologist with such an extreme dislike of children that he can't even endure being in the same car with one. Yet, throughout most of the film, when two youngsters, in a throwback to earlier horror traditions, become prime prey for prehistoric creatures, Neill will risk his own life and limb in order to save theirs.

In the generally antigross-out context of *Jurassic Park*, there is nonetheless one odd scene toward the beginning of the film that suggests the ambivalence of gross-out, although the film finally pulls back from this. In response to a prepubescent boy who sarcastically questions how monstrous dinosaurs might have been, Neill conjures up the image of a predatory dinosaur in graphic detail. All through his description, Neill menacingly circles about the boy, holding out the lethal claw of a velociraptor as if he himself intended to do the boy harm. As a kind of graphic peroration, he makes a final gesture toward the boy with the claw that threatens evisceration. Later in the film when the children are threatened by live dinosaurs, however, Neill tosses away the claw, and an insert shot of the claw lying on the ground signals its expressive meaning as an act of renunciation. In abandoning his own identification with the agressive dinosaurs, Neill reveals to himself and to the audience as well that he is a good father after all.

It wouldn't be hard to imagine how all this might develop in a work of gross-out horror where the prehistoric monsters could become agents of Neill's inexplicable rage against children, while his subsequent acceptance of the children would, at best, always be compromised by the ambivalence of an ongoing threat from the monsters. In fact, Spielberg's *E.T.* (1982), concurrent with the gross-out horror cycle, presents an ambivalent father-figure who is also defined metonymically by an insert shot. In place of the father who has abandoned the family, an ominous male authority figure, signified by a repeated insert shot of dangling keys (the character is in fact named *Keys* in the end credits), comes on the scene threatening to destroy the good father fantasy figured by the extraterrestrial. By the time of *Jurassic Park*, however, no ambivalence may be admitted. The actuality of children in danger instantaneously transforms Neill, draining him of all hostility as he unquestioningly leaps to their defense. As in *Home Alone* and *Silence of the Lambs*, a fissure has been opened solely to be covered over. We must come to know, as postgross-out films assure us, that all parents—even if they seem to be absent or downright hostile—are actually strong, protective, and 100 percent devoted to their children.

Index

Designer:	Teresa Bonner
Text:	ITC Garamond Light
Compositor:	Impressions, *a division of* Edwards Brothers
Printer:	Edwards Brothers
Binder:	Edwards Brothers